USING
MODULA-2
An
Introduction To
Computer Science I

Programming books from boyd & fraser

Structuring Programs in Microsoft BASIC
BASIC Fundamentals and Style
Applesoft BASIC Fundamentals and Style
Complete BASIC: For the Short Course
Fundamentals of Structured COBOL
Advanced Structured COBOL: Batch and Interactive
Comprehensive Structured COBOL
Pascal
WATFIV-S Fundamentals and Style
VAX Fortran
Fortran 77 Fundamentals and Style
Learning Computer Programming: Structured Logic, Algorithms, and Flowcharting

Also available from boyd & fraser

Database Systems: Management and Design
Using Pascal: An Introduction to Computer Science I
Using Modula-2: An Introduction to Computer Science I
Data Abstraction and Structures: An Introduction to Computer Science II
Fundamentals of Systems Analysis with Application Design
Data Communications for Business
Data Communications Software Design
Microcomputer Applications: Using Small Systems Software
The Art of Using Computers
Using Microcomputers: A Hands-On Introduction

Shelly, Cashman and Forsythe books from boyd & fraser

Computer Fundamentals with Application Software
Workbook and Study Guide to accompany Computer Fundamentals with Application Software
Learning to Use SUPERCALC®3, dBASE III®, and WORDSTAR® 3.3: An Introduction
Learning to Use SUPERCALC®3: An Introduction
Learning to Use dBASE III®: An Introduction
Learning to Use WORDSTAR® 3.3: An Introduction
BASIC Programming for the IBM Personal Computer
Structured COBOL — Flowchart Edition
Structured COBOL — Pseudocode Edition
Introduction to Turbo Pascal Programming

USING
MODULA-2

An
Introduction To
Computer Science I

DAVID D. RILEY

University of Wisconsin
La Crosse

THE SOUTHEAST BOOK COMPANY
BOYD & FRASER PUBLISHING COMPANY
BOSTON

Dedication

To my wife

Sandra

who has encouraged, sacrificed, sustained, sympathized, cooperated, typed, edited, and most importantly inspired; and to our children

Kasandra and Derek

who have demonstrated patience beyond their years.

臺內著字第　　　號

發 行 人：卓　　　鑫　　　淼
發 行 所：東　南　書　報　社
地　　址：台北市博愛路１０５號
登 記 證：局版臺業字第０７２５號
總 經 銷：新月圖書股份有限公司
郵政劃撥：１０７７５７３－８號
地　　址：台北市重慶南路一段143號3樓
電　　話：三　三　一　七　八　五　六　號
印 刷 所：合興彩色印刷有限公司
地　　址：西園路2段261巷34弄44號
中華民國七十六年　　月　　日第　　版

CREDITS:

Editor: Tom Walker
Director of Production: Becky Herrington
Ancillaries Editor: Donna Villanucci
Manufacturing Director: Erek Smith

COVER PHOTOGRAPHY AND DESIGN:

Tom Norton – TOM NORTON DESIGNS

© 1987 by Boyd & Fraser Publishing Company

Manufactured in the United States of America

Library of Congress Cataloging-in-Publication Data

```
Riley, David D., 1951-
   Using Modula-2.

   Includes index.
   1. Modula-2 (Computer program language)  I. Title.
QA76.73.M63R55  1987          005.13'3          86-28358
ISBN 0-87835-236-8
```

TABLE OF CONTENTS

Chapter 4 – (CONTROL) STRUCTURED PROGRAMMING

Chapter 5 – MORE STRUCTURED PROGRAMMING

Chapter 6 – LOGIC AND PROGRAMMING

Chapter 7 – THE PROCEDURE

Chapter 11 – INTRODUCTION TO DATA ABSTRACTION (TYPE, CONST, ENUMERATED DATA TYPES, AND SUBRANGES)

Chapter 12 – INTRODUCTION TO STRUCTURED DATA: THE ONE-DIMENSIONAL ARRAY

Chapter 13 – THE MULTIDIMENSIONAL ARRAY

Chapter 14 – THE RECORD DATA STRUCTURE

Chapter 15 – MORE PROGRAMMING TOOLS

PREFACE

Recent developments in computer hardware and software are driving a change in introductory computer science courses. These developments range from new computer workstations that provide a productive environment for software design to new programming languages, such as Modula-2, that incorporate up-to-date facilities for software engineering. The introductory computer science course must mature along with the profession. New techniques for software development must be integrated into sound pedagogical experience.

ABOUT THIS BOOK

Using Modula-2: An Introduction to Computer Science I is an examination of today's computer science fundamentals, consistent with the ACM's 1984 guidelines for a CS 1 course. This text recognizes that tomorrow's software designer will require knowledge that goes beyond mere familiarity with programming languages. The use of Modula-2 conforms to Niklaus Wirth's own opinion that Modula-2 is a tool for thinking that just coincidentally happens to be a programming language.

This text also reflects a philosophy that students' performance is closely related to the instructor's expectations. Student feedback, based on class testing of preliminary editions of this book, suggests that this presentation is both challenging and realistic.

Since many students entering college have some familiarity with programming in high-level languages, the organization of this text is based on programming tools and techniques, rather than the features of some programming language. These tools include intelligent use of control structures, data structures, design, good programming style, and debugging techniques.

DISTINGUISHING FEATURES

Development of Tools and Techniques

Every programmer needs a toolbox. This book includes numerous *tools* for the developing software engineer. Among these tools are syntax diagrams, debugging techniques, assertions, procedure hierarchy charts, block structure diagrams, control flow diagrams, pseudolanguages, and numerous widely-used algorithms.

Attention to Programming Style and Design

To highlight the importance of good programming style, many separate "Programming with Style" sections are sprinkled throughout the text. Each describes the **how** and the **why** of some aspect of competent program design. Issues of good algorithmic design are similarly highlighted in "Designing with Wisdom" sections appearing throughout the book.

Extensive, Well-Chosen Examples

Many students learn by example. Therefore, the text includes numerous carefully selected examples, averaging over two complete programs per chapter, with many other algorithms and procedures. The programs have all been compiled and executed. Each major concept is illustrated by one or more examples. Programmers often model their programs from examples drawn from texts. A concerted effort has been made to choose examples that not only support the material, but serve as good models for reference use as well.

Assertions

In this text, assertions are introduced immediately and used throughout. Pre- and postconditions are included in procedures. Loop invariants are shown as a means for designing loops. Assertions are among the most important documentation and design tools currently available and represent a disciplined, precise approach to software development. Students have found this approach both challenging and rewarding.

Problem Definition Form

A six-part problem definition form is used to illustrate the importance of precise and complete definitions. This form includes input specifications, output specifications, error handling, and a sample program execution. Major programming examples and programming project assignments are consistently presented in this form.

Terminology

The computer scientist needs an extensive vocabulary. Terms are boldfaced and listed at the end of every chapter. An extensive glossary at the end of the text includes the definitions of boldfaced as well as other important terms.

Modula-2

The Modula-2 programming language, designed by Niklaus Wirth, incorporates features that have come to prominence after Wirth's earlier creation: Pascal. Modula-2 is accessible and straightforward, incorporating facilities for modern program design and implementation. In addition, this language is an excellent tool for further study in computer science.

Exercises

Each chapter contains numerous student exercises that form a review of the chapter. Selected answers appear in the back of the book for student review. The solutions to all unanswered exercises are in the Instructor's Manual.

Class Tested

Preliminary versions of this text were used successfully in classes at the University of Wisconsin–La Crosse over two semesters. Student suggestions have resulted in important improvements in pedagogy and accuracy.

PCollier Systems Compiler

All programs have been compiled and executed using the Modula-2PC™ compiler and library. An educational version of Modula-2PC, including the compiler, PCollier Systems Editor + Environment™ and associated library modules is available **free of charge** to instructors upon request from Boyd & Fraser. This software may be duplicated as required by schools using this textbook.

ANCILLARY MATERIALS

A comprehensive instructor's support package accompanies **Using Modula-2: An Introduction to Computer Science I**. These ancillaries are available upon request from Boyd & Fraser.

Instructor's Manual

Material in the Instructor's Manual follows the organization of the text. Each chapter of the Instructor's Manual includes:

- Lecture Outline
- General Comments
- Chapter Goals
- Solutions to Exercises
- Programming Project Solutions
- Quick Challenge Questions (including solutions)

Included in the Instructor's Manual is an extensive collection of 135 transparency masters. These masters include selected figures, tables, and program segments from the text.

ProTest

Boyd & Fraser's fourth-generation test-generating program, ProTest, has been designed specifically to accompany this text.

DATA ABSTRACTION AND STRUCTURES: AN INTRODUCTION TO COMPUTER SCIENCE II

Using Modula-2: An Introduction to Computer Science I is the first of a pair of texts covering the ACM recommendations for CS 1 and CS 2. The second book, entitled **Data Abstraction and Structures: An Introduction to Computer Science II**, is also available from Boyd & Fraser. This second text explores the use of data abstraction in software design. The presentation in the text includes abstract data types, external modules, generic data types, and object-oriented design. Numerous data structures, such as stacks, queues, sequences, strings, linked lists, and trees, are examined as strategies for implementing abstractions.

ORGANIZATION

The Programming Process

From the very first chapter, programming is presented as a four-step process. Chapter 1 defines this process as

1) Problem definition
2) Algorithm design
3) Program coding
4) Program maintenance

The importance of problem definitions is emphasized in the first chapter and continually reinforced throughout the text.

An Introduction to the Complete Modula-2 Program

Chapter 2 focuses on data. Introductory data types are presented in terms of their domain and operations, consistent with modern forms for defining abstract data types. This chapter also presents syntax diagrams, a formalism used throughout the text to define language structures. The subset of Modula-2 presented within Chapter 2 is sufficient for students to write elementary programs.

Program Design Techniques

Chapter 3 is an introduction to software design. Several examples illustrate top down design using a careful stepwise refinement. This chapter also explores alternative pseudolanguages and begins the study of debugging issues that continues throughout the remainder of the book.

(Control) Structured Programmi

Chapter 4 begins the examination of structured programming. The topics of sequential execution and abstraction (in the form of procedures with parameters) are presented. The focal point of this presentation is top down design using these control structures. This emphasis is continued in Chapter 5.

More Structured Programming

Chapter 5 completes the survey of control structures by examining selection (in the form of the IF instruction) and repetition (the WHILE instruction). As in Chapter 4, this presentation concentrates on the use of these forms of control in top down design. The early presentation of the basic control structures from Chapters 4 and 5 allows ample opportunity for students to exercise their programming skills.

Logic and Programming

Programming is rooted in logic. The current trends in software engineering and new language design suggest that these roots are becoming even more important. Chapter 6 is a brief look at the direct application of logic to programming in a procedural language, such as Modula-2. This chapter incorporates critical material often omitted from introductory computer science texts.

The Procedure

Chapter 7 expands on the earlier presentation of procedures by including an extensive look at intelligent use of parameter passage and scope of variables in software design. Functions and built-in procedures are also discussed in this chapter.

Input and Output of Test Files

Chapter 8 concentrates on the topic of text I/O. This chapter examines both interactive I/O and files, using the InOut module.

More About Selection

Chapter 9 completes the presentation of selection control structures. This chapter looks at ELSIF clauses and the CASE instruction. An examination of how to choose from alternate selection structures is included.

More About Repetition

Chapter 10 covers repetition, including the REPEAT and LOOP instructions. Loop invariants are presented, and a straightforward six-step procedure for using invariants to design loops is utilized.

Introduction to Data Abstraction

Chapter 11 is an introduction to data abstraction, using the CONST and TYPE declarations. Subranges and enumerated types are presented.

Introduction to Structured Data: The One-Dimensional Array

The structures, algorithms and applications of one-dimensional arrays are examined in Chapter 12. Included in this presentation are the FOR instruction, buffering, searching, simple sorting, strings and table-driven code.

The Multidimensional Array

The discussion of arrays is expanded to include multidimensional structures in Chapter 13. This chapter also explores using arrays as functions and methods for debugging code.

The Record Data Structure

Chapter 14 completes this introduction to structured data by examining record structures. Significant topics of this chapter include arrays of records, sorting records, the WITH statement and variant records.

More Programming Tools

The final chapter is a collection of five major topics: recursion, pointers and dynamic data, stacks, queues and sets. Recursive procedures and functions are both examined. Recursion is also compared to repetition, as a form of control. The dynamic data facilities of Modula-2 are used to illustrate linked list structures. Linked lists implementations of stacks and queues are given.

ACKNOWLEDGEMENTS

Many people have played important roles in the development of this text including Boyd & Fraser: Boston, under the direction of President Tom Walker and the incomparable production crew in California, under the direction of Becky Herrington.

I am grateful to the following reviewers for their helpful suggestions: Gary Cutler, Peter J. Gingo, John M. Lloyd, Michael Michaelson, Allen Tucker, Terry A. Ward, John A. Wenzel, and Ron Willard. I also thank my colleagues at the University of Wisconsin–La Crosse who have contributed to this effort in countless ways.

A special acknowledgement is due to all of the people involved with the IBM University Program courses. Participation in the CSF2 and CSF3 courses shaped many of my beliefs regarding an introduction to this discipline. I thank the people who developed or maintain this educational material — Debra Baker, Tony Baxter, John Bentley, Elaine Rich and Mary Shaw. I also thank those with whom I have taught these courses, especially Albert Baker. In addition, I must express my gratitude to Nancy Morrison, who has made a significant contribution to the success of this program and who is responsible for my interest and involvement.

I also thank Peter Collier, President of PCollier Systems, for developing a student version of Modula-2 PC™. His forward thinking has provided educators convenient access to a modern Modula-2 implementation of highest quality.

1 ||| THE PROGRAMMING PROCESS

1.1 WHAT IS PROGRAMMING?

A **program** is a sequence of instructions that, when performed, causes a particular task to be carried out by a computer. **Software** can be defined as a collection of programs. The individuals who create programs, or software, are **programmers**. This book examines the programmer's craft.

Programming is best described as **problem solving**. Writing a program is similar to writing a recipe for preparing chocolate chip cookies. In each case, a specific problem is presented, such as "How do you make chocolate chip cookies?" The object is to produce a

> Complete
> Correct
> Understandable

solution to the problem.

The fundamental difference between writing a recipe and programming is that a recipe is used by a person, while a program is executed by a computer. Early programmers had few programming rules. Gradually, computer programming evolved from an art form to an engineering process. This change was caused largely by the enormous difficulties that occur when non-engineered software was used. A program should be designed like a bridge, to perform a specified task correctly and to be maintainable for the future. Like bridge builders, programmers must follow carefully-established engineering procedures in performing their craft.

1.2 THE STEPS OF THE PROGRAMMING PROCESS

Programming has four distinct steps. These four steps are shown in Figure 1.1. First, a programmer must **define the problem** in order to obtain an adequate idea of what task the program must perform. The second step is to **design a solution** to the defined problem. This solution is generally somewhat less formal than the final program. Third, after the solution is designed, the programmer must **code the program**.

This step is a translation from the designed solution into a program that can be executed on a computer. The fourth and final step is to **maintain the program**. This is an ongoing process of correcting program deficiencies and adding new features.

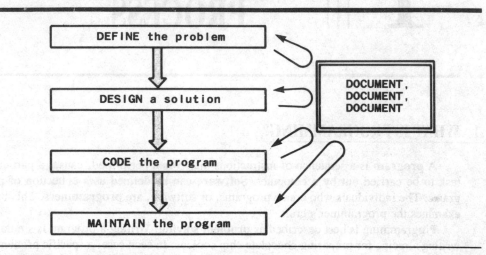

FIGURE 1.1 *The four steps of programming*

This process starts with a **user**, an individual who uses programs. A user who needs a new program to solve a problem begins by presenting the problem to a **systems analyst**. The systems analyst must understand both the user's problem and computer programming. Together, the user and the systems analyst define the problem. The **problem definition** is then forwarded to the **designer**, who is responsible for designing a solution. This solution, an **algorithm**, is a sequence of instructions that specify a solution to the problem. But algorithms are often not suited for execution by a computer, so the completed algorithm is translated by a **coder** into a computer program. Future alterations to the program are the responsibility of a **maintenance programmer**. Systems analysts, designers, coders, and maintenance programmers are all programmers.

The programming process is rarely this straightforward. Many users, systems analysts, designers, and coders may be required to complete a large programming project. Furthermore, it is often necessary to back up to an earlier step because of unforeseen developments. All of this complexity adds further justification for the careful engineering of software. With large numbers of programmers involved in the creation of a program, it is imperative that the efforts at each step are complete, correct, and understandable.

1.3 DEFINING THE PROBLEM

Defining the problem may be the most important step of the programming process. The problem definition serves as the *contract* between the user and programmer(s). As with any legal contract, a poorly written problem definition is useless. A good problem definition must communicate the task to be performed clearly and precisely, and it must do so to both the user and the programmer.

A carefully written problem definition protects the interests of both the user and the programmer. The user may begin plans for using the resulting software based on knowledge of what that software will do. When the programming project enters the design step, a good problem definition forms the foundation for design of a solution.

A problem definition (**program specification**) is a precise, complete, and understandable description of what happens when a particular program executes. To understand this definition from the user's perspective, it is necessary to examine what occurs when a program executes. The user typically views the computer as a **black box**. That is to say, it is not *how* the computer works, but rather *what* it does that is of interest to the user.

The user's black-box view of the computer naturally focuses on how humans communicate with an executing program. They do so through **input** and **output**. Certain information must be input into the computer in order for the computer to produce the desired results as output. For example, a data entry person may have to type hourly wage, number of hours worked, and payroll deductions as input to some program. In response the program will output payroll checks. Computer programs are also used to control the trajectory of a space flight. Input to such a program might come from sensors that detect current speed, direction, location, and gravitational force. The output of such a program would likely be electrical signals to control the space shuttle engines.

*P*rogramming-with-*S*tyle

Characteristics of a Good Problem Definition

A good problem definition always has three characteristics. It must be

> PRECISE
> COMPLETE
> UNDERSTANDABLE

These three factors determine the quality of a problem definition. A *precise* definition removes all ambiguity. There should be no question as to what output is expected from a program for any particular input. A *complete* definition considers all possibilities for input and specifies the associated output. Even erroneous or unexpected input should be addressed for completeness. Because the problem definition is the only contract between user and programmer, both the user and the systems analyst must be able to understand the problem definition if it is to be meaningful.

Often precision, completeness, and understandability are in conflict. Many legal documents are difficult to understand because they are written in a formal language designed for precision. Some exam questions are so precise that the student can spend more time reading than answering. Even worse, the student may miss the intent of the question because of the massive amount of detail. The best problem definitions must achieve a balance among all three qualities.

1.4 A STANDARD PROBLEM DEFINITION FORM

Consider the following problem definition.

"Input three numbers and output the numbers in order."

This definition fails all three tests for a problem definition: It is neither precise, complete, nor understandable. Should values be input one number per line, or all three on a single line? What happens if fewer or more than three numbers are input or if input is nonnumeric? Does "in order" mean greatest to least, least to greatest, or the same order as input?

Clearly, this definition leaves too many questions unanswered. Answering all the questions increases specificity, but it makes the definition wordy and hard to read. Throughout this text, problems will be defined using a standard form which maximizes precision, completeness, and understandability. Using this form, every problem definition consists of six parts.

1) The problem title
2) The general description
3) The input form
4) The output form
5) Errors
6) An example

The standard problem definition is illustrated below.

TITLE
> Sort three integers

DESCRIPTION
> Input three integers, and output the same three integers sorted from least to greatest.

INPUT
> Three integers (see definition below) are to be input, one per line.
> Integer: One or more consecutive decimal digits, optionally preceded by a plus sign, " + ", or a minus sign, "-".

OUTPUT
> The same three integers that are input are output. All three integers are output on the same line, with a single blank separating adjacent integers. The output values are sorted with the smallest value on the left.

ERRORS
> 1) Fewer than three integers input will cause the program to wait for additional input.
> 2) Lines of input after the first three are ignored.

3) If any of the first three lines does not contain a single integer, then the program terminates with the following message:

INVALID INPUT – only a single integer per line allowed.

EXAMPLE

input → -3

2

+17

output → -3 2 +17

There are several ways to use this definition. The problem is summarized in the "description" section. To comprehend the problem, it is necessary to consider the "description," "output," "input," and "error" sections as a unit. Anyone who wanted to find the details of input or output form would choose to consult the appropriate section. In addition, the unexpected input cases are clearly enumerated to tell users and programmers what action the program will take in these instances. The "title" section provides a quick and sketchy definition that may be useful for someone who already knows, or is not interested in, the details.

The "example" section may be the most useful section of the entire problem definition form. A well chosen example can quickly convey the essence of the problem, as well as illustrate different cases. When writing a problem definition, it is important to take care to illustrate expected input and as many options as possible.

1.5 DESIGNING A SOLUTION

The second step of programming is designing a solution. This is the most difficult step in programming. At this stage, the problem definition must be transformed into the algorithm. A good designer must be proficient in all aspects of programming. A good designer must also be a talented problem solver, capable of approaching each new problem based on well established design techniques. A good designer must be experienced. Finally, a good designer must be capable of working with other designers, since only the smallest programs are designed by a single individual.

Unfortunately, all large programs today contain errors — sometimes several hundred errors. Most of these errors can be traced to poor designs. Poor designs, in turn, result from complex problems and inadequate design techniques. Designers must use rigorously developed engineering procedures based on the rules of logical reasoning if error-free programs are ever to exist.

There are two principal models for reasoning. The first model is known as **deductive reasoning**. The fictional detective Sherlock Holmes immortalized this form of logical thinking. Deductive reasoning applies general rules to specific cases. For example, Holmes might have deduced the specific fact "The butler is the murderer" from the more general information "The murderer is blond" and "The butler is the only possible blond suspect." **Inductive reasoning** is the opposite of deductive reasoning. It draws general conclusions from specific cases. For example, inductive reasoning might be used to base the general conclusion "the sun rises in the east" from many specific observations that it has always risen in the east.

These two processes of deducing from the general to the specific and inducing from the specific to the general correspond closely to the two most widely used design techniques, **top-down design,** and **bottom-up design**. Like deduction, top-down design begins with a large task and decomposes this task into subtasks. Bottom-up design applies already designed specific tasks to the solution of a larger task.

For example, consider the designer of a new refrigerator/freezer. This designer is given an initial set of specifications for the unit (i.e., the problem definition) and is asked to produce detailed diagrams and specifications for the resulting product (i.e., the design). The designer might apply top-down design by decomposing a single design task into two smaller design tasks.

1) Designing the refrigerator unit
2) Designing the freezer

The same designer may choose to design the refrigeration compressor before designing the coolant tubes, cabinet or shelving. This choice will place certain constraints on the rest of the design. Designing the specific compressor before designing its surroundings is an instance of bottom-up design.

The goal of the designer is to produce an **algorithm**. The algorithm is the connection between problem definition and executable program. The systems analyst will likely review the algorithm to be sure that it reflects the problem definition. Therefore, systems analyst, designer, and coder must all read and understand the algorithm.

Every algorithm is expressed in some **pseudolanguage**. Algorithms, also referred as **pseudocode**, cannot be executed on any computer.

1.6 CODING THE ALGORITHM

The coder's job is to translate an algorithm into a program. Since the goal is to produce a complete, correct, and understandable program, there must be a good technique for expressing programs. Recipes are usually expressed in some **natural language** such as English, French, Russian, or Japanese. Correspondingly, programs are expressed in some **programming language**. Today it is not possible to use any natural language as a programming language because natural languages are too complex to be "understood" by computers. Unlike natural languages, programming languages are designed specifically for expressing problem solutions that can be executed by a computer.

The earliest programs were coded in **machine languages**. Machine language programs are a collection of numbers, each number representing a single computer instruction. Each computer is capable of executing only one machine language, and most different computers use machine languages that are incompatible with one another. Therefore, coding in a machine language restricts the program to one particular computer model.

In addition to machine languages, most computers use or support **assembler languages**. An assembler language is similar to machine language in that each instruction in an assembler language roughly corresponds to a single instruction that the computer is capable of executing. An assembler language differs from a machine language in that instructions use **mnemonics**. For example, the instructions below might be used on the PDP-11 computer to decrement (DEC) or subtract a value 1 from the value stored in location 1024 of the memory of the computer.

Machine Instruction	Assembler Instruction
005337 002000	DEC #1024

(this is an octal,
base 8, number)

Machine languages and assembler languages are structured around the primitive instructions that a computer can execute. For this reason they are referred to as **low-level languages**. Many programs have been written, and continue to be written, in low-level languages. There are difficulties with coding in assembler or machine languages that restrict their use today.

The difficulties with low-level languages led to the creation of **high-level languages**. A high-level language is more like a natural language than a machine language. Typically, a single high-level instruction requires several low-level instructions to perform the same function. Computers can directly execute only those programs written in machine language. Assembler and high-level language programs must be translated before they can be executed.

There have been many different high-level programming languages created since the invention of the computer. Figure 1.2 lists a some of the more notable ones.

Language	Brief Description
COBOL	– An early language designed for business applications, still widely used
FORTRAN	– An early language, used largely by scientists and engineers
ALGOL 60	– A general-purpose language of the 1960s
BASIC	– An early language much used for teaching
PL/1	– A general purpose language designed in the early 1960s
Lisp	– A language used widely for "artificial intelligence" applications
Pascal	– A language with widespread acceptance, especially in colleges and universities
C	– A language designed for writing software like that of an operating system
Ada	– A recent language designed by the U S Department of Defense, now required for many DOD applications
Modula-2	– A recent language gaining acceptance as a successor to Pascal
Prolog	– A recent language based on the rules of mathematical logic

FIGURE 1.2 Some notable high-level programming languages

Modula-2 is the creation of one man, **Niklaus Wirth**. In the 1960s several versions of ALGOL were designed as general purpose languages. Because they encompassed many important computer science concepts of the time, these languages were often used to teach computer science. In the early 1970s Wirth created **Pascal**, which is based largely on ALGOL 60. Designed with programming education in mind, Pascal has become the language of choice for most computer science programs today.

Niklaus Wirth researched programming languages while working with the Mesa system at Xerox Palo Alto Research Center. Complaints regarding certain inadequacies of Pascal, the absence of several new concepts in Pascal, and Wirth's own experience with the Mesa system prompted the creation of Modula-2. The language was completed as part of a research project begun in 1977 at the Institut fur Infomatik of ETH Zurich.

Every language requires a precise "standard" definition. The original definition of Modula-2 appeared in *Programming in Modula-2*, written by Niklaus Wirth. The language was revised in 1985. The third edition of Wirth's book contains the current definition of Modula-2 as it is described in this text.

1.7 MAINTAINING THE PROGRAM

In order to complete a job, the coder must be convinced that the program matches the pseudocode when it is executed correctly on the computer. The systems analyst, designer, and most importantly, the user must then test and verify that the program is correct. Finally, the product (the program) is ready for shipment, complete with all necessary documentation. However, this is not the end of the programming process; it is the beginning of the maintenance step.

An error in a program is a **bug**. Program bugs may be the result of an inadequate problem definition, a design that does not satisfy the problem definition, or a program that does not match the design. Regardless of the cause, the user's response is "the program was not supposed to do that!" The correction of bugs is a major component of program maintenance.

The other major component of program maintenance is the modification of the program to include new features or to change existing features. The user may have a change of heart about how the program is to work, requiring a rewrite of the program. The complexity of the program maintenance effort depends upon the types of changes to be made. In the worst case, a complete revision of the program from definition to code may be required. It is not unusual for more programming time to be devoted to maintenance than to the creation of the program.

1.8 PROGRAM DOCUMENTATION

The final component of the programming process to be described is **documentation**. Documentation refers to a wide variety of written descriptions that facilitate the programming process and enhance the resulting programs. Documentation is an ongoing effort that must be an integral part of each step of programming. Problem specification, design documents, algorithms, and programs are all documents. Within programs, **inter-**

nal documentation assists anyone reading the code. **Tutorial manuals**, another form of documentation, teach a user about a new program. **Reference manuals** are a resource for describing software commands.

1.9 THE FUTURE OF PROGRAMMING

In an effort to correct the errors of the past, much has been done to ensure the correctness of the code produced by programmers. Rigorous rules and the laws of mathematics are being applied to assist programmers with their craft. Today there are a few large programs that have been formally defined and rigorously proven to be correct. In addition, there are programming tools to assist in algorithm design and program debugging.

It is already possible for the designer to work in conjunction with a computer to produce the code. This integration and automation of the design and coding steps of programming is likely to continue. It is also possible that some day computers may be able to program themselves. In this case, the programmer would continue to define the problem, probably in some very formal language. The computer could accept the definition and translate it into the appropriate program.

It is not possible to predict the future of programming accurately. Many changes to the craft of programming are likely. Whatever the future brings, programmers must be equipped to deal with this task called "programming." This book attempts to present an introduction to the best programming tools and techniques of today. Every programmer has a responsibility to keep current by learning new tools and techniques when they become available.

1.10 SUMMARY

The model presented in this chapter divides the programming process into four steps.

1) Defining the problem
2) Designing a solution
3) Coding the program
4) Maintaining the program

Additionally, program documentation is included in the model as an effort that continues throughout the programming process. It is important to remember that the programming process is extremely complex. However, this model establishes the important components that must be considered for effective engineering of all software, regardless of complexity.

The remainder of this text will propose numerous problems, some small and some large. Clearly, the programming model is designed especially for large problems, because large problems are of interest to computer scientists. Regardless of the size of the problem, it is important to practice careful engineering techniques. Habits formed through experience with smaller problems can be retained for application on larger ones.

Remember that good programming is *not* just coding a quick solution, using whatever technique is expedient. Instead, good programming is a carefully orchestrated engineering procedure for the creation of software that is complete, correct, and understandable.

||| KEY TERMS

program	coder	machine language
software	maintenance programmer	assembler language
programmer	program specification	mnemonic
problem solving	black box	low-level language
problem definition	input	high-level language
design (of programs)	output	Niklaus Wirth
coding	deductive reasoning	Pascal
program maintenance	inductive reasoning	bug
user	algorithm	documentation
systems analyst	pseudolanguage	internal documentation
problem definition	pseudocode	tutorial manual
designer	natural language	reference manual
algorithm	programming language	

||| EXERCISES

1. Consider the model of the programming process presented in Sections 1.2 through 1.7

   a) List the four steps of this process in the order in which they are performed.

   b) What are the titles given to the individuals involved at each step of the process?

   c) Between each two consecutive steps of the programming process there is a product created by the earlier step and used in the following step. It has been suggested that each of these products can be thought of as programs, except that computers that ca execute them may not exist. What are the three intermediate products?

   d) What is the fifth component of the programming process, and why is it not included as one of the steps?

   e) "Haste makes waste" is a proverb worth remembering. Briefly, describe how this proverb might apply to the programming process.

2. Describe how pseudocode differs from a program.

3. To illustrate the difficulty of using English definitions, write an English sentence that could be interpreted to have two entirely different meanings.

4. Identify the three main goals that every problem definition should achieve.

5. Enumerate the six parts of the standard problem definition form used in this text.
   a) Describe what is contained in each.
   b) For each, indicate how the definition would suffer from omitting that part.

6. What are the three most desirable qualities in a program?

7. For each of the following, identify whether it represents a top-down, or a bottom-up, approach.
   a) Designing the floorplan of a house, then selecting locations for window and doors.
   b) Selecting a particular hubcap you like, then purchasing an automobile the hubcap fits.
   c) Selecting a tape drive for a stereo system, then selecting other hi-fi components the effectively complement the tape drive.
   d) Deciding upon a company's management structure by first dividing the company into divisions, then dividing the divisions into subdivisions.
   e) Alphabetizing names by placing all the A's in one group, all the B's in a second group, etc.; then alphabetizing within each group.
   f) Outlining a research paper before writing it.
   g) Selecting a choice location in an undeveloped piece of property on which you would like to build a house, then plotting all streets and lots in the property to maximize the value of your own house.
   h) Enrolling in a favorite class for next semester, then deciding which other courses to take based on their compatibility with this favorite.

8. Section 1.6 described natural languages and programming languages.
   a) List as many similarities between natural and programming languages as you can.
   b) List as many differences between natural and programming languages as you can.

9. Errors that occur during programming have various effects on other steps of the process. Briefly, identify the main effect of each of the following.
   a) The effect of a poor problem definition upon the user
   b) The effect of a poor problem definition upon the systems analyst
   c) The effect of a poor problem definition upon the designer
   d) The effect of an erroneous design on the systems analyst
   e) The effect of an erroneous design on the coder
   f) The effect of an erroneous design on the maintenance programmer
   g) The effect of a program bug upon the user
   h) The effect of a program bug upon the maintenance programmer

10. For each part of Exercise 9 identify what action the indicated individual is likely to take.

| | | PROGRAMMING PROJECTS

An editor is a program that allows a computer to function somewhat like a typewriter. If possible, use the editor from your computer to complete the problems that follow.

1. Below is a general description and an example for a particular formal problem definiti
   Supply input and output specifications that are consistent.

   TITLE
   > Identify Values Within a Specified Range

   DESCRIPTION
   > This program accepts two integers representing an upper and lower bound
   > for a range of integers. Next, several other integers will be input (up to an
   > integer with a value of zero). The program will identify all of these last
   > integers that are within the range.

   EXAMPLE

   ```
   input   →    -1        output →    The range is -1 to 5
                5                     3 is within the range
                3                     -1 is within the range
                -3                    5 is within the range
                -1
                5
                7
                0
   ```

2. Below is a general description and an example for a particular formal problem
   definition. Supply input and output specifications.

   TITLE
   > Interactive Textual Analyzer

   DESCRIPTION
   > This problem represents an interactive textual analyzer for English sentences.
   > This analyzer calculates the following information for each file to be
   > analyzed:
   > 1) total number of sentences,
   > 2) total number of words,
   > 3) average (mean) number of words per sentence, and
   > 4) average (mean) word length.
   >
   > The required input is menu driven. The user specifies one of three menu
   > choices to:
   > 1) analyze a different file
   > 2) display the results of the analysis on the screen
   > 3) terminate the execution of the program
   >
   > All data to be analyzed is assumed to have been previously stored in some
   > computer file.

   EXAMPLE
   > NOTES: 1) The left side of the page, entitled "DISPLAY", shows a current
   >   snapshot of the computer display screen. The right side, entitled
   >   "INPUT", shows the input that is specified between snapshots.
   >   2) <<return>>
   >   symbolizes the user striking the carriage return key.

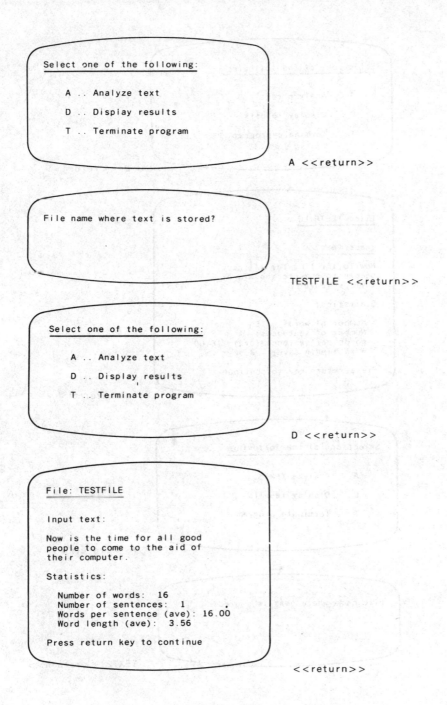

Select one of the following:

    A .. Analyze text

    D .. Display results

    T .. Terminate program

A <<return>>

File name where text is stored?

TESTFILE <<return>>

Select one of the following:

    A .. Analyze text

    D .. Display results

    T .. Terminate program

D <<return>>

File: TESTFILE

Input text:

Now is the time for all good
people to come to the aid of
their computer.

Statistics:

    Number of words: 16
    Number of sentences: 1
    Words per sentence (ave): 16.00
    Word length (ave): 3.56

Press return key to continue

<<return>>

Select one of the following:

    A .. Analyze text

    D .. Display results

    T .. Terminate program

D <<return>>

File: TESTFILE

Input text:

Now is the time for all good
people to come to the aid of
their computer.

Statistics:

  Number of words: 16
  Number of sentences: 1
  Words per sentence (ave): 16.00
  Word length (ave): 3.56

Press return key to continue

<<return>>

Select one of the following:

    A .. Analyze text

    D .. Display results

    T .: Terminate program

A <<return>>

File name where text is stored?

TEXT2 <<return>>

```
Select one of the following:

    A .. Analyze text

    D .. Display results

    T .. Terminate program
```

                                                          D <<return>>

```
File: TEXT2

Input text:

Professor Nocompute desperately needs
a mechanized grading procedure. He
teaches classes of up to 40 students
and evaluates a class using the
scores from one to four exams. Each
of Nocompute's exams may have a
different number of maximum points
possible. For each student he likes
to record a last name, social security
number, and total points (the raw
score) for each exam. Nocompute
calculates grades by translating all
raw scores into 'percentages of the
possible score and averaging these
percentages to obtain an overall
average for the student.

Statistics:

  Number of words:  89
  Number of sentences:    5
  Words per sentence (ave): 17.80
  Word length (ave):  5.07

Press return key to continue
```

                                                          <<return>>

```
Select one of the following:

    A .. Analyze text

    D .. Display results

    T .. Terminate program
```

                                                          T <<return>>

        END OF ANALYSIS

3. Write an EXAMPLE section for the following problem definition.

TITLE
Coach Brown's Roundball Stats

DESCRIPTION
The basketball coach, Bill Brown, wants the ID numbers of all male students who are over six feet tall and also who weigh at least two hundred pounds. He also wants the ID number of the tallest male and the heaviest male.

INPUT
Each student's data will be contained on a single line, with four items on the line. The first item is a gender code, either F or M. The second item is an integer representing the student's height in inches. The third item on the line is an integer representing the student's weight in pounds. The fourth item on the line is a two-digit ID number for the student. Each item is separated from the item following by exactly two blanks. Following all of the student input lines, there is one line with a Z as a gender code. This last line indicates the end of input.

OUTPUT
The output consists of the following six parts:
1) A header line with " ID HEIGHT WEIGHT "
2) A blank line
3) On consecutive lines matching the input order the ID, height and weight of all male students over 6 feet tall and weighing at least 200 pounds are listed.
4) A blank line
5) A line like "The tallest player is < id > ." where "< id >"is the ID of the tallest male student input.
6) A line like "The heaviest player is < id >" where "< id >" is the ID of the heaviest male student.

ERRORS
1. If too few values are input per line (fewer than 4), then undefined results occur.
2. If the first value per line is not a character or the last three values are not integers then undefined results occur.
3. Any additional input on a line or additional lines after the line with the gender code of Z is ignored.
4. Any gender code other than M or F produces the following message: "INVALID GENDER CODE" and the entire input line is ignored.
5. If the last input line does not contain a Z gender code then undefined results occur.
6. There is no attempt to detect unrealistic height and weight values.

4. Write a problem definition to complete the problem below.

TITLE
Room Area Calculation

DESCRIPTION

A building contractor needs a program to make rough cost estimates for apartment building costs. This program should accept as input the number of rooms in the building, followed by the length and width of each room. The cost of the building is approximated to be $500 per room plus $40 per square foot. The contractor wants the program to output the number of rooms, total square footage of all rooms, and the total cost of the building.

5. Write a problem definition to complete the problem below.

TITLE
Simple Character Graphics Program

DESCRIPTION
This program is designed to permit the user to draw a limited number of pictures in an interactive environment. The user must be operating a keyboard and viewing a screen. Input to the program consists of single keystrokes. The following is a list of valid keystrokes and their corresponding action:

keystroke	action
C	Clear the screen and begin at top.
B	Move down two lines (leaving blank lines).
S	Print 3 blanks followed by a plus (+) on the current line and move down one line
F	Print 1 blank followed by 5 pluses (+ + + + +) on the current line and move down one line.
T	Print a triangle while moving down 4 consecutive lines (1st line - 3 blanks and +, 2nd line - 2 blanks and + + +, 3rd line -1 blank and + + + + +, 4th line - + + + + + + + +).
L	This terminates the program execution.

2

THE CONCEPT OF DATA

2.1 STORAGE OF INFORMATION

Information that is stored within a computer is **data**. The execution of a program involves considerable data manipulation. Most programming languages contain input instructions to input data, output instructions to output data, and assignment instructions to manipulate data. All of these instructions require that the computer support a method for storing data. Likewise, the programming language provides a mechanism for referring to stored data. Any data stored by the execution of a program is stored in a **variable**, and groups of variables are referred to as **data structures**.

Every variable has two important aspects.

1) Its **name**
2) Its **value**

The name of a variable is the **identifier** that is used to refer to that variable within a program. The value of a variable is the data stored by that variable. For example, suppose a program is written to maintain the inventory of a grocery store. This program contains a variable, *named* NumberOfJellyJars, that stores the *value* 100.

A variable can store only one value. Suppose that a new delivery of one thousand jars of jelly were added to the inventory by the program. This would cause the the value 1100 to be assigned to NumberOfJellyJars. The fact that NumberOfJellyJars used to have a value of 100 cannot be ascertained from this single variable.

Many programming languages, including Modula-2, require that every variable be **declared**. Modula-2 declarations are signified by the identifier VAR. Below is a segment of a program in Modula-2 that declares the variable NumberOfJellyJars.

```
VAR NumberOfJellyJars : INTEGER;
```

A VAR declaration specifies two characteristics of the variable.

1) The *name* of the variable
2) The *type* of the variable

In this case the name of the variable is NumberOfJellyJars and the type is INTE-GER.

Programming-with-Style

Choosing Meaningful Identifiers

One of the most important characteristics of a well written program is carefully chosen identifiers. Since variable names are identifiers, it is important to choose good variable names. Suppose the identifier J had been used in place of NumberOfJellyJars. It is unlikely that anyone but the coder would be able to understand what is meant by J. In time even the coder is likely to forget. Reading, debugging and maintaining programs with such obscure identifiers is a difficult task. It is important to choose good identifiers, but it isn't always easy. A well chosen name reflects the identifier's purpose. There are no absolute rules for selecting good identifiers, but the guidelines below can be helpful.

Some Guidelines for Selecting Meaningful Identifiers

1. Don't use single character identifiers unless no better name exists.
2. Try to make the identifiers as short as possible and still maintain the meaning.
3. Capitalize the first letter of each English word within an identifier, but do not capitalize the other letters.
4. Don't include spaces in identifiers, since they are not allowed.

Below are pairs of identifiers. The better identifier in each pair is indicated, along with the reason it is better.

Poor Identifier	Better Identifier	Reason
Z	NumberOfZsSold	Z is meaningless
maximumage	MaximumAge	better use of caps
TotalNumberPainted	NumberPainted	more succinct

2.2 SYNTAX DIAGRAMS

Communicating to a computer via a program is far more demanding than communicating with another person. A person might find any of the following lines to be an acceptable replacement for the declaration of NumberOfJellyJars given in Section 2.1.

```
VARIABLE  NumberOfJellyJars : INTEGER;

VAR NumberOfJellyJars - INTEGER;

NumberOfJellyJars is an INTEGER;
```

However, in Modula-2 all three of these attempts to declare NumberOfJellyJars are totally unrecognizable.

The **syntax** of a program is its grammatical form. There are rules for every programming language that define the permissible syntax of programs written in that language. Natural languages also have syntactic rules. The syntax of natural languages is defined by rules of grammar and spelling. The syntax of a programming language is much less complex than that of a natural language, but more strictly enforced.

A **character** can be defined to be a single input or output symbol. Most of the keys on a computer keyboard represent single characters. Uppercase alphabetic letters (i.e. "A", "B", ..., "Z"), lowercase alphabetic letters (i.e. "a", "b", ..., "z"), and decimal digits (i.e. "0", "1", ..., "9") are all characters. There are many other symbols that are also characters, such as "?", "<", and "$". Even a single space or blank is a character (in this book a space will often be symbolized as b over-slash, "Ƀ". A **character string** is a sequence of consecutive characters. For example, the declaration

VAR NumberOfJellyJars : INTEGER,

consists of a string of thirty-two characters. The first four characters of the string are "V", "A", "R" and "Ƀ".

Syntax diagrams are graphic structures used to describe a collection of character strings. Any valid path through a syntax diagram represents a syntactically acceptable character string. One can trace a path by following the sequence of characters and arrows, beginning with the arrow entering at the left and ending at the arrow leaving on the right. Using syntax diagrams is like playing a board game — moving from square to square by following the arrows.

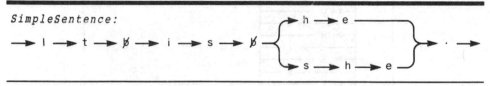

SimpleSentence:

FIGURE 2.1 *An example of a syntax diagram*

Figure 2.1 describes two syntactically correct character strings. The string described by the upper path is

It is he.

The string described by the lower path is

It is she.

No other character strings are syntactically correct for this diagram. It is helpful to name different syntax diagrams. The diagram in Figure 2.1 is named "SimpleSentence."

The syntax of a Modula-2 identifier is defined in Figure 2.2 on the following page. This syntax diagram shows that an identifier must begin with an alphabetic letter followed by zero or more letters and/or numeric digits.

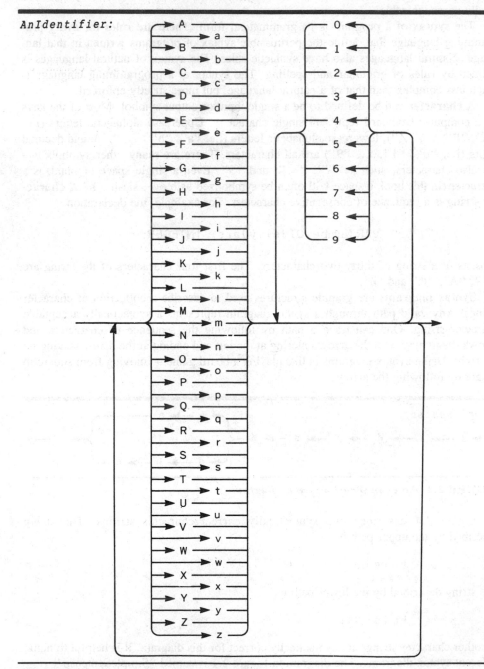

FIGURE 2.2 *Syntax diagram for identifier*

Figure 2.3 defines Identifier, AlphaChar, and Digit in three separate syntax diagrams. AlphaChar is defined as any single uppercase or lowercase alphabetic character.

Digit is defined as any single decimal digit. Identifier is defined in terms of of Alpha-Char and Digit. The *name* of one syntax diagram can replace the diagram when used within another diagram. In this case, the syntax for Identifier is defined to be a single AlphaChar followed by zero or more AlphaChars and/or Digits.

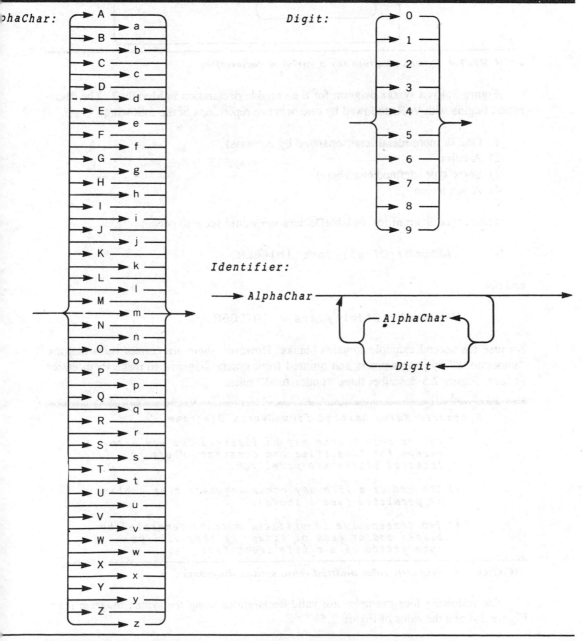

FIGURE 2.3 *Syntax diagram for Identifier, AlphaChar, and Digit*

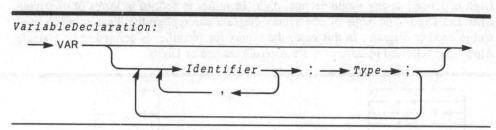

VariableDeclaration:

FIGURE 2.4 *Syntax diagram for a variable declaration*

Figure 2.4 is a syntax diagram for the variable declaration in Modula-2. The declaration begins with VAR, followed by one or more repetitions of the following.

1) One or more identifiers (separated by commas)
2) A colon
3) Some type (defined elsewhere)
4) A semicolon

The syntax diagram for VariableDeclaration would seem to permit

VARNumberOfJellyJars:INTEGER;

and not

VAR NumberOfJellyJars : INTEGER;

because the second example contains blanks. However, there are certain rules that are "understood" by programmers and omitted from syntax diagrams to make them easier to read. Figure 2.5 describes three "understood" rules.

Syntactic Rules Omitted from Syntax Diagrams

1) One or more blanks may be inserted for any arrow except for Identifier and Constant, where no internal blanks are permitted.

2) The end of a line may occur anywhere that a blank is permitted (see 1 above).

3) Two consecutive identifiers must be separated by blanks and/or ends of lines, or they will be interpreted as a single identifier.

FIGURE 2.5 *Syntactic rules omitted from syntax diagrams*

The following four examples are valid declarations using the syntax diagram from Figure 2.4 and the rules of Figure 2.5.

```
VAR NumberOfJellyJars : INTEGER;
VAR NumberOfJellyJars : INTEGER;
VAR NumberOfJellyJars : INTEGER ;
VAR
    NumberOfJellyJars : INTEGER;
```

The character string

```
VARNumberOfJellyJars:INTEGER;
```

is not a syntactically correct VariableDeclaration because it violates Rule 3 of the rules stated in Figure 2.5. This rule requires that VAR and NumberOfJellyJars be separated in order to be two identifiers.

2.3 SEMANTICS

Programs, like English sentences, have both form and meaning. The meaning of a program is called its **semantics**. The semantics of the Modula-2 character string

```
VAR NumberOfJellyJars : INTEGER;
```

tell us that this is a declaration of a variable whose name is NumberOfJellyJars and whose value is to be of type INTEGER. Syntax diagrams specify only syntax; a description of semantics needs to be added for a thorough definition. A complete definition for the variable declaration of Modula-2 is given in Figure 2.6. Notice how the semantic portion describes the purpose of the syntax and adds other important details.

VariableDeclaration:

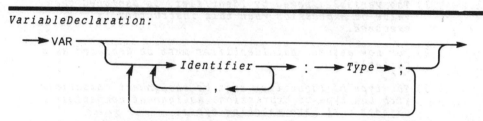

Semantics of VariableDeclaration:

1) All Identifiers specified in a list before the colon are declared to be the names of individual variables that store values of the identical Type specified after the colon.

2) No identifer may be included in a VariableDeclaration that has been previously declared within the same program unit.

3) Certain identifiers, known as reserved words, cannot be declared as variables. Appendix B contains a complete list of the reserved words for Modula-2.

FIGURE 2.6 *Syntax and semantics of VariableDeclaration*

Humans might be satisfied using "No.OfJellyJars", "NumberOfJarsOfJelly", "JellyJarCount" or, "NumberOfJellyJars" as the name of the variable previously declared. However, Modula-2 will not accept any of these options. If a variable name is declared to be NumberOfJellyJars, then anything else is viewed as a misspelling for this variable.

Many programming languages do not recognize any difference between uppercase and lowercase letters. Modula-2 is different; it is said to be a **case sensitive** language. In Modula-2 every lower-case letter is different from every upper-case letter. This case sensitivity means that NumberOfJellyJars, NUMBEROFJELLYJARS, and numberofjellyjars represent three *different* identifiers.

Modula-2 is a **strongly typed** language; different types of data are carefully distinguished from each other. Every variable of a strongly typed language is restricted to storing values of a single type. The type of the variable also limits the different places where it may be used. NumberOfJellyJars may only be used where integer variables are allowed, when it is declared with an INTEGER type.

2.4 THE ASSIGNMENT INSTRUCTION

An **assignment instruction** can be used to assign a value to any previously declared variable. The syntax and semantics of the Modula-2 assignment instruction are specified in Figure 2.7.

AssignmentInstr:

⟶ Identifier ⟶ := ⟶ Expression ⟶

Semantics of AssignmentInstr:

1) The variable, named by Identifier, is assigned the value of Expression when this instruction is executed.

2) For now assume that Identifier must be declared as a variable.

3) The type of Identifier must be assignment compatible with the type of Expression. Assignment compatible objects must have matching types.

FIGURE 2.7 *The syntax and semantics of AssignmentInstr*

Suppose that a Modula-2 program contained the following declarations:

```
VAR
    JarsOfJelly : INTEGER;
    JarsOfPeanutButter : INTEGER;
    LoavesOfBread : INTEGER;

VAR
    QuartsOfMilk : INTEGER;
    PintsOfCottageCheese : INTEGER;
```

This program contains six variables of type INTEGER. Below are three assignment instructions that are valid following the above declarations:

$$JarsOfJelly := 17;$$

$$CupsOfYogurt := 0;$$

$$QuartsOfMilk := -3;$$

In the first assignment `JarsOfJelly` is assigned the value 17. In the second assignment `CupsOfYogurt` is assigned 0. In the last instruction, QuartsOfMilk is assigned -3 (perhaps to indicate a back order in inventory). Figure 2.8 contains several incorrect attempted at assignment instructions, illustrating common programming errors.

Incorrect Instruction	Reason
JarsOfJam := 17;	JarsOfJam *is not a declared variable.*
LoavesOfBread = 0;	*"=" appears where ":=" is required.*
74 := JarsOfPeanutButter;	*The variable must appear on the left side of the ":=".*
PintsOfCottageCheese:=75.32;	*"75.32" is not an integer.*

FIGURE 2.8 *Invalid attempted assignment instructions*

2.5 INTEGER: A SCALAR DATA TYPE

The data types used in programming languages can be classified into either of two categories.

scalar data types
structured data types

Scalar data types are the simplest possible data types. By contrast, **structured data types** consist of some combination of scalar data types. A typical structured data type consists of many individual scalar pieces. The pieces may be of scalar type or of another structured type. Any data type has three associated components.

1) Its name
2) A set of constants of that type
3) A set of operations upon that type

The **name** of a type is the identifier used to designate the type in declarations. A **constant** is a symbol for a value that may be assigned to a variable of compatible type.

Operations are used to construct expressions for the type. For example, Modula-2 includes an integer data type, and

1) INTEGER is the name of the type.
2) 32 is a constant of the integer type.
3) Addition(+) is one operation permitted on integer data.

Modula-2 supports nine built-in scalar data types: INTEGER, CARDINAL, REAL, CHAR, BOOLEAN, POINTER, BITSET, enumerated, and subrange. The first four scalar types are presented in this chapter.

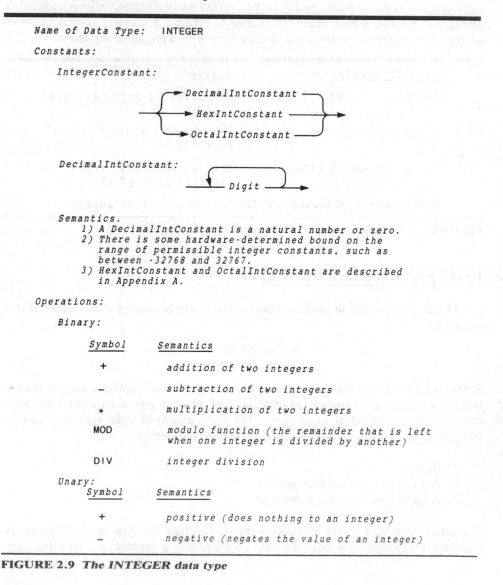

```
Name of Data Type:    INTEGER

Constants:

    IntegerConstant:

                        ┌──► DecimalIntConstant ──┐
                    ───┤ ──► HexIntConstant ───────├──►
                        └──► OctalIntConstant ────┘

    DecimalIntConstant:

                    ──────── Digit ───────►

Semantics.
    1) A DecimalIntConstant is a natural number or zero.
    2) There is some hardware-determined bound on the
       range of permissible integer constants, such as
       between -32768 and 32767.
    3) HexIntConstant and OctalIntConstant are described
       in Appendix A.

Operations:

    Binary:

        Symbol      Semantics

          +         addition of two integers

          -         subtraction of two integers

          *         multiplication of two integers

         MOD        modulo function (the remainder that is left
                    when one integer is divided by another)

         DIV        integer division

    Unary:
        Symbol      Semantics

          +         positive (does nothing to an integer)

          -         negative (negates the value of an integer)
```

FIGURE 2.9 *The INTEGER data type*

Figure 2.9 specifies important details about the **INTEGER** data type. Constants of this type are similar to those used in arithmetic. Below are four syntactically correct Modula-2 INTEGER constants.

<u>Valid INTEGER constants</u>

7534

32

0

0001

Below are two invalid INTEGER constants.

<u>Invalid INTEGER constants</u>

32.7 ← decimal point not permitted

7,645 ← commas not permitted

INTEGER operations may be use to combine INTEGER values into INTEGER expressions. For example

66 + 13

is an INTEGER expression that uses the INTEGER operation +. The + symbol is used in Modula-2 to denote addition, so the value of this expression is 79.

One place where expressions are used extensively is the assignment instruction. Below are several assignment instructions which assign the value of an INTEGER expression to an INTEGER variable.

LoavesOfBread : = 24 * 10   assigns 240 to LoavesOfBread

JarsOfJelly : = 100 + 1000   assigns 1100 to JarsOfJelly

QuartsOfMilk : = 2000 − 2016   assigns -16 to QuartsOfMilk

JarsOfPeanutButter : = −3   assigns -3 to JarsOfPeanutButter

CupsOfYogurt : = +4   assigns 4 to CupsOfYogurt

Most of the INTEGER operations are commonly used in mathematics. Two operations, DIV and MOD, are more unusual. DIV symbolizes integer division, the integer portion of the result from dividing two integers. For example 14 DIV 3 has the value 4 and −9 DIV 2 has the value -4.

MOD is the Modula-2 operator that denotes the remainder of an integer division. The value of 14 MOD 3 is 2, because 14 divided by 3 is 4 with a remainder of 2. The MOD operation is more complicated when negative values are used.

Wirth defined MOD this way:

$$x \ MOD \ y \ = \ x - ((x \ DIV \ y) * y)$$

when he defined Modula-2.

2.6 INTEGER EXPRESSIONS

INTEGER expressions may be far more complicated than a single operator and two INTEGER constants. The complete syntax for an integer expression is defined as SimpleIntegerExpression in Figure 2.10.

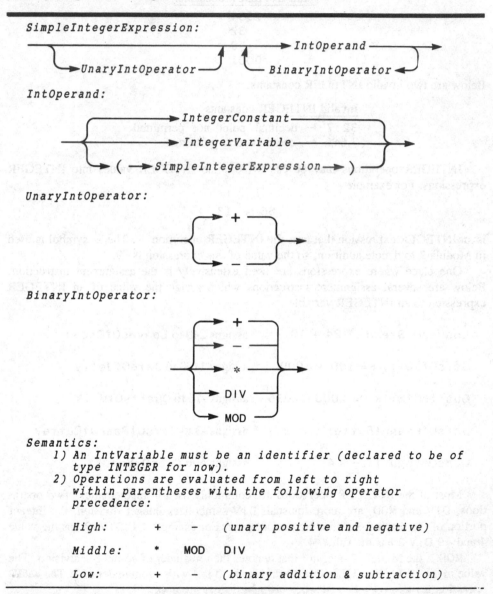

```
SimpleIntegerExpression:
```

```
IntOperand:
```

```
UnaryIntOperator:
```

```
BinaryIntOperator:
```

```
Semantics:
    1) An IntVariable must be an identifier (declared to be of
       type INTEGER for now).
    2) Operations are evaluated from left to right
       within parentheses with the following operator
       precedence:

    High:        +      -      (unary positive and negative)

    Middle:      *    MOD  DIV

    Low:         +      -      (binary addition & subtraction)
```

FIGURE 2.10 Description of SimpleIntegerExpression

The order in which operations are performed determines the value of an expression.

Suppose the expression 3 + 2 * 4 is to be evaluated. If the " + " operation is performed first, then the resulting value is

$$(3 + 2) * 4 \ = \ 5 * 4 \ = \ 20$$

If the "*" is the first operation performed, then the expression evaluates as

$$3 + (2 * 4) \ = \ 3 + 8 \ = \ 11$$

The rules for expression evaluation in Modula-2 are like mathematical rules, making use of **operator precedence**.

1) Expressions within parentheses are evaluated first (beginning with the innermost parentheses).
2) Within an unparenthesized expression all operations of higher precedence are performed before any with lower precedence (see Figure 2.10).
3) Within an unparenthesized expression all operations of equal precedence are performed left to right.

An example of an evaluation of an INTEGER expression is shown in Figure 2.11. This expression is evaluated operation by operation in the same order as Modula-2.

Expression	Operation performed
(-1 + 2 * (3 - 4 * ((6 - 3) DIV 2)) * 7) - 8)	
(-1 + 2 * (3 - 4 * ([3] DIV 2) * 7) - 8)	6 - 3
(-1 + 2 * (3 - 4 * [1] * 7) - 8)	3 DIV 2
(-1 + 2 * (3 - [4] * 7) - 8)	4 * 1
(-1 + 2 * (3 - [28]) - 8)	4 * 7
(-1 + 2 * [-25] - 8)	3 - 28
([-1]+2 * (-25) - 8)	-1 (unary)
(-1 + [-50] - 8)	2 * (-25)
([-51] - 8)	-1 + (-50)
[-59]	-51 - 8

FIGURE 2.11 *Example expression evaluation*

INTEGER expressions may include INTEGER variables, as well as constants. When a variable is used in an expression, then the variable's value is used during evaluation. Suppose the value of NumberOfJarsOfJelly is 100, then the value of the expression NumberOfJarsOfJelly * 3 is 100 * 3, or 300.

2.7 MORE SCALAR TYPES

In addition to INTEGER, Modula-2 supports two other numeric data types, the **CARDINAL** data type is described in Figure 2.12 and the **REAL** data type in Figure 2.13.

```
Name of Data Type:  CARDINAL

Constants:

   CardinalConstant:
```

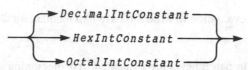

```
   Semantics:
       1) A CardinalConstant is a positive integer or zero.
       2) There is some hardware-determined upper bound on
          the range of permissible CARDINAL constants, such
          as 65535.

   Operations:

       Binary:
```

Symbol	Semantics
+	addition of two cardinals
–	subtraction of two cardinals
*	multiplication of two cardinals
MOD	modulo function (the remainder left when one cardinal is divided by another)
DIV	cardinal division

```
       Unary:
```

Symbol	Semantics
+	positive (does nothing to a cardinal)

FIGURE 2.12 *The CARDINAL data type*

CARDINAL and INTEGER data types are very similar. CARDINAL values are restricted to positive integers, while INTEGERs may be positive or negative. Because they do not store negatives, CARDINALs can usually store larger numbers than INTEGERs. A typical Modula-2 implementation restricts INTEGER values to the range from -32,768 through 32,767, while CARDINAL values are restricted to 0 through 65,535. These restrictions on the size of a value of type INTEGER and CARDINAL do not apply to REAL values. In addition REAL values can store decimal, fractional, values.

```
Name of Data Type:   REAL

Constants:

    RealConstant:
```

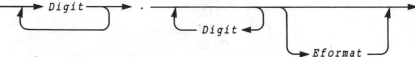

```
    Eformat:
```

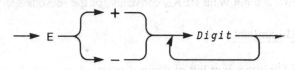

```
    Semantics:
        1) A RealConstant is a positive or negative decimal
           number.
        2) Eformat is a form of scientific notation, where
           "E+n" is interpreted as "times ten raised to the
           nth power."

Operations:

    Binary:

        Symbol      Semantics

          +              addition of two reals

          -              subtraction of two reals

          *              multiplication of two reals

          /              division of two reals
                         (one real divided by another)

    Unary:
        Symbol      Semantics

          +              positive (does nothing to a real )

          -              negative (negates the value of a real)


    Expression evaluation: same as INTEGER with "/"
                           precedence equal to "*"
```

FIGURE 2.13 The REAL data type

Some valid REAL constants are given below.

<u>Valid REAL constants</u>

75.4
0.25
(272.)
-63.4
99.E3

The numbers below are not valid REAL constants for the reasons specified.

<u>Invalid REAL constants</u>

.7   ← one Digit required left of decimal point
28   ← CARDINAL or INTEGER constant
7A.25   ← "A" not a Digit

The rules for expression evaluation of CARDINAL and REAL expressions are like those of INTEGER expressions. Because of the way that REAL values are stored, they are not always exact. Instead, they approximate the precise value as accurately as possible.

Programming-with-Style

How to Choose Among CARDINAL, INTEGER, and REAL

The Modula-2 programmer has three numeric data types from which to choose: INTEGER. CARDINAL and REAL. Below is the best order to choose from.

1) CARDINAL
2) INTEGER
3) REAL

There are advantages to each of the three types that make them all useful. Since REAI values store approximations, they are usually chosen last. However, when a decimal value mus be stored a REAL is required. CARDINAL is preferred over INTEGER when the data is known to always be positive.

Programs process much data that is non-numeric. An employer might wish to store the name, age, sex, education, and experience of an employee. Of these five pieces of employee information, only age is necessarily numeric data. One non-numeric data type supported by Modula-2 is the **CHAR** data type, as defined in Figure 2.14. A CHAR is a data type for a single character.

Name of Data Type: CHAR

Constants:

   CharConstant:

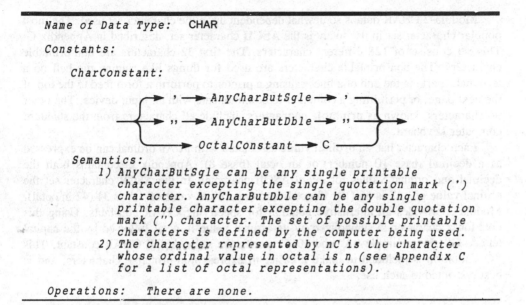

   Semantics:
     1) AnyCharButSgle can be any single printable
       character excepting the single quotation mark (')
       character. AnyCharButDble can be any single
       printable character excepting the double quotation
       mark (") character. The set of possible printable
       characters is defined by the computer being used.
     2) The character represented by nC is the character
       whose ordinal value in octal is n (see Appendix C
       for a list of octal representations).

Operations: *There are none.*

FIGURE 2.14 *The CHAR data type*

A CHAR constant is generally symbolized as a single character within single quotation marks or a single character within double quotation marks. Below are several examples of CHAR constants.

Valid CHAR constants
"A"
'b'
"$"
" ' "
"3"
" " — a blank or space

The following erroneous CHAR constants illustrate some common problems in writing CHAR constants.

Invalid CHAR constant	Reason
"ab"	← more than one character within quotes
' '	← no characters within quotes
" " "	← enclosing quotes cannot be the same as the character within
"a'	← must begin and end with same type quote mark (either single or double)

Modula-2 CHAR data is somewhat dependent upon the character set used. The most popular character set in use today is the **ASCII** character set, described in Appendix C. This set consists of 128 different characters. The first 32 characters are non-printable characters. The non-printable characters are used for things like ringing the bell on a terminal, marking the end of a line, causing a printer to perform a form feed to the top of the next page, or permitting a computer to communicate with an input device. The other 96 characters, known as **printable characters**, include all characters from the standard computer keyboard.

Each character has an **ordinal value** associated with it. An ordinal can be expressed as a decimal (base 10 number) or an octal (base 8). Appendix C contains both the decimal and ordinal values for every ASCII character. In the ASCII character set the ordinal value of "A" is 65 (101 in octal) and the ordinal value of "!" is 34 (42 in octal). Modula-2 provides an alternative notation for specifying CHAR constants. Using this notation a character is symbolized by its ordinal value in octal followed by the capital letter "C". For example "A" and 101C specify the same ASCII CHAR constant. This "C" notation is included to make it easier to express non-printable characters, and is best restricted to such use.

2.8 STRONG DATA TYPING

The *type* of every constant, variable, and expression is important in a strongly typed language. Programs must declare the type of every variable. In addition, strict compatibility rules must be followed. Three of these rules for Modula-2 are.

1) In every assignment instruction, the variable and expression to be assigned must be **assignment compatible**, either identical or one is CARDINAL and the other INTEGER.
2) Every operation is defined for particular types of operands.
3) Two operands joined by an operator must have **compatible** type. For now, compatible operands must have identical type.

Modula-2 allows one expression to be assigned to a variable as long as the expression and variable have the same type. For example, the INTEGER variable NumberOfJellyJars may be used as follows

```
NumberOfJellyJars := 3
```

because 3 is an INTEGER expression. On the other hand, the following two assignment instructions are not permissible, since 2.1 is a REAL and "A" is a CHAR constant.

```
NumberOfJellyJars := 2.1

NumberOfJellyJars := "A"
```

The following instruction may appear to be valid

```
NumberOfJellyJars := "5"
```

but it is not. The expression in this case is of type CHAR. The fact that the particular character is "5" is irrelevant.

Initially, the strongly typed nature of Modula-2 may seem awkward for numeric expressions. In mathematics there is often no distinction among REAL, INTEGER and CARDINAL, but Modula-2 does not allow such freedom. It is possible to multiply either two INTEGER expressions, or two CARDINAL expressions, or two REAL expressions, but no other combinations are allowed.

The main source of confusion in sorting out "what can be multiplied by what" seems to stem from the use of **overloaded** operators. An overloaded operator is one that can express different functions. The asterisk, "*", is overloaded because it can symbolize any of three operations.

1) INTEGER multiplication (the multiplication of two INTEGER expressions)
2) CARDINAL multiplication (the multiplication of two CARDINALs)
3) REAL multiplication (the multiplication of two REALs)

The " + " operator is overloaded with six different operations — the unary positive operation and the binary addition operation for all three numeric types. Interestingly, the "/" operator is not overloaded, because CARDINALs and INTEGERs use the integer division operator, DIV. Figure 2.15 summarizes overloading for all numeric operations.

The following operations are permitted for all three numeric types (INTEGER, CARDINAL and REAL) so long as operands have identical type.

```
    +   (unary positive)
    -   (unary negative)
    +   (addition)
    -   (subtraction)
    *   (multiplication)
```

The following operations are permitted when both operands have INTEGER or both CARDINAL type.

```
    DIV (integer division)
    MOD (modulo — integer remainder)
```

The following operation is permitted only when both operands have REAL type.

```
    /   (real division)
```

FIGURE 2.15 *Permissible numeric operations*

On the following page is a list of valid Modula-2 expressions and the type of the values of these expressions, assuming that the variable AstronautCount is of type CARDINAL, TimeToLiftoff is REAL, and ControlCode is INTEGER.

Valid Modula-2 Expressions

Expression	Type
AstronautCount + 1	CARDINAL
ControlCode * 17	INTEGER
TimeToLiftoff + 60.0	REAL

The table below illustrates erroneous expressions.

Expression	Reason
ControlCode / 2	"/" requires operands to be REAL and 2 is not (see Figure 2.13)
ControlCode / 2.0	"/" requires both operands to be REAL and ControlCode is not
AstronautCount + ControlCode	the two variables are of different types
AstronautCount – 1.0	the variable is CARDINAL and the constant is REAL
TimeToLiftoff + 60	the variable is REAL and the constant is either INTEGER of CARDINAL

The principles of strong typing in numeric expressions are slightly relaxed for INTEGER and CARDINAL. Modula-2 allows a positive constant within the range of the INTEGER values to be treated as either an INTEGER or a CARDINAL. This means that both

ControlCode + 7

and

AstronautCount + 7

are permissible. Modula-2 also allows an INTEGER expression to be assigned to a CARDINAL variable or a CARDINAL expression to be assigned to an INTEGER variable.

Sometimes a coder needs to mix expressions of different types. Modula-2 provides for this possibility with **type conversion functions**. A type conversion function translates an expression of one type into a value of another type. The syntax of type conversion functions is defined in Figure 2.16.

`NumericTypeConversionFunction:`

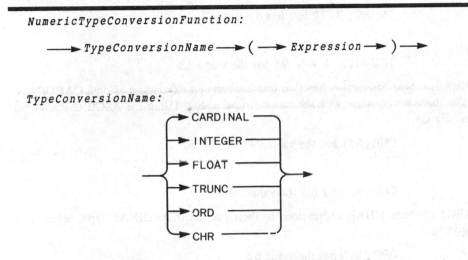

`TypeConversionName:`

Note: *Each type conversion function is designed to convert an expression of one type into another, as follows.*

Function	Initial type	Resulting type
CARDINAL	INTEGER	CARDINAL
INTEGER	CARDINAL	INTEGER
FLOAT	CARDINAL	REAL
TRUNC	REAL	CARDINAL
CHR	CARDINAL	CHAR
ORD	CHARACTER *or* INTEGER *or* CARDINAL *or* enumerated	CARDINAL

FIGURE 2.16 *The syntax of type conversion functions*

The following invalid expression:

        AstronautCount + ControlCode

can be corrected as

        AstronautCount + CARDINAL(ControlCode)

or

$$INTEGER(AstronautCount) + ControlCode$$

The CARDINAL, INTEGER, and FLOAT type conversion functions translate a numeric value to its equivalent value as a different type. The TRUNC function converts from REAL to CARDINAL by **truncating** the expression to its integer portion. For example

$$TRUNC(3.7256) \text{ has the value } 3$$

and

$$TRUNC(7.7 + 5.9) \text{ has the value } 13$$

CHR is a type conversion function that converts an expression of type CARDINAL into the character constant with the same ordinal value. Using the ASCII character set (Appendix C)

$$CHR(52) \text{ has the value "4"}$$

and

$$CHR(60+5) \text{ has the value "A".}$$

ORD converts CHR expressions to their ordinal, CARDINAL type, value. For example

$$ORD("A") \text{ has the value } 65$$

Using type conversion functions require that the value to be converted fall within permissible bounds. For example, CARDINAL(-3) produces an error since -3 is negative and CARDINAL values must be positive. Such an error is called a **type conversion error** or **bounds violation**.

2.9 SEQUENCES OF INSTRUCTIONS

Suppose that the following declarations are included in a Modula-2 program.

```
VAR
    Snowflakes:     CARDINAL;
    WaterContent:   REAL;
    Snowball:       CARDINAL;
    MoreFlakes:     CARDINAL;
```

If the following three assignments are executed in order

```
Snowflakes  := 4;
WaterContent := 3.4;
Snowflakes  := 7;
```

then WaterContent stores the value 3.4, and Snowflakes stores the value 7. The **control flow**, order of execution, is important. If the first and last instructions were executed in the opposite order, then Snowflakes would store 4 afterwards.

The control flow in Modula-2 defines that at most one instruction will be executing at any time. Normal control flow is **sequential** because it proceeds from one instruction to the next. In later chapters, instructions that alter this sequential flow will be examined. Figure 2.17 defines the syntax for a sequence of instructions.

InstructionSequence:

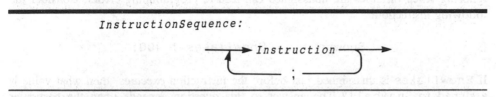

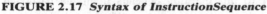

FIGURE 2.17 *Syntax of InstructionSequence*

Thus far, the only Modula-2 instruction discussed is the assignment instruction. Another valid Modula-2 instruction is called the **null instruction.** The null instruction gets its name from the fact that it has no characters and represents nothing to be executed. The null instruction is significant because it simplifies the rules for placing semicolons in programs. Figure 2.17 specifies that two consecutive instructions must be *separated* by a semicolon. The inclusion of a null instruction allows a semicolon at the end of any sequence of instructions. In this instruction sequence:

```
Snowflakes  := 7;
WaterContents := 3.4;
Snowflakes  := 4;
```

the semicolons after the first two assignments are required separators, but the semicolon after the last instruction is optional. It signifies a separation from an invisible final null instruction.

A programmer must be able to **trace** the execution of a section of code, imitating how a computer executes. One technique that is useful in tracing is to examine the values of variables throughout execution. Figure 2.18 traces the execution of the previous sequence of instructions.

Instruction Executed	Snowflakes	WaterContents
Snowflakes := 7;	7	
WaterContents := 3.4;		3.4
Snowflakes := 4;	4	

FIGURE 2.18 *A trace of a sequence of assignment instructions*

A programmer begins a trace by listing variable names across a page. Next each instruction is examined, one at a time, in the order of execution. As the first instruction, Snowflakes:=7;, is traced, a "7" is placed in the column under Snowflakes. This records that the variable now stores 7. Similarly, "3.4" is placed under the WaterContents column when the second instruction is traced. Tracing the final instruction, Snowflakes:=4; causes the programmer to place the number "4" under the earlier value of 7. At any time during a trace the bottom-most value in a column records what is stored in the variable. Therefore, after the instruction sequence, Snow-flakes stores 4 and `WaterContents` stores 3.4.

Variables are not assigned any value before a program begins to execute. A newly declared variable must be assumed to be **unassigned**, because its value is **undefined**. Ignoring when variables are unassigned can lead to programming errors. Consider the following instruction:

$$\text{Snowball} := \text{Snowflakes} * 400;$$

If `Snowflakes` is unassigned just before the instruction executes, then what value is assigned to `Snowball`? The answer to this question depends upon the particular Modula-2 system. Many systems will display some message to notify the programmer of the error. Other systems permit the assignment to execute, but cause some meaningless value to be stored in `Snowball`. In either case the programmer has committed an error. It is important to be certain that a variable is assigned before including the variable in some expression. Such errors can be detected by a trace.

Programs frequently swap the contents of two variables. For example, suppose that `Snowflakes` and `MoreFlakes` are both assigned variables whose values must be interchanged. The following instruction sequence may look like the correct solution, but it isn't.

$$\text{Snowflakes} := \text{MoreFlakes};$$
$$\text{MoreFlakes} := \text{Snowflakes}$$

The error in this code is uncovered by tracing its execution. Assume that the initial value of Snowflakes is 1 and MoreFlakes is 3.

Instruction Executed	Snowflakes	MoreFlakes
	1	3
Snowflakes := MoreFlakes;	3	
MoreFlakes := Snowflakes;		3

The problem with this attempted swapping code is that assigning a value to Snow-flakes causes the previous value of Snowflakes to be lost. The correct code requires a third cardinal variable, call it TempFlakes, to store the original value of Snowflakes temporarily. The solution is

$$\text{TempFlakes} := \text{Snowflakes};$$
$$\text{Snowflakes} := \text{MoreFlakes};$$
$$\text{MoreFlakes} := \text{TempFlakes}$$

Another trace illustrates how the code has been corrected.

Instruction Executed	Snowflakes	MoreFlakes	TempFlakes
	1	3	
TempFlakes : = Snowflakes;			1
Snowflakes : = MoreFlakes;	3		
MoreFlakes : = TempFlakes;		1	

*P*rogramming-with-*S*tyle

There are two very simple but important rules to remember when writing a list of sequential instructions.

1) List one instruction per line unless there is a *very* good reason for doing otherwise.
2) *Indentation* is critical for code readability. Begin each instruction of a sequence in the same column.

2.10 THE COMMENT

A **comment** is a character string inserted anywhere within a program in order to aid with reading the code. Comments have no effect on the execution. They serve as internal documentation.

The syntax of the Modula-2 comment, as specified in Figure 2.19, consists of a character string bracketed by (* and *). It may be placed anywhere that a blank is permitted, and may be as short as a few characters or as long as several lines.

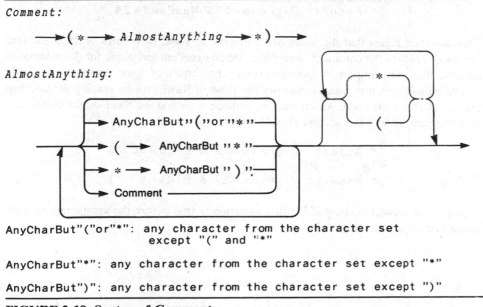

Comment:

AlmostAnything:

AnyCharBut"("or"*": any character from the character set
            except "(" and "*"

AnyCharBut"*": any character from the character set except "*"

AnyCharBut")": any character from the character set except ")"

FIGURE 2.19 *Syntax of Comment*

It is possible to **nest** comments. Comments or other structures are considered to be nested whenever one is entirely enclosed within another. Below is an example of a nested comment.

```
(* A nested comment follows: (* This is nested *) *)
```

Every comment must be closed with the two character sequence *). A common programming error is forgetting to close a comment.

Comments are useful to programmers in many ways. Frequently, a short comment is included to describe an identifier when it is declared. Such a use of comments is exemplified below:

```
VAR
    Pigs : CARDINAL;     (* total number of pigs for 12/5/86 *)
    PigPens : CARDINAL;  (* count as of 12/5/86 *)
    NewPens : CARDINAL;  (* pigpens on order as of 12/5/86 *)
```

Comments are also useful just before a particularly difficult piece of code in order to clarify its purpose.

Perhaps the most important style of commenting that a programmer can use is called an **assertion**. Assertions are comments that describe variable contents. An assertion is placed at the location in the program where it will be true at the time of execution. An assertion identifies "what is true at this point in the program execution" and not "how this situation occurred." Below is one example of an assertion.

```
PigPens := 5;
NewPens := (PigPens+3) * (2+1)
(* Assert: PigPens=5 & NewPens=24 *)
```

This assertion states that the value of PigPens is 5 and NewPens is 24 at the time execution reaches the comment. Assertions are an excellent technique for documentation because they state important facts describing the results of some computation. In the preceding example it is easier to identify the value of NewPens by reading the assertion tnan it is to trace the code. Assertions also provide a method for checking the correctness of a program. Below is a section of code with two assertions.

```
(* Assert: PigPens=20 & Pigs=50 *)
Pigs := Pigs + 10;
(* Assert: PigPens=20 & Pigs=60 *)
```

This code is correct because if the first assertion is true before the assignment then the second must be true afterwards.

*P*rogramming-with-*S*tyle

Some Hints on How to Use Comments Effectively

It should be considered mandatory to include comments in code. Comments enhance the *readability* of any program regardless of the task or programming language used. There are no concrete rules for using comments, but there are a few guidelines that should be followed.

1) Include enough comments. Remember that a program always seems readable when it is being written. Comments are included for later and/or for persons other than the original coder. A good goal is for 30% of a program to be comments.
2) Be careful not to include too many comments. It is possible to write a program with so many comments that they hide the code. If something is obvious without a comment, don't comment!
3) Comments ought to be included in such a way that they can be read with the code. Their indentation should be consistent with the code they describe. They should not obscure the code nor be hidden in a corner.
4) Good places to comment:
   - descriptions of identifiers when they are declared (on the same line when possible)
   - passages of code that are difficult to read
   - at the beginning of every major program segment a comment should be included to describe the purpose of the segment
   - as assertions at key checkpoints in the code (assertions should be fairly evenly spaced in the code and need only state the most important facts)

It seems ironic that the most important instruction in a programming language may be one that performs absolutely no function at the time of execution — the COMMENT!

2.11 STANDARD MODULA-2 OUTPUT VIA INOUT

Programs must interact with the "real world" in order to perform useful functions. This interaction takes the form of input and output (**I/O**). Any useful program outputs information in some form. Many programs also permit input.

Modula-2 is somewhat unusual because there are no standard I/O instructions included. The language is designed in this way to permit flexibility in supporting different kinds of I/O and different I/O devices. To allow such flexibility and still provide some standards, Niklaus Wirth included several "standard" I/O modules in the design of Modula-2. The most common of these is **InOut**. InOut is designed to perform I/O on devices like a standard computer terminal (keyboard and associated video display). The InOut module includes the following **procedures**.

Write to output one character
WriteInt to output one integer
WriteCard to output one cardinal
WriteString to output a string of characters
WriteLn to end a line of output and begin the next
Read to input one character
ReadInt to input one integer
ReadCard to input one cardinal

Each of these procedures performs a different task. The write procedures perform output of a single value. The read procedures input a single value into a variable. Furthermore, each procedure requires a specific data type. For example, the Write procedure outputs the value of a single CHAR on the computer display. Figure 2.20 describes this procedure.

WriteCall:

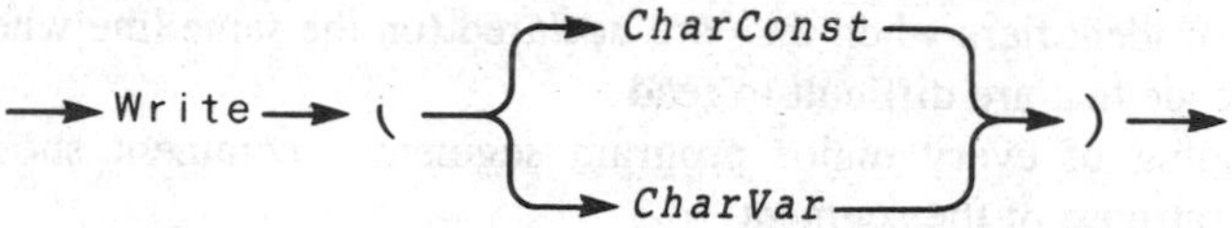

Semantics:

If CharConst (i.e., any character constant) is specified then the value of this constant is output to the display. If CharVar (i.e., any variable declared to be of type CHAR) is specified then the character last assigned to the variable is output.

FIGURE 2.20 *The Write procedure call*

Like other Modula-2 program units, procedures enforce strong data typing. The InOut Write procedure can be used to display a single character. The character value may be specified either by a character constant or a data structure of type CHAR. In order to display the value of other data types it is necessary to use a different procedure.

Computer video screens, and other similar character-oriented output devices, display characters in horizontal lines. A typical such video display is capable of forming twenty-four lines of eighty characters. Each execution of a Write procedure causes another character to be displayed on the same output line, immediately to the right of the previous character output. For example, the following sequence of procedure calls produce the output line Where's Sam?

```
Write( "W" );
Write( "h" );
Write( "e" );
Write( "r" );
Write( "e" );
Write( "'" );
Write( "s" );
Write( " " );
Write( "S" );
Write( "a" );
Write( "m" );
Write( "?" );
```

The above sequence of instructions is tedious. To avoid such lengthy sequences InOut includes another procedure called WriteString, defined in Figure 2.21.

WriteSringCall:

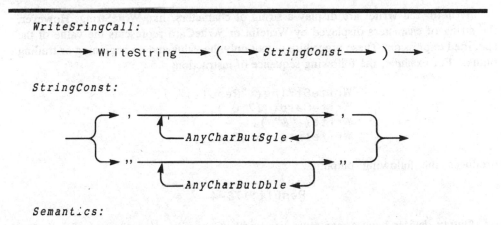

StringConst:

Semantics:

> *The characters specified between the quotes or double quotes are displayed in order.*

FIGURE 2.21 *The WriteString procedure call*

The previous example required eleven Write procedure calls to display the Where's Sam message. This same task can more appropriately be performed by the single WriteString instruction:.

WriteString("Where's Sam?")

WriteInt and WriteCard are included in InOut for the display of integer and cardinal expressions. These two procedure calls are defined in Figure 2.22.

WriteIntCall:

$\longrightarrow$ WriteInt $\longrightarrow$ ($\longrightarrow$ *IntegerExpression* $\longrightarrow$, $\longrightarrow$ 0 $\longrightarrow$) $\longrightarrow$

WriteCardCall:

$\longrightarrow$ WriteCard $\longrightarrow$ ($\longrightarrow$ *CardExpression* $\longrightarrow$, $\longrightarrow$ 0 $\longrightarrow$) $\longrightarrow$

Semantics:

IntegerExpression is a valid expression of type INTEGER.
CardExpression is a valid expression of type CARDINAL.
When one of these procedures is called the value of the
expression is displayed.

FIGURE 2.22 *The WriteInt and WriteCard procedure calls*

WriteInt and WriteCard display a string of characters, like WriteString. However, the string of characters displayed by WriteInt or WriteCard represents the value of the specified expression. These procedure output only the value and no beginning or trailing blanks. For example, the following sequence of instructions

```
WriteString( "Result:" );
WriteCard( 17,0 );
Write( "&" );
WriteInt( 16-20,0 );
```

produces the following output:

Result:17&-4

Output devices have a maximum line width. Generally, when the end of a display line is reached an output device will cause the output to be continued at the beginning of the next line. In practice, it is poor planning to permit this to occur. A better alternative is for the programmer explicitly to cause the output to proceed to the next line. In the InOut module from Modula-2 the facility that provides this carriage return capability is called WriteLn, described in Figure 2.23.

WriteLnCall:

$\longrightarrow$ WriteLn $\longrightarrow$

Semantics:

WriteLn causes succeeding output to begin on the next output
line.

FIGURE 2.23 *The WriteLn procedure call*

The execution of the sequences of instructions is traced below. "Resulting Output" indicates the exact form of output resulting from the execution. It is assumed that the output for each example begins at the left end of the first output line. Mileage is an INTEGER variable.

Instructions

```
Mileage := 17;

WriteString( "The mileage for this trip was ");
WriteInt( Mileage,0 );
Write( "." );
WriteLn;

WriteString( "Have a nice day!" );
WriteLn;
```

Resulting Output

```
The mileage for this trip was 17.
Have a nice day!
```

This example illustrates the useful technique of including a blank character at the end of the string constant and before the output of an integer. This forces a blank to precede the value of Mileage displayed by the next call. Without this blank, the first line of output would be:

```
The mileage for this trip was-17.
```

2.12 STANDARD INPUT VIA INOUT

Write, WriteString, WriteInt, WriteCard and WriteLn provide simple facilities for displaying character output from a Modula-2 program. However, the user of a program often needs to include *input* to the program as well. The most common of all computer input occurs when a user types at a keyboard. The executing program must input these keystrokes and store them in some variable(s).

Three of the procedures supplied in the InOut module for supporting input are Read, ReadInt and ReadCard. Each of these procedures inputs a single value (one or more characters) and assigns the value to a specified variable. The syntax for invoking these procedures is indicated in Figure 2.24.

ReadCalls:

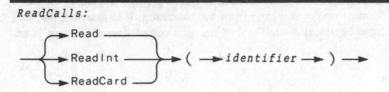

Semantics:

> *One data value specified in the form of a constant (see below) with appropriate type is received from the input device and assigned to the variable "identifier." The variable "identifier" must have type compatible with the particular call (i.e., CHAR for* Read*, INTEGER for* ReadInt*, and CARDINAL for* ReadCard*).*

> *Input data form:*

>> *ReadInputForm:*

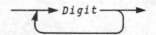

>> *ReadCardInputForm:*

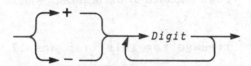

>> *ReadIntInputForm:*

FIGURE 2.24 *Description of Read, ReadInt, and ReadCard*

Each of these three procedures inputs, or reads, a single value from the input device. A Read inputs a single character; ReadCard inputs an unsigned integer; ReadInt inputs an optionally signed integer. A variable name must be supplied whenever one of the input procedures is called. The procedure assigns the value input to this variable.

Many I/O devices automatically **echo** the input. That is to say, when a user supplies input, the device displays the input as output. In some Modula-2 systems only the numeric digits supplied to ReadCard or ReadInt are echoed, and Read characters are not echoed at all.

Below is an example section of Modula-2 code using input and output.

```
WriteString( "How much do you weigh (in pounds)?" );
WriteLn;
ReadCard( PoundWeight);
```

To illustrate the execution of the above code assume that the user is using a video display terminal with attached keyboard for an I/O device. The execution of the first two instructions causes a single line of output to be produced with the indicated question. In order to complete the execution of the ReadCard instruction the program requires that the user type an appropriate value. A program *suspends execution* whenever input is needed until the input can be received. Suppose that the user wishes to respond with a weight of 200 pounds. An appropriate input would be for the user to strike four keys: The "2" key, the "0" key, the "0" again, and the "return" key. Since input is assumed to be echoed, the video display should appear as indicated in the following snapshot.

```
How much do you weigh (in pounds)?
200
```

Just as Modula-2 variables must be declared in a program prior to their use, so also InOut procedures must be declared. InOut procedure declaration is most conveniently accomplished via a special case of an IMPORT declaration. This special declaration is defined in Figure 2.25 as "InOutImportDecl".

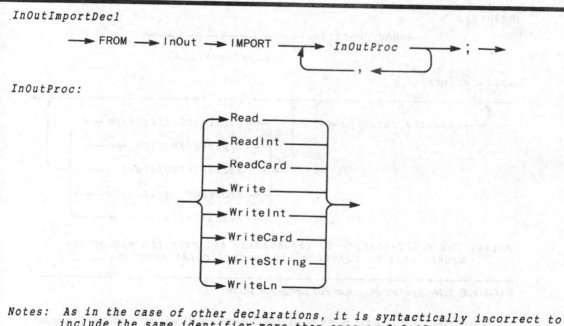

InOutImportDecl

InOutProc:

Notes: As in the case of other declarations, it is syntactically incorrect to include the same identifier more than once as InOutProc.

FIGURE 2.25 InOut import declaration form

A program that utilizes the Read, Write, WriteInt, and WriteLn procedures would require a declaration such as:

```
FROM InOut IMPORT Read, Write, WriteInt, WriteLn;
```

Each InOut procedure that is used within a program must be included exactly once in such a declaration within a program.

2.13 THE SHELL OF A MODULA-2 PROGRAM MODULE

The common form, or **shell**, of a Modula-2 program is described in Figure 2.26.

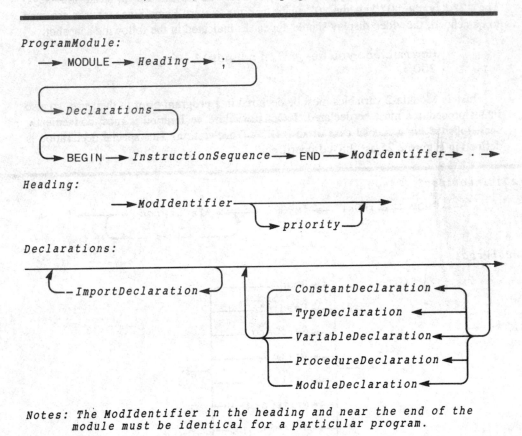

Notes: The ModIdentifier in the heading and near the end of the
module must be identical for a particular program.

FIGURE 2.26 Syntax diagram for program shell

Throughout this text the portions of this program shell will be elaborated. Figure 2.27 contains a reduced shell that contains only the portions of a Modula-2 program that have been discussed thus far.

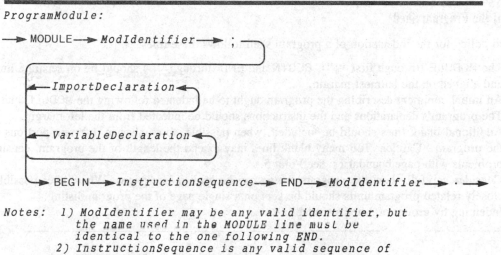

ProgramModule:

Notes: 1) *ModIdentifier may be any valid identifier, but*
        the name used in the MODULE line must be
        identical to the one following END.
        2) *InstructionSequence is any valid sequence of*
        Modula-2 instructions.

FIGURE 2.27 *A reduced shell of a Modula-2 program module*

As an illustration Figure 2.28 contains a complete Modula-2 program to input a weight in pounds, convert and round this weight to the nearest kilogram and print the result.

```
MODULE PoundsToKilograms;
      (* This program inputs a single value representing a  *)
      (* weight in pounds and outputs the equivalent weight *)
      (* in kilograms.                                      *)
      FROM InOut IMPORT WriteString, WriteLn, WriteCard, ReadCard;

   VAR
      PoundWeight : CARDINAL;
      KgWeight    : CARDINAL;

BEGIN
   WriteString( "How much do you weigh (in pounds)?" );
   WriteLn;
   ReadCard( PoundWeight);

   KgWeight := TRUNC( (0.45359237 * FLOAT(PoundWeight)) + 0.5 );
   (* Assert: KgWeight = Kilogram equivalent of PoundWeight   *)
   (*                    rounded to the nearest kg.           *)

   WriteLn;
   WriteLn;
   WriteString( "Your mass in Kilograms is ");
   WriteCard( KgWeight,0 );
   WriteString(" (to the nearest Kg.)");
   WriteLn;
END PoundsToKilograms.
```

FIGURE 2.28 *The PoundsToKilograms program*

Programming-with-Styl

Style of the Program Shell

A good policy for the indentation of a program shell follows these rules.

1) The MODULE (through first ";"), BEGIN and END (through "."), should be on separate lines and aligned on the leftmost margin.
2) An initial comment describing the program ought to be indented following the MODULE line.
3) The program's declarations and the instructions should be indented from the left margin.
4) Additional blank lines should be included, when possible, to emphasize different portions of the program. (Caution: Too many blank lines may extend the length of the program, causing problems with page boundaries; see Point 5.)
5) Consider carefully how the program listing can be broken into pages. Where ever possible, closely related program units should be kept on a single page of the program listing.
6) Indenting by groups of 3 helps readability.

Many of the older programming languages are **line oriented**. A line-oriented language uses the end of a program line as a means of separating program units. Modula-2 utilizes punctuation symbols (e.g., semicolons, commas, BEGIN, END) as separators. This permits the programmer to write program units that are spread over several lines, or to include several program units on a single line. However, Modula-2 does require that an identifier or constant be placed entirely on a single line.

Programming-with-Style-

The Declaration Section

There are a few good rules to follow when writing program declarations.

1) It is best to separate different types of declarations, such as IMPORT and VAR, by blank lines.
2) It is best to group related declarations, such as variables that are used together in some manner.
3) IMPORT (and EXPORT) declarations may list items in a short, concise list, continued over as many lines as necessary.
4) Individual variables in a VAR declaration ought to appear each on a separate line, with the same amount of indentation.
5) Identifiers with names that do not indicate their intended use require the inclusion of a comment after the declaration and on the same line.
6) If large numbers of identifiers are declared, it is often a good idea to alphabetize within groups.

2.14 AN EXAMPLE OF A PROGRAM

The entire process, from problem definition to program, can be illustrated by an example. Figure 2.29 contains a problem definition for reversing four input characters. The program to solve this problem is contained in Figure 2.30.

TITLE

Reverse the order of four characters

DESCRIPTION

This is an interactive program that prompts the user to input four characters; it then outputs the characters in reverse order.

INPUT

Input consists of four characters on a single line followed by a carriage return.

OUTPUT

The first output consists of a message to prompt the user for input. This message is Please type four characters. Following the prompt, the user must input the four characters. Next a blank line is output, followed by the message Your four characters in reverse order are: followed on the same line by the four input characters in reverse order.

ERRORS

1) The program waits for at least four characters to be input.
2) Any extra input is ignored.

EXAMPLE

Below is a snapshot of the display after the program has executed. The input characters are highlighted.

```
        Please type four characters.
        EDIT

        Your four characters in reverse order are: TIDE
```

FIGURE 2.29 *Problem definition of ReverseFourChars*

```
MODULE ReverseFourChars;
      (* This program inputs four characters and reverses *)
      (* their order.                                      *)
      FROM InOut IMPORT Read, Write, WriteString, WriteLn;

      VAR
          FirstChar   : CHAR;
          SecondChar  : CHAR;
          ThirdChar   : CHAR;
          FourthChar  : CHAR;
BEGIN
    WriteString( "Please type four characters." );
    WriteLn;

    Read( FirstChar );
    Read( SecondChar );
    Read( ThirdChar );
    Read( FourthChar );

    WriteLn;
    WriteString( "Your four characters in reverse order are: " );
    Write( FourthChar );
    Write( ThirdChar );
    Write( SecondChar );
    Write( FirstChar );
    WriteLn;
END ReverseFourChars.
```

FIGURE 2.30 *The ReverseFourChars program*

ReverseFourChars has the general shape of a Modula-2 program. The indentation pattern separates the declarations from the code with the BEGIN line. In this program four variables are declared, FirstChar, SecondChar, ThirdChar and FourthChar. An IMPORT declaration appears at the beginning of the program because InOut procedures are used in the program body. The code of the program consists of several input and output instructions.

2.15 THE CODER'S VIEW OF PROGRAMMING

Today's programmer follows a distinct sequence of steps in order to transfer a Modula-2 program from brain to execution. These steps are depicted in Figure 2.31.

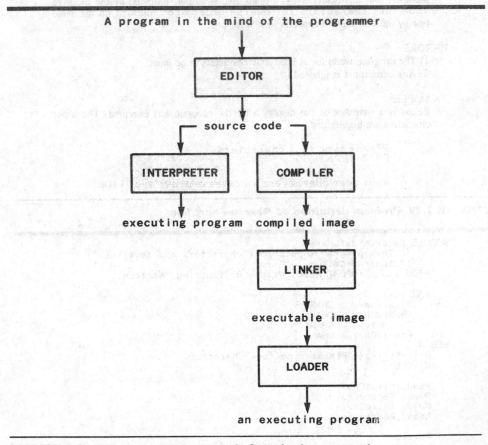

FIGURE 2.31 *How a program proceeds from brain to execution*

In preparing a program for execution, there are several software tools (i.e., othe programs) that the coder may use:

an editor
a compiler
an interpreter
a linker
a loader

These tools define the steps of the process of bringing code to execution.

In the first step the coder must enter the program into the computer. Most use a program, called an **editor**, to help build a program. An editor allows a coder to type program text. When a program has been entered, using the editor, it can be saved. The saved program is called the **source code**. The source code is stored in a **file** under some **file name**, the identifier by which the file may be accessed.

Most Modula-2 systems include a **compiler**. A compiler accepts, as input, a source program, and produces as output a **compiled image**, sometimes referred to as the **object code**. A compiled image is a translation of the source program into a low-level language that can be understood by the hardware. The compiler performs its task by examining the entire source program for syntactic correctness and translating it if no errors are detected. The compiled image is stored in a file that is different from the source file.

In addition to the compiled image file, some compilers may produce **listing** files. A listing is a copy of the source code along with error messages and other useful information.

Compiled images usually require **linking** prior to execution. Another program, called a **linker** performs the necessary linking of the compiled image to produce an **executable image**. The compiler examines only the source file, but does not attempt to resolve facilities imported from external modules. Therefore, it is the linker's task to resolve any references to InOut (or other imported external modules) within the program. The executable image, resulting from linking, contains the complete collection of machine code combined from all necessary modules. This executable image will be saved in another separate file.

In the final step a **loader** retrieves the machine code from the executable image file. The loader places, or loads, this machine code into the memory of the computer at the appropriate location and begins execution.

Using a compiler results in a three-step process:

1) Compile
2) Link
3) Load and execute

This process is often referred to as **compile, link, and go**. In some systems one or more of these steps may be hidden from the user, making the process appear simpler than it is. In other systems the user must issue commands to initiate each step separately.

Some Modula-2 systems use an **interpreter**, instead of a compiler and linker. An interpreter works the way a human does, tracing through code execution. It examines each instruction just before it is to be executed. After checking the syntax and decoding the semantics of an instruction, the interpreter causes the task performed by the instruction to occur.

An **operating system** is the collection of software that, together with the hardware, forms a nucleus of facilities upon which all other software relies. File systems, for example, are managed by the operating system. The file system portion of the operating system provides operations to make it convenient for other programs or the user to create, locate, modify and delete files. The processes of editing, interpreting, compiling, linking, and loading are also an integral part of a modern operating system.

2.16 ERRORS THAT MAY OCCUR

The coder is likely to experience numerous errors while creating a sizable program. These errors can be classified into three classes.

Syntax errors
Execution errors
Logic errors

Syntax errors occur from incorrect program syntax. Such errors may be detected by a compiler, interpreter, or linker. The detecting software usually displays a diagnostic to indicate the place in the source code where the error is detected and some information about the type of error. If a Modula-2 programmer spelled MODULE as Module, the compiler would detect a syntax error. Most compilers do not create a compiled image after detecting one or more syntax errors. Interpreters usually terminate execution when a syntax error is located.

An **execution error** occurs when an executing program causes something to happen that can be detected to be incorrect. The error may be detected by the interpreter or by the machine code produced by the compiler/linker or by the operating system in severe cases. For example, an execution error would occur if

```
WriteCard( GolfBalls, 0 )
```

is executed prior to assigning GolfBalls a value. The WriteCard call instruction is syntactically correct, but an attempt to output an unassigned variable is erroneous. (Note: Not all Modula-2 systems can detect such an error.) Other execution errors occur when the result of the evaluation of a numeric expression is too large or too small to be represented on the computer, or a division by 0 is attempted.

Generally, a detected execution error is **fatal**. When a fatal error occurs the execution of the program is immediately terminated and some error message displayed.

Even when there are no syntax errors and no execution errors there may still be a problem. It is possible for a program to execute properly but produce the wrong results. This type of error is known as a **logic error**. A logic error occurs when a calculation requires a division by 3.0, but the program specifies a division of 2.5. Unless programmers carefully examine their code and its output, logic errors can easily go unnoticed.

Syntax error diagnostics and execution error messages differ from system to system. A good coder becomes familiar with the messages generated by a system to make the most of often sparsely provided information.

2.17 SUMMARY

All programs have two elements.

1) Data
2) Instructions

Modula-2 separates data into different types. This chapter examines INTEGER, CARDINAL, REAL, and CHAR data types. Data can be stored in variables, declared at the beginning of the program. In addition, data can be manipulated by expressions.

Modula-2 also includes many instructions. Assignment instructions assign values to variables. Output instructions display the value of expressions. Input instructions assign values to variables, using data that is read from the user.

The operating system assists a programmer in designing and executing software. Editors are for writing programs, while compilers, linkers, and interpreters allow the program to execute.

||| KEY TERMS

data	case sensitive	ASCII
variable	strongly typed	printable character
data structure	assignment instruction	ordinal value
variable name	scalar data types	assignment compatible
variable value	structured data types	compatible
identifier	constant	operator overloading
declaration	operation	type conversion functions
syntax	expression	truncate (a real value)
character	INTEGER	type conversion error
character string	operator precedence	bounds violation
syntax diagram	CARDINAL	control flow
semantics	REAL	sequential execution
reserved word	CHAR	null instruction

KEY TERMS *(continued)*

execution trace
unassigned variable (undefined
  value)
comment
nesting of code
assertion
I/O
InOut
procedure
Write, WriteCard, WriteInt,
  WriteString, WriteLn
Read, ReadCard, ReadInt

echo
program shell
line oriented (programming
  language)
editor
source code
file
file name
compiler
compiled image
object code
listing

linking
linker
executable image
loader
compile, link and go
interpreter
operating system
syntax error
execution error
fatal error
logic error

III EXERCISES

1. Use one sentence to describe what it means for a variable to be unassigned.

Use the declarations below when answering the questions that follow:

```
(* These variables are used in a program that maintains the
   inventory and various related statistics for a small com-
   puter store.  The company sells just one brand of personal
   computers - HAL PCs.  In addition the store also sells three
   popular programs: DIFICALC, dBASED 0, and WORDPOLYGON.   *)

    VAR
        HALsSold :      CARDINAL;
        HALsOnHand :    CARDINAL;
        HALsOnOrder :   CARDINAL;
        HALCost :       INTEGER;     (* cost to the store in
                                        cents for one HAL *)
        HALRetail :     INTEGER;     (* retail cost in dollars
                                        of one HAL *)

    VAR
        dBsSold, dBsOnHand :       CARDINAL;
        DIFIsSold, DIFIsOnHand :   CARDINAL;
        WORDsSold, WORDsOnHand :   CARDINAL;
```

```
VAR
    dBCode  :    CHAR;    (* These codes are single letter *)
    DIFICode : CHAR;      (* codes used by the store to    *)
    HALCode :    CHAR;    (* identify inventory items.     *)
    WORDCode : CHAR;
    TempCode : CHAR;      (* temporary storage *)

VAR
    Days :            CARDINAL;  (* number business days
                                    that have passed *)
    IncomePerDay :  REAL;  (* average amount in dollars *)
    IncomePerWeek : REAL;  (* average amount in dollars
                              for the most recent week *)
    TotalIncome :    INTEGER ; (* in dollars *)
```

2. Below are several attempted assignment instructions. All of these instructions contain errors. Precisely identify each error. You should assume that every variable used has been assigned a prior value and that results remain within the appropriate ranges.
   a) halcost : = 2016
   b) HAL Retail : = 7500
   c) 33 + 4 : = HalsOnHand
   d) WORDsSold = 24
   e) HALsOnOrder : = −4
   f) dBCode : = D
   g) dBsSold : = 3 ** 4
   h) TotalIncome : = (HALsSold * HALCost) + (dBsSold * 500)
      + (DIFIsSold * 200) + (WORDsSold * 300)
   i) Days : = 17 * 2.0
   j) IncomePerDay : = TotalIncome DIV INTEGER(Days)
   k) Days : = CARDINAL(TotalIncome/IncomePerDay)

3. Write a VAR declaration to declare three variables: Answer should be of type CHAR, Profit should be of type REAL, and StoreNum should be of type CARDINAL.

4. Name the best data type for a variable that must meet the specifications from each part below:
   a) a variable representing the number of store employees
   b) a variable representing the first initial of the owner's last name
   c) a variable representing the number of whole shopping days before your birthday
   d) a variable representing the total profit (in cents) that the store has made (it may be possible to be "in the red")
   e) a variable representing the average employee salary, as accurately as possible

5. Each of the following is an attempt to specify a constant of type INTEGER, CARDINAL, REAL or CHAR. Some are correct and some are incorrect. Indicate which ones are incorrect and include a correction that seems to capture the intent. For those that are correct indicate their type.
   a) "'"
   b) 75
   c) 75.0
   d) 1,700
   e) 103C
   f) 65.
   g) .13

6. Write the ordinal value of each of the following CHAR constants, using the ASCII character set:
   a) "B"
   b) 't'
   c) "7"
   d) 105C

7. Show the evaluation order of each expression below by placing integers beneath the operators (1 for the first operation performed, 2 for the second, etc.)
   a) 1.1 + 2.25 * 4.0 + (- 6.4) * 5.0 / 3.2 * 3.7 - 2.8
   b) 7 DIV 6 * 3 + 4 * 7 MOD 3
   c) (((6 + 2) * (7 - 3)) MOD (5 + (6 + 4))) + 3
   d) (7 + 34) DIV (1 - (- (3 + 2)) * 2) * 4

8. Calculate the value of each expression from Exercise 7.

9. Using the given assertions as preconditions for each sequence of instructions, trace the execution of the code. Indicate the final values assigned to each variable referred to in the section:
   a) (* ASSERT: dBsSold = 12 & dBsOnHand = 4 & DIFIsSold = 0 *)
      dBsSold : = dBsSold + 3;
      dBsOnHand : = dBsOnHand – 3;
      DIFIsSold : = dBsSold * 2;
   b) (*ASSERT: Days = 10 & IncomePerDay = 100 *)
      (*   & IncomePerWeek = 200.   *)
      Days : = Days + 1;
      IncomePerDay : = IncomePerDay + 78. ;
      IncomePerWeek : = IncomePerDay +
               FLOAT(TRUNC(IncomePerDay/2));

10. Write a Modula-2 expression to yield each of the following values:
    a) the value of TotalIncome plus 17
    b) the greatest integer value that is less than or equal to IncomePerWeek's value
    c) the value of IncomePerDay rounded to the nearest INTEGER
    d) the sum of the ordinal values of all five "Code variables."

11. Write a correct assignment instruction to assign...
    a) IncomePerDay the correct value (i.e., the average using TotalIncome and Days)
    b) DIFIsSold the result of multiplying the sum of dBsSold plus 3 and the value of WORDsSold
    c) HALRetail a 50% markup from HALCost (remember that HALCost represents cents and HALRetail dollars)

12. Write a sequence of assignment statements that exchanges the previously assigned values of dBCode, WORDCode and DIFICode in the following manner:
    DIFICode takes on the value dBCode had before the exchange.
    dBCode takes on the value WORDCode had before the exchange.
    WORDCode takes on the value DIFICode had before the exchange.

13. The syntax of RealConstant requires at least one digit to the left of a decimal point, but zero or more to the right. Rewrite the syntax diagram so that one or more digits would be required on both the left and the right.

14. Each part below specifies a list of I/O needs for a particular program. Indicate an IMPORT declaration that declares the procedures from the InOut module that are necessary (and no additional procedures) for the program.
    a) A program that inputs five integer values and outputs three characters.
    b) A program that outputs several lines of messages and has no input.
    c) A program that inputs two cardinal values and outputs two characters on separate lines.

15. Specify precisely the output that is produced by the execution of each of the following code segments, using the I/O procedures from InOut.
    a) Write("!");
       Write("?");
       WriteLn;
       WriteString("XXX");
       WriteString("YY");
       WriteLn;
    b) WriteString("RESULT =");
       WriteInt(-75 * 3, 0);
       WriteCard(4321, 0);
       WriteCard(9876, 0);

16. Specify the name of the file that serves as input and the name of the file that stores the resulting output for each of the following programs. (If there is no input file, indicate the source of input. If there is no output file, indicate the action performed by the software).
    a) a compiler
    b) an editor
    c) a linker
    d) a loader
    e) an interpreter

17. Classify each of the following errors as either syntax errors, execution errors, or logical errors:
    a) a division by some variable with a value of 0
    b) a VAR declaration with a semicolon omitted from the end
    c) attempting to add to the value of some variable that has not been assigned a value
    d) misspelling BEGIN as BGIN
    e) failing to declare a variable that is used in a program module
    f) outputing an employee's name where a Social Security Number was supposed to be output
    g) omitting WriteString from the IMPORT declaration, but attempting to call it in the code

18. For each of the errors indicated in Problem 4, state whether the error is detected by the compiler, by the linker, by the executing code, or not detected (i.e., no error message is generated).

||| PROGRAMMING PROJECTS

1. Use the editor and interpreter (or the editor, compiler, linker, and loader) on your system to create and execute the PoundsToKilograms program from this chapter.

2. Use the editor and interpreter (or editor, compiler, linker, and loader) on your system to create and execute the ReverseFourChars program from this chapter.

3. Below is a Modula-2 program that uses about the worst style imaginable. Using an editor, create the same program formatted so that the indentation is reasonable.

```
MODULE Doubler;

    (* This is program inputs an integer and outputs the
       integer multiplied by two *)

FROM InOut IMPORT  WriteString, WriteLn, WriteInt,
ReadInt; VAR  SomeInteger : INTEGER; BEGIN
WriteString("Please type an integer"); WriteLn; ReadInt(
SomeInteger ); WriteString ("Your integer doubled is: ");
WriteInt( SomeInteger*2, 0 ); WriteLn; END Doubler.
```

3 ||| PROGRAM DESIGN TECHNIQUES

3.1 FROM DEFINITION TO CODE

Programming is the process of nurturing a problem from an abstract idea to an executable piece of code. It is a four step process: (1) defining the problem, (2) designing the solution, (3) coding the solution, and (4) maintaining the solution. This chapter examines the second step, designing the solution, which is an algorithm.

A good algorithm has three characteristics.

1 It must be **precise**.
2) It must be **complete**.
3) It must be **correct** with respect to the defined problem.

A computer is an instrument that demands precision. An imprecise algorithm results in difficulties later in the programming process. Completeness is also important. It is often more expedient for a designer to provide a partial algorithm, but filling in the missing portions is invariably more difficult after the design process.

A designer must devote sufficient time to ensure that the algorithm is correct. Most logic errors in the final code can be traced back to incorrect algorithms. It is more time consuming for the coder to correct these bugs than for the designer to do so.

An algorithm is written in the form of some **pseudolanguage**. A pseudolanguage is similar to a programming language in that it provides a means for expressing a problem solution. The primary distinction is that programs (written in programming languages) can be translated and executed by some computer, while algorithms (written in pseudolanguages) cannot. The main advantage to using a pseudolanguage is avoiding some of the unnecessary syntactic detail required by the programming language.

Designing-with-Wisdom-

A Design Must be PRECISE, COMPLETE, and CORRECT

At each step of design a designer should repeat three questions regarding the designed algorithm.

1) Is the algorithm as precise as possible?
2) Is the algorithm a complete solution to the problem at hand?
3) Does the algorithm solve the problem correctly?

Any change made to an algorithm to improve its precision, completeness or correctness will almost assuredly result in a better algorithm.

3.2 HOW TO BEGIN THE DESIGN

There are two important pieces of knowledge that good designers must have to begin their designs.

1) They must understand the problem.
2) They must understand the options for expressing the solution (ultimately the programming language).

Every design begins with a careful consideration of the problem. Each detail of the problem must be understood if there is any chance for an algorithm to be complete and correct. Since the ultimate goal of design is to produce a program, designers must also be aware of the programming language to be used. In fact, many designers use pseudo-languages that closely resemble programming languages.

Figure 3.1 on the opposite page, is a problem definition that illustrates the basic nature of the design process. The problem is one of moving a computer-controlled robot about a factory.

At the outset, this robot cart problem seems simple. Everyone has given directions to other people before. It is tempting to suggest that the robot should "go that direction for a while" or to offer the infamous "You can't miss it!" However, these typical human directions are too imprecise to be useful.

Good design is rooted in a solid understanding of the problem to be solved. It is easy to understand the problem superficially. The superficial understanding of the robot cart problem from Figure 3.1 is something like:

Move the robot cart from Location 1 to Location 3.

Designers cannot be satisfied with such superficial understanding. It is necessary to dig more deeply into the problem definition to unearth the essential details of the problem. Such digging identifies the following facts.

TITLE
Moving a robot cart from Point 1 to Point 3.

DESCRIPTION
The factory has just installed robot carts to move small items about in certain parts of the factory. Below is a map of the factory corridors that may be traversed by the robot cart. The grid in the map specifies units of ten foot increments and the numbers indicate possible locations for the robot cart to stop for loading/unloading. This particular program assumes the robot cart to be located at Location 1 headed south and causes it to move to Location 3.

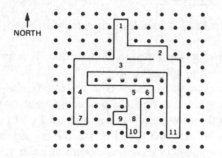

INPUT
There is no input. When this program is executed, the robot cart will move without human input.

OUTPUT
The robot cart beeps when it arrives at its destination. Otherwise there is no output.

ERRORS
If the robot cart does not begin from Location 1 headed south, then undefined results occur when this program is executed.

EXAMPLE
The robot cart proceeds as detailed below, emitting an audible beep upon arriving at Location 3.

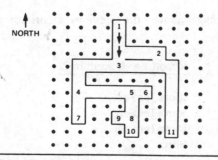

FIGURE 3.1 *Definition of robot cart problem*

1) Initially the robot cart is at Location 1 and heading south (this information comes from the DESCRIPTION section).
2) Location 3 is exactly thirty feet due south of Location 1 (this information comes from the diagram in the DESCRIPTION and/or EXAMPLE sections).
3) The cart must emit a beep upon arriving at Location 3 (this information comes from the DESCRIPTION and/or OUTPUT sections).

With these details unearthed it should be obvious that the following algorithm is suitable for this problem.

RobotCart Algorithm 1:

Move the cart headed south exactly thirty feet, stop, and beep.

This meets the stated criterion for a good algorithm. It is precise, and it correctly states the complete algorithm to solve the problem.

The second step in beginning to design is to understand the options for expressing the algorithm. Remember that the designer is producing an algorithm to assist the coder to produce code. Perhaps the programming language used on the robot cart's computer contains only instructions to vary the speed of the motors driving the cart. In such a language a determination of speed of travel and length of travel time is more appropriate than distance traveled. It might be that the programming language expresses movement in terms of north/south/east/west rather than forward/backward. In any event the quality of the algorithm will depend to an extent upon the programming language that is ultimately used.

To complete this problem assume that the designer has chosen to express the algorithm using the following pseudolanguage.

Instruction	Semantics
MoveTenFeet	causes the cart to move forward exactly 10 feet and then come to a stop
RightTurn	causes the cart to rotate exactly 90 degrees to the right (i.e., clockwise)
Beep	causes the cart to beep

Using the pseudolanguage above, the previous algorithm can be expressed as follows.

RobotCart Algorithm 2:

```
MoveTenFeet
MoveTenFeet
MoveTenFeet
Beep
```

This algorithm has four instructions. The first three instructions cause the cart to move from Location 1 to Location 3. It is unnecessary to indicate stopping the cart, since the activity of stopping is incorporated into the MoveTenFeet pseudoinstruction. Algorithm 2 is precise, complete, and correct.

Designing-with-Wisdom

Two Beginning Issues for Any Design

Before proceeding with the design process, a designer must confront two issues.

1) How should algorithms be expressed? The designer must choose a pseudolanguage before anything else can occur.
2) What is the problem to be solved? It is a drastic (and all too common) mistake to proceed with design before fully understanding the problem to be solved. Often listing details of the problem or tracing through an example of the problem can be helpful. It is best to examine the problem both for overlooked details and for the general tasks to be performed. If a design stalls, reexamining the problem definition never hurts.

3.3 TOP DOWN DESIGN

Programmers must never forget their frailty. From the robot cart problem it is possible to conclude that the design of an algorithm is an easy task. It is wrong to draw such a conclusion. Humans are capable of solving small problems, like the robot cart, quite effectively. However, every good designer knows that humans cannot easily solve the big problems. Even the best minds cannot manage the volume of detail necessary to solve large problems.

We can imagine that long ago humans found the easiest way to break a bundle of sticks in half was to remove each stick and break it in half individually. Often referred to as "divide and conquer," the solution to managing big problems is to break them into smaller problems and solve the small problems. So it is with algorithm design. Whenever a problem seems too big, a designer instinctively **decomposes**, or **refines**, the problem into subproblems. If necessary the subproblems may be further refined into their own subproblems.

This process of beginning with a single large problem and refining it repeatedly is called **top down design**. The "top" level of the process is the entire problem to be solved. The "bottom" level is the final algorithm. The process of decomposing problems into ever smaller subproblems is known as **stepwise refinement**. The term "refinement" means to divide large problems into smaller ones. The process is called "stepwise" because refinement occurs as a sequence of small steps. The design of a refrigerator/freezer, discussed in Chapter 1, proceeded top down when the complete problem was refined into two subproblems, the design of the refrigerator unit and the design of the freezer unit.

Figure 3.2 on the following page, is a robot cart problem that illustrates the process of top down design and stepwise refinement.

TITLE
Moving a robot cart from Point 1 to Point 9.

DESCRIPTION
The factory has just installed robot carts to move small items about in certain parts of the factory. Below is a map of the factory corridors that may be traversed by the robot cart. The grid in the map specifies units of ten foot increments and the numbers indicate possible locations for the robot cart to stop for loading/ unloading. This particular program assumes the robot cart to be located at Location 1 and causes it to move to Location 9.

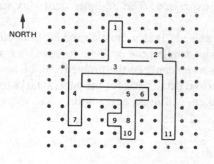

INPUT
There is no input. When this program is executed the robot cart will move without human input.

OUTPUT
There is no output.

ERRORS
If the robot cart does not begin from Location 1 headed south then undefined results occur when this program is executed.

EXAMPLE
The robot cart proceeds as detailed below, stopping at Location 9.

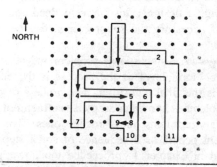

FIGURE 3.2 A second robot cart problem

This second robot cart problem may seem simple, but it contains more complexity than the earlier problem. The trip from Location 1 to 9 involves various corridors of different lengths. Applying top down design helps to manage the complexity. The first step in a top down design could appear as shown in Figure 3.3.

```
RobotCart2 Step 1:

    (* Move cart initially headed south from 1 to 3 *)
    (* Move cart initially headed south from 3 to 4 *)
    (* Move cart initially headed south from 4 to 5 *)
    (* Move cart initially headed east from 5 to 9  *)
```

FIGURE 3.3 *Design Step 1 of RobotCart2*

These new pseudoinstructions are written as Modula-2 comments to indicate their informality and to facilitate top down design. Each comment describes a task (a subproblem to be solved) somewhat informally. In the case of Step 1, the comments indicate four specific tasks that need to be performed in sequence. This is not the only way to refine the problem, but it gives a precise, complete, and correct algorithm. It is precise because each comment unambiguously indicates a particular task. The algorithm is complete because the sequence of instructions solves the problem. The algorithm is correct as long as each comment is correctly interpreted.

The algorithm of Step 1 is only a high level refinement, not the final algorithm. The process of top down design can be described as translating the comment pseudoinstructions into more precise pseudoinstructions. The final algorithm of the design phase should not include any comments that require refinement.

The next step of the top down design results from treating each of the four comment pseudoinstructions as separate problems. Each of these four problems is simpler than the original problem. Examination of the first comment reveals that this is a similar problem to the robot cart problem solved in the past section, except that a final beep is not produced. A designer need not, and should not, reinvent a solution. Therefore, the following refinement of the first pseudoinstruction is natural.

(* Move cart initially headed south from 1 to 3 *)

is refined to

MoveTenFeet
MoveTenFeetMoveTenFeet

The second comment in Step 1 is to move the cart, initially southbound, from Location 3 to Location 4. To solve this problem the designer should return to the problem definition. A careful examination of the problem definition yields the following facts.

1) The appropriate corridor leaving 3 goes west.
2) After 30 feet, this corridor makes a 90 degree turn to the south.
3) It is 20 feet from the turn to Location 4.

From these facts the following refinement of this comment can be made:

(* Move cart initially headed south from 3 to 4 *)

is refined to

RightTurn
(* Move cart forward 30 feet *)
(* Turn cart left 90 degrees   *)
(* Move cart forward 20 feet *)

The above refinement is one of many choices. It is acceptable because it is precise, complete, and correct. The last three pseudoinstructions in this refinement are left as comments. The designer could have chosen to write this refinement without the use of comment pseudoinstructions. However, such a refinement would contain several more instructions. The above refinement into four pseudoinstructions has the advantage of simplicity. It is clearly correct and understandable.

The third pseudoinstruction from Step 1 was to move the cart, now headed south, from Location 4 to Location 5. From the diagram in the problem definition, it can be seen that Location 5 is 40 feet straight west of Location 4. Therefore, the following refinement of this comment seems appropriate.

(* Move cart initially headed south from 4 to 5 *)

is refined to

(* Turn cart left 90 degrees *)
MoveTenFeet
MoveTenFeet
MoveTenFeet
MoveTenFeet

The reason that the left turn is left as a comment is because it seems somewhat difficult. Remember that the pseudocode being used has a RightTurn instruction, but no equivalent for a left turn. Whenever a subtask seems somewhat difficult, it is often a good idea to procrastinate its solution to the next step.

The final comment from Step 1 is refined below.

(* Move cart initially headed east from 5 to 9 *)

is refined to

(* Move cart initially headed east from 5 to 8   *)
(* Move cart initially headed south from 8 to 9 *)

The second step of the top down design results from combining all of the individual refinements into a single algorithm. This algorithm is shown in Figure 3.4. The underlined comments in this figure are not necessary for the algorithm of Step 2, but are included to illustrate the progression from the first to the second step.

RobotCart2 Step 2:

```
(* Move cart initially headed south from 1 to 3 *)
            MoveTenFeet
            MoveTenFeet
            MoveTenFeet

(* Move cart initially headed south from 3 to 4 *)
            RightTurn
        (* Move cart forward 30 feet *)
        (* Turn cart left 90 degrees *)
        (* Move cart forward 20 feet *)

(* Move cart initially headed south from 4 to 5 *)
        (* Turn cart left 90 degrees *)
            MoveTenFeet
            MoveTenFeet
            MoveTenFeet
            MoveTenFeet


(* Move cart initially headed east from 5 to 9 *)
(* Move cart initially headed east from 5 to 8 *)
(* Move cart initially headed south from 8 to 9*)
```

FIGURE 3.4 *Design Step 2 of RobotCart2*

Step 2 has increased the number of pseudoinstructions from the four large tasks of Step 1 to a total of fourteen subtasks. Some of these subtasks can be performed by the RightTurn and MoveTenFeet pseudoinstructions. Such subtasks are now refined in sufficient detail. However, there are still six comment pseudoinstructions that require a third step to refine. The first of these should be refined as indicated below:

(* Move cart forward 30 feet *)

is refined to

MoveTenFeet
MoveTenFeet
MoveTenFeet

The second comment is "(* Turn cart left 90 degrees *)". This can be accomplishe' as follows:

(* Turn cart left 90 degrees *)

is refined to

RightTurn
RightTurn
RightTurn

Refinements for the third and fourth comments in Step 2 should be obvious. They are shown below.

(* Move cart forward 20 feet *)

is refined to

MoveTenFeet
MoveTenFeet

(* Turn cart left 90 degrees *)

is refined to

RightTurn
RightTurn
RightTurn

To perform the fifth comment from Step 2 it is necessary to reexamine the problem definition for more detail. The following refinement is appropriate:

(* Move cart initially headed east from 5 to 8 *)

is refined to

RightTurn
MoveTenFeet
MoveTenFeet

The refinement of the final comment in Step 2 is like the one above. The initial direction of travel is found in the comment, and the distance and direction of travel are found in the problem definition. With this information, the refinement proceeds as shown:

(* Move cart initially headed south from 8 to 9 *)

is refined to

RightTurn
MoveTenFeet

RobotCart2 Step 3:

```
          MoveTenFeet
          MoveTenFeet
          MoveTenFeet

          RightTurn
          MoveTenFeet
          MoveTenFeet
          MoveTenFeet
          RightTurn
          RightTurn
          RightTurn
          MoveTenFeet
          MoveTenFeet

          RightTurn
          RightTurn
          RightTurn
          MoveTenFeet
          MoveTenFeet
          MoveTenFeet
          MoveTenFeet

          RightTurn
          MoveTenFeet
          MoveTenFeet
          RightTurn
          MoveTenFeet
```

FIGURE 3.5 *RobotCart2 Design Step 3*

The pseudocode resulting in Step 3, shown in Figure 3.5, consists of 24 instructions in sequence. The complexity of deriving all of these instructions is reduced by considering only small subproblems during top down design. At this point it is clear that the design is complete, because no further comments remain to be refined.

Designing with Wisdom

Refinement - How Much? How Fast?

When proceeding to refine a complex task into subtasks, many degrees of refinement are possible. Psychologists suggest that humans can usefully manage seven (plus or minus two) independent concepts at one time. This suggests that a single task should be refined into no more than seven (plus or minus two) subtasks. An inexperienced designer should try to refine into five or fewer subtasks at a time. This may take a little longer, but generally saves time in the long run.

3.4 ALTERNATE FORMS FOR TOP DOWN DESIGN

There are several ways to express top down design. The form used thus far is a listing of pseudoinstructions, one per line. The design process consists of repeatedly refining the comments of an algorithm in stepwise fashion. The final algorithm contains no comments that have not been refined.

Sometimes it is helpful for the designer to see a complete top down design. There are many techniques that can illustrate the organization of a top down design. Two techniques will be demonstrated in this section.

The first technique is an outline. The outline consists of the pseudoinstructions of the algorithm in the proper sequence. The headings of the outline indicate higher levels in the design, and the subheadings under a heading indicate the subtasks of the task. To illustrate this concept an outline of the second robot cart problem is shown in Figure 3.6.

```
1. (* Move cart initially headed south from 1 to 3 *)
   1.1  MoveTenFeet
   1.2  MoveTenFeet
   1.3  MoveTenFeet

2. (* Move cart initially headed south from 3 to 4 *)
   2.1  RightTurn
   2.2  (* Move cart forward 30 feet *)
        2.2.1  MoveTenFeet
        2.2.2  MoveTenFeet
        2.2.3  MoveTenFeet
   2.3  (* Turn cart left 90 degrees *)
        2.3.1  RightTurn
        2.3.2  RightTurn
        2.3.3  RightTurn
   2.4  (* Move cart forward 20 feet *)
        2.4.1  MoveTenFeet
        2.4.2  MoveTenFeet

3. (* Move cart initially headed south from 4 to 5 *)
   3.1  (* Turn cart left 90 degrees *)
        3.1.1  RightTurn
        3.1.2  RightTurn
        3.1.3  RightTurn
   3.2  MoveTenFeet
   3.3  MoveTenFeet
   3.4  MoveTenFeet
   3.5  MoveTenFeet

4. (* Move cart initially headed east from 5 to 9 *)
   4.1  (* Move cart initially headed east from 5 to 8 *)
        4.1.1 RightTurn
        4.1.2 MoveTenFeet
        4.1.3 MoveTenFeet
   4.2  (* Move cart initially headed south from 8 to 9 *)
        4.2.1 RightTurn
        4.2.2 MoveTenFeet
```

FIGURE 3.6 *Outline form of RobotCart2 Design*

Every detail of the stepwise refinement process for this problem is visible in the outline. We can see how many steps there were in the process, how many separate refinements were necessary, and exactly what the result of each refinement was. Unfortunately, it is difficult to find the final algorithm because it is spread throughout the outline.

Another form for expressing the top down design is to diagram the process in rectangles. The second robot cart design would be diagramed as given in Figure 3.7.

(* Move cart initially headed south from 1 to 3 *)	MoveTenFeet	
	MoveTenFeet	
	MoveTenFeet	
(* Move cart initially headed south from 3 to 4 *)	RightTurn	
	(* Move cart forward 30 feet *)	MoveTenFeet
		MoveTenFeet
		MoveTenFeet
	(* Turn cart left 90 degrees *)	RightTurn
		RightTurn
		RightTurn
	(* Move cart forward 20 feet *)	MoveTenFeet
		MoveTenFeet
(* Move cart initially headed south from 4 to 5 *)	(* Turn cart left 90 degrees *)	RightTurn
		RightTurn
		RightTurn
	MoveTenFeet	
	MoveTenFeet	
	MoveTenFeet	
	MoveTenFeet	
(* Move cart initially headed east from 5 to 9 *)	(* Move cart initially headed east from 5 to 8 *)	RightTurn
		MoveTenFeet
		MoveTenFeet
	(* Move cart initially headed south from 8 to 9 *)	RightTurn
		MoveTenFeet

FIGURE 3.7 *Rectangular Algorithm Form for RobotCart2 Design*

3.5 ANOTHER EXAMPLE OF TOP-DOWN DESIGN

The final example of design in this chapter creates a change-making algorithm. The details are specified in the problem definition of Figure 3.8.

TITLE
    Monetary change making

DESCRIPTION

The problem is to mimic the change-making activity of a store clerk. Given the cost of an item (the clerk must add 5% for sales tax) and the amount of money paid, the clerk returns the appropriate change in the largest monetary denominations possible. All change must be made in terms of quarters, dimes, nickels, and pennies.

INPUT

Two positive integers are input interactively in response to prompts (see OUTPUT section). The first integer represents the cost of the item (prior to sales tax). The second integer represents the amount of money paid to the clerk for the item. Both values represent money in cents.

OUTPUT

Two output lines prompt for interactive input. These are as follows:

```
Specify cost (in cents):
```

and

```
Specify amount paid (in cents):
```

One blank line follows the two prompt lines. After the blank line the following three lines occur:

```
Total cost (5% tax incl.): <t>
Amount remitted: <r>
Amount returned: <c>
```

Note that "$<t>$" denotes the value of the input cost (in cents) of the item (from the first value input) plus an additional 5% and rounded to the nearest cent; "$<r>$" denotes the amount (in cents) paid by the customer (the second number input); and "$<c>$" denotes the total amount (in cents) to be returned to the customer in change.

Following the above three lines another blank line is output followed by the four lines below.

```
Quarters returned: <q>
Dimes returned: <d>
Nickels returned: <n>
Pennies returned: <p>
```

Note that "$<q>$" "$<d>$" "$<n>$" and "$<p>$" all denote cardinal values and represent the change made in quarters, dimes, nickels and pennies. Change is made by returning the largest denominations possible.

(continued)

ERRORS

1) Any input not in the prescribed form (i.e., positive integers) produces undefined results.

2) If the amount paid to the clerk is less than the cost (including sales tax), then undefined results occur.

EXAMPLE

Below is a snapshot after the execution of the program. Output proceeds down the screen from left to right on each line. Input is highlighted.

```
Specify cost (in cents): 137
Specify amount paid (in cents): 200

Total cost (5% tax incl.): 144
Amount remitted: 200
Amount returned: 56

Quarters returned: 2
Dimes returned: 0
Nickels returned: 1
Pennies returned: 1
```

FIGURE 3.8 *Problem Definition for Change Making*

Sometimes it is convenient to use a subset of the implementation language as a pseudolanguage. Since the pseudolanguage does not need to be executable code, this language subset can be somewhat informal. In the case of the change maker problem the pseudolanguage is a subset of Modula-2 including I/O instructions, assignment instructions and comments. Because this is a pseudolanguage, the required Modula-2 declarations will be ignored for now.

Design can proceed once the pseudolanguage is chosen. The first step is often the most difficult in top down design. In this case, the problem contains lots of detail, so it is best to concentrate on general aspects of the problem. One important aspect of any program solution is its **flow**. The flow of a program is the order in which operations (or instructions) are executed. On a gross level, programs can perform only three tasks.

1) Input data
2) Output results
3) Process data

The tasks "input data" and "output data" obviously refer to I/O operations in a program. "Process data" is a reference to various types of calculations. A top level of design can often be constructed from some combination of these three general tasks.

The change maker problem can be solved with a top level algorithm combining the three tasks as follows:

first ..... input data
next ...... process data
finally ... output results

This sequence is identifiable, since all input (with prompting) occurs at the beginning of execution and the resulting output is at the end. Between the input and the output some processing must occur. This general algorithm pattern can be referred to as **input/ process/output**. The input/process/output pattern is among the most common of the execution flows exhibited by algorithm sequences.

Step 1, the topmost level of the top down design for the change-making problem, is shown in Figure 3.9. This step results from the identification of an input/process/output algorithm and from adding a bit more precision based on the problem definition.

```
(* prompt & input the cost and amount paid *)
(* calculate results for output *)
(* output totals and output change *)
```

FIGURE 3.9 *Design Step 1 for change making (to be improved)*

While the design Step 1 presented in Figure 3.9 is a workable starting algorithm, it is not the best choice for a topmost algorithm. A hint of this fact can be found in the last pseudoinstruction in the algorithm. The fact that there are two general collections of output (i.e., "totals" and "change") suggests that two output comments might be preferable. A better version of this first step of design is shown in Figure 3.10.

```
(* prompt & input the cost and amount paid *)
(* calculate results for output *)
(* output totals *)
(* output change to be returned *)
```

FIGURE 3.10 *Modified Step 1 for change making (to be improved)*

A second improvement in this first step can be made by keeping related tasks close (see "Designing with Wisdom" on the next page). The "calculate results" task from Figure 3.10 is lumped into one group even though two different collections of output have now been identified. It is preferable to perform calculations for each collection of output in closer proximity to that output. The resulting modifications are reflected in Figure 3.11. This algorithm is a good choice for the topmost refinement of the problem.

```
(* prompt & input the cost and amount paid *)
(* calculate totals *)
(* output totals *)
(* calculate change to be returned *)
(* output change to be returned *)
```

FIGURE 3.11 *Acceptable Step 1 for change making*

*D*esigning-with-*W*isdom

Keep Related Tasks Close Together

It is always best to group tasks or operations that are closely related as close together as possible. For example, perform any calculations that are used in other calculations just prior to their use. Likewise, it is best to perform processing for results to be output as close to the output operation(s) as possible.

The next step of the design of this algorithm requires the refinement of the comments from this first step. Refinement of the first comment of Step 1, "Prompt & input cost and amount paid," suggests two prompts and two inputs. Examination of the INPUT and OUTPUT sections of the problem definition provide the necessary detail for the following refinement:

(* prompt & input the cost and amount paid *)

is refined to

WriteString("Specify cost (in cents): ");
ReadCard(ItemCost);
WriteLn; (* to complete the first line *)
WriteString("Specify amount paid (in cents): ");
ReadCard(AmountPaid);

It is important to remember that the above refinement uses a pseudolanguage. Variable declarations that are required in Modula-2 are omitted to simplify the algorithm.

The second comment in the Step 1 algorithm also requires examination of the problem definition. The OUTPUT section of the problem definition clarifies that "totals" to be calculated include the TotalCost, AmountPaid, and AmountToReturn as given by the following postcondition (assertion following calculations).

Postcondition (for "calculate totals"):
(* ASSERT: TotalCost = Round(ItemCost increased by 5%) *)
(*   AND   *)
(*   AmountToReturn = AmountPaid − TotalCost   *)

A bit of translation is required to fit the above assertion into Modula-2 assignment instructions. The phrase ItemCost increased by 5% can be translated into 105% of ItemCost and then into 1.05 * ItemCost. Likewise Round(x) translates into TRUNC(x+0.5). Accounting for these translations and maintaining type compatibility results in the following refinement:

(* calculate totals *)

is refined to

```
TotalCost := TRUNC( FLOAT(ItemCost)*1.05 + 0.5 );
AmountToReturn := AmountPaid - TotalCost;
(* ASSERT: TotalCost =  Round(ItemCost increased by 5%)*)
(*            AND                                         *)
(*          AmountToReturn = AmountPaid - TotalCost       *)
```

The information needed to complete the refinement of "output totals" is immediately available from the OUTPUT section of the problem definition. A possible refinement is shown below:

(* output totals *)

is refined to

```
WriteLn;
(* the blank line prior to totals *)
(* output TotalCost line *)
(* output AmountPaid line *)
(* output AmountToReturn line *)
```

The justification for leaving the three comments unrefined above relates back to a previous "Designing with Wisdom" that suggests it is better to refine slowly. To expand these three output comments completely requires three output instructions each. The number of pseudoinstructions refined from a single comment would then total ten. Even though it might be acceptable to complete the refinement into ten instructions, based on the premise that there are really only four output lines, the above refinement still appears to be preferable.

The fourth comment pseudoinstruction from the Step 1 algorithm is "Calculate the change to be returned." The problem description indicates that change is to be made in quarters, dimes, nickels, and pennies and in the largest denominations possible. A quick thought about how people make change (see "Designing with Wisdom" on the next page) suggests that a person would first identify how many quarters could be returned, then how many dimes, then nickels, and finally pennies. After deciding how much of each denomination to return, the person must also subtract the value of the returned denomination from the amount of change yet to be returned. This algorithm is further elaborated by the refinement below:

(* calculate change to be returned *)

is refined to

```
(* calculate QuartersToReturn and subtract from AmountToReturn *)
(* calculate DimesToReturn and subtract from AmountToReturn *)
(* calculate NickelsToReturn and subtract from AmountToReturn *)
(* calculate PenniesToReturn *)
```

Designing-with-Wisdom

Many Algorithms Come from Human Activities

Many algorithms are based on human activity. Often designers create algorithms by thinking of how they would perform the task (or some closely related task) in real life. Such examination of real life activities requires a careful tracing of an activity that is performed. For example, if the task is to alphabetize a list of names, then a logical approach is to consider how humans alphabetize lists. However, most individuals cannot immediately relate with the necessary precision how they would alphabetize a list. The ability to relate such an algorithm effectively is an important skill for a programmer.

The refinement of "Output change to be returned" parallels that of the previously refined "Output totals." Below is the refinement for the second step of the design.

(* output change to be returned *)

is refined to

WriteLn;
(* output QuartersToReturn line *)
(* output DimesToReturn line *)
(* output NickelsToReturn line *)
(* output PenniesToReturn line *)

The complete Step 2 refinement of the change-making problem is shown in Figure 3.12. Examining the length of the algorithm for the Step 2 again reinforces the importance of top down design. This would also be a good time to review the correctness, precision and completeness of the algorithm.

```
WriteString( "Specify cost (in cents): ");
ReadCard( ItemCost );
WriteLn;
WriteString( "Specify amount paid (in cents): ");
ReadCard( AmountPaid );

TotalCost := TRUNC( FLOAT(ItemCost)*1.05 + 0.5 );
AmountToReturn := AmountPaid - TotalCost;
  (* ASSERT: TotalCost  =  Round(ItemCost increased by 5%)*)
  (*           AND                                         *)
  (*           AmountToReturn = AmountPaid - TotalCost     *)

WriteLn; (* the blank line prior to totals *)
(* output TotalCost line *)
(* output AmountPaid line *)
(* output AmountToReturn line *)
```

(continued)

```
(* calculate QuartersToReturn and subtract from AmountToReturn *)
(* calculate DimesToReturn and subtract from AmountToReturn    *)
(* calculate NickelsToReturn and subtract from AmountToReturn  *)
(* calculate PenniesToReturn *)

WriteLn;
(* output QuartersToReturn line *)
(* output DimesToReturn line    *)
(* output NickelsToReturn line  *)
(* output PenniesToReturn line  *)
```

FIGURE 3.12 *Design Step 2 for change making*

The design process for the change-making problem can be completed in the third step. There are several output comments that require refinement. These refinements should be straightforward when following the rules of Modula-2. The only remaining comments requiring refinement are of the form Calculate SomeDenomToReturn and subtract from AmountToReturn. To refine these comments requires more thinking about how humans make change. Tracing through an actual instance might be helpful. Suppose that change had been made through the quarters and that AmountToReturn = 23. In order to make change in dimes, a human answers the question:

How many dimes are there in 23 cents?

This question translates into:

How many times does 10 divide into 23 evenly?

The Modula-2 translation of the answer to these questions is the cardinal value resulting from dividing 23 by 10 or

23 DIV 10

Likewise,

subtract from AmountToReturn

translates into

the remainder after dividing 23 by 10

In Modula-2 the "remainder" function is MOD so

23 MOD 10

yields the correct new AmountToReturn after making change in dimes. The complete Step 3 is contained in Figure 3.13.

```
WriteString( "Specify cost (in cents): " );
ReadCard( ItemCost );
WriteLn;
WriteString( "Specify amount paid (in cents): " );
ReadCard( AmountPaid );

TotalCost := TRUNC( FLOAT(ItemCost)*1.05 + 0.5 );
AmountToReturn := AmountPaid - TotalCost;
(* ASSERT: TotalCost =  Round(ItemCost increased by 5%)*)
(*           AND                                         *)
(*         AmountToReturn = AmountPaid - TotalCost       *)

WriteLn (* the blank line prior to totals *);
WriteString( "Total cost (5% tax incl.): " );
WriteCard( TotalCost,0 );
WriteLn;
WriteString( "Amount remitted: " );
WriteCard( AmountPaid,0 );
WriteLn;
WriteString( "Amount returned: ");
WriteCard( AmountToReturn,0 );
WriteLn;

QuartersToReturn := AmountToReturn DIV 25;
AmountToReturn := AmountToReturn MOD 25;

DimesToReturn := AmountToReturn DIV 10;
AmountToReturn := AmountToReturn MOD 10;

NickelsToReturn := AmountToReturn DIV 5;
AmountToReturn := AmountToReturn MOD 5;

PenniesToReturn := AmountToReturn;

WriteLn;
WriteString( "Quarters returned: ");
WriteCard( QuartersToReturn,0 );
WriteLn;
WriteString( "Dimes returned: "):
WriteCard( DimesToReturn,0 );
WriteLn;
WriteString( "Nickels returned: ");
WriteCard( NickelsToReturn,0 );
WriteLn;
WriteString( "Pennies returned: ");
WriteCard( PenniesToReturn,0 );
WriteLn;
```

FIGURE 3.13 *Design Step 3 (final step) for change making*

A properly completed design can be conveniently translated into code by a coder. The change-making algorithm from Step 3 illustrates this. The coder has yet to complete only the declarations and check for correct syntax to generate the Modula-2 program equivalent to this algorithm. Such a program is shown in Figure 3.14.

```
MODULE ChangeMaker;

        (* This program inputs an item cost and an amount paid *)
        (* and calculates change in quarters, dimes, nickels   *)
        (* pennies                                             *)

    FROM InOut IMPORT ReadCard, WriteString, WriteCard, WriteLn;

    VAR
        AmountPaid        : CARDINAL;
        AmountToReturn    : CARDINAL;
        DimesToReturn     : CARDINAL;
        ItemCost          : CARDINAL;
        NickelsToReturn   : CARDINAL;
        PenniesToReturn   : CARDINAL;
        QuartersToReturn  : CARDINAL;
        TotalCost         : CARDINAL;

BEGIN
    WriteString( "Specify cost (in cents): " );
    ReadCard( ItemCost );      WriteLn;
    WriteString( "Specify amount paid (in cents): " );
    ReadCard( AmountPaid );

    TotalCost := TRUNC( FLOAT(ItemCost)*1.05 + 0.5 );
    AmountToReturn := AmountPaid – TotalCost;
    (* ASSERT: TotalCost =  Round(ItemCost increased by 5%)*)
    (*           AND                                        *)
    (*           AmountToReturn = AmountPaid – TotalCost    *)

    WriteLn (* the blank line prior to totals *);
    WriteString( "Total cost (5% tax incl.): " );
    WriteCard( TotalCost,0 );
    WriteLn;
    WriteString( "Amount remitted: " );
    WriteCard( AmountPaid,0 );
    WriteLn;
    WriteString( "Amount returned: ");
    WriteCard( AmountToReturn,0 );
    WriteLn;

    QuartersToReturn := AmountToReturn DIV 25;
    AmountToReturn := AmountToReturn MOD 25;

    DimesToReturn := AmountToReturn DIV 10;
    AmountToReturn := AmountToReturn MOD 10;

    NickelsToReturn := AmountToReturn DIV 5;
    AmountToReturn := AmountToReturn MOD 5;

    PenniesToReturn := AmountToReturn;
```

(continued)

```
      WriteLn;
      WriteString( "Quarters returned: ");
      WriteCard( QuartersToReturn,0 );
      WriteLn;
      WriteString( "Dimes returned: ");
      WriteCard( DimesToReturn,0 );
      WriteLn;
      WriteString( "Nickels returned: ");
      WriteCard( NickelsToReturn,0 );
      WriteLn;
      WriteString( "Pennies returned: ");
      WriteCard( PenniesToReturn,0 );
      WriteLn;

   END ChangeMaker.
```

FIGURE 3.14 *The ChangeMaker program*

*D*esigning-with-*W*isdom

Top Down Design Is a Natural for a Good Editor

Some designers resist top down design because it requires too much time and paper to write each step fully. However, the correct way to design is using a text editor. It is best to complete the top level design in the editor, then print and review it. If this algorithm is satisfactory, then use the editor to replace each comment with its refinement, print and review the next step. This process is repeated until no more refinement is necessary. A good editor makes inserting new lines for a refinement a snap, and the final algorithm can easily be translated into a program!

3.6 INTRODUCTION TO DEBUGGING

Errors are possible in every part of the programming process. Experienced coders know that code just translated from an algorithm must undergo testing. Therefore it is important that a new program be adequately tested for bugs. The simplest form of testing begins with a **test oracle**. A test oracle is a collection of acceptable program input along with the associated output. The "example" section of the problem definition form can provide a good test oracle.

Once a test oracle has been identified, the coder supplies the input from the test oracle to the executing program. The output produced by this execution is then compared to the calculated output of the oracle. If the actual output disagrees with the oracle output, then the coder must search the code for the discrepancy, or program bug. This process of searching for the bug is known as **debugging**.

The oracle plays a crucial role in the debugging process. If the oracle contains an error (that is, the output specified is incorrect for the given input), then a coder may waste time searching for a bug in the code that doesn't exist.

On the other hand, a test oracle does not ensure correctness. All that can be said about a program that works for one collection of input is that it succeeds or fails in that one circumstance. It is very possible that the program will perform differently for a different collection of input. Coders often conclude that a program is correct based on a single test. Such a conclusion is as absurd as the judgment that all horses are black based on the viewing a single black horse. Still, it is important to test a program, and the first few tests often reveal program bugs.

3.7 SUMMARY

Design quiescence is defined to be the time at which the job of a designer is complete. The results of design quiescence should be a precise, complete and correct algorithm. The goal of the past design examples is to illustrate a design quiescence resulting in an algorithm that is very nearly code. Such design quiescence makes the job of the coder simpler.

In a larger programming shop, design quiescence is not so easily defined. Typically, large programs are the project of a team of many designers and coders. The process of top down design is also an effective tool for reaching quiescence in this environment. A more experienced designer, often called a **lead designer** generally designs the topmost levels. The lead designer's experience suggests the time at which design quiescence (for this high level design) is reached. The result of the lead designer's design quiescence is several tasks that are subtasks of the original problem found through top down design. These individual tasks form the set of problems to be solved by other designers on the team. The entire process is built on the hierarchical structure of top down design. In the hierarchy are many situations where the design quiescence for one designer results in problem definitions for other designers. The best designers are those who can refine problems into subproblems that are conveniently utilized at the succeeding level of programming.

The change-making design from the Section 3.5 illustrates the great amount of detail present in the design of a single program. There are many separate tasks that must be refined and problem definition details to be examined. This design also suggests that the advantage of top down design is in problem simplification. Solving the change-making problem is reduced to solving several much simpler problems that together constitute the larger task.

The process of careful top down design sometimes seems to be a slow and tedious procedure. Such lengthy design is viewed by some programmers as a source of unnecessary delay in the creation of programs. Ironically, an effort to rush the design of algorithms almost invariably slows down the project rather than speeds it up. Hasty design tends to produce imprecision, incompleteness and ultimately incorrectness. Incorrect algorithms translate into incorrect programs. The manifestation of this incorrectness is in the form of costly logic errors in the program. A true software engineer always takes the necessary time to produce algorithms that are correct, precise, and complete.

||| KEY TERMS

precise algorithm

complete algorithm

correct algorithm

pseudolanguage

top down design

stepwise refinement

outline style pseudocode

rectangular style pseudocode

flow (of control)

input/process/output algorithm

test oracle

debugging

design quiescence

lead designer

||| EXERCISES

1. Each part below is a general description of some task. Perform a single refinement of this task into subtasks such that the algorithm consisting of the subtasks is correct and complete with respect to the original task.
   a) evaluating a job applicant applying for an opening as a programmer
   b) milking a cow
   c) controlling a space shuttle mission to the moon and back
   d) constructing a house
   e) selecting the "best" personal computer
   f) drinking a glass of water
   g) planting a vegetable garden
   h) watching a baseball game

2. Consider the change making design as discussed in the chapter.
   a) Rewrite this algorithm using the outline form presented.
   b) Rewrite this algorithm using the rectangular form presented.

3. On the following page is a third robot cart design problem. Using the pseudolanguage presented for the earlier robot cart problems, perform a complete top down design of the solution.

4. Discuss how the top down design of the RobotCart2 algorithm from Chapter 3 would have been different if the pseudolanguage included an additional LeftTurn pseudoinstruction. You may assume the LeftTurn causes the robot to rotate 90 degrees to the left.

TITLE
Moving a robot cart from Point 9 to Point 11.

DESCRIPTION
The factory has just installed robot carts to move small items about in certain parts of the factory. Below is a map of the factory corridors that may be traversed by the robot cart. The grid in the map specifies units of ten foot increments and the numbers indicate possible locations for the robot cart to stop for loading/unloading. This particular program assumes the robot cart to be located at Location 9, headed east, and causes it to move to Location 11.

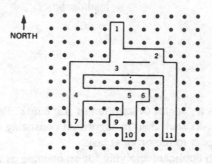

INPUT
There is no input. When this program is executed the robot cart will move without human input.

OUTPUT
There is no output.

ERRORS
In the event that the robot cart is not located at Location 9 prior and headed east immediately prior to executing this program, then undefined results occur.

EXAMPLE
The robot cart proceeds as detailed below, stopping at Location 11.

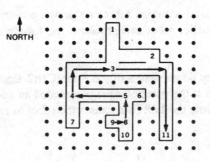

| | | PROGRAMMING PROJECTS

1. Perform a complete top down design for the following problem, showing the complete algorithm at each step of the refinement process. Code the final solution in Modula-2.

TITLE
Counting change

DESCRIPTION
A parking meter money collector has the responsibility of counting all coins collected in the meters and total the sum. In order to simplify this task, a program is required to input the number of coins (quarters, dimes, and nickels) and output the total amount.

INPUT
There are three cardinal values input. Each is input interactively in response to a prompt (see OUTPUT). The input values represent, respectively, the number of quarters, dimes and nickels collected from the parking meters.

OUTPUT
The first portion of the output consists of three prompts, one for each input value. Each prompt is on a separate line, with the input value on the next line. There are no blank lines separating input values and prompts. The three prompt lines are as follows:

```
No. of Quarters?"
No. of Dimes?"
No. of Nickels?"
```

Following the prompted input two blank lines are output. The final line output has the form specified below, where " <$> " represents the total amount (cardinal value) of dollars collected and " <C> " represents the remaining cents from the total.

```
Amount collected: <$> Dollars & <C> cents
```

ERRORS
Any input that does not meet the specifications produces undefined results.

EXAMPLE
Below is a single snapshot that illustrates a single execution of the program. The input is highlighted.

```
No. of Quarters?
20
No. of Dimes?
15
No. of Nickels?
3
Amount collected:  6 Dollars & 65 cents
```

2. Perform a complete top down design for the following problem, showing the complete algorithm at each step of the refinement process. Code the final solution in Modula-2.

TITLE
    Output all combinations of three characters

DESCRIPTION
    A study is being conducted regarding three character words. In order to assist with the study a program is needed to display all possible combinations of particular three character combinations.

INPUT
    After an initial prompt line (see OUTPUT), three consecutive characters are to be input.

OUTPUT
    The first line output is a prompt line as follows:

        Type three characters on the next line.

    Following the prompt line the input occurs on the next line. Two blank lines follow the input line. After the blank lines is a heading line as follows:

        Below are all combinations of the above characters:

    This header line is followed by a single blank line. The final six lines of output consist of all six possible orderings of the three input characters. These six lines each contain a single ordering of the three characters written consecutively and indented 20 characters.

ERRORS
    The program waits until three input characters have been struck (followed by the return key). There are no possible erroneous inputs. It is unusual if two or more of the input characters are the same, but in such a case the program will still output six combinations of characters, although some will be duplicates.

EXAMPLE
    Below is a single snapshot that illustrates a single execution of the program. The input is highlighted.

    Type three characters on the next line.

    ETA

    Below are all possible combinations of the above characters:

        ETA
        EAT
        TEA
        TAE
        AET
        ATE

3. Perform a complete top down design for the following problem, showing the complete algorithm at each step of the refinement process. Code the final solution in Modula-2.

TITLE

Estimate programming time for Acme Programming Ltd

DESCRIPTION

Acme Programming Ltd. (APL) is having difficulty with their programmers. It seems that a recent audit revealed that APL's programmers spent their time in the following proportions:

         5% problem definition
         8% designing
        24% coding
        63% maintaining

The company wants to estimate the number of hours per week spent in each area of programming by the staff. Every programmer on APL's staff works 40 hours per week.

INPUT

After an initial prompt line (see OUTPUT), a single cardinal is input to specify the total number of programmers currently working for the company.

OUTPUT

The first line output is a prompt line as follows:

                Number of programmers:

Following the prompt line the input occurs on the same line. One blank line follow the input line. After the blank line are the following four lines, where "<D>" denotes total programming hours per week devoted to problem definition, "<d>" denotes the total hours/week of designing, "<c>" denotes the total hours/week of coding, and "<m>" denote the total hours/week of code maintenance. All output values are rounded to the nearest cardinal.

        Defining hours per week: <D>
        Designing hours per week: <d>
        Coding hours per week: <c>
        Maintaining hours per week: <m>

ERRORS

If a non cardinal value is input, then undefined results occur. Extra input is ignored.

EXAMPLE

Below is a single snapshot that illustrates a single execution of the program. The input is highlighted.

```
Number of programmers: 3
Defining hours per week: 6
Designing hours per week: 10
Coding hours per week: 29
Maintaining hours per week: 76
```

4. Perform a complete top down design for the following problem, showing the complete algorithm at each step of the refinement process. Code the final solution in Modula-2.

TITLE

Income tax prototype program

DESCRIPTION

An accounting firm wants to attract customers by placing a personal computer on display in a local shopping mall. The computer needs a program to assist any shopping mall patron in estimating their net income after income taxes. In order to demonstrate the idea a rough prototype program is required. This prototype needn't contain the exacting detail of the final program. The prototype must permit the user to specify total income (in a cardinal number of dollars) and number of dependents. The prototype should then estimate federal and state income taxes based on a deduction of $800 for each dependent. Federal tax is calculated at 20% of income less deductions. State tax is calculated at 10% of income less deductions.

INPUT

Input consists of two cardinal values as typed in response to prompts (see OUTPUT). The first cardinal represents the user's annual income before taxes and the second cardinal represents the number of dependents claimed by the user.

OUTPUT

There are two prompt lines output with input accepted from each line. The two prompts are as follows:

```
Specify income before taxes:
Specify number of dependents:
```

One blank line follows the input lines. After the blank line are the following four lines, where "<F>" denotes the amount of federal tax (computed at 20% of income [after subtracting $800 per dependent]), "<S>" denotes the amount of state tax (computed at 10% of income [after subtracting $800 per dependent]), "<T>" denotes the total taxes (i.e. federal plus state tax) and "<N>" denotes the net amount (i.e. the income less $800 per depedent and less total taxes). All values are rounded to the nearest dollar.

```
Federal Tax: <F>
State Tax: <S>
Total taxes: <T>
Net Income: <N>
```

ERRORS

If a non cardinal value is input, then undefined results occur. Extra input is ignored.

EXAMPLE

Below is a single snapshot that illustrates a single execution of the program. The input is highlighted.

```
Specify income before taxes: 25000
Specify number of dependents:4
Federal Tax: 4360
State Tax: 2180
Total taxes: 6540
Net Income: 15260
```

4 ||| (CONTROL) STRUCTURED PROGRAMMING

.1   THE FOUR FUNDAMENTAL ELEMENTS OF CONTROL

The **control flow**, or order of instructions, defines the task performed by an algorithm. Algorithms with correct pseudoinstructions in an incorrect order are of no value. Suppose the robot cart algorithms of Chapter 3 are modified by rearranging the order of instructions. There is little chance that a rearranged algorithm will cause the robot cart to move correctly from one place to another. It is more likely that the robot will crash into a wall.

Every algorithm is composed from four forms of control flow:

> Sequence
> Abstraction
> Selection
> Repetition

A **sequence** is a list of instructions performed one after another in order. An instruction sequence is like a chain. Each link of a chain, except the first, follows after exactly one other link. Likewise, each instruction in a sequence must be performed after the instruction that precedes it. This is referred to as **sequential execution**.

People are unable to solve large problems without special problem-solving techniques. **Abstraction** is one technique used to help manage the complexity of large problems. Abstraction relies upon emphasizing important concepts, while hiding (abstracting) unnecessary detail.

Top down design relies upon abstraction. Each step of a top down design refines an algorithm (an abstraction) into a more detailed version. For example, the pseudoinstruction

(* calculate TotalOfSalaries *)

is an abstraction. This abstraction captures the important concept of the task. At the same time, there are many details omitted, such as which salaries are to be totaled. In this pseudoinstruction the designer has decided that more information about which salaries are to be totaled is unnecessary detail.

Subprograms provide control abstraction. Each subprogram performs a single part, or **subtask**, of the complete program.

Selection permits an algorithm to specify a choice between alternatives. An operating system *selects* whether to allow a user access to the computer or not, according to the identification code that is input.

The greatest potential of a computer lies in its ability to perform many instructions with speed and accuracy. **Repetition** is a technique for capitalizing on this potential. Repetition causes some task to be performed over and over again. For example, a program to output a blank page of 66 lines outputs a single blank line repeatedly.

Sequence, abstraction, selection and repetition control are fundamental to all algorithms, even those not normally executed by computers. For example, consider the following recipe for chocolate mousse.

If large eggs are used, then 4 eggs are required; 5 medium eggs may be used instead. Separate an egg, placing the white and yolk in separate mixing bowls. Repeat this separation for the remaining eggs. Beat egg whites until they are frothy. Add one teaspoon of sugar to egg whites and beat until well mixed; continue to add and mix sugar similarly until 2 tablespoons have been mixed. Beat mixture until stiff peaks form. Repeat (add a tablespoon of sugar, then beat) until mixture is lightly colored. Stir egg yolk mixture over simmering water; continue to beat until thick and creamy. Fold egg yolk mixture into egg white mixture. Beat whipping cream until stiff peaks form. Combine chocolate, powdered sugar, and vanilla with whipping cream. Combine whipping cream mixture and egg mixture. Serve when mousse is completely chilled.

As an algorithm, this recipe illustrates all of the fundamental elements of control. The sentences of the recipe represent individual subtasks that are performed in a sequence. To illustrate the sequence of subtasks more clearly, the recipe is rewritten in Figure 4.1 with each subtask separately numbered in the order in which it is performed.

```
1) If large eggs are used, then 4 are required; 5 medium eggs
   may be used instead.
2) Separate an egg, placing the whites and yolks in to two individual
   mixing bowls.
3) Repeat this separation for the remaining eggs.
4) Beat egg whites until they are frothy.
5) Add one teaspoon of sugar to egg whites and beat until well
   mixed; continue to add and mix sugar similarly until 2
   tablespoons have been mixed.
6) Beat mixture until stiff peaks form.
7) Repeat (add a tablespoon of sugar, then beat) until mixture
   is lightly colored.
8) Stir egg yolk mixture over simmering water; continue to beat
   until thick and creamy.
9) Fold egg yolk mixture into egg white mixture.
10) Beat whipping cream until stiff peaks form.
11) Combine chocolate, powdered sugar, and vanilla with whipping
    cream. 12) Combine whipping cream mixture and egg mixture.
13) Serve when mousse is completely chilled.
```

FIGURE 4.1 *Recipe for making chocolate mousse*

Abstraction occurs several times in this recipe. Instruction 2 says to separate egg whites from egg yolks and place in two individual bowls. Instruction 3 does not repeat all of the detail, but abstractly refers to the process as:

> this separation

Another abstraction occurs in Instruction 5, where

> add and mix sugar similarly

is an abstraction for

> Add one teaspoon of sugar to egg whites and beat until well mixed.

Selection occurs in this recipe as well. Instruction 1 specifies alternatives (to use 4 eggs or to use 5 eggs) to be selected according to the size of the eggs. The final instruction is a selection of whether or not to serve the mousse. The option of serving is chosen based on whether the mixture is completely chilled.

Repetition is specified in many of the recipe instructions. Instruction 3 is one example.

> Repeat this separation for the remaining eggs.

The mousse recipe also illustrates **composition of control**. In several instances different elements of control are combined. Instruction 3 combines repetition

> Repeat this separation for the remaining eggs.

with abstraction

> Repeat this separation for the remaining eggs.

Even the entire list of recipe instructions is an example of control composition, because it combines many different forms of control in a single sequence.

4.2 SEQUENCES

In a programming language, a sequence of instructions is a list of instructions that appear one after another. To perform, or execute, the sequence means to perform each individual instruction one at a time. Each instruction in a sequence begins immediately after the previous instruction completes.

Programming-with-Style

Punctuation of Sequences

The Modula-2 rules for punctuation of sequences are as follows.

1) In a sequence of instructions, every two consecutive instructions *must* be separated by a semicolon.
2) A semicolon following a sequence of instructions is *optional*.

4.3 CONTROL ABSTRACTION IN ALGORITHMS

A complex problem results in an algorithm that is too long and detailed to comprehend as a single unit. When this occurs, it is better to refine the problem into separate subtasks called **routines**. Figure 4.2 defines a problem that illustrates the use of routines to perform control abstraction.

TITLE
Draw a stick figure with asterisks

GENERAL
As a part of an entertainment (game) program, a stick figure is needed. Several forms are being drawn on the computer experimentally. This program draws one particular form out of asterisk ("*") characters.

INPUT
There is no input.

OUTPUT
The program is to output a stick figure with the following output (under the "Stick Figure" heading):

```
Stick Figure   Line by Line Description
   *****        (10-"b"s, 5-"*"s)
   *   *        (10-"b"s, "*", 3-"b"s, "*")
   *****        (10-"b"s, 5-"*"s)
 *     *     *  (6-"b"s, "*", 5-"b"s, "*", 5-"b"s, "*")
**    *    **   (7-"b"s, 2-"*"s, 3-"b"s, "*", 3-"b"s, 2-"*"s)
  *******      (9-"b"s, 7-"*"s)
    ***        (11-"b"s, 3-"*"s)
    ***        (11-"b"s, 3-"*"s)
    ***        (11-"b"s, 3-"*"s)
    ***        (11-"b"s, 3-"*"s)
   *   *       (10-"b"s, "*", 3-"b"s, "*")
   *   *       (10-"b"s, "*", 3-"b"s, "*")
  *     *      (9-"b"s, "*", 5-"b"s, "*")
  *     *      (9-"b"s, "*", 5-"b"s, "*")
 ***   ***     (7-"b"s, 3-"*"s, 5-"b"s, 3-"*"s)
 ***   ***     (7-"b"s, 3-"*"s, 5-"b"s, 3-"*"s)
```
(continued)

ERRORS

Since there is no input, there are no errors that can occur.

EXAMPLE

Below is the output of the stick figure as produced by this program:

preceded by ten spaces

FIGURE 4.2 *Problem definition for the stick figure drawing*

```
(* output the lines for the head of the stick figure *)
(* output the lines for the arms of the stick figure *)
(* output the lines for the body of the stick figure *)
(* output the lines for the legs of the stick figure *)
(* output the lines for the feet of the stick figure *)
```

FIGURE 4.3 *Step 1 of refining the stick figure drawing*

Figure 4.3 indicates a top level refinement of the stick figure problem. The task of drawing a stick figure is decomposed into a sequence of five subtasks. Each of these subtasks can be refined. For example:

(* output the lines for the head of the stick figure *)

is refined to

```
WriteString( "          *****" );
WriteLn;
WriteString( "          *   *" );
WriteLn;
WriteString( "          *****" );
WriteLn;
```

After refining all of the comments from Step 1, the designer has an important choice to make. The designer can complete Step 2 by replacing all comments from Step 1 with their refinements. This solution results in the algorithm from Figure 4.4.

```
WriteString( "              •••••" );
WriteLn;
WriteString( "          •      •" );
WriteLn;
WriteString( "             •••••" );
WriteLn;

WriteString( "        •      •     •" );
WriteLn;
WriteString( "       ••    •    ••" );
WriteLn;
WriteString( "          •••••••••" )
WriteLn;

WriteString( "             •••");
WriteLn;
WriteString( "             •••");
WriteLn;
WriteString( "             •••");
WriteLn;
WriteString( "             •••");
WriteLn;

WriteString( "          •    •" );
WriteLn;
WriteString( "          •    •" );
WriteLn;
WriteString( "          •    •" );
WriteLn;
WriteString( "          •    •" );
WriteLn;

WriteString( "        •••     •••" );
WriteLn;
WriteString( "        •••     •••" );
WriteLn;
```

FIGURE 4.4 *First option for Step 2 of the design of the stick figure drawing*

The second option available to the designer at Step 2 is to treat some or all of the comments from Step 1 as separate routines; see Figure 4.5. The algorithm in this figure is divided into six routines. The last routine is the main algorithm. It is called the **mainline routine**.

```
OutputHead routine:
        WriteString( "              •••••" );
        WriteLn;
        WriteString( "          •      •" );
        WriteLn;
        WriteString( "             •••••" );
        WriteLn;
```

(continued)

```
OutputArms routine:
      WriteString( "        •        •      •" );
      WriteLn;
      WriteString( "         ••      •   ••" );
      WriteLn;
      WriteString( "           •••••••••" );
      WriteLn;

OutputBody routine:
      WriteString( "▲            •••");
      WriteLn;
      WriteString( "             •••");
      WriteLn;
      WriteString( "             •••");
      WriteLn;
      WriteString( "             •••");
      WriteLn;

OutputLegs routine:
      WriteString( "        •     •" );
      WriteLn;
      WriteString( "       •       •" );
      WriteLn;
      WriteString( "      •         •" );
      WriteLn;
      WriteString( "     •           •" );
      WriteLn;

OutputFeet routine:
      WriteString( "    •••       •••" );
      WriteLn;
      WriteString( "   •••         •••" );
      WriteLn;

Mainline routine (driver):
      OutputHead;
      OutputArms;
      OutputBody;
      OutputLegs;
      OutputFeet;
```

FIGURE 4.5 *Second option for Step 2 of the design of the stick figure drawing*

The mainline routine in Figure 4.5 is similar to the algorithm of Step 1 of the design. Every comment pseudoinstruction from Step 1 is abbreviated in Figure 4.5, and the comment form "(* ... *)" is replaced by a **routine invocation**. Routine invocations indicate when to execute a routine. Each invocation consists of the name of the routine, a single identifier. This mainline consists of a sequence of five routine invocations, representing the five subtasks to be performed.

The two options for Step 2 of the stick figure drawing reveal the basic advantage of abstraction: keeping algorithms simple. The mainline routine of the second option is much shorter and more descriptive than the complete algorithm of the first option. It more clearly states that the output consists of a head, arms, body, legs, and feet. By contrast, the earlier algorithm, without separate routines, describes this algorithm as a sequence of 32 output instructions.

Figure 4.5 also points out a disadvantage of abstraction: separation of the algorithm. Whenever a routine invocation instruction is included, it references a subtask described in a separate algorithm. This means that the complete algorithm must be read in parts instead of a complete single unit. In the case of the stick figure drawing, it is necessary to examine six separate algorithms, or routines, in order to view the complete algorithm. Still, this disadvantage is minor by comparison to the usefulness of abstraction for the solution of large problems. See "Designing with Wisdom" for some hints on how to utilize abstraction effectively.

Designing-with-Wisdom

Some Ideas on When to use Abstraction (routines)

A routine separates the details of the abstraction's subtask from its use or invocation. This has the advantage of keeping the "using" routine uncluttered. However, this also has the disadvantage of forcing anyone examining the algorithm to look to another location to find the details of an abstraction.

There are no clearcut rules for when to use a separate routine. However, there are a few guidelines to remember.

1) The goal of abstraction is to reduce complexity. One good measure of this form of complexity is readability. If separate routines will make the algorithm more readable, use them.
2) The maximum length of an individual routine should depend upon the length of the complete algorithm. For a 50 line algorithm, a 10 line limit on the length of routines might make sense. However, if every routine of a 2000 line algorithm is 10 lines long, then there are 200 separate routines! Remember that complexity is caused by the length of a routine, but complexity is also caused by the number of routines.
3) A single routine should not be longer than one page (50 to 60 lines) except under unusual circumstances.
4) Any nontrivial task that is performed in several different places of an algorithm is a candidate to become a separate routine.

4.4 CONTROL ABSTRACTION IN MODULA-2: THE PROCEDURE

The coded form of a routine is a **subprogram**. Subprograms are also known by many other names, such as **function** and **subroutine**. In Modula-2 subprograms are called **procedures**. Invoking a Modula-2 **parameterless procedure** is accomplished by using the name of the procedure as an instruction. The WriteLn procedure may be invoked anywhere within a program by specifying the following instruction:

WriteLn

Each time this procedure is invoked, the WriteLn procedure produces the end of another output line.

The WriteLn procedure is a standard portion of the InOut module. Therefore, the code for this procedure already exists and is not included in a program that uses WriteLn.

Programmers may also declare their own procedures. The form of a declaration of a programmer supplied parameterless procedure is shown in Figure 4.6. In Modula-2, procedure declarations may be placed wherever a VAR declaration is allowed.

ParameterlessProcDeclaration:

→ PROCEDURE ——▶ *ProcIdentifier* ——▶ ; ——▶*ProcDeclarations*——

▶ BEGIN ——▶*InstructionSequence*——▶END ——▶*ProcIdentifier*——▶ ; ——▶

ProcDeclarations:

>   For now *ProcDeclarations consists of zero or more VAR declarations.*

Note: The ProcIdentifier following PROCEDURE *must be identical to the corresponding one before the final* ";" *of the procedure.*

FIGURE 4.6 *Syntax diagram for ParameterlessProcedure*

There is a strong similarity between the form of a procedure declaration and the shell of a program. Each contains a declaration section and a code section. The only differences between these two forms is that the procedure declaration begins with PRO-CEDURE instead of MODULE, ends in a semicolon rather than a period, and cannot contain IMPORT declarations. The philosophy behind the similarity between program module and procedure declaration is that both define tasks. The procedure's task is merely a subtask of the complete program.

The code section of the procedure, also called the **procedure body**, specifies the task performed by the procedure. When the procedure is invoked or **called** the result is the execution of the procedure body. A procedure invocation causes a **transfer of control** from the currently executing code to the instructions of the procedure body. After this transfer the procedure executes until its last instruction is finished, then there is an implicit transfer of control back to the instruction sequence from which invocation occurred, as shown in Figure 4.7.

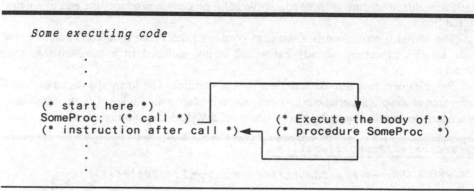

```
Some executing code
         .
         .
         .
(* start here *)
SomeProc;  (* call *)              (* Execute the body of *)
(* instruction after call *)       (* procedure SomeProc  *)
         .
         .
         .
```

FIGURE 4.7 *An example of procedure control transfer*

Figure 4.8 shows the earlier stick figure algorithm in the form of a complete Modula-2 program. In this program, procedures replace the routines of the algorithm.

```
MODULE StickFigure;
    (* This program creates a display of a stick figure *)

FROM InOut IMPORT WriteString, WriteLn;

    PROCEDURE OutputHead;
        (* POST: The head of the stick figure has been displayed *)
    BEGIN
        WriteString( "          *****" );
        WriteLn;
        WriteString( "          *   *" );
        WriteLn;
        WriteString( "          *****" );
        WriteLn
    END OutputHead;

    PROCEDURE OutputArms;
        (* POST: The lines containing the arms of a stick figure *)
        (*        have been displayed                            *)
    BEGIN
        WriteString( "       *    *    *" );
        WriteLn;
        WriteString( "        **   *   **" );
        WriteLn;
        WriteString( "         **********" );
        WriteLn
    END OutputArms;

    PROCEDURE OutputBody;
        (* POST: The body of the stick figure has been displayed *)
    BEGIN
        WriteString( "          ***");
        WriteLn;
        WriteString( "          ***");
        WriteLn;
        WriteString( "          ***");
        WriteLn;
        WriteString( "          ***");
        WriteLn
    END OutputBody;
```

(continued)

```
        PROCEDURE OutputLegs;
            (* POST: The legs of the stick figure have been displayed *)
        BEGIN
                WriteString( "          *    *" );
                WriteLn;
                WriteString( "          *    *" );
                WriteLn;
                WriteString( "          *      *" );
                WriteLn;
                WriteString( "        *        *" );
                WriteLn
        END OutputLegs;

        PROCEDURE OutputFeet;
            (* POST: The feet of the stick figure have been displayed *)
        BEGIN
                WriteString( "      ***        ***" );
                WriteLn;
                WriteString( "      ***        ***" );
                WriteLn
        END OutputFeet;

    BEGIN (* StickFigure mainline *)
        OutputHead;
        OutputArms;
        OutputBody;
        OutputLegs;
        OutputFeet
    END StickFigure.
```

FIGURE 4.8 *The StickFigure program*

The declarations of the five procedures, OutputHead, OutputArms, Output-Body, OutputLegs, and OutputFeet are placed near the beginning of the program. The body (mainline code) of the program follows all the declarations. When the program executes it begins with the mainline. Figure 4.9 traces the execution of the program, showing the output that occurs.

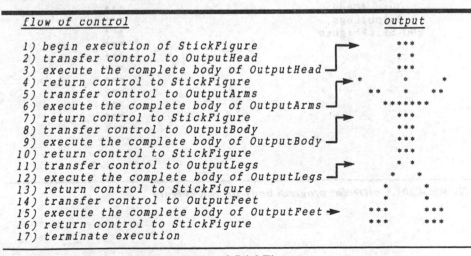

flow of control	*output*
1) begin execution of StickFigure	
2) transfer control to OutputHead	
3) execute the complete body of OutputHead	
4) return control to StickFigure	
5) transfer control to OutputArms	
6) execute the complete body of OutputArms	
7) return control to StickFigure	
8) transfer control to OutputBody	
9) execute the complete body of OutputBody	
10) return control to StickFigure	
11) transfer control to OutputLegs	
12) execute the complete body of OutputLegs	
13) return control to StickFigure	
14) transfer control to OutputFeet	
15) execute the complete body of OutputFeet	
16) return control to StickFigure	
17) terminate execution	

FIGURE 4.9 *Trace of the execution of StickFigure*

The use of procedure postconditions and preconditions is an effective means of communicating the function performed by the procedure. The **procedure precondition and postcondition** are assertions that define a procedure in the form of a contract. The terms of this contract state :

IF the precondition is true when the procedure is invoked, THEN the postcondition will be true when the procedure finishes.

A precondition and postcondition pair completely describe the task performed by a procedure. In the StickFigure program, each procedure includes a postcondition, labelled "POST" that describes the task performed by that procedure.

Sometimes a procedure works regardless of the conditions at the time of invocation. In this case the precondition is omitted. The StickFigure procedures have no preconditions, because each will output its portion of the stick figure regardless of the conditions at the time it is called.

Procedures may be invoked many times within a single program. For example, Figure 4.10 contains a different module body that could be substituted for the one in the StickFigure program of Figure 4.8. This diagram illustrates the importance of the order of procedure invocations.

The code below could be substituted for the body in the program in Figure 4.8

Resulting output

```
BEGIN (* New mainline *)
    OutputArms;
    OutputBody;
    OutputHead;
    OutputHead;
    OutputBody;
    OutputLegs;
END StickFigure
```

FIGURE 4.10 *A different program body for StickFigure*

*P*rogramming-with-*S*tyle

Style of the Procedure

Rules for good procedure style are similar to rules for good program style. Below is a collection of the most important rules to remember.

1) Selecting a good procedure name may be even more important than choosing other good identifiers. Remember that a procedure is an abstraction used to reduce complexity. If the procedure name is not meaningful, then instead of reducing complexity the procedure introduces confusion.
2) The PROCEDURE line (through first ";"), BEGIN line, and END line (through ".") should begin in the same column.
3) The declarations and the instructions of the procedure body should be indented from the PROCEDURE, BEGIN, and END lines.
4) Every procedure should include a comment describing the precondition and the postcondition. These comments should be indented on separate lines just after the PROCEDURE line and marked as PRE and POST. If there is no precondition, then this comment may be omitted.

A second example of a design that utilizes abstraction is defined in Figure 4.11.

TITLE
Process weekly employee information for three employees

GENERAL
A small company, consisting of three employees, needs to print weekly employee information forms to be in compliance with new federal guidelines. The information forms must contain job title, employee initials, Social Security number, hours worked and gross wage. This information must be printed according to a very specific format. The company computes all wages based on hours worked, with no overtime.

INPUT
Input to the program consists of three lines, one per employee. The first line is information for the company president, the second for the company vice president, and the last is for the company flunky. Each of these lines has the following form:

- four characters for initials (first initial followed by "." followed by last initial followed by ".")
- one or more blanks
- the last four digits of the Social Security number
- one or more blanks
- a cardinal value (representing hourly wage, in dollars)
- one or more blanks
- a cardinal value (representing hours worked)

(continued)

OUTPUT

Before to the three input lines, there are five output lines written as a comment to the user. The form of these lines is shown below.

```
Specify info for pres., v.p., and flunky on 3 lines. Each
line should contain initials (4 chars), last four digits
of social security number, hourly wage (cardinal
value) and hours worked the past week (cardinal value).
Following each input the correct info form will be
displayed.
```

The above prompt is followed by a blank line, prior to the prompt for the first input line. Each input line is prompted with an output line as shown below. The expression " <job title> " stands for "President" for the first input line, "Vice Pres." for the second and "Flunky" for the third.

```
Input <job title> info below:
```

After each input line there is one blank line and then the following information form.

```
ƀƀƀInitials:ƀƀƀ<first and last initials without periods>
ƀƀƀS.S.#:ƀƀƀƀƀƀ<last 4 digits of employee's soc. sec. #>
ƀƀƀwage/hr:ƀƀƀƀ<employee's hourly wage>
ƀƀƀhours:ƀƀƀƀƀƀ<number of hours worked this week>
ƀƀƀweekly wage:ƀƀ<weekly wage (wage/hr times hours)>
< a blank line >
< a blank line >
```

The notation " < a blank line > " symbolizes a blank line of output. In general, the use of " < ... > " denotes the output of the information described; this output should be left-justified.

ERRORS

The program assumes all input to be of the form specified and will produce undefined results for any other input.

EXAMPLE

Below is a snapshot of the execution of this program.

```
Specify info for pres., v.p. and flunky on 3 lines. Each
line should contain initials (4 chars), last four digits
of social security number, hourly wage (cardinal
value) and hours worked the past week (cardinal value).
Following each input the correct info form will be
displayed.

Input President info below:

R.R. 7234   123 21

    Initials:    RR
    S.S.#:       7234
    wage/hr:     123
    hours:       21
    weekly wage:   2583
```

```
Input Vice Pres. info below:

G.B. 2348 27  35

     Initials:     GB
     S.S.#:        2348
     wage/hr:      27
     hours:        35
     weekly wage:  945

Input Flunky info below:

D.R. 3896  4  50

     Initials:     DR
     S.S.#:        3896
     wage/hr:      4
     hours:        50
     weekly wage:  200
```

FIGURE 4.11 *Problem definition for weekly employee information problem*

Figure 4.12 contains an algorithm, consisting of four subtasks, for this problem.

```
(' output the initial description ')
(' input/output/process info for the president ')
(' input/output/process info for the v.p. ')
(' input/output/process info for the flunky ')
```

FIGURE 4.12 *Design Step 1 of weekly employee information*

Abstraction can be a very effecti /e tool whenever the same subtask is performed in multiple places within an algorithm. In this instance the subtasks for the last three comment pseudoinstructions are nearly identical. When the same subtask or a very similar one occurs many times, it is wise to make it into a routine. The second step of the top down design results in the algorithm shown in Figure 4.13. A separate "Process-OneEmployee" routine has been used to capture the common task performed for each employee.

```
ProcessOneEmployee routine:
      (' input info and output form for one employee ')


mainline routine:
    WriteString("Specify info for pres., v.p. and flunky on 3 lines. Each");
    WriteLn;
    WriteString("line should contain initials (4 chars), last four digits of");
    WriteLn;
    WriteString("social security number, hourly wage (cardinal value) and");
    WriteLn;
    WriteString("hours worked the past week (cardinal value). Following each");
    WriteLn;WriteString("input the correct info form will be displayed.");
    WriteLn;
    WriteLn;                                              (continued)
```

```
WriteString( "Input President info below:" );
WriteLn;
ProcessOneEmployee;

WriteString( "Input Vice Pres. info below:" );
WriteLn;
ProcessOneEmployee;

WriteString( "Input Flunky info below:" );
WriteLn;
ProcessOneEmployee;
```

FIGURE 4.13 *Design Step 2 of weekly employee information*

The ProcessOneEmployee routine from Figure 4.13 is the only portion of the algorithm remaining to be refined. Figure 4.14 shows Step 3 of the design, including the refinement of ProcessOneEmployee.

```
ProcessOneEmployee routine:
    (' input initials, S.S.#, wage/hour, and hours ')
    (' output initials ')
    (' output S.S.# ')
    (' output wage/hour ')
    (' output hours ')
    (' calculate and output weekly wage ')
    WriteLn;
    WriteLn;

mainline routine:
    WriteString("Specify info for pres., v.p. and flunky on 3 lines. Each");
    WriteLn;
    WriteString("line should contain initials (4 chars), last four digits of");
    WriteLn;
    WriteString("social security number, hourly wage (cardinal value) and");
    WriteLn;
    WriteString("hours worked the past week (cardinal value). Following each");
    WriteLn;
    WriteString("input the correct info form will be displayed.");
    WriteLn;
    WriteLn;

    WriteString( "Input President info below:" );
    WriteLn;
    ProcessOneEmployee;

    WriteString( "Input Vice Pres. info below:" );
    WriteLn;ProcessOneEmployee;

    WriteString( "Input Flunky info below:" );
    WriteLn;
    ProcessOneEmployee;
```

FIGURE 4.14 *Design Step 3 of weekly employee information*

The remaining six comments from Step 3 can be refined into non-comment pseudoin-struction in a single refinement. The resulting algorithm (Step 4) is shown in Figure 4.15.

```
ProcessOneEmployee routine:
        Read( FirstInitial );
        Read( Period );  (* "." expected *)
        Read( LastInitial );
        Read( Period );  (* "." expected *)
        ReadCard( SocSecNum );
        ReadCard( WagePerHr );
        ReadCard( HoursWorked );
        WriteLn;

        WriteString( "    Initials:    " );
        Write( FirstInitial );
        Write( LastInitial );
        WriteLn;

        WriteString( "    S.S.#:" );
        WriteCard( SocSecNum, 0 );
        WriteLn;

        WriteString( "    wage/hr:    " );
        WriteCard( WagePerHr, 0 );
        WriteLn;

        WriteString( "    hours:      " );
        WriteCard( HoursWorked, 0 );
        WriteLn;

        WeeklyWage := WagePerHr * HoursWorked;
        WriteString( "    weekly wage:  " );
        WriteCard( WeeklyWage, 0 );

        WriteLn;
        WriteLn;

mainline routine:
        WriteString("Specify info for pres., v.p. and flunky on 3 lines. Each");
        WriteLn;
        WriteString("line should contain initials (4 chars), last four digits of");
        WriteLn;
        WriteString("social security number, hourly wage (cardinal value) and");WriteLn;
        WriteString("hours worked the past week (cardinal value). Following each");
        WriteLn;
        WriteString("input the correct info form will be displayed.");
        WriteLn;
        WriteLn;

        WriteString( "Input President info below:" );
        WriteLn;
        ProcessOneEmployee;

        WriteString( "Input Vice Pres. info below:" );
        WriteLn;
        ProcessOneEmployee;

        WriteString( "Input Flunky info below" );
        WriteLn;
        ProcessOneEmployee;
```

FIGURE 4.15 *Design Step 4 of weekly employee information*

When pseudocode is translated into a Modula-2 program all variable and procedure declarations must be supplied. In·this case there are three CHAR variables (F i r - s t I n i t i a l, Second I n i t i a l, and Per i od), as well as four CARDINAL variables (SocSecNum, WagePerHr, HoursWorked, and Week l yWage).

There are two possible places to declare these variables:

1) Within the procedure
2) Within the outer program module

Identifiers, including variables, declared within a procedure are said to be **local identifiers**. These identifiers are known only within the procedure in which they are declared and may not be used outside the procedure. The **scope of visibility**, sometimes called "the scope" of an identifier, is the program region in which it can be referenced (used). The scope of a local variable is the body of the procedure in which it is declared.

Variables ·and other identifiers declared in the program module declaration section are called **global identifiers**. A global identifier is known within the entire module and all of its procedures (i.e., those with their bodies fully specified within the module). The scope of visibility of a global variable is the entire module, including all of its procedures. This means that a global variable may be accessed by the body of the program module and by the bodies of procedures contained within the program module. There is one exception to this scope rule for global identifiers: The scope of visibility ·of a global identifier is restricted whenever the same identifier is declared local to some procedure. For example, consider the program skeleton in Figure 4.16.

```
MODULE ExampleOfGlobalIDRestriction;
    VAR SocSecNum : CARDINAL;
        HoursWorked : CARDINAL;

    PROCEDURE DisplayCompanyLogo;
    BEGIN
        (* the procedure's code goes here *)
    END DisplayCompanyLogo;

    PROCEDURE CalculatePay;
        VAR WeeklyWage :CARDINAL;
            HoursWorked :CARDINAL;
    BEGIN
        (* the procedure's code goes here *)
    END CalculatePay;

BEGIN
    (* the module's code goes here *)
END ExampleOfGlobalIDRestriction.
```

FIGURE 4.16 *Outline of a program with global and local variables*

In this program skeleton, SocSecNum and HoursWorked are the only global variables. The scope of these global variables includes the mainline and all procedures. Therefore, either variable may be used within the mainline code or the code of D i s - p l ayCompanyLogo.

Within the CalculatePay procedure are two local variables, WeeklyWage and HoursWorked. The scope of these variables is restricted to the code for the procedure in which they are declared. These variables cannot be accessed in the mainline nor within DisplayCompanyLogo.

The CalculatePay procedure may also use SocSecNum because this variable is global. However, the global variable called HoursWorked is not accessible within CalculatePay because there is a local variable declared with the same name. Within CalculatePay any reference to HoursWorked will be to the local variable, *not* the global.

The coder of the algorithm from Figure 4.15 must decide whether to use local or global variables. The rule that any competent programmer follows is to use local variables whenever possible (see "Programming with Style"). The resulting program is shown in Figure 4.17.

```
MODULE ProcessWeeklyEmployeeInfo,
        (* This program inputs weekly employee info and *)
        (* produces the government required form.       *)
     FROM InOut IMPORT Read, ReadCard, Write, WriteString,
                  WriteCard, WriteLn;

     PROCEDURE ProcessOneEmployee;
        (* POST: one line of input is consumed and the   *)
        (*       corresponding output produced for a      *)
        (*       single employee (see problem definition  *)
        (*       for details                              *)

        VAR  FirstInitial : CHAR;
             LastInitial  : CHAR;
             Period       : CHAR;
             HoursWorked  : CARDINAL;
             SocSecNum    : CARDINAL;
             WagePerHr    : CARDINAL;
             WeeklyWage   : CARDINAL;
     BEGIN
         Read( FirstInitial );
         Read( Period ) (* "." expected *);
         Read( LastInitial );
         Read( Period ) (* "." expected *);,
         ReadCard( SocSecNum );
         ReadCard( WagePerHr );
         ReadCard( HoursWorked );
         WriteLn;

         WriteString( "   Initials:   " );
         Write( FirstInitial );
         Write( LastInitial );
         WriteLn;

         WriteString( "   S.S.#:" );
         WriteCard( SocSecNum, 0 );
         WriteLn;

         WriteString( "   wage/hr:   " );
         WriteCard( WagePerHr, 0 );
         WriteLn;                                    (continued)
```

```
        WriteString( "    hours:          " );
        WriteCard( HoursWorked, 0 );
        WriteLn;

        WeeklyWage := WagePerHr * HoursWorked;
        WriteString( "    weekly wage:   " );
        WriteCard( WeeklyWage, 0 );

        WriteLn;
        WriteLn
    END ProcessOneEmployee;

BEGIN (* ProcessWeeklyEmployee program module *)

    WriteString( "Specify info for pres., " );
    WriteString( "v.p. and flunky on 3 lines. Each");
    WriteLn;   WriteString( "line should contain initials " );
    WriteString( "(4 chars), last four digits of" );
    WriteLn;
    WriteString( "social security number, " );
    WriteString( "hourly wage (cardinal value) and" );
    WriteLn;
    WriteString( "hours worked the past week " );
    WriteString( "(cardinal value). Following each" );
    WriteLn;
    WriteString( "input the correct info form " );
    WriteString( "will be displayed." );
    WriteLn;
    WriteLn;

    WriteString( "Input President info below:" );
    WriteLn;
    ProcessOneEmployee;

    WriteString( "Input Vice Pres. info below:" );
    WriteLn;
    ProcessOneEmployee;

    WriteString( "Input Flunky info below:" );
    WriteLn;
    ProcessOneEmployee

END ProcessWeeklyEmployeeInfo.
```

FIGURE 4.17 *Code for the weekly employee information problem*

*P*rogramming-with-*S*tyle

The Local vs. Global Controversy

Many coders prefer to make all identifiers global. They attempt to justify such practice by claiming that it saves coding time. However, using global declarations as a default is shortsighted. Identifiers should be local whenever possible. The thought processes that are avoided by making all identifiers global are among the most important a coder must consider. By avoiding the choice and initially defaulting to global identifiers, the coder may save some initial coding time, but almost invariably he or she will lose considerable coding time in later stages (especially during program maintenance). The use of local identifiers restricts access. The best rule is as follows:

Never use a global identifier unless you are fully prepared to justify your action!

Global identifiers can sometimes be justified for the following reasons.

1) The mainline uses the variable.
2) Local declaration would be highly inefficient.
3) The identifier is shared by many procedures.

Before using such justification, it is always best to consider whether a non-global alternative exists. If it does, it is probably superior to the global alternative.

4.5 PARAMETER PASSAGE

There are many times when parameterless procedures are inadequate. Suppose that WriteChar is a parameterless procedure that can output any single character. The mainline program that invokes WriteChar must have some method for selecting the character to be output. One possible solution is for the mainline to assign this character to a global variable, then WriteChar outputs the variable's value.

This is an awkward solution at best. Every invocation of WriteChar requires an additional assignment instruction. Furthermore, it is a bad programming practice to access global variables directly from a procedure.

Modula-2 already includes a procedure, called Write, that solves this problem. When this procedure is invoked as shown below

```
Write("?");
```

then the question mark character is output. If the procedure is invoked as shown below

```
Write("Q");
```

then a different character, the letter "Q", is output.

The Write procedure uses a technique known as **parameter passage**. Whenever Write is invoked, a **parameter** must be included to specify the character to be output. In the first invocation above, the character constant "?" is the parameter. In the second example, the parameter is "Q".

Modula-2 requires precise declarations for the use of parameter passage. When a procedure is declared, it must include a declaration for each parameter of the procedure that specifies:

1) The parameter's formal name
2) The parameter's type
3) The method of parameter passage to be used

Figure 4.18 contains a complete syntactic definition for procedure declarations, and Figure 4.19 defines procedure invocation syntax.

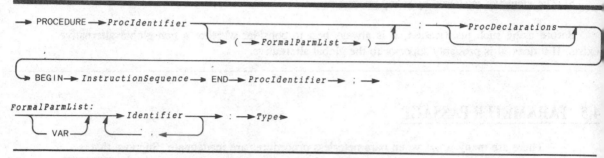

FIGURE 4.18 *Syntax diagram for ProcDeclaration*

The identifiers declared as parameters in the procedure are known as **formal parameters**. A formal parameter specifies the parameter name to be used within the code of the procedure. Prior to any list of formal parameters, a single VAR prefix may be included to determine the method of parameter passage.

When the procedure is invoked, a separate expression, called the **actual parameter**, must be supplied for every formal parameter. If a procedure is called many times, it may have a different actual parameter for the same formal parameter at each invocation.

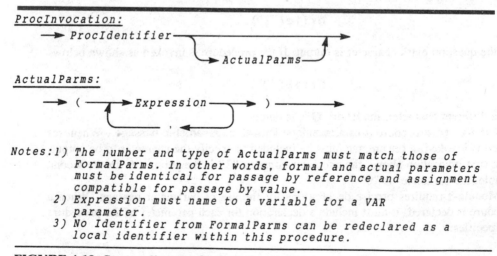

```
Notes:1) The number and type of ActualParms must match those of
         FormalParms. In other words, formal and actual parameters
         must be identical for passage by reference and assignment
         compatible for passage by value.
      2) Expression must name to a variable for a VAR
         parameter.
      3) No Identifier from FormalParms can be redeclared as a
         local identifier within this procedure.
```

FIGURE 4.19 *Syntax diagram for ProcInvocation*

Figure 4.20 contains an example WriteSquaredLine procedure. This procedure has a single formal parameter called CardVal.

```
PROCEDURE WriteSquaredLine(CardVal : CARDINAL);
   (* PRE:  CardVal is assigned              *)
   (* POST: A line is output that contains the value of *)
   (*       CardVal squared.                 *)
BEGIN
   WriteString("The value of ");
   WriteCard(CardVal,0);
   WriteString(" squared is ");
   WriteCard(CardVal*CardVal,0);
   WriteLn;
END WriteSquaredLine;
```

FIGURE 4.20 *The WriteSquaredLine procedure*

If the procedure above is invoked with the instruction

> WriteSquaredLine(5);

the following output line is written:

> The value of 5 squared is 25

The actual parameter can be any expression of CARDINAL type. For example

> WriteSquaredLine(3*4);

produces the output

> The value of 12 squared is 144

A CARDINAL variable can also be used as the actual parameter. For example

> WriteSquaredLine(SomeCard);

is a valid invocation as long as SomeCard is an assigned CARDINAL variable. The name of the actual parameter may or may not be the same as the formal parameter.

The WriteSquaredLine procedure uses a technique known as **parameter passage by value**. When a parameter is passed by value, the invoked procedure receives a *copy* of the value of the actual parameter. This is the preferred way to pass parameters when the data is only passed *to* the procedure. Sometimes it is necessary to pass data back *from* the invoked procedure. This requires the other parameter passage technique called **parameter passage by reference**.

The Modula-2 Read procedure uses parameter passage by reference. An invocation like

> Read(SomeChar)

causes a value to be input and assigned to the CHAR variable SomeChar. In this case, the Read procedure must pass *back* a value through its parameter. This is impossible with parameter passage by value.

When a parameter is passed by reference, the actual parameter *must be a variable*, not a constant or some other expression. The invoked procedure is given shared access to this variable. The procedure can examine the value of the variable and/or assign it a new value.

Figure 4.21 contains a GetPercent procedure. This procedure outputs a prompt to the user and inputs a cardinal value.

```
PROCEDURE GetPercent( VAR UserInput : CARDINAL );
   (* POST: A value, input from the user, is assigned to UserInput *)
BEGIN
   WriteString("Please input a value between 1 and 100: ");
   ReadCard(UserInput);
END GetPercent;
```

FIGURE 4.21 *The GetPercent procedure*

The UserInput parameter is passed by reference. This is denoted in Modula-2 by prefixing the formal parameter declaration with VAR. When GetPercent is invoked as shown below

GetPercent(SomeCard);

the CARDINAL variable SomeCard is shared with the procedure. The procedure refers to this shared variable with the formal parameter name, UserInput. When GetPercent inputs a value for UserInput, this value is really assigned to the actual parameter SomeCard.

Procedures often contain several parameters. The exact number and type of each parameter are specified in the procedure declaration. For example, Figure 4.22 contains a procedure called AnnualInterest with four parameters.

```
PROCEDURE AnnualInterest(    Principal : CARDINAL;
                             Rate : REAL;
                         VAR Interest : REAL;
                         VAR Total : CARDINAL );
      (* PRE:  Principal and Rate are assigned       *)
      (* POST: Interest = Principal * Rate           *)
      (*       & Total = Principal + Interest,  rounded *)
BEGIN
   Interest := FLOAT(Principal) * Rate;
   Total := TRUNC( FLOAT(Principal)+Interest+0.5 );
END AnnualInterest;
```

FIGURE 4.22 *The AnnualInterest procedure*

The first and last parameters are of type CARDINAL, and the two middle parameters are REAL. When AnnualInterest is invoked, actual parameters are associated with formal parameters by their position. In this case, the first and fourth actual parameters must be CARDINAL in type, while the second and third must be REAL.

Annual Interest also illustrates a mixture of the two parameter passage techniques. Values are supplied at invocation for original principal and interest rate, so Principal and Rate are passed by value. Annual Interest calculates and returns both an annual interest amount and the sum of the principal and this interest, so Interest and Total are passed by reference. An invocation like

    Annual Interest(1000,0.09,Int,NewPrincipal)

causes the REAL variable Int to be assigned the value 90.0 and the CARDINAL variable NewPrincipal to be assigned the value 1090.

Programming-with-Style

Style of formal parameter declarations

It is best to adopt the same style for declaring formal parameters as for declaring variables. Every formal parameter should be declared on a separate line and with matching indentation.

4.6   AN EXAMPLE OF A DESIGN USING PROCEDURES

Figure 4.23 contains a problem definition that makes use of parameter passage. The first step in the top down design for this problem is pictured in Figure 4.24.

TITLE
    Fence and sod calculation
DESCRIPTION
    Fisher Fencing Firm contracts to lay new sod and install fences. A single crew can complete two homes (both sod and fence) per week. This program prompts the user to input the dimensions of two lawns and outputs the total and average perimeters and areas for both lawns. The company intends to use this program to assist in ordering materials.
INPUT
    The user is prompted twice to enter two cardinal values per line. Each pair of input values consists of the length and width of a single lawn.
OUTPUT
    Each input pair is preceded by a separate prompt line as follows:

    Please type the length and width of a lawn.

    Following all input a blank line is output followed by the following four lines:

                                                             (continued)

```
Total fence length: <p>
Total sod area: <ta>
Average fence length: <ap>
Average sod area: <aa>
```

where <tp>, <ta>, <ap> and <aa> all denote cardinal values and <tp> is the total perimeter of both lawns, <ap> is the average perimeter (truncated), <ts> is the total square feet of both lawns and <aa> is the average (truncated.)

ERRORS

Any input not in the prescribed form produces undefined results.

EXAMPLE

The diagram below shows a snapshot of an execution of this program with all input highlighted:

```
Please type the length and width of a lawn.
50 100
Please type the length and width of a lawn.
101 99
Total fence length: 700
Total sod area: 14999
Average fence length: 350
Average sod area: 7499
```

FIGURE 4.23 *The fence and sod calculation problem definition*

```
PROCEDURE GetAreaAndPerimeter( VAR Area : CARDINAL;
                               VAR Perimeter : CARDINAL);
    (' POST: Two cardinals are prompted and input      ')
    ('      & Area is the product of these cardinals   ')
    ('      & Perimeter is their sum times 2           ')
mainline routine
        TotalArea := 0;
        TotalPerimeter := 0;
        GetAreaAndPerimeter(LawnArea,LawnPerimeter);
        (' update TotalArea and TotalPerimeter ')
        GetAreaAndPerimeter(LawnArea,LawnPerimeter);
        (' update TotalArea and TotalPerimeter ')
        (' output results ')
```

FIGURE 4.24 *Design Step 1 for fence and sod calculation*

In the top level of design, a procedure called GetAreaAndPerimeter is defined. This routine will prompt the user for the length and width of a lawn, then return the lawn's area and perimeter. The notation for this routine in Step 1 is borrowed from Modula-2. This notation is useful for specifying the parameter information (i.e., both Area and Perimeter are CARDINAL parameters passed by reference). The choice to pass both parameters by reference is necessary, since they must return data to the mainline.

The remaining details can be completed in just one more design step. The result of this design is shown in the final program given in Figure 4.25.

```
MODULE FenceAndSodCalculator;
      (* This program totals and averages the perimeter and *)
      (* area of two user-input lawns.                       *)
    FROM InOut IMPORT WriteString, WriteLn, ReadCard, WriteCard;

    VAR
        TotalArea : CARDINAL;
        TotalPerimeter : CARDINAL;
        LawnArea : CARDINAL;
        LawnPerimeter : CARDINAL;

    PROCEDURE GetAreaAndPerimeter( VAR Area : CARDINAL;
                                   VAR Perimeter : CARDINAL);
          (* POST: Two cardinals are prompted and input   *)
          (*       & Area is the product of these cardinals *)
          (*       & Perimeter is their sum times 2         *)
        VAR
            Length : CARDINAL;
            Width : CARDINAL;
    BEGIN
        WriteString("Please type the length and width of a lawn.");
        WriteLn;
        ReadCard(Length);
        ReadCard(Width);
        WriteLn;
        Area := Length * Width;
        Perimeter := (Length + Width) * 2;
    END GetAreaAndPerimeter;

BEGIN  (* FenceAndSodCalculator mainline *)
    TotalArea := 0;
    TotalPerimeter := 0;
    GetAreaAndPerimeter(LawnArea,LawnPerimeter);
    TotalArea := TotalArea + LawnArea;
    TotalPerimeter := TotalPerimeter + LawnPerimeter;
    GetAreaAndPerimeter(LawnArea,LawnPerimeter);
    TotalArea := TotalArea + LawnArea;
    TotalPerimeter := TotalPerimeter + LawnPerimeter;
    (* Assert: TotalArea = total area for both input lawns *)
    (*        & TotalPerimeter = total perimeter for both   *)
    WriteLn;
    WriteString("Total fence length: ");
    WriteCard(TotalPerimeter,0);  WriteLn;
    WriteString("Total sod area: ");
    WriteCard(TotalArea,0);  WriteLn;
    WriteString("Average fence length: ");
    WriteCard(TotalPerimeter DIV 2, 0);  WriteLn;
    WriteString("Average sod area: ");
    WriteCard(TotalArea DIV 2, 0);  WriteLn;
END FenceAndSodCalculator.
```

FIGURE 4.25 *FenceAndSodCalculator program*

4.7 SUMMARY

Top down design begins with a problem definition. Step by step this problem definition is molded into a program. At each step the algorithm is decomposed into more detailed control structures.

There are four major forms of control to be considered in design: sequences, abstraction, selection, and repetition. This chapter concentrates on sequences and abstraction.

Instructions such as assignment statements and I/O invocations form sequential control flow. Each instruction is executed in order.

In Modula-2, abstraction in control takes the form of a PROCEDURE. Procedures are like programs within programs. They may have their own local variables, and data may be communicated with them through parameter passage.

Many programs can be written using just sequences and procedures, but a complete set of design tools must include selection and repetition. The next chapter considers these issues.

||| KEY TERMS

control flow
sequence
sequential execution
abstraction
subprogram
subtask
selection
repetition
composition of control
routine
mainline routine

invocation (of routines
  or procedures)
function
subroutine
procedure
parameterless procedure
procedure body
call (routines or procedures)
transfer of control
procedure precondition

procedure postcondition
local identifier
scope of visibility
global identifiers
parameter passage
parameter
formal parameter
actual parameter
parameter passage by value
parameter passage by referen

||| EXERCISES

1. Below are two English descriptions of particular tasks. Part (a) specifies the task of chang ing a flat tire. Part (b) contains part of the directions for assembling a model airplane.
   For each part state at least one instance of sequence, abstraction, selection, and repetition
   a) The first step is to remove the flat tire. This can be accomplished by jacking up the car and removing the hubcap if necessary. Next, all lug nuts connecting the wheel to the car must be removed. (In order to remove a lug nut, use the tire iron from the trunk to turn the nut counterclockwise.) Finally, the wheel with the flat tire may be

removed from the car.

The second step is to attach the spare tire. This tire must be removed from the trunk and mounted in place of the flat. All lug nuts must be replaced. If a hubcap was removed it should be replaced. Finally, the car can be lowered and the jack, tire iron, and flat tire inserted in the trunk.

b) When the paint has dried on the airplane tail section, the tail should be inserted in the fuselage. The five fuselage decals should be applied next. These decals may be applied one at a time by soaking them in water, removing them from their paper backing, and attaching them in the desired locations.

2. Trace the execution of each of the following algorithms and indicate the precise lines of output produced:

a) PROCEDURE WriteHERE;
```
        WriteString("HERE");
```

mainline routine:
```
        Write( "X" );
        WriteHere;
        WriteLn;
        Write("T");
        WriteHere;
        WriteLn;
```

b) PROCEDURE Write2Cards(Card1 : CARDINAL;
                         Card2 : CARDINAL);
```
        WriteCard(Card1,0);
        WriteCard(Card2,0);
        WriteLn;
```

mainline routine:
```
        Write2Cards(11,22);
        Write2Cards(10+34,11*5);
```

c) PROCEDURE SumOfOrds(Char1 : CHAR;
                           Char2 : CHAR;
                        VAR Sum : CARDINAL);
```
        Sum := ORD(Char1) + ORD(Char2);
```

mainline routine:
```
        SumOfOrds("A", "B", Total);
        WriteCard(Total,0);
        WriteLn;
```

d) PROCEDURE HalfLife(Orig : CARDINAL;
                      VAR Half : CARDINAL);
```
        Half := Orig DIV 2;
```

mailine routine:
```
        SomeCard := 100;
        HalfLife(SomeCard,AnotherCard);
        WriteCard(SomeCard,0);
        WriteCard(AnotherCard,0);
        WriteLn;              HalfLife(SomeCard,AnotherCard);
        WriteCard(SomeCard,0);
        WriteCard(AnotherCard,0);
        WriteLn;
        HalfLife(AnotherCard,SomeCard);
        WriteCard(SomeCard,0);
        WriteCard(AnotherCard,0);
        WriteLn;
```

3. a) List all of the formal parameters for each part of Exercise 2.
   b) List all of the actual parameters for each part of Exercise 2.

4. a) List all of the formal parameters from Exercise 2 that are passed by value.
   b) List all of the formal parameters from Exercise 2 that are passed by reference.

5. Write an appropriate precondition for each procedure in Exercise 2.

6. Write an appropriate postcondition for each procedure in Exercise 2.

||| PROGRAMMING PROJECTS

1. The program below averages three pairs of input cardinals. Supply the missing Aver geEm procedure, using parameter passage by value as much as possible.

```
MODULE Ave3Pair;
      (* This module averages 3 pair of input values *)
      .(* NOTE: This module is missing a procedure *)

   FROM InOut IMPORT ReadCard, WriteCard, WriteString, WriteLn;

   VAR
      Val1 : CARDINAL;
      Val2 : CARDINAL;
      Average : CARDINAL;

BEGIN (* Ave3Pair mainline *)
   WriteString( "1st pair? ");
   ReadCard(Val1);
   ReadCard(Val2);         WriteLn;
   AverageEm(Val1, Val2, Average);
   WriteString("Average of last 2 input numbers is: ");
   WriteCard(Average,0);
   WriteLn; WriteLn; WriteLn;
   WriteString( "2nd pair? ");
   ReadCard(Val1);
   ReadCard(Val2);
   WriteLn;
   AverageEm(Val1, Val2, Average);
   WriteString("Average of last 2 input numbers is: ");
   WriteCard(Average,0);
   WriteLn; WriteLn; WriteLn;
   WriteString( "3rd pair? ");
   ReadCard(Val1);
   ReadCard(Val2);
   WriteLn;
   AverageEm(Val1, Val2, Average);
   WriteString("Average of last 2 input numbers is: ");
   WriteCard(Average,0);
   WriteLn; WriteLn; WriteLn;
END Ave3Pair.
```

2. Modify the Ave3Pair program from Project 1 so that another separate procedure prompts and inputs each pair. You may change each input prompt to "Input pair?"

3. Below is a problem definition. Perform a complete top down design for this problem. Your final algorithm should include procedures. Code your algorithm in Modula-2 and test its correctness.

TITLE
 Mileage for Ed's Trip

DESCRIPTION
 Ed is going to drive to his next sales meeting. He wants a program to calculate his gas mileage. The trip is made in three legs, and the car is refueled after each leg.

INPUT
 The program prompts and inputs three pairs of cardinal values, one per leg of the trip. The first value in each input pair is the number of miles for the leg and the second is the number of gallons of gasoline used to refuel.

OUTPUT
 The prompt on a separate line before each input pair is as follows:

                Miles&Fuel?

 Input should come from the same line as the prompt. After each input pair the gas mileage for that leg is output as follows:

                M.P.G. (for this leg): <m>

 where <m> denotes the miles per gallon rounded to the nearest cardinal. A blank line follows each of these gas mileage lines.

 After all input completes, the final output is:

                Total Mileage: <M>
                Total Gallons of Gas: <G>
                Average M.P.G.: <A>

 where <M> denotes the combined mileage for all three legs, <G> denotes the combined gasoline refuelings and <A> denotes the combined average miles per gallon rounded to the nearest cardinal.

ERRORS
 All input not conforming to the above specifications produces undefined results.

EXAMPLE
 Below is a complete sample program execution. All input is highlighted:

                Miles & Fuel? 300 10
                M.P.G. (for this leg): 30

                Miles & Fuel? 340 11
                M.P.G. (for this leg): 31

                Miles & Fuel? 300 9
                M.P.G. (for this leg): 33

                Total Mileage: 940
                Total Gallons of Gas: 30
                Average M.P.G.: 31

4. Below is a problem definition. Perform a complete top down design for this problem. Your final algorithm should include procedures. Code your algorithm in Modula-2 and test its correctness.

TITLE

Hockey Statistics

DESCRIPTION

Three of the best Olympic Hockey teams are those of the Soviet Union, Czechoslovakia, and the United States. The United States coach would like a program to keep track of the number of goals scored by each of these teams in the four matches just before the Olympics.

INPUT

The coach inputs three lines, one for each team. Each line contains four cardinal scores, one for the number of goals scored by that team in each of its last four matches.

OUTPUT

An initial prompt like the two lines below precedes all input lines:

```
Please input three lines of 4 scores. The lines should
be in this order: Soviet U., Czech., USA
```

Following the three input lines, a blank line is output followed by the lines below:

```
                    Soviet Union: <SU>
                    Czechoslovakia: <CZ>
                    United States: <US>

                    Total Ave: <A>
```

where <SU>, <CZ> and <US> are the average number of goals scored in the matches rounded to the nearest tenth of a goal. <A> denotes the average number of goals for all twelve scores, also rounded to the nearest tenth of a goal. (Note: One of your procedures should output real numbers so they appear rounded to the nearest tenth.)

ERRORS

All input not conforming to the above specifications produces undefined results.

EXAMPLE

Below is a complete sample program execution. All input is highlighted:

```
Please input three lines of 4 scores. The lines should
be in this order: Soviet U., Czech., USA.

9 8 5 7
5 5 5 5
3 2 9 1

Soviet Union: 7.3
Czechoslovakia: 5.0
United States: 3.8

Total Ave: 5.3
```

5 ||| MORE STRUCTURED PROGRAMMING

5.1 THE NEED FOR MORE CONTROL

A full set of design control structures includes:

1) Sequences
2) Abstraction (the procedure)
3) Selection
4) Repetition

The last chapter considered the first two structures. This chapter considers the remaining pair.

An algorithm needs to make choices. If the problem is to select the largest from some collection of values, then there needs to be a control structure to choose. **Selection** control structures are used to make choices.

Often times an algorithm repeats the same task over and over. The **repetition** control structures makes this possible.

5.2 SELECTION: THE IF CONTROL STRUCTURE

The most commonly used form of selection in algorithms and programming languages is an **IF instruction**. An IF instruction has two basic forms. The first form is referred to as an **IF-THEN instruction**. The second form of the IF is called **IF-THEN-ELSE instruction**. Both of these forms are illustrated in Figure 5.1 on the following page.

IF instruction (first form - without ELSE)

```
IF (* condition *) THEN
    (* pseudoinstructions *)
END
```

IF instruction (second form - with ELSE)

```
IF (* condition *) THEN
    (* pseudoinstructions *)
ELSE
    (* other pseudoinstructions *)
END
```

FIGURE 5.1 *IF-THEN and IF-THEN-ELSE pseudoinstructions*

In both the IF-THEN and IF-THEN-ELSE pseudoinstructions (* condition *) represents some designer-supplied **selection condition**. The selection condition is a logical expression that can be evaluated to be either true or false. The indented pseudocode comments from Figure 5.1 may be replaced by any sequence of pseudoinstructions desired. The (* pseudoinstructions *) immediately following THEN is referred to as the **THEN clause**, while the (* other pseudoinstructions *) immediately following the ELSE is called the **ELSE clause**.

An IF-THEN (without ELSE) specifies a portion of pseudocode that is to be optionally performed. When an IF-THEN instruction is performed, two things happen. First, the selection condition, (* condition *), is evaluated and found to be either true or false. Second, a choice is made based on the selection condition value. If this condition is true, the THEN clause is performed. If (* condition *) is false, the THEN clause is not performed. As an example, consider the algorithm below.

```
Read( Period );
IF Period#"." THEN
    WriteString( "ERRONEOUS INPUT _ period expected");
    WriteLn;
END;
Read( LastInitial );
```

When the algorithm above is performed, the Read instruction is performed first. Next, the selection condition, Period# " . " , is evaluated. This condition tests the value stored in Period to see whether or not it is the period character, "." (the symbol "#" means "not equal to").

After the character is input and stored in Period, a selection is made. If Period does not store "." then the THEN clause is performed, writing out the error message. If the character stored in Period is ".", the THEN clause is not performed. After executing the IF, the final Read instruction is always performed. The general flow of control for the IF-THEN instruction is diagrammed in Figure 5.2.

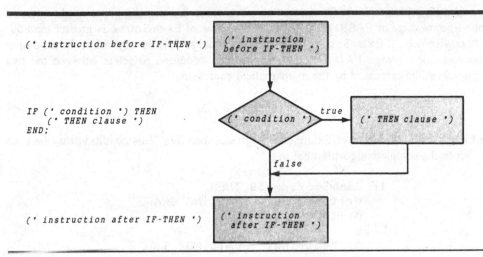

FIGURE 5.2 *Control flow of the IF-THEN instruction*

The IF-THEN instruction is a type of **control structure**. A control structure is an instruction that controls the execution sequence of other instructions. Control structures may cause different control flow depending upon various conditions at execution time.

The IF-THEN-ELSE is another selection control structure. This instruction contains a THEN clause and an ELSE clause. When an IF-THEN-ELSE is performed it selects one of the two clauses to perform. The control flow for the IF-THEN-ELSE is diagrammed in Figure 5.3.

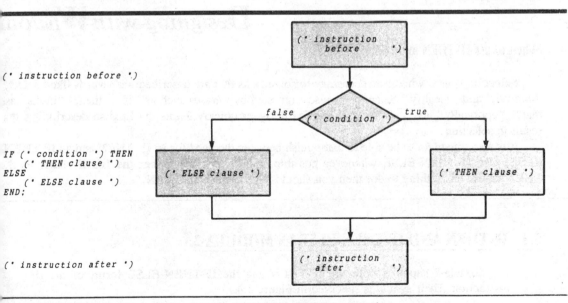

FIGURE 5.3 *Control flow of the IF-THEN-ELSE instruction*

An algorithm to identify whether an exam score is a passing grade might output a one line message of PASSING GRADE, if the value of ExamScore is greater than 59. Otherwise (i.e., if ExamScore is less than or equal to 59), the algorithm should output the one line message FAILING. An appropriate condition to select between the two options can be expressed by the mathematical expression:

$$ExamScore > 59$$

which is read "the value of ExamScore is greater than 59." This condition may be used to write the complete algorithm below.

```
IF ExamScore > 59 THEN
    WriteString( "PASSING GRADE" );
    WriteLn;
ELSE
    WriteString( "FAILING" );
    WriteLn;
END
```

Sometimes selection control structures are referred to as **branches** because they allow the control flow to branch to one collection of instructions or another. The IF-THEN is called a **one-armed branch** because its control flow appears diagramatically to have one arm which passes through the optional THEN clause. The IF-THEN-ELSE is called a **two-armed branch** since its control flow diagram appears to have one arm passing through the THEN clause and another passing through the ELSE clause.

Designing-with-Wisdom

When to use IF-THEN and IF-THEN-ELSE

Selection is used when it is necessary to solve tasks that are described with words like "select," "choose," and "identify." Selection is also suggested by phrases such as "if ... then," "in the case that," "optionally," and "whenever." A good designer quickly learns the English descriptions that result in selection.

It is also important to be able to distinguish between the need for an IF-THEN and an IF-THEN-ELSE. Use IF-THEN-ELSE whenever possible. If you find that either the ELSE clause or the THEN clause has nothing to do, then you should have used an IF-THEN.

5.3   IF-THEN AND IF-THEN-ELSE IN MODULA-2

Modula-2 supports both the IF-THEN and the IF-THEN-ELSE forms of the IF instruction. Their syntax is specified in Figure 5.4.

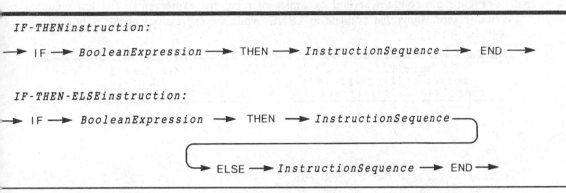

IF-THENinstruction:

IF-THEN-ELSEinstruction:

FIGURE 5.4 *Syntax diagram for IF-THEN instruction and IF-THEN-ELSE instruction*

The "BooleanExpression" from Figure 5.4 stands for any valid Modula-2 expression that is of type BOOLEAN, a logical expression. A complete discussion of the Modula-2 BooleanExpression is presented in Chapter 6. In this chapter a simple version of logical expression, called a **relational expression** is examined.

Relational expressions (see Figure 5.5 for the Modula-2 definition) are so named because they are a comparison of two expressions. The two expressions compared must be of compatible type, both either INTEGER, CHAR, CARDINAL, or REAL.

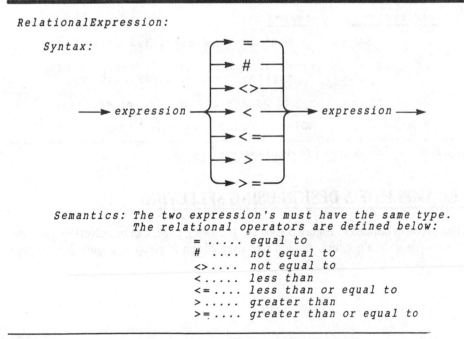

RelationalExpression:

   Syntax:

```
Semantics: The two expression's must have the same type.
           The relational operators are defined below:
               = ..... equal to
               # .... not equal to
               <>.... not equal to
               < ..... less than
               <= .... less than or equal to
               > ..... greater than
               >= .... greater than or equal to
```

FIGURE 5.5 *Syntax and semantics of RelationalExpression*

Figure 5.6 contains several examples of relational expressions. The left column contains expressions that evaluate to TRUE, while the expressions of the right column evaluate to FALSE.

True Valued *RelationalExpressions* *(Assume Total=3 & Initial="F")*	*False Valued* *RelationalExpressions* *(Assume Total=3 & Initial="F")*
17 < 34	17 > 17
"?" <= "?"	"B" <= "A"
65.3 – 1.2 >= (–3.2) * 1.75	71 + 3 <> 77 – 3
Initial < "Z"	Initial = "9"
Total = TRUNC(2.1) + 1	Total * 2 = Total * 4
(Total * 2) # 74	(Total + 2) >= 123

FIGURE 5.6 *Samples of relational expressions*

The invalid relational expressions in Figure 5.7 illustrate possible syntax errors that can occur.

syntactically *invalid* *expression*	*reason*
17 < > 34	<> *must be two consecutive characters*
"A" < 25	*type incompatibility (comparing a CHAR* *expression, "A", to a CARDINAL, 25)*
75 => 23	=> *is an invalid relational operator*
3 NOT= 4	NOT= *is not a relational operator*

FIGURE 5.7 *Syntactic errors in relational expressions*

5.4   AN EXAMPLE OF A DESIGN USING SELECTION

The problem defined in Figure 5.8 on the following page, can be solved by an input/ process/output style algorithm. Such a top level design is given in Figure 5.9 on page 136.

TITLE
Identify high temperature

DESCRIPTION
A meteorologist needs a program to assist in weather processing for the evening weather report. The meteorologist always collects three temperature readings between the mid-day and evening weather reports. The program should input the three temperatures (they are expressed in degrees Fahrenheit) and output the highest temperature. This program should also print the message FREEZE WARNING if the highest of these temperatures is lower than 40 degrees.

INPUT
The three temperatures are input, one per line, as INTEGER constants. Each input is given in response to a prompt (see OUTPUT section).

OUTPUT
Three prompt lines preceed the input. These prompt lines are:

```
Please enter first reading:
Please enter second reading:
Please enter third reading:
```

Following the prompted input are two blank lines followed by the line below, where <h> denotes the value of the greatest of the three input values:

```
High temperature since mid-day: <h>
```

If the value of the greatest of the three input temperatures is less than 40 degrees, then an additional blank line followed by the following line is output:

```
FREEZE WARNING
```

ERRORS
Any input not in the prescribed form produces undefined results.

EXAMPLE
The diagram below shows a snapshot of an execution of this program, with all input highlighted.

```
Please enter first reading: -1
Please enter second reading: 15
Please enter third reading: 10

High temperature since mid-day: 15

FREEZE WARNING
```

FIGURE 5.8 *Problem definition for three temperature analysis*

```
(* prompt and input the three temperatures *)
(* output two blank lines *)
(* identify highest of the three temperatures *)
(* output the highest temperature *)
(* output freeze warning if necessary *)
```

FIGURE 5.9 *Design Step 1 for three temperature analysis*

The two comments from design Step 1 that will require selection are the third comment:

(* identify highest of the three temperatures *)

and the last comment:

(* output freeze warning if necessary *)

Deciding how to perform the selection required by (* identify highest of the three temperatures *) is best done by considering how to select the largest of three values. One possibility is to compare the first two items and discard the smaller. Next, the larger from the first comparison can be compared to the third to find the largest of all. Translating this informal algorithm into a refinement for the pseudoinstruction yields the following.

(* identify highest of the three temperatures *)

is initially refined as

(* assign HighTemp the greater of FirstTemp and SecondTemp *)
(* assign HighTemp the greater of HighTemp and ThirdTemp   *)

At this stage of refinement, the general algorithm for selecting the largest of three values has been refined into two subtasks. These subtasks are refined as follows.

(* assign HighTemp the greater of FirstTemp and SecondTemp *)

is refined as

```
IF FirstTemp > SecondTemp THEN
    HighTemp : = FirstTemp
ELSE
    HighTemp : = SecondTemp
END
(* ASSERT: HighTemp is the largest of FirstTemp & SecondTemp   *)
(*              assign HighTemp the greater of HighTemp and ThirdTemp *)
```

is refined as

```
IF ThirdTemp > HighTemp THEN
   HighTemp : = ThirdTemp
END
(* ASSERT: HighTemp is the largest of FirstTemp, *)
(*            SecondTemp and ThirdTemp            *)
```

The final pseudoinstruction from Step 1 is (* output freeze warning if necessary *). The word "if", of course, calls for selection. In this case, an IF-THEN instruction is appropriate. The correct refinement is given below.

(* output freeze warning if necessary *)

is refined as

```
IF HighTemp < 40 THEN
   WriteLn;
   WriteString( "FREEZE WARNING" );
   WriteLn;
END
```

The completed design for the three temperature analysis appears in Step 2. This algorithm is in Figure 5.10. The corresponding Modula-2 program is given in Figure 5.11.

```
WriteString( "Please enter first reading: " );
ReadInt( FirstTemp );
WriteLn;
WriteString( "Please enter second reading: " );
ReadInt( SecondTemp );
WriteLn;
WriteString( "Please enter third reading: " );
ReadInt( ThirdTemp );
WriteLn;
WriteLn;
WriteLn;

IF  FirstTemp > SecondTemp   THEN
   HighTemp := FirstTemp
ELSE
    HighTemp := SecondTemp
END
IF  ThirdTemp > HighTemp   THEN
   HighTemp := ThirdTemp
END

(* ASSERT: HighTemp is the largest of FirstTemp, *)
(*            SecondTemp and ThirdTemp            *)

WriteString( "High temperature since mid-day: " );
WriteInt( HighTemp, 0 );
WriteLn;
IF  HighTemp < 40  THEN
   WriteLn;
   WriteString( "FREEZE WARNING" );
   WriteLn;
END
```

FIGURE 5.10 *Final design step for three temperature analysis*

```
MODULE AnalyzeThreeTemps;
    (* This program inputs three temperature integers, outputs    *)
    (* the largest, and outputs a freze warning when the largest  *)
    (* is less than 40 degrees F.                                  *)

    FROM InOut IMPORT WriteString, WriteInt, WriteLn, ReadInt;

    VAR
        FirstTemp   : INTEGER;
        SecondTemp  : INTEGER;
        ThirdTemp   : INTEGER;
        HighTemp    : INTEGER;

BEGIN
    WriteString( "Please enter first reading: " );
    ReadInt( FirstTemp );
    WriteLn;
    WriteString( "Please enter second reading:" );
    ReadInt( SecondTemp );
    WriteLn;
    WriteString( "Please enter third reading: " );
    ReadInt( ThirdTemp );
    WriteLn;
    WriteLn;
    WriteLn;

    IF  FirstTemp > SecondTemp  THEN
        HighTemp := FirstTemp
    ELSE
        HighTemp := SecondTemp
    END;
    IF  ThirdTemp > HighTemp  THEN
        HighTemp := ThirdTemp
    END;
    (* ASSERT: HighTemp is the largest of FirstTemp, *)
    (*         SecondTemp, and ThirdTemp             *)

    WriteString( "High temperature since mid-day: " );
    WriteInt( HighTemp, 0 );
    WriteLn;

    IF  HighTemp < 40  THEN
        WriteLn;
        WriteString( "FREEZE WARNING" );
        WriteLn;
    END

END AnalyzeThreeTemps.
```

FIGURE 5.11 *Program for three temperature analysis*

Programming-with-Style

IF Punctuation

The IF instruction imposes no additional punctuation requirements. A semicolon is *optional* after any THEN clause or ELSE clause.

Indentation of the IF instruction

Indentation is critical to the readability of control structures. Below are two instances of the same Modula-2 code, with and without proper indentation:

```
Poor indentation                    Good indentation

IF Max = Min THEN                   IF Max = Min THEN
Middle . = Max;                       Middle := Max;
WriteCard( Middle, 0 )                WriteCard( Middle, 0 )
ELSE                                ELSE
Middle := (Max+Min) DIV 2             Middle := (Max+Min) DIV 2
END;                                END;
   IF Middle = Final THEN           IF Middle = Final THEN
WriteString( "fini" )                 WriteString( "fini" )
      END                           END
```

The key to good control-structure indentation is to distinguish the control structure from its component instructions. In the IF instruction, the bodies of the THEN clause and the ELSE clause should be indented. There are two currently accepted practices for IF: one that indents everything from the IF, and one that indents only the THEN and ELSE clauses.

```
IF (* condition *) THEN        IF (* condition *)
   (* THEN clause *)           THEN
ELSE                              (* THEN clause *)
   (* ELSE clause *)           ELSE
END                               (* ELSE clause *)
                               END
```

5.5 REPETITION: THE WHILE CONTROL STRUCUTRE

Computers are often thought of as faithful servants because they perform large numbers of instructions with accuracy and without protest. This characteristic equips computers well for performing repetitive tasks. The most widely accepted repetition control structure for program design is WHILE. Sometimes called a **WHILE instruction** or **WHILE loop**, this control structure is described in Figure 5.12.

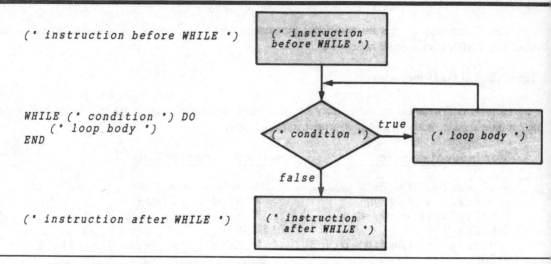

```
(* instruction before WHILE *)


WHILE (* condition *) DO
     (* loop body *)
END


(* instruction after WHILE *)
```

FIGURE 5.12 *Control flow of the WHILE instruction*

A WHILE loop has two parts:

1) a loop condition
2) a loop body

The **loop condition**, (* condition *) from Figure 5.12, is a logical expression that controls how often the loop is performed. The loop body contains the instructions of the task performed each time the loop is repeated.

WHILE begins executing with the evaluation of the loop condition. If the condition is found to be false, then the execution of the WHILE is terminated and control passes to the next instruction after the WHILE. However, if the loop condition evaluates to true, then the body of the loop is performed. Performing the body once is called an **iteration** of the loop. After each loop iteration, this process is repeated, beginning with a reevaluation of the loop condition.

Below is an example of a WHILE loop. This loop uses the CARDINAL variable PowerOfTwo to display the value of 2 raised to several integer powers. The comments following the lines of the algorithm are included for tracing purposes only.

```
PowerOfTwo := 2;                      (* (1) *)
WHILE PowerOfTwo < 10 DO              (* (2) *)
    WriteCard( PowerOfTwo, 0 );       (* (3) *)
    WriteLn;
    PowerOfTwo := PowerOfTwo * 2      (* (4) *)
END;
WriteString( "the end" );            (* (5) *)
```

A trace of this algorithm is shown in Figure 5.13. The value of the variable PowerOfTwo after the loop is terminated is 16.

Line no.	Action	PowerOfTwo	Output
(1)	PowerOfTwo := 2	2	
(2)	condition is 2<10 = true		
(3)	output WriteCard(...		2
(4)	PowerOfTwo := 2*2	4	
(2)	condition is 4<10 = true		
(3)	output WriteCard(...		4
(4)	PowerOfTwo := 4*2	8	
(2)	condition is 8<10 = true		
(3)	output WriteCard(...		8
(4)	PowerOfTwo := 8*2	16	
(2)	condition is 16<10 = false		
(5)	output WriteString(...		the end

FIGURE 5.13 *Trace of a sample WHILE Loop*

The most annoying logical error known to programmers is the **infinite loop**. An infinite WHILE loop is one for which the loop condition nevers becomes false, so the loop is performed over and over. The infinite loop below is the result of a small change to the previous WHILE.

```
(* WARNING - infinite loop below *)
PowerOfTwo := 2;
WHILE PowerOfTwo > 1 DO
    WriteCard( PowerOfTwo, 0 );
    WriteLn;
    PowerOfTwo := PowerOfTwo * 2
END;
WriteString( "the end" );
```

The loop condition has been changed to PowerOfTwo > 1. This condition is true the first time it is tested (2>1). Since the value of PowerOfTwo *increases*, is *incremented*, with each iteration, the loop condition will remain true forever.

Of course most computer programs with infinite loops don't really execute forever. If the above algorithm were coded and executed, the value of PowerOfTwo would eventually become too large for the computer to store. At that time the computer would generate a **run-time error**. There are infinite loops that do not produce any errors. For example, suppose the PowerOfTwo := PowerOfTwo * 2 instruction is removed from the above algorithm. In this case it is up to the user or a computer operator to intervene. Most Modula-2 systems provide some keystroke that will terminate program execution. A programmer may need this keystroke to halt an infinite loop execution. Before attempting to write any programs containing loops, it is always a good idea to find out how to terminate an executing program from the keyboard!

5.6   COUNTER AND TRAILER STYLE LOOPS

Two general forms of the WHILE loop are so common they are given special names:

Counter loops

Trailer loops

A **counter loop** is so named because it counts how many iterations have been performed and terminates the loop when the count is sufficient. Counter loops would be used in the following:

- Read a list of *20* album titles.
- Read a sequence of *5* lap times for a race car.
- Process a collection of *thirty* bank transactions.
- Input and process a group of *five thousand* module identifiers.

A counter loop requires that a variable be used to count the number of loop iterations performed. This variable is referred to as a **counter variable**. Each iteration must cause the counter variable to be incremented, and the loop condition tests the final value. A counter loop that iterates 50 times is shown below.

```
Counter := 1;
WHILE Counter<=50 DO
    (* the task to be performed goes here *)
    Counter := Counter + 1
END
```

Two operations must be included for a counter loop to work correctly. It is essential to initialize the value of the counter variable before starting the loop (see `Counter := 1` above). If this initialization is not performed, `Counter` may be undefined. It is also necessary to alter the value of the counter variable within the loop body (see `Counter := Counter + 1` above). Failure to change the value of the loop counter within the loop body will most likely result in an infinite loop.

Trailer loops continue for values up to some particular value. This final value is called a **trailer value**. Samples of problems that require trailer loops include:

- Read a list of album titles *until "??"* is encountered
- Read a sequence of lap times *followed by a time of 0*
- Input all bank transactions *prior to an XXX* code
- Input a group of module identifiers *until a syntactically invalid indentifier* is input

The trailer loop below inputs integers until the first negative value is read:

```
ReadInt( SomeInt );
WHILE SomeInt >= 0 DO
  (* process SomeInt *)
  ReadInt( SomeInt )
END
```

Trailer loops require two operations, as do counter loops. It is often essential to perform a **priming read**, that is to read the first item value, before starting the loop. Failure to perform the first ReadInt in the example may leave SomeInt as an unassigned variable when it is first tested in the loop condition. It is also essential that a new item be input before the next loop condition is evaluated. Failure to do so generally results in an infinite loop. The trailer loop form above is typical. The value of SomeInt is input at the very end of one iteration and not processed until the next iteration.

The syntax of the Modula-2 WHILE instruction is shown in Figure 5.14. As with the IF instruction, "BooleanExpression" will be taken for now to mean "RelationalExpression."

WHILEinstruction:

→ WHILE ──→ *BooleanExpression* ──→ DO ──→ *InstructionSequence* ──→ END ──→

FIGURE 5.14 *Syntax diagram for WHILE instruction*

Designing-with-Wisdom

The Three Questions for a WHILE Loop

When using a WHILE loop in a design, the designer must answer three questions.

1) What task is to be performed in a single loop iteration? (The answer to this question becomes the body of the loop.)
2) Under what conditions should repetition continue? (The answer to this question becomes the loop condition.)
3) What is required for the loop condition to be tested and the loop body to execute the first time? (The answer to this produces initialization code preceding the loop.)

.7 AN EXAMPLE OF A DESIGN USING REPETITION

The problem from Figure 5.15 on the following page is used to illustrate a complete top down design requiring repetition.

TITLE

Count words in a single sentence

DESCRIPTION

One method of analyzing the reading level of written material is to examine the length of sentences. In this problem a single sentence will be input. The input sentence must end with a period. The program counts the number of words in the sentence.

INPUT

There is a single line of input consisting of an English sentence with no leading or trailing blanks. Consecutive words are separated by a single blank. The final word of the sentence is followed immediately by a period.

OUTPUT

A single prompt line of the following form precedes the input line:

Please specify sentence to be analyzed below:

Following the prompted input line are two blank lines followed by the line below, where <w> denotes the value of the number of words in the input sentence:

Word count = <w>

ERRORS

1) If no period is included, undefined results occur.
2) Any input following the first period is ignored.
3) Additional blanks in the input line produce erroneous wordcounts.
4) Omitted blanks in the input line produce erroneous word counts.

EXAMPLE

The diagram below shows a snapshot of an execution of this program with all input highlighted.

Please specify sentence to be analyzed below:

Now is the time for all good computers to come to
              the aid of the coder.

Word count = 16

FIGURE 5.15 *Problem definition for word count*

The key item to note in the word count problem is that blanks can be used to count words. An input sentence must contain exactly one blank between two consecutive words. This means that every word, except the last, is followed by a blank. Therefore, counting words is equivalent to counting blanks and adding one (for the last word).

Another important aspect of this problem is that the input can be any number of characters. This input terminates with a period. These two facts suggest a trailer loop. The three questions to be answered regarding this loop (see "Designing with Wisdom" earlier in this section), along with the appropriate answers, are given (opposite).

Question: What task is to be performed in a single loop iteration?

Answer: Check the input character and update word count (if necessary); then input the next character.

Question: Under what conditions should repetition continue?

Answer: As long as the input character is not a period.

Question: What is required for the loop condition to be tested and the loop body to execute for the first time?

Answer: The first character must be input (priming read) and word count initialized to 0.

The algorithm resulting from these answers is shown in Design Step 1 in Figure 5.16.

```
WordCount := 0;
(' output prompt ')

Read( NextChar );
WHILE NextChar#"." DO
    (' update WordCount if at the end of a word ')
    Read( NextChar )
END;

(' count the last word ')
(' output WordCount ')
```

FIGURE 5.16 *Design Step 1 for word count*

The major portion of this algorithm is a trailer loop that executes again and again until a period is input. The body of the loop processes the character that was read in the preceding iteration (or before the loop started) and reads the next character.

The next refinement step is pictured in Figure 5.17. The body of the loop uses an IF-THEN instruction to select when to update the count of input words appropriately.

```
WordCount := 0;
WriteString( "Please specify sentence to be analyzed below:" );
WriteLn;

Read( NextChar );
WHILE NextChar#"." DO
    IF  NextChar=" "  THEN
        WordCount := WordCount + 1
    END;
    Read( NextChar )
END

WordCount := WordCount + 1   (' count the last word ');
WriteLn;
WriteLn;
WriteString( "Word count = ");
WriteCard( WordCount,0 );
WriteLn;
```

FIGURE 5.17 *Design Step 2 for word count*

Figure 5.18 contains the complete Modula-2 program for this word counting problem.

```
MODULE WordCount;
    (* This program inputs a single line sentence and counts  *)
    (* the words in the sentence. Note: Sentence must end      *)
    (* in a period, with exactly one blank separating words.   *)

    FROM InOut IMPORT WriteString, WriteCard, WriteLn, Read, Write;

    VAR
        WordCount : CARDINAL;
        NextChar  : CHAR;

BEGIN
    WordCount := 0;
    WriteString( "Please specify sentence to be analyzed below:" );
    WriteLn;

    Read( NextChar );
    Write( NextChar );   (* echo input character *)
    WHILE NextChar#"." DO
      IF  NextChar=" "  THEN
          WordCount := WordCount + 1
      END;
      Read( NextChar );
      Write( NextChar );   (* echo input character *)
    END;

    WordCount := WordCount + 1;    (* count the last word *)
    WriteLn;
    WriteLn;
    WriteString( "Word count = " );
    WriteCard( WordCount,0 );
    WriteLn
END WordCount.
```

FIGURE 5.18 *Modula-2 program for word count*

Designing-with-Wisdom

When to Initialize

The word count problem illustrates how important it is to initialize certain variables (Word-Count & NextChar). Any variable whose value is necessary for output or evaluation of some expression must have been previously assigned some value. It is best to examine all variables within a module to see if they require initial values, and try to place these initializations as close as possible to where they are required. Good candidates for such required initialization are counter variables, variables input by a loop, and variables used to accumulate sums.

Delay Clause and Body Refinement Until the Next Step

During the process of top down design it is always necessary to fight the temptation to fill in too much detail too early. One good beginning rule is to delay refining THEN clauses, ELSE clauses and loop bodies until the next step after the IF or WHILE is created. A minor exception to this policy should be made for counter and trailer loops where the counter or trailer variable update required in the loop body should be specified when the loop is introduced.

Programming-with-Style

WHILE Punctuation

The WHILE instruction does not add any new punctuation requirements. A semicolon is optional following the body of the loop.

Indentation of the WHILE instruction

Like the clauses of an IF instruction, the body of a WHILE loop must always be indented for readability. The preferred form of such indentation is shown below.

```
WHILE (* condition *) DO
    (* loop body *)
END
```

5.8 ANOTHER DESIGN

This section summarizes the ideas of the chapter by considering another example of a design problem. The problem definition is contained in Figure 5.19.

TITLE
Rectangle/parallelogram display

DESCRIPTION
This program is an example of interactive generation of pictures. The program is capable of producing two different pictures, a parallelogram or a rectangle. It repeatedly prompts the user to indicate which picture is desired, then outputs it.

INPUT
For each iteration, a single character is input in response to the initial Which diagram? prompt. This input should be either a P, an R, or an X (uppercase letters only). When R is specified (a rectangle is to be output) the user will also be prompted to specify the height of the rectangle. This height of rectangle input must be a cardinal constant in the range from (and including) 2 to 20.

(continued)

OUTPUT

The prompt prior to each picture selection is as follows:

Which diagram? ("P" or "R" or "X")

Following this prompt, it is assumed that either a P an R or an X will be input. An X signals the end of execution.

In response to a P the following parallelogram is output:

```
11111
 11111
  11111
   11111
    11111
```

An R response to the picture prompt specifies that a rectangle is to be output. The program prompts for a height in this instance. This prompt is shown below:

Rectangle height? (2 to 20)

The rectangle produced should be as follows. (Note that the number of +'s in height should be the number input in reponse to the height prompt and the width is always 10.) The illustration assumes height to be six.

```
+ + + + + + + + + +
+                 +
+                 +
+                 +
+                 +
+ + + + + + + + + +
```

ADDITIONAL details of output:
1) Input should be accepted from the line following the prompt.
2) There should be 1 to 4 blanks lines separating pictures and prompted input, but the exact number is not critical.

ERRORS
1) Any input to the picture prompt other than P, R, or X causes the rectangle option to be chosen.
2) Any non-cardinal input in response to the rectangle height prompt produces undefined results.
3) Any value input for this purpose that is greater than 20 causes the following message to be displayed and no picture to be produced for this case:

INPUT MUST BE FROM 2 to 20

4) The specification of a rectangle height of 0 or 1 produces undefined results.

(continued)

EXAMPLE

Below is a series of snapshots depicting a sample execution of this program. All input is highlighted.

```
Which diagram? ("P" or "R" or "X")
R

Rectangle height? (2 to 20)
3

+ + + + + + + + +
+               +
+ + + + + + + + +


Which diagram? ("P" or "R" or "X")
P

11111
 11111
  11111
   11111
    11111


Which diagram? ("P" or "R" or "X")
p

Rectangle height? (2 to 20)
2

+ + + + + + + + +
+ + + + + + + + +


Which diagram? ("P" or "R" or "X")
R

Rectangle height? (2 to 20)
21

INPUT MUST BE FROM 2 to 20


Which diagram? ("P" or "R" or "X")
X
```

FIGURE 5.19 *Problem description for rectangle/parallelogram display*

The top level algorithm for the rectangle/parallelogram display problem must use repetition, repeatedly requesting the user for information and displaying the appropriate picture. The designer proceeds by answering the three questions for a WHILE loop.

Question: What task is to be performed in a single loop iteration?
Answer: Display the picture for the current user choice and input user's next choice.
Question: Under what conditions should repetition continue?
Answer: As long as the user's choice is not X.
Question: What is required for the loop condition to be tested and the loop body to execute for the first time?
Answer: The first user choice is input (priming read).

These answers suggest a trailer loop. Figure 5.20 contains the first step of the design that results. The output instructions of this step are required to perform the prompting of input.

```
WriteString( 'Which diagram? ("P" or "R" or "X")' );
WriteLn;
Read( DiagramChar );

WHILE  DiagramChar<>"X" DO

    (* display picture *)

    WriteString( 'Which diagram? ("P" or "R" or "X")' );
    WriteLn;
    Read( DiagramChar )
END
```

FIGURE 5.20 *Design Step 1 for rectangle/parallelogram display (initial version)*

Before the designer proceeds to Step 2, a **design review** is in order. A good design review consists of scanning through an algorithm to ensure that it is precise, complete, and correct.

A design review of this algorithm should reveal that it is basically correct. The (* display picture *) comment is a bit vague, making the algorithm somewhat imprecise. In addition, the designer seems to have overlooked the blank lines that were required to separate portions of output. The omission of these blank lines makes the algorithm incomplete. The best time to correct these deficiencies is now. Figure 5.21 on the opposite page, contains another version of Step 1 that has been improved after the design review.

```
WriteString( 'Which diagram? ("P" or "R" or "X")' );
WriteLn;
Read( DiagramChar );

WHILE  DiagramChar<>"X" DO
   WriteLn;
   WriteLn;

   (* display user chosen rectangle or parallelogram *)

   WriteLn;
   WriteLn;
   WriteString( 'Which diagram? ("P" or "R" or "X")' );
   WriteLn;
   Read( DiagramChar )
END
```

FIGURE 5.21 *Design Step 1 for rectangle/parallelogram display (second version)*

This algorithm can be simplified a bit by combining the prompt and input of DiagramChar in a separate procedure. This makes the mainline a bit more compact, as shown in Figure 5.22.

```
PROCEDURE GetDiagramChar( VAR DiagramChar : CHAR );
    (* POST: DiagramChar is assigned from input *)
   WriteString( 'Which diagram? ("P" or "R" or "X")' );
   WriteLn;
   Read( DiagramChar );

mainline routine:
   GetDiagramChar(DiagramChar);
   WHILE  DiagramChar<>"X" DO
      WriteLn;
      WriteLn;

      (* display user chosen rectangle or parallelogram *)

      WriteLn;
      WriteLn;
      GetDiagramChar(DiagramChar);
   END
```

FIGURE 5.22 *Design Step 1 for rectangle/parallelogram display (final version)*

Step 1 contains only a single unrefined comment, (* display user chosen rectangle or parallelogram *). The word "chosen" suggests the use of an IF-THEN-ELSE selection. A careful reading of the input, output and error sections of the problem clarify that the two display options are a parallelogram (for DiagramChar = "P") and a rectangle (for DiagramChar#"P"). This results in the following refinement.

(* display user chosen rectangle or parallelogram *)

is refined as

```
        IF DiagramChar = "P" THEN
            (* display parallelogram *)
        ELSE
            (* display rectangle with user specified height *)
        END
```

At this point the designer may also recognize that the two comments above, (* display parallelogram *) and (* display rectangle with user specified height *), are going to refine into rather lengthy algorithms. It is probably wise to treat both of these comments as routines and refine them separately from the main algorithm. The resulting Step 2 of this design is shown in Figure 5.23.

```
PROCEDURE GetDiagramChar( VAR DiagramChar : CHAR );
        (* POST: DiagramChar is assigned from input *)

    WriteString( 'Which diagram? ("P" or "R" or "X")' );
    WriteLn;
    Read( DiagramChar );
PROCEDURE DisplayParallelogram;
        (* display parallelogram *)

PROCEDURE DisplayRectangle;
        (* display rectangle with user specified height *)

mainline routine:
    GetDiagramChar(DiagramChar);
    WHILE  DiagramChar<>"X" DO
        WriteLn;
        WriteLn;

        IF DiagramChar="P" THEN
            DisplayParallelogram
        ELSE
            DisplayRectangle
        END;

        WriteLn;
        WriteLn;
        GetDiagramChar(DiagramChar);
    END
```

FIGURE 5.23 *Design Step 2 for rectangle/parallelogram display*

This example also raises a point about consistency in refinement. Displaying a rectangle is going to be more complex than displaying a parallelogram. A designer might notice this fact. Still, these two tasks are very similar. If the designer chooses to treat one of the tasks as a separate routine then it is best to be consistent and treat the other task similarly.

A design review of Step 2 should also be performed. A thorough review of this design should discover imprecision regarding the task performed by the routines. This algorithm can be improved by including procedure preconditions and postconditions. Figure 5.24 on the opposite page, contains the improved design Step 2.

```
PROCEDURE GetDiagramChar( VAR DiagramChar : CHAR );
   (* POST: DiagramChar is assigned from input *)

   WriteString( 'Which diagram? ("P" or "R" or "X")' );
   WriteLn;
   Read( DiagramChar );

PROCEDURE DisplayParallelogram;
      (* POST: the following picture is output: *)
      (*            11111                       *)
      (*           11111                        *)
      (*          11111                         *)
      (*         11111                          *)
      (*        11111                           *)
   (* display parallelogram *)

PROCEDURE DisplayRectangle;
      (* POST: A picture of a rectangle made of +'s  *)
      (*       is output. The width of the rectangle *)
      (*       is ten chars and the height is supplied *)
      (*       via user input.                        *)
   (* display rectangle with user specified height  *)

mainline routine:
   GetDiagramChar(DiagramChar);
   WHILE  DiagramChar<>"X" DO
      WriteLn;
      WriteLn;

      IF DiagramChar="P" THEN
         DisplayParallelogram
      ELSE
         DisplayRectangle
      END;

      WriteLn;
      WriteLn;
      GetDiagramChar(DiagramChar);
   END
```

FIGURE 5.24 *Improved design Step 2 for rectangle/parallelogram display*

Refinement of (* display parallelogram *) requires the output of five lines as shown below.

(* display parallelogram *)

is refined as

```
WriteString( "11111");          WriteLn;
WriteLn;                        WriteString( "  11111");
WriteString( " 11111");         WriteLn;
WriteLn;                        WriteString( "   11111");
WriteString( "  11111");        WriteLn;
```

The comment (* display rectangle with user specified height *) is more complicated to refine than (* display parallelogram *). The difficulty with this task is that the user is permitted to specify a height for the rectangle. Once the height has been specified, the algorithm must either display the rectangle or display an error message (see the errors section of the problem definition). This choice translates into a selection (IF-THEN-ELSE) that is based upon whether the height specified is greater than 20 or not. The entire refinement is shown below:

(* display a rectangle with user specified height *)

is refined as

```
WriteString( "Rectangle height? (2 to 20)");
WriteLn;
ReadCard( Height );
IF Height > 20 THEN
    WriteString( "INPUT MUST BE FROM 2 TO 20");
    WriteLn
ELSE
    (* display rectangle *)
END
```

Figure 5.25 contains the completed Step 3 of the parallelogram/rectangle display problem. A design review at this stage should concentrate on the two abstractions, because they contain the only refinements made after the design review for Step 2. This simplifies the design review.

```
PROCEDURE GetDiagramChar( VAR DiagramChar : CHAR );
    (* POST: DiagramChar is assigned from input *)

    WriteString( 'Which diagram? ("P" or "R" or "X")' );
    WriteLn;
    Read( DiagramChar );

PROCEDURE DisplayParallelogram;
    (* POST: the following picture is output: *)
    (*                11111                   *)
    (*               11111                    *)
    (*              11111                     *)
    (*             11111                      *)
    (*            11111                       *)

    WriteString("11111");
    WriteLn;
    WriteString(" 11111");
    WriteLn;
    WriteString("  11111");
    WriteLn;
    WriteString("   11111");
    WriteLn;
    WriteString("    11111");
    WriteLn;                                          (continued)
```

```
PROCEDURE DisplayRectangle;
    (* POST: A picture of a rectangle made of +'s    *)
    (*         is output. The width of the rectangle  *)
    (*         is ten chars and the height is supplied *)
    (*         via user input.                        *)

    WriteString( "Rectangle height? (2 to 20)");
    WriteLn;
    ReadCard( Height );
    IF Height > 20 THEN
        WriteString( "INPUT MUST BE FROM 2 TO 20");
        WriteLn
    ELSE
        (* display rectangle *)
    END

mainline routine:
    GetDiagramChar(DiagramChar);
    WHILE  DiagramChar<>"X" DO
        WriteLn;
        WriteLn;
        IF DiagramChar="P" THEN
            DisplayParallelogram
        ELSE
            DisplayRectangle
        END;
        WriteLn;
        WriteLn;
        GetDiagramChar(DiagramChar);
    END
```

FIGURE 5.25 *Design Step 3 for rectangle/parallelogram display*

The final step of the design process may be completed by refining (* display rectangle *). Returning to the problem definition, a rectangle can be more carefully described as being ten characters wide and 2 to 20 (as specified by the variable, Height) characters high. Further examination shows that displaying a rectangle actually consists of displaying its top line, its middle lines, and then its bottom line. There may be zero or more middle lines, and the middle lines are different from the top and the bottom. Furthermore, the number of middle lines to be displayed should equal Height-2. A designer knows that the following form of counting loop performs a task exactly N times, where N is some cardinal.

```
Counter : = 1;
WHILE Counter < = N DO
    (* perform desired task *)
    Counter : = Counter + 1
END
```

In order to display the middle lines of the loop, it is necessary to perform a single line output Height–2 times. The resulting refinement is contained within the final algorithm of Figure 5.26.

```
PROCEDURE GetDiagramChar( VAR DiagramChar : CHAR );
    (* POST: DiagramChar is assigned from input *)

    WriteString( 'Which diagram? ("P" or "R" or "X")' );
    WriteLn;
    Read( DiagramChar );

PROCEDURE DisplayParallelogram
    (* POST: the following picture is output: *)
    (*            11111                       *)
    (*           11111                        *)
    (*          11111                         *)
    (*         11111                          *)
    (*        11111                           *)

    WriteString("11111");
    WriteLn;
    WriteString(" 11111");
    WriteLn;
    WriteString("  11111");
    WriteLn;
    WriteString("   11111");
    WriteLn;
    WriteString("    11111");
    WriteLn;

PROCEDURE DisplayRectangle;
    (* POST: A picture of a rectangle made of +'s   *)
    (*       is output. The width of the rectangle  *)
    (*       is ten chars and the height is supplied *)
    (*       via user input.                        *)

    WriteString( "Rectangle height? (2 to 20)");
    WriteLn;
    ReadCard( Height );
    IF Height>20 THEN
        WriteString( "INPUT MUST BE FROM 2 TO 20");
        WriteLn
    ELSE
        WriteString( "++++++++++" );
        WriteLn;
        MiddleLineCount := 1;
        WHILE MiddleLineCount<=Height-2 DO
            WriteString( "+        +" );
            WriteLn;
            MiddleLineCount := MiddleLineCount + 1
        END;
        WriteString( "++++++++++" );
        WriteLn
    END
```

(continued)

```
mainline routine:
    GetDiagramChar(DiagramChar);
    WHILE  DiagramChar<>"X" DO
        WriteLn;
        WriteLn;

        IF DiagramChar="P" THEN
            DisplayParallelogram
        ELSE
            DisplayRectangle
        END;

        WriteLn;
        WriteLn;
        GetDiagramChar(DiagramChar);
    END
```

FIGURE 5.26 *Design Step 4 for rectangle/parallelogram display*

In coding this algorithm, the most important decision is where to declare the variables. There are three variables used, DiagramChar, Height, and MiddleLine-Count. DiagramChar is used in the mainline, and must therefore be declared global to the module. Height and MiddleLineCount are best declared local to Display-Rectangle, since they are not used elsewhere. The completed Modula-2 program is given in Figure 5.27.

```
MODULE ParallelogramRectangleDisplay;
    (* This program allows the user to repeatedly specify *)
    (* a choice between parallelogram and rectangle.       *)
    (* The user's selection is then displayed. Also,       *)
    (* rectangle's height must be user specified.          *)

FROM InOut IMPORT Read, ReadCard,
                  Write, WriteLn, WriteString, WriteCard;
VAR
    DiagramChar : CHAR;    (* specifies user choice *)

PROCEDURE GetDiagramChar( VAR DiagramChar : CHAR );
    (* POST: DiagramChar is assigned from input *)
BEGIN
    WriteString( 'Which diagram? ("P" or "R" or "X")' );
    WriteLn;
    Read( DiagramChar );
END GetDiagramChar;
```

(continued)

```
      PROCEDURE DisplayParallelogram;
            (* POST: the following picture is output: *)
            (*                11111                   *)
            (*                11111                   *)
            (*                 11111                  *)
            (*                  11111                 *)
            (*                   11111                *)
      BEGIN
         WriteString("11111");
         WriteLn;
         WriteString(" 11111");
         WriteLn;
         WriteString("  11111");
         WriteLn;
         WriteString("   11111");
         WriteLn;
         WriteString("    11111");
         WriteLn;
      END DisplayParallelogram;


      PROCEDURE DisplayRectangle;
            (* POST: A picture of a rectangle made of +'s   *)
            (*         is output. The width of the rectangle *)
            (*         is ten chars and the height is supplied *)
            (*         via user input.                       *)
         VAR
            Height : CARDINAL;
            MiddleLineCount : CARDINAL;
      BEGIN
         WriteString( "Rectangle height? (2 to 20)");
         WriteLn;
         ReadCard( Height );
         WriteLn;
         WriteLn;
         IF Height>20 THEN
            WriteString( "INPUT MUST BE FROM 2 TO 20");
            WriteLn
         ELSE
            WriteString( "++++++++++" );
            WriteLn;
            MiddleLineCount := 1;
            WHILE MiddleLineCount<=Height-2 DO
               WriteString( "+        +" );
               WriteLn;
               MiddleLineCount := MiddleLineCount + 1
            END;
            WriteString( "++++++++++" );
            WriteLn
         END
      END DisplayRectangle;

   BEGIN (* ParallelogramRectangleDisplay mainline *)
      GetDiagramChar(DiagramChar);
      WHILE  DiagramChar<>"X" DO
         WriteLn;
         WriteLn;
         IF DiagramChar="P" THEN
            DisplayParallelogram
         ELSE
            DisplayRectangle                          (continued)
         END;
```

```
        WriteLn;
        WriteLn;
        GetDiagramChar(DiagramChar);
     END
 END ParallelogramRectangleDisplay.
```

FIGURE 5.27 *ParallelogramRectangleDisplay program*

5.9 SUMMARY

Top down design is driven by a decomposition according to control structures. This chapter has examined two of the fundamental tools of top down design: selection and repetition.

Modula-2 includes several control structures for selection and repetition. This chapter examines the IF-THEN and IF-THEN-ELSE for selection and the WHILE for repetition.

It is relatively simple to construct an algorithm and convert it to Modula-2 code by using a text editor. This merger of design and coding streamlines the programming process without sacrificing the quality of resulting programs.

As a design progresses, every algorithm must be complete, precise, and correct. Periodic design reviews during the design process can help to ensure these qualities and to save time later in the programming process.

The techniques examined in the last two chapters are collectively referred to as **structured programming**. Structured programming is a programming concept that emerged in the 1970s. It is widely accepted today as a preferred approach to program design. Instead of a particular tool or technique, structured programming is a combination of ideas. Structured programming concentrates on the control flow of an algorithm, using a restrictive set of sequence, abstraction, selection, and repetition control structures like those presented. Structured programming relies upon top down design and stepwise refinement to guide the creation of an algorithm. Structured programming represents a disciplined style of program development.

| | | KEY TERMS

selection	control structure	iteration
repetition	branch instruction	infinite loop
IF instruction	one armed branch	counter loop
IF-THEN instruction	two armed branch	counter variable
IF-THEN-ELSE instruction	relational expression	trailer loop
selection condition	WHILE instruction	design review
THEN clause	WHILE loop	structured programming
ELSE clause	loop condition	

|||Exercises

1. Trace the execution of each of the following algorithms and indicate the precise line of output produced:

a)
```
IF 2>2 THEN
     Write( "A" );
     Write( "B" )
ELSE
     Write( "C" );
     Write( "D" )
END;
LettersOut := 1;
WHILE LettersOut<=6 DO
     Write( "X" );
     Write( "Y" );
     LettersOut := LettersOut + 1
END;
```

b)
```
Looped := 0;
WHILE Looped<1 DO
     Write( "D" );
     Looped := 1
END;
IF Looped=1 THEN
     Write( "R" )
END;
```

c)
```
OutputZap routine:
     Write( "Z" );
     Write( "A" );
     Write( "P" );

mainline routine:
     OutputZap;
     OutputZap;
     IF 0=0 THEN
          Write( "?" );
          OutputZap;
          Write( "!" )
     ELSE
          Write( "$" )
     END;
     Write( "*" );
```

d)
```
FourQuestions routine:
     Counter := 1;
     WHILE Counter<=4 DO
          Write( "?" );
          Counter := Counter + 1
     END;
     Write( "+" );

mainline routine:
     Write( "A" );
     MainCounter := 1;
     WHILE MainCounter<=3 DO
          Write( "B" );
          FourQuestions;
          Write( "C" );
          MainCounter := MainCounter + 1
     END;
```

2. For each of the following tasks, indicate whether the task is more nearly represented by an IF-THEN or an IF-THEN-ELSE. Write an IF-THEN or IF-THEN-ELSE to describe the algorithm.
   a) calculating wages at time and a half for overtime or at the regular hourly wage without overtime
   b) displaying an error message when the balance gets below zero
   c) discounting the cost for persons over 65 years old
   d) using separate tax tables for single and married taxpayers
   e) assigning the smallest value of AppleCount and OrangeCount to a variable called MinCount
   f) placing an order when the inventory gets below the reorder point
   g) cutting class on the day a programming assignment is due
3. There are three WHILE loops below. Indicate the differences between them.

```
Loop 1:
    OutCount := 5;
    WHILE OutCount <- 10 DO
        WriteCard( OutCount, 0 );
        WriteLn;
        OutCount := OutCount + 1;
    END

Loop 2:
    OutCount := 5;
    WHILE OutCount < 10 DO
        WriteCard( OutCount, 0 );
        WriteLn;
        OutCount := OutCount + 1;
    END

Loop 3:
    OutCount := 5;
    WHILE OutCount <= 10 DO
        WriteCard( OutCount, 0 );
        WriteLn;
    END
```

4. The following loop prints the values from 0 to 7 on consecutive lines (as shown to the right of the loop). For parts (a) through (d) modify this loop to produce the indicated output.

```
Sample Loop                          Output of Sample Loop

Counter := 0;                                  0
WHILE Counter<=7 DO                            1
    WriteCard( Counter, 0 );                   2
    WriteLn;                                    3
END                                            5
                                               6
                                               7
```

a) Desired loop output:

```
5
6
7
8
9
10
11
12
```

b) Desired loop output:

```
0
2
4
6
8
10
```

c) Desired loop output:

```
2
4
8
16
32
64
```

d) Desired loop output:

```
7
6
5
4
3
2
1
0
```

5. Use the informally described algorithms of (i) through (iv) below to respond to parts (a) through (d).

   i) Input characters from a single line until a blank is encountered.
   ii) Input integers until a value greater than 99 is input.
   iii) Input 50 characters
   iv) Input characters until a ? is encountered, and count how many characters precede the ?.

   a) For each of (i) through (iv), indicate whether the task suggests a counter loop or a trailer loop.
   b) For each of (i) through (iv), indicate an appropriate loop condition.
   c) For each of (i) through (iv), specify the required body of the loop.
   d) For each of (i) through (iv), specify any necessary initializations prior to the loop.

|||PROGRAMMING PROJECTS

1. Below is an algorithm to input 5 lists of integers and to average each list. Write the
   Modula-2 program for this algorithm, taking care to declare variables appropriately.

```
InputAndAverage routine:
    (* POST: IF one or more integer values are input *)
    (*          followed by a value = MaxInt          *)
    (*        THEN                                     *)
    (*          the average of the values before       *)
    (*          MaxInt is output                        *)
    (*        ELSE IF the first input value = -9999     *)
    (*        THEN an error message is displayed        *)
    SumOfInput := 0;
    NumberInput := 0;
    ReadInt( CurrentInput );
    WHILE CurrentInput<>-9999 DO
        NumberInput := NumberInput + 1;
        SumOfInput := SumOfInput + CurrentInput;
        ReadInt( CurrentInput );
    END;

    (* ASSERT: SumOfInput = the total of all input      *)
    (*                    values preceding the last     *)
    (*               AND                                 *)
    (*         NumberInput = the count of integers that  *)
    (*                    were input preceding the last  *)

    WriteLn;
    WriteLn;
    IF NumberInput=0 THEN
        WriteString( "ERROR - cannot average zero values");
        WriteLn;
    ELSE
        WriteString( "Number of values input: " );
        WriteInt( NumberInput, 0 );
        WriteLn;
        WriteString( "Average of values input: " );
        WriteInt( SumOfInput DIV NumberInput, 0 );
        WriteLn;
    END

mainline routine:
    WriteString( "You will be asked to input five lists" );
    WriteLn;
    WriteString( "of integers after appropriate prompts." );
    WriteLn;
    WriteString( "Each list must be trailed by an integer" );
    WriteLn;
    WriteString( "with the value: -9999");
    WriteLn;
    WriteLn;
```

```
ListsProcessed := 1;
WHILE ListsProcessed<=5 DO
    WriteLn;
    WriteLn;
    WriteLn;
    WriteString( "Specify values for list #" );
    WriteInt( ListsProcessed, 0 );
    WriteString( " below:" );
    WriteLn;
    InputAndAverage;
    ListsProcessed := ListsProcessed + 1;
END
```

2. The algorithm below is a demo of vertical block letter printing. This simple demo can display only the words "SPA" and "SAP". The user repeatedly selects which word to display from a menu. Write the corresponding Modula-2 program, taking care to decl variables appropriately.

```
OutputBlockA routine:
(* POST: The following is output:  *)
(*                                 *)
(*      AAAAAA                     *)
(*      A    A                     *)
(*      AAAAAA                     *)
(*      A    A                     *)
(*      A    A                     *)

        WriteString( "AAAAAA" );
        WriteLn;
        WriteString( "A    A" );
        WriteLn;
        WriteString( "AAAAAA" );
        WriteLn;
        WriteString( "A    A" );
        WriteLn;
        WriteString( "A    A" );
        WriteLn;
        WriteLn;

OutputBlockP routine:
(* POST: The following is output:  *)
(*                                 *)
(*      AAAAAA                     *)
(*      A    A                     *)
(*      AAAAAA                     *)
(*      A                          *)
(*      A                          *)

        WriteString( "AAAAAA" );
        WriteLn;
        WriteString( "A    A" );
        WriteLn;
        WriteString( "AAAAAA" );
        WriteLn;
        WriteString( "A     " );
        WriteLn;
        WriteString( "A     " );
        WriteLn;
        WriteLn;
```

```
OutputBlockS routine:
    (' POST: The following is output: ')
    ('                                ')
    ('      AAAAAA                     ')
    ('      A                          ')
    ('      AAAAAA                     ')
    ('           A                     ')
    ('      AAAAAA                     ')

        WriteLn;
        WriteString( "AAAAAA" );
        WriteLn;
        WriteString( "A     " );
        WriteLn;
        WriteString( "AAAAAA" );
        WriteLn;
        WriteString( "     A" );
        WriteLn;
        WriteString( "AAAAAA" );
        WriteLn;
        WriteLn;

mainline routine:
    WriteString( "This program demos the output of" );
    WriteLn;
    WriteString( "words made out of block letters." );
    WriteLn;
    WriteString( "Only two words are now possible 'SPA' & 'SAP'" );
    WriteLn;
    WriteLn;

    WriteString( "Would you like to continue? (Y or N)" );
    Read( ContinueResponse );
    WriteLn;
    WriteLn;
    IF ContinueResponse = "Y" THEN
       MessagesDisplayed := 0;
       WriteString( "Select keystroke: 0...SPA, 1...SAP, 2...exit" );
       WriteLn;
       ReadCard( MenuSelection );
       WHILE MenuSelection#2 DO
          WriteLn;
          WriteLn;
          WriteLn;
          IF MenuSelection = 0 THEN
             OutputBlockS;
             OutputBlockP;
             OutputBlockA;
          ELSE
             OutputBlockS;
             OutputBlockA;
             OutputBlockP;
          END;
          WriteLn;
          WriteString( "Select keystroke: 0...SPA, 1...SAP, 2...exit" );
          WriteLn;
          ReadCard( MenuSelection );
       END
    END
```

3. Below is a problem definition. Perform a complete top down design for this problem. Your final algorithm should display all four fundamental elements of control. Code your algorithm in Modula-2 and test its correctness. (Hint: Use a separate routine to input/process/output a single golfer's score.)

TITLE

> Total golf round score

DESCRIPTION

> Professional golfers have been known to lose tournaments because they failed to total their score at the end of a round correctly. This program is to help golfers avoid such problems. The program repeatedly inputs scores for a nine hole round and outputs the total score.

INPUT

> The program repeatedly totals scores. Before each repetition, a golfer is prompted to continue or to terminate the program (see output section for this prompt). In response, the user types a "C" (capital C) to proceed (any other keystroke causes program termination). Next the programmer is prompted to input nine cardinal values. These nine values are the scores from nine holes. After the program displays results, it repeats the entire process.

OUTPUT

> For each repetition of the process, the following are output:
> - An initial prompt as shown below:

```
This is the PGA official score tally program.
You will be asked for your scores for nine
holes and your total score for the round will
be automatically calculated.
(Type "C" to continue - anything else to terminate)
```

> - Following the input keystroke, two blank lines are output
> - Following the blank lines the following prompt is output:

```
Specify the 9 scores below (separated by blanks):
```

> - Following the nine input cardinals, a blank line is output, followed by the following line, where <t> is the total of the nine input cardinals:

```
Your total score is <t>
```

> - When the total score, <t>, is greater than 60, the following message is also output:

```
Congratulations, you duffer
```

> - Three blank lines are output prior to the next repetition.

ERRORS

> All input not conforming to the above specifications produces undefined results.

EXAMPLE

Below is a complete sample program execution. All input is highlighted:

```
This is the PGA official score tally program.
You will be asked for your scores for nine
holes, and your total score for the round
will be automatically calculated.
(Type "C" to continue, anything else to terminate.)
C

Specify the 9 scores below (separated by blanks):
 5 7 3 4 8 5 4 5 6

Your total score is 47.

This is the PGA official score tally program.
You will be asked for your scores for nine
holes, and your total score for the round will
be automatically calculated.
(Type "C" to continue, anything else to terminate.)
C

Specify the 9 scores below (separated by blanks):
 10 7 8 9 8 9 7 8 12

Your total score is 78.
Congratulations, you duffer

This is the PGA official score tally program.
You will be asked for your scores for nine
holes, and your total score for the round will
be automatically calculated.
(Type "C" to continue, anything else to terminate)
X
```

4. Below is a problem definition. Perform a complete top down design for this problem. Your final algorithm should display all four fundamental elements of control. Code your algorithm in Modula-2 and test its correctness. Hint: use a separate routine to display the portion of the calculator image below the display ("<R>" in output section).

TITLE

The two-function integer calculator

DESCRIPTION

This program simulates the activity of a two-function calculator. This calculator can manipulate only integer values, and its only two functions are addition and subtraction. The user may specify any unparenthesized sequence of integers separated by + or -. All calculations are made in the order the operations are specified. The result is displayed in a calculator graphic when the user enters an "equals" sign.

INPUT

After an initial prompt (see output section), the user must specify an integer on the next line. On subsequent lines, the user must type (alternately) operations (either + or -), then integers. Each operation and each integer must be on a separate line. Input is terminated by typing a line containing an = in place of an operator line.

OUTPUT

The following initial prompt is displayed.

```
This is a two-function calculator. Type your
integer expression on the following lines:
```

Before each value (operand) input the user is prompted with:

```
Value?
```

Before each operation input the user is prompted with:

```
Operation (+, - or =)?
```

Following the input lines two blank lines are displayed. After the blank lines the following calculator graphic is output. Note that <R> symbolizes the result of the calculation input.

```
------------------------
|  ------------------   |
| |        <R>       |  |
|  ------------------   |
|                       |
|   7    8    9    -    |
|                       |
|   4    5    6    +    |
|                       |
|   1    2    3        |
|                       |
|   0              =    |
|                       |
------------------------
```

ERRORS

All input not conforming to the above specifications produces undefined results.

EXAMPLE

Below is a complete sample program execution. All input is highlighted.

```
This is a two-function calculator. Type your
integer expression on the following lines:
Value? 10
Operation (+, - or =)? +
Value? 5
Operation (+, - or =)? -
Value? 12
Operation (+, - or =)? +
Value? -8
Operation (+, - or =)? =
```

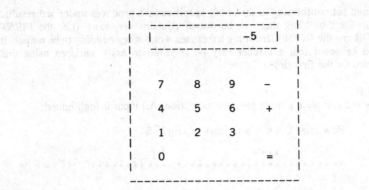

5. Below is a problem definition. Perform a complete top down design for this problem. Your final algorithm should display all four fundamental elements of control. Code your algorithm in Modula-2 and test its correctness.

TITLE
   The tall building builder

DESCRIPTION
   A kindergarten teacher needs a program that will demonstrate to children the relative size of different numbers. The teacher's idea is to use a program to ask a child to input a number and then displays a building with as many stories as the child has specified.'

INPUT
   After an initial prompt (see output section) the child must specify a cardinal on the same line.

OUTPUT
   The following initial prompt is displayed:

   How tall is your building?

   Following the input lines two blank lines are displayed. After the blank lines a picture of a building like the one below is output. Notice that the section marked ONE STORY will be included as many times as the input value specifies.

```
                              ****              | |
ROOF    {  ***********************************************
           *                                           *
           *       --           --          --         *
ONE        *      | |          | |         | |         *
STORY      *       --           --          --         *
           *                                           *
           *       --           --          --         *
ONE        *      | |          | |         | |         *
STORY      *       --           --          --         *
           *                                           *
           *     _____        __       _____        *
FIRST      *    |      |      | |      |      |       *
FLOOR      *    |_____|      | |      |_____|       *
           *  _____| |_____
```

ERRORS

All input not conforming to the above specifications produces undefined results. The smallest building that can be drawn contains one story (i.e. the FIRST FLOOR and the ROOF). Inputting a 0 causes a one-story building to be output. It should be noted that a teacher may be required to assist children using this program for the first time.

EXAMPLE

Below is a complete sample program execution. All input is highlighted:

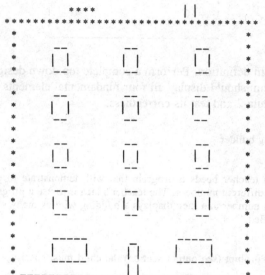

```
How tall is your building? 5
```

6. Below is a problem definition. Perform a complete top down design for this problem. Your final algorithm should display all four fundamental elements of control. Code your algorithm in Modula-2 and test its correctness.

TITLE

The insurance cost estimator

DESCRIPTION

A computer program is needed to give users an estimate of their cost for home-owner's or renter's insurance. The program accepts user input and calculates the correct annual premium cost. Renter's insurance cost depends upon the total amount insured. The charge for up to (and including) $25,000 worth of insurance is $30. The insurance cost is $40 when total insured property exceeds $25,000.

Homeowner's insurance also has two possible fees. If the house being insured is worth $100,000 or less then the base homeowner's cost is $100. If the house being insured is worth more than $100,000 then the base cost is $130.

The home-owner's insurance has two features not available for renters. Off-premises items may be insured for an additional fee of 1% of their total value (only increments in thousands of dollars are permitted). Finally, the homeowner's policy offers a 10% discount on the total (the base cost plus any charge for off-premises items) if a $250 deductible option is chosen.

INPUT

In response to an initial prompt, the user strikes any key. An R keystroke specifies a choice to calculate renter's insurance, while any other keystroke specifies homeowner's insurance. Next the user is prompted to input either the value of the belongings to be insured (for the renter) or the value of the house being insured (for the homeowner). Whichever value is input, it must be a cardinal in thousands. For the homeowner, two more inputs are required.

In response to a prompt for off-premises items, the homeowner should input a cardinal representing the amount to insure in thousands. Finally, the homeowner is prompted to consider a $250 deductible clause. To choose such a clause the homeowner must type a Y. Any other response does not calculate this deductible.

OUTPUT

Below are the prompts described in the input section. Each prompt should be displayed on a separate line with a blank line above it. Input is specified on the line following the prompt.

Initial prompt:

```
Please type "R" for renter, or any letter for home-owner
```

Renter value prompt:

```
Type total value of your belongings (in thousands of $s).
```

Homeowner value prompt:

```
Type total value of your house (in thousands of $s).
```

Homeowner off-premises prompt:

```
Type value of off-premises items to insure (in
thousands of $s).
```

Homeowner $250 deductible prompt:

```
Do you wish to insure at $250 deductible?
("Y" or "N")
```

The final line of output follows three blank lines and indicates the insurance cost. The first line below is the renter form, while the second is the home-owner form. In either case <c> represents the insurance premium cost for one month (see description for how to calculate).

```
Monthly renter's premium is $<c>

Monthly home-owner's premium is $<c>
```

ERRORS

All input not conforming to the above specifications produces undefined results.

EXAMPLE

Below is a complete sample program execution. All input is highlighted.

```
Please type "R" for renter, or any letter for home-owner
H

Type total value of your house (in thousands of $s).
85

Type value of off-premises items to insure (in
thousands of $s).
2

Do you wish to insure at $250 deductible?
("Y" or "N")
Y

Monthly home-owner's premium is $108
```

6

LOGIC AND PROGRAMMING

.1 LOGICAL VALUES AND EXPRESSIONS

The concepts of **logic** are used throughout computer science. Computer hardware is constructed from circuits that are based on logic. The conditional expressions used in selection and repetition instructions are logical expressions that control program flow. Assertions are logical statements used to describe a state of computation. Virtually every aspect of computer hardware and software has its foundations in logic.

In a logical system, there are only two possible values: True and False. In Boolean algebra, the most common symbol for "true" is "1"; for "false", "0". Electronically, a positive voltage is often interpreted as "true" and a ground is interpreted as "false." In Modula-2 there is a Boolean data type for which the two valid constants are **TRUE** and **FALSE**.

A **logical expression** is a statement that can be evaluated as being either TRUE or FALSE. Logical expressions are constructed from logical constants, logical variables, and logical operators. For example, the logical expression

NOT TRUE

consists of the logical operator **NOT**, and the logical constant TRUE, and it has a logical value of FALSE.

Logical expressions may contain **logical variables**. A logical variable is restricted to storing either TRUE or FALSE. Below is an example.

NOT IsFinished

The value of NOT IsFinished is TRUE whenever the logical variable IsFinished has a FALSE value and FALSE whenever IsFinished has a TRUE value.

Two other useful logical operators are called **AND** and **OR**. The expression

IsFinished AND IsPositive

is TRUE only when both variables IsFinished and IsPositive are TRUE. The expression

IsFinished OR IsPositive

is TRUE except when both IsFinished and IsPositive are FALSE. This OR operation is called an **inclusive OR**. The value of an inclusive OR operation is TRUE whenever either *one or both* of the expressions operated on by OR is TRUE.

The NOT, AND, and OR operations are the most commonly used of all logical functions. NOT is referred to as **logical negation**; AND is called **conjunction**; and OR is known as **disjunction**. Numerous other symbols are used for the basic operations of NOT, AND, and OR. Two alternate notations are shown in Figure 6.1. The labels "Boolean algebra" and "math logic" are used because these notations are often associated with these disciplines of study.

Modula-2	Boolean algebra	Math logic
NOT P ~ P	$\overline{P}$	$\neg P$
P AND Q P & Q	PQ	$P \wedge Q$
P OR Q	$P + Q$	$P \vee Q$

FIGURE 6.1 *Alternate notation for NOT, AND, and OR (where P and Q denote logical expressions)*

One universal method for describing the values of logical expressions is a **truth table**. A truth table is an exhaustive listing of all possible values for the logical expression being described. Figure 6.2 contains truth tables that define the three logical operations NOT, AND, and OR, using P and Q as logical variables.

NEGATION		CONJUNCTION			DISJUNCTION		
P	NOT P	P	Q	P AND Q	P	Q	P OR Q
FALSE	TRUE	FALSE	FALSE	FALSE	FALSE	FALSE	FALSE
TRUE	FALSE	FALSE	TRUE	FALSE	FALSE	TRUE	TRUE
		TRUE	FALSE	FALSE	TRUE	FALSE	TRUE
		TRUE	TRUE	TRUE	TRUE	TRUE	TRUE

FIGURE 6.2 *Truth tables for NOT, AND, and OR*

In a truth table, the right-hand column contains the expression defined by the table. An additional column is included on the left for every logical variable in the expression. Each row of the table describes one possibility. For example, the third row of the AND table in Figure 6.2 describes the case where P has the value TRUE, and Q has the value

FALSE. The truth table defines the value of "P AND Q" to be FALSE for these values of P and Q. This is correct because P AND Q is defined as false when either part is false. There are four rows in the table for AND, so that all four combinations of values for P and Q are described.

Logical expressions constructed from other logical expressions are known as **compound logical expressions**. Just as in other expressions, parentheses are used to specify operations that must be performed first. The truth table for P AND (Q OR R) is shown in Figure 6.3.

P	Q	R	Q OR R	P AND (Q OR R)
FALSE	FALSE	FALSE	FALSE	FALSE
FALSE	FALSE	TRUE	TRUE	FALSE
FALSE	TRUE	FALSE	TRUE	FALSE
FALSE	TRUE	TRUE	TRUE	FALSE
TRUE	FALSE	FALSE	FALSE	FALSE
TRUE	FALSE	TRUE	TRUE	TRUE
TRUE	TRUE	FALSE	TRUE	TRUE
TRUE	TRUE	TRUE	TRUE	TRUE

FIGURE 6.3 *Truth table for P AND (Q OR R)*

6.2 IMPLICATION AND EQUIVALENCE

Two additional logical operators of importance are **implication**, "→", and **equivalence**, " = ". These two operators can be described via truth tables as shown in Figure 6.4.

IMPLICATION			EQUIVALENCE		
P	Q	P → Q	P	Q	P = Q
FALSE	FALSE	TRUE	FALSE	FALSE	TRUE
FALSE	TRUE	TRUE	FALSE	TRUE	FALSE
TRUE	FALSE	FALSE	TRUE	FALSE	FALSE
TRUE	TRUE	TRUE	TRUE	TRUE	TRUE

FIGURE 6.4 *Truth tables defining implication and equivalence*

Logical implication appears in many different forms in English. Some of the phrases indicating implication are "if - then," "whenever," "implies," "is necessary," "is sufficient." As an example, let P represent the statement "The sky is gray" and Q represent "It is raining." The logical expression

$$P \rightarrow Q$$

or

$$(\text{the sky is gray}) \rightarrow (\text{it is raining})$$

can be used to symbolize any of the following English sentences.

The sky is gray **implies** it is raining.

If the sky is gray, **then** it is raining.

When the sky is gray, it rains.

The sky being gray **is sufficient for** it to rain.

It is raining **is necessary when** the sky is gray.

6.3 BOOLEAN DATA TYPES IN MODULA-2

Modula-2 permits and often requires the use of logical expressions. **BOOLEAN** is the Modula-2 data type of logical expressions and variables. The BOOLEAN constants are

TRUE
FALSE

and the permissible operators are

NOT (or ~)
AND (or &)
OR
=, #, <>, < =, <, >=, >

There is no explicit operator in Modula-2 that is equivalent to "→" (The relational operator < = performs the same operation when applied to Boolean expressions, but this notation is difficult to read.)

The following instructions are example uses of Modula-2 Boolean expressions assuming IsHappy, IsLucky, ItsFriday and IsFinished are all assigned variables of type BOOLEAN.

```
IsFinished := (IsHappy OR IsLucky) AND ItsFriday;
IF IsFinished THEN
    WriteString( "Fini")
END;
```

A more complete description of the Boolean data type is contained in Figure 6.5.

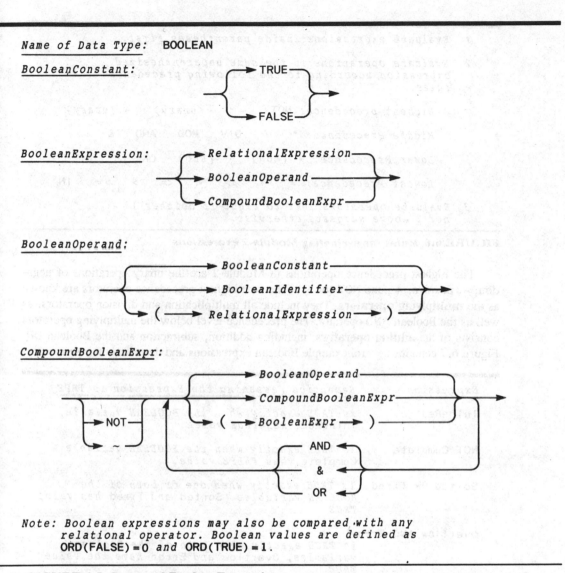

Name of Data Type: BOOLEAN

BooleanConstant: TRUE / FALSE

BooleanExpression: RelationalExpression / BooleanOperand / CompoundBooleanExpr

BooleanOperand: BooleanConstant / BooleanIdentifier / (RelationalExpression)

CompoundBooleanExpr: NOT ~ / BooleanOperand / CompoundBooleanExpr / (BooleanExpr) / AND / & / OR

Note: Boolean expressions may also be compared ·with any
relational operator. Boolean values are defined as
ORD(FALSE) = 0 *and* ORD(TRUE) = 1 .

FIGURE 6.5 *Syntax of BooleanExpression*

Figure 6.6 describes the complete rules for evaluating expressions, including Boolean operations.

1. *Evaluate expression's inside parentheses first.*

2. *Evaluate operations in the same unparenthesized expression according to the following precedence rules.*

   Highest precedence: NOT   ~   – *(unary)*   + *(unary)*

   Middle Precedence: *   /   DIV   MOD   AND   &

   Lower Precedence: + *(add)*   – *(sub)*   OR

   Lowest Precedence: =   #   <>   <   <=   >   >=   IN

3. *Evaluate operators left to right if neither 1 nor 2 above suggests otherwise.*

FIGURE 6.6 *Rules for evaluating Modula-2 expressions*

The highest precedence operations in Modula-2 are the unary operations of negation, –, positive, +, and NOT (or ~). The next highest precedence operators are known as the **multiplying operators**. They include all multiplication and division operators, as well as the Boolean AND operator. The precedence level below the multiplying operators consists of the **adding operators**, including addition, subtraction and the Boolean OR. Figure 6.7 contains several example Boolean expressions and describes their semantics.

Expression	*Semantics (assuming the Expression is TRUE)*
InTheRed	*is TRUE exactly when the BOOLEAN variable,* InTheRed, *has TRUE value*
NOT Complete	*is TRUE exactly when the BOOLEAN variable,* Complete, *has FALSE value*
Sorted OR Tired	*is TRUE exactly when one or both of the BOOLEAN variables,* Sorted *and* Tired *has value TRUE*
Overflow AND Error	*is TRUE exactly when both of the Boolean variables,* Overflow *and* Error *have the value TRUE*
Joe<= Sam	*is TRUE exactly when the value of variable* Joe *is less than or equal to the value of* Sam
(Mel < Tim) AND (Tim < Jim)	*is TRUE exactly when the value of Mel is less than* Tim *and* Tim *is less than Jim*

FIGURE 6.7 *Samples of BOOLEAN expressions*

One common difficulty with the precedence rules of Modula-2 is caused by the low precedence of relational operators. The following two Boolean expressions both result in syntax errors.

SomeCard = 3 AND SomeChar = "?" (* incorrect syntax *)

SomeCard = 3 OR SomeChar = "?" (* incorrect syntax *)

The problem with these expressions is that AND and OR have a higher precedence than =, or any other relational operator. This difficulty is corrected by inserting parentheses around relational expressions as shown below.

(SomeCard = 3) AND (SomeChar = "?")

(SomeCard = 3) OR (SomeChar = "?")

Another standard mathematical notation that does *not* work in Modula-2 is

a < b < c (* incorrect syntax *)

This expression is syntactically invalid in Modula-2, but it can be expressed as

(a < b) & (b < c)

Still another difficulty with the use of the Boolean operators AND and OR is the temptation to apply them to non-Boolean expressions. For example the following expression is invalid for INTEGER expressions a, b, and c.

(a OR b) < c (* incorrect syntax *)

At first glance the expression above *appears* to mean that either a is less than c or b is less than c. However, the expression is syntactically invalid, because ORing two INTEGER expressions is improper. The correct Modula-2 expression is:

(a < c) OR (b < c)

6.4 SIMPLIFYING BOOLEAN EXPRESSIONS

There are many alternative ways of expressing most Boolean expressions. The Boolean expression below

((Home = 0) OR (Vistor = 0)) AND NOT ((Home = 0) AND (Visitor = 0))

means that exactly one of the variables Home and Vistor stores the value 0. This expression may also be stated as:

$$((Home = 0) \text{ \& } (Visitor \# 0)) \text{ OR } ((Vistor = 0) \text{ \& } (Home \# 0))$$

These two expressions are **equivalent** because one is TRUE exactly when the other is TRUE.

There are many logical rules, called **axioms** and **theorems**, that can be used to convert from one expression into an equivalent alternative. Often the alternative is **simplified**, shorter and easier to read.

For programmers two of the more important logical rules are the **distributive axioms** and **DeMorgan's laws**. Figure 6.8 defines these rules.

Distributive Axioms

$$(P \text{ OR } Q) \text{ \& } (P \text{ OR } R) \;=\; P \text{ OR } (Q \text{ \& } R)$$

$$(P \text{ \& } Q) \text{ OR } (P \text{ \& } R) \;=\; P \text{ \& } (Q \text{ OR } R)$$

DeMorgan's Laws

$$(NOT \; P) \text{ \& } (NOT \; Q) \;=\; NOT \; (P \text{ OR } Q)$$

$$(NOT \; P) \text{ OR } (NOT \; Q) \;=\; NOT \; (P \text{ \& } Q)$$

FIGURE 6.8 *Distributive axioms and DeMorgan's laws*

The logical expression

$$((Home = 3) \text{ \& } (Vistor > 1)) \text{ OR } ((Home = 3) \text{ \& } (Home > Visitor))$$

can be simplified to

$$(Home = 3) \text{ \& } ((Vistor > 1) \text{ OR } (Home > Visitor))$$

using a distributive axiom. Similarly the following expression

$$NOT \; ((Int1 > = 0) \text{ \& } (Int2 > = 0))$$

can be simplified as

$$(Int1 < 0) \text{ OR } (Int2 < 0)$$

using DeMorgan's laws.

There are many other logical rules that can be used to manipulate and simplify Boolean expressions. Appendix D contains a more extensive collection.

*P*rogramming-with-*S*tyle

The Use of Logic in Programs

A programmer must make every effort to become proficient with the rules of logic and their use in programming languages. Misunderstanding of these ideas often leads to clumsy, or even incorrect, code.

Below are three specific rules that enhance the readability of programs using Boolean expressions.

Simplify expressions:
Use the rules of logic to translate expressions into less complex expressions whenever possible. For example

Overdrawn OR (Balance = 0)

is better than

NOT(NOT Overdrawn AND (Balance#0))

even though they are equivalent logical expressions.

Avoid the use of negatives
Try to use Boolean variables that are stated in the affirmative and avoid the use of the NOT operator. Consider which of the following two WHILEs is easier to read.

WHILE NOT OutOfData DO ...

or the alternative

WHILE MoreData DO ....

Don't compare to TRUE *or* FALSE
Consider the following examples where a comparison to a Boolean constant is unnecessarily made.

(A>B) = TRUE should be A>B
Sorted = FALSE should be NOT Sorted
(Empty = TRUE) AND (Finished = FALSE) should be Empty AND (NOT Finished)

6.5 HOW BOOLEAN EXPRESSIONS ARE EVALUATED IN MODULA-2

Modula-2 uses a technique to evaluate Boolean expressions called **conditional evaluation** (AND, &, and OR are known as **conditional operators**). Conditional, or **short circuit**, evaluation of an expression always evaluates the left operand, but only if necessary evaluates the right operand. For example, when the following Modula-2 Boolean expression

(StudentCount = 0) OR PassingGrade

is evaluated, the left operand, (Student = 0), is evaluated first. If this left operand is found to be TRUE, then there is no reason to check the right operand. Conditional evaluation uses this fact and only evaluates the right operand when necessary. Figure 6.9 describes this form of evaluation.

```
The expression:

        LeftOperand   OR   RightOperand

is performed as follows.

        IF LeftOperand THEN
            (* expression is TRUE *)
        ELSE
            IF RightOperand THEN
                (* expression is TRUE *)
            ELSE
                (* expression is FALSE *)
            END
        END

Note: LeftOperand and RightOperand can be any
      Boolean expression
```

FIGURE 6.9 *Evaluation of the Modula-2 conditional OR*

Evaluation of AND (or &) also makes use of conditional evaluation. If the first operand in an AND operation is FALSE, then the operation is FALSE, and the second operand is not evaluated. Figure 6.10 summarizes evaluation of the conditional AND.

```
The expressions:
        LeftOperand   AND   RightOperand

        LeftOperand   &   RightOperand

are evaluated:
        IF NOT LeftOperand THEN
            (* expression is FALSE *)
        ELSE
            IF RightOperand THEN
                (* expression is TRUE *)
            ELSE
                (* expression is FALSE *)
            END
        END                                   (continued)
```

> *Note:* LeftOperand *and* RightOperand *can be any*
>   *Boolean expression*

FIGURE 6.10 *Evaluation of the Modula-2 conditional AND*

Boolean expressions have the same value regardless of whether conditional evaluation is used, but there are two advantages to conditional evalution.

1) The executing program is potentially faster because rightmost operands are evaluated only when necessary.
2) The omitted evaluation of a rightmost operand sometimes can be used to simplify code.

The first advantage raises an issue that most programmers must be aware of, namely **program efficiency**. A user is always pleased if a program can execute faster. Many compilers are capable of assisting the programmer by **optimizing** programs. An optimized program should be expected to execute faster, occupy less computer storage space, or both. By defining AND and OR as conditional operators, Modula-2 has built into the language a simple form of optimization.

The second advantage of conditional Boolean expression evaluation is more subtle. An example illustrates this advantage. The code segment below outputs a warning whenever the average exam score (ExamTotal DIV ExamCount) is less than 75.

```
IF ExamCount#0 THEN
   IF (ExamTotal DIV ExamCount) < 75 THEN
      WriteString( "WARNING – Exam average under 75" )
   END
END
```

The above code works properly with, or without, conditional evaluation. However, the simplified code below performs the same task as long as conditional evaluation is used.

```
IF (ExamCount#0) & ((ExamTotal DIV ExamCount) < 75) THEN
   WriteString( "WARNING – Exam average under 75" )
END
```

This second version may not work without conditional evaluation. Suppose Exam–Count stores 0, and then evaluating ExamTotal DIV ExamCount attempts a division by zero (an execution error). Conditional evaluation avoids this difficulty because the division is never attempted when ExamCount#0 is FALSE.

While this use of conditional evaluation is convenient for avoiding such things as division by zero and unassigned variable errors, it must be used cautiously. A programmer must always be mindful that the *left* operand gets evaluated first. If the two relational expressions in the second option above were reversed as follows:

```
IF ((ExamTotal DIV ExamCount) < 75) & (ExamCount#0) THEN
    WriteString( "WARNING - Exam average under 75" )
END
```

then conditional evaluation would not help, since the division is performed before checking the value of `ExamCount`.

6.6 APPLICATIONS OF LOGIC

BOOLEAN variables are powerful tools that can enhance readability. For example, the following algorithm processes triplets of input characters as long as all three are upper-case alphabetic letters and the second character is strictly between the first and third.

```
(* Assume Char1, Char2 and Char3 are CHAR variables *)

Read(Char1); Read(Char2); Read(Char3);
WHILE ("A"<=Char1) & (Char1<="Z") &
      ("A"<=Char2) & (Char2<="Z") &
      ("A"<=Char3) & (Char3<="Z") &
      (((Char1<Char2) & (Char2<Char3)) OR
      ((Char3<Char2) & (Char2<Char1))) DO
   (* Process Char1, Char2 and Char3 *)
   Read(Char1); Read(Char2); Read(Char3);
END;
```

The reason this code is so difficult to read is that the loop condition is too complicated. The following alternative expresses the same algorithm, using two BOOLEAN variables, `Char2Between1and3` and `CharsAreAlpha`. This code is a bit longer, but it is easier to understand.

```
(* Assume Char1, Char2 and Char3 are CHAR variables *)

Read(Char1); Read(Char2); Read(Char3);
Char2Between1and3 := ((Char1<Char2) & (Char2<Char3))
             OR ((Char3<Char2) & (Char2<Char1));
CharsAreAlpha := ("A"<=Char1) & (Char1<="Z")
          & ("A"<=Char2) & (Char2<="Z");
          & ("A"<=Char3) & (Char3<="Z");

WHILE CharsAreAlpha AND Char2Between1and3 DO
   (* Process Char1, Char2 and Char3 *)
   Read(Char1); Read(Char2); Read(Char3);
   Char2Between1and3 := ((Char1<Char2) & (Char2<Char3))
             OR ((Char3<Char2) & (Char2<Char1));
   CharsAreAlpha := ("A"<=Char1) & (Char1<="Z")
          & ("A"<=Char2) & (Char2<="Z");
          & ("A"<=Char3) & (Char3<="Z");
END;
```

For a second example, suppose that a bank is monitoring six particular savings accounts; call them AccountA, AccountB, AccountC, AccountD, AccountE and AccountF. A BOOLEAN variable, called AreSolventAtoF could be used to ensure that each of the six accounts contains a value greater or equal to zero. This variable is assigned the appropriate value as follows.

```
AreSolventAtoF  :=    (AccountA>=0) & (AccountB>=0)
                    & (AccountC>=0) & (AccountD>=0)
                    & (AccountE>=0) & (AccountF>=0);
```

After the above assignment, the Boolean variable AreSolventAtoF can be used in a WHILE or IF condition to abbreviate the lengthy Boolean expression. Of course AreSolventAtoF may need updating whenever the values of the six accounts are changed.

6.7 ROBUST PROGRAMS

A **robust** program is a program that produces reasonable error messages for unreasonable input. A truly robust program will accept almost any input and detect errors, rather than permitting the operating system to produce severe run time errors. Phrases in problem definitions like "produces undefined results" are usually undesirable from the user's perspective and do not encourage a robust solution.

Different implementations of a language handle execution errors in various ways. For example, if a program attempts to use the value of an unassigned variable, some Modula-2 systems will detect the error and terminate execution with an error message. Other implementations of Modula-2 may ignore the error but use some meaningless value for the variable contents. Regardless of the system's response to such errors, a programmer must consider them as errors that make a program less robust.

Locating all potential execution errors is a complicated task. Execution errors may be produced by attempting to use unassigned variables, or by the use of any arithmetic operation that has a result too large or small for the computer. Division by zero is another source of execution errors. To create truly robust programs, the programmer must examine all variable accesses and operations for potential errors.

One technique often used to make code more robust is to utilize Boolean parameters as **error signals**. For example, the Modula-2 CHR function (for ASCII) is defined to translate CARDINAL values in the range from 0 through 127 into CHAR values. When the actual parameter has a value 128 or greater, an invocation of CHR produces a **bounds violation** (an error that occurs whenever a value is outside some prescribed bounds).

The CardToChar procedure of Figure 6.11 contains a parameter called Success that serves as an error signal. CardToChar performs a translation similar to CHR. However, CardToChar checks the value to be translated, OrdVal. If OrdVal is greater than 127, then CardToChar avoids a bounds violation by not attempting a type conversion. Success is assigned TRUE or FALSE to signal whether the conversion is successful. This parameter allows the invoking routine to test for valid translations.

```
PROCEDURE CardToChar(      OrdVal  : CARDINAL;
                       VAR CharVal : CHAR;
                       VAR Success : BOOLEAN );
     (* PRE:  OrdVal is assigned                   *)
     (* POST: Success = TRUE,  if OrdVal<=127      *)
     (*               = FALSE, otherwise           *)
     (*      & CharVal = CHR(OrdVal), if Success   *)
BEGIN
    IF  OrdVal>=128  THEN
        Success := FALSE
    ELSE
        Success := TRUE;
        CharVal := CHR(OrdVal)
    END
END CardToChar;
```

FIGURE 6.11 *The CardToChar procedure*

A similar use of error signals is shown in Figure 6.12. In this instance, the error signal, Underflow, is used, preventing an invalid subtraction.

```
PROCEDURE SubtractCard(     LeftOprnd  :  CARDINAL;
                            RghtOprnd  :  CARDINAL;
                        VAR Difference:  CARDINAL;
                        VAR Underflow :  BOOLEAN  );
     (* PRE:  LeftOprnd and RghtOprnd are assigned      *)
     (* POST: Underflow = TRUE,  if RghtOprnd>LeftOprnd *)
     (*                 = FALSE, otherwise              *)
     (*      & Difference = LeftOprnd-RghtOprnd, if     *)
     (*                                NOT Underflow *)
BEGIN
    IF  RghtOprnd>LeftOprnd  THEN
        Underflow := TRUE
    ELSE
        Underflow := FALSE;
        Difference := LeftOprnd - RghtOprnd
    END
END SubtractCard;
```

FIGURE 6.12 *The SubtractCard procedure*

6.8 USING LOGICAL ASSERTIONS AS PROGRAM DOCUMENTATION

Many times programmers include comments to prefix a section of code. These comments translate roughly into a statement such as "I am about to do the following...". This type of comment is questionable for two reasons.

1) The person reading the code should know the programming language and can, therefore, read the code without an informal English translation.

2) The fact that a comment has been included to describe the code implies that the programmer expects the code to be difficult to read. Since programmers must strive for readability, this kind of a comment is an admission that the code that follows is probably not very good.

Instead of using comments as prefixes to code, programmers can just as easily suffix code. It may seem unnusual to place a comment after the code it describes. However, humans have limited memories. A large program is complex reading material, and it is difficult to know which details are important. Placing comments after a passage of code reminds a reader of important facts. If properly written, these comments can be used for a sort of "speed reading" where the programmer skips the details of code passages and examines only each of the comments that follow.

The best type of suffix comment is the **logical assertion**. Such a comment contains important information about the **state of computation**, a snapshot of data values, at the specified point of execution.

Assertions are best written as Boolean expressions. One example of an assertion is

```
(* Assert: Busy OR (Users=0) *)
```

This assertion states that at the time where the comment would be executed the value of the Boolean variable Busy is TRUE or the value of Users is 0, or both.

The reason for using *logical* assertions to document programs is that logic is a kind of language that can be used for careful reasoning. Mathematicians have been using logical expressions in proofs for many centuries. Logical assertions provide a concise and precise means for expressing program execution facts.

Assertions may be written in many ways. The IF instruction below can be used to calculate a purchase price (assume that all variables are of type REAL).

```
IF TotalPurchase>400.0 THEN
    Cost := TotalPurchase * 0.9
ELSE
    Cost := TotalPurchase
END
```

The following assertion could be placed after this code to describe its result.

```
(* Assert: (TotalPurchase>400)  →  Cost=TotalPurchase*0.9  *)
(*    AND (TotalPurchase<=400)  →  Cost=TotalPurchase      *)
```

An alternate, but logically equivalent, method for expressing this assertion is:

```
(* Assert: Cost = TotalPurchase*0.9, if TotalPurchase>400 *)
(*              = TotalPurchase,      otherwise           *)
```

This second assertion form more clearly documents the code by emphasizing the main point of the assertion, that Cost has been assigned some value. Assertions must be readable for other programmers. If techniques like the notation used in this second example improve readability, they should be used.

Programming-with-Style

Managing the Complexity of Assertions

Assertions are the most important form of program documentation, but they must be used carefully. A careless programmer can easily obscure the code by including too many assertions. Such obscurity can also result from assertions that are too complex or poorly written.

Three ways of reducing assertion complexity are:

1) Carefully select a few places to locate assertions. A few well-placed assertions are much better than large numbers of assertions.
2) Select only the important facts to include in an assertion. Don't include every known detail, or assertions will become cluttered and unreadable.
3) Try expressing an assertion in a different logical form if doing so improves readability without sacrificing precision.

6.9 DEBUGGING AND THE LOGICAL EXPRESSION

Debugging is made easier when assertions are included in programs. The programmer can debug by checking the code to ensure that the assertions are correct. If there is a bug in the code, then either the code and the assertions do not agree or the assertions are too incomplete to capture the necessary information.

There are two important rules to remember when checking assertions.

1) *Check the code in segments.* Code can be divided into segments, where assertions separate each segment from the next. Each segment can be examined separately by assuming the assertion preceding the segment is true and arguing that executing the segment ensures that the assertion following the segment will result.
2) *Consider all possible control paths.* When the checking discussed in (1) is performed, it is essential that every possible execution path of control from the beginning to the end of the segment be considered. It must be shown that the final assertion is true for all such paths.

Checking all assertions carefully can be an extremely time-consuming task in a large program. In practice, such total checking is seldom performed. Instead, programmers carefully examine segments they believe have the greatest potential for bugs. This sort of checking can be used to discover bugs in a design review, as well as the final code.

6.10   THE ASSERT PROCEDURE

Another technique for testing is to utilize a procedure to test program assertions *during* the execution of the program. This is possible if assertions are written as Boolean expressions of the programming language. Figure 6.13 contains a procedure, called `Assert`, that can be used as an assertion checker within any Modula-2 program.

In order to test any assertion, it is supplied as the first actual parameter to `Assert`. Of course this actual parameter must be a valid Modula-2 Boolean expression. When the `Assert` procedure is invoked, it examines the evaluated assertion. If the assertion is TRUE, then `Assert` performs no further task. If the assertion parameter is found to be FALSE, then presumably the program has a bug. `Assert` prints a warning message whenever it is invoked with a FALSE assertion. Furthermore, this warning message includes a cardinal value passed as the second `Assert` parameter. The programmer is expected to use a different number for each `Assert` invocation so that the warning will indicate the location of the FALSE assertion. The program of Figure 6.13 is a typical use of Assert.

```
MODULE AssertExample;
    (* This module exemplifies the use of the Assert procedure *)
    FROM InOut IMPORT WriteString, WriteLn, WriteCard;

    VAR
        Retail : CARDINAL;
        Wholesale : CARDINAL;

    PROCEDURE Assert( BooExpr : BOOLEAN;
                      CodeLoc : CARDINAL );
        (* PRE:  BooExpr and CodeLoc are assigned           *)
        (* POST: If BooExpr is FALSE, then a WARNING message *)
        (*       containing the value of CodeLoc is output.  *)
    BEGIN
        IF NOT BooExpr THEN
            WriteLn;
            WriteString ( "WARNING - Assertion Is false at location " );
            WriteCard( CodeLoc, 0 );
            WriteLn
        END
    END Assert;

  BEGIN (* AssertExample mainline *)
    Retail := 100;
    Wholesale := 80;
    Assert( (Retail=100) & (Wholesale=80), 11 );

    DEC( Retail, 20 );
    DEC( Wholesale, 30 );
    Assert( (Retail=80) & (Wholesale=60), 12 );
  END AssertExample.
```

FIGURE 6.13 *Assert procedure and example of its use*

The first invocation of `Assert` will evaluate a TRUE assertion. The second invocation of Assert will evaluate a FALSE assertion and display the message:

WARNING – Assertion is false at Location 12

This indicates to the user that a bug exists in the program and was identified at Assertion 12 in the code.

The Assert routine is a handy facility for program testing. It must be remembered that the Assert procedure performs "assertion testing" and not "assertion verification". The fact that no assertion warnings have been found ensures only that the program works correctly for those particular conditions. There may still be bugs.

6.11 SUMMARY

The rules of logic form the foundation upon which computer science is constructed. This chapter has taken a brief look at some of the applications of logic in programming, including the use of Boolean variables and expressions. Issues of the evaluation and uses for the Modula-2 Boolean type are explored. A demonstration of how Boolean variables could be used to enhance code readability and improve robustness is included.

This chapter also examines the importance of logic in program documentation. A programmer who uses assertions supplies the "watch points" to permit rigorous program examination. Programs can be informally reviewed and debugged using these watch points. Accomplished programmers can even go through formal proofs to guarantee the correctness of code based on assertions. There is little doubt that a competent programmer must understand logic.

||| KEY TERMS

logic	disjunction	DeMorgan's laws
TRUE	truth table	conditional evaluation
FALSE	compound logical expression	conditional operators
logical expression	implication	short circuit
NOT	equivalence	program efficiency
logical variable	Boolean type	optimizing (a program)
AND	multiplying operators	robust (programs)
&	adding operators	error signals
OR	equivalent logical expressions	bounds violation
inclusive OR	logical axioms	logical assertion
logical negation	logical theorems	state of computation
conjunction	distributive axioms	

||| EXERCISES

1. Supply completed truth tables for each of the following logical expressions.
   a) (NOT P) OR (P & Q)
   b) (P & Q) OR ((NOT Q) & P)
   c) (P → Q) & ((Q → P) OR R)
   d) (P & (NOT Q)) = ((NOT P) OR Q)
   e) (NOT Q → P) = (P → NOT Q)
   f) P → (Q → R)

2. Let ZeroCounter represent the assertion "Counter = 0" and Max99 represent the assertion "Max = 99" and InOrder represent the statement "Min < Max". Express each of the following statements using only ZeroCounter, Max99, Inorder, and the appropriate logical operators.
   a) The variable Counter has a value of zero and the variable Max has a value of 99.
   b) Either Max equals 99 or Min is less than Max or both.
   c) Either Max equals 99 or Min is less than Max, but not both.
   d) Both Max equals 99 and Min is less than Max are true.
   e) Either counter equals zero or Max is not 99.
   f) If Counter is nonzero then Max equals ninety-nine.

3. For each of the logical equivalences below the expression on each side of the " = " can be argued to be equivalent using a single axiom. Name the axiom for each.
   a) Fried OR (Broiled & (NOT Greasy)) = (Fried OR Broiled) & (Fried OR (NOT Greasy))
   b) NOT((A > B) & (B > C)) = NOT(A > B) OR NOT(B > C)
   c) (NOT Lobster) AND (NOT Shrimp) = NOT(Lobster OR Shrimp)
   d) (Total > 0) & ((Salary < 100) OR (Salary > 200)) = ((Total > 0) & (Salary < 100)) OR ((Total > 0) & (Salary > 200))

4. The logical-implication operator is not included as an operator in Modula-2. Write a Modula-2 expression that is equivalent to the follownning:

   P → Q

   assuming that P and Q are some valid Boolean expressions. Do not use any relational operators.

5. The logical operation of exclusive OR is not included in Modula-2. The expression

   P exclusive OR Q

   is TRUE when either P or Q is TRUE, but not both. Write a Modula-2 expression that is equivalent to this. Do not use any relational operators.

6. Write Modula-2 Boolean expressions to express each of the following.
   a) The values of variables A, B, C, and D store values that are strictly decreasing from left to right.
   b) Exactly two of the variables FirstChar, ScndChar, and ThrdChar have a question mark as their value.
   c) If IsRound is TRUE then Count equals 17; otherwise Count equals zero.
   d) I, J, and K all have unique values and Mid equals the value of the variable between the other two.
   e) If Ted, Ed, Ned and Red all have the same value, then none of Martha, Mavis, Mabel, or Mae have a value of zero.

||| PROGRAMMING PROJECTS

1. Write a program to solve the following problem.

   TITLE
   Capitalize words

   DESCRIPTION
   This program inputs a collection of words. The output of this program is the same text as input, but with the first letter of every word capitalized. A word is defined to be any string of characters following a sequence of blanks.

   INPUT
   The user must specify a single line of input that terminates with a period.

   OUTPUT
   The user is prompted for the input line as follows:

   Specify a sentence (end with a period)

   After a blank line, the input lines are displayed on the screen just as they are input (up through the period) except that the first letter of every word is capitalized.

   ERRORS
   There are no forms of invalid input, so no errors can be detected.

   EXAMPLE
   Below is a sample execution with interactive input highlighted.

   Specify a sentence (end with a period)

   The ANTS go marching one by one – Hurrah, Hurrah.
   The ANTS Go Marching One By One – Hurrah, Hurrah.

2. The problem definition below is a more robust variation of a problem from Chapter 5. Write a Modula-2 program to solve this problem.

TITLE

The robust two-function integer calculator

DESCRIPTION

This program simulates the activity of a two-function calculator. This calculator can manipulate only integer values, and its only two functions are addition and subtraction. The user may specify any unparenthesized sequence of integers separated by + or -. All calculations are made in the order in which the operations are specified. The result is displayed in a calculator graphic when the user enters an equals sign.

INPUT

After an initial prompt (see output section), the user must specify an integer on the next line. On subsequent lines, the user must type (alternately) operations (either + or -) then integers. Each operation and each integer must be on a separate line. Input is terminated by typing a line containing an = in place of an operator line.

OUTPUT

The following initial prompt is displayed:

> This is a two-function calculator. Type your
> integer expression on the following lines.

Before each value (operand) input the user is prompted with:

> Value?

Before each operation input the user is prompted with:

> Operation (+, - or =)?

Following the input lines two blank lines are displayed. After the blank lines the following calculator graphic is output. Note that <R> symbolizes the result of the calculation input.

```
 ---------------------------
|   -----------------------   |
|  |              <R>      |  |
|   -----------------------   |
|                             |
|                             |
|    7      8      9      -    |
|                             |
|    4      5      6      +    |
|                             |
|    1      2      3          |
|                             |
|    0                   =    |
|                             |
 ---------------------------
```

ERRORS

1) Any value that would cause the result to be too large (i.e., greater than MAX(INTEGER)) or too small (i.e., less than MIN(INTEGER)) causes no change in the calculated value and the following message is displayed: RESULT OUT OF BOUNDS.

2) If any symbol other than " + ", "-" or " = " is entered as an operation then the program continues prompting for an operation until a valid operation is entered.

EXAMPLE

Below is a complete sample of a program execution. For this example MAX(INTEGER) = 32,767 and MIN(INTEGER) = -32,768 are assumed. All input is highlighted.

```
This is a two-function calculator. Type your
integer expression on the following lines:

Value? 20000
Operation (+, - or =)? +
Value? 20000
RESULT OUT OF BOUNDS
Operation (+, - or =)? -
Value? -20000
RESULT OUT OF BOUNDS
Operation (+, - or =)? -
Value? 20000
Operation (+, - or =)? -
Value? 20000
Operation (+, - or =)? -
Value? 20000
RESULT OUT OF BOUNDS
Operation (+, - or =)? +
Value? -20000
RESULT OUT OF BOUNDS
Operation (+, - or =)? Z
Operation (+, - or =)? ?
Operation (+, - or =)? x
Operation (+, - or =)? +
Value? 20000
Operation (+, - or =)? =
```

```
 ------------------------
|  -------------------   |
| |             <0>  |   |
|  -------------------   |
|                        |
|                        |
|    7    8    9    -     |
|                        |
|    4    5    6    +     |
|                        |
|    1    2    3          |
|                        |
|    0              =     |
|                        |
 ------------------------
```

7 ||| THE PROCEDURE

7.1 THE IMPORTANCE OF PARAMETERS

Procedures, even parameterless ones, are an effective programming tool for abstraction. However, parameterless procedures do not include enough facilities for solving many problems.

For example, Figure 7.1 contains a program to display a table of some positive integers, their squares (value raised to the second power) and cubes (value raised to the third power).

```
MODULE SqrCube;
        (* This program outputs a table of cardinals,    *)
        (* squares, and cubes over the range from 0 to 7. *)
        (* This solution is improved in Figure 7.2.       *)
    FROM InOut IMPORT WriteString, WriteLn, WriteCard;

    VAR
        TheCard : CARDINAL;
BEGIN
    WriteString( "Value...Square...Cube" );
    WriteLn;
    WriteString( "--------------------------" );
    WriteLn;
    TheCard := 0;
    WHILE TheCard<=7 DO
        WriteCard( TheCard,0 );
        WriteString( "..." );
        WriteCard( TheCard*TheCard,0 );
        WriteString( "..." );
        WriteCard( TheCard*TheCard*TheCard,0 );
        WriteLn;
        TheCard := TheCard + 1:
    END;
END SqrCube.
```

FIGURE 7.1 *SqrCube program to output table of square and cubes*

The output produced when SqrCube is executed is shown below.

```
Value...Square...Cube
   0...0...0
   1...1...1
   2...4...8
   3...9...27
   4...16...64
   5...25...125
   6...36...216
   7...49...343
```

This program, like so many Modula-2 programs that use InOut, is somewhat cluttered with I/O procedure invocations. It would be better to output an entire row of the table with a single procedure; call it WriteCardSqrCubeLn. A program using this alternative is shown in Figure 7.2.

```
MODULE SqrCubeWithProc;
        (* This program outputs a table of cardinals,     *)
        (* squares, and cubes over the range from 0 to 7. *)
    FROM InOut IMPORT WriteString, WriteLn, WriteCard;

    VAR
        TheCard : CARDINAL;

    PROCEDURE WriteCardSqrCubeLn( SomeCard : CARDINAL );
        (* POST: SomeCard, its square, and its cube are displayed *)
        (*       on a single output line, ending with WriteLn     *)
    BEGIN
        WriteCard( SomeCard,0 );
        WriteString( "..." );
        WriteCard( SomeCard*SomeCard,0 );
        WriteString( "..." );
        WriteCard( SomeCard*SomeCard*SomeCard,0 );
        WriteLn
    END WriteCardSqrCubeLn;

BEGIN (* SqrCubeWithProc mainline *)
    WriteString( "Value...Square...Cube" );
    WriteLn;
    WriteString( "---------------------" );
    WriteLn;
    TheCard := 0;
    WHILE TheCard<=7 DO
        WriteCardSqrCubeLn( TheCard );
        TheCard := TheCard + 1
    END
END SqrCubeWithProc.
```

FIGURE 7.2 *SqrCubeWithProc procedure*

This new program includes a single procedure, WriteSqrCubeLn. This modification makes the mainline more compact and readable. The designer of this code made an important decision in selecting TheCard to be a parameter passed by value. The same problem can be solved using parameter passage by reference or a global variable in place of TheCard. However, the designer has made the best decision in this case.

Avoiding global variables is always wise. To appreciate the potential problem caused by allowing shared access to global identifiers, suppose five programmers are working together on a single program. These five have decided to divide the program, top down style, into five separate procedures, one for each programmer. If all data communication between procedures occurs in global variables, the project is in trouble. The usual result is that one procedure alters some global variable that another procedure expects to be unaltered.

The real source of the problem with global data is that there are no restrictions on how or when it is accessed. It isn't enough for each programmer to design correct procedures. The combination of procedures must also result in a correct program. It is often harder to make the procedures work together than to design them.

Consider the problem of how to control access to the safety deposit boxes at a bank. Below are four possible security policies for controlling access to security box contents individually.

1) Permit any patron or the bank president to examine and/or alter the contents of all safety deposit boxes.
2) Permit patrons to examine and/or alter the contents of the safety deposit boxes they rent and the bank president to examine and alter all boxes.
3) Permit patrons to examine (but not alter) the contents of the boxes they rent and the bank president to examine and/or alter all boxes.
4) Permit patrons exclusive right to examine and/or alter the contents of the boxes they rent.

Option 1 seems an undesirable method for managing "safety" deposit boxes. Under this option theft of valuables appears likely. Option 2 is more reasonable, but many patrons may not like the bank president to have access to their belongings. Option 3 seems like an unusual security policy. Option 4 is the most realistic and acceptable alternative.

These four safety deposit box security policies are listed in order of increased access restrictions. In Option 1, access to the boxes is virtually unrestricted. In Option 2, access has been restricted to two parties, a patron and a president. In Option 3, two parties have access, but the patron's access is limited solely to examination. In Option 4, only a single patron has access.

Now imagine the bank president to be a program module, and the patrons to be procedures of the program. Option 1 corresponds to the use of global variables with unrestricted access. This lack of security is as bad a policy in programs as it is in the banking community.

Option 4, above, corresponds to the use of local variables in programs. Only the procedure that declares the variable locally has access to it. This option imposes the most severe restrictions on data access of any option and is every programmer's first choice.

Safety deposit box Options 2 and 3 are acceptable compromises in security. The programming analogy to Option 2 is **parameter passage by reference**. The procedure has direct access to selected variables passed as actual parameters. Option 3 corresponds to **parameter passage by value**. When a parameter is passed by value, the procedure may examine, but not alter, its contents.

7.2 PARAMETER PASSAGE BY VALUE REVISITED

Parameter passage is a programming mechanism that allows one routine to pass selective access to data to a procedure it invokes. The two methods of parameter passage used in Modula-2 are parameter passage by value and parameter passage by reference.

When a parameter is passed by value, *a copy of the value of the actual parameter is assigned to the formal parameter at invocation.* During the procedure execution that follows the invocation, the formal parameter behaves like a local variable.

InOut does not include a procedure to output REAL data. However it is possible to write a Modula-2 procedure to output a REAL, call it OutputReal. This procedure writes a real value as truncated to a specific number of digits to the right of the decimal point.

Procedure design should begin with a consideration of parameters. In this case two values need to be shared by the calling routine and OutputReal. The first value is the real number to be displayed and the second is the accuracy. These formal parameters are called SomeReal and Accuracy. Both parameters can be passed by value because OutputReal need not (and should not) alter the values of either actual parameter. The resulting procedure declaration begins as follows.

```
PROCEDURE OutputReal( SomeReal : REAL;
                      Accuracy : CARDINAL );
```

The order in which parameters are declared is important. For any invocation of OutputReal the first actual parameter's value will be copied into SomeReal and the second copied into Accuracy. An invocation such as

```
OutputReal(3.2, 1) (* valid invocation *)
```

is valid syntax, but

```
OutputReal(1,3.2)(* invalid invocation *)
```

is incorrect syntax, because 1 is not a REAL value and 3.2 is not CARDINAL.

Designing a procedure is like designing a program. Neither can proceed without a careful problem definition. Figure 7.3 defines the problem for OutputReal and Figure 7.4 contains an acceptable first step of refining the procedure.

Like every good procedure design, this one begins with a precondition and a postcondition. The refinement of OutputReal continues by separating the procedure body into three tasks.

TITLE
OutputReal procedure

DESCRIPTION
OutputReal will display a real value, given by its first parameter, as truncated to a specific number of digits, given by its second parameter.

OUTPUT
The output of an invocation of OutputReal(SomeReal,Accuracy) is a single real value, SomeReal, on the current line of output with as many digits left of the decimal point as necessary, and as many digits right of the decimal point as specified by Accuracy. The output value shall always be truncated to the specified accuracy.

ERRORS
If SomeReal and Accuracy are unassigned values, then undefined results occur.

EXAMPLE
Below are several examples of invocations of this procedure with the corresponding output to their right.

Invocation	Output
OutputReal(3.2, 1)	3.2
OutputReal(7.221, 1)	7.2
OutputReal(−75.32, 0)	−75.
OutputReal(3.2, 4)	3.2000
OutputReal(3.25, 1)	3.2
OutputReal(3.02, 2)	3.02
OutputReal(3.76, 0)	3.

FIGURE 7.3 *Problem definition for the OutputReal procedure*

```
PROCEDURE OutputReal( SomeReal:REAL;
                      Accuracy:CARDINAL)
   (* PRE:  SomeReal and Accuracy are assigned            *)
   (* POST: A single real value, from SomeReal, is output on  *)
   (*       the current line of output with as many digits left *)
   (*       of the decimal point as necessary, and as many    *)
   (*       digits right of the decimal point as specified by  *)
   (*       Accuracy.  The output value shall always be       *)
   (*       truncated to the specified accuracy.             *)

   (* output SomeReal truncated to Accuracy digits right of the
      decimal point   *)
```

FIGURE 7.4 *Design Step 1 of OutputReal*

1) Output the digits left of the decimal point.
2) Output the decimal point.
3) Output the digits right of the decimal point.

Figure 7.5 Illustrates this step of the refinement.

```
PROCEDURE OutputReal( SomeReal:REAL;
                      Accuracy:CARDINAL)
   (* PRE:  SomeReal and Accuracy are assigned            *)
   (* POST: A single real value, from SomeReal, is output on   *)
   (*       the current line of output with as many digits left *)
   (*       of the decimal point as necessary, and as many     *)
   (*       digits right of the decimal point as specified by   *)
   (*       Accuracy. The output value shall always be         *)
   (*       truncated to the specified accuracy.               *)
BEGIN
   (* output the whole portion of SomeReal *)
   Write( "." );
   (* output the digits from SomeReal right of the decimal point
      and truncated to Accuracy digits *)
END OutputReal
```

FIGURE 7.5 *Design Step 2 of OutputReal*

Remember that the Modula-2 TRUNC function translates from REAL to CARDI-NAL. Since the value of SomeReal might be negative, the following refinement is required.

(* output the whole portion of SomeReal *)

is refined as

```
IF SomeReal < 0.0 THEN
   SomeReal : = -SomeReal;
   Write( "-" );
END;
WriteCard( TRUNC(SomeReal), 0 );
```

One method for displaying the digits to the right of the decimal is to calculate each digit, one at a time, as shown below.

(* output the digits from SomeReal right of the decimal point
and truncated to Accuracy digits *)

is refined as

```
WHILE Accuracy > 0 DO
   (* Calculate and output next digit from left *)
   Accuracy : = Accuracy - 1
END
```

Filling in body of this loop and an appropriate initialization yields the complete procedure shown in Figure 7.6.

```
PROCEDURE OutputReal( SomeReal:REAL;
                      Accuracy:CARDINAL);
  (* PRE:   SomeReal and Accuracy are assigned            *)
  (* POST:  A single real value, from SomeReal, is output on *)
  (*        the current line of output with as many digits left *)
  (*        of the decimal point as necessary, and as many    *)
  (*        digits right of the decimal point as specified by  *)
  (*        Accuracy.  The output value shall always be      *)
  (*        truncated to the specified accuracy.             *)
BEGIN
   IF SomeReal < 0.0 THEN
      SomeReal := -SomeReal;
      Write( "-" );
   END;
   WriteCard( TRUNC(SomeReal), 0 );

   Write( "." );

   SomeReal := SomeReal - FLOAT(TRUNC(SomeReal));
   WHILE Accuracy>0 DO
      SomeReal := SomeReal * 10.0;
      WriteCard( TRUNC(SomeReal),0 );
      SomeReal := SomeReal - FLOAT(TRUNC(SomeReal));
      Accuracy := Accuracy - 1
   END;
END OutputReal;
```

FIGURE 7.6 *The complete OutputReal procedure*

The OutputReal procedure relies on the fact that SomeReal and Accuracy are passed by value. Within this procedure, these parameters are assigned new values. Such assignments are made to the copies, leaving the original actual parameters unaltered. This characteristic of value parameters is shown by using a tracing technique where invoked procedures have their parameters traced like local variables. The use of this technique can be illustrated by a mainline with variables MainReal and MainCard and code as shown below.

```
OutputReal( -8.5, 0 );
WriteLn;
MainReal := 7.25;
MainCard := 1;
OutputReal( MainReal, MainCard );
WriteLn;
```

Tracing the execution of this code proceeds as indicated in Figure 7.7 on the following page.

Instruction	mainline		OutputReal		Output
	MainReal	MainCard	SomeReal	Accuracy	Produced
OutputReal(-8.5,0)	-	-	-8.5	0	
(* transfer control					
to OuputReal *)					
SomeReal:=-SomeReal			8.5		
Write("-")					-
WriteCard(TRUNC(SomeReal),0)					8
Write(".")					
SomeReal:=SomeReal-FLOAT(...			0.5		
(* return from OutputReal *)					
WriteLn					
MainReal := 7.25	7.25	-			
MainCard := 1		1			
OutputReal(MainReal,MainCard)			7.25	1	
(* transfer control					
to OutputReal *)					
WriteCard(TRUNC(SomeReal),0)					7
Write(".")					
SomeReal:=SomeReal-FLOAT(...			0.25	1	
SomeReal:=SomeReal*10.0			2.5		
WriteCard(TRUNC(SomeReal),0)					2
SomeReal:=SomeReal-FLOAT(...			0.5		
Accuracy:=Accuracy-1				0	
(* return from OutputReal *)					
WriteLn					

FIGURE 7.7 *A trace of OutputReal*

Tracing through the sample execution reveals how parameters passed by value can be used by a calling routine to pass data *to* the called procedure. When

_OutputReal(MainReal,MainCard)

is executed the value of MainReal is copied into SomeReal and the value of Main-Card into Accuracy. Parameter passage by value does not allow the calling routine to receive any data back from the procedure after it returns. Throughout the execution of OutputReal, any change to SomeReal or Accuracy has no effect upon MainReal or MainCard.

7.3   PARAMETER PASSAGE BY REFERENCE REVISITED

Parameter passage by value can be too constraining, because the invoked procedure cannot share results back to the calling routine. Parameter passage by reference is more flexible. A parameter passed by reference is also known as a **VAR parameter**, because the formal parameter declaration must be preceded by VAR. VAR parameters allow the procedure to access to the original variable, instead of just a copy.

Like a value parameter, a VAR parameter requires that the actual parameter and formal parameter be of the same type. Unlike the value parameter, an actual VAR parameter cannot be an expression; a variable must be used.

Figure 7.8 contains a Modula-2 procedure called SwapChars. SwapChars is designed to accept two variables of type CHAR and swap, or interchange, their contents. Both of the formal parameters of SwapChar, (FrstChar and SecdChar), are VAR parameters.

```
PROCEDURE SwapChars( VAR FrstChar : CHAR;
                     VAR SecdChar : CHAR );
        (* PRE:  FrstChar and SecdChar must be assigned *)
        (* POST: The values of FrstChar & SecdChar from *)
        (*          invocation time are interchanged      *)
    VAR OldFrst : CHAR;
    BEGIN
        OldFrst  := FrstChar;
        FrstChar := SecdChar;
        SecdChar := OldFrst;
    END SwapChars;
```

FIGURE 7.8 *The SwapChars procedure*

A procedure invocation such as

SwapChars(CharI,CharII)

causes the SwapChars procedure to be called and the parameter correspondence established. Each formal VAR parameter is linked to the storage used by the corresponding actual parameter. In this invocation, FrstChar is linked to CharI, and SecdChar is linked to CharII. Throughout this invocation of SwapChar, any access of Frst-Char is actually an access of CharI and any access of SecdChar is actually an access of CharII. Figure 7.9 contains a program that utilizes SwapChars to input and sort three characters.

```
MODULE SortThreeChars;
    (* This program sorts three input characters from *)
    (* least to greatest.                             *)
    FROM InOut IMPORT Read, Write, WriteString, WriteLn;

    VAR CharI  : CHAR;
        CharII : CHAR;
        CharIII : CHAR;

    PROCEDURE SwapChars( VAR FrstChar : CHAR;
                         VAR SecdChar : CHAR );
            (* PRE:  FrstChar and SecdChar must be assigned *)
            (* POST: The values of FrstChar & SecdChar from *)
            (*          invocation time are interchanged.    *)
        VAR OldFrst : CHAR;
        BEGIN
            OldFrst  := FrstChar;
            FrstChar := SecdChar;
            SecdChar := OldFrst;
        END SwapChars;
```

(continued)

```
BEGIN (* SortThreeChars mainline *)
    WriteString( "Please type 3 letters on the line below:" );
    WriteLn;
    Read( CharI );
    Read( CharII );
    Read( CharIII );
    WriteLn;

    IF CharI>CharII THEN
        SwapChars(CharI,CharII)
    END;
    (* ASSERT: CharI <= CharII *)

    IF CharI>CharIII THEN
        SwapChars(CharI,CharIII)
    END;
    (* ASSERT: CharI <= CharII   AND *)
    (*         CharI <= CharIII      *)

    IF CharII>CharIII THEN
        SwapChars(CharII,CharIII)
    END;
    (* ASSERT: CharI<=CharII<=CharIII *)

    WriteLn;
    WriteString( 'Your input characters sorted are: "');
    Write( CharI );
    Write( CharII );
    Write( CharIII );
    Write( '"' );
    WriteLn;
END SortThreeChars.
```

FIGURE 7.9 *SortThreeChars program*

Figure 7.10 is a trace of a sample execution of SortThreeChars. The distinction between the tracing of parameters passed by reference from those passed by value is illustrated. In the first procedure invocation

$$SwapChars(CharI, CharII)$$

references are established from FrstChar and SecdChar to CharI and CharII. Each reference is denoted by an "@" symbol and an arrow pointing to the variable referenced. Any access of FrstChar during this invocation is actually an access of CharI because of this reference. Likewise, any access of SecdChar is an access of CharII. Formal VAR parameters, like FrstChar and SecdChar, behave like parasites with no independent storage. Whenever access of a formal VAR parameter is specified, the access must be to the actual parameter which serves as the parasite's host.

This example also illustrates how each invocation establishes its own parameter linkages. The second procedure invocation from SortThreeChars is

$$SwapChars(CharII,CharIII)$$

During this invocation the parameter referenced by FrstChar is CharII and the parameter referenced by SecdChar is CharIII.

Instruction	mainline Charl	CharII	CharIII	SwapChars FrstChar	SecdChar	OldFrst
(' skip prompt instructions ')	-	-	-			
Read(CharI) ('assume "C" input')	"C"	-	-			
Read(CharII) ('assume "A"')	"C"	"A"	-			
Read(CharIII) ('assume "B"')	"C"	"A"	"B"			
SwapChars(CharI,CharII)				@	@	
(' transfer control to ')						
(' SwapChars - note parm ')	"C"	"A"	"B"			
(' passage by reference ')						
OldFrst := FrstChar	"C"	"A"	"B"			"C"
FrstChar := SecdChar	"A"	"A"	"B"			"C"
SecdChar := OldFrst	"A"	"C"	"B"			"C"
(' return from SwapChars ')						
(' CharI<CharIIIso second ')						
(' then-clause is skipped ')						
SwapChars(CharII,CharIII)				@	@	
(' transfer control to ')						
(' SwapChars ')	"A"	"C"	"B"			
OldFrst := FrstChar	"A"	"C"	"B"			"C"
FrstChar := SecdChar	"A"	"B"	"B"			"C"
SecdChar := OldFrst	"A"	"B"	"C"			"C"
(' return from SwapChars ')						

(' the resulting output is displayed from the mainline ').

FIGURE 7.10 *A trace of SortThreeChars*

The choice between the two parameter passage techniques should be based upon the type of data sharing that is needed. If the calling routine needs to pass data, but does not need to receive any data back, then parameter passage by value is appropriate. Figure 7.11 pictures this one-way "flow of data" as an arrow from the calling routine to the invoked procedure.

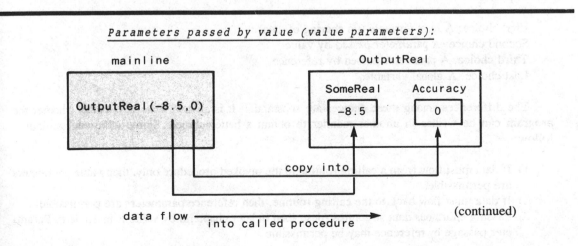

Parameters passed by value (value parameters):

(continued)

Parameters passed by reference (VAR parameters):

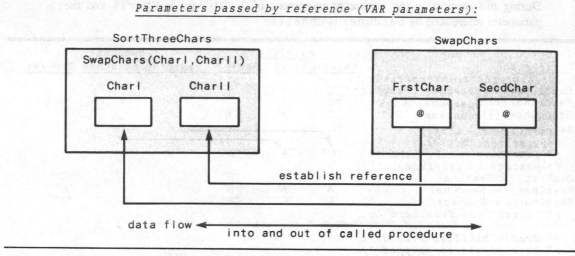

FIGURE 7.11 *Direction of data flow for value and VAR parameters*

Parameter passage by reference must be used whenever data resulting from a procedure execution needs to be passed back to tha calling routine. VAR parameters allow data to flow to and/or from the invoked procedure. Figure 7.11 shows this with arrows going both directions.

Programming-with-Style

Which Parameter Passage Technique is Best?

In large programming projects many errors can be traced to difficulties with the data transfer between different routines. Restricting the "data interfaces" tends to minimize such problems. Below is a prioritized list for how to select variables. The topmost options should always be chosen first if possible.

First choice: A local variable (no sharing of data)
Second choice: A parameter passed by value
Third choice: A parameter passed by reference
Last choice: A global variable

The differences among these choices are substantial. It is always wise to consider whether the program can be written in another manner to obtain a better choice. Some additional guidelines follow:

1) If data must flow from a calling routine to the invoked procedure only, then value parameters are permissible.
2) If data must flow back to the calling routine, then reference parameters are permissible.
3) Passing enormous data structures (described in later chapters) by value is inefficient. Parameter passage by reference may be permissible.

4) There are very few acceptable justifications for direct access of global variables by different routines. Sometimes if parameter lists are so long that readability is destroyed, then such access is a permissable alternative. Every routine that directly accesses globals should clearly indicate this fact in an initial comment.

7.4 FUNCTIONS

Sometimes, a procedure is written for the express purpose of returning a single piece of data. Such procedures correspond to the mathematical notion of a **function**. Typical mathematical functions include square root, and trigonometric functions such as sine, cosine, and logarithms. Most programming languages also make extensive use of functions. The first evidence of functions in Modula-2 was presented earlier in the form of type-conversion functions. For example, the instruction

$$SomeCard := TRUNC(7.5)$$

makes use of a Modula-2 function, called TRUNC.

Functions may be created in any program using a modification of the procedure declaration syntax shown in Figure 7.12.

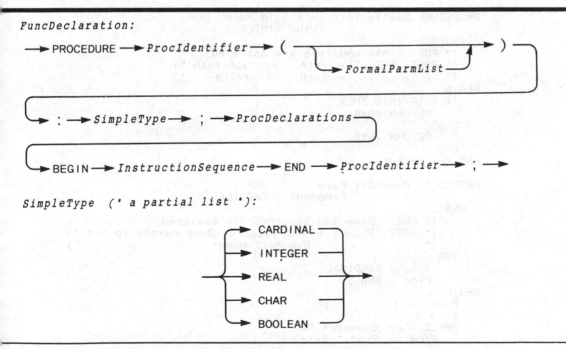

```
FuncDeclaration:

──► PROCEDURE ──► ProcIdentifier ──► ( ──────────────────► ) ──┐
                                       └─► FormalParmList ──┘

  └─► : ──► SimpleType ──► ; ──► ProcDeclarations ──┐

  └─► BEGIN ──► InstructionSequence ──► END ──► ProcIdentifier ──► ; ──►

SimpleType (' a partial list '):

                          ──► CARDINAL
                          ──► INTEGER
                          ──► REAL ──►
                          ──► CHAR
                          ──► BOOLEAN
```

FIGURE 7.12 *Syntax diagram for FuncDeclaration*

The major distinction between a procedure and a function declaration is the inclusion of a type after the parameter list of a function. This type declares the form of the value returned by the function. This **function type** must be a simple type (i.e., CARDI-NAL, INTEGER, REAL, CHAR, BOOLEAN for now). A minor syntactic difference between procedures and functions is that the parentheses enclosing the parameter list are always required (even when there are no parameters) for functions.

Three different Modula-2 function declarations are given in Figure 7.13. The function called RoundRealToInt is a type conversion function to convert a REAL valued parameter by rounding to the appropriate INTEGER. The SmallerInt function is designed to return the smaller of its two integer parameters. PowerOf is a function that returns a REAL value that is the value of its first parameter raised to the power specified by its second parameter.

```
PROCEDURE RoundRealToInt( aReal : REAL )
: INTEGER;
    (* PRE:  smallest integer <= aReal <= largest integer *)
    (* POST: RESULT = aReal rounded to nearest integer    *)
BEGIN
    IF aReal<0 THEN
        RETURN -INTEGER(TRUNC((-aReal)+0.5))
    ELSE
        RETURN INTEGER(TRUNC(aReal+0.5))
    END
END RoundRealToInt;


PROCEDURE SmallerInt( IntA : INTEGER;
                      IntB : INTEGER )
: INTEGER;
    (* PRE:  IntA and IntB are assigned    *)
    (* POST: RESULT = IntA,  if IntA<IntB *)
    (*              = IntB,  otherwise     *)
BEGIN
    IF IntA<IntB THEN
        RETURN IntA
    ELSE
        RETURN IntB
    END
END SmallerInt;

PROCEDURE PowerOf( Base     : REAL;
                   Exponent : CARDINAL )
: REAL;
        (* PRE:  Base and Exponent are assigned         *)
        (* POST: RESULT = the value of Base raised to the *)
        (*                Exponent power                  *)
    VAR
        I    : CARDINAL;
        Prod : REAL;
BEGIN
    Prod := 1;
    I := 1;
    WHILE I <= Exponent DO
        Prod := Prod * Base;
        I := I + 1;
    END;
    RETURN Prod
END PowerOf;
```

FIGURE 7.13 *Three functions (RoundRealToInt, SmallerInt, and PowerOf)*

These examples demonstrate several features common to functions. Every function must complete its execution by returning to the invoking routine. This return is accomplished by a RETURN instruction. The syntax of a function RETURN instruction is given in Figure 7.14. In addition to specifying the transfer of control back to the calling routine, the RETURN instruction also specifies some expression that is the value returned by the function. This expression must be assignment compatible with the function type.

$$\longrightarrow \text{RETURN} \longrightarrow \textit{Expression} \longrightarrow$$

Note: Expression may be any valid Modula-2 expression with type assignment compatible with the function

FIGURE 7.14 *Syntax of a function RETURN instruction*

Function postconditions need some method of denoting the value returned by the function (the value of the expression from the RETURN instruction). In this text, **RESULT** is used to represent the function value. This convention is used *only* within assertions.

Programming-with-Style

The Notation of Preconditions and Postconditions

Sometimes it is necessary to develop special notation in order to write effective pre- and post-conditions. Throughout this book the following notations are used.

1) RESULT is used in functions to denote the value that is returned by the function.
2) <entry> is used as a suffix to a variable to denote the value of that variable at the time the procedure was invoked. This notation is unnecessary for preconditions or value parameters.

An example of these two notations is given below.

```
PROCEDURE Zero()
: CARDINAL;
      (* POST:  RESULT = 0 *)
BEGIN
    RETURN 0;
END Zero;

PROCEDURE Add2( VAR Dest : INTEGER;
                    Oprnd : INTEGER );
    (* PRE:  Dest and Oprnd are assigned  *)
    (* POST: Dest = Dest<entry> + Oprnd *)
BEGIN
    Dest := Dest + Oprnd;
END Add2;
```

While the syntax of procedure and function calls is nearly identical, the way in which they are invoked is different. A procedure is invoked as a separate instruction. A function is invoked within an expression. Anywhere that an expression of type T can be placed, a function of type T is also syntactically correct. The function is invoked at precisely the same time an expression in its place would be evaluated. For example, the WriteInt procedure outputs the value of some integer expression. This integer expression may be an integer function, such as:

```
WriteInt( RoundRealToInt(-33.6), 0 )
```

This instruction causes the RoundRealToInt function to be invoked and its result (-34) to be output. Similarly, the assignment instruction

```
E := M * PowerOf(C,2)
```

utilizes the PowerOf function. Executing this instruction consists of multiplying the REAL variable, M, times the value returned by PowerOf and assigning the result to the REAL variable, E. The code segment that follows invokes the SmallerInt function (CostInFrancs, CostInPounds, Cost, FrenchExchangeRate and BritishExchangeRate may all be assumed to be INTEGER variables.)

```
ReadInt( CostInFrancs );
ReadInt( CostInPounds );
Cost := 2 * SmallerInt( CostInFrancs * FrenchExchangeRate,
                CostInPounds * BritishExchangeRate );
(* ASSERT: Cost = twice the best price in the U.S. dollars *)
```

7.5 STANDARD MODULA-2 PROCEDURES AND FUNCTIONS

High level programming languages usually incorporate several procedures and functions that are predefined. A programmer may use these functions without declaration. Such routines are referred to as **standard procedures**, **built in procedures**, or **intrinsic procedures**. The complete list of Modula-2 standard procedures is included in Appendix E. Figure 7.15 contains a brief description of some of the more significant standard procedures and functions.

```
Type conversion & transfer functions
    CARDINAL .... from INTEGER to CARDINAL
    CHR ........ from CARDINAL to CHAR
    FLOAT ...... from CARDINAL to REAL
    INTEGER ..... from CARDINAL to INTEGER
    ORD ........ from CHAR to CARDINAL
    TRUNC ...... from REAL to CARDINAL
```

(continued)

Increment and decrement procedures

DEC *(single parm.)* ... *decrement the actual parameter*
                               by 1

DEC *(two parms.)* ..... *decrement first actual parameter*
                                by the value of the second

INC *(single parm.)* ... *increment the actual parameter*
                                by 1

INC *(two parms.)* ..... *increment first actual parameter*
                                by the value of the second

NOTE: The first parameter of DEC *or* INC *may be of any scalar type, including* CARDINAL, CHAR *and* INTEGER *but not* REAL. *The optional second parameter must be* CARDINAL.

MAX *and* MIN *functions*

MAX .... *returns the largest possible value for type specified by actual parameter*

MIN .... *returns the smallest possible value for type specified by actual parameter*

NOTE: The actual parameter must be an identifier naming a scalar type, such as CARDINAL, CHAR, INTEGER *or* REAL.

Miscellaneous functions

ABS .... *Returns the absolute value of its parameter (may be* INTEGER *or* REAL*).*

CAP .... *Parameter must be* CHAR. *Returns the upper-case equivalent for any alphabetic parameter; otherwise returns the parameter.*

ODD .... *Parameter must be* CARDINAL. *Returns* TRUE *if parameter is an odd number; otherwise returns* FALSE.

FIGURE 7.15 *Summary of some standard procedures and functions*

The standard procedures and functions include some routines that could declared by the programmer. For example, Figure 7.16 includes a function called UpperCase that duplicates the task performed by the standard CAP function.

```
PROCEDURE UpperCase( SomeChar : CHAR )
: CHAR;
   (* PRE:  SomeChar is assigned                          *)
   (* POST: RESULT = upper-case equivalent of SomeChar,   *)
   (*                   if SomeChar is a lower-case letter *) ,
   (*                SomeChar, otherwise                   *)
BEGIN
   IF ("a"<=SomeChar) & (SomeChar<="z") THEN
      RETURN  CHR( ORD(SomeChar) - ORD("a") + ORD("A") )
   ELSE
      RETURN  SomeChar
   END
END UpperCase;
```

FIGURE 7.16 *UpperCase function (equivalent to CAP)*

Other standard procedures cannot be duplicated in a program. For example, the standard procedures ABS, DEC, and INC are **generic procedures**. They are called "generic" because they work for actual parameters of more than one type. ABS is a function that accepts a single parameter and returns its absolute value (unsigned numeric value). The actual parameter for ABS may be either an INTEGER or a REAL; the result returned will match the actual parameter type. Similarly, DEC and INC are generic procedures because their first parameter may be of type CARDINAL, CHAR or INTEGER. The following invocation:

    INC(SomeVar);

causes the value of the variable SomeVar to be increased by 1. If SomeVar is a CARDINAL or INTEGER, this operation is an addition of 1 to the actual parameter. If SomeVar is CHAR, then this operation assigns to the actual parameter the character with the next higher ordinal value.

INC and DEC make use of a second sort of generic quality because they have an optional second parameter. A CARDINAL expression may be supplied as a second actual parameter for these procedures. If the second parameter is included, it specifies the amount to decrement or increment. For example

    (* Assert: SomeChar="T" & SomeCard=7 *)
    INC(SomeChar,3);
    DEC(SomeCard,2+2);
    (* Assert: SomeChar="W" & SomeCard=3 *)

The MAX and MIN functions are also impossible for a programmer to duplicate. These functions return the largest and smallest possible values of any scalar type. When calling these functions, a type identifier, rather than a variable or expression, is supplied as an actual parameter. For example

    MAX(CARDINAL)

is an expression that returns the largest CARDINAL value that is possible for the current Modula-2 system. Likewise,

    MIN(REAL)

returns the smallest possible REAL value.

7.6 RETURN AND HALT

Modula-2 supports two additional methods for initiating transfer of control: RETURN and HALT. These two have somewhat similar purposes, but are implemented differently. RETURN is an instruction in Modula-2, while HALT is a standard procedure. This distinction is of little importance in practice, since either may be executed by simply specifying its name.

The RETURN instruction was presented previously as the means by which a function must specify a value to return. RETURN with no expression following it may also be used in procedures that are not functions. When a RETURN is executed, control transfers immediately back to the calling routine. If no RETURN is executed, a procedure returns when it has completely executed its body.

HALT is a parameterless procedure that terminates the execution of the entire program upon invocation. Executing HALT may also cause information to be output in some Modula-2 implementations.

RETURN and HALT are extremely useful features of Modula-2 when used properly. However, RETURN and HALT should be used with caution. Modula-2 programmers expect procedures and programs to terminate at the bottom of their code. RETURN and HALT instructions are more difficult to locate because they may be embedded anywhere in the code.

One appropriate use of RETURN is shown in Figure 7.17. The problem is to write a procedure to calculate the winnings of a game show contestant. This procedure must input a sequence of integer values that represent a contestant's winnings in dollars for each individual game. The sequence is terminated by the first negative input. A contestant plays the first three games at the "beginning level." When contestants have won three games they reach the "intermediate level." A contestant who wins five games at the intermediate level (for a total of eight games) begins playing at the "expert level." To calculate a contestant's total winnings, it is necessary to sum the winnings from all beginning level games, then add twice the value of the winnings from the intermediate level games, and finally add triple the winnings from the expert level. A contestant may lose at any time, in which case no more games are played (a negative value is input).

There are three loops in the Winnings procedure, one for each level of the game show. The first two loops are terminated when the maximum number of games at that level have been won. The final loop exhausts any remaining input. A RETURN is a convenient method for exiting the procedure from inside either of the first two loops.

```
PROCEDURE Winnings( VAR TotWinnings : INTEGER );
    (* POST: TotWinnings = Beg + (Int * 2) + (Exp * 3) *)
    (*                                                   *)
    (*            where Beg is the sum of the first 3    *)
    (*    inputs, Int is the sum of the next 5 inputs    *)
    (*    and Exp is the sum of the remaining inputs.    *)
    (*    Input is terminated by a zero.  If <8 inputs,  *)
    (*    then Exp=0.  If <3 inputs then Int=0.          *)
    VAR
        OneGame : INTEGER;
        GamesAtThisLevel : CARDINAL;
    BEGIN
        TotWinnings := 0;
        WriteString( 'Input winnings at the beginning level');
        WriteLn;
        GamesAtThisLevel := 1;
        WHILE GamesAtThisLevel<=3 DO
            ReadInt( OneGame );
            IF OneGame<0 THEN
                RETURN  (* procedure exit when game lost *)
            ELSE
                TotWinnings := TotWinnings + OneGame
            END;
            INC( GamesAtThisLevel );
        END;
```

(continued)

```
     (* ASSERT: TotWinnings = total winnings at beginning level *)
     WriteString( 'Input winnings at the intermediate level');
     WriteLn;
     GamesAtThisLevel := 1;
     WHILE GamesAtThisLevel<=5 DO
         ReadInt( OneGame );
         IF OneGame<0 THEN
             RETURN   (* procedure exit when game lost *)
         ELSE
             TotWinnings := TotWinnings + (2*OneGame)
         END;
         INC( GamesAtThisLevel );
     END;

     (* ASSERT: TotWinnings = total winnings through the *)
     (*                       intermediate level          *)
     WriteString( 'Input winnings at the expert level');
     WriteLn;
     ReadInt( OneGame );
     WHILE OneGame>=0 DO
         TotWinnings := TotWinnings + (3*OneGame);
         ReadInt( OneGame );
     END;
END Winnings;
```

FIGURE 7.17 *Winnings procedure*

If RETURN instructions are not utilized to solve this problem, then the code suffers. Figure 7.18 illustrates this issue in another procedure that performs the same task. This new procedure is called WinningsWithout RETURN. In order to avoid the use of RETURN instructions, four major changes are made.

1) The first two loops require compound Boolean expressions for conditions, because OneGame > = 0 must also be included.
2) Two additional IF-THEN instructions are used to prevent executing either of the last two loops when a negative value has been input.
3) An additional IF-THEN is used in each the first two loops to prevent inappropriate prompting of the first input for the loop that follows.
4) The first two loops have been modified to input a value in one iteration, but not process it until the next iteration.

All of these four changes make this second procedure more complex and harder to read than Winnings.

```
PROCEDURE WinningsWithoutRETURN( VAR TotWinnings : INTEGER );
     (* POST: TotWinnings = Beg + (Int * 2) + (Exp * 3) *)
     (*                                                  *)
     (*           where Beg is the sum of the first 3    *)
     (*   inputs, Int is the sum of the next 5 inputs,   *)
     (*   and Exp is the sum of the remaining inputs.    *)
     (*   Input is terminated by a zero. If <8 inputs    *)
     (*   then Exp=0. If <3 inputs then Int=0.           *)
```

(continued)

```
        VAR OneGame : INTEGER;
            GamesAtThisLevel : CARDINAL;
BEGIN
        TotWinnings := 0;
        WriteString( 'Input winnings at the beginning level');
        WriteLn;
        GamesAtThisLevel := 1;
        ReadInt( OneGame );
        WHILE (GamesAtThisLevel<=3) AND (OneGame>=0) DO
            TotWinnings := TotWinnings + OneGame;
            IF GamesAtThisLevel<3 THEN
                ReadInt( OneGame );
            END;
            INC( GamesAtThisLevel );
        END;


        (* ASSERT: TotWinnings = total winnings at beginning level *)
        (*             AND                                          *)
        (*             OneGame<0 IMPLIES no games played at higher  *)
        (*                                 levels                   *)
        IF OneGame>=0 THEN
            WriteString( 'Input winnings at the intermediate level');
            WriteLn;
            GamesAtThisLevel := 1;
            ReadInt( OneGame );
            WHILE (GamesAtThisLevel<=5) AND (OneGame>=0) DO
                TotWinnings := TotWinnings + (2*OneGame);
                IF GamesAtThisLevel<5 THEN
                    ReadInt( OneGame );
                END;
                INC( GamesAtThisLevel );
            END;


            (* ASSERT: TotWinnings = total winnings through the *)
            (*                       intermediate level         *)
            (*             AND                                  *)
            (*             OneGame<0 IMPLIES no games played at *)
            (*                                 expert level     *)
            IF OneGame>=0 THEN
                WriteString( 'Input winnings at the expert level');
                WriteLn;
                ReadInt( OneGame );
                WHILE OneGame>=0 DO
                    TotWinnings := TotWinnings + (3*OneGame);
                    ReadInt( OneGame );
                END;
            END;
        END;
END WinningsWithoutRETURN;
```

FIGURE 7.18 *WinningsWithoutRETURN procedure*

*P*rogramming-with-*S*tyle

When to Use RETURN or HALT

It is generally a good policy to avoid overuse of RETURN and HALT. They are often difficult to locate for someone reading the code. However, their use is justifiable when the alternative is several more complex logical expressions and/or many additional layers of control structures. One common use for these structures is a type of error return, where an error is detected inside of some control structure and an immediate exit is in order. Other events that are similar in nature to this error exit may also be considered.

7.7 SCOPE, VISIBILTY, AND BINDING

Every identifier has two important qualities: its **scope of visibility** and its **range of existence**. The scope of visibility (or just "scope") of an identifier was defined previously as the program region where the identifier may be accessed. Variables declared in the program module are globally visible, while variables declared in a procedure are locally visible to that procedure.

The range of existence of an identifier, or data structure, can be measured only at run time. Variables are created and destroyed during the execution of a program. The process of creating a previously non-existent variable is known as **allocation**, and the process of destroying the variable is called **deallocation**. The time of execution during which an identifier has been allocated but not deallocated is known as its "range of existence." In many cases the range of existence is the same as the scope of visibility. In other situations, an identifier may be allocated, but not visible.

The title **block structured language** is given to programming languages that define identifier scope according to program "blocks." In Modula-2 the blocks are programs (modules) and procedures, including functions. The scope of an identifier in a block structured language is defined by the location of its declaration. The scope of every identifier can be determined even before the program executes by examining the blocks surrounding the identifier. This is called **static scope** because the scope does not change during the execution of the program.

A simple technique for determining the scope of identifiers is to list the declarations from a program and draw rectangles around every block (procedure, function or module). Any procedure (or function) declared within another procedure, function or program, must be symbolized as a rectangle entirely within the rectangle for the routine in which it is declared. An example of this use of rectangles is shown in Figure 7.19.

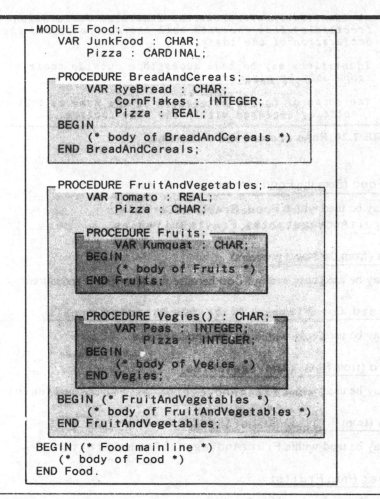

```
┌─ MODULE Food; ──────────────────────────────────┐
│    VAR JunkFood : CHAR;                          │
│        Pizza : CARDINAL;                         │
│   ┌─ PROCEDURE BreadAndCereals; ──────────────┐  │
│   │     VAR RyeBread : CHAR;                   │  │
│   │         CornFlakes : INTEGER;             │  │
│   │         Pizza : REAL;                      │  │
│   │ BEGIN                                      │  │
│   │     (* body of BreadAndCereals *)          │  │
│   │ END BreadAndCereals;                       │  │
│   └────────────────────────────────────────────┘  │
│                                                  │
│   ┌─ PROCEDURE FruitAndVegetables; ───────────┐  │
│   │     VAR Tomato : REAL;                     │  │
│   │         Pizza : CHAR;                      │  │
│   │   ┌─ PROCEDURE Fruits; ──────────────┐    │  │
│   │   │     VAR Kumquat : CHAR;           │    │  │
│   │   │ BEGIN                             │    │  │
│   │   │     (* body of Fruits *)          │    │  │
│   │   │ END Fruits;                       │    │  │
│   │   └────────────────────────────────────┘    │  │
│   │                                            │  │
│   │   ┌─ PROCEDURE Vegies() : CHAR; ─────┐    │  │
│   │   │     VAR Peas : INTEGER;           │    │  │
│   │   │         Pizza : INTEGER;          │    │  │
│   │   │ BEGIN                             │    │  │
│   │   │     (* body of Vegies *)          │    │  │
│   │   │ END Vegies;                       │    │  │
│   │   └────────────────────────────────────┘    │  │
│   │ BEGIN (* FruitAndVegetables *)            │  │
│   │     (* body of FruitAndVegetables *)       │  │
│   │ END FruitAndVegetables;                    │  │
│   └────────────────────────────────────────────┘  │
│ BEGIN (* Food mainline *)                        │
│     (* body of Food *)                           │
│ END Food.                                        │
└──────────────────────────────────────────────────┘
```

FIGURE 7.19 *Scope diagram example*

The Food program illustrates scope of visibility via the rectangular enclosure technique. The rules of scope for this form of diagram are summarized in Figure 7.20.

Applying these scope rules to the example from Figure 7.19 yields the following:

1) The scope of an identifier includes the rectangle in which it is declared. This scope also includes any rectangle inside.

2) The scope of an identifier does not extend beyond the rectangle in which it is declared.

3) An identifier may be redeclared only if the declarations occur in different immediately enclosing rectangles.

(continued)

4) An identifier references the innermost declaration (rectangle) that encloses both the reference and the declaration of the identifier.

5) Identifiers may be made accessible outside their scope only by parameter passage.

6) The scope of formal parameters is the same as that of any identifier declared within the same routine.

FIGURE 7.20 *Rules of scope and declaration*

JunkFood (from the Food program)

> may be used within Food, BreadAndCereals, FruitAndVegetables, Fruits and Vegies

Pizza (from the Food program)

> may be used only within Food because this identifier is redeclared

Ryebread, CornFlakes & Pizza (from BreadAndCereals)

> may be used only within BreadAndCereals

Tomato (from FruitAndVegetables)

> may be used within FruitAndVegetables, Fruits and Vegies

Pizza (from FruitAndVegetables)

> may be used within FruitAndVegetables and Fruits

Kumquat (from Fruits)

> may be used only within Fruits

Peas and Pizza (from Vegies)

> may be used only within Vegies

The rules of scope apply to all identifiers declared within some rectangle. Procedure and function names are included in these identifiers. Notice that the rectangles surrounding each procedure do not enclose the name of the procedure. This is done to indicate that a procedure is declared within the scope immediately outside their own rectangles. In this example BreadAndCereals and FruitAndVegetables are both declared globally within the Food program module, while Fruit and Vegies are declared local to the FruitAndVegetables procedure. When the scope rules say that a procedure A is "within the scope of" or "accessible to" procedure B, this means that an invocation of A is allowed in the body of B.

It is also instructive to view scope from the perspective of the routine. Figure 7.21 lists the identifiers that are accessible to each routine.

The Food *program body has access to*

variables:	JunkFood *(from* Food)
	Pizza *(from* Food)
procedures:	BreadAndCereals
	FruitAndVegetables

The BreadAndCereals *procedure body has access to*

variables:	JunkFood *(from* Food)
	RyeBread *(from* BreadAndCereals)
	CornFlakes *(from* BreadAndCereals)
	Pizza *(from* BreadAndCereals)
procedures:	BreadAndCereals
	FruitAndVegetables

The FruitAndVegetables *procedure body has access to*

variables:	JunkFood *(from* Food)
	Tomato *(from* FruitAndVegetables)
	Pizza *(from* FruitAndVegetables)
procedures:	BreadAndCereals
	FruitAndVegetables
	Fruits
	Vegies

The Fruits *procedure body has access to*

variables:	JunkFood *(from* Food)
	Tomato *(from* FruitAndVegetables)
	Pizza *(from* FruitAndVegetables)
	Kumquat *(from* Fruits)
procedures:	BreadAndCereals
	FruitAndVegetables
	Fruits
	Vegies

The Vegies *function body has access to*

variables:	JunkFood *(from* Food)
	Tomato *(from* FruitAndVegetables)
	Peas *(from* Vegies)
	Pizza *(from* Vegies)
procedures:	BreadAndCereals
	FruitAndVegetables
	Fruits
	Vegies

FIGURE 7.21 *Data accessible to each routing of Food*

Parameter passage by reference can be used to pass access from one scope to another. This provides a kind of indirect access to data that might otherwise be outside the scope of the invoked procedure.

While all the rules defining static scoping are important, they add complexity to the programmer's task. This complexity can be significantly reduced if the programmer accesses only local variables and parameters.

The range of existence rules for the data structures examined thus far in the text are straightforward. A data structure is allocated (comes into existence) when the declaring routine is invoked and is deallocated (ceases to exist) when the declaring routine returns. These rules for existence describe **automatic variables**. The name "automatic variables" is used because the variables are automatically allocated at routine invocation and deallocated at routine exit. All variables that are local to a routine and all formal parameters are automatic variables.

The most important thing to remember about automatic variables is that local data structures do not remain in existence between consecutive invocations of the same routine. Suppose Fruits is invoked two times consecutively. When a procedure is invoked, its local variables are initially unassigned. This means even though the first execution of Fruits may assign some value to Kumquat, a second invocation begins with a newly-allocated Kumquat variable that is unassigned. The value of Kumquat from the first invocation is lost when Fruits returns, and the variable is automatically deallocated.

One of the advantages to block structured languages is that the rules for scope of visibility and range of existence are consistent. Because of the manner in which variables are allocated and deallocated, a programmer is guaranteed that if a variable is accessible, then it will have been allocated.

A contrived example of the complexities of static scope and parameter passage is contained in Figure 7.22. The Stooges program does not perform any particularly useful task, but rather shows the possibilities for confusion of data access using block structured language. It is nearly impossible to read this program because of its complex accesses. However, tracing the code execution is instructive.

```
MODULE Stooges;
        (* This program performs no useful task, except *)
        (* to illustrate data access that is far too     *)
        (* complex.  Let this be a lesson regarding the  *)
        (* need for careful control of data access.      *)

    FROM InOut IMPORT WriteString, WriteLn, Write;

    VAR Moe  : CHAR;
        Joe  : CHAR;
        Curly : CHAR;

    PROCEDURE WriteInfo( RoutineID : CHAR;
                         MoeVal  : CHAR;
                         JoeVal  : CHAR;
                         CurlyVal : CHAR );
    BEGIN
        WriteString( ' output from routine: ' );
        Write( RoutineID );
        WriteLn;
        WriteString( '    values of Moe, Joe and Curly -> ' );
        Write( MoeVal );
        Write( JoeVal );
        Write( CurlyVal );
        WriteLn;
        WriteLn;
    END WriteInfo;
```

(continued)

```
            PROCEDURE ZZZ( Harpo : CHAR );
            BEGIN
                Harpo := "Z";
                WriteInfo( "Z", Moe, Joe, Curly )
            END ZZZ;

            PROCEDURE AAA( VAR Chico : CHAR );
                VAR Curly : CHAR;
            BEGIN
                Curly := Chico;
                Chico := "A";
                WriteInfo( "A", Moe, Joe, Curly )
            END AAA;

            PROCEDURE Joker( VAR Zeppo : CHAR;
                                  Moe : CHAR    );
                PROCEDURE Groucho( VAR Chico : CHAR );
                BEGIN
                    Chico := "F";
                    Moe  := "U";
                    Joe  := "N";
                    WriteInfo( "G", Moe, Joe, Curly )
                END Groucho;

            BEGIN (* Joker *)
                Zeppo := "T";
                Moe := "I";
                Groucho( Zeppo );
                Moe := "L";
                Groucho( Moe );
                WriteInfo( "J", Moe, Joe, Curly )
            END Joker;

        BEGIN (* Stooges mainline *)
            Moe := "M";
            Joe := "J";
            Curly := "C";
            ZZZ( Moe );
            WriteInfo( "1", Moe, Joe, Curly );
            Moe := "M";
            Joe := "J";
            Curly := "C";
            AAA( Moe );
            WriteInfo( "2", Moe, Joe, Curly );
            Moe := "M";
            Curly := "C";
            Joker( Moe, Joe );
            WriteInfo( "3", Moe, Joe, Curly );
            WriteString("Where is Larry?"); WriteLn;
        END Stooges.
```

FIGURE 7.22 *Example of scope and parameter passage — the Stooges program*

Figure 7.23 is a complete trace of the execution of Stooges.

```
Control flow                              Data

                              Stooges
                              Moe Joe Curly
(' up to ZZZ(Moe) ')          "M"  "J"  "C"
ZZZ(Moe) . . . . . . . . . . . . . . . .  ZZZ
                                      .   Harpo
                                      .    "M"
       Harpo := "Z"                   .    "Z"
       (' RETURN ')  . . . . . . . . . . . (·deallocate·)

(' up to AAA(Moe) ')      "M"  "J"  "C"
AAA(Moe) . . . . . . . . . . . . . . . .  AAA
                          "M" ←           Chico Curly
                                            @      -
       Curly := Chico                              "M"
       Chico := "A"       "A"          .
       (' RETURN ')  . . . . . . . . . . . (·deallocate·)

(' up to Joker(etc. ')  "M"  "J"  "C"
Joker(Moe, Joe) . . . . . . . . . . .     Joker
                                          Zeppo Moe
                          "M" ←             @     "J"
       Zeppo := "T"       "T"       .
       Moe := "I"                           "I"
       Groucho(Zeppo) . . . . . . . . . . . . . . Groucho
                                    .             Chico
                                                    @
          Chico := "F"    "F"       .
          Moe := "U"                        "U"
          Joe := "N"          "N"   .
          (' RETURN ')  . . . . . . . . . . . . . (·deallocate·)

       Moe := "L"                       .    "L"
       Groucho(Moe) . . . . . . . . . . . . . . . Groucho
                                    .             Chico
                                                    @
          Chico := "F"               .    "L" ←
          Moe := "U"                      "F"
          Joe := "N"          "N"         "U"
          (' RETURN ')  . . . . . . . . . . . . . (·deallocate·)

       (' RETURN ')  . . . . . . . . . . . (·deallocate·)

(' HALT ')            (·deallocate·)


       Notation used above:

          - Program instructions are on the left.
          - Only selected instructions are included.
          - Each invocation is indented.
          - (' RETURN ') denotes an implicit procedure return
          - The values of variables and parameter are under "Data."
          - The procedure name is above the its data.
          - "-" denotes an unassigned value.
          - Data deallocation is denoted (·deallocate·).
```

FIGURE 7.23 A trace of Stooges

The call of ZZZ passes the actual parameter Moe by value to the formal parameter Harpo. When this occurs a copy of the value of Moe, "M", is assigned to Harpo. However, since Moe is passed by value, no change occurs to this variable throughout the execution of ZZZ. The invocation of AAA also uses Moe as its actual parameter. In this case Moe is passed by reference to Chico. So when Chico is assigned a new value via Chico := "A" it is actually Moe that receives the value "A". AAA also has a local variable, Curly. Therefore the assignment of "M" to Curly assigns the value to the local Curly, rather than the global variable with the same name.

When Joker is invoked from the mainline, a reference to the actual parameter Moe is passed to the formal parameter Zeppo. Also, a copy of the value of the actual parameter Joe is passed to the formal parameter Moe. The first invocation of Groucho from Joker passes by reference the actual parameter Zeppo to the formal parameter Chico. Since Zeppo is itself a reference to the global variable Moe, Chico also references Moe. The assignment of "F" to Chico, is actually an assignment to the global Moe that is referenced through two consecutive procedure calls and VAR parameters. In the second invocation of Groucho, Chico is passed a reference to Moe.

The Stooges program is difficult to read and to trace because prudent rules for sharing data have been ignored. There are several instances where non-local data is accessed without parameter passage. Altering non-local and non-parameter access is often called a **side effect**. Side effects are a dangerous practice that promotes bugs. As evidence of this consider how difficult a side effect makes the process of tracing. The Groucho procedure assigns "N" to Joe. In order to locate Joe, a programmer must notice that Joe is neither a local variable nor formal parameter of Groucho. The next outer scope from Groucho is the Joker routine, but it too has neither a local variable nor formal parameter called Joe. The final enclosing scope is the Stooges program module. Here a global variable called Joe is found, and is therefore the object of the access within Groucho.

In addition to being difficult to trace, side effects are troublesome for program maintenance. A maintenance programmer often begins with the knowledge that some variable has been erroneously assigned a value. A reasonable methodology for eliminating the bug is first to locate all places in the code where the variable is altered. This location task is far more complicated when side effects are present.

Programming-with-Style

Avoidance of Side Effects

A side effect occurs whenever a procedure or function assigns a value to a variable that is neither a local variable nor a formal parameter of the current routine. Side effects always increase the potential for program bugs. One technique for identifying side effects is to draw scope of visibility rectangles around routines. A side effect occurs for any assignment to an identifier reference that crosses a rectangle boundary. The rule below should be followed carefully.

BE PREPARED TO OFFER SUBSTANTIAL
JUSTIFICATION FOR A SIDE EFFECT, OR DON'T USE IT!

7.8 PROCEDURE HIERARCHY CHARTS

The scope of visibility diagrams and parameter tracing techniques proposed in earlier sections are helpful in the study of data flow. However, they are of minimal assistance in studying the control flow of procedures. Scope rules indicate only which routines are *permitted* to invoke other routines, and not which routines *do* invoke others.

A **procedure hierarchy chart** is a tool used to diagram the control relationships among the routines of a program. Procedure hierarchy charts are pictorial images of a program where procedures and functions are symbolized as boxes. These boxes are interconnected to indicate potential invocations from one routine to another. Within this diagram there is a single separate arrow from the calling routine to any routine that it directly invokes. If possible, the calling routine is located above the routine it invokes. Figure 7.24 is one such hierarchy chart. This example illustrates a program called Inventory. The program contains an instruction to invoke the SumryReprt procedure.

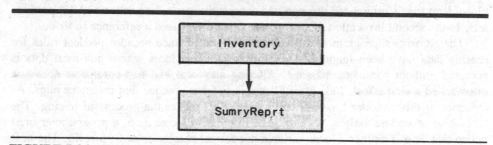

FIGURE 7.24 *An initial procedure hierarchy chart*

Procedure hierarchy charts, also known as **module hierarchy charts**, do not specify actual execution time invocations, but rather the possibility of an invocation. In other words, there exists at least one invocation instruction for SumryReprt within the Inventory mainline, but there is no guarantee that this call ever occurs during the actual execution.

Hierarchy charts also fail to show the number of times that a procedure is, or can be, invoked. The chart in Figure 7.24 correctly represents the relationship between Inventory and SumryReprt regardless of the number of times that Inventory invokes SumryReport and regardless of the number of different invocation instructions for SumryReprt.

Figure 7.25 on the opposite page, contains a procedure hierarchy chart for the Stooges program in the previous section. The hierarchy chart contains the information:

```
Stooges calls ZZZ, AAA, WriteInfo and Joker
Joker calls both Groucho and WriteInfo
ZZZ calls only WriteInfo
WriteInfo does not call any other procedures, except
              I/O instructions
```

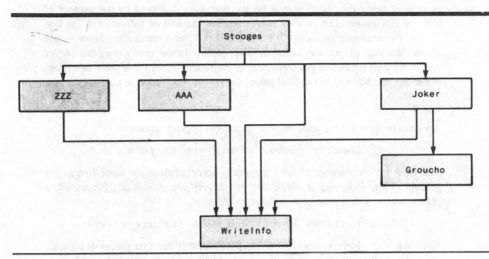

FIGURE 7.25 *Hierarchy chart for Stooges example*

7.9 AN EXAMPLE OF PROCEDURES

Figure 7.26 describes a problem for calculating batting averages for a baseball team. The basic problem is to write a program that will calculate the individual batting averages of team members, as well as the team average.

TITLE
Baseball batting averages

DESCRIPTION
This program calculates baseball averages for each individual player, as well as a team average. Input to the program is done for the entire baseball team, one player at a time. Batting information includes the results from all games in which a player participated. The batting average for each player is calculated by summing the number of hits and dividing by the total number of times at bat. The team batting average is calculated similarly by using the total number of hits and times at bat for all team members. All batting averages are expressed in terms of a cardinal value that is the truncated average number of hits per thousand times at bat.

INPUT
An initial prompt requests the total number of players on the team. In response to this request, the user must input a cardinal greater than 0. For each team member the user will be prompted to input batting information. The information for a player consists of a sequence of pairs of cardinals for every game in which that player had at least one time at bat followed by a pair of zeros. Each pair of cardinals preceding the trailing pair of zeros consists of a value representing the

(continued)

number of times the player was at bat for that game followed by the number of hits for that game. The pair of zeros signifies the end of information for that player. For example an input of 4 3 5 1 6 0 0 0 for a particular player would signify that this player was at bat in three games. In the first game, this player was at bat four times and got three hits; in the second game there were five times at bat and one hit; and in the final game, the player was hitless in six times at bat.

OUTPUT

An intial prompt for the total number of players appears as below.

       Specify number of players on team:

The input for the number of team players is accepted from the same line as the prompt. Then following a blank line all players are processed. Processing a player begins with a prompt as follows.

     Specify times at bat and hits for player <i>:

Note that <i> above symbolizes a sequence number for that player (i.e. 1, 2, etc.). After all input for a single player, one blank line is output followed by:

```
            Info for player: <i>
            times at bat: <pab>
            total hits: <ph>
            batting average: <pba>
```

The symbolism above uses <i> for the player sequence number, <pab> for the total number of times at bat for the player, <ph> for the total player hits and <pba> for the player's batting average (expressed as a truncated cardinal average hits per thousand times at bat). Following the entire list of players, two blank lines are output followed by the line below, where <p>, <tab>, <th> and <tba> are the team statistics for number of players, total times at bat, hits and batting average, respectively.

```
            Team Totals
            number of players: <p>
            times at bat: <tab>
            total hits: <th>
            batting average: <tba>
```

ERRORS

1) If the number of players is specified to be zero, then the program terminates with the following message.

             NO PLAYERS ON TEAM!!

2) If any player has no times at bat, then the following message is output in place of the three lines including times at bat, total hits, and player's batting average.

             BENCH WARMER!!

3) If input does not conform to the input specifications, or if no player on the entire team has a single time at bat, then undefined results occur.

(continued)

EXAMPLE

Below is a sample execution of the entire program with all input highlighted. Only five players are included to keep the example simple.

```
Specify number of players on team: 5

Specify times at bat and hits for player: 1
5 1   0 0

Info for player: 1
    times at bat: 5
    total hits: 1
    batting average: 200

Specify times at bat and hits for player: 2
5 1   4 4  1 0  0 0

Info for player: 2
    times at bat: 10          total hits: 5
    batting average: 500

Specify times at bat and hits for player: 3
3 0   5 0  2 0  0 0

Info for player: 3
    times at bat: 10
    total hits: 0
    batting average: 0

Specify times at bat and hits for player: 4
0 0

Info for player: 4
    BENCH WARMER!

Specify times at bat and hits for player: 5
1 0   2 1  1 1  1 0  0 0

Info for player: 5
    times at bat: 5
    total hits: 2
    batting average: 400


Team Totals
    number of players: 5
    times at bat: 30
    total hits: 8
    batting average: 266
```

FIGURE 7.26 *Definition for batting statistics problem*

The BaseballStats program of Figure 7.27 is a solution to this problem. BaseballStats makes use of two procedures, OutputStats and Process-Player. OutputStats displays one set of statistics and is invoked by both BaseballStats and ProcessPlayer. The statistics displayed by OutputStats includes a number of times at bat, total hits and batting average. OutputStats is designed solely for displaying information so all parameters to it are passed by value.

ProcessPlayer is a procedure to accumulate batting information for a single player. This procedure inputs data from several baseball games for the specified player and accumulates the number of times the player was at bat and number of hits. Because the mainline is responsible for accumulating the overall team statistics, ProcessPlayer must return the accumulated statistics for each player. Wisely, the programmer has chosen to accomplish this return of information via VAR parameters, rather than using global variables.

One additional parameter, PlayerNum, is used in ProcessPlayer. This parameter is required so that ProcessPlayer can display the appropriate heading prior to displaying totals for a player. Since ProcessPlayer does not alter this number, PlayerNum is passed by value.

```
MODULE BaseballStats;
    (* See problem description from Figure 7.26 *)
    FROM InOut IMPORT WriteString, WriteCard, WriteLn, ReadCard;
    VAR
        PlayerCount   : CARDINAL; (* total number of players *)
        PlayerNum     : CARDINAL;
        PlayerAtBats  : CARDINAL;
        PlayerHits    : CARDINAL;
        TeamAtBats    : CARDINAL;
        TeamHits      : CARDINAL;

    PROCEDURE OutputStats( AtBats : CARDINAL;
                           Hits   : CARDINAL );
        (* PRE:  AtBats > 0                                        *)
        (* POST: The following lines are output:                   *)
        (*              times at bat: <AtBats>                     *)
        (*              total hits: <Hits>                         *)
        (*              batting average: <1000 * Hits/AtBats> *)
    BEGIN
        WriteString( "   times at bat: " );
        WriteCard( AtBats, 0 );
        WriteLn;
        WriteString(" total hits: " );
        WriteCard( Hits, 0 );
        WriteLn;
        WriteString( " batting average: " );
        WriteCard( 1000*Hits DIV AtBats, 0 );
        WriteLn;
    END OutputStats;

    PROCEDURE ProcessPlayer(     PlayerNum : CARDINAL;
                             VAR TotAtBats : CARDINAL;
                             VAR TotHits   : CARDINAL );

        (* PRE:  PlayerNum is assigned                              *)
        (* POST: The following lines are output according to the    *)
        (*       input total hits, <ph>, and total times at bat,    *)
        (*       <pab> for player PlayerNum.  <pba> = 1000 * <ph> / *)
        (*       <pab> (and rounded):                               *)
        (*                         Info for player: <PlayerNum> *)
        (*                             times at bat: <pab>       *)
        (*                             total hits: <ph>          *)
        (*                             batting average: <pba>    *)
        (*       & TotAtBats = total at bats for player PlayerNum   *)
        (*       & TotHits = total hits for player PlayerNum        *)
```

(continued)

```
        VAR OneGameAtBats : CARDINAL;
            OneGameHits   : CARDINAL;
    BEGIN
        WriteString( "Info for player: " );
        WriteCard( PlayerNum, 0 );
        WriteLn;
        TotAtBats := 0;
        TotHits := 0;
        ReadCard( OneGameAtBats );
        ReadCard( OneGameHits );
        WHILE OneGameAtBats#0 DO
            TotAtBats := TotAtBats + OneGameAtBats;
            TotHits := TotHits + OneGameHits;
            ReadCard( OneGameAtBats );
            ReadCard( OneGameHits );
        END;
        WriteLn;
        IF TotAtBats=0 THEN
            WriteString( "BENCH WARMER!!" );
            WriteLn;
        ELSE
            OutputStats( TotAtBats, TotHits );
        END;
    END ProcessPlayer;

  BEGIN (* BaseballStats mainline *)
      WriteString( "Specify number of players on team:" );
      ReadCard( PlayerCount );    WriteLn;
      IF PlayerCount=0 THEN
          WriteString( "NO PLAYERS ON TEAM!" );
          WriteLn;
      ELSE
          TeamAtBats := 0;
          TeamHits := 0;
          PlayerNum := 1;
          WHILE  PlayerNum<=PlayerCount  DO
              WriteLn;
              ProcessPlayer(PlayerNum,PlayerAtBats,PlayerHits) ;
              TeamAtBats := TeamAtBats + PlayerAtBats;
              TeamHits := TeamHits + PlayerHits;
              PlayerNum := PlayerNum + 1;
          END;
          (* ASSERT: TeamAtBats = sum of all player at bats  *)
          (*         AND                                     *)
          (*         TeamHits = sum of hits from all players *)

          (* output team statistics *)
          WriteLn;
          WriteLn;
          WriteString( "Team Totals: " );
          WriteLn;
          WriteString( "   number of players: " );
          WriteCard( PlayerCount, 0 );
          WriteLn;
          OutputStats( TeamAtBats, TeamHits );
      END
  END BaseballStats.
```

FIGURE 7.27 *The BaseballStats program*

The two major criteria for evaluating the quality of a program are the quality of its data flow and the quality of its control flow. A scope of visibility diagram for Baseball Stats reveals that no side effects occur. In addition, it can be concluded that the parameter lists of this program are short, and parameter passage by reference is used only when necessary. These observations suggest sound data flow choices.

A procedure hierarchy chart can be used to evaluate the control flow between procedures. The hierarchy chart for this program, shown in Figure 7.28, is uncomplicated with a clear hierarchy. These are hierarchy chart qualities of a good control flow.

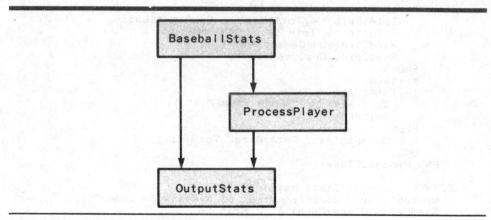

FIGURE 7.28 *Hierarchy chart for BaseballStats*

7.10 IMPROVING READABILITY WITH PROCEDURES

Boolean functions can be used to abbreviate part of a particularly complicated Boolean expression. Suppose three INTEGER variables, called Side1, Side2, and Side3 are supposed to store the lengths of the sides of a triangle. The sum of any two of the sides of a triangle must be less than the third, and all sides must be greater than 0. An IF instruction like the one below can test for valid sides.

```
IF (Side1<=0) OR (Side2<=0) OR (Side3<=0)
   OR (Side1+Side2 >= Side3)
   OR (Side1+Side3 >= Side2)
   OR (Side2+Side3 >= Side1)
THEN
   WriteString( "These sides do not represent a triangle" )
END;
```

A Boolean function, IsValidTriangle, is used below to improve the readability of the code. The declaration of this function is in Figure 7.29.

```
IF NOT IsValidTriangle(Side1, Side2, Side3) THEN
   WriteString( "These sides do not represent a triangle" )
END;
```

```
PROCEDURE IsValidTriangle( Side1 : INTEGER;
                           Side2 : INTEGER;
                           Side3 : INTEGER)
  : BOOLEAN;
     (* PRE:  Side1, Side2 & Side3 all assigned            *)
     (* POST: RESULT = TRUE, if parameters represent valid  *)
     (*                      lengths for sides of a triangle *)
     (*              = FALSE, otherwise                      *)
BEGIN
   RETURN (Side1>0) & (Side2>0) & (Side3>0)
          & (Side1+Side2 < Side3)
          & (Side1+Side3 < Side2)
          & (Side2+Side3 < Side1)
END IsValidTriangle;
```

FIGURE 7.29 *IsValidTriangle Boolean function*

7.11 DEBUGGING AND THE PROCEDURE: STUBS AND DRIVERS

There are two important techniques used by programmers in order to test and debug programs containing procedures. The first technique uses **procedure stubs**. A procedure stub is an unrefined shell of a procedure. This shell performs the simplest possible task that still supplies sensible results to a calling routine. The most important use of a stub is for testing during earlier levels of top down design. Suppose a programmer has completed the design of an algorithm except for three procedures that still require refinement. The existing design can be tested by supplying procedure stubs for these unrefined procedures and observing the execution of the refined code.

The BaseballStats program may well have been designed and tested in this manner. Assume that the designer refined and coded the mainline and OutputStats routines. It would be reasonable to test these portions of the program before designing ProcessPlayer. This can be done by providing a procedure stub for Process-Player that "fakes" the unrefined procedure so the rest of the program can execute. An examination of the code suggests that ProcessPlayer need only return reasonable values for its TotAtBats and TotHits parameters. One simple procedure stub that provides for useful testing is shown in Figure 7.30.

```
PROCEDURE ProcessPlayer(     PlayerNum : CARDINAL;
                         VAR TotAtBats : CARDINAL;
                         VAR TotHits   : CARDINAL );
     (* STUB *)
   BEGIN
      TotAtBats := 10;
      TotHits := 5
   END ProcessPlayer;
```

FIGURE 7.30 *A procedure stub for ProcessPlayer*

This procedure stub includes the two assignment instructions because its parameters must return some sensible values. Furthermore, the values 10 and 5 make for easy calculation of the desired output when testing the mainline.

The key to using procedure stubs is to keep them simple. A programmer should never include more in a stub than is absolutely necessary to perform the desired testing. When the code in the stub becomes complex, it may be less work to design the actual procedure.

The other technique for debugging code with procedures is to test completed routines individually. In this approach, a routine like OutputStats has been completely coded. A separate mainline is the written for the express purpose of testing OutputStats. This mainline is referred to as a **test driver** because its sole purpose is to drive the invocation for testing. Figure 7.31 contains a test driver for OutputStats procedure.

```
MODULE TestOutputStats;
    (* Test driver for the OutputStats procedure *)
    FROM InOut IMPORT WriteString, WriteCard, WriteLn;

    PROCEDURE OutputStats( AtBats : CARDINAL;
                           Hits   : CARDINAL );
        (* PRE:  AtBats > 0                                    *)
        (* POST: The following lines are output:               *)
        (*              times at bat: <AtBats>                 *)
        (*              total hits: <Hits>                     *)
        (*              batting average: <1000 * Hits/AtBats> *)
    BEGIN
        WriteString( "    times at bat: " );
        WriteCard( AtBats, 0 );
        WriteLn;
        WriteString( "    total hits: " );
        WriteCard( Hits, 0 );
        WriteLn;
        WriteString( "    batting average: " );
        WriteCard( 1000*Hits DIV AtBats, 0 );
        WriteLn
    END OutputStats;

BEGIN (* test driver for OutputStats *)
    WriteString('+++++++++++++++++++++');
    WriteLn;
    OutputStats( 6, 4 );
    OutputStats( 3, 0 );
END TestOutputStats.
```

FIGURE 7.31 *TestOutputStats, a procedure test driver*

As with the procedure stub, a test driver should be as simple to code as possible. In Figure 7.31 the test driver calls OutputStats with parameters selected to test various options and to provide for easy checking of output. Displaying the initial line of + 's is included to check for the appropriate output spacing. Testing with procedure stubs is the opposite of testing with test drivers. When procedure stubs are used the higher levels of the code are developed and tested by supplying "fake" lower level procedure stubs. Using a test driver, one tests the lower level procedures with an artificial top level. Ironically, both of these techniques are very useful for software design.

7.12 SUMMARY

The Modula-2 tool for control abstraction is the procedure. There are two forms of procedures, those without a value and functions that return a value.

In order to use procedures, a programmer must fully understand many issues. The techniques used for parameter passage by value and reference (VAR) provide for data flow between calling and called routine. The rules of static scoping and range of existence define the semantic behavior of variables that are local to procedures.

A programmer must always seek new programming tools. Tools such as the standard procedures and functions of Modula-2 can assist with coding. Tools like diagramming scope prove helpful in examining data flow and locating side effects. Tools like procedure hierarchy charts provide a means for examining invocation structures and relationships among major components of a program. Debugging techniques like procedure stubs, and test drivers assist in software development.

Procedure preconditions and postconditions are very special tools. These assertions serve as the bolts that connect procedure body and invocation. They aid the designer by presenting explicit definition of the task to be performed. They help the coder check code. They provide maintenance programmers with the specifications necessary for locating errors and making program modifications.

This chapter has demonstrated that abstraction via Modula-2 procedures is a powerful and flexible resource. Mastery of this resource is not easy, but it is critical to the mastery of programming.

||| KEY TERMS

parameter passage	intrinsic procedure	block structured language
parameter passage by value	generic procedure	static scope
parameter passage by reference	RETURN instruction	automatic variable
VAR parameter	HALT procedure	side effect
function	scope of visibility	procedure hierarchy chart
RESULT	range of existence	module hierarchy chart
standard procedure	allocation (of data)	procedure stub
built in procedure	deallocation (of data)	test driver

||| EXERCISES

1. Use the procedure below to complete parts (a) through (f):

```
PROCEDURE ParmExample(     FrstParm : CHAR;
                           ScndParm : CHAR;
                       VAR ThrdParm : CHAR;
                       VAR FrthParm : CHAR );
      (* PRE:  ? *)
      (* POST: ? *)
      VAR LocalVar : CARDINAL;
BEGIN
      ScndParm := "2";
      ThrdParm := "3";
      LocalVar := FrstParm;
      FrstParm := FrthParm;
      FrthPrm := LocalVar;
      Write(FrstParm); Write(ScndParm);
      Write(ThrdParm); Write(FrthParm);  WriteLn;
END ParmExample;
```

a) List all formal parameters that are passed by value.
b) List all formal parameters that are passed by reference.
c) Indicate the output that is produced by the execution of the code below:

```
VarA := "A";
VarB := "B";
VarC := "C";
VarD := "D";
ParmExample( VarA, VarB, VarC, VarD );
Write( VarA );
Write( VarB );
Write( VarC );
Write( VarD );
```

d) Describe explicitly why the following invocation of ParmExample results in a synta
error: ParmExample("1", "2", "3", "4")

   ParmExample("1", "2", "3", "4")

e) A precondition for ParmExample should specify all parameters that must be assigned
prior to the invocation. List all such parameters, but do not include those that do not
require assignment for ParmExample to work properly.

f) Specify an appropriate postcondition for this ParmExample. Postconditions should
be as explicit as possible.

2. Use the procedure below to complete parts (a) through (e):

```
PROCEDURE AnotherExample( VAR FrstParm : CARDINAL;
                              ScndParm : CARDINAL;
                          VAR ThrdParm : CARDINAL;
                              FrthParm : CARDINAL );
      (* PRE:  ? *)
      (* POST: ? *)
      VAR LocalVar : CARDINAL;
    BEGIN
      ScndParm := FrstParm;
      ThrdParm := FrthParm
      LocalVar := FrstParm + ScndParm;
      ThrdParm := ThrdParm + 1;
      FrthPrm := LocalVar + ScndParm
      Write(FrstParm); Write(ScndParm);
      Write(ThrdParm); Write(FrthParm);   WriteLn;
    END AnotherExample;
```

a) List all formal parameters that are passed by value.

b) List all formal parameters that are passed by reference.

c) Indicate the output that is produced by the execution of the code below:

```
VarI   := 1;
VarII  := 2;
VarIII := 3;
VarIV := 4;
AnotherExample( VarI, VarII, VarIII, VarIV );
WriteCard( VarI, 0 );
WriteCard( VarII, 0 );
WriteCard( VarIII, 0 );
WriteCard( VarIV, 0 );
```

d) A precondition for ParmExample should specify all parameters that must be assigned prior to the invocation. List all such parameters, but do not include those that do not require assignment for ParmExample to work properly.

e) Specify an appropriate postcondition for this ParmExample. Postconditions should not specify information about final values of data structures that have no effect after return. Postconditions should also be as explicit as possible.

3. Specify the value of each of the following function calls:

a) ABS((−7) * 2)

b) CAP("r")

c) CAP("G")

d) CAP(CHR(ORD("T")))

4. Use the function procedure written below to complete parts (a) through (e):

```
PROCEDURE Increase( SomeVal : INTEGER )
  : INTEGER;
      (* PRE:  ? *)
      (* POST: ? *)
    BEGIN
      RETURN (SomeVal + 1)
    END Increase;
```

a) What is the value of Increase(3)?

b) How is Increase similar to the standard INC procedure when no second parameter is used)?

c) List all of the differences between Increase and INC.

d) Indicate an appropriate precondition for Increase.

e) Indicate an appropriate postcondition for Increase.

5. Consider the Stooges program from this chapter.

a) Diagram the static scoping of this program.

b) List all of the side effects from this program.

c) Specify the exact output produced by an execution of this program.

The program below is used in Exercise 6:

```
MODULE MoreStooges;
     (* This module does not perform any useful task *)
     (* except to illustrate data access that is far *)
     (* too complex.                                  *)
   FROM InOut IMPORT WriteString, WriteLn, WriteCard,
                      Write;
   VAR
      Moe  : CARDINAL;
      Joe  : CARDINAL;
      Curly : CARDINAL;

   PROCEDURE WriteInfo( RoutineID : CHAR;
                        MoeVal  : CARDINAL;
                        JoeVal  : CARDINAL;
                        CurlyVal  : CARDINAL );
   BEGIN
      WriteString( ' output from routine: ' );
      Write( RoutineID );
      WriteLn;
      WriteString( '    values of Moe, Joe and Curly → ' );
      WriteCard( MoeVal,6 );
      WriteCard( JoeVal,6 );
      WriteCard( CurlyVal,6 );
      WriteLn;
      WriteLn;
   END WriteInfo;

   PROCEDURE IncEm( VAR Harpo: CARDINAL;
                        Chico: CARDINAL  );
      VAR Moe  : CARDINAL;
   BEGIN
      Harpo := Harpo + 1;
      Chico := Chico + 1;
      Moe  := Moe + 1;
      Joe  := Joe + 1;
      WriteInfo( "I", Moe, Joe, Curly )
   END IncEm;

   PROCEDURE MessEm( VAR Chico : CARDINAL;
                         Harpo : CARDINAL;
                         VAR Zeppo : CARDINAL  );
       VAR
          Curly : CARDINAL;
```

```
            PROCEDURE TangleEm(      Groucho : CARDINAL;
                                VAR Harpo   : CARDINAL );
            BEGIN
                Harpo := Groucho;
                Groucho := 0;
                WriteInfo( "T", Moe, Joe, Curly )
            END TangleEm;

            PROCEDURE FlogEm( Zeppo : CARDINAL );
                VAR Joe : CARDINAL;
            BEGIN
                Joe := 100;
                IncEm( Zeppo, Joe );
                TangleEm( Curly, Moe );
                WriteInfo( "F", Moe, Joe, Curly )
            END FlogEm;

        BEGIN (* MessEm *)
            Curly := 1000;
            Joe := 2000 + Moe;
            TangleEm( Curly, Moe );
            FlogEm( Zeppo );
            WriteInfo( "M", Moe, Joe, Curly )
        END MessEm;

    BEGIN (* MoreStooges mainline *)
        Moe := 1;
        Joe := 2;
        Curly := 3;
        IncEm( Curly, Joe );
        WriteInfo( "1", Moe, Joe, Curly );

        Moe := 1;
        Joe := 2;
        Curly := 3;
        IncEm( Curly, Moe );
        WriteInfo( "2", Moe, Joe, Curly );

        Moe := 1;
        Joe := 2;
        Curly := 3;
        IncEm( Curly, Curly );
        WriteInfo( "3", Moe, Joe, Curly );

        Moe := 1;
        Joe := 2;
        Curly := 3;
        MessEm( Moe, Joe, Curly );
        WriteInfo( "4", Moe, Joe, Curly )
    END MoreStooges.
```

6. Use the useless MoreStooges program above to complete the following:
   a) Diagram the procedure hierarchy for this program.
   b) Diagram the static scope of this program.
   c) For each procedure in this program specify which other procedures it can invoke directly.
   d) Indicate precisely what output is produced by the execution of this program.

7. Write the code for the procedure below. Consider which type of selection is best suited to the problem. Examine your solution to ensure correctness.

TITLE

A procedure called `DollarsToPounds`

DESCRIPTION

This procedure has the following heading:

```
PROCEDURE DollarsToPounds(    Cents      : CARDINAL;
                          VAR Pounds     : CARDINAL;
                          VAR Shillings  : CARDINAL;
                          VAR Pence      : CARDINAL  );
```

The procedure translates U.S. money (Cents) into the old British standard (Pounds, Shillings and Pence). The exchange rate is assumed to be $1.98 per pound sterling. Upon return from this procedure, Pounds, Shillings, and Pence should all be assigned the appropriate values so that the British equivalent of Cents is returned in the largest denominations possible. The British monetary system defines one pound to be 20 shillings and one shilling to be 12 pence.

INPUT

None from InOut

The Cents parameter serves as the input value amount of U.S. money in cents.

OUTPUT

None from InOut

The Pounds, Shillings and Pence parameters return the British equivalent of Cents expressed in the largest denominations possible.

ERRORS

If Cents is unassigned, then undefined results occur.

EXAMPLE

Value of Cents	Corresponding values of Pounds, Shillings and Pence
240	1, 0, 0
100	0, 8, 4
425	1, 15, 5

||| PROGRAMMING PROJECTS

1. Write a routine to perform the indicated task. You should test your procedure with an appropriate test driver.

   a) Write a function with two parameters, Altitude and Height, representing the altitude and height of a triangle. Below are the precondition and postcondition for this function:

   > PRE: Altitude and Height are assigned
   > POST: RESULT = Altitude*Height/2, rounded

   b) Write a function with three parameters. If the first parameter is a "T", then the function should use the remaining two parameters and behave as described in a) above. If the first parameter is not "T", then the remaining two parameters should be taken to represent the length and width of a rectangle and the function should return the area.

   c) TITLE
   > A function called BoardFeet

   DESCRIPTION
   > Write a function with three parameters, representing the length, width and height of a board in inches. The function must return the truncated number of board feet in this board. Note: one board foot is defined as 144 cubic inches.

   INPUT
   > None

   OUTPUT
   > None

   ERRORS
   > Any parameters which produce an area larger than MAX(CARDINAL) produce undefined results.

   EXAMPLE
   > BoardFeet(12, 24, 1) returns the value 2.

   d) Write a procedure, called WriteMoney, with a single CARDINAL parameter, called Money, and the following precondition and postcondition:

   > PRE: Money is assigned
   > POST: Money is output as $D.CC

   Where D denotes the number of whole dollars (1 or more digits) and CC denotes the number of cents beyond a whole dollar (exactly 2 digits). For example WriteMoney(325) outputs "$3.25", WriteMoney(200) outputs "$2.00", and WriteMoney(20) outputs "$0.20".

e) A function called CompoundedVal that returns the amount due on a loan that is compounded annually. The function's three parameters are the original principle, a interest rate, and the number of years in the loan.

f) TITLE

A procedure called LumberCost

DESCRIPTION

Write a procedure that inputs four triplets of cardinal values. Each triplet represents the length, width and height (in inches) of a single board. The procedure should output the individual cost of each board and return the combined board feet and combined cost of the four boards. The first parameter of LumberCost is used to pass the cost (in cents per board foot) of lumber into the LumberCost procedure. The last two parameters are used to return the combined board feet and lumber cost, respectively. Note: The use of BoardFeet from part (c) and WriteMoney from part (d) are suggested as local routines within Lumber-Cost.

INPUT

Input consists of four sets of three consecutive cardinal constants (triplets), where each triplet is the length width and height (in inches) of a single board).

OUTPUT

Each input triplet is preceded by a single line consisting of the following prompt:
Input board dimensions (in inches).
Following the input for each board, these three items are output:

1) A line of the form Board feet . . . . . <bf> where <bf> denotes the number of board feet in the particular board just input
2) A line of the form Cost . . . . <cb> where <cb> is the cost of this particular board (displayed with a leading dollar sign and exactly two digits right of the decimal point)
3) One blank line

ERRORS

Any input inconsistent with the above input specifications produce undefined results.

EXAMPLE

The following snapshots represent the input (highlighted) and output of a single call of the form:

```
LumberCost( 20, TotBoardfeet, TotCost )
```

Note that the final values of TotBoardFeet and TotCost will be 20 and 400, respectively, for this invocation.

```
Input board dimensions (in inches)
       12 12 1
Board Feet . . . . . 1
Cost . . . . . . . . . . $0.20
```

```
Input board dimensions (in inches)
   120 1 6
Board Feet ..... 5
Cost .......... $1.00

Input board dimensions (in inches)
   0 0 0
Board Feet ..... 0
Cost .......... $0.00

Input board dimensions (in inches)
   168 2 6
Board Feet ..... 14
Cost .......... $2.80
```

g) TITLE

A procedure called WriteRoman

DESCRIPTION

The WriteRoman procedure has a single parameter with value in the range from 1 to 39. This procedure outputs on the current output line the Roman Numeral representation of its parameter.

INPUT

None

OUTPUT

From one to seven characters forming the Roman Numeral representation of the parameter. Roman numerals count as follows: (I, II, III, IV, V, VI, VII, VIII, IX, X, XI, XII, ..., XXXIX).

ERRORS

A parameter value less than 1 or greater than 39 produces the following error message:

CAN'T OUTPUT ROMAN NUMERALS <1 OR >39

EXAMPLES

WriteRoman(3) outputs III
WriteRoman(38) outputs XXXVIII

2. Write a program to solve the following problem. You must use procedures in this program.

TITLE

Carpet Yardage Calculator

DESCRIPTION

A Carpet seller needs a program to calculate the amount of carpet to be ordered for carpeting houses. Input to the program consists of dimensions (in feet) of each room of a single house to be carpeted. The program calculates the total amount of carpet to be ordered by totaling the square footage for all rooms and adding ten percent (assumed wastage). The resulting square footage is rounded to the next higher square yard and output. Note: There are nine square feet in one square yard.

INPUT

All input is prompted (see output for prompt details). The first input is a cardinal constant indicating the number of rooms to be carpeted alike. Following this input are the indicated number of pairs of cardinal constants, where each pair represents the length and width of one room (in feet).

OUTPUT

The initial prompt line is Number of rooms?. The prompt output prior to each room is Length & width (in feet)? After the input for a room the following is output followed by a blank line:

    Square footage of this room is <S>

where <S> is the amount of square footage for the room.

The final output consists of the following lines:

    Total square feet in all rooms: <F>
    Number of square yards to order: <Y>

where <F> is the sum of all the <S> values and <Y> is <F> in square yards plus 10% and rounded to the nearest cardinal.

ERRORS

Any input not conforming to specifications produces undefined results.

EXAMPLE

Below is a sample execution where all input is highlighted.

    Number of rooms?   3
    Length & width (in feet)?   10 10
    Square footage of this room is 100

    Length & width (in feet)?   5 12
    Square footage of this room is 60

    Length & width (in feet)?   14 15
    Square footage of this room is 210

    Total square feet in all rooms: 370
    Number of square yards to order: 45

3. Write a program to solve the following problem. You must use procedures in this pr gram.

TITLE
    Checkbook program

DESCRIPTION
    This program is designed to manage a checkbook for the First International Bank. The program inputs transactions and outputs the balance for a single account. Each transaction can be either a deposit or withdrawal in any whole dollar-amount (First International believes pennies to be inconsequential). First International adds an extra $2 to any account when the amount of a deposit exceeds $2000. First International also has a policy of permitting overdrawn accounts, but there is a $5 charge placed on any withdrawal for which the resulting account becomes or remains overdrawn. No withdrawal transactions are permitted for an account that is overdrawn by more than $2000, but the $5 fee is still charged for such attempts.

INPUT
    An initial input in response to a prompt is a cardinal value that is the initial checkbook balance. Transaction input consists of a single character for the transaction (either "W" for withdrawal, "D" for deposit or "X" for the end of input) followed by a cardinal value that is the amount of the transaction (this amount does not follow the "X" input, but only the "W" and the "D"). The last input is the "X". Prior to each input a prompt is specified and after each input the resulting balance and any necessary messages (see output and errors sections below).

OUTPUT
    The initial balance request prompt is as follows:

    Specify initial balance:

    Prior to each transaction, the following two line prompt is output:

    Specify a transaction:
    "W" – withdrawal "D" – deposit "X" quit

    Following the input transaction character for either a withdrawal or a deposit, the following prompt precedes the entered amount:

    Amount of transaction (in whole dollars):

    Following the input the following line is output indicating the balance, <b>, after the transaction.

    Resulting balance: <b>

    A blank line separates each balance from the prompt for the next transaction.

ERRORS
    1) Input not conforming to specifications produces undefined results.
    2) Whenever a deposit of $2000 or greater is made, there is an automatic $2 bonus added immediately to the balance.

3) Whenever the balance resulting from a withdrawal is below 0, there is an additional $5 overdraft charge subtracted immediately from the balance.

4) Whenever a withdrawal is attempted from an account that is $2000 or more overdrawn, then the following message is output (following the balance line), the withdrawal is not permitted, and $5 is charged against the account.

OVERDRAFT IN EXCESS OF $2000

EXAMPLE

Below is a sample execution with input highlighted.

```
Specify initial balance:
     100
Specify a transaction:
 "W" – withdrawal  "D" – deposit    "X" quit
D
Amount of transaction (in whole dollars):
100
Resulting balance: 200

Specify a transaction:
 "W" – withdrawal  "D" – deposit    "X" quit
W
Amount of transaction (in whole dollars):
500
Resulting balance: –305

Specify a transaction:
 "W" – withdrawal  "D" – deposit    "X" quit
W
Amount of transaction (in whole dollars):
1800
Resulting balance: –2110

Specify a transaction:
 "W" – withdrawal  "D" – deposit    "X" quit
W
Amount of transaction (in whole dollars):
100
Resulting balance: –2115
OVERDRAFT IN EXCESS OF $2000

Specify a transaction:
 "W" – withdrawal  "D" – deposit    "X" quit
D
Amount of transaction (in whole dollars):
3000
Resulting balance: 887

Specify a transaction:
 "W" – withdrawal  "D" – deposit    "X" quit
X
```

4. Solve the following problem with a program containing procedures. You may wish to program stubs in the design process for this program.

TITLE

Utilities invoice program

DESCRIPTION

A natural gas and electrical company needs a program to calculate invoices for utilities charges. This company makes all calculations based on CCF (100 cubic feet) of natural gas and KW (kilowatt-hour) of electricity consumed. The company's fee for all electrical use is as follows:

10 cents per KW for the first 1000KW
9 cents per KW for the next 500KW
8 cents per KW for anything over 1500KW

Costs for natural gas differ for residential and industrial customers. Residential customers pay 50 cents per CCF for all natural gas. Industrial customers pay 45 cents per CCF for the first 500CCF and 40 cents per CCF for any use in excess of 500CCF.

INPUT

The program must be interactive, and it must permit the printing of several invoices per program execution. All input requires prompting (see output section).

For each invoice the user is first prompted as to whether the customer is a residential customer or industrial ("I" signifies industrial; anything else is residential). Next the user inputs two cardinals for the number of KW of electricity and the number of CCF of natural gas consumed during the month. Following output of the invoice, the user is required to type a "Y" to continue to process another invoice.

OUTPUT

Below is the output produced (prompts and all) for a single customer, where <R or I> is either the character "R" for residential customer or "I" for industrial, <e> is the cardinal amount of electricity consumed, <e$> is the cost for electricity, <n> is the amount of natural gas consumed, <n$> is the cost for natural gas, and <t$> is the sum of <e$> and <n$>.

```
Customer type? ("I" for industrial, anything otherwise)
Electrical use? (in KW)
Natural gas use? (in CCF)

INVOICE:   Customer type: <R or I>

           Electricity consumed: <e>KW
           Electrical charge:    <e$>

           Natural gas consumed: <n>CCF
           Natural gas charge:   <n$>

           Total amount due .... <t$>
```
<<two blank lines>>
```
Another invoice? (Y or N)
```

ERRORS
Any input not of the above form produces undefined results.

EXAMPLE
Below is a sample execution with all input highlighted.

```
Customer type? ("I" for industrial, anything otherwise) R
Electrical use? (in KW)  100
Natural gas use? (in CCF)  100

INVOICE:   Customer type: R

           Electricity consumed: 100KW
           Electrical charge:    $10.00

           Natural gas consumed: 100CCF
           Natural gas charge:   $50.00
           ------------------------------
           Total amount due .... $60.00


Another invoice? (Y or N)  Y
Customer type? ("I" for industrial, anything otherwise) II
Electrical use? (in KW)  2000
Natural gas use? (in CCF)  1000

INVOICE:  Customer type: I

           Electricity consumed: 2000KW
           Electrical charge:    $185.00

           Natural gas consumed: 1000CCF
           Natural gas charge:  $425.00
           ------------------------------
           Total amount due .... $610.00


Another invoice? (Y or N) Y
Customer type? ("I" for industrial, anything otherwise) ii
Electrical use? (in KW)  1003
Natural gas use? (in CCF)  0

INVOICE:  Customer type: I

           Electricity consumed: 1003KW
           Electrical charge:    $100.27

           Natural gas consumed: 0CCF
           Natural gas charge:  $0.00
           ------------------------------
           Total amount due .... $100.27


Another invoice? (Y or N)  N
```

8 ||| INPUT AND OUTPUT OF TEXT FILES

8.1 TEXT FILES

Variables can be thought of as a form of "short term memory." They store data reliably for the short time that the program executes, but are then deallocated. Many computer applications require a method for storing data after a program has terminated. In other words, they need a "long term memory." Such memory is called **secondary storage**.

Secondary storage makes use of physical media such as **floppy diskettes**, **hard disks**, and **magnetic tape**. Information is recorded on the medium for later use. For example, a floppy disk consists of a thin platter on which magnetic encodings can be stored and later retrieved. The magnetic encoding remains unchanged unless another magnetic field alters it. A single floppy disk can be used to store data used by a single program during different executions, or shared between different programs. The floppy can also be moved from one computer to another to transport data.

From the programmer's perspective, the data stored in secondary storage is divided into collections of data called **files**. A major part of any operating system is a "file manager" that is responsible for assisting with the creation, update, and retrieval of files.

It is impossible to use a computer without encountering files. When a program is created, using the editor, the resulting source code is stored in a file. Compiling a program creates a second file containing the compiled code. The linker creates still another file. The compiler and linker, themselves, are stored in files.

Files are divided into two classes.

Text Files
Binary Files

A **text file** contains only characters. These are files designed for human consumption. Editors create text files. Files transferred directly to a printer or computer display must be text files.

Binary files come in an infinite number of different forms, but all share the common feature that they are designed to be consumed by computers rather than humans. A binary file uses numeric encodings that are difficult, if not impossible, for humans to read. Compilers and linkers are good examples of binary files. If either of these files is transferred directly to a computer display, the result is a useless collection of what looks like random characters.

The Modula-2 program facilities for manipulating binary files vary from one implementation of Modula-2 to the next. To some extent this variation exists to allow for differences between installations. Such facilities are often described as "Files modules" or "FileSystem modules".

8.2 MORE ABOUT INOUT

Storing and retrieving data from a file is analogous to transmitting characters to a display or reading from a keyboard. Both are forms of input and output (I/0). An input operation may read (retrieve values) from the keyboard or from a file. Similarly, an output operation may write (transmit data) to a display or to a file. The term **interactive I/O** refers to the I/O style in which input comes from a keyboard and output goes to a display. Any form of input using files is called **file I/O**.

Because of the similarities between interactive I/O and file I/O on text files, **InOut** is designed to combine facilities for both. This is possible by treating a text file as one long stream of characters, similar to the stream of characters written to a display or the stream of keystrokes (characters) read from a keyboard.

The complete collection of facilities available in InOut is summarized in Figure 8.1. These include procedures to read input, either from a keyboard or a file, and procedures to write output, either to a display or file.

The Facilities Provided by InOut

```
Input
    Read ........ a procedure to input a single character
    ReadCard ..... a procedure to input a string of characters
                   representing a single cardinal
    ReadInt ...... a procedure to input a string of characters
                   representing a single integer
    Done ........ a BOOLEAN variable indicating the status
                   after any input (Done=TRUE means I/O ok)
    ReadString ... a procedure to input a string of characters
                   into an array)
    termCH ....... a variable used in conjunction with ReadString
    OpenInput .... a procedure to open a new input file
    CloseInput ... a procedure to close the current input file
                   and revert to the standard input device

Output
    Write ........ a procedure to output a single character
    WriteCard .... a procedure to output the value of a single
                   cardinal as a string of characters
    WriteInt ..... a procedure to output the value of a single
                   integer as a string of characters       (continued)
```

```
WriteString .. a procedure to output a string of characters
WriteLn....... a procedure to output the EOL character
OpenOutput ... a procedure to open a new output file ·
CloseOutput .. a procedure to close the current output file
               and revert to the standard output device

A related constant
    EOL .......... a character constant that is the special
                   character used to signify the end of a line
                   for both input and output
```

FIGURE 8.1 *The facilities of InOut*

InOut consists of six input procedures, seven output procedures, two variables, and a constant. A programmer may use any or all of these facilities within a program, as long as an appropriate IMPORT declaration is included to specify exactly which facilities are used. A sample such declaration is given below.

```
FROM InOut IMPORT Read, Write, ReadCard, WriteLn, Done;
```

```
(* The above declaration permits the use of the *)
(* four procedures and one variable listed.     *)
```

It is important to understand precisely what occurs when various types of input are supplied. Figure 8.2 contains a more detailed description of the read procedures in terms of postconditions.

```
PROCEDURE Read( VAR InChar : CHAR );
   (* POST: InChar = next input character              *)
   (*       & Done = TRUE,  if successful input occurred *)
   (*              = FALSE, if end of file at entry      *)
   (* NOTE: In many systems no output echo is produced  *)

PROCEDURE ReadCard( VAR InCard : CARDINAL );
   (* POST: InCard = cardinal value of input string    *)
   (*       & Done = TRUE,  if cardinal is read          *)
   (* NOTE: This procedure causes all leading blanks and *)
   (*       control characters to be consumed. A valid   *)
   (*       cardinal input consists of all consecutive   *)
   (*       characters in the range from "0" through "9". *)
   (*       In many systems only numeric digits are      *)
   (*       output echoed.                               *)

PROCEDURE ReadInt( VAR InInt : INTEGER );
   (* POST: InInt = integer value of input string       *)
   (*       & Done = TRUE, if cardinal is read           *)
   (* NOTE: This procedure causes all leading blanks and *)
   (*       control characters to be consumed. A valid   *)
   (*       integer input consists of all consecutive    *)
   (*       characters in the range from "0" through "9"  *)
   (*       optionally preceded by "+" or "-".           *)
   (*       In many systems only numeric constant        *)
   (*       characters are output echoed.                *)
```

(continued)

```
PROCEDURE ReadString( VAR InString : ARRAY OF CHAR );
    (* POST: InString = next non-blank sequence of chars *)
    (*       & Done = TRUE,  if string is read            *)
    (* NOTE: This procedure skips all leading blanks and  *)
    (*       control characters. The character sequence   *)
    (*       that follows up to the next blank or control *)
    (*       character is input to InString and this      *)
    (*       last charcter assigned to termCH. See        *)
    (*       Chapter 11 for a discussion of arrays.       *)
    (*       In many systems no output echo is produced.  *)
```

FIGURE 8.2 *Description of Read, ReadCard, ReadInt, and ReadString*

All input procedures have the side effect of assigning the Done variable a value before returning. An invocation of Read assigns Done the value TRUE when at least one input character remains in the file at the time of invocation.

The ReadCard and ReadInt procedures perform parallel tasks. Each is designed to input a string of characters representing a numeric value and to assign the value to the parameter. They both perform somewhat of a type conversion, to transfer from a character string to a numeric value. When ReadCard is executed, the user may specify a sequence of keystrokes (characters). This character sequence is translated into the unsigned integer value it represents and this value is assigned to the ReadCard parameter.

Both ReadCard and ReadInt cause all blanks or **control characters** (any character with ordinal value < 32 in ASCII) preceding the numeric string to be consumed and ignored. The character string following leading blanks and control characters should be an integer constant (signed for ReadInt and unsigned for ReadCard). If so, then all consecutive decimal digits characters that follow are consumed and taken as part of this input value. Different implementations of Modula-2 behave in various ways when executing ReadCard or ReadInt for unexpected input. It is best to be careful of input form and include an additional blank after each cardinal or integer input string. This blank will be the last character consumed by the input procedure.

To illustrate the actions performed by these input procedures, assume that the next input to be supplied is the line pictured below (arrows point to the next input character).

$$\downarrow$$

Next input:　ЬЬЬЬЬ–133ЬB725

(Before)　$\uparrow$

Further assume that the following procedure invocation is executed.

ReadInt(SomeInt)

Since this input operation was successful, the following results occur due to this invocation.

SomeInt = –133 AND Done = TRUE

and the remaining input can be pictured as

Next input: ꟸꟸꟸꟸꟸ–133ꟸB725
(After)

There are some differences when input is interactive, rather than from a file. For interactive input, the user is always presumed to be able to supply another keystroke, so Done is always assigned TRUE after an interactive Read. Additionally, interactive ReadCard and ReadInt cause the keystrokes input as cardinal or integer values to be echoed to the output display as they are struck in most Modula-2 systems. This echo is not produced for file I/O.

Another input feature that is important for a keyboard is a special treatment of backspacing. Keyboards have a backspace key. Striking this key produces an input character (CHR(8) = 10C for ASCII). Backspace characters encountered for interactive input in ReadCard and ReadInt only are treated as erase keys, erasing past keystrokes. This facility of InOut permits the user of a program to backspace consistently with other computer applications.

Designing-with-Wisdom-

The Done Variable of InOut

InOut input procedures do not produce execution errors. Instead, the variable Done is assigned a value to indicate a successful input operation (Done = TRUE) or an unsuccessful one (Done = FALSE). The value assigned to the parameter of a Read, ReadCard, ReadInt or Reads-String is meaningless whenever Done = FALSE upon return.

The output procedures for InOut, are described in Figure 8.3.

```
PROCEDURE Write( OutChar : CHAR );
    (' PRE: OutChar is assigned.                    ')
    (' Post: OutChar appended to previous output ')

PROCEDURE WriteCard( OutCard : CARDINAL;
                     FieldWidth : CARDINAL )
    (' PRE:  OutCard and FieldWidth are assigned.        ')
    (' POST: The value of OutCard as a string of decimal  ')
    ('       digit characters is appended to previous output ')
    ('       within a field specified by FieldWidth       ')
    ('                                                     ')
    (' FieldWidth: specifies the minimum number of         ')
    ('       characters that are output. OutCard is        ')
    ('       preceded by blanks as necessary.              ')
```

(continued)

```
      PROCEDURE WriteInt( OutInt : INTEGER;
                         FieldWidth : CARDINAL );
          (* PRE:  OutInt and FieldWidth are assigned.              *)
          (* POST: The value of OutInt as a string of decimal digit*)
          (*       characters (preceded by "-" for a negative) is  *)
          (*       appended to previous output within a field       *)
          (*       specified by FieldWidth.                         *)
          (*                                                        *)
          (* FieldWidth: specifies the minimum number of           *)
          (*       characters that are output. OutInt is           *)
          (*       preceded by blanks as necessary.                *)

      PROCEDURE WriteString( OutString : ARRAY OF CHAR );
          (* PRE:  OutString is assigned.                          *)
          (* POST: The characters from OutString are appended      *)
          (*       to previous output.                             *)
          (* NOTE: ARRAY OF CHAR is compatible with any            *)
          (*       string constant.                                *)

      PROCEDURE WriteLn;
          (* POST: The EOL character is appended to previous       *)
          (*       output.                                         *)
          (* NOTE: In some Modula-2 systems, the output of a       *)
          (*       line does not occur until WriteLn executes.     *)
```

FIGURE 8.3 *Description of Write, WriteCard, WriteInt, WriteString, and WriteLn*

Output of numeric values is performed by WriteCard and WriteInt. Both of these procedures must translate the numeric value of their first parameter into a string of characters. For WriteCard, this string consists solely of characters in the range from "0" through "9", while WriteInt must begin with "-" when the value is negative. The rules for FieldWidth, the second parameter, usage are specified below.

1) If the number of characters in the numeric string is greater than or equal to FieldWidth, then the numeric string is merely output, unaltered.

2) If the number of characters in the numeric string is less than FieldWidth, then blanks are inserted as a prefix so that a total of FieldWidth characters are output.

Examples of the output produced by various WriteInt and WriteCard instructions are shown in Figure 8.4.

Procedure Call	Corresponding Output 123456789 (* position numbers *)
WriteInt(25+3,2)	28
WriteCard(25+3,4)	28
WriteInt(25+3,0)	28
WriteInt(7−15,2+1)	−8
WriteInt(−765,0)	−765
WriteCard(0,3)	0

FIGURE 8.4 *Example invocations of WriteInt and WriteCard*

Output displays and printers work with **output lines**. Therefore, the I/O character stream is divided into "lines" by InOut. Each line is followed by a special control character. Inout makes this character available in the form of the character constant EOL. The procedure invocation

WriteLn;

is identical to

Write(EOL);

Even for input from a keyboard, ends of lines are used. From the keyboard an end of a line is signified by striking a "Carriage Return" key. This treatment of text files as lines of characters permits processing input or output as either a stream of lines or a stream of characters.

Designing-with-Wisdom

The Subtle WriteLn

In many Modula-2 systems, none of the characters on a line are output until a WriteLn is invoked. Sometimes program execution is traced by using embedded write instructions. Even though several Write, WriteString, WriteCard, and/or WriteInt instructions may have executed, the program will not display results until a WriteLn is invoked.

8.3 FILE PROCESSING USING INOUT

InOut is designed to work with a single input source and a single output destination at a time. When a program begins execution, input is assumed to come from the **standard input device** and output is assumed to go to the **standard output device**. Generally, the standard input and output devices are the user's keyboard and display; InOut defaults to interactive I/O.

In order to utilize InOut for file I/O, it is necessary to use the procedures OpenInput, OpenOutput, CloseInput and CloseOutput. Figure 8.5 describes these procedures in more detail.

```
PROCEDURE OpenInput( DefExt : ARRAY OF CHAR );
  (* Post: A user-specified file is opened for input.      *)
  (*       After a successful open, subsequent input comes *)
  (*       from this file, beginning with the first        *)
  (*       character of the file.                          *)
  (*       Done = TRUE,   if open is successful            *)
  (*            = FALSE,  if file cannot be opened          *)
```

(continued)

```
PROCEDURE OpenOutput( DefExt : ARRAY OF CHAR );
    (* Post: A user specified file is opened for output.        *)
    (*       After a successful open, a new file is created,    *)
    (*       and subsequent output goes to this file.           *)
    (*       Done = TRUE,   if open is successful               *)
    (*            = FALSE,  if file cannot be opened             *)

PROCEDURE CloseInput;
    (* Post: The input file is closed, and subsequent input     *)
    (*       comes from the standard input device.              *)

PROCEDURE CloseOutput;
    (* Post: The output file is closed, and subsequent output   *)
    (*       goes to the standard output device.                *)
```

FIGURE 8.5 *Description of OpenInput, OpenOutput, CloseInput, and CloseOutput*

Before a file can be used by any program, that file must be **opened**. Opening a file is accomplished by invoking OpenInput, for a new input file, or OpenOutput, for a new output file. When a new input file is opened, the file is always reset so that reading begins with the first character of the file. When a file is opened for output, this causes a new file to be created that is initially empty.

An invocation of either OpenInput or OpenOutput requires the name of a file. This name is supplied by the user from the standard input device. When either of the open procedures is invoked it causes the user to be prompted to supply a file name. If the specified file cannot be opened successfully, then the open procedure assigns FALSE to Done and returns without having opened any file. This might occur if the user specified the name of a non-existent file in response to an OpenInput prompt.

The DefExt parameter of the open procedures can be used to supply a default "file extension" that is useful for some operating systems. For example, suppose the following procedure invocation is executed.

OpenOutput("TXT");

If the user responds to this prompt with

MyFile

the program attempts to open a file named "MyFile.TXT" for output. Throughout this text there are no default file extensions used. To eliminate such a default a pair of consecutive double quotes is supplied as the open parameter as shown below.

OpenOutput("");

If the user responds to this invoation with

MyFile

then the program attempts to open a file named "MyFile" for output. If an operating system allows extensions on file names, then a user may override the default by specifying a file name including an extension.

It is always a good idea to **close** any open file when a program is finished with the file. CloseInput or CloseOutput must be invoked to close files from InOut. It is particularly important to close output files, since part of the file may be lost otherwise.

Figure 8.6 contains a sample WirthMessage program that creates a file. This file will store the three lines:

> Niklaus Wirth claims that Modula-2
> is a tool for thinking that is only
> coincidentally a programming language.

```
MODULE WirthMessage;
    (* This program creates a new file with a user-   *)
    (* specified name that contains a 3 line message. *)
    FROM InOut IMPORT OpenOutput, CloseOutput, Done,
                    WriteString, WriteLn;
BEGIN
    WriteString( "Please specify a name for a new file:");
    OpenOutput( "" );
    IF  NOT Done  THEN
        WriteString( "ERROR in file name!");
        WriteLn;
        HALT;
    END;

    WriteString( "Niklaus Wirth claims that Modula-2" ); WriteLn;
    WriteString( "is a tool for thinking that is only"); WriteLn;
    WriteString( "coincidentally a programming language."); WriteLn;
    CloseOutput;
END WirthMessage.
```

FIGURE 8.6 *WirthMessage program to create a message file*

When WirthMessage executes, the user is prompted with the following line.

> Please specify a name for a new file:

If the user types a valid file name, then a new file with that name will be created, and the three-line message will be stored as the contents of this file. The Done variable is used to detect any erroneous file specification and to terminate the program with an error message.

Figure 8.7 contains a second example program, called DisplayFile. This program reads all of the contents of some user-specified file and copies these contents to the standard output device. If the user executes the WirthMessage program followed by DisplayFile and types the same file name for each, then the three line message will be placed in the file and also copied to the output display.

Another program that is similar to DisplayFile demonstrates both input from and output to files. The InOutCopy program from Figure 8.8 makes an exact copy of any file into a newly created file.

```
      MODULE DisplayFile;
          (* This program copies a user-specified file onto *)
          (* the standard output device.                    *)
          FROM InOut IMPORT OpenInput, CloseInput, Done,
                           Read, Write, WriteString, WriteLn;
          VAR
             InChar : CHAR;
      BEGIN
          WriteString( "Please specify a file:");
          OpenInput( "" );
          WriteLn;
          IF  NOT Done  THEN
             WriteString( "ERROR in file name!");
             WriteLn;
             HALT;
          END;

          Read( InChar );
          WHILE  Done  DO     (* Done = MoreInput *)
             Write( InChar );
             Read( InChar );
          END;
          CloseInput;
      END DisplayFile.
```

FIGURE 8.7 *DisplayFile program to display a file*

```
MODULE InOutCopy;
      (* This program makes a copy of one file into another.     *)
      (* The user is prompted to specify source and destination *)
      (* file names.                                             *)
      FROM InOut IMPORT Read, Write, WriteLn, WriteString, Done,
                       OpenInput, OpenOutput, CloseInput, CloseOutput;

      VAR OneChar : CHAR;
          MoreInputRemains : BOOLEAN;

BEGIN
      WriteString( "Please specify name of original file:");
      OpenInput( "" );
      WriteLn;
      IF  NOT Done  THEN
          WriteString( "ERROR in file name _ program terminating.");
          WriteLn;
          HALT;
      END;
      (* ASSERT: input file appropriately opened *)

      WriteString( "Please specify name of new copy of original file:");
      OpenOutput( "" );
      IF  NOT Done  THEN
          WriteLn;
          WriteString( "ERROR in file name _ program terminating.");
          WriteLn;
          HALT;
      END;
      (* ASSERT: output file appropriate opened *)                    (continued)
```

```
    Read( OneChar );
    MoreInputRemains := Done;
    WHILE MoreInputRemains DO
        Write( OneChar );
        Read( OneChar );
        MoreInputRemains := Done
    END;
    (* ASSERT: output file is exact copy of input file *)

    CloseInput;
    CloseOutput;
END InOutCopy.
```

FIGURE 8.8 *InOutCopy program*

An execution of the InOutCopy program produces the following interactive I/O with the user. (Note that user input is highlighted.)

```
Please specify name of original file: FILE1
Please specify name of new copy of original file: FILE2
```

Having been provided the names of the files, the program will read all input, including EOL characters, from the file named FILE1 and copy each into a newly created file, called FILE2. The Done variable is used to detect when input has been exhausted.

The requirement that InOut is restricted in simultaneous access to a single input file and a single output file means that the following are all impossible.

- Two or more input files both open at the same time
- Two or more output files both open at the same time
- An input file open, together with the standard input device
- An output file open, together with the standard output device
- A file opened for both input and output at the same time

However, it is possible to input (or output) from multiple files within a single program so long as the previous file has been closed. Furthermore, invoking either the CloseInput or CloseOutput procedure closes the associated file and also reverts to the appropriate standard I/O device. In a single program, it is possible to switch input sources or output destinations many times, and even to reuse a source or destination. Figure 8.9 contains a sequence of instructions to illustrate.

An instruction sequence	*User supplied input*
`(* input coming from std input device *)` `(* output going to std output device  *)`	
`OpenOutput("");`	OUTFOO
`(* input coming from std input device *)` `(* output going to new "OUTFOO" file  *)`	

(continued)

An instruction sequence	*User supplied input*
OpenInput("");	INFOO
(* input coming from file "INFOO" *)	
(* output going to "OUTFOO" file *)	
CloseInput;	
(* input coming from std input device *)	
(* output going to "OUTFOO" file *)	
OpenInput("");	INFOOTOO
(* input coming from file "INFOOTOO" *)	
(* output going to "OUTFOO" file *)	
CloseInput;	
OpenInput("");	INFOO
(* input coming from file "INFOO" *)	
(* output going to "OUTFOO" file *)	
CloseOutput;	
OpenOutput("");	OUTFOO
(* input coming from file "INFOO" *)	
(* output going to new "OUTFOO" file *)	
CloseInput;	
CloseOutput;	
(* input coming from std input device *)	
(* output going to std output device *)	

FIGURE 8.9 *Example of consecutive file opens and closes*

Initially the program in the figure is accepting input from the standard input device and sending output to the standard output device. Next the file OUTFOO is opened for output and INFOO for input. Executing CloseInput closes INFOO; input will once again be accepted from the keyboard. Next file INFOOTOO is opened for input and closed. After that INFOO is opened for a second time. Every time a file is opened for input, reading begins from the start of the file. Therefore, the second time INFOO is opened, reading begins with the first character of the file, regardless of whether reads occurred the previous time it was open.

As the execution proceeds, the output file, OUTFOO is closed and then reopened. This second open for the same file creates a new file with the same name as a previously created file. For many operating systems, this results in the loss of the first file named OUTFOO. Other operating systems keep track of different **file versions**. Such a system automatically numbers or renames older files of the same name so that they are not lost. In an operating system, supporting file versions two versions of OUTFOO would be created by the code from Figure 8.9.

InOut performs a variety of I/O known as **sequential I/O**. This name comes from the manner in which input or output is processed — sequentially. In order to input a particular value from a file, all of the characters preceding it must first be input. There is no mechanism provided by InOut to skip forward or backward within the input, or output, instead files are viewed as one continuous stream of characters.

ANOTHER FILE MANIPULATION PROGRAM

Many text files have large numbers of blanks within them. Consider the numbers of blanks caused by indentation in Modula-2 program files. Several techniques can be employed to compress a file by removing some of the blanks. One technique is to replace any string of 3 or more consecutive blanks by some control character, say 7C, followed by a cardinal constant equalling the number of blanks and a trailing blank. This would replace a string such as:

"ƀƀƀƀƀƀHiƀMom,ƀƀƀƀƀƀƀƀƀƀƀƀSendƀƀmoney.ƀƀƀƀƀ"

with

"<7C>6ƀHiƀMom,<7C>12ƀSendƀƀmoney.<7C>5ƀ"

where "<7C>" denotes the single control character with ordinal value of 7.

Figure 8.10 contains a program that inputs one user-specified file and copies it into another using this form of blank compression.

```
MODULE CompressBlanks;
    (* This program filters a file, producing another file   *)
    (* with blanks compressed (3 or more consecutive blanks) *)
    (* are replaced by "<7C>n " where "n" is the number of   *)
    (* blanks replaced. The user is required to specify       *)
    (* both the source and destination files upon execution. *)

    FROM InOut IMPORT Read, Write, WriteLn, WriteString, WriteCard,
                Done, OpenInput, OpenOutput, CloseInput, CloseOutput;

    PROCEDURE CopyCompressed;
            (* PRE:  An input file has been successfully opened *)
            (* POST: The contents of the input file are copied  *)
            (*       to the output file with sequences of 3 or  *)
            (*       more blanks compressed.                    *)
        VAR
            OneChar : CHAR;
            BlankCount : CARDINAL;
            MoreInFile : BOOLEAN;
            CompressChar: CHAR;
```

(continued)

```
    BEGIN
        Compress Char:=7c;
        Read( OneChar );
        MoreInFile := Done;
        WHILE MoreInFile DO
            IF OneChar#" " THEN
                Write( OneChar );
                Read( OneChar );
            ELSE   (* OneChar=" " *)
                BlankCount := 0;
                WHILE Done AND (OneChar=" ") DO
                    INC( BlankCount );
                    Read( OneChar );
                END;
                IF BlankCount<3 THEN
                    IF BlankCount=1 THEN
                        Write( " " );
                    ELSE   (* BlankCount=2 *)
                        WriteString( "  " );
                    END;
                ELSE (* BlankCount>=3 *)
                    Write( CompressChar );
                    WriteCard( BlankCount,0 );
                    Write( " " );
                END;
            END;
            MoreInFile := Done;
        END;
    END CopyCompressed;

BEGIN
    WriteString( "Specify name of file to compress:");
    OpenInput( "" );
    IF  NOT Done  THEN
        WriteLn;
        WriteString( "ERROR in file name _ program terminating.");
        WriteLn;
        HALT;
    END;
    (* ASSERT: input file appropriately opened *)

    WriteLn;
    WriteString( "Specify file name for compressed version:");
    OpenOutput( "" );
    IF  NOT Done  THEN
        WriteLn;
        WriteString( "ERROR in file name _ program terminating.");
        WriteLn;
        HALT;
    END;
    (* ASSERT: output file appropriate opened *)

    CopyCompressed;

    CloseInput;
    CloseOutput;
END CompressBlanks.
```

FIGURE 8.10 *The CompressBlanks program*

The CompressBlanks program makes use of a procedure called CopyCompressed to perform the copying of one file in compressed form. CopyCompressed requires an open input file as a precondition. (If input comes from the standard input device, then Done is always TRUE and this procedure will never terminate.)

8.5 SUMMARY

File processing is an activity that consumes a large percentage of all computer time. It is neccesary to create files, to write data into them, and to read data from them. This chapter concentrates on text files: those consisting of a single stream of characters.

Modula-2 provides a collection of facilities, known as the "InOut module," for performing simple file processing. InOut incorporates procedures for reading and writing characters, strings, cardinals and integers in character form. Files may be opened and closed flexibly via InOut. InOut is restricted to sequential file access and a single input and a single output file opened simultaneously.

The InOut module also has special provisions for supporting interactive I/O. Interactive I/O allows backspacing and echoing of numeric input, and handles the Done variable differently than for files.

Most of the discussion within an introductory programming text necessarily centers around data within the program. Still, it is important for a programmer to be able to manage the vast collection of information that exists outside the program in the form of files on secondary storage devices.

||| KEY TERMS

secondary storage	binary file	standard input device
floppy diskette	interactive I/O	standard output device
hard disk	file I/O	open (a file)
magnetic tape	InOut	close (a file)
file	control character	file versions
text file	output line	sequential I/O

||| EXERCISES

1. Show the precise output that would occur following the execution of each code segment below.

    a)
```
Write( "U" );
Write( "s" );
WriteLn;
WriteString( "Them" );
WriteLn;
```

```
    b)  WriteCard( 75 DIV 3, 0 );
        WriteInt( 13-24, 0 );
        WriteLn;

    c)  WriteCard( 987,4 );
        WriteCard( 987,3 );
        WriteCard( 987,2 );
        WriteCard( 987,1 );
        WriteCard( 987,0 );
        WriteLn;

    d)  WriteInt( -13,4 );  WriteLn;
        WriteInt( -13,3 );   WriteLn;
        WriteInt( -13,2 );   WriteLn;
        WriteInt( -13,1 );  WriteLn;

    e)  Write( "?" );
        WriteString( "testing" )  WriteLn;
        WriteString( "testing" );
        WriteString( "This is only a test." );
        WriteCard( 17+3,6 );
        WriteString( "hmmmm" );
        WriteInt( 8*(-11),0 );
        WriteLn;
        WriteInt( 12,4 );
        WriteString( "ZZZZ" );
        WriteLn;
```

2. Which of the following statements are TRUE using InOut I/O?
    a) Only one file may be opened for input at a time.
    b) When any program begins to execute a file called INPUT is automatically opened for input.
    c) When a program begins to execute, immediate output goes to the standard output device.
    d) Regardless of whether or not any files are opened the name for a new file to open must always come from the standard input device.
    e) The field width specification provided as an actual parameter to a WriteCard invocation must have a value greater than or equal to the length of the required output string.
    f) It is possible for several consecutive Write instructions to have been executed to the display and yet have no output appear on the display.
    g) After CloseOutput is invoked, Write instructions output to the standard output device.
    h) If a single program opens an input file, reads some characters, closes the file, then reopens it, the second time the file is opened, input picks up at the point it left off when closed.
    i) Done is assigned TRUE after every Read from the standard input device.
    j) Done is assigned TRUE when a Read is attempted on a file that has had all input consumed.

3. Each part below contains a sequence of instructions, along with appropriate user input. Show the exact contents of all files after the code is executed. Also show all output transmitted to the standard output device.

a) An instruction sequence   User supplied input

```
OpenOutput("");                    OUT1
WriteString( "Info for one." );
WriteLn;
OpenInput("");                     IN1
CloseInput;
CloseOutput;
OpenOutput("");                    OUT2
WriteString( "Info for two." );
CloseOutput;
```

b) An instruction sequence   User supplied input

```
OpenOutput("");                    FileA
WriteString( "Ah-one" );
WriteLn;
CloseOutput;
WriteString( "Ah-two" );
WriteLn;
OpenOutpqut("");                   FileB
WriteString( "Ah-three" );
WriteLn;
CloseOutput;
WriteString( "Ah-four" );
WriteLn;
```

c) An instruction sequence   User supplied input

```
OpenOutput("");                    File1
WriteString( "Some stuff" );
WriteLn;
CloseOutput;
WriteString( "More stuff" );
WriteLn;
OpenOutput("");                    File1
WriteString( "Still more stuff" );
WriteLn;
CloseOutput;
WriteString( "Enough stuff" );
WriteLn;
```

4. Test your Modula-2 system out by answering the following questions.
   a) What is echoed when an interactive Read, ReadCard or ReadInt is invoked (be sure to test for leading and invalid characters (non-numeric))?
   b) Is Done ever FALSE when a ReadInt or ReadCard is invoked? Try typing invalid characters or a return.
   c) Does the system produce any prompt when OpenInput or OpenOutput are invoked?
   d) Under what circumstances does OpenInput set Done to FALSE? Test for invalid file names or non-existent files.
   e) What occurs when OpenOutput opens a fiie with the same name as a previously-created file?

| | | PROGRAMMING PROJECTS

1. The CompressBlanks program from Figure 8.10 translates a file into another form by compressing long sequences of blanks. Write a similar program, called ExpandBlanks, that accepts a file of the form generated by CompressBlanks and returns it into its original form.

2. Modify the CompressBlanks program from Figure 8.10 so that it reads from one file and returns the compressed version back to that same file. Notice that it may be necessary to use a second file on a temporary basis, and prompt the user to specify file names more than once.

3. Write a different type of blank compression program, similar to CompressBlanks from Figure 8.10. This program should replace all strings of five consecutive blanks with a tab character (11C). Also write the corresponding program to return files compressed in this way to their original form.

4. Write a program to solve the following problem.

    TITLE
      Capitalize words

    DESCRIPTION
      This program inputs a text file and processes it as a collection of words. The output of this program is the same text as the input, but with the first letter of every word capitalized. A word is defined to be any string of characters following a sequence of blanks. The output must be sent to the display.

    INPUT
      Interactively the user is prompted for the name of the input file of words. The input from the word file should consist only of strings of alphabetic characters (words) that are always preceded by one or more blanks.

    OUTPUT
      Output begins with the following prompt on a separate line:

          Input file name?

      After a blank line, the input file lines are displayed on the screen just as they appear in the input file, excepting that the first letter of every word is capitalized.

    ERRORS
      Attempting to read from a file that cannot be opened results in the following error message and immediate program termination:

          UNABLE TO OPEN SPECIFIED FILE

      All other errors produce undefined results.

EXAMPLE

Below are the contents of a file called LOGWORDS.

```
AND    conjunction Disjunction    axioms
NOT   all right       assertions
```

Below is a sample execution with interactive input highlighted.

```
Input file name? LOGWORDS

AND    Conjunction Disjunction    Axioms
NOT   All Right       Assertions
```

5. Write a program to solve the following problem.

TITLE

Concatenate two text files

DESCRIPTION

This program inputs two text files and creates a third file from the concatenation of the two input files.

INPUT

Interactively the user is prompted for the name of the input files. These files must be text files.

OUTPUT

Output begins with the following prompt on a separate line:

```
First input file name?
```

After a blank line the the second prompt is displayed as below:

```
Result file name?
```

There is no prompt for the second file name other than that generated by the system for an OpenInput.

After program execution, a result file (specified by the user in response to the second prompt) is created. The contents of the result file consist of the contents of the first input file followed immediately by the contents of the second input file.

ERRORS

Attempting to read from a file that cannot be opened results in the following error message and immediate program termination:

```
UNABLE TO OPEN SPECIFIED FILE
```

EXAMPLE

Below is a sample execution with interactive input highlighted.

```
First input file name? HE
Result file name? THEY
<System prompt> SHE
```

Below are the contents of the text file, HE, as input during the execution of the program.

```
Now is the time for a good man to come
to the aid of his country.
```

Below are the contents of the text file, SHE, as input during the execution of the program.

```
Now is the time for a good woman to come
to the aid of her country.
```

Below are the contents of the text file, THEY, as created and output during the execution of the program.

```
Now is the time for a good man to come
to the aid of his country.
Now is the time for a good woman to come
to the aid of her country.
```

6. Write a program to solve the following problem.

TITLE
    Single Command Line Editor

DESCRIPTION
    This program can delete a user-specified line from a file.

INPUT and OUTPUT
    Interactively the user is prompted, before starting the process, as follows:

```
Delete(D), or Quit(anything else)
```

The user should type a D to delete a line or any other character to terminate the program.
After the delete command, the user is prompted to specify a cardinal line number with the prompt below:

```
Which line?
```

Next the user is prompted for the original file and the file to copy into (less the deleted line). These prompts are as follows:

```
Source File?
```

and

```
Destination File?
```

ERRORS
    If either specified file cannot be correctly opened, then the program terminates with the following message:

```
INVALID FILE NAME
```

If a line number is specified that is greater than the number of lines in the updated file, then the program copies the file without the deletion and the following message is issued:

```
Invalid Line Number!
```

EXAMPLE

All input is highlighted in the example below. The original contents of the file, called EdFile, are as follows:

```
AAAAA aaaaa AAAAA
bbbbb BBBBB bbbbb
CCCCC ccccc CCCCC
```

Program Execution:

```
Delete(D), or Quit(anything else)  D
Which line?  2
Source File?  EdFile
Destination File?  ResFile
```

The Resulting ResFile is shown below:

```
AAAAA aaaaa AAAAA
CCCCC ccccc CCCCC
```

9 ||| MORE ABOUT SELECTION

9.1 REVIEW OF THE IF INSTRUCTION

Selection control structures make choices. When an IF instruction is executed, a choice between possible control flows is made. The simplest selection instruction is IF-THEN (See Figure 9.1). The choice made in the execution of an IF-THEN instruction is whether or not to execute the optional THEN clause.

The IF-THEN in code:

```
IF ('BooleanExpression') THEN
    (' THEN clause ')
END ,
```

The IF-THEN control flow:

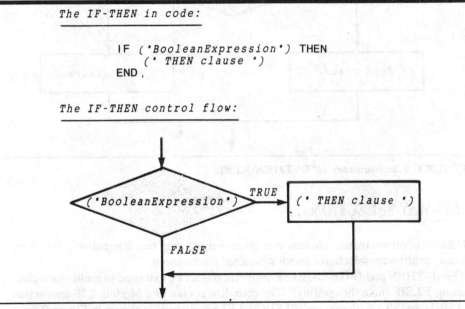

FIGURE 9.1 Summary of IF-THEN

Slightly more complex than the IF-THEN is the IF-THEN-ELSE. The IF-THEN-ELSE offers a single choice with two alternatives: the THEN clause and the ELSE clause. Figure 9.2 summarizes the IF-THEN-ELSE control structure.

Both IF-THEN and IF-THEN-ELSE are referred to as **two-way selections**, because each selects one of two control paths to execute. The IF-THEN alternatives are to execute or not to execute the THEN clause. The IF-THEN-ELSE alternatives are to execute the THEN clause or to execute the ELSE clause.

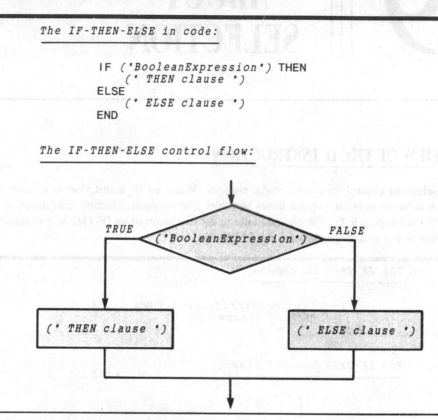

```
The IF-THEN-ELSE in code:

        IF ('BooleanExpression') THEN
                (' THEN clause ')
        ELSE
                (' ELSE clause ')
        END


The IF-THEN-ELSE control flow:
```

FIGURE 9.2 *Summary of IF-THEN-ELSE*

9.2 MULTI-WAY SELECTION

Often algorithms require choices that involve more than two alternatives. For these problems, **multi-way selection** control structures are required.

The IF-THEN and IF-THEN-ELSE instructions can be extended to multi-way selection using **ELSIF** (note the spelling). The complete syntax of a Modula-2 IF instruction with THEN and also with optional ELSIF and ELSE clauses, is shown in Figure 9.3.

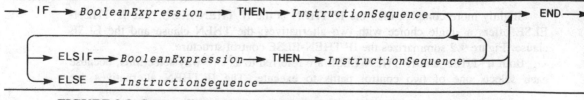

FIGURE 9.3 *Syntax diagram of the complete IF instruction*

A complete IF instruction must contain a THEN clause. It may contain zero or more ELSIF clauses, and it is optionally followed by an ELSE clause. ELSIFs should be indented as THEN and ELSE are. The control flows for an IF instruction are diagrammed in Figures 9.4 and 9.5.

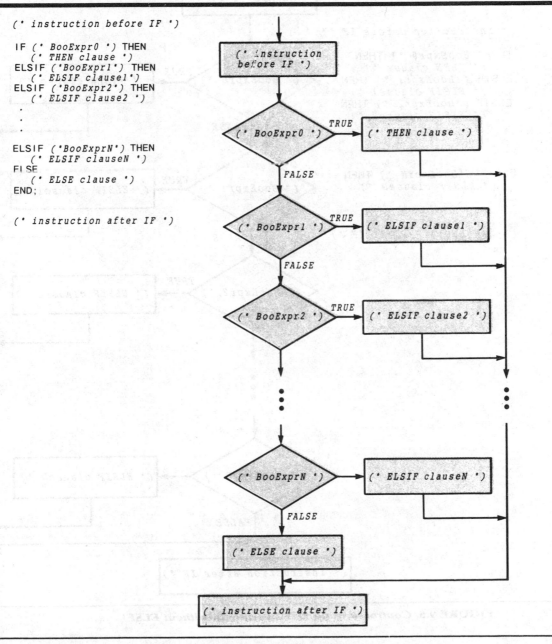

```
(* instruction before IF *)

IF (* BooExpr0 *) THEN
    (* THEN clause *)
ELSIF ('BooExpr1') THEN
    (* ELSIF clause1 *)
ELSIF ('BooExpr2') THEN
    (* ELSIF clause2 *)
    .
    .
    .

ELSIF ('BooExprN') THEN
    (* ELSIF clauseN *)
ELSE
    (* ELSE clause *)
END;


(* instruction after IF *)
```

FIGURE 9.4 *Control flow of the IF instruction (with ELSE)*

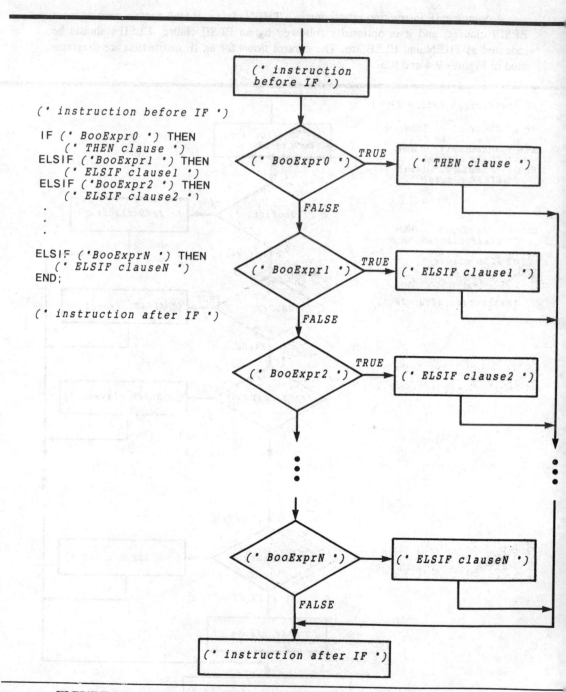

```
(' instruction before IF ')

IF (' BooExpr0 ') THEN
     (' THEN clause ')
ELSIF ('BooExpr1 ') THEN
     (' ELSIF clause1 ')
ELSIF ('BooExpr2 ') THEN
     (' ELSIF clause2 ')
  .
  .
  .
ELSIF ('BooExprN ') THEN
     (' ELSIF clauseN ')
END;

(' instruction after IF ')
```

FIGURE 9.5 *Control flow of the IF instruction (without ELSE)*

Both ELSIF and THEN clauses are preceded by boolean expressions that are used in the selection. These boolean expressions are often referred to as **guards**. The name "guard" is used because the condition "guards" the clause, allowing its execution only when the condition is TRUE. The complete semantics of an IF instruction can be described as follows.

1) If the guard for the THEN clause is TRUE, then the THEN clause is selected.
2) If the guard for an ELSIF clause is TRUE, and all preceding guards of the same IF are FALSE, then the ELSIF is selected.
3) If all guards of an IF are FALSE, then the ELSE, if present, is selected.
4) If all guards of an IF are FALSE and there is no ELSE, then no clauses are selected.

Figure 9.6 defines an example function where multi-way selection is useful.

TITLE

Function to calculate used-car salesman's commission

DESCRIPTION

This is a function that returns the used-car salesman's commission on car sales for the week. A single cardinal value parameter specifies the total dollar sales used to calculate commission. The function returns the cardinal dollar commission truncated to the nearest dollar. Commission is calculated according to the following formula:

Total Sales	Commission %
Up to $5000	1.0%
$5001 to $10000	1.8%
$10001 to $20000	2.5%
Over $20000	3.0%

INPUT

There is no input, but a single parameter serves to specify the total dollars sales.

OUTPUT

There is no output, but the value returned by the function is the truncated commission in dollars.

ERRORS

If the total dollar sales is unassigned then undefined results occur.

EXAMPLES

```
UsedCarCommission( 1000 ) returns 10
UsedCarCommission( 10000 ) returns 180
UsedCarCommission( 20001 ) returns 600
```

FIGURE 9.6 *UsedCarCommission function definition*

The `UsedCarCommission` function problem refines into a four-way selection, where each of the four alternatives in the selection yields a different commission percentage. The guards for `UsedCarCommission` are determined by the amount of total sales. The solution for this problem is completed in Figure 9.7.

```
PROCEDURE UsedCarCommission( TotSales : CARDINAL )
: CARDINAL;
    (* PRE:  TotSales is assigned                             *)
    (* POST: RESULT = TotSales*.01,  if TotSales<=5000         *)
    (*              = TotSales*.018, if 5000<TotSales<=10000   *)
    (*              = TotSales*.025, if 10000<TotSales<=20000  *)
    (*              = TotSales*.03,  if 20000<TotSales         *)
BEGIN
    IF  TotSales<=5000  THEN
        RETURN TRUNC( FLOAT(TotSales) * 0.01 );
    ELSIF  TotSales<=10000  THEN
        RETURN TRUNC( FLOAT(TotSales) * 0.018 );
    ELSIF  TotSales<=20000  THEN
        RETURN TRUNC( FLOAT(TotSales) * 0.025 );
    ELSE  (*TotSales>20000*)
        RETURN TRUNC( FLOAT(TotSales) * 0.03 );
    END;
END UsedCarCommission;
```

FIGURE 9.7 *UsedCarCommission function*

Because of the order of guard evaluation, there is no need to check the lower bound on `TotSales` in any of the ELSIF conditions from `UsedCarCommission`. For example, the first ELSIF guard is not

$$(5001<=TotSales) \ \& \ (TotSales<=10000)$$

but rather

$$TotSales<=10000$$

This simpler guard is equivalent to the compound one in the sense that the ELSIF guard is never tested when `TotSales<=5000`, because the guard on the preceding THEN clause performs the task. Another example use of ELSIF clauses is shown in Figure 9.8.

```
WriteString( "Do you like ELSIFs (Y or N)?" ); WriteLn;
Read( Answer );
IF  CAP(Answer)="Y"  THEN
    WriteString( 'You answered "yes".' ); WriteLn;
    WriteString( "Your friendly computer agrees!"); WriteLn;
ELSIF  CAP(Answer)="N"  THEN
    WriteString('You answered "no".' ); WriteLn;
    WriteString( "Perhaps you should consider the alternative." ); WriteLn;
ELSE
    WriteString('I interpret your response as a "maybe".'); WriteLn;
END;
WriteString( "Now for your next question..." );
```

FIGURE 9.8 *Code segment using ELSIF*

In this last example, a character is input into Answer. This character is to be interpreted as a "yes," a "no," or a "maybe" response to some question. An upper case or lower case "Y" represents "yes"; an upper case or lower case "N" means "no"; and any other character is interpreted as "maybe".

9.3 THE RELATIONSHIP OF ELSIF, NESTED IFS, AND OPTIONAL ELSES

Any program may be written without the ELSIF option, even when multi-way selection is required. However, it is often clumsy to express complex selections using only IF-THENs or IF-THEN-ELSEs. The previous UsedCarCommission function is rewritten in Figure 9.9 without any ELSIF clauses.

```
PROCEDURE UsedCarCommission( TotSales : CARDINAL )
: CARDINAL;
    (* PRE:   TotSales is assigned                          *)
    (* POST: RESULT = TotSales*.01,  if TotSales<=5000       *)
    (*               = TotSales*.018, if 5000<TotSales<=10000 *)
    (*               = TotSales*.025, if 10000<TotSales<=20000 *)
    (*               = TotSales*.03,  if 20000<TotSales       *)
BEGIN
    IF  TotSales<=5000  THEN
        RETURN TRUNC( FLOAT(TotSales) * 0.01 );
    ELSE
        IF  TotSales<=10000  THEN
            RETURN TRUNC( FLOAT(TotSales) * 0.018 );
        ELSE
            IF  TotSales<=20000  THEN
                RETURN TRUNC( FLOAT(TotSales) * 0.025 );
            ELSE  (*TotSales>20000*)
                RETURN TRUNC( FLOAT(TotSales) * 0.03 );
            END;
        END;
    END;
END UsedCarCommission;
```

FIGURE 9.9 *UsedCarCommission function using nested IF-THEN-ELSEs: an inferior solution*

This new UsedCarCommission solution uses IF-THEN-ELSE instructions within other ELSE clauses, in place of ELSIFs. This placement of one control structure (an IF-THEN-ELSE) within the body (ELSE clause) of another is called **nested** control structures.

The nested version from Figure 9.9 demonstrates the sequence of execution for the ELSIF. However, the ELSIF version shows better programming style, because it more clearly captures a four-way selection.

It is also possible to express `UsedCarCommission` using only one-armed IFs. Such a solution appears in Figure 9.10.

```
PROCEDURE UsedCarCommission( TotSales : CARDINAL )
: CARDINAL;
    (* PRE:   TotSales is assigned                             *)
    (* POST: RESULT = TotSales*.01,   if TotSales<=5000         *)
    (*               = TotSales*.018, if 5000<TotSales<=10000   *)
    (*               = TotSales*.025, if 10000<TotSales<=20000  *)
    (*               = TotSales*.03,  if 20000<TotSales         *)
BEGIN
    IF  TotSales<=5000  THEN
        RETURN TRUNC( FLOAT(TotSales) * 0.01 );
    END;
    IF  (TotSales>=5001) & (TotSales<=10000)  THEN
        RETURN TRUNC( FLOAT(TotSales) * 0.018 );
    END;
    IF  (TotSales>=10001) & (TotSales<=20000)  THEN
        RETURN TRUNC( FLOAT(TotSales) * 0.025 );
    END;
    IF  TotSales>20000  THEN
        RETURN TRUNC( FLOAT(TotSales) * 0.03 );
    END;
END UsedCarCommission;
```

FIGURE 9.10 *UsedCarCommission function using only IF-THENs: an inferior solution*

This `UsedCarCommission` function in Figure 9.10 is correct, because the guards for the four THEN clauses are written in such a way that exactly one can be TRUE at any instant in time. However, this version is the worst of the three, because readability is impaired by the additional ENDs and by the compound Boolean expressions. In addition, the correctness of this solution depends upon the fact that exactly one guard must be TRUE.

The Figure 9.10 version of `UsedCarCommission` is also less efficient than the preceding two solutions. They did not require compound conditions as did the third. Furthermore, the earlier versions evaluated guards only until one was found to be TRUE. The solution in Figure 9.10 will evaluate all four guards under any circumstances.

There is one additional important, and very subtle, deficiency caused by implementing a multi-way selection with only one-armed IFs. This deficiency lies in the interdependence of all the consecutive IF-THENs. Suppose a maintenance programmer found it necessary to alter `TotSales` within `UsedCarCommission`. This alteration might cause the function to execute multiple clauses of the IF erroneously. The control structures of the first two versions of `UsedCarCommission` ensure that exactly one alternative is selected.

*P*rogramming-with-*S*tyle—

The Choice of ELSIF, Nested IF-THEN-ELSE, or IF-THEN

When implementing a multi-way selection with more than two alternatives, it is always possible to use a two-way selection control structure. However, doing so is usually unwise.

If the code naturally requires a *n-way selection*, then a more readable solution is produced from an n-way branch. A good general solution to multi-way selection is the use of the ELSIF clause. Under no circumstances should IF-THEN instructions be used to express a control that is naturally a selection with more than two alternatives. Such a solution is harder to read, and to debug, and it is usually inefficient.

Sometimes nested IF structures produce good code, even when a selection with more alternatives is possible. Figure 9.11 contains a problem definition for a Weekly-Wage procedure for calculating the wage of one of the six employees of a computer store.

TITLE
WeeklyWage procedure

DESCRIPTION
The WeeklyWage procedure calculates the wage for a single computer store employee. A computer store has six employees (two managers, three clerks, and a go-fer). In order to keep information confidential, the information given to this routine is controlled by three parameters. The first parameter indicates the job classification of the employee ("M" for manager, "C" for clerk, and "G" for go-fer). The second parameter is an employee number within each job class (i.e. the two managers are numbered 1 and 2, the clerks are numbered 1, 2, and 3). The third parameter is used to pass the number of hours worked to the procedure for hourly employees. Pay, a cardinal, is returned via the fourth parameter to the routine in terms of the gross dollar salary for the week. Pay is calculated according to the following:

> Manager #1 .....Straight salary of $900
>
> Manager #2 .....Straight salary of $825
> Clerk #1 ....$6 per hour (no increase for overtime)
> Clerk #2 ....$5 per hour (no increase for overtime)
> Clerk #3 ....$5 per hour (no increase for overtime)
> Go-fer #1 ....Straight salary of $80

INPUT
None from InOut.

(continued)

Parameter info passed to the procedure:

Parm #	Type	Semantics
1	CHAR	Job classification ("M" for manager, "C" for clerk, "G" for go-fer)
2	CARDINAL	Employee identification number within the job class
3	CARDINAL	Number of hours worked (meaningful only for employees paid by the hour)

OUTPUT

Depending on the particular job class input, one of the following three messages is displayed:

For manager: `Paycheck for manager #i`
For clerk: `Paycheck for clerk #i`
For go-fer: `Paycheck for general assistant`

Note: i denotes the employee number in the above output. The procedure returns the weekly wage, in dollars, of the employee in its fourth parameter (CARDINAL type).

ERRORS

If the initial values of the first two parameters are not as described, then the following message is displayed, and the program halts:

`INVALID CALL OF WeeklyWage`

EXAMPLE

Invocation	Output	Value of Wage as returned
`WeeklyWage("M",1,0,Wage)`	`Paycheck for manager #1`	900
`WeeklyWage("C",2,20,Wage)`	`Paycheck for clerk #2`	100
`WeeklyWage("Z",3,0,Wage)`	`INVALID CALL OF WeeklyWage`	–

FIGURE 9.11 *Definition of the WeeklyWage procedure*

The main design issue of the `WeeklyWage` procedure is how to subdivide the alternatives to form the appropriate selection structure. The three most reasonable top level selections are:

1) A seven-way selection, one for each employee and one for errors (see Figure 9.12).
2) A two-way selection, one for hourly-waged employees and another one for straight salaried employees (see Figure 9.13).
3) A three-way selection based on job classification (see Figure 9.14).

```
PROCEDURE WeeklyWage(      EmpClass : CHAR;
                           EmpNum : CARDINAL;
                           HoursWorked : CARDINAL;
                    VAR Wage : CARDINAL        );
  (* PRE:  Assigned(EmpClass) AND Assigned(EmpNum)           *)
  (*       AND                                               *)
  (*       (EmpClass="C"  ->  Assigned(HoursWorked)          *)
  (* POST: InValidParameters -> error message and HALT       *)
  (*       AND                                               *)
  (*       ValidParameters -> employee job class and number  *)
  (*                          displayed AND Wage=appropriate  *)
  (*                          weekly wage                     *)
BEGIN
  IF  (EmpClass="M") & (EmpNum=1)  THEN
      WriteString( "Paycheck for manager #1" );
      WriteLn;
      Wage := 900;
  ELSIF  (EmpClass="M") & (EmpNum=2)  THEN
      WritoString( "Paycheck for manager #2" );
      WriteLn;
      Wage := 825;
  ELSIF  (EmpClass="C") & (EmpNum=1)  THEN
      WriteString( "Paycheck for clerk #1" );
      WriteLn;
      Wage := HoursWorked * 6;
  ELSIF  (EmpClass="C") & (EmpNum=2)  THEN
      WriteString( "Paycheck for clerk #2" );
      WriteLn;
      Wage := HoursWorked * 5;
  ELSIF  (EmpClass="C") & (EmpNum=3)  THEN
      WriteString( "Paycheck for clerk #3" );
      WriteLn;
      Wage := HoursWorked * 5;
  ELSIF  EmpClass="G"  THEN
      WriteString( "Paycheck for general assistant" );
      WriteLn;
      Wage := 80;
  ELSE  (* invalid parameters *)
      WriteString( "INVALID CALL OF WeeklyWage" );
      HALT;
  END;
END WeeklyWage;
```

FIGURE 9.12 *WeeklyWage procedure split by employee (too verbose)*

The solution in Figure 9.12 is a based on a seven-way selection for the six employees plus the error case. The resulting code from such an approach is lengthy and repetitive. This repetition is most evident for Clerks 2 and 3, where the ELSIF clauses are identical except for the clerk number.

This kind of repetitive code is not only inelegant, but also inefficient. Whenever EmpClass is invalid, all six guards, most of them compound Boolean expressions, must be evaluated.

The option of combining employees according to their type of salary, shown in Figure 9.13, removes the repetition from the clerk cases. However, the code for managers is nested four levels. *It is always good to avoid nesting when possible.* This second alternative is less readable than the first, because the IF nesting complicates the structure.

```
PROCEDURE WeeklyWage(      EmpClass : CHAR;
                          EmpNum : CARDINAL;
                          HoursWorked : CARDINAL;
                 VAR Wage : CARDINAL        );
   (* PRE:  Assigned(EmpClass)  AND  Assigned(EmpNum)       *)
   (*       AND                                             *)
   (*       (EmpClass="C"  ->  Assigned(HoursWorked)        *)
   (* POST: InValidParameters -> error message and HALT     *)
   (*       AND                                             *)
   (*       ValidParameters -> employee job class and number *)
   (*                          displayed AND Wage=appropriate *)
   (*                          weekly wage                  *)
BEGIN
   IF  ((EmpClass#"M") & (EmpClass#"C") & (EmpClass#"G"))
       OR  ((EmpClass="M") & (EmpNum#1) & (EmpNum#2))
       OR  ((EmpClass="C") & ((EmpNum=0) OR (EmpNum>3)))  THEN
      WriteString( "INVALID CALL OF WeeklyWage" );
      HALT
   ELSE  (* valid parameters *)
      IF  EmpClass="C"  THEN
         WriteString( "Paycheck for clerk #" );
         WriteCard( EmpNum, 0 );
         WriteLn;
         IF  Empum=1 THEN
            Wage := HoursWorked * 6;
         ELSE
            Wage := HoursWorked * 5;
         END;
      ELSE  (* EmpClass="M" or EmpClass="G" *)
         IF  EmpClass="M"  THEN
            WriteString( "Paycheck for manager#" );
            WriteCard( EmpNum, 0 );
            WriteLn;
            IF  EmpNum=1  THEN
               Wage := 900;
            ELSE
               Wage := 825;
            END
         ELSE  (* EmpClass="G" *)
            WriteString( "Paycheck for general assistant" );
            WriteLn;
            Wage := 80;
         END;
      END;
   END;
END WeeklyWage;
```

FIGURE 9.13 *WeeklyWage procedure split by wage type (messy and difficult to read)*

```
PROCEDURE WeeklyWage(      EmpClass : CHAR;
                           EmpNum : CARDINAL;
                           HoursWorked : CARDINAL;
                  VAR Wage : CARDINAL          );
  (* PRE:  Assigned(EmpClass)   AND  Assigned(EmpNum)         *)
  (*       AND                                                *)
  (*       (EmpClass="C"  ->  Assigned(HoursWorked)           *)
  (* POST: InValidParameters -> error message and HALT        *)
  (*       AND                                                *)
  (*       ValidParameters -> employee job class and number   *)
  (*                          displayed AND Wage=appropriate  *)
  (*                          weekly wage                     *)
BEGIN
   IF  EmpClass="C"  THEN
    IF  EmpNum=1 THEN
       Wage  := HoursWorked * 6;
    ELSIF  (EmpNum=2) OR (EmpNum=3)  THEN
       Wage  := HoursWorked * 5;
    ELSE  (* erroneous EmpNum *)
       WriteString( "INVALID CALL OF WeeklyWage" );
       HALT;
    END;
    WriteString( "Paycheck for clerk #" );
    WriteCard( EmpNum, 0 );
    WriteLn;
   ELSIF  EmpClass="M"  THEN
    IF  EmpNum=1  THEN
       Wage  := 900;
    ELSIF  EmpNum=2  THEN
       Wage  := 825;
    ELSE  (* erroneous EmpNum *)
       WriteString( "INVALID CALL OF WeeklyWage" );
       HALT;
    END;
    WriteString( "Paycheck for manager#" );
    WriteCard( EmpNum, 0 );
    WriteLn;
   ELSIF  EmpClass="G"  THEN
    WriteString( "Paycheck for general assistant" );
    WriteLn;
    Wage  := 80;
   ELSE  (* erroneous EmpClass *)
    WriteString( "INVALID CALL OF WeeklyWage" );
    HALT;
   END;
END WeeklyWage;
```

FIGURE 9.14 *WeeklyWage procedure split by job classification*

The third WeeklyWage option, selecting according to job classification, is far more readable than the second. Even though both of the last two solutions have an identical number of lines of code, the last has at most two levels of nested IFs. The elimination of so many compound Boolean expressions also makes it more readable and more efficient than the first option.

The solution in Figure 9.14 distributes the error-handling into three locations, for invalid clerk number, invalid manager number and invalid employee classification. This provides a readable means for indicating where errors occur. This solution also allows for easy modification of printing different error messages in each situation. This too is better than the earlier two versions.

Programming-with-Styl

Refining a Selection

The key issues to remember about refining selection control structures are these:

1) Consider the maximum number of individual alternatives possible (such as Option 1 of Week l yWage). For some problems this is the best solution. Even when this isn't the best form of refinement, this mode of thought often leads to better options.
2) Consider the logical (humanly natural) means for grouping the alternatives (Options 2 and 3 of Week l yWage are natural groupings).
3) Try to keep the nesting levels low. Deep nesting makes for difficult reading.
4) Try to keep the guards as simple as possible. Complicated guards are difficult to read.
5) Try not to reevaluate guards or portions of guards, since reevaluation is inefficient, and it often suggests that unnatural grouping has occurred.

9.4 THE CASE INSTRUCTION

Sometimes a single expression can be used to separate all of the cases in a multi-way selection. In these instances the **CASE** control structure may be useful. The syntax diagram of the Modula-2 CASE is shown in Figure 9.15.

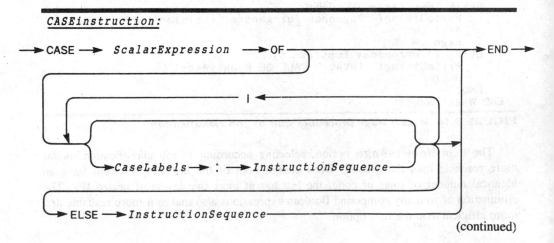

CASEinstruction:

(continued)

CaseLabels:

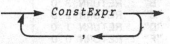

Notes:

- *"ScalarExpression" is an expression of any scalar type, including CARDINAL, INTEGER, CHAR, and BOOLEAN.*
- *"ConstExpr" is some expression of the same type as ScalarExpression and where all operands are constants.*
- *Each "ConstExpr" must represent a constant that is different from all other ConstExpr values in the same CASE.*

FIGURE 9.15 *Syntax diagram for CASEinstruction*

A CASE instruction is executed by first evaluating the ScalarExpression, sometimes called the **case expression**. The "ConstExprs" within the case, referred to as **case labels**, are searched. When a CASE instruction executes, one of the following events occurs next.

1) If a case label equal to the value of *ScalarExpression* is present, then the corresponding **case clause** (the code immediately after the label list) is executed.
2) If no case label is equal to *ScalarExpression*, the ELSE clause, if present, is executed.
3) If no case label is equal to *ScalarExpression*, and no ELSE clause is included, then the behavior of the CASE is undefined (an unpleasant alternative).

An example of a CASE instruction is found in the GradePoint function from Figure 9.16. GradePoint has a single parameter, representing a letter grade (either "A", "B", "C", "D", or "F"). The function returns the associated grade point value, using the standard four-point scale given below:

Letter Grade	Grade Point Equiv.
A	4.0
B	3.0
C	2.0
D	1.0
F	0.0

```
PROCEDURE GradePoint( LetterGrade : CHAR )
: REAL;
   (* PRE:  LetterGrade is either "A", "B", "C", "D", or "F"   *)
   (* POST: RESULT = 4.0,  if LetterGrade="A"                  *)
   (*              = 3.0,  if LetterGrade="B"                  *)
   (*              = 2.0,  if LetterGrade="C"                  *)
   (*              = 1.0,  if LetterGrade="D"                  *)
   (*              = 0.0,  if LetterGrade="F"                  *)
```

(continued)

```
            BEGIN
              CASE LetterGrade OF
                "A" : RETURN 4.0  |
                "B" : RETURN 3.0  |
                "C" : RETURN 2.0  |
                "D" : RETURN 1.0  |
                "F" : RETURN 0.0
              END
            END GradePoint;
```

FIGURE 9.16 *GradePoint function*

Figure 9.17 contains a slightly more complicated use of the CASE. The Classi-fyChar procedure can be used to classify the characters of a simple numeric expression. There are three possible classifications for characters.

1) The characters " + ", "–", "*", and "/" are *operators*.
2) The decimal digits are *digits*.
3) Anything else is *other*.

A Boolean parameter is used to identify each of the classifications.

```
PROCEDURE ClassifyChar(    C : CHAR;
                      VAR IsOperator : BOOLEAN;
                      VAR IsDigit : BOOLEAN;
                      VAR IsOther : BOOLEAN  );
  (* PRE:  C is Assigned                                        *)
  (* POST: IsOperator = TRUE,  if C is any of "+", "–",         *)
  (*                               "*", or "/"                  *)
  (*                  = FALSE,  otherwise                       *)
  (*          IsDigit = TRUE,   if "0"<=C<="9"                  *)
  (*                  = FALSE,  otherwise                       *)
  (*          IsOther = TRUE,   if NOT (IsOperator OR IsDigit)  *)
  (*                  = FALSE,  otherwise                       *)
BEGIN
  IsOperator := FALSE;
  IsDigit := FALSE;
  IsOther := FALSE;

  (* ASSERT: (NOT IsOperator) & (NOT IsDigit) & (NOT IsOther) *)
  CASE C OF
    "+", "–", "*", "/" :
        IsOperator := TRUE  |
    "0","1","2","3","4","5","6","7","8","9" :
        IsDigit := TRUE
    ELSE
        IsOther := TRUE
  END
END ClassifyChar;
```

FIGURE 9.17 *ClassifyChar procedure*

*P*rogramming-with-*S*tyle

Indenting the CASE Instruction

There is no one best technique for indenting CASE instructions. Different indentation styles are useful in different situations. A few guidelines are proposed below.

1) Always begin the CASE and its END in the same column.
2) Always indent the label lists preceding each case alternative.
3) ELSE may be begun in the same column as CASE or the label lists; this is a matter of personal taste.
4) If label lists are short, then instructions may follow on the same line.
5) If some of the label lists are long, then it may be preferable to begin the case clause indented on the line after the label list.
6) A " |" must follow each case clause, except that " |" is optional after the last case clause.

9.5 THE CHOICE BETWEEN IF AND CASE

The CASE instruction is preferred over an IF with ELSIFs for multi-way selection. This preference follows the global style rule of favoring the most restrictive alternative. CASE instructions are more restrictive than IFs, because the guard expression in an IF is a Boolean expression, while labels on CASE alternatives are limited to constant expressions of scalar type. Often the form of the CASE is also more readable.

For example, consider a `TransDialLetter` procedure, designed to translate an uppercase alphabetic letter into the numeric digit that corresponds to the letter on a push button telephone dial. Figure 9.18 contains a picture of a push button telephone face that indicates the correspondence. The push buttons "1," "*," "0," and "#" do not have any alphabetic letters on them. Also the alphabetic letters "Q" and "Z" do not correspond to any of the push buttons.

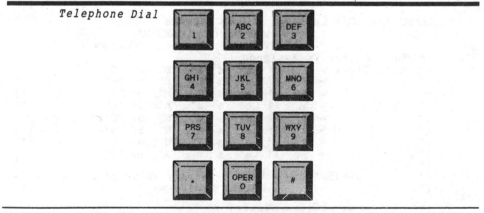

Telephone Dial

FIGURE 9.18 *Telephone Dial used by TransDialLetter*

Figure 9.19 contains two options for implementing `TransDialLetter`. The first option uses a CASE instruction, while the second uses a multi-way IF. The CASE option is the more readable and, therefore, the better choice.

```
PROCEDURE TransDialLetter(     Let : CHAR;
                            VAR Digit : CARDINAL;
                            VAR ValidButton : BOOLEAN );
    (* PRE:  Letter is Assigned                           *)
    (* POST: Digit = 2,   if Let is "A", "B", or "C"      *)
    (*             = 3,   if Let is "D", "E", or "F"      *)
    (*             = 4,   if Let is "G", "H", or "I"      *)
    (*             = 5,   if Let is "J", "K", or "L"      *)
    (*             = 6,   if Let is "M", "N", or "O"      *)
    (*             = 7,   if Let is "P", "R", or "S"      *)
    (*             = 8,   if Let is "T", "U", or "V"      *)
    (*             = 9,   if Let is "W", "X", or "Y"      *)
    (*                                                    *)
    (*      ValidButton = TRUE,  for any value of Let above *)
    (*                  = FALSE, otherwise                *)

    (*----------------------------*)
    (*  Option #1 -- Using CASE  *)
    (*----------------------------*)
BEGIN
    ValidButton := TRUE;
    CASE  Let  OF
      "A", "B", "C" :  Digit := 2 |
      "D", "E", "F" :  Digit := 3 |
      "G", "H", "I" :  Digit := 4 |
      "J", "K", "L" :  Digit := 5 |
      "M", "N", "O" :  Digit := 6 |
      "P", "R", "S" :  Digit := 7 |
      "T", "U", "V" :  Digit := 8 |
      "W", "X", "Y" :  Digit := 9
    ELSE
      ValidButton := FALSE
    END
END TransDialLetter;


PROCEDURE TransDialLetter(     Let : CHAR;
                            VAR Digit : CARDINAL;
                            VAR ValidButton : BOOLEAN );
    (* PRE:  Letter is Assigned                           *)
    (* POST: Digit = 2,   if Let is "A", "B", or "C"      *)
    (*             = 3,   if Let is "D", "E", or "F"      *)
    (*             = 4,   if Let is "G", "H", or "I"      *)
    (*             = 5,   if Let is "J", "K", or "L"      *)
    (*             = 6,   if Let is "M", "N", or "O"      *)
    (*             = 7,   if Let is "P", "R", or "S"      *)
    (*             = 8,   if Let is "T", "U", or "V"      *)
    (*             = 9,   if Let is "W", "X", or "Y"      *)
    (*                                                    *)
    (*      ValidButton = TRUE,  for any value of Let above *)
    (*                  = FALSE, otherwise                *)

    (*----------------------------*)
    (*  Option #2 -- Using IF    *)
    (*----------------------------*)
```

(continued)

```
BEGIN
    ValidButton : = TRUE;
    IF  (Let>="A") AND (Let<="C")  THEN
        Digit : = 2;
    ELSIF (Let>="D") AND (Let<="F") THEN
        Digit : = 3;
    ELSIF (Let>="G") AND (Let<="I") THEN
        Digit : = 4;
    ELSIF (Let>="J") AND (Let<="L") THEN
        Digit : = 5;
    ELSIF (Let>="M") AND (Let<="O") THEN
        Digit : = 6;
    ELSIF (Let="P") OR (Let="R") OR (Let="S") THEN
        Digit : = 7;
    ELSIF (Let>="T") AND (Let<="V") THEN
        Digit : = 8;
    ELSIF (Let>="W") AND (Let<="Y") THEN
        Digit : = 9;
    ELSE
        ValidButton : = FALSE;
    END;
END TransDialLetter;
```

FIGURE 9.19 *Two options for TransDialLetter procedure*

There are times when the CASE instruction is impractical. Figure 9.20 contains a function to identify alphabetic characters (both lower case and upper case) from all other characters. The first option (using a CASE instruction) is cluttered with case labels. The second option (using an IF) abbreviates the selection guards by making using of the fact that the alphabetic characters are consecutive.

```
PROCEDURE  IsAlpha( C : CHAR )
  : BOOLEAN;
    (* PRE:  C is Assigned                                      *)
    (* POST: RESULT = TRUE,    if "a"<=C<="z" OR "A"<=C<="Z"    *)
    (*                = FALSE,  otherwise                        *)

    (*---------------------------------*)
    (*  Option #1 -- using CASE  *)
    (*---------------------------------*)
BEGIN
    CASE  C  OF
       "a", "b", "c", "d", "e", "f", "g", "h", "i",
       "j", "k", "l", "m", "n", "o", "p", "q", "r",
       "s", "t", "u", "v", "w", "x", "y", "z",
       "A", "B", "C", "D", "E", "F", "G", "H", "I",
       "J", "K", "L", "M", "N", "O", "P", "Q", "R",
       "S", "T", "U", "V", "W", "X", "Y", "Z":
            RETURN TRUE
    ELSE
            RETURN FALSE
    END
END IsAlpha;
```

(continued)

```
PROCEDURE    IsAlpha( C : CHAR )
: BOOLEAN;
    (* PRE:   C is Assigned                                    *)
    (* POST: RESULT = TRUE,    if "a"<=C<="z" OR "A"<=C<="Z" *)
    (*                = FALSE,  otherwise                       *)

    (*-------------------------*)
    (*   Option #2 -- using IF  *)
    (*-------------------------*)
BEGIN
    IF   (("a"<=C) & (C<="z")) OR (("A"<=C) & (C<="Z"))   THEN
        RETURN TRUE;
    ELSE
        RETURN FALSE;
    END;
END IsAlpha;
```

FIGURE 9.20 *Two options for IsAlpha procedure*

The CASE instruction is impractical for IsAlpha because of the long label lists. Sometimes the CASE cannot be used at all. This occurs whenever the number of possible case labels becomes infinite. The WaterCondition procedure from Figure 9.21 is one such example. This procedure selects an option based on the value of a REAL parameter which makes a CASE implementation impossible.

```
PROCEDURE WaterCondition( Temperature : REAL );
    (* PRE:   Temperature is Assigned                     *)
    (* POST: An appropriate message is output.  This     *)
    (*        message one of the following:               *)
    (*        "Water is frozen,"  if Temperature<32       *)
    (*        "Water is liquid,", if 32<=Temperature<212  *)
    (*        "Water is boiling," otherwise               *)
BEGIN
    IF  Temperature<32.0  THEN
        WriteString( "Water is frozen" );
    ELSIF  Temperature<=212.0  THEN
        WriteString( "Water is liquid" );
    ELSE  (* Temperature>212.0 *)
        WriteString( "Water is boiling" );
    END;
END WaterCondition;
```

FIGURE 9.21 *WaterCondition procedure*

9.6 DEBUGGING SELECTION

If a program is correct, then it must work properly for all possibilities. Selection control structures provide alternative paths for control flow. The correctness of selection requires an exhaustive examination of all possible paths. One established method of testing is to execute a program with various test data until every different clause of every control structure has been executed at least once. This technique ensures that every instruction has been executed, but does not consider all possible combinations of alternative clauses. Still, this is a far better testing strategy than trying only one or two randomly chosen sets of test data.

One important feature of the selection control structures contained in Modula-2 is their **single entry/single exit** nature. An IF instruction always begins execution with the evaluation of the guard preceding the THEN clause. This guard evaluation represents the single entry point. An IF terminates execution (unless RETURNs or HALTs are executed) at a single exit point. This exit point corresponds to the END. The instruction executed after an IF is the same regardless of which IF alternative is executed. Likewise, the CASE instruction has a single entry point in the evaluation of the case expression and a single exit point, symbolized by the END.

This single entry/single exit selection property permits debugging by identifying assertions that immediately precede and follow a selection structure. The assertion before the selection becomes a precondition for the structure and the assertion after is a postcondition. For debugging, all of the alternatives through the control structure should be examined to guarantee the correctness of the structure with respect to these preconditions and postconditions. For example, the IF instruction below has been bracketed by its precondition and postcondition.

```
(* ASSERT: A & B are Assigned) *)
IF A>B THEN
    Max := A;
ELSE
    Max := B;
END;
(* ASSERT: Max>=A & Max>=B *)
```

In order to ensure the correctness of this code, all possible control paths beginning at the first assertion and ending at the final must be considered. The two cases are:

> _CASE 1:_ $A > B$ If $A > B$ is TRUE, the THEN clause is executed, causing Max = A. In this case, the postcondition is correct because $A > B$ and Max = A.

> _CASE 2:_ NOT $A > B$ If the guard expression is FALSE, then $A < = B$ and the ELSE clause is executed. The ELSE clause guarantees the postcondition by setting Max = B when $A < = B$.

In similar fashion, all of the alternatives of a selection must be considered as individual cases. Overlooked possibilities are a frequent source of program bugs.

.7 SUMMARY

The number of alternative selection control structures in modern high level languages is modest. In Modula-2 there are only two selection control structures, IF and CASE. These two control structures have the flexibility to provide a wide range of readable applications.

It is not always easy to choose the "best" form of selection for a particular algorithm. Sometimes an IF is preferable to a CASE, and at other times the opposite is true. Sometimes there is a choice of how many different alternatives to represent at some level in refinement. It is better to use multi-way selection rather than two-way in some instances. Other times, grouping alternatives together reduces repetitive and inefficient code. Examining the complexity of guard expressions is another factor in this decision, as are nesting level considerations.

The wide choice in selection application and use causes variety in programs. In many instances, the quality of a particular piece of code can be traced to the quality of the selection structures.

||| KEY TERMS

selection	CASE instruction
two-way selection	case expression
multi-way selection	case label
ELSIF	single entry/single exit structure
guard	case clause
nested control structures	

||| EXERCISES

1. Use the Modula-2 code below to complete parts (a) through (e).

```
ReadInt( SomeInt );
IF  SomeInt>0  THEN
    WriteString( "positive");
ELSIF  SomeInt=0  THEN
    WriteString( "zero" );
ELSE
    WriteString( "negative");
END;
WriteLn;
```

   a) Trace the execution of this code if the value 17 is input.
   b) Write an appropriate precondition and a postcondition for the IF instruction.
   c) Why is it not possible to replace the IF with a CASE in this code?

2. Rewrite the ClassifyChar procedure from Figure 9.14 of this chapter by using a multi-way IF instruction to replace the CASE. Why is the version with the CASE the better choice?

3. The hexadecimal numbering system is often used by computer scientists. Hexadecimal numbers use the base 16 number system and have sixteen digits, rather than 10 as in the decimal system. The sixteen digits of the hexadecimal system are 0, 1, 2, 3, 4, 5, 6, 7, 8, 9, A, B, C, D, E, and F. The value of each hexadecimal digit increases by one in the indicated order. So the decimal value of the hexadecimal digit "8" is also 8, the value of "A" is 10, the value of "C" is 12, etc. Below is a procedure that converts a hexadecimal digit (stored in a CHAR parameter) into a CARDINAL value.

```
PROCEDURE HexDigitToCard(     HexDigit : CHAR;
                          VAR CardDigit : CARDINAL;
                          VAR ValidConversion : BOOLEAN );
   (* PRE:  HexDigit is Assigned                        *)
   (* POST: CardDigit = hexadecimal value of HexDigit, if   *)
   (*                   HexDigit is a valid hexadecimal  *)
   (*         ValidConversion = TRUE, if HexDigit is a valid *)
   (*                                  hexadecimal        *)
   (*                         = FALSE, otherwise          *)
   (* NOTE: "0"<=HexDigit<="9"  OR  "A"<=HexDigit<="F"     *)
   (*       means that HexDigit is a valid hexadecimal    *)
BEGIN
   IF  ("0" <= HexDigit) AND (HexDigit <= "9")  THEN
      CardDigit := ORD(HexDigit) - ORD("0");
      ValidConversion := TRUE;
   ELSIF  ("A" <= HexDigit) AND (HexDigit <= "F")  THEN
      CardDigit := ORD(HexDigit) - ORD("A") + 10;
      ValidConversion := TRUE;
   ELSE
      ValidConversion := FALSE;
   END;
END HexDigitToCard;
```

a) Rewrite the HexDigitToCard procedure using a CASE in place of the IF.

b) Briefly compare the solution proposed to the one written for (a). Which is better? Why?

c) Enumerate all of the control flow paths that must be considered to verify the correctness of the code shown above.

d) Enumerate all of the control flow paths that must be considered to verify the correctness of the CASE solution written for Part (a) above.

4. Write the code for the function below. Consider which type of selection is best suited to the problem. Examine your solution to ensure correctness.

```
PROCEDURE ResponseVal( Answer : CARDINAL )
   : CARDINAL;
      (* PRE:  Answer is Assigned                  *)
      (* POST: RESULT = 0,  if 0<=Answer<=2)  *)
      (*              = 1,  if Answer = 5     *)
      (*              = 2,  if Answer = 4     *)
      (*              = 3,  if Answer = 3     *)
      (*              = 4,  otherwise         *)
```

5. Write the code for the function below. Consider which type of selection is best suited the problem. Examine your solution to ensure correctness.

TITLE

A function called InsurancePremium for auto insurance

DESCRIPTION

This function has the following heading:

```
PROCEDURE InsurancePremium (  BaseCost : CARDINAL;
                              Age      : CARDINAL)
    : CARDINAL;
```

The function accepts a base monthly premium cost BaseCost and returns the actual premium for a driver of a specified age Age. The company calculates premiums such that most drivers pay the base rate. All premiums are truncated to the next lower dollar value. Only drivers of the following ages have the rates specified below:

Age	Premium
16	2.8 times the base rate
17	2.8 times the base rate
18	2.1 times the base rate
19	1.7 times the base rate
20	1.5 times the base rate
21	1.3 times the base rate
22	1.3 times the base rate

INPUT

None from InOut

The BaseCost parameter serves as the input base premium cost (in dollars) and the Age parameter serves to specify the age of the policy applicant.

OUTPUT

None from InOut

The result returned by this routine consists of the base cost multiplied by the appropriate factor and truncated to the nearest cardinal.

ERRORS

If BaseCost or Age are unassigned, then undefined results occur.

EXAMPLE

Below are several function invocations along with their value.

```
InsurancePremium(100, 16) = 280
InsurancePremium(100, 45) = 100
InsurancePremium(141, 21) = 183
InsurancePremium(157, 19) = 266
```

6. Assuming that Some I nt is an assigned INTEGER variable prior to each of the following code segments, write an assertion that is true after the code and that completely incorporates the task performed by the code.

a)
```
CASE  SomeInt  OF
   1 :  SomeChar := "T"  |
   7 :  SomeChar := "Y"
ELSE
   SomeChar := "D";
END
```

b)
```
CASE  SomeInt  OF
   7,3,2 :  AlsoInt := -3  |
   25,26 :  AlsoInt := SomeInt  |
   1001  :  AlsoInt := 0;
END
```

c)
```
IF  SomeInt = 3  THEN
   SomeChar := "3";
ELSIF  SomeInt <= 2  THEN
   SomeChar := "-";
ELSIF  SomeInt >= 100  THEN
   SomeChar := "+";
ELSE
   SomeChar := "?";
END
```

d)
```
IF  SomeInt = 2  THEN
   AlsoInt := 102;
ELSIF  SomeInt < 10  THEN
   AlsoInt := 10;
ELSIF  SomeInt < 20  THEN
   AlsoInt := 20;
END
```

7. One common scheme for classifying college students is to use the number of semesters in attendance. With this scheme, classifications of 1 and 2 are used for freshmen, 3 and 4 for sophomores, 5 and 6 for juniors, and 7, 8, and 9 for seniors. The function below is designed to translate such a classification into a cardinal representing years of attendance. Specify the precondition and postcondition for this function.

```
PROCEDURE YearAttending( SemesterAttending: CARDINAL )
   : CARDINAL;
      (* PRE:  ? *)
      (* POST: ? *)
BEGIN
   CASE  SemesterAttending  OF
      1,2   :  RETURN 1  |
      3,4   :  RETURN 2  |
      5,6   :  RETURN 3  |
      7,8,9 :  RETURN 4
   ELSE
      RETURN 0
   END
END YearAttending;
```

8. Write a precondition and a postcondition for the following procedure.

```
PROCEDURE QuantityDiscount( RetailCost : REAL;
                           Quantity : CARDINAL   )
: CARDINAL;
    (* PRE:  ? *)
    (* POST: ? *)
BEGIN
   IF  Quantity <= 1  THEN
      RETURN TRUNC( RetailCost );
   ELSIF  Quantity <= 10  THEN
      RETURN TRUNC( RetailCost * .80 );
   ELSIF  Quantity <= 100  THEN
      RETURN TRUNC( RetailCost * .70 );
   ELSIF  Quantity <= 250  THEN
      RETURN TRUNC( RetailCost * .68 );
   ELSE
      RETURN TRUNC( RetailCost * .66 );
   END;
END QuantityDiscount;
```

||| PROGRAMMING PROJECTS

1. Write a program for the following problem definition.

TITLE

Classify triangles by lengths of sides

DESCRIPTION

A triangle can be classified according to the length of its three sides. If all three sides of a triangle have the same length, then the triangle is said to be "equilateral." If just two sides have the same length, then the triangle is "isosceles." Triangles that have sides with three different lengths are called "scalene." In addition, it is impossible for a triangle to have one side that has a length that is greater than the sum of the other two sides. This program inputs triples of cardinals that represent the lengths of the three sides of a triangle. For each triple, the program outputs either "EQUILATERAL", "ISOSCELES", "SCALENE", or "IMPOSSIBLE". The end of input is signified by a triple in which one of the values is zero (0). After all triples are input, the program also outputs the total number of each class of triangle processed.

INPUT

Prompted input consists of groups of three consecutive cardinal constants (triples) separated by one or more blanks. The last triple contains a 0. Each triple, except the last, represents the lengths of the sides of a single triangle.

OUTPUT

Before each input triple the following two line prompt is displayed.

```
Input lengths of triangle sides.
(0 signifies input termination)
```

Following the input of a triplet, the line from the four below that is appropriate for this triplet, is output.

```
Equilateral (3 equal sides)
Isosceles (2 equal sides)
Scalene (3 different sides)
Invalid (a side is longer than sum of others)
```

Following the output line for each triple two blank lines precede the next prompt.

Following the last input triple (where one value is 0) is a blank line and the following four summary lines. The symbolism assumes that "<E>" is the total count of equilateral triangles input, "<I>" is the number of isosceles, "<S>" is the number of scalene, and "<X>" is the number of invalid.

```
Equilateral total = <E>
Isosceles total = <I>
Scalene total = <S>
Invalid total = <X>
```

ERRORS

The only error identified is the input of a triangle that is invalid (i.e. any one side is longer than the sum of the other two). Invalid triangles are so counted.

EXAMPLE

Below is a sample execution with all input highlighted.

```
Input lengths of triangle sides.
(0 signifies input termination)

5 3 4
Scalene (3 different sides)


Input lengths of triangle sides.
(0 signifies input termination)

7 3 7
Isosceles (2 equal sides)


Input lengths of triangle sides.
(0 signifies input termination)

1 4 4
Isosceles (2 equal sides)
```

```
Input lengths of triangle sides.
(0 signifies input termination)

2 4 1
Invalid (a side is longer than sum of others)


Input lengths of triangle sides.
(0 signifies input termination)

3 4 20
Invalid (a side is longer than sum of others)


Input lengths of triangle sides.
(0 signifies input termination)

1 0 8

Equilateral total = 0
Isosceles total = 2
Scalene total = 1
Invalid total = 2
```

2. Write a program for the following problem definition.

TITLE
Average quiz grades for instructor Letterman

DESCRIPTION
An instructor, known by the students as "Quiz Letterman," has a habit of giving many quizzes in a course. Letterman records all quiz scores as letter grades of "A," "B," "C," "D," or "F." At semester end, Letterman averages the quiz grades of each student by translating them to a 4.0 grading system (A = 4.0, B = 3.0, C = 2.0, D = 1.0, and F = 0.0). Letterman averages the points corresponding to quiz grades for each student, then translates the resulting average by rounding it to the nearest letter grade. The problem is to write a program to automate Letterman's grade averaging. Letterman will place student grades in a file where all quiz scores for a single student are stored consecutively.

INPUT
The user is prompted only for the file name, where remaining input resides.

Input from the file consists of five sets of letter grades. All grades for one student are together and are followed by an exclamation point (!) The grades are single uppercase letters, either "A", "B", "C", "D", or "F". Each student may have a different number of grades.

OUTPUT

The request for the input file name is prompted by the following line:

Quiz grade file name?

After each of the five input lines is input, the following line is output. Note that <i> signifies the sequence number of the input line and <g> signifies the letter grade that is the average for the given line.

Student #<i> -- Grade: <g>

ERRORS

1) If there is an error opening the specified file, then the program terminates with the following error message:

INVALID INPUT FILE!

2) Characters other than "A", "B", "C", "D", "F", or "!" arc ignored.
3) If there are no letter grades for a student, then "X" is output for the student's grade.
4) If too few input lines (fewer than five) exist, then undefined results occur.

EXAMPLE

Below is the prompt and highlighted response for a particular execution.

Quiz grade file name?
MYCLASS

Below are the contents of the file called "MYCLASS".

AAB!
!
AABCBAAF!
DaB!
A B!

Below is the output produced, using the above file:

Student #1 -- Grade: A
Student #2 -- Grade: X
Student #3 -- Grade: B
Student #4 -- Grade: C
Student #5 -- Grade: A

3. Write a program for the following problem definition.

TITLE
Summarize constant numeric expressions.

DESCRIPTION
This problem is to perform a simple translation of a numeric expression to summarize its form. Input to the program will consist of lines from a file containing the original expressions. For each input line, a single output line will summarize the expression. The summary results from the following modifications to the expression.

1) Each cardinal constant is replaced by X.
2) Each operator is replaced by +.
3) All blanks are deleted.
4) Parentheses remain unmodified.
5) Certain invalid characters are replaced by !.

INPUT
The user is prompted to specify a file name. All of the input line for translation come from this file. Each input line consists of a sequence of characters representing constant numeric expressions. Each expression consists of a sequence of operands, operators, parentheses (both "(" and ")") and blanks. An operand must be an unsigned decimal number (cardinal constant). The permissible operators are " +," "-," "*," and "/." Lines may consist of zero or more operands operators, parentheses and/or blanks in any order and combination. The final input line is signified by a single "?" as the first character. No other input lines may begin with "?".

OUTPUT
Each file name is prompted by the following:

Please specify file of expressions

A blank line follows the user's input. The rest of the output consists of the translated lines input from the file. The translation occurs as follows:

1) Each operand (cardinal constant) is replaced by "X".
2) Each operator is replaced by " + ".
3) All blanks are removed.
4) Each left and right parenthesis remains unchanged.
5) All other characters are replaced by "!".

Prior to each input prompt a blank line is output.

ERRORS
None other than the unexpected characters replaced by "!".

EXAMPLE

The contents of a file named ExprFile are given below:

```
123 + (7 – 32 * 64 / (3 + 2764))
7464646
* * *
((        88    //    88    (
74aBD76 + ? – 7P + (
?
```

Below is a sample execution with input highlighted

```
Please specify file of expressions:
ExprFile

X + (X + X + X + (X + X))
X
+ + +
((X + + X(
X!!!X+!+X!+(
```

4. Write a program for the following problem definition.

TITLE

Determine the value of a three-card poker hand.

DESCRIPTION

This program inputs a three-card poker hand and outputs the value of the hand. For this version of three-card poker the following hands are recognized (listed from highest hand to lowest):

PokerHand	Desription
Three of a kind	All three cards have the same value (e.g., three Aces or three seven's)
Flush	All three cards are the same suit (e.g., all three are hearts or spades)
Pair	Two cards the same and the other different (e.g., two Aces and a two)
HighCard	None of the above apply

The program must indicate the value of the highest card if the HighCard hand is found. Cards arranged from least to greatest value are: 2, 3, 4, 5, 6, 7, 8, 9, 10, Jack, Queen, King, Ace.

INPUT

Input consists of repetitions of poker hands.

Each input hand consists of three pairs of two consecutive characters. Each pair is prompted; it represents one card of the hand. The first character of the pair is the value of the card (either a digit from "2" to "9," or "0" for 10, or "J" for

Jack, "Q" for Queen, "K" for King, or "A" for Ace. The second character of the pair indicates the suit of the card "H" for hearts, "D" for diamonds, "C" for clubs, or "S" for spades.

After each hand is processed, the user will be prompted to respond for continued program use. A response of uppercase "Y" initiates repetition of the process. Anything else terminates the program.

OUTPUT

The cards of each hand are prompted by the following line:

```
Enter next poker card:
```

Following the three cards of the hand, a blank line is output followed by the single line from the four below that is appropriate:

```
PokerValue: 3 of a kind
PokerValue: Flush
PokerValue: Pair
PokerValue: HighCard
```

A blank line follows the line above, then the following prompt checks for another iteration:

```
Input another? (Y or N)
```

If an uppercase "Y" is input in response to this last prompt, then two blank lines are output and the process repeats.

ERRORS

Undefined results occur for erroneous input.

EXAMPLE

Below is a sample execution, where all input has been highlighted.

```
Enter next poker card: 5H
Enter next poker card: 3C
Enter next poker card: 5D

PokerValue: Pair

Input another? (Y or N) Y

Enter next poker card: 3D
Enter next poker card: 2H
Enter next poker card: 8D

PokerValue: HighCard

Input another? (Y or N) Y
```

> Enter next poker card: JS
> Enter next poker card: OS
> Enter next poker card: AS
>
> PokerValue: Flush
>
> Input another? (Y or N) x

5. Modify your program for Project 4 so that it also recognizes straights. A poker hand is a straight when the three cards form a consecutive sequence, such as 8, 9 and 10 or Jack, Queen, and King. (Note: The Ace is in both the straight: Queen, King, Ace and the straight: Ace, 2, 3). A straight should be recognized as a hand just better than a flush.

6. Write a program for the following problem definition.

TITLE
   Translate Roman numerals into cardinal constants

DESCRIPTION
   This program inputs one Roman numeral per line and outputs the corresponding cardinal constant in the next line. Roman numerals are defined to include the following symbols with the given meaning:

Roman symbol	Decimal value
X	10
V	5
I	1

INPUT
   Input consists of six lines of Roman numerals. Each line must contain only the characters "X," "V," and/or "I." The largest Roman numeral that the program need accept is XXXIX, 39.

OUTPUT
   Prior to all input, the following message is displayed:

   Specify six Roman numerals below.

   A blank line follows the prompt.
   After each input line, the decimal equivalent of the input Roman numeral is displayed. The value of a Roman numeral is found by summing the value of individual characters except for the following pairs of characters with special meaning.

   "IX" represents 9.
   "IV" represents 4.

The output line containing the decimal value, <d>, has the form shown below:

Decimal value = <d>

A blank line separates each output line from the next input line.

ERRORS

Any input Roman numeral not conforming to the input rules causes the output line specified above to be replaced by:

Decimal value = unknown (ERROR)

EXAMPLE

Below is a sample execution with input highlighted.

Specify six Roman numerals below.

X
Decimal value = 10

IX
Decimal value = 9

XXIV
Decimal value = 24

XXXVIII
Decimal value = 38

XVIV
Decimal value = unknown (ERROR)

XXXXI
Decimal value = unknown (ERROR)

7. Write a program for the following problem definition.

TITLE

Score one bowling game

DESCRIPTION

This program inputs the number of pins knocked down by each consecutive ball rolled in a single bowling game and outputs the score for each frame of the game.

Bowling is scored as follows. One game consists of ten frames. Each frame has an associated score, and each frame's score is used to calculate the score of the frame that follows (a score of zero precedes the first frame). For each frame a bowler rolls the first ball and may knock down 0 to 10 of the ten pins standing. If the bowler knocks down all ten pins, it is called a "strike." Otherwise the bowler rolls a second ball at the remainder of the ten pins. If all pins are knocked down after the second ball then is is called a spare. The score for each frame is calculated as follows.

a) if the frame is a strike then the score is the sum of the current frame plus the number of pins knocked down on the two rolls after the strike plus ten. Note: Except for the tenth frame, the two rolls included come from following frame(s).
b) If the frame is a spare then the score is the sum of the current frame plus the number of pins knocked down on the roll after the spare plus ten.
c) If the frame is neither a strike nor a spare, then the score is the sum of the current frame plus the total pins knocked down in the two rolls of the current frame.

The tenth frame is unique in that if a strike or a spare occurs in the tenth frame, then the bowler must bowl three times, starting with ten pins any time all pins have been knocked down.

INPUT

Prompted input consists of the file name that contains the input for a single game. This file consists of a sequence of cardinal constants separated by blanks that represent, respectively, the number of pins knocked down by each consecutive roll during the bowling game.

OUTPUT

The following message prompts the name of the input file.

Name of file containing bowling game?

A blank line follows the above prompt.
Ten consecutive lines are output. They contain the scores for each frame of the game. The form of these lines is as follows, where <f> is the frame number and <s> is the score for that frame:

Frame: <f> Score: <s>

ERRORS

All erroneous input produces undefined results.

EXAMPLE

Below is the interactive I/O with input highlighted.

Name of file containing bowling game?

SCORE1.DAT

Contents of the file named "SCORE1.DAT"

1 2 1 9 2 8 10 10 10 5 1 10 10 10 9 1

Output resulting from use of the SCORE1.DAT file:

```
Frame:  1 Score:   3
Frame:  2 Score:  15
Frame:  3 Score:  35
Frame:  4 Score:  65
Frame:  5 Score:  90
Frame:  6 Score: 106
Frame:  7 Score: 112
Frame:  8 Score: 142
Frame:  9 Score: 171
Frame: 10 Score: 191
```

10

MORE ABOUT REPETITION

10.1 REVIEW OF THE WHILE INSTRUCTION

Repetition is a convenience for the programmer. A loop just a few lines long can cause thousands of individual instructions to be executed. Modula-2 supports four different types of **repetition** control structures, referred to as **loops**:

The **WHILE** loop
The **REPEAT** loop
The **LOOP** loop
The **FOR** loop

Every loop consists of two features.

1) A **loop body** consisting of a group of instructions to be executed repeatedly.
2) Some **loop condition** that determines when to terminate the repetition.

The body of the loop specifies *what* is to be executed in every **iteration**—each time the loop is repeated. The loop condition specifies *when* to repeat the body.

An algorithm to print the Fibonacci sequence makes use of loops. Fibonacci numbers were discovered by a Thirteenth Century mathematician, Leonardo Fibonacci. They consist of an infinite sequence of cardinals. The first two values in the sequence are both 1. Thereafter, each value in the sequence can be calculated by summing the two Fibonacci values that immediately precede it. The first ten values in the Fibonacci number sequence are 1, 1, 2, 3, 5, 8, 13, 21, 34, and 55. Figure 10.1 contains a program that calculates and outputs the Fibonacci numbers smaller than $MaxFib$.

```
MODULE FibNums;
    (* This program outputs Fibonacci numbers through some *)
    (* user-specified maximum.                             *)
    FROM InOut IMPORT ReadCard, WriteCard, WriteString,WriteLn;

    VAR
        OneFib : CARDINAL;
        NextFib : CARDINAL;
        NewFib : CARDINAL;
        MaxFib : CARDINAL;
BEGIN
    WriteString( "Largest desired Fibonacci number? ");
    ReadCard( MaxFib );  WriteLn;                          (continued)
```

```
OneFib := 1;
NextFib := 1;
WriteCard( OneFib,9 ); WriteLn;
WHILE NextFib < MaxFib DO      (* loop condition *)
     (* ASSERT: The sequence of Fibonaccis prior  *)
     (*         to NextFib has been output.       *)
     (*    AND  OneFib, NextFib are consecutive    *)
     (*         Fibonacci numbers.                 *)
     WriteCard( NextFib,9 );        (* --------- *)
     WriteLn;                       (*     ^     *)
     NewFib := OneFib + NextFib;    (* loop body *)
     OneFib := NextFib;             (*     v     *)
     NextFib := NewFib;             (* --------- *)
END;
(* ASSERT: The sequence of Fibonaccis through *)
(*         MaxFib has been output.            *)
END FibNums.
```

FIGURE 10.1 *Program FibNums to output Fibonacci numbers*

The FibNums program is an example of a WHILE loop. Figure 10.2 contains a review of the WHILE construct.

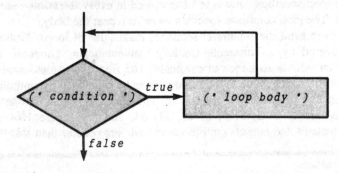

Syntax Diagram for WHILE:

→ WHILE ⟶ *BooleanExpression* ⟶ DO ⟶ *InstructionSequence* ⟶ END →

The WHILE *in code:*

```
WHILE (* condition *) DO
   (* loop body *)
END
```

The WHILE *control flow:*

FIGURE 10.2 *Summary of WHILE*

10.2 THE REPEAT LOOP

The body of a WHILE loop is executed only if the loop condition is found to be TRUE. Because the loop condition is tested prior to executing the loop, it is said that a WHILE loop performs its **test at the top of the loop**. It is also possible to use loops that perform the **test at the bottom of the loop**. A REPEAT loop is the Modula-2 version of repetition that performs the test at the bottom. The body of a REPEAT loop is always executed once before evaluating the loop condition for the first time. Figure 10.3 summarizes the syntax and semantics of this loop for Modula-2.

Syntax Diagram for REPEAT:

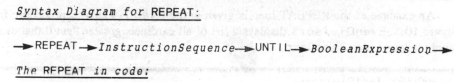

The REPEAT *in code:*

```
REPEAT
    (' loop body ')
UNTIL (' condition ')
```

The REPEAT *control flow:*

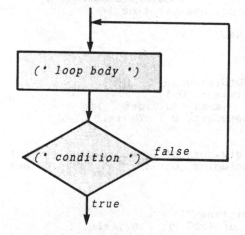

FIGURE 10.3 *Summary of REPEAT*

In addition to performing the test at the bottom of the loop, there is one other difference between the REPEAT loop and the WHILE. REPEAT loops terminate when their loop condition is TRUE, just the opposite of a WHILE loop.

Figure 10.4 on the following page, compares REPEAT and WHILE loops with two loops that both perform the same task. Both of these loops are counting loops that are iterated ten times.

Two counting loops (from one to ten)

The WHILE version	The REPEAT version
`Counter := 1;`	`Counter := 1;`
`WHILE  Counter <= 10  DO`	`REPEAT`
`   (* perform some task *)`	`   (* perform some task *)`
`   INC( Counter );`	`   INC( Counter );`
`END`	`UNTIL  Counter > 10`

FIGURE 10.4 *WHILE and REPEAT counting loops*

An example of the REPEAT loop is given in the EvenDivisors procedure from Figure 10.5. EvenDivisors displays a list of all cardinals greater than 0 that evenly divide its parameter SomeCard.

```
MODULE TestDivisors;
     (* This program is a test driver for Divisors *)
   FROM InOut IMPORT WriteCard, WriteLn, WriteString;

   PROCEDURE Divisors( SomeCard : CARDINAL );
        (* PRE:  SomeCard >= 1                       *)
        (* POST: All divisors of SomeCard down to 1  *)
        (*       are output one per line.            *)
      VAR
        Divisor : CARDINAL;
   BEGIN
      Divisor := SomeCard;
      REPEAT
        IF  SomeCard MOD Divisor = 0  THEN
           WriteCard( Divisor, 0 );
           WriteString( " evenly divides " );
           WriteCard( SomeCard, 0 ); WriteLn;
        END;
        DEC( Divisor )
        (* ASSERT: All divisors of SomeCard down to, but *)
        (*         not including, Divisor have been output *)
      UNTIL Divisor < 1
   END Divisors;

BEGIN (* TestDivisors mainline *)
   WriteString("Divisors of 4500:");   WriteLn;
   Divisors( 4500 );
   WriteLn;
   WriteString("Divisors of 1:");   WriteLn;
   Divisors( 1 );
END TestDivisors.
```

FIGURE 10.5 *TestDivisors program*

10.3 THE LOOP LOOP AND EXIT INSTRUCTION

The LOOP control structure of Modula-2 is more flexible than WHILE or REPEAT. LOOP loops can test the loop condition at the top of the loop, the bottom of the loop, or anywhere within the loop. A LOOP can even include several loop conditions.

In its simplest form, the LOOP control structure is an infinite loop. The syntax and semantics of this form are shown in Figure 10.6.

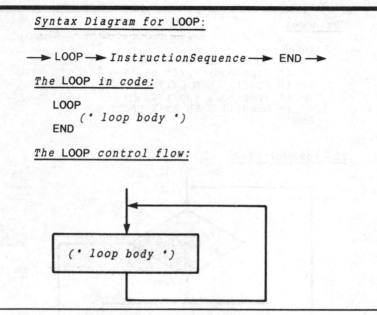

Syntax Diagram for LOOP:

⟶ LOOP ⟶ *InstructionSequence* ⟶ END ⟶

The LOOP *in code:*

```
LOOP
    (' loop body ')
END
```

The LOOP *control flow:*

```
(' loop body ')
```

FIGURE 10.6 *Summary of LOOP*

Programs like those used to control the operating system or to monitor air traffic control may be written to execute indefinitely. However, for most programs, an infinite loop is an error. Modula-2 includes an **EXIT instruction** as a method for terminating the infinite execution of a LOOP. Figure 10.7 describes the syntax and semantics of the EXIT instruction.

Syntax Diagram for EXIT:

⟶ EXIT ⟶

Semantics of EXIT:

> *Execution of an* EXIT *causes immediate termination of the innermost enclosing* LOOP *construct.*

FIGURE 10.7 *Syntax and semantics of EXIT*

In practice, an EXIT instruction is usually guarded by enclosing it within a selection instruction. The instruction

IF Condition THEN EXIT END

is the most common form of providing a loop condition within a LOOP. One or more such instructions may be placed anywhere within a LOOP body.

Figure 10.8 contains a sample LOOP. In this example, there are three loop conditions that may terminate the execution of the loop.

The code:

```
LOOP
    IF Condl THEN EXIT END;
    (* loop body (part 1) *)
    IF CondII THEN EXIT END;
    (* loop body (part 2) *)
    IF CondIII THEN EXIT END;
END
```

The control flow:

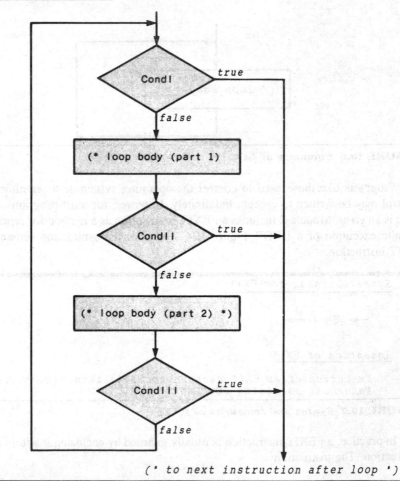

FIGURE 10.8 *An example of LOOP and its semantics*

The EXIT instruction within a LOOP behaves similar to the RETURN instruction of a procedure. Just as the RETURN could be placed anywhere within a procedure, the EXIT can be placed anywhere within a loop. The RETURN causes immediate procedure termination; the EXIT causes immediate loop termination. The RETURN is useful for "error handling" within procedures, and the EXIT can be used similarly in loops.

Figure 10.9 contains a program, TotalTenTriples, that inputs cardinals three at a time. After each triplet, its sum is printed. When all ten triplets are processed, the total of the 30 cardinals is output. Any detected input error causes immediate program termination with an error message.

```
MODULE TotalTenTriples;
        (* This program inputs ten triplets of cardinals.   *)
        (* The sum of each triplet is output along with      *)
        (* the sum of all ten triplets (30 cardinals).       *)
        (*                                                    *)
        (* NOTE: if any error is detected during input then  *)
        (*       the program terminates immediately with an  *)
        (*       error message.                               *)
    FROM InOut IMPORT WriteString, WriteCard, WriteLn,
                      ReadCard, Done;
    VAR
        Card1 : CARDINAL;
        Card2 : CARDINAL;
        Card3 : CARDINAL;
        Sum : CARDINAL;
        TripleCount : CARDINAL;
BEGIN
    WriteString( "Please type 30 cardinals " );
    WriteString( "separated by blanks:" );  WriteLn;
    Sum := 0;
    TripleCount := 0;
    LOOP
        ReadCard( Card1 );
        IF NOT Done THEN
            EXIT      (* LOOP TERMINATION CONDITION *)
        END;
        Sum := Sum + Card1;

        ReadCard( Card2 );
        IF NOT Done THEN
            EXIT      (* LOOP TERMINATION CONDITION *)
        END;
        Sum := Sum + Card2;

        ReadCard( Card3 );
        IF NOT Done THEN
            EXIT      (* LOOP TERMINATION CONDITION *)
        END;
        Sum := Sum + Card3;

        WriteString( "The next triple sum = " );
        WriteCard( Card1+Card2+Card3, 0 );  WriteLn;
        INC( TripleCount );
        IF  TripleCount = 10  THEN
            EXIT      (* LOOP TERMINATION CONDITION *)
        END
    END;
```

(continued)

```
(* Assert: All ten triplets processed  *)
(*         OR an input error has occurred *)
WriteLn;

IF  TripleCount<10  THEN
    WriteString( "Input error - premature termination!" );
    WriteLn
END;
WriteString( "Total sum = " );
WriteCard( Sum, 0 );  WriteLn;
END TotalTenTriples.
```

FIGURE 10.9 *The TotalTenTriples program*

A LOOP control structure works well for the `TotalTenTriples` program because loop termination may occur for one of four reasons.

1) An error occurs reading the first cardinal of a triplet.
2) An error occurs reading the second cardinal of a triplet.
3) An error occurs reading the third cardinal of a triplet.
4) All 10 triplets have been processed.

For the sake of comparison, the loop from `TotalTenTriples` has been written using LOOP, WHILE, and REPEAT control structures in Figure 10.10. All three versions produce identical output for the same input.

```
The LOOP version:
LOOP
    ReadCard( Card1 );
    IF NOT Done THEN
        EXIT        (* LOOP TERMINATION CONDITION *)
    END;
    Sum := Sum + Card1;

    ReadCard( Card2 );
    IF NOT Done THEN
        EXIT        (* LOOP TERMINATION CONDITION *)
    END;
    Sum := Sum + Card2;

    ReadCard( Card3 );
    IF NOT Done THEN
        EXIT        (* LOOP TERMINATION CONDITION *)
    END;
    Sum := Sum + Card3;

    WriteString( "The next triple sum = " );
    WriteCard( Card1+Card2+Card3, 0 );  WriteLn;
    INC( TripleCount );
    IF  TripleCount = 10  THEN
        EXIT        (* LOOP TERMINATION CONDITION *)
    END
END;
```

(continued)

```
The REPEAT version:
   REPEAT
      ReadCard( Card1 );
      IF  Done  THEN
         Sum := Sum + Card1;

         ReadCard( Card2 );
         IF  Done  THEN
            Sum := Sum + Card2;

            ReadCard( Card3 );
            IF  Done  THEN
               Sum := Sum + Card3;

               WriteString( "The next triple sum = " );
               WriteCard( Card1+Card2+Card3, 0 );
               WriteLn;
               INC( TripleCount )
            END
         END
      END
   UNTIL (NOT Done) OR (TripleCount = 10);

The WHILE version:
   ReadCard( Card1 );
   WHILE  Done AND (TripleCount < 10)  DO
      Sum := Sum + Card1;

      ReadCard( Card2 );
      IF  Done  THEN
         Sum := Sum + Card2;

         ReadCard( Card3 );
         IF  Done  THEN
            Sum := Sum + Card3;

            WriteString( "The next triple sum = " );
            WriteCard( Card1+Card2+Card3, 0 );
            WriteLn;
            INC( TripleCount ;

            IF  TripleCount < 10  THEN
               ReadCard( Card1 )
            END
         END
      END
   END;
```

FIGURE 10.10 **LOOP, REPEAT, and WHILE versions of the loop from** *Total Ten Triples*

The three loops of Figure 10.10 illustrate the utility of the LOOP control structure. The LOOP version uses an EXIT to "skip" the remainder of the loop, while the REPEAT and WHILE versions must include guards for this purpose. The result is nested control structures. The LOOP version is somewhat longer, but easier to read because it shows how one iteration consists of three similar operations to process Card1, Card2 and Card3. The nested control IF instructions of the REPEAT and WHILE versions tend to obscure what the loop is doing.

The REPEAT and WHILE versions from Figure 10.10 can also be shown to be less efficient than the LOOP version. Notice that the LOOP loop always checks the value of Done once, immediately after each ReadCard. In the REPEAT and WHILE versions, Done is tested within the loop body and as the loop condition, one additional test per loop iteration.

Programming-with-Style

Which Loop to Choose?

The programmer must often decide whether to use WHILE, REPEAT, or LOOP. Each of the styles of looping is useful in different circumstances. Below are a few guidelines to remember when choosing.

1) The WHILE loop is most general and probably the safest choice under most conditions.
2) The REPEAT loop is preferable to the WHILE if the loop body must be executed at least once.
3) The REPEAT loop is preferable to the WHILE when it eliminates the need for loop initializations such as priming reads.
4) The LOOP loop is generally the most unreadable choice, because loop termination points are buried inside the body of the loop.
5) The advantages of REPEAT and WHILE over LOOP may be nullified by a loop that requires multiple exits from different locations in the body. The most common instance of this occurs in the form of loop exit for error conditions.
6) Using the LOOP is a last resort. The programmer should carefully consider the alternatives before a LOOP is used.

10.4 THE RELATIONSHIP OF WHILE, REPEAT, AND LOOP CONSTRUCT

Two collections of control structures are said to be **functionally equivalent** if any program that can be written using either collection can also be written using the other. The WHILE, REPEAT and LOOP loops are all functionally equivalent when an IF instruction is permitted. For example, Figure 10.11 on the opposite page, shows how to express a WHILE loop or a REPEAT loop, using a LOOP, IF, and EXIT.

Translating a LOOP instruction into functionally equivalent code using WHILE (or REPEAT) is more difficult. This translation is performed by using a new Boolean variable, call it LoopComplete, not used elsewhere in the original code. LoopComplete keeps track of when an EXIT would occur in a LOOP. A typical functionally equivalent translation from LOOP to WHILE is shown in Figure 10.12 on the opposite page.

It is always *possible* to express one of the looping structures in terms of another. However, sometimes one option is far more readable than another. A good programmer is proficient with all options and able to choose the best one for a particular algorithm.

A WHILE loop	*Functionally Equivalent LOOP loop*

WHILE SomeCondition DO
   SomeBody
END
	LOOP
	   IF NOT SomeCondition THEN
	      EXIT
	   END;
	   SomeBody
	END

A REPEAT loop	*Functionally Equivalent LOOP loop*

REPEAT
   AnotherBody
UNTIL AnotherCondition
	LOOP
	   AnotherBody;
	   IF AnotherCondition THEN
	      EXIT
	   END
	END

FIGURE 10.11 *Using LOOP to express WHILE and REPEAT loops*

An Example LOOP	*A Functionally Equivalent WHILE*

LOOP
   InstructionA;
   IF CondA THEN
      EXIT
   END;
   InstructionB;
   IF CondB THEN
      EXIT
   ELSE
      InstructionC;
      IF CondC THEN
         EXIT
      END
   END
END
	LoopComplete := FALSE;
	WHILE NOT LoopComplete DO
	   InstructionA;
	   IF CondA THEN
	      LoopComplete := TRUE
	   ELSE
	      InstructionB;
	      IF CondB THEN
	         LoopComplete := TRUE
	      ELSE
	         InstructionC;
	         IF CondC THEN
	            LoopComplete := TRUE
	         END
	      END
	   END
	END

FIGURE 10.12 *An example of use of WHILE to express a LOOP*

10.5 THE LOOP INVARIANT

An assertion placed within a loop is called a **loop invariant**. Because loops are executed repeatedly, the loop invariant is encountered repeatedly. Each time a loop invariant is encountered it must be TRUE. In other words, the loop invariant must be "invariantly" true with respect to its location in the loop.

Loop invariants are most useful when placed immediately before the test of the loop condition. This means that the loop invariant is always true just before the decision is made to iterate or terminate the loop. Figure 10.13 contains a REPEAT loop with an appropriate loop invariant.

```
Count := 1;
Factorial := 1;
(* ASSERT: Count=1 & Factorial=1 *)
REPEAT
    INC( Count );
    Factorial := Factorial * Count;
    (* INV: Factorial=1*2*...*Count & Count<=5 *)
UNTIL Count>=5;
(* ASSERT: Factorial = 1*2*3*4*5 *)
```

FIGURE 10.13 *An example of a loop invariant calculating 5!*

The loop invariant in Figure 10.13 is identified as a comment prefixed by "INV:". (This notation will be used throughout the remainder of the text.) A good loop invariant:

1) Captures what is happening in the loop by expressing what is true just before testing the loop condition
2) Includes enough information to guarantee the desired result when the loop terminates

The loop invariant from Figure 10.13 captures what the loop is doing by stating that Factorial = (1*2*..*Count) after each loop iteration.

This loop also guarantees the desired postcondition. From the portion of the invariant, Count<=5, and the loop condition terminating this loop, Count>=5, it is clear that Count must store the value 5 when the loop ends. If Count=5 and the loop invariant are true, then the assertion following the loop has to be true.

The example in Figure 10.8 calculates the value of 5 factorial (also written "5!") and stores the result in Factorial. Figure 10.14 contains a different algorithm for this same calculation.

```
CountDown := 5;
Factorial := 5;
(* ASSERT: CountDown=5 & Factorial=5 *)
REPEAT
    DEC( CountDown );
    Factorial := Factorial * CountDown;
    (* INV: Factorial=5*4*...*CountDown & CountDown>=1 *)
UNTIL Count<=1;
(* ASSERT: Factorial = 5*4*3*2*1 & CountDown=1 *)
```

FIGURE 10.14 *A second example of loop invariant calculating 5!*

The power of a loop invariant lies in its ability to describe loop semantics. Comparing these two loop invariants illustrates this point. The first loop calculates a factorial by increasing Count from 1 to 5. The loop invariant states it this way:

$$Factorial = 1*2*...*Count \ \& \ Count<=5$$

The second algorithm calculates a factorial by decreasing CountDown from 5 to 1. This is expressed in the invariant

$$Factorial = 5*4*...*CountDown \& CountDown >= 1$$

In both cases, the loop invariant supplies a concise summary of the task performed within the body.

In these previous examples, the loop invariant has been placed just before the UNTIL, because this is just before the loop condition test for a REPEAT. The invariant must be placed at the top of the loop for a WHILE. Figure 10.15 show this use of invariants with two algorithms that calculate N! (Assuming that N is a CARDINAL variable.)

```
C := 1;
Factorial := 1;
(* ASSERT: C=1 & Factorial=1 *)
WHILE   (* INV: Factorial = (C-1)! & C<=N+1 *)
(C<=N) DO
    Factorial := Factorial * C;
    INC( C )
END
(* ASSERT: Factorial = N! *)

J := 0;
Factorial := 1;
(* ASSERT: J=0 & Factorial=1 *)
WHILE   (* INV: Factorial=J! & J<=N *)
(J<N) DO
    INC( J );
    Factorial := Factorial * J
END
(* ASSERT: Factorial = N! *)

(* NOTE: X! = 1*2*3*...*X,   if X>=1   *)
(*            = 1,            if X=0    *)
```

FIGURE 10.15 *Two examples of loops for calculating N!*

The placement of the loop invariant in these WHILE loops may appear unusual at first. Since the loop invariant must be true immediately before the test of the loop condition, the invariant in a WHILE is shown between the WHILE and the loop condition. The loop condition is moved down one line.

The differences in the two loops in Figure 10.15 are very slight. In the first loop the loop invariant is:

$$Factorial = (C-1)! \& C <= N+1$$

In other words, at the top of the loop the value of C is always 1 greater than the last number multiplied times Factorial. By contrast, the second loop invariant states:

$$Factorial = J! \& J <= N$$

In this case the loop counter is J, instead of C. Furthermore, at the top of the loop the value of J has been multiplied times Factorial.

The loop conditions must be different for these two loops to be correct. When the first loop terminates, $C = N+1$. This fact can be drawn from knowledge that the loop invariant (C< = N + 1) is true and that the loop condition is false (meaning C>N). Since C = N + 1 upon loop termination, the portion of the loop invariant that indicates Factorial = (C−1) ! becomes N! by substituting N + 1 for C.

*P*rogramming-with-*S*tyle

Loop Invariants in Code

Every loop should be documented with a loop invariant assertion. This assertion should indicate an expression that is true just prior to the evaluation of a loop condition. The preferred style for this documentation is shown below for WHILE and REPEAT loops:

```
WHILE (*INV: TheLoopInvariant *)
LoopCondition DO
  LoopBody
END

REPEAT
  LoopBody
  (* INV: TheLoopInvariant *)
UNTIL LoopCondition
```

For the LOOP loop, a separate loop invariant is required immediately preceding every condition guarding an EXIT. These multiple loop invariants may all be different assertions.

Writing loop invariants takes some practice. Below are a few helpful hints:

1) Begin with the question: *What has happened so far in the loop?* An answer to this question that is true every time the loop has iterated is the loop invariant.
2) Examine what is supposed to be true as a result of the completion of the loop. The loop invariant usually states some partial progress toward this goal.
3) Draw a picture of what happens during a typical loop iteration. The loop invariant must capture what is true before and after the iteration.
4) The best time to identify the loop invariant is when the loop is designed. If you know how to design the loop, you already know the loop invariant!

Loop invariants very often have the following general form:

For all values from previous loop iterations some particular condition is true.

This type of loop invariant is shown in some sample loops from Figure 10.16 on the opposite page.

A loop to skip blank characters on an input line:

```
REPEAT
    Read( SomeChar )
    (* INV: All previous characters input from this *)
    (*       line were blank                        *)
UNTIL (NOT Done) OR (SomeChar<>" ")
(* ASSERT: (NOT Done)  OR  SomeChar is the first non-blank *)
(*                     character from the input line       *)
```

A loop to find tne greatest whole divisor of Number:

```
    (* ASSERT: Number is a cardinal & Number>1 *)
    Divisor := Number - 1;
    WHILE (* INV: No cardinal in the range between Divisor *)
          (*      and Number evenly divides Number         *)
          (*   & 1<=Divisor<Number                         *)
    Number MOD Divisor # 0 DO
        DEC( Divisor )
    END
    (* ASSERT: Divisor is the greatest whole divisor of *)
    (*         Number, except Number itself             *)
```

A loop to find the smallest input integer:

```
    (* ASSERT: The first input value is a valid integer *)
    ReadInt( Min );
    WHILE   (* INV: Of all input thusfar Min stores the *)
            (*      smallest value                       *)
    Done DO
        ReadInt( SomeVal );
        IF  Done & (SomeVal<Min)  THEN
            Min := SomeVal
        END
    END
    (* ASSERT: Of all input through the end of the file *)
    (*         Min stores the smallest value            *)
```

FIGURE 10.16 *Examples of loops with invariants*

Designing-with-Wisdom-

Loop Invariants and Design

The best designers construct loops by reasoning from invariants. For example, consider the design of a loop to search for some particular value, SearchVal, among the input. At run time, if the loop is being iterated, SearchVal has not been found. A proper loop invariant must indicate this fact. One possibile loop invariant would be:

All previous input values did not = SearchVal

Selecting a loop invariant begins the way all other design begins, by examining the desired result. Once the designer decides what needs to be true upon loop termination, the loop invariant and the algorithm follow.

The process of verifying the correctness of a loop can be reduced to the verification of four loop properties.

1) The loop must be properly initialized (loop **initialization**).
2) Each iteration must perform the desired task (loop **preservation**).
3) Upon loop exit the desired results are true (loop **finalization**).
4) The loop will eventually terminate execution (loop **termination**).

All four loop properties must be guaranteed in order to be sure that the loop is correct. Guaranteeing initialization is the same as verifying that the loop is properly set up to execute for the first iteration. Initialization holds if the loop invariant is true the first time it is encountered during loop execution. Forgetting to initialize variables properly before entering a loop is a common programming error. A careful consideration of initialization will detect such bugs.

Proving loop preservation is the same as showing that loop iteration performs the desired task. Since the loop invariant defines what must be true for each loop iteration, the easiest proof of preservation is to show that executing the body of the loop once always preserves the invariant. In this case, "preserves the invariant" means that if the loop invariant is true, and the loop body is executed once then the loop invariant is true afterwards.

When the loop terminates, two pieces of information may be assumed.

1) The loop condition has caused termination.
2) The loop invariant is still true.

Proving loop finalization amounts to arguing that these two pieces of information are sufficient to guarantee the desired loop postcondition.

The loop finalization argument ensures only that the desired results occur *if* the loop terminates. Loop termination argues that the loop *does* terminate. Verification of loop termination is a matter of examining the loop to ensure that each iteration makes progress toward a situation that causes the loop to terminate execution. If termination cannot be shown, then the potential for an infinite loop exists.

It is possible to verify the correctness of loops formally by proving each of these four properties. It is also possible to debug programs by mentally considering all four properties for each loop. Every loop must be properly initialized, preserved, finalized, and terminated for the program to be correct.

Designing-with-Wisdom-

Six Steps for Designing a Loop

The six steps below should be followed to design a loop.

1) Select the type of loop (WHILE, REPEAT, or LOOP).
2) Select the invariant (general algorithm).
3) Use the invariant to determine the loop condition.

4) Use the invariant to determine any initializations that are required prior to the loop.
5) Use the invariant to guide the design of the loop body.
6) Review the resulting loop for correct initialization, finalization, preservation, and termination.

Any loop can be designed correctly and reliably if these six steps are employed by the designer. In the next section, two examples are shown using these steps.

10.6 DESIGNING LOOPS

This section presents two examples that utilize the six-step loop design procedure suggested in the previous "Designing with Wisdom." These examples demonstrate the usefulness of loop invariants in designing and debugging loops. The first problem to be solved is defined in Figure 10.17.

TITLE
   Asterisk Double Characters

DESCRIPTION
   This program scans a user-specified input file for consecutive pairs of the same character. While the file is being processed, it is output to the standard output device. Any time that two consecutive occurrences of the same character are encountered they are displayed as a single asterisk, "*."

INPUT
   The only input from the user is a prompted reply to specify a file for processing. This entire file will be input.

OUTPUT
   The prompt for specifying the input file is:

                    Input file?

Following the user's response, two blank lines are output. Next the specified input file is copied to the standard output device with only the following change: Each time that a consecutive pair of the same character is found, it is replaced by a single "*" (Note that a character cannot be in two consecutive pairs so AAA is output as *A and not **).

ERRORS
   The program need not attempt error checking of any kind.

                                                          (continued)

EXAMPLE

Below is an sample execution. The user input is highlighted in the example. The contents of the "SHEEPISH" file, used by the program, are shown below.

Input file "SHEEPISH":

```
As the moon came up over the moor, the sheep bleated "Baa baa."
One enthusiastic ewe got carried away and bellowed "Baaa
Baaaaa!"
```

Execution summary:

```
Input file? SHEEPISH
```

```
As the m*n came up over the m*r, the sh*p bleated "B* B*".One
enthusiastic ewe got ca*ied away and be*owed "B*a B**a!"
```

FIGURE 10.17 *Asterisk double characters problem definition*

A top level algorithm for solving the asterisk double characters problem is shown in Figure 10.18.

```
WriteString( "Input file? " );
OpenInput("");
WriteLn; WriteLn; WriteLn;
(* Echo input file to output, replacing double chars with * *)
CloseInput;
```

FIGURE 10.18 *Top level algorithm for asterisk double characters*

The comment left to be refined in Figure 10.18 can be best accomplished by a loop. This is evident from the need to input repeatedly, examine and output characters. This loop can be designed using the earlier six step process. Figures 10.19 through 10.24 describe this six step approach to the design of the asterisk double characters problem.

Step 1 - Select the type of loop

Either a WHILE or REPEAT loop should be used whenever possible. The choice between these two is based upon whether the loop executes 0 or more times (a WHILE) or 1 or more times (a REPEAT). In this case there may be no characters in the file so the loop should be 0 or more times. The resulting algorithm is:

```
WriteString( "Input file? " );
OpenInput("");
WriteLn; WriteLn; WriteLn;

(* loop initialization? *)
WHILE (* INV: loop invariant *)
(* loop condition *) DO
    (* loop body *)
END;
CloseInput;
```

FIGURE 10.19 *Step 1 of loop design for asterisk double characters*

Step 2 - Select the invariant

Selecting an invariant is equivalent to deciding upon the basic algorithm for the loop. For this problem, the logical algorithm is to process another input character for each loop iteration. Assuming that the last input character is stored in the variable LastIn, an appropriate loop invariant would be as follows:

All input characters before LastIn have been echoed with double characters replaced by "*".

The resulting algorithm is:

```
WriteString( "Input file? " );
OpenInput("");
WriteLn; WriteLn; WriteLn;

(* loop initialization? *)
WHILE (* INV: All input characters before LastIn have been  *)
      (*       echoed with double characters replaced by "*" *)
(* loop condition *) DO
   (* loop body *)
END;
CloseInput;
```

FIGURE 10.20 *Step 2 of loop design for asterisk double characters*

Step 3 - Use the invariant to determine the loop condition

When the loop terminates, all of the characters from the input file must have been processed. Since the loop invariant states that all characters "before LastIn" have been processed, the loop must terminate when a read operation has encountered the end of the input file. For InOut the Done variable indicates if more input exists. The appropriate algorithm is:

```
WriteString( "Input file? " );
OpenInput("");
WriteLn; WriteLn; WriteLn;

(* loop initialization? *)
WHILE (* INV: All input characters before LastIn have been  *)
      (*       echoed with double characters replaced by "*" *)
Done DO
   (* loop body *)
END;
CloseInput;
```

FIGURE 10.21 *Step 3 of loop design for asterisk double characters*

Step 4 - Use the invariant to determine any initializations that are required prior to the loop

There are two things that should be considered when providing instructions to initialize a WHILE loop:

1) The loop invariant must be TRUE just before the loop executes.
2) All portions of the loop condition must be assigned.

In this case, the loop invariant is meaningful only if some character has been input into LastIn. Furthermore, the loop condition is assigned only if some input operation has occurred. Both of these requirements can be satisfied with an initial priming read. The resulting code is:

```
WriteString( "Input file? " );
OpenInput("");
WriteLn; WriteLn; WriteLn;

Read( LastIn );
WHILE (* INV: All input characters before LastIn have been  *)
      (*      echoed with double characters replaced by "*" *)
Done DO
   (* loop body *)
END;
CloseInput;
```

FIGURE 10.22 *Step 4 of loop design for asterisk double characters*

Step 5 - Use the invariant to guide the design of the loop body

This is generally the most difficult of the steps of loop design because some loop bodies are complicated algorithms. When designing the body of any loop a programmer must remember two points.

1) The loop invariant must be preserved.
2) A loop iteration must make progress toward loop completion.

For this problem, "progress toward loop completion" suggests that at least one new character should be input and processed for each iteration. In order to "preserve the invariant" it is necessary to compare the new character to the previous one, checking for double characters, before echoing. The code below appropriately completes this task.

```
WriteString( "Input file? " );
OpenInput("");
WriteLn; WriteLn; WriteLn;
```

(continued)

```
Read( LastIn );
WHILE (* INV: All input characters before LastIn have been  *)
      (*       echoed with double characters replaced by "*" *)
Done DO
    PreviousIn := LastIn;
    Read( LastIn );
    IF NOT Done THEN  (* no more input is available *)
        Write( PreviousIn )
    ELSIF PreviousIn=LastIn   (* a double character *)
        Write( "*" );
        Read( LastIn )      (* start with the next character *)
    ELSE
        Write( PreviousIn )
    END
END;
CloseInput;
```

FIGURE 10.23 *Step 5 of loop design for asterisk double characters*

Step 6 - Review the resulting loop for correct initialization,
       preservation, finalization, and termination

This last step is included to check correctness one last time. If all of the other steps were followed carefully this is merely a repetition of earlier thought processes. The appropriate questions to consider, and their answers for this solution, are given below:

Is the loop invariant TRUE initially (just before the loop)?
   Yes, because the first character has been read into
   LastIn.

If the loop invariant is TRUE and the loop condition is FALSE
(for a WHILE loop), is the necessary condition after the loop
guaranteed?
   Yes, because Done can be FALSE only when an attempt to
   input another character for LastIn has failed
   bacause no characters remain. The loop invariant states
   that all prior input characters have been appropriately
   processed.

Is the loop invariant preserved for each loop iteration?
   Yes, because the loop condition must be TRUE (for a WHILE)
   prior to each loop iteration. Therefore, LastIn stores
   some valid file character. If another read is attempted
   three possible cases exist.

      1) There are no more characters in the file.
      2) The new input character matches the previous one.
      3) The new input character differs from the previous one.

   Each of these cases can be shown to be handled correctly
   by the loop body, so the invariant is always preserved.

Is the loop required to terminate?
   Yes, because each loop iteration reads at least one more
   character from the file. At some point, the characters of
   the file must be completely consumed so the loop condition
   will become FALSE and the loop will terminate.

FIGURE 10.24 *Step 6 of loop design for asterisk double characters*

A complete program, called AsterDoubleChars, for this algorithm is shown in Figure 10.25.

```
MODULE AsterDoubleChars;
    (* This program echoes a user specified input file on  *)
    (* standard output device, replacing double occurrences *)
    (* of the same character with "*"                       *)
    FROM InOut IMPORT WriteString, Read, Write, WriteLn, Done,
                    OpenInput, CloseInput;
    VAR
        LastIn : CHAR;
        PreviousIn : CHAR;
BEGIN
    WriteString( "Input file? " );
    OpenInput("");
    WriteLn; WriteLn; WriteLn;

    Read( LastIn );
    WHILE (* INV: All input characters before LastIn have been  *)
          (*      echoed with double characters replaced by "*" *)
    Done DO
        PreviousIn := LastIn;
        Read( LastIn );
        IF NOT Done THEN
            Write( PreviousIn );
        ELSIF PreviousIn=LastIn THEN
            Write( "*" );
            Read( LastIn )
        ELSE
            Write( PreviousIn )
        END
    END;
    CloseInput;
END AsterDoubleChars.
```

FIGURE 10.25 *AsterDoubleChars program*

The second example problem involves examining the properties of a bouncing ball. Figure 10.26 contains the problem definition.

TITLE
    Bouncing Ball

DESCRIPTION
    When a ball bounces, the height of each bounce can be described by the following equation:

$$BounceHeight = DropHeight * BouncinessFactor$$

    Every ball bounces a little differently from any other. The "BouncinessFactor" describes how bouncy the ball is. "DropHeight" is the height from which the ball was dropped.

(continued)

This program requires the user to input a bounciness factor and beginning height for a bouncing ball (in centimeters). The program then graphs subsequent bounces of the ball until a bounce under 1 centimeter has occurred.

INPUT

The user is prompted to input two cardinal values. The first input is the bounciness factor times 1000 (for example, an input of 788 denotes a bounciness factor of 0.788). The second input denotes the height of the original bounce in centimeters.

OUTPUT

The prompts for specifying the two input values are given on separate lines as follows:

```
Bounciness factor (x1000)?
Original drop height (in cm.)?
```

Following a blank line, a separate output line is produced for every subsequent ball bounce. The line contains the cardinal height of the bounce rounded to the nearest cm. (right justified in a seven character field) followed by two blanks followed by "*" characters (one for each cm. of bounce height). These lines continue for subsequent ball bounces until the height of a bounce is less than 1 cm.

A blank line is output following the above. Finally, the accumulated total of count and distance of all bounces is displayed on two separate lines as follows (where <cnt> denotes the total number of bounces and <dis> denotes the total distance of fall for all bounces to the nearest cm.):

```
Number of bounces: <cnt>
Total distance bounced: <dis>
```

ERRORS

The program need not attempt error checking of any kind.

EXAMPLE

Below is an sample execution. The user input is highlighted in the example.

```
Bounciness factor (x1000)? 800
Original drop height (in cm.)? 10

      8  ********
      6  ******
      5  *****
      4  ****
      3  ***
      3  ***
      2  **
      2  **
      1  *
      1  *
      1  *

Number of bounces: 11
Total distance bounced: 3/
```

FIGURE 10.26 *Bouncing ball problem*

A top level algorithm for solving the bouncing ball problem is shown in Figure 27.

```
WriteString( "Bounciness factor (x1000)? " );
ReadCard( BounceFactor );   WriteLn;
WriteString( "Original drop height (in cm.)? " );
ReadCard( FirstHeight ); WriteLn;

WriteLn;

(* Calculate & display all bounces down to 1 cm. *)
WriteLn;
WriteString( "Number of bounces: ");
WriteCard( BounceCnt,0 );   WriteLn;
WriteString( "Total distance bounced: " );
WriteCard( TRUNC(BounceDist+0.5),0 );   WriteLn;
```

FIGURE 10.27 *Top level algorithm for bouncing ball*

Again, the unrefined portion of the algorithm requires a loop. The design of this loop is shown in Figures 10.28 through 10.33.

Step 1 - Select the type of loop

For this problem, the ball is allowed to bounce through the first bounce less than 1 cm. Therefore, the loop will be executed one or more times, suggesting a REPEAT. This results in:

```
WriteString( "Bounciness factor (x1000)? " );
ReadCard( BounceFactor );   WriteLn;
WriteString( "Original drop height (in cm.)? " );
ReadCard( FirstHeight );   WriteLn;
WriteLn;
(* loop initialization? *)
REPEAT
    (* loop body *)
    (* INV: loop invariant *)
UNTIL (* loop condition *);

WriteLn;
WriteString( "Number of bounces: ");
WriteCard( BounceCnt,0 );   WriteLn;
WriteString( "Total distance bounced: " );
WriteCard( TRUNC(BounceDist+0.5),0 );   WriteLn;
```

FIGURE 10.28 *Step 1 of loop design for bouncing ball*

Step 2 - Select the invariant

It is often best to supply a postcondition for the loop in order to determine what the loop invariant should be. For the loop from Figure 10.28 the following postcondition is required:

```
(* Loop post: All bounces through LastHeight have been    *)
(*            processed.                                    *)
(*         & LastHeight is the height of the first          *)
(*            bounce under 1 cm.                            *)
(*         & BounceCnt is the count of all bounces.         *)
(*         & BounceDist is the total bounce height.         *)
```

(continued

The most straightforward solution is a loop that processes another bounce for each loop iteration. An appropriate invariant can be found by expressing partial progress toward the loop postcondition as shown below

```
(* INV: All bounces through LastHeight have been      *)
(*      processed.                                      *)
(*      & All bounces prior to the last had height >= 1 cm.*)
(*      & BounceCnt is the count of all bounces processed.*)
(*      & BounceDist is the total bounce height thus far. *)
```

The resulting algorithm is:

```
WriteString( "Bounciness factor (x1000)? " );
ReadCard( BounceFactor );  WriteLn;
WriteString( "Original drop height (in cm.)? " );
ReadCard( FirstHeight );  WriteLn;
WriteLn;
(* loop initialization? *)
REPEAT
   (* loop body *)
   (* INV: All bounces through LastHeight have been      *)
   (*      processed                                      *)
   (*      & All bounces prior to the last had height >= 1 cm.*)
   (*      & BounceCnt is the count of all bounces processed *)
   (*      & BounceDist is the total bounce height thus far *)
UNTIL (* loop condition *);
(* Loop post: All bounces through LastHeight have been *)
(*            processed                                 *)
(*            & LastHeight is the height of the first   *)
(*            bounce under 1 cm.                        *)
(*            & BounceCnt is the count of all bounces   *)
(*            & BounceDist is the total bounce height   *)

WriteLn;
WriteString( "Number of bounces: ");
WriteCard( BounceCnt,0 );  WriteLn;
WriteString( "Total distance bounced: " );
WriteCard( TRUNC(BounceDist+0.5),0 );  WriteLn;
```

FIGURE 10.29 *Step 2 of loop design for bouncing ball*

Step 3 - Use the invariant to determine the loop condition

The loop invariant requires only one thing to be equivalent to the loop postcondition.

LastHeight must be less than 1 cm.

This results in the following algorithm.

```
WriteString( "Bounciness factor (x1000)? " );
ReadCard( BounceFactor );  WriteLn;
WriteString( "Original drop height (in cm.)? " );
ReadCard( FirstHeight );  WriteLn;
WriteLn;
(* loop initialization? *)
```

(continued)

```
REPEAT
    (* loop body *)
    (* INV: All bounces through LastHeight have been          *)
    (*       processed                                        *)
    (*     & All bounces prior to the last had height >= 1 cm.*)
    (*     & BounceCnt is the count of all bounces processed  *)
    (*     & BounceDist is the total bounce height thusfar    *)
UNTIL LastHeight<1.0;
(* Loop post: All bounces through LastHeight have been  *)
(*            processed                                 *)
(*          & LastHeight is the height of the first     *)
(*            bounce under 1 cm.                        *)
(*          & BounceCnt is the count of all bounces     *)
(*          & BounceDist is the total bounce height     *)

WriteLn;
WriteString( "Number of bounces: ");
WriteCard( BounceCnt,0 );  WriteLn;
WriteString( "Total distance bounced: " );
WriteCard( TRUNC(BounceDist+0.5),0 );  WriteLn;
```

FIGURE 10.30 *Step 3 of loop design for bouncing ball*

---

*Step 4 - Use the invariant to determine any initializations that
         are required prior to the loop.*

Initialization is somewhat more difficult to determine for a REPEAT loop, because both
the loop invariant and loop condition occur at the bottom of the loop. However, the
invariant includes three variables, LastHeight, BounceCnt and BounceDist.
With the information that no previous bounces have been processed, these three variables
are correctly initialized as shown below:

```
WriteString( "Bounciness factor (x1000)? " );
ReadCard( BounceFactor );  WriteLn;
WriteString( "Original drop height (in cm.)? " );
ReadCard( FirstHeight );  WriteLn;
WriteLn;
LastHeight := FLOAT(FirstHeight);
BounceCnt := 0;
BounceDist := 0.0;
REPEAT
    (* loop body *)
    (* INV: All bounces through LastHeight have been          *)
    (*       processed                                        *)
    (*     & All bounces prior to the last had height >= 1 cm.*)
    (*     & BounceCnt is the count of all bounces processed  *)
    (*     & BounceDist is the total bounce height thusfar    *)
UNTIL LastHeight<1.0;
(* Loop post: All bounces through LastHeight have been  *)
(*            processed                                 *)
(*          & LastHeight is the height of the first     *)
(*            bounce under 1 cm.                        *)
(*          & BounceCnt is the count of all bounces     *)
(*          & BounceDist is the total bounce height     *)
```

(continued)

```
WriteLn;
WriteString( "Number of bounces: ");
WriteCard( BounceCnt,0 );  WriteLn;
WriteString( "Total distanced bounced: " );
WriteCard( TRUNC(BounceDist+0.5),0 );  WriteLn;
```

FIGURE 10.31 *Step 4 of loop design for bouncing ball*

Step 5 - Use the invariant to guide the design of the loop body

Each loop iteration must first calculate a new bounce height and then process this height. The loop body shown below performs the correct task.

```
WriteString( "Bounciness factor (x1000)? " );
ReadCard( BounceFactor );  WriteLn;
WriteString( "Original drop height (in cm.)? " );
ReadCard( FirstHeight );  WriteLn;
WriteLn;
LastHeight := FLOAT(FirstHeight);
BounceCnt := 0;
BounceDist := 0.0;
REPEAT
    LastHeight := LastHeight * FLOAT(BounceFactor)/1000.0;
    WriteAsterLine( TRUNC(LastHeight+0.5) );
    BounceCnt := BounceCnt + 1;
    BounceDist := BounceDist + LastHeight;
    (* INV: All bounces through LastHeight have been     *)
    (*        processed                                  *)
    (*      & All bounces prior to the last had height >= 1 cm.*)
    (*      & BounceCnt is the count of all bounces processed  *)
    (*      & BounceDist is the total bounce height thusfar    *)
UNTIL LastHeight<1.0;
(* Loop post: All bounces through LastHeight have been  *)
(*            processed                                 *)
(*        &   LastHeight is the height of the first     *)
(*            bounce under 1 cm.                         *)
(*        &   BounceCnt is the count of all bounces     *)
(*        &   BounceDist is the total bounce height     *)

WriteLn;
WriteString( "Number of bounces: ");
WriteCard( BounceCnt,0 );  WriteLn;
WriteString( "Total distance bounced: " );
WriteCard( TRUNC(BounceDist+0.5),0 );  WriteLn;
```

FIGURE 10.32 *Step 5 of loop design for bouncing ball*

Step 6 - Review the resulting loop for correct initialization, preservation, finalization, and termination

The questions to be considered are only slightly different for a REPEAT than for a WHILE loop.

(continued)

Is the loop invariant TRUE initially (after the 1st iteration)?
  Yes, because the distance after the first bounce has been processed and all variables have been updated appropriately.
If the loop invariant is TRUE and the loop condition is TRUE, (for a REPEAT loop) is the necessary condition after the loop guaranteed?
  Yes, because if the loop condition is TRUE, then LastHeight *is less than 1 cm., and the loop condition guarantees that all previous bounces processed were greater than or equal to 1 cm.*

Is the loop invariant preserved for each loop iteration?
  Yes, because another complete bounce is processed, and all variables mentioned in the invariant are correctly updated.

Is the loop required to terminate?
  Only if the user inputs a bounciness factor lower than 1000. This is all right, because the problem definition states that all input may be assumed correct. However, this does make the program less robust and perhaps should be modified.

FIGURE 10.33 *Step 6 of loop design for bouncingball*

A complete program, called Ba l lBounce, for this algorithm is shown in Figure 10.34. This program includes the WriteAsterLine procedure omitted from the algorithm. It also checks for a bounciness factor that would result in an infinite loop.

```
MODULE BallBounce;
     (* This program simulates a bouncing ball *)
   FROM InOut IMPORT WriteString, WriteCard, Write, WriteLn,
                     ReadCard;
   VAR
      BounceFactor : CARDINAL;
      FirstHeight : CARDINAL;
      LastHeight. : REAL;
      BounceCnt : CARDINAL;
      BounceDist : REAL;

   PROCEDURE WriteAsterLine( AsterCount : CARDINAL );
        (* PRE:  AsterCount is assigned                       *)
        (* POST: One line containing the value of AsterCount  *)
        (*       followed by that many asterisks is output    *)
   BEGIN
      WriteCard( AsterCount,7 );
      WriteString( "  " );
      WHILE  AsterCount>0 DO
         Write ( "*" );
         DEC( AsterCount );
      END;
      WriteLn;
   END WriteAsterLine;
```

(continued)

```
BEGIN   (* BallBounce *)
   WriteString( "Bounciness factor (x1000)? " );
   ReadCard( BounceFactor );   WriteLn;
   IF BounceFactor>=1000 THEN
      WriteString( "Bounciness must be < 1000 - FATAL ERROR" );
      WriteLn;
      HALT;
   END;
   WriteString( "Original drop height (in cm.)? " );
   ReadCard( FirstHeight );   WriteLn;
   WriteLn;
   LastHeight := FLOAT(FirstHeight);
   BounceCnt := 0;
   BounceDist := 0.0;
   REPEAT
      LastHeight := LastHeight * FLOAT(BounceFactor)/1000.0;
      WriteAsterLine( TRUNC(LastHeight+0.5) );
      BounceCnt := BounceCnt + 1;
      BounceDist := BounceDist + LastHeight;
      (* INV: All bounces through LastHeight have been      *)
      (*        processed                                   *)
      (*    AND All bounces prior to the last had height >= 1 cm.*)
      (*    AND BounceCnt is the count of all bounces processed *)
      (*    AND  BounceDist is the total bounce height thus far *)
   UNTIL LastHeight<1.0;
   (* Loop post: All bounces through LastHeight have been  *)
   (*              processed                               *)
   (*         AND  LastHeight is the height of the first   *)
   (*              bounce under 1 cm.                       *)
   (*         AND  BounceCnt is the count of all bounces   *)
   (*         AND  BounceDist is the total bounce height   *)

   WriteLn;
   WriteString( "Number of bounces: " );
   WriteCard( BounceCnt,0 );   WriteLn;
   WriteString( "Total distance bounced: " );
   WriteCard( TRUNC(BounceDist+0.5),0 );   WriteLn;

END BallBounce.
```

FIGURE 10.34 *BallBounce program*

10.7 DEBUGGING LOOPS

The best technique for debugging an existing loop is found in Step 6 of the process for designing a loop. To debug a loop requires a consideration of the four essential loop properties. These properties can be restated as the following questions:

> Is the loop invariant properly initialized?
> Is the loop invariant preserved?
> Do the loop invariant and loop condition properly finalize?
> Does the loop terminate?

In order to consider these questions, the programmer needs to know the loop invariant. If the original programmer did not specify an invariant, then it is necessary to pick an appropriate one. It is usually more difficult to supply a loop invariant for an existing piece of code than to do so when the code is designed. However, many bugs can be uncovered just by trying to identify a loop invariant.

Consideration of the four essential loop properties can be performed on many levels. A very rigorous mathematical proof of correctness can be performed. Such a proof requires extremely formal assertions and loop invariants. This is time consuming and prone to human error.

A less formal method of debugging uses code tracing techniques. The four essential properties of a loop suggest the following traces for each loop:

1) Trace the code up to the first time the loop invariant is encountered, and ensure that the invariant is TRUE.
2) Trace a "typical" loop iteration, beginning with the assumption that the loop invariant is TRUE, and show that it remains TRUE after the iteration.
3) Trace the final execution of the loop to see if the desired results are ensured after the loop.
4) Trace the loop a few consecutive times and examine the results to be certain that loop termination must occur.

Another debugging technique is to output the value of the invariant while the program executes. Since many invariants are complex logical expressions, this technique may best be accomplished by displaying the values of the variables that play important roles in the loop invariant. For example the loop from the BallBounce program could include internal write instructions to output the values of LastHeight, BounceCnt, and BounceDist each time the loop body is executed.

10.8 SUMMARY

Loops are used to perform repetitive execution of a task. The task to be repeated is known as the loop body. The situation that causes repetition to terminate is known as the loop condition.

Designing loops starts in the same way as designing other types of code. The best design technique begins by examining the goal or postcondition. A careful, six-step process is presented for completing loop design.

Loop design and loop correctness go hand in hand. The four essential properties for loop correctness are:

Initialization
Preservation
Finalization
Termination

These properties rely upon the loop invariant. Designers should design from a loop invariant and debuggers should debug from the loop invariant.

Many programming errors occur within loops. This results from the fact that loops are more complicated to understand and design than sequences or selection. Short cuts of the six-step loop design process are dangerous and likely to result in bugs. Following the established design techniques and considering initialization, preservation, finalization and termination of all loops results in code that works the *first time*.

||| KEY TERMS

repetition	test at the top of the loop
loop	test at the bottom of the loop
WHILE loop	EXIT instruction
REPEAT loop	functionally equivalent
LOOP loop	loop invariant
FOR loop	loop initialization
loop body	loop preservation
loop condition	loop finalization
iteration	loop termination

||| EXERCISES

1. Specify the output for each of the loops below:

    a)
    ```
    CountByTwo := 0;
    WHILE CountByTwo<20 DO
        WriteCard( CountByTwo, 0 );
        CountByTwo := CountByTwo + 2;
    END
    ```

    b)
    ```
    Counter := 3;
    REPEAT
        WriteCard( Counter, 0 );
        INC( Counter );
    UNTIL Counter>4
    ```

    c)
    ```
    CountAgain := 28;
    WHILE CountAgain>20 DO
        CountAgain := CountAgain - 1;
        WriteCard( CountAgain, 0 );
    END
    ```

    d)
    ```
    Count := 33;
    REPEAT
        INC( Count );
        WriteCard( Count, 0 );
        INC( Count );
    UNTIL Counter>4
    ```

e)
```
AnotherCount := 42;
WHILE AnotherCount>20 DO
    WriteCard( AnotherCount, 0 );
    INC( AnotherCount );
END
```

2. Supply postconditions for each of the loops below:

   a)
   ```
   Suma := 0;
   CountByTwo := 0;
   WHILE CountByTwo<20 DO
       Suma := Suma + CountByTwo;
       CountByTwo := CountByTwo + 2;
   END
   ```

   b)
   ```
   Sumb := 0;
   Counter := 3;
   REPEAT
       Sumb := Sumb + Counter;
       INC( Counter );
   UNTIL Counter>4
   ```

   c)
   ```
   Sumc := 0;
   CountAgain := 28;
   WHILE CountAgain>20 DO
       CountAgain := CountAgain - 1;
       Sumc := Sumc + CountAgain;
   END
   ```

   d)
   ```
   Sumd := 0;
   Count := 33;
   REPEAT
       INC( Count );
       Sumd := Sumd + Count;
       INC( Count );
   UNTIL Counter>4
   ```

3. Supply loop invariants for all of the loops from Exercise 2.

4. Consider the code to calculate five factorial (5!) from Figure 10.13.
   a) Rewrite this code to produce code that is functionally equivalent, but uses a WHILE instead of a REPEAT loop (you may use IFs also).
   b) Rewrite this code to produce code that is functionally equivalent, but that uses a LOOP instead of a REPEAT loop (you may use IFs and EXITs also).

5. Consider the three loops contained in Figure 10.16.
   a) Rewrite the code from the first REPEAT loop (the code to skip blank characters on an input line) to produce code that is functionally equivalent, but that uses a WHILE instead of a REPEAT loop (you may use IFs also).
   b) Rewrite the code from the first WHILE loop (the code to find the greatest whole divisor of Number) to produce code that is functionally equivalent, but that uses a REPEAT instead of a WHILE loop (you may use IFs also).

c) Rewrite the code from the second WHILE loop (the code to find the smallest input integer) to produce code that is functionally equivalent, but that uses a REPEAT instead of a WHILE loop (you may use IFs also).

6. Consider the TotalTenTriples procedure from Figure 10.9.
   a) How many invariants does this loop require?
   b) Supply the loop invariants for this loop.

7. Each part below specifies a loop postcondition and loop invariant. Write the corresponding loop (you may use all WHILE loops).
   a) POST: LastIn is the last input integer & LastIn = -33 & All input prior to LastIn < > -33
      INV: LastIn is the last input integer & All input prior to LastIn < > -33
   b) POST: MaxNeg is the largest of all input integers that are negative (MaxNeg = MIN(INTEGER) if no negatives have been input) AND Done
      INV: MaxNeg is the largest of all input integers that are negative (MaxNeg = MIN(INTEGER) if no negatives have been input)
   c) POST: OddSum = $1 + 3 + \ldots + 99$
      INV: (OddSum = $1 + 3 + \ldots + J$) & ($0 < J < 100$) & (J MOD 2 = 1)
   d) POST: EvenSum = $0 + 2 + \ldots + 1000$
      INV: (EvenSum = $I + (I + 2) + (I + 4) + \ldots + 1000$) & ($0 < = I < = 1000$) & (I MOD 2) = 0

8. Identify which style of loop (WHILE, REPEAT, or LOOP) is the best choice for each of the following algorithms:
   a) Summing all cardinals from 1 to 1000.
   b) Summing all cardinals from 0 to N, where N could be any value from 0 to MAX (CARDINAL).
   c) Outputting all input characters up to, but not including, the first period.
   d) Outputting all input characters up to, and including, the first exclamation point.

||| PROGRAMMING PROJECTS

1. Write and test the GreatestCommonFactor function defined below.

```
PROCEDURE GreatestCommonFactor( ValA : CARDINAL;
                                ValB : CARDINAL )
   CARDINAL;
      (* PRE:  ValA>=1 & ValB>=1                        *)
      (* POST: (ValA MOD RESULT = 0)     AND            *)
      (*       (ValB MOD RESULT = 0)     AND            *)
      (*       No value greater than RESULT makes the   *)
      (*       above two conditions TRUE                *)
```

2. Write and test the LeastCommonMultiple function defined below.

```
PROCEDURE LeastCommonMultiple( ValA : CARDINAL;
                               ValB : CARDINAL )
  CARDINAL;
  (* PRE:  ValA>=1 & ValB>=1                          *)
  (* POST: (RESULT MOD ValA = 0)     AND              *)
  (*        (RESULT MOD ValB = 0)     AND             *)
  (*        No value smaller than RESULT makes the    *)
  (*        above two conditions TRUE                 *)
```

3. Write a program to solve the following problem.

TITLE
Pythagorean Triples

DESCRIPTION
Pythagorean triples, named after the Greek philosopher and mathematician, are three cardinal values such that the square of the largest exactly equals the sum of the squares of the other two. The triple (3,4,5) is a Pythagorean triple, because $5*5 = (4*4) + (3*3)$. The Pythagorean Theorem guarantees that all right triangles with sides of integral length have sides that form a Pythagorean triple. This program outputs all Pythagorean triples where each of the three cardinals of the triple is less than or equal to some user-specified value.

INPUT
A single cardinal is input in response to the prompt. This value is the maximum for each of the three values of the triple.

OUTPUT
The input prompt is as follows:

Please specify maximum short side length:

Following the prompt is a blank line followed by all Pythagorean triples, one per line in the form shown below.

< FirstVal,SecondVal,ThirdVal >

In order to reduce repetitious output, each triple should be output so that First Val < = SecondVal < = ThirdVal.

ERRORS
Non-cardinal input produces undefined results. No attempt is made to verify that the triple represents valid triangle sides.

EXAMPLE

Input is highlighted in the example execution below:

Please specify maximum short side length: 20

        < 3/4/5 >
        < 5/12/13 >
        < 6/8/10 >
        < 8/15/17 >
        < 9/12/15 >
        < 12/16/20 >

4. Write a program to solve the following problem.

TITLE

Histogram from File Data

DESCRIPTION

This program inputs a sequence of cardinal values from a user-specified file and outputs a horizontal histogram with one bar output for each cardinal. The user can specify the histogram size.

INPUT

The user must supply two pieces of information in response to prompts. The first input is a size factor, a cardinal value greater than one. The size factor indicates how big to make the histogram. For example a size factor of 10 means to plot one histogram character for every 10 units of input data. The second input is the name of a file containing the data to be plotted in the histogram.

Input from the user-specified file must consist of zero or more cardinal values to be plotted. All input to be plotted should be followed with the value 0.

OUTPUT

The user prompt preceding the input size factor is:

Specify size factor (units/char):

The user prompt preceding the file name input is:

Please specify data file name:

Following two blank lines, each consecutive cardinal input from the user-specified file produces a horizontal bar of asterisks. The number of asterisks in the bar is the cardinal value divided by the size factor and truncated to the next lower cardinal. Following each bar line a blank line is output.

ERRORS
1) An invalid file name causes the program to halt with the following message INVALID FILE!
2) A size factor of zero produces undefined results.
3) Any non-cardinal values in the input file produce undefined results.
4) Any non-cardinal input for a size factor produces undefined results.
5) No bar line may contain more than 50 asterisks. If the value of the input cardinal results in an output line that exceeds this limitation, then a line with 49 asterisks and a question mark is output.

EXAMPLE
The file below is used as input to the example:

File name: HISTODAT
File contents: 73 85 99 137 66 2000 153 0

For the example below, all user input is highlighted.

```
Specify size factor (units/char): 10
Please specify data file name: HISTODAT
```

```
*******

********

*********

*************

******

****************************************************?

**************
```

5. Write the histogram program from Project 4 with the following change.

Prompt the user for a another input (prompted just before file name prompt). This input must be a cardinal that specifies the number of bar lines for the width of each bar. For example, if the user specifies 3, then each cardinal produces three consecuti horizontal lines of asterisks of the same length for each bar of the histogram. Consec tive bars should still be separated by a single blank line.

6. Write a program to solve the following problem.

DESCRIPTION

A golf pro shop has just installed a new personal computer to total golf scores for an upcoming tournament. For this golf tournament, every player will play nine holes and turn in the completed scorecard to the pro shop. The owner of the pro shop will enter scores for each of the nine holes. The program needs to display the total for each nine hole score so the total calculated by the player can be verified. The program must also keep track of the best round (lowest score) and the number of rounds lower than par (36 for this course).

INPUT

A prompt is made on the screen prior to data entry for each contestant. The owner may then input nine cardinal values separated by blanks. After the last player is entered, an input consisting of a 0 for the first hole is entered.

OUTPUT

Prior to the input for a player the following prompt is displayed.

Next Player?

Following the input for a player a separate output line, like the one below, is output to display the player's score, $<S>$, for the round (total of all nine input cardinals):

Round Score : $<S>$

After all players are processed, the following two lines are output, where $<L>$ is the lowest of all round scores input and $<N>$ is the count of round scores that were less than 36:

Best Round: $<L>$
Number of Players Under Par: $<N>$

ERRORS

No attempt is made to verify any score's validity.

EXAMPLE

Input is highlighted in the example execution below.

Next Player? 5 4 5 6 4 3 5 4 6
Round Score: 42

Next Player? 5 3 4 4 4 3 4 3 5
Round Score: 35

Next Player? 4 3 4 3 4 3 4 3 5
Round Score: 33

Next Player? 6 3 4 3 4 2 4 4 4
Round Score: 34

Next Player? 5 4 5 4 4 2 4 4 5
Round Score: 37

Next Player? 0

Best Round: 33
Number of Players Under Par: 3

7. Write a program to solve the following problem.

TITLE
Parity Checker

DESCRIPTION
When digital data is communicated via telephone lines, it is often transmitted in 8-bit parcels. Each of the 8 bits can be interpreted as either a zero (0) or a one (1). Many times the first seven bits of the parcel are data and the eighth bit is a "parity bit." The transmitter uses this eighth bit to force the eight bit parcel to be either even or odd parity. The receiver is able to check the validity of transmission by ensuring that the correct parity has been transmitted. To have even parity, the number of "1" bits in the 8-bit parcel must be even; for odd parity the number of 1s must be odd. If the transmitter is sending with odd parity, then it forces the eighth bit to "0" when the first seven have odd parity and to "1" when the first seven have even parity.

This program inputs 8-bit parcels, stored as character strings, from a user-specified input file. After each parcel, the program displays the its parity.

INPUT
The user is prompted to specify the file name of the 8-bit parcels for input. This file is expected to contain zero or more lines of parcels. Each line should contain exactly one 8-bit parcel as a character string of consecutive 0s and 1s.

OUTPUT
The prompt for the user-specified file is as follows:

Specify data parcel file name:

Each input line from the file is displayed exactly as it appears in the file. At the end of the line either after a single blank, " < <even> > " or " < <odd> > " is displayed to indicate even or odd parity, respectively, for the parcel. Output lines continue until the has been entirely processed.

ERRORS
Leading bits that are not "0" or "1" are ignored on each line and input begins with the first "0" or "1".

All input errors cause the following message after the display of the input line and in place of " < <even> > " or " < <odd> > ":

[[ERROR]]

These errors include too few bits in the parcel, more than eight characters on the input line and any bit character that is not "0" or "1".

EXAMPLE

Below is the file used for the example:

> File Name: TRANSDAT1
> File Contents: 00011101
> 11111110
> 10101011
> 000X0000
> 11011011
> 11b10101
> 110

Below is a sample program execution with user input highlighted.

```
Specify data parcel file name: TRANSDAT1

    00011101 <<even>>
    11111110 <<odd>>
    10101011 <<odd>>
    000X0000 [[ERROR]]
    11011011 <<even>>
    11b10101 [[ERROR]]
    110 [[ERROR]]
```

8. Write a program to solve the following problem.

TITLE

Merit Evaluation Summary

DESCRIPTION

Betatest International is a large corporation that believes strongly in peer merit evaluation of employees. Every company employee is evaluated annually via a questionnaire consisting of seven questions. For each of the questions the valid responses are integers from 5 (for the highest recommendation) to 1 (for the lowest). The respondent may leave any question blank to indicate "no opinion." The Director of Personnel selects several peers that must complete the evaluation questionnaire for each employee. The Personnel Office collects the questionnaire responses on computer mark-sensitive forms. All information is stored automatically so that all responses for a single employee are in a separate file with one line of the file for each of the seven questions.

The purpose of this program is to process the questionnaire files and output summary information for one or more employees. The user of this program must specify the name(s) of one or more employee questionnaire files. The program must report summary scores for each question and an average evaluation for all seven questions.

INPUT

The only two inputs from the user's perspective are prompted requests to continue and for a file name to process. In response to the request to continue, only an uppercase "Y" is an acceptable affirmative response. This program makes no attempt to identify invalid file names.

The data in each of the input files must consist of exactly seven lines of data. (Each line corresponds to the collection of all responses to one question for the employee.) On each line, the responses are consecutive characters from 1 to 5 and each line must be terminated by a "*" character. The number of responses on a single line may vary because a blank response from a respondent is not recorded in the file.

OUTPUT

The prompt for continuation is as follows:

Process a file (Y or N)?

The prompt for a file name is as follows:

Specify employee file for processing:

This prompt is followed by a blank line and then by the eight lines of summary information below:

Question #1: <ave1>
Question #2: <ave2>
Question #3: <ave3>
Question #4: <ave4>
Question #5: <ave5>
Question #6: <ave6>
Question #7: <ave7>
Summary evaluation: <FinAve>

The notation above uses <ave1>, <ave2>, ..., <ave7> to symbolize the average (mean) of all responses to the corresponding question. <FinAve> symbolizes the average of the seven response averages [(<ave1> + <ave2> + ... + <ave7>) / 7]. All averages output are rounded to the nearest cardinal value.

Following the output for one file, there are two blank lines before the user input prompt is repeated.

ERRORS

Since the input files are generated by a different program, there are very few errors possible. Only the three forms of erroneous input listed below can occur in a file.

1) If there are no responses to a particular question, then the input line will contain only EOL. In this event, both this question output line and the "Summary evaluation" line should specify the following in place of the average: NO RESPONSES.

2) The other program that creates these input files occasionally places a 6 or 7 as a response. Such responses should be ignored for calculating averages.

3) If asterisks are omitted from the end of lines the program will be unreliable.

EXAMPLE

Below is a sample execution. The user input is highlighted in the example. The two files used for input are "John" and "Sue". The data in these files is summarized below.

Input file "John":   Input file "Sue":

```
1212*           55*
33333*            4655*
4*            3*
241333*             *
22*            44*
233*            555*
4*            5*
```

Execution summary:

```
Process a file (Y or N)? Y
Specify employee file for processing: John

Question #1: 2
Question #2: 3
Question #3: 4
Question #4: 3
Question #5: 2
Question #6: 3
Question #7: 4
Summary evaluation: 3

Process a file (Y or N)? Y
Specify employee file for processing: Sue

Question #1: 5
Question #2: 5
Question #3: 3
Question #4: NO RESPONSES
Question #5: 4
Question #6: 5
Question #7: 5
Summary evaluation: NO RESPONSES

Process a file (Y or N)? N
```

11

INTRODUCTION TO DATA ABSTRACTION

|1.1 MORE ABSTRACTION

Control structures are important in programming, but programming is more than control structures. **Data structures**, the program units for storing information, are just as important.

One of the most powerful design tools is control abstraction. Since abstraction is a good idea for control structures, it makes sense that abstraction is also a good idea for data structures. The name given to the related collection of programming techniques is **data abstraction**. As with control abstraction, data abstraction emphasizes the important features and suppresses (abstracts) certain details.

Data abstraction occurs in many forms. Wisely chosen variable names are a simple form of data abstraction. The variable name CurrentTemperature is a better choice than T. The emphasis conveyed by CurrentTemperature is that it stores a value representing the current temperature. The variable name T does not convey the same message.

Modern high level programming languages include numerous facilities specifically to support data abstraction. In this chapter, four Modula-2 language features supporting data abstraction are presented. Two of these features are program objects—constants and types. The other two features are data types—enumerated types and subranges.

11.2 CONSTANTS

Variables are used in programs to represent data. The value of a variable is not determined until a program executes. During execution, the variable's value may change many times.

Constants also appear frequently in programs. The following are all valid Modula-2 constants:

```
7.3   (* type REAL *)
3     (* type CARDINAL *)
"$"   (* type CHAR *)
TRUE(* type BOOLEAN *)
```

A constant differs from a variable in two important ways.

1) The value of the constant is known when the program is written
   (at **compile time**).
2) The value of a constant does *not* change during program execution.

Variables in Modula-2 are named by identifiers. These names are declared in a VAR declaration and used, within the appropriate scope, to refer to the variable.

Modula-2 also permits the programmer to declare constants. **Programmer-defined constants** are also named by identifiers and declared in a **CONST** declaration that is similar to the VAR declaration. A CONST declaration specifies the name of the constant and the associated value. Figure 11.1 contains the syntax diagram for a CONST declaration.

```
ConstantDeclaration:

    CONST ──────▶ ConstIdentifier ──▶ = ──▶ ConstExpression ──▶ ; ──▶
                └──────────────────────────────────────────────┘

ConstIdentifier:

    (* Can be any valid identifier not previously declared *)
    (* locally within the same scope                       *)

ConstExpression:

    (* Can be any expression where all of *)
    (* the operands are constants         *)

NOTE: The type of a constant expression can be
      BOOLEAN, CARDINAL, CHAR, INTEGER, REAL, SET,
      enumerated, or string
```

FIGURE 11.1 *Syntax diagram for ConstantDeclaration*

Modula-2 constants are restricted to be of certain types (BOOLEAN, CARDINAL, CHAR, INTEGER, REAL, SET, enumerated, or string). Some example CONST declarations are shown in Figure 11.2.

```
CONST Pi = 3.14159;

CONST T = TRUE;
      Blank = " ";
      BestGrade = "A";

CONST NamePrompt = "Please specify your last name: ";
      MyAge = 34;

CONST Freezing = 32;
      Boiling = 212;
```

(continued)

```
CONST SalesTaxRate = 0.05;
      Star = "*";
      LastYear = 1986;

CONST InchesPerMeter = 39.370;
      MetersPerFoot = 1.0 / (InchesPerMeter * 12.0);
      WeeksPerYear = 52;
      DaysPerYear = WeeksPerYear * 7 + 1;
```

FIGURE 11.2 *Example CONST declarations*

The CONST declaration can be thought of as a method for renaming a constant with an identifier. The first example declaration of Figure 11.2 causes 3.14159 to be renamed as Pi. Within the scope of this declaration, 3.14159 and Pi can be used interchangeably.

This type of renaming is a form of abstraction. By using the identifier Pi, the programmer can emphasize that the mathematical constant Pi is being used and suppress the detail of its precise value. Similarly, NamePrompt can be used in a instruction such as

WriteString(NamePrompt)

to abstract the details of the exact prompt message.

Once a constant identifier is declared, its value is established, and it remains the same throughout its scope. The identifier Star, declared in Figure 11.2, will always represent the character "*" throughout the procedure or module in which it is so declared. Any instruction that attempts to assign a value to Star results in a syntax error. Furthermore, Star is not permissible as a VAR type actual parameter.

Programmer-defined constants can improve program readability. The following assignment instruction code might appear within a program to add sales tax to the cost of an item:

CustomerCharge := Cost + Cost * SalesTaxRate;

Such an instruction is more descriptive than

CustomerCharge := Cost + Cost * 0.05;

There are different degrees of "constantness." Some constants, such as Pi, Blank, Freezing, or WeeksPerYear are forever constant by their definition. There will always be 52 weeks in a year in the way we define time. However, some constants do not always have the same value. Constants such as MyAge, NamePrompt, SalesTaxRate, and LastYear are constant throughout a single program execution, but may change from one time the program is executed to the next.

Using a user-defined constant for these changing constants is also a good idea. It is easier to locate a constant within a CONST declaration than one embedded in the code. This makes it easier to update constants periodically. If LastYear is declared as a CONST, a maintenance programmer can quickly identify a needed change that may be otherwise obscured by including 1986 within the program. Furthermore, it could be that the program uses the same constant more than once. If a programmer-defined constant is used, then only a single CONST declaration needs to be found and updated.

Programming-with-Style

Style and the Use of Programmer-Defined Constants

A programmer-defined constant should be considered as an alternative for every constant within a program. If a more meaningful identifier improves readability, it should be used.

A second reason for using programmer-defined constants is to provide for ease of program modification for constant values that may need to be updated for a future program execution. These types of constants should be either clearly identified or else declared globally to make them easier to find.

Sometimes programmer-defined constants are overused. It is always possible to rename 2 as Two or 1.0/2.0 as OneHalf, but such names impair, rather than enhance, readability.

The style of CONST declarations should follow the style of VAR declarations, including one declaration per line and consistent indentation. It is probably wisest to place CONST declarations before VAR declarations if both are present within the same scope.

11.3 TYPES

A **programmer-defined type** is a more powerful tool for data abstraction than the programmer-defined constant. Modula-2 supports many **standard types**. A standard type, or **intrinsic type**, is recognized by the language without a type declaration. BOOLEAN, CARDINAL, CHAR, INTEGER and REAL are all standard types in Modula-2.

In Modula-2, programmer-defined types are declared by a **TYPE declaration**. Each programmer-defined type must derive its form from known types (standard types or other programmer-defined types). The TYPE declaration must specify this derivation. Figure 11.3 contains a syntax diagram for the TYPE declaration.

```
TypeDeclaration:

──▶ TYPE ──────▶ TypeIdentifier ──▶ = ──▶ KnownType ──▶ ; ──────▶
            ▲─────────────────────────────────────────────┘


TypeIdentifier:
        (* Can be any valid identifier not previously declared *)
        (* locally within the same scope                        *)

KnownType:
        (* Can be any standard Modula-2 type or any       *)
        (* user-defined type previously declared in a     *)
        (* scope containing the current declaration       *)

NOTE: Standard Modula-2 types include all simple types and all structured types
```

FIGURE 11.3 *Syntax diagram for TypeDeclaration*

In its simplest usage, a TYPE declaration is a renaming device. Any standard Modula-2 type can be renamed with an identifier chosen by the programmer. Any programmer-defined type that is known within the current scope can also be renamed. Figure 11.4 contains sample uses of programmer-defined types for renaming.

```
TYPE Logical = BOOLEAN;

TYPE FloatingPoint = REAL;
     FixedPoint = INTEGER;

TYPE WholeNumber = CARDINAL;
     PosInteger = WholeNumber;
```

FIGURE 11.4 *Examples of TYPE declarations for renaming*

After the declarations from Figure 11.4, the identifiers Logical, FloatingPoint, FixedPoint, WholeNumber and PosInteger are known as types. They can be used in VAR declarations or parameter declarations just like any standard type. In addition, the rules of scope apply to programmer-defined types the same as they apply to declared variables or programmer-defined constants.

Since Modula-2 is a strongly typed language, the relationship of a programmer-defined type and the standard types is an important issue. Each programmer-defined type is derived from one or more other types. In Figure 11.4, Logical is derived from BOOLEAN, FloatingPoint is derived from REAL, and so on. PosInteger is directly derived from WholeNumber, and WholeNumber is derived from CARDI-NAL, so indirectly PosInteger is derived from CARDINAL.

There are four possible *compatibility relationships* between two data types in Modula-2. These four relationships govern the manner in which variables of various types can be used in Modula-2 programs. Figure 11.5 describes the four compatibility relationships for simple types.

```
Identical - Two types are exactly the same (must use the same
            identifier).

Compatible - The two types must be
            a) identical, or...
            b) one is declared = to the other, or...
            c) one is a subrange of the other, or...
            d) they are both subranges of the same
               underlying standard type.

Assignment compatible - The two types must be
            a) compatible, or ...
            b) one is compatible with INTEGER and the
               other is compatible with CARDINAL, or ...
            c) one is CHAR and the other is a string of
               length one.

Incompatible - Any two types that are not assignment compatible
            are incompatible.
```

FIGURE 11.5 *Compatiblity relationships for simple types*

The requirements for type compatibility in Modula-2 are slightly different for various operations. For example, an expression may be assigned to any **assignment compatible** variable, while two numeric expressions may be added together only if they are **compatible**. Some of the rules for Modula-2 type compatibility are summarized in Figure 11.6.

Operation	Compatibility requirements
assignment (:=)	assignment compatible variable & expression types
numerical, logical, relational	compatible operand types
value parameter passage	assignment compatible formal and actual parameter types
VAR parameter passage	identical formal and actual parameter types

FIGURE 11.6 Compatibility requirements of simple Modula-2 types

The renaming facility of TYPE declarations should be used on occasion, but not overused. Programmer-defined types are *compatible*, but not *identical*, to the types from which they are derived. This can make VAR parameter passage of values with programmer-defined types difficult. It is reasonable to expect a programmer to know the standard types of a language. It is more difficult for that same programmer to read unfamiliar programmer-defined types.

The primary use for the TYPE declaration is not for renaming, but rather for creating new types that are not among the standard ones. This usage will be detailed as the enumerated, subrange, and structured types are presented.

*P*rogramming–with–*S*tyle

Style and the Use of Programmer-Defined Types

Programmer-defined types are used primarily for creating new types, not available in the standard types of the programming language. These types are, however, derived from the standard types.

Any one of the reasons below would be sufficient for using programmer-defined types.

1) The desired type is not standard in the language (Examples of this include all enumerated, subrange, and structured types.)
2) The actual type from which the programmer-defined type is derived may be changed in later versions of the program (For example, the type Money may be derived from CARDINAL until some later time when negative amounts must be kept, requiring Money to be derived from INTEGER.)

3) The standard type is less readable (For example, WholeNumber may be more meaningful to some people than CARDINAL.) (Note: This last reason is always debatable. Even though WholeNumber may be more meaningful, CARDINAL is a standard part of the language and is more likely to be known by another programmer.)

The form of TYPE declarations should follow the style of VAR declarations: one declaration per line, consistent indentation, and so on. It is often the case that programmer-defined constants are used to declare types and that programmer-defined types are used to declare variables. For this reason, it is customary to place declarations in the following order: CONST, then TYPE, then VAR.

11.4 ENUMERATED DATA TYPES

The standard types of any programming language are limited. Suppose a programmer is writing a program to maintain statistics on automobile manufacturers, including American Motors Corporation, Ford Motor Company, General Motors Corporation, and Chrysler Corporation. One particular variable, called Manufacturer, is used in this program to store the manufacturer's name. Since no programming language includes a standard data type called AutoManufacturer, the programmer has to find another way to represent this information.

Encoding data of one type to represent something else is one creative way to solve the dilemma of the Manufacturer variable. In this case, it is possible to encode auto manufacturers as cardinals and represent each manufacturer as shown below.

Representation	Manufacturer
0	American Motors Corporation
1	Chrysler Corporation
2	Ford Motor Company
3	General Motors Corporation

Manufacturer is declared to be of type CARDINAL. Assigning the appropriate corporation to Manufacturer is accomplished by use of the corresponding cardinal constant.

The ways of encoding information are limited only by the programmer's imagination. There is no particular reason to represent American Motor Corporation as 0 and Ford Motor Company as 2. The programmer could just as easily reverse these representations. The programmer could also choose to encode the manufactures as character constants and declare Manufacturer of type CHAR.

Encoding is an effective programming tool, but it can lead to obscurity if used carelessly. A programmer choosing to encode Manufacturer with the cardinal representations above can improve readability by also using the following programmer-defined constants:

```
                    CONST
                      AMC = 0;
                      Chrysler = 1;
                      Ford = 2;
                      GM = 3;
```

After this declaration the following assignment instruction is possible:

`Manufacturer := Ford`

The above assignment is more readable than

`Manufacturer:=2`

even though both instructions are equivalent.

Some forms of encoding are incorporated into programming languages. The CHAR data type in Modula-2 is nothing more than an encoding that is standard to Modula-2. A programmer can decode a CHAR constant using the ORD function to find its cardinal representation (ordinal value).

The following questions illustrate some shortcomings of encoding.

- What does it mean for `Manufacturer` to be assigned the value 4?

- What does it mean if the constant AMC is assigned to the variable `NumberOfJellyJars`?

- What if a programmer does not document the encoding scheme carefully?

Modula-2 includes a feature known as the **enumerated type** to eliminate some of the shortcomings of encodings. An enumerated type is not a single standard type, but rather a set of rules for creating new types. The syntax and semantics for this type are shown in Figure 11.7.

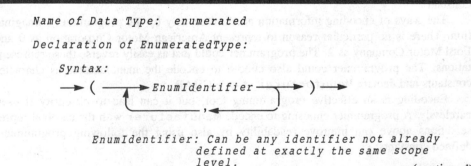

Name of Data Type: enumerated

Declaration of EnumeratedType:

Syntax:

*EnumIdentifier: Can be any identifier not already
                defined at exactly the same scope
                level.*

(continued)

Semantics: Each EnumIdentifier is a constant of this particular enumerated type and must not be declared ambiguously. These constants are ordered with ordinal values beginning at 0 for the first EnumIdentifier and continuing with consecutive cardinal values for additional EnumIdentifiers

Constants: Any EnumIdentifier used in the declaration

Operations: assignment (:=) and relational operations

Note: Enumerated types are Modula-2 simple types. They share the properties of this class.

FIGURE 11.7 *The enumerated data type*

An enumerated type is created by listing (enumerating) the constants for the type. These constants must all be identifiers. Furthermore, these identifiers may not be ambiguously defined with the same scope. Figure 11.8 contains several example enumerated type declarations.

```
TYPE Gender = (Male, Female);

TYPE AppleVariety = (Baldwin, Cortland, Delicious,
                     Jonathon, McIntosh, Wealthy,
                     Winesap);

TYPE ColorSpectrum = (Infrared, Red, Orange, Yellow,
                      Green, Blue, Violet, Ultraviolet);

TYPE AnimalGroup = (Bird, Fish, Insect, Mammal, Reptile);

     AnimalPart = (Blood, Brain, Ear, Eye, Hand, Heart,
                   Hoof, Horn, Tail, Tooth, Tentacle,
                   Tongue);
```

FIGURE 11.8 *Examples of enumerated type declarations*

A declaration, like that of ColorSpectrum, creates a new type. The name of this type is ColorSpectrum. The permissible constants of the type are the eight identifiers Infrared, Red, ..., Ultraviolet. These identifiers are programmer-defined constants, implicitly declared by the enumeration. The scope of visibility for ColorSpectrum and its eight constants is the procedure or module in which the declaration occurs. Once ColorSpectrum has been declared in this manner, it becomes a valid type that is available within its scope. The following declaration is now acceptable.

```
VAR
     ForegroundHue : ColorSpectrum;
     BackgroundHue : ColorSpectrum;
```

This declaration creates two variables of type ColorSpectrum. These variables may be assigned values through instructions like the following.

```
ForegroundHue := Blue;
BackgroundHue := ForegroundHue;
(* ASSERT: ForegroundHue = BackgroundHue = Blue *)
```

The only valid expressions that may be assigned to ForegroundHue are constants declared within the ColorSpectrum type, such as Blue; or variables or functions that are of assignment compatible type.

The declaration of ColorSpectrum also defines an order for its constants. Enumerated constants are ordered by increasing value from left to right in their declaration. Any two compatible enumerated expressions can be compared with relational operators.

```
Red < Blue                 (* a TRUE expression *)
Ultraviolet >= Green       (* a TRUE expression *)
Orange # Yellow            (* a TRUE expression *)
ForegroundHue <> Yellow
BackgroundHue <= ForegroundHue
```

All statements above are valid relational expressions that use the declarations from Figure 11.8.

The ORD function can be used on enumerated expressions. The leftmost identifier constant in every enumeration has the ordinal value 0, the second from the left has ordinal value 1. After the Figure 11.8 declarations, the following assertion is correct.

```
(* ASSERT: ORD(Infrared)=0  &  ORD(Yellow)=3   *)
(*         &   ORD(Hand)=4   &  ORD(Cortland)=1 *)
```

Several other standard Modula-2 procedures and functions are useful with enumerated types. The VAL function can be used as an inverse function to ORD. The first parameter of VAL is the type desired for the result, and the second is an expression for the ordinal value of the result. Below are several example uses of VAL.

```
(* ASSERT: VAL(ColorSpectrum,1) = Red                            *)
(*     & VAL(ColorSpectrum,ORD(Green)) = Green                   *)
(*     & VAL(ColorSpectrum,ORD(ForegroundHue))=ForeGroundHue     *)
(*     & VAL(ColorSpectrum,25) → run-time ERROR                  *)
(*     & VAL(AnimalGroup,1) = Fish                               *)
```

Both of the standard procedures INC and DEC can be used on variables of enumerated type. An INCremented enumerated variable is assigned the value of a succeeding enumerated constant, while a DECremented variable is assigned the preceeding constant.

```
(* ASSERT: ForegroundHue=Blue & BackgroundHue=Green *)
INC( ForegroundHue );
DEC( BackgroundHue,2 );
(* ASSERT: ForegroundHue=Violet & BackgroundHue=Orange *)
```

*P*rogramming-with-*S*tyle

Using Enumerated Data Types

The enumerated data type is a very useful tool for data abstraction. An enumerated type can use meaningful identifiers as constants, rather than a meaningless encoding.

Enumerated types are best declared in a TYPE declaration as programmer-defined types, even though it is possible to include an enumeration in a VAR declaration. Using a separate declaration for each enumerated type makes it possible to declare several variables, parameters, and/or other types. In addition, variables and parameters of identical type are otherwise impossible.

11.5 SUBRANGE DATA TYPES

There are many times when the range of values stored by a variable is known to be more restrictive than the range of the constants of an available type. For example, variables storing integer percentages are usually restricted to the range from 0 to 100 (representing 0% to 100%). The Modula-2 CARDINAL type can be used to store whole percentages, but the range of CARDINAL, 0 to MAX(CARDINAL), is much larger than needed. Using a type with excess constant values doesn't necessarily produce bugs, but it seems less than ideal.

Modula-2 provides a method for declaring types that permits the programmer to specify a range of allowed values. The result is known as a **subrange data type**, described in Figure 11.9.

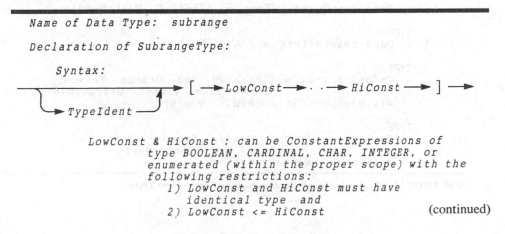

```
Name of Data Type:  subrange

Declaration of SubrangeType:

    Syntax:
                              [ ─→LowConst─→ · · ─→HiConst─→ ] ─→
        └─→ TypeIdent ─┘

        LowConst & HiConst : can be ConstantExpressions of
                    type BOOLEAN, CARDINAL, CHAR, INTEGER, or
                    enumerated (within the proper scope) with the
                    following restrictions:
                    1) LowConst and HiConst must have
                       identical type  and
                    2) LowConst <= HiConst              (continued)
```

> *TypeIdent : a standard type identifier that is*
> *assignment compatible with HiConst and LowConst*

> *Semantics: A subrange type is compatible with the type of*
> *its HiConst and LowConst. If both HiConst and*
> *LowConst are CARDINAL, then the new type is*
> *compatible with CARDINAL. If one or both of*
> *HiConst and LowConst are INTEGER, then the new*
> *type is compatible with INTEGER.*

> *The "TypeIdent" option permits declarations*
> *such as INTEGER[1..10] to force the type to be*
> *compatible with INTEGER, rather than CARDINAL.*

> *Constants: Any constant of the same type as LowConst, with a*
> *value greater than or equal to LowConst and less*
> *than or equal to HiConst.*

> *Operations: All operations permitted for the type of LowConst*
> *and HiConst*

> *Note: Subrange types are Modula-2 simple types that share the*
> *the properties of this class.*

FIGURE 11.9 *The subrange data type*

Subrange data types are declared by specifying the lower and upper bound constants of the desired range. Modula-2 allows subranges of the types BOOLEAN, CARDINAL, CHAR, INTEGER, or an enumerated type (within their scope of visibility). Figure 11.10 shows several example subrange declarations.

```
TYPE
    Percentage = [0..100];

CONST
    MaxOnHand = 1000;
TYPE
    WarehouseQuantityType = INTEGER[0..MaxOnHand];

TYPE
    UppercaseLetters = ["A".."Z"];

TYPE
    ColorSpectrum = (Infrared, Red, Orange, Yellow,
                     Green, Blue, Violet, Ultraviolet)
    VisibleSpectrum = [Red .. Violet];

TYPE
    DayType = (Sunday, Monday, Tuesday, Wednesaay,
               Thursday, Friday, Saturday);
    WeekDay = [Monday..Friday];
```

FIGURE 11.10 *Example of declarations of subrange types*

Subranges *inherit* all of the operations of the type from which they are derived. If the program declares variables of type `Percentage`, then all of the CARDINAL operations are permitted. Furthermore, these `Percentage` type variables are type compatible with CARDINAL data.

Subrange data types can be very useful for program debugging. Many compilers generate code that performs **bounds checking** when executed. Executing a program with bounds checking causes the code to perform a special test each time a new value is assigned to a variable of subrange type. This check examines the value *assigned* to the variable to see that it is within the proper range. If the variable is outside the range, then' a run-time error occurs.

Programming with Style

Why Use Subrange Data Types?

Subranges should be used when a type is known to have a fixed range of some appropriate type. One advantage of a subrange type is the additional information provided to the reader of the program regarding restrictions on permissible value assignments. Another advantage given by subranges is provided through the debugging support of bounds checking.

11.6 SUBRANGES AS CASE LABELS

Modula-2 has one additional feature that makes use of the notation of subranges. In a CASE instruction, subranges of constant expressions may be used in place of constant expressions for case label. This syntax does not allow the "[" and "]", square brackets. Figure 11.11 contains a new version of the IsAlpha function presented in Chapter 9 that uses this notation.

```
PROCEDURE  IsAlpha( C : CHAR )
 : BOOLEAN;
    (* PRE:  C is Assigned                                    *)
    (* POST: RESULT = TRUE,    if "a"<=C<="z" OR "A"<=C<="Z" *)
    (*                = FALSE, otherwise                      *)
BEGIN
    CASE  C  OF
      "a".."z", "A".."Z" :  RETURN TRUE
    ELSE
        RETURN FALSE
    END
END IsAlpha;
```

FIGURE 11.11 *An example of subranges in the CASE instruction: the IsAlpha function*

11.7 AN EXAMPLE OF USE OF DATA ABSTRACTION

A program that benefits from the use of the data abstraction techniques shown in this chapter is described in Figure 11.12. The problem is to calculate the difference between two dates from the last half of the Twentieth Century.

TITLE

    Date Differences

DESCRIPTION

    Americans often write dates using an abbreviation such as 3/27/51. This notation describes a date as a three-number sequence with slashes ("/") separating consecutive numbers. The first number of the sequence is the sequence number of the month, the second is the sequence number of the day within the month, and the final number is the last two digits of the year. In other words, "3/27/51" can be translated as "March 27, 1951."

    This program inputs pairs of dates from the last half of the Twentieth Century written in this form and outputs the number of days separating the two dates.

INPUT

    The program processes pairs of dates repetitiously. Prior to each iteration, the user is prompted for a choice of whether to continue or stop. A response of "Y" or "y" causes the program to continue; any other response terminates execution.

    For each iteration, the programmer must enter two dates on separate lines. The exact form of each line is one or two decimal digits followed by "/" followed by one or two decimal digits followed by "/" followed by one or two decimal digits followed by EOL. There may be no blanks or other additional characters included.

OUTPUT

    Below is the complete form of a single iteration, where input is denoted by enclosure within "< * ... * >", and <difference> denotes the cardinal number of days between the two input dates.

        Do you wish to continue (Y or N)? <*answer*>
        Please specify two dates (form MM/DD/YY) below:
        `<*date1*>`
        `<*date2*>`

    The number of days between is <difference>

    Two blank lines of output separate consecutive iterations.

ERRORS

    Input not of the prescribed form produces undefined results. No attempt is made to verify that the date is realistic (i.e., any two-digit day such as 99 is accepted, but erroneous dates produce undefined results).

(continued)

EXAMPLE

The example below illustrates a single excution. All input is highlighted.

```
Do you wish to continue (Y or N)? Y
Please specify two dates (form DD/MM/YY) below:
3/27/51
3/30/51

The number of days between is 3

Do you wish to continue (Y or N)? y
Please specify two dates (form DD/MM/YY) below:
12/31/86
11/30/86

The number of days between is 31

Do you wish to continue (Y or N)? y
Please specify two dates (form DD/MM/YY) below:
10/9/79
11/17/81

The number of days between is 770

Do you wish to continue (Y or N)? n
```

FIGURE 11.12 *Problem description for DateDifference*

A complete program, called `DateDifference`, to solve this problem, is shown in Figure 11.13. The mainline of this program consists largely of a loop to input pairs of dates, output their differences and check whether the user wishes to continue or not.

```
MODULE DateDifference;
      (* This program reads pairs of dates in the form *)
      (* MM/DD/YY and outputs the days separating the   *)
      (* dates of the pair.  The dates must be from     *)
      (* the last half of the 20th century.             *)

    FROM InOut IMPORT Read, Write, WriteString, WriteCard, WriteLn, EOL;

    CONST DaysInHalfCentury = 365*50 + 12;

    TYPE MonthType = (Jan, Feb, Mar, Apr, May, Jun,
                      Jul, Aug, Sep, Oct, Nov, Dec);
        DayRange = [1..31];   (* day of the month *)
        YearRange = [50..99];  (* representing 1950 .. 1999 *)
        HalfCenturyDayRange = [0 .. DaysInHalfCentury-1];
        TwoDigitCard = [0..99];
```

(continued)

```
VAR ContinueResponse : CHAR;
    DayI   : DayRange;
    DayII  : DayRange;
    MonthI   : MonthType;
    MonthII  : MonthType;
    YearI    : YearRange;
    YearII   : YearRange;
    DaysInHalfCenturyI  : HalfCenturyDayRange;
    DaysInHalfCenturyII : HalfCenturyDayRange;


PROCEDURE InputDate( VAR Day : DayRange;
                     VAR Month : MonthType;
                     VAR Year : YearRange );
(* PRE:  The next input line is of the form MM/DD/YY      *)
(* POST: (Day = the numeric value of DD )   AND           *)
(*       (Month = a MonthType constant with ORD = MM-1) AND *)
(*       (Year = the numeric value of YY) AND             *)
(*       (the input line has been echoed)                 *)

PROCEDURE ValueOfNextInput()
: TwoDigitCard;
    (* PRE:  The next input is of the form ddX, where "dd" *)
    (*       is a 1 or 2 digit number & X is "/" or EOL    *)
    (* POST: (the ddX input has been read and echoed)  AND *)
    (*       (RESULT = numeric value of DD)                *)
    VAR
        FirstChar : CHAR;
        SecndChar : CHAR;
        ThirdChar : CHAR;
    BEGIN (* ValueOfNextInput *)
        Read( FirstChar );
        Write( FirstChar );
        Read( SecndChar );
        IF  SecndChar=EOL   THEN
            WriteLn
        ELSE
            Write( SecndChar )
        END;
        IF   (SecndChar="/") OR (SecndChar=EOL)   THEN
            RETURN( ORD(FirstChar)-ORD("0") )
        ELSE
            Read( ThirdChar );   (* this should read "/" or EOL *)
            IF  ThirdChar=EOL   THEN
                WriteLn
            ELSE
                Write( ThirdChar )
            END;
            RETURN( (ORD(FirstChar)-ORD("0"))*10 +
                    ORD(SecndChar)-ORD("0") )
        END
    END ValueOfNextInput;

BEGIN  (* InputDate *)
    Month := VAL( MonthType, CARDINAL(ValueOfNextInput()-1) );
    Day := ValueOfNextInput();
    Year := ValueOfNextInput()
END InputDate;
```

(continued)

```
PROCEDURE DaysPast1950( Day   : DayRange;
                        Month : MonthType;
                        Year  : YearRange )
  : HalfCenturyDayRange;
        (* PRE:  Month/Day/Year represents a valid twentieth *)
        (*       century date                                *)
        (* POST: RESULT = number of days from Jan. 1, 1950   *)
        (*       to the date Month/Day/Year                  *)
    CONST PastYearsDaysMax = DaysInHalfCentury-365;
    TYPE DaysFromPriorMonthsRange = [0 .. 365-31];
    VAR DaysFromPastYears : [0..PastYearsDaysMax];

    PROCEDURE DaysFromPriorMonths( Month : MonthType;
                                   Year  : YearRange )
      : DaysFromPriorMonthsRange;
        (* POST: RESULT = the number of days in the year Year *)
        (*                from months preceding Month         *)
      VAR DaysPassed : DaysFromPriorMonthsRange;
      BEGIN
        CASE Month OF
            Jan : DaysPassed :=   0 |
            Feb : DaysPassed :=  31 |
            Mar : DaysPassed :=  59 |
            Apr : DaysPassed :=  90 |
            May : DaysPassed := 120 |
            Jun : DaysPassed := 151 |
            Jul : DaysPassed := 181 |
            Aug : DaysPassed := 212 |
            Sep : DaysPassed := 243 |
            Oct : DaysPassed := 273 |
            Nov : DaysPassed := 304 |
            Dec : DaysPassed := 334
        END;
        (* ASSERT: DaysPassed is correct except for leap years *)
        IF  ((Year MOD 4) = 0) AND (Month > Feb)  THEN
            RETURN( DaysPassed + 1 )
        ELSE
            RETURN( DaysPassed )          END
      END DaysFromPriorMonths;

BEGIN (* DaysPast1950 *)
   IF  Year=0  THEN
       DaysFromPastYears := 0
   ELSE
       DaysFromPastYears := (Year-50)*365 + ((Year-1) DIV 4) + 1;
   END;
   RETURN( DaysFromPastYears +
           DaysFromPriorMonths(Month,Year) +
           Day - 1)
END DaysPast1950;
```

(continued)

```
BEGIN (* DateDifference mainline *)
  WriteString( "Do you wish to continue (Y or N)? " );
  Read( ContinueResponse );
  WriteLn;
  WHILE   (* INV: PreviousDatesProcessed *)
    CAP(ContinueResponse)="Y" DO
      WriteString( "Please specify two dates (form MM/DD/YY) below:"
      WriteLn;
      InputDate( DayI, MonthI, YearI );
      InputDate( DayII, MonthII, YearII );
      WriteString( "The number of days between is " );
      DaysInHalfCenturyI  := DaysPast1950(DayI,MonthI,YearI);
      DaysInHalfCenturyII := DaysPast1950(DayII,MonthII,YearII);
      IF  DaysInHalfCenturyI > DaysInHalfCenturyII  THEN
          WriteCard( DaysInHalfCenturyI-DaysInHalfCenturyII, 0 )
      ELSE
          WriteCard( DaysInHalfCenturyII-DaysInHalfCenturyI, 0 )
      END;
      WriteLn; WriteLn; WriteLn;
      WriteString( "Do you wish to continue (Y or N)? " );
      Read( ContinueResponse );
      WriteLn;
  END

  (*------------------------------------------------------------*)
  (*                      DEFINITIONS                           *)
  (*------------------------------------------------------------*)
  (* PreviousDatesProcessed  is                                 *)
  (*     all prior input pairs have been processed              *)
  (*     as specified by the problem description                *)
  (* The form MM/DD/YY  is                                      *)
  (*     three one-digit or two-digit numbers separated         *)
  (*     by single slashes ("/") and followed by a              *)
  (*     EOL character (no other characters are                 *)
  (*     permitted)                                             *)
  (*------------------------------------------------------------*)
END DateDifference.
```

FIGURE 11.13 *The DateDifference program*

Each date in a pair is stored in three variables. The first date of the pair is stored in variables DayI, MonthI, and YearI. The second date is stored in DayII, MonthII, and YearII.

DateDifference makes use of subranges in several places. Since DayI and DayII store a day of the month, they are of type DayRange which is [1..31]. Likewise, YearI and YearII store the last two digits of the year. The acceptable range of 50 to 99 is specified by the subrange type YearRange.

Enumerated data types are also used in DateDifference. MonthType is an enumerated type with twelve constants consisting of abbreviations for the 12 months of a year. MonthI and MonthII are variables of type MonthType.

The mainline of DatesDifference utilizes a procedure called InputDate to input each date of a pair. The InputDate routine scans an input line of the form "MM/DD/YY", where MM, DD, and YY are each one-digit or two-digit numbers. InputDate analyzes and translates the input line into the corresponding values for its parameters Month, Day, and Year. InputDate calls ValueOfNextInput to input each of the three parts of a date input.

For each invocation, `ValueOfNextInput` looks for an input string consisting of one or two decimal digits followed by either / or <EOL>. The string input is echoed as output. The value returned by `ValueOfNextInput` is the numeric value of the first one or two characters (digits). Since the value returned by this function must be the numeric value of a one-digit or two-digit cardinal, it is declared as type `TwoDigit-Card`.

`InputDate` uses three assignment instructions to assign input values to `Month`, `Day` and `Year`. For the assignment of `Month` a VAL function is used, translating from an ordinal to the corresponding enumerated constant.

`DateDifference` calculates the number of days separating two dates by first calculating the number of days between each date and Jan. 1, 1950. `DaysPast1950` is a function that returns this value for a given date. A cardinal subrange, called `Half-CenturyDayRange` provides a type that includes the range of possible numbers of days in the twentieth century. The value of `DaysInHalfCentury` comes from 50 years of 365 days per year plus 12 leap years for a total of 365*50 + 12 days.

There are two primary reasons for using data abstraction in a program. The first reason is to improve readability. Using an enumerated type for `MonthType` results in a CASE instruction within the procedure `DaysFromPriorMonths` that is very readable. Any programmer reading the CASE should be able to understand its purpose quickly. Furthermore, any bug in this CASE instruction should be detected easily.

The second reason for using data abstraction is to provide additional bounds checking. Suppose a programmer erroneously reverses the order of the first two assignment instructions of `InputDate`. The result is a program that interprets a date abbreviation more like the common European date form (listing day before month.) This error will be detected any time a day greater than 12 is input, because a bounds violation will occur. Since subranges are used, a few test executions of the program should be able to point out such a bug, and where it occurs.

Another advantage to data abstraction comes from forcing the programmer to think. A programmer who makes the extensive use of subranges present in the `DateDif-ference` program is forced into considering what the actual ranges should be. This kind of thought is likely to uncover many potential bounds violations before the design is complete.

1.8 COMMON PITFALLS OF CONST, TYPE, ENUMERATED TYPE, AND SUBRANGE

The Modula-2 facilities discussed in this chapter are not without difficulties. Becoming accustomed to the interrelationships of CONST, VAR, and TYPE or the limitations of enumerated and subrange declarations requires some practice. This section includes some common pitfalls waiting to snare the unsuspecting programmer.

THE CONVOLUTED DECLARATION ORDER PITFALL

Two rules must be remembered for all declarations, including CONST, TYPE, and VAR. The first rule is that the scope of visibility rules are the same for every declared identifier, regardless of whether it names a constant, type, or variable. The second rule is that any object used within the declaration of another should textually precede its use. This means that a constant used in a subrange declaration should be declared *before* the subrange declaration. Likewise, if both an enumerated type and a subrange of it are to be declared, the enumerated type should be first. Not all Modula-2 systems require this order, but it improves readability.

THE MISTAKEN CONSTANT IDENTITY PITFALL

The programmer-defined constant is just that, *constant*! It is unacceptable to assign a value to programmer-defined constant through assignment or input instructions. Furthermore, a programmer-defined constant cannot be used as an actual parameter for a VAR parameter.

THE CONFUSION OVER VARIABLES AND TYPES PITFALL

Variables store values; types cannot store values. Programmer-defined types are used only to declare variables, parameters, function values, or other types. Sometimes it is less confusing to pick type identifiers that clarify their usage. For example Month-Type and YearRange suggest types, whereas Month and Year suggest variables.

THE USE OF NON-IDENTIFIERS AS ENUMERATED CONSTANTS PITFALL

This pitfall occurs when a programmer attempts to assign a non-enumerated value, such as a cardinal, integer, or string, to a variable of enumerated data type. Enumerated variables can store constants of their own type only (i.e., identifiers from the declaration list). The following declaration

```
TYPE
    MoneyDenominations = (Penny, Nickel, Dime, Quarter,
                          Half, 1, 2, 5, 10, 50, 100) ;
    (* incorrect syntax in this TYPE declaration *)
```

is incorrect, because the values 1, 2, 5, 10, 50, and 100 are not identifiers and may not be included as constants of an enumerated type.

Furthermore, identifiers are *not* strings. Assuming that Month is a variable of MonthType from the DateDifference program the following assignment is allowed.

```
                    Month : = May;
```

On the other hand, this next instruction is not allowed.

```
        Month : = "May"; (* incorrect syntax *)
```

Only three expressions of enumerated type exist.

1) A constant (identifier) declared within the enumeration list of the declaration of the type.
2) A variable declared to be of assignment compatible type.
3) A function declared to return a value of the enumerated type.

The Use of Non-identifiers as Enumerated Constants Pitfall is a common malady. This illness, if left unattended, can lead to the next more serious ailment...

THE WHAT IN THE WORLD IS AN ENUMERATED TYPE PITFALL

Enumerated types often seem unnusual. They are the only way in Modula-2 to create a new type along with constants of the type. However, enumerated data types are no more unusual than Booleans. The Modula-2 BOOLEAN type can be thought of as:

```
TYPE
    BOOLEAN = (FALSE,TRUE);   (* not valid Modula-2 *)
```

The only difference between this declaration and the standard BOOLEAN type is that logical operations (AND, &, OR, NOT and ~) are not allowed for programmer-declared enumerated types.

THE MULTIPLE DECLARATION OF ENUMERATED TYPE CONSTANTS PITFALL

Any identifier that is within the enumeration list in the declaration of an enumerated type is declared as a constant of this type. A CONST declaration could not have done more! The following declaration is illegal.

```
TYPE
    CarModel = (FourDoor, TwoDoor, Wagon, Other);
    TruckType = (Pickup, EighteenWheeler, Other);
(* compile time error - multiple declaration of Other *)
```

The subtle error above is that Other is declared twice, both as a constant of type CarModel and a constant of type TruckType. Modula-2 compilers will *not* accept such an ambiguous declaration of Other, even if the ordinal values are identical.

THE FAILURE TO INCLUDE AN "EXTRA" ENUMERATED CONSTANT PITFALL

When a variable of enumerated type is used as the counter of a loop, an additional dummy constant is sometimes required. Suppose the following loop is to be executed using Month, a variable of the enumerated type, MonthType:

```
Month := Jan;
REPEAT
    (* Perform some task *)
UNTIL Month > Dec;
(* above code works only with Month of certain types *)
```

If the declaration of MonthType from DateDifference is used, then this code produces a bounds violation the last time INC is invoked (i.e., when Month is incremented from Dec). A declaration, like the one below, that includes an extra constant in the enumeration corrects the problem.

```
TYPE
    MonthType = (Jan, Feb, Mar, Apr, May, Jun, Jul,
                 Aug, Sep, Oct, Nov, Dec, UndefinedMonth);
```

The UndefinedMonth style dummy constant does not enhance the abstraction and should be avoided when possible.

THE I NEED TO PERFORM I/O ON ENUMERATED TYPE DATA PITFALL

There are countless occasions when being able to input or output data of enumerated type would be convenient. For example, debugging is more convenient if variables of enumerated type can be output. Unfortunately, there are *no standard I/O routines for enumerated type data* in Modula-2. Programmers must write their own I/O routines to read or write strings and perform conversions to or from the associated enumerated type. The InputDate procedure from DateDifference performs one such input operation of months by reading characters, converting them to cardinals, and cardinals to enumerated type data using the VAL function.

THE ATTEMPT TO SUBRANGE A REAL PITFALL

It is tempting to form a subrange of real values, such as the one below:

```
TYPE
    RiverStageRange = [0.0 .. 21.5];
    (* an illegal Modula-2 declaration *)
```

This might be a convenient feature, but it is *not* a part of Modula-2.

THE FORGOTTEN RULES OF SUBRANGE COMPATIBILITY PITFALL

Subranges are *compatible*, not identical to, the types from which they are derived. The only difficulty this poses is for parameter passage by reference, where *identical* types are required. This is a particular problem for input procedures, because they use parameter passage by reference. For example, the invocation

```
            ReadCard( SomeSubrange )
```

is illegal for any SomeSubrange that has a subrange type.

THE I WANT AN ARBITRARY SET, NOT A SUBRANGE PITFALL

It is sometimes convenient to select various nonconsecutive constants of some type and try to form a new type. It is also *impossible* in Modula-2. For example, there is no way to declare a new type MathOperators to include just the character constants "+", "–", "*", and "/". Both of the declarations below fail. The first attempt falls into The Use of Non-identifiers as Enumerated Constants Pitfall. The second attempt is an abuse of the subrange brackets for something other than a subrange.

```
(* Incorrect attempt 1 *)
TYPE
    MathOperators = ("+", "–", "*", "/");
(* Incorrect attempt 2 *)
TYPE
    MathOperators = ["+", "–", "*", "/"];
```

A subrange must be only a single consecutive collection of constants.

THE CONSTRUCT BIG TYPES OUT OF LITTLE TYPES PITFALL

Modula-2 supports breaking larger (a larger collection of permissible values) simple types into smaller through a subrange. There is no corresponding facility for constructing larger simple types out of smaller ones. The following example validly declares a type and three subrange types:

```
TYPE
    AutoMakers = (AMC, Chrysler, Ford, GM,
                  Audi, BMW, Mercedes, VW,
                  Honda, Nissan, Mitsubishi, Toyota);
    USautoMakers = [AMC .. GM];
    GermanAutoMakers = [Audi .. VW];
    JapanAutoMakers = [Honda .. Toyota];
```

However, suppose a programmer wishes to initially declare USautomakers, GermanAutoMakers and JapanAutoMakers as enumerated types as below:

```
TYPE
    USautoMakers = (AMC, Chrysler, Ford, GM);
    GermanAutoMakers = (Audi, BMW, Mercedes, VW);
    JapanAutoMakers = (Honda, Nissan, Mitsubishi, Toyota);
```

There is no method for combining these three types to declare the enumerated type AutoMakers. It is always necessary to begin with the most general type and to use subranges to subdivide.

Programmer-defined constants, programmer-defined types, enumerated types, and subrange types are very powerful tools. The pitfalls of this section are intended to clarify their limitations.

11.9 SUMMARY

Abstraction can transform obscure notation into meaningful statements. This chapter introduces the concept of data abstraction. Four Modula-2 tools are presented to provide methods of extending the data facilities of Modula-2 beyond the standard features of the language.

The programmer-defined constant permits the creation of new constants. These constants take the form of identifiers that rename some existing constant. This renaming is a simple form of abstraction.

The programmer-defined type allows a programmer to create new data types freely. These newly created types become data templates with properties similar to those of the standard types of Modula-2. The TYPE declaration is a key tool, if not *the* key tool, in data abstraction.

The TYPE declaration creates new types from existing ones. Much of the power of the programmer-defined type is, therefore, derived from the standard types of the language. Two Modula-2 data types that enhance the flexibility of TYPE declarations are the enumerated type and the subrange type.

An enumerated type is a tool for making the language fit the data, instead of the other way around. Once declared, an enumerated type is an ordered simple type. The number of standard language features for manipulating enumerated types is small, but the programmer can easily extend them through the use of procedures and functions.

A subrange data type is formed from a consecutive subset of constants from some available simple type. Subrange data types afford the opportunity to clarify the actual range of permissible values for data. Subranges also provide improved bounds checking.

||| KEY TERMS

data structure	intrinsic type	incompatible type
data abstraction	TYPE	encoding (of data)
programmer-defined constant	identical type	enumerated type
CONST	compatible type	subrange type
programmer-defined type	assignment compatible	bounds checking
standard type	type	

||| EXERCISES

1. Use the declarations below to complete parts (a) through (g).

```
CONST
    SOS = " ... --- ...";
    MerchantFleetMax = 6000;

TYPE
    ShipType = (Trawler, Freighter, OilTanker,
                TowBoat, Cargo, Liner, PTboat,
                Cruiser, Destroyer, Battleship);
    MilitaryShip = [PTboat .. Battleship];
    FamousVessel = (Clermont, Constitution, Lusitania,
                    Maine, Monitor, Merrimack,
                    Titanic);
    MerchantFleetRange = [0..MerchantFleetMax];

VAR
    ShipA : ShipType;
    ShipB : FamousVessel;
    Warship : MilitaryShip;
    USMerchantFleetSize : MerchantFleetRange;
    JapanMerchantFleetSize : MerchantFleetRange;
```

a) List all programmer-defined types resulting from these declarations.

b) List all constants that have been created by the above CONST and TYPE declarations.

c) For each variable below, list all of the permissable constants that it may store.

```
                    ShipA
                    ShipB
                    Warship
```

d) Write an assignment instruction that causes the variable ShipA to store the value TowBoat.

e) Specify a sequence of InOut procedure invocations that would output the S.O.S. signal, "... --- ...", three consecutive times (be certain to use the programmer- defined constant, SOS).

f) Specify an appropriate declaration for MerchantShipType that could be included in these declarations as a programmer-defined type for all ships of ShipType that are not of type MilitaryShip.

g) What is the value of the expression ORD(PTboat)?

Use the following collection of declarations to complete Exercises 2 through 4.

```
CONST
    Nickel = 5;
    Dollar = 100;

TYPE
    CentType = (Large, Indian, Eagle,
                Wheat, Steel, Washington);
    OldCents = [Large..Eagle];
    QuarterType = (Barber, Liberty, Washington, Clad);
    NewQuarterRange = [Liberty..Clad];
    UnderADollar = [0..Dollar];

VAR
    Quarter : QuarterType;
    Cent : CentType;
    NewQuarter : NewQuarterRange;
    PrewarCent : OldCents;
    Int : INTEGER;
    Card : CARDINAL;
    Change : UnderADollar;
```

2. Given the above declarations, list all of the instructions below that are invalid and indicate why. (Assume that all variables are assigned values.)

a) `Cent := "Steel";`

b) `Int := Nickel;`

c) `Card := Dollar;`

d) `Change := Nickel;`

e) `Dollar := 1;`

f) `Int := ORD(Cent);`

g) `Card := ORD(Quarter);`

h) `Int := ORD(CentType);`

i) `INC( QuarterType );`

j) `DEC( PrewarCent );`

k) `Cent := VAL(Cent,1);`

l) `Quarter := ORD(QuarterType);`

m) `NewQuarter := [Barber..Clad];`

n) `PrewarCent := Large;`

o) `NewQuarter := Barber;`

p) `Change := Dollar - Nickel;`

q) `Int := Change;`

r) `Int := Nickel + Cent;`

s) `Int := Nickel + Large;`

t) `Int := Dollar + CentType;`

u) `QuarterType := Barber;`

3. For each of the instructions below, indicate whether the instruction execution *definitely* results in a bounds violation, *may* result in a violation (depending upon particular value assignments), or *never* results in a bounds violation.

a) Quarter : = Quarter;

b) NewQuarter : = Clad;

c) NewQuarter : = Barber;

d) NewQuarter : = Liberty;

e) Int : = Dollar;

f) Card : = Nickel;

g) PrewarCent : = Cent;

h) Cent : = PrewarCent;

i) Int : = ORD(Cent);

j) Card : = ORD(NewQuarter);

k) INC(Change) :

l) DEC(Cent);

m) DEC(PrewarCent);

n) DEC(Card);

o) DEC(Int);

p) Change : = Nickel + Dollar;

q) Change : = Card;

r) Card : = Change;

s) Card : = Int;

t) Int : = Card;

u) Quarter : = VAL(QuarterType,2);

v) Cent : = VAL(CentType,0);

w) PrewarCent: =VAL(CentType,3);

x) PrewarCent: =VAL(CentType,Card);

4. For each pair of expressions below, indicate whether their type is *incompatible*, *assignment compatible*, *compatible*, or *identical*.

a) Quarter and Cent

b) NewQuarter and Quarter

c) ORD(Quarter) and Card

d) ORD(Cent) and Change

e) Nickel and Int

f) Change and Int

g) Change and Card

h) VAL(QuarterType,Card) and Quarter

i) VAL(QuarterType,Change) and NewQuarter

Use the following declarations to complete Exercise 5.

```
CONST
    Quartet = 4;
    OrchestraSeats = 105;

TYPE
    StringFamily = ( Guitar, Harp, Violin,
                     Viola, Cello, Bass );
    BrassFamily = ( Bugle, Trumpet, Coronet, FrenchHorn,
                    Trombone, Baritone, Tuba );
    ViolinFamily = [Violin..Bass];

VAR
    FirstStringInstr : StringFamily;
    SecondStringInstr : StringFamily;
```

5. For each declaration below assume that it follows immediately after the above declarations. Indicate if the new declaration is invalid in Modula-2 and if so why.

a) VAR BrassInstrument : BrassFamily;

b) VAR OrchestraSize : OrchestraSeats;

c) VAR StringInstr : ViolinFamily;

d) CONST BiggerOrchestra = OrchestraSeats + 4;

e) CONST SandrasInstrument = Violin;

f) CONST QuartetInstruments = ViolinFamily

g) CONST BrassSection = [2..25];

h) CONST Logo = "Modula Philharmonic";

i) TYPE Percussion = (KettleDrum, SnareDrum, Bongo, BassDrum, Tamborine, Claves, WoodBlocks);

j) TYPE LowBrass = [Trombone..Tuba];

k) TYPE MaxOrchestra = OrchestraSeats;

l) TYPE IntroMessage = "We proudly present our orchestra."

m) TYPE OrchestraRange = [1..OrchestraSeats];

n) TYPE HiBrowStrings = ViolinFamily;

o) TYPE OrchestralStrings = ViolinFamily + (Harp);

p) TYPE BobCanPlayThese = (Guitar, Bass);

q) TYPE SueCanPlayThese = [Harp, Cello];

r) TYPE BrassAndStrings = [BrassFamily..StringFamily];

s) TYPE BrassAndStrings = (BrassFamily,StringFamily);

t) TYPE BrassAndStrings = BrassFamily + StringFamily;

u) TYPE BandInstruments = (Woodwinds, Drums, Coronet, Trombone,
                            Tuba, Others);

v) TYPE RockInstruments = (Guitar, Organ, Piano, Drums);

6. Below are two techniques for declaring variables with and without separate programmer
    defined types. What are the advantages to the use of separate types (the first declarations)?

```
(* declarations with separate types *)
TYPE
  TurtleType = (Leatherback, Snapping, Sea,
        Painted, Softshell );
VAR
  Turtle : TurtleType;


(* declaration without separate types *)
VAR Turtle : (Leatherback, Snapping, Sea,
        Painted, Softshell );
```

7. Add another declaration to the one below to create a user-defined type, called Deci-
    duousVarieties, with the appropriate permissable constants.

```
TYPE TreeVarieties = (Ash, Elm, Oak,
                Walnut, Maple, Pine);
```

8. Add another declaration to the one below to create a user-defined type, called Wet-
    Weather, with the appropriate permissable constants.

```
TYPE Precipitation = (Rain, Sleet, Hail,
                Snow, Drizzle, Dry);
```

9. The following declarations specify the desired constants for the types OldLanguages and NewLanguages. Specify a complete collection of declarations that will declare a variable, called ProgLang such that ProgLang can store any from either of the types OldLanguages and NewLanguages (Note: Don't use the declarations below if you don't need them).

```
OldLanguage = ( FORTRAN, COBOL, PLI, Algol );
NewLanguage = ( Pascal, C, Ada, Modula );
```

10. Write appropriate declarations for the following programmer-defined constants.

a) LitersPerGallon

b) QuestionMark

c) TwentyBlanks

d) MyName

e) MyAge

f) RowsOfCharsOnComputerDisplay

g) NumberOfCharsOnComputerDisplay

11. Write appropriate declarations for the following programmer-defined types.

a) PlanetType

b) Seasons

c) FabricType

d) HumanAgeRange

e) NaturalNumber (* Natural numbers are integers *)
   (* greater than 0   *)

f) SmallLetters

g) HumanBodyTemperatureRange

h) OvenTemperatureRange

12. Write a Modula-2 procedure, called ReadDirection that will input the next character and return via a single parameter a value of type Directions (declared below). If the input character matches the first letter (either uppercase or lowercase) of a Directions constant, then that should be the value returned. If the input character does not match the first character of any Directions constant, then DirectionUnknown should be returned.

```
TYPE Directions = ( North, East, South,
                    West, DirectionUnknown);
```

13. Write a Modula-2 procedure, called WriteShark, with a two value type parameters. The first parameter is of type SharkVariety (declared below). The second parameter is of type CARDINAL. WriteShark must output the string of characters corresponding to the identifier name of the value of the first parameter. The second parameter specifies the field width for output. If this field width exceeds the length of the identifier name, then the output is right justified with blanks filling the field on the left.

```
TYPE SharkVariety = ( Blue, Hammerhead, GreatWhite,
                      Leopard, Tiger, Whale );
```

||| PROGRAMMING PROJECTS

1. Figure 11.11 contains a problem definition for the DateDifference program in Figure 11.12. This program does very little error checking, allowing bounds checking to capture most input errors. Modify the program so that the following two errors are handled as indicated.

   1) Any "MM" specification (the one or two digits representing the month number) that are greater than 12 or equal to 0 produces the following error message:

   ERROR – Month specification out of bounds

   2) Any "DD" specification (the one or two digits representing the date) that is erroneous for the given month and year produces the following error message:

   ERROR – Date invalid for given month

   In the event of either of these errors, the program does not output the day difference message, but simply proceeds to the next prompt for continuation.

2. Write a program to solve the following problem. Be certain to make effective use of the data abstraction tools presented in this chapter.

TITLE
Metric to U.S. Weight Conversion

DESCRIPTION
In the Roman/U.S. system of measurement, one ton is 2000 pounds, and one pound is 16 ounces. In the metric system mass can be measured in Kilograms. In the earth's gravitational pull, one pound equals approximately 0.4535924 Kilograms.

This program inputs five cardinals representing the mass (in kilograms) of five objects. The equivalent weight of the object is then output in the largest U.S. whole units possible. Any fraction less than one ounce is ignored.

INPUT
Five input cardinals representing the mass of five objects in kilograms. The maximum permissible input mass is 5000.

OUTPUT
Prior to each input value, two blank lines are output followed by the input prompt below:

Specify the mass of an object (0 – 5000):

The three lines below specify the converted weight of the object. Weight is output in the largest whole units possible with $<t>$, $<p>$, and $<o>$ representing the number of tons, pounds and ounces, respectively. Fractions of an ounce are ignored.

```
Tons : <t>
Lbs  : <p>
Ozs  : <o>
```

ERRORS
Any input greater than 5000 produces the following error message, and no equivalent weight output is produced:

Weight specification must be under 5000!

EXAMPLE
Below is an example execution, where all input has been highlighted.

```
Specify the mass of an object (0 – 5000): 100
Tons : 0
Lbs  : 220
Ozs  : 7


Specify the mass of an object (0 – 5000): 999
Tons : 1
Lbs  : 202
Ozs  : 6
```

```
Specify the mass of an object (0 – 5000) : 0
Tons : 0
Lbs  : 0
Ozs  : 0


Specify the mass of an object (0 – 5000) : 10000
Weight specification must be under 5000!


Specify the mass of an object (0 – 5000) : 4500
Tons : 4
Lbs  : 1920
Ozs  : 12
```

3. Write a program to solve the following problem. Be certain to make effective use of the data abstraction tools presented in this chapter.

TITLE

Fruit Shipper Invoicing

DESCRIPTION

A fresh-fruit distributor needs a program to produce invoices for orders. The distributor handles only four items, delicious apples, bananas, navel oranges and peaches. Each item is shipped to retail stores in large cases with only one case size for each type of fruit. The distributor's prices for the next two months are as follows:

$$\text{apples (per case)} = \$25$$
$$\text{bananas (per case)} = \$18$$
$$\text{oranges (per case)} = \$29$$
$$\text{peaches (per case)} = \$38$$

All produce is delivered in refrigerated trucks. A truck can hold a maximum of 500 cases. This program is incapable of handling orders in excess of one truck-load. In addition, retailers are given a 5% discount for orders larger than 80% of a truckload.

The distributor has a special phone line to process orders. The employee who answers the phone inputs the order into this program immediately. Therefore, the program interactively prompts and also accepts input.

INPUT

For each order, the input occurs as a sequence of pairs of input. Each pair of input data consists of an input fruit type followed by a quantity ordered for that type. Each input of the pair is prompted. The valid inputs for fruit type are any of the following single characters (lower case letters are also permissible):

Fruit type input char	Meaning
A	apples
B	bananas
O	oranges
P	peaches
E	end of this order
X	cancel this order

Any cardinal value is a valid entry for the quantity of the input pair.

Input pairs continue to be accepted for a single order until either an E or X input is specified. A terminating input of E signifies the normal end of an order, while a terminating input of X signifies that the order should be voided.

The quantities ordered accumulate, so that if two orange orders occur during a single sequence of input pairs, then the total quantity is the sum of the two. Upon normal end of an order, and only then, an invoice is output. This program continues infinitely processing invoices.

OUTPUT

The prompts for the two inputs of each pair as as shown below:

```
Fruit Type? (A,B,O,P,E,X) >>
Quantity? >>
```

The prompted input continues, with blank lines separating consecutive input pair prompts, until an "E" or an "X" is input as fruit type. If an "X" is input, all accumulations are zeroed out and the program is ready to accept a subsequent order. In this case, the following message is displayed followed by a return to the input prompt sequence:

```
Order Voided!
```

If the order is terminated normally, then two blank lines are output followed by the invoice below:

Item	Quantity	Cost
Apples	$<qA>$	$<cA>$
Bananas	$<qB>$	$<cB>$
Oranges	$<qO>$	$<cO>$
Peaches	$<qP>$	$<cP>$

```
Total     <cT>
Discount  <d>
Amount due <cF>
```

In the invoice $<qA>$, $<qB>$, $<qO>$, and $<qP>$ are used to represent, respectively, the sum of all quantities from a single order for apples, bananas, oranges and peaches. $<cA>$, $<cB>$, $<cO>$, and $<cP>$ represent the corresponding cost for the given quantity of the item. <cT> symbolizes the total charge for this order. <d> represents the 5% discount (if applicable). <d> is rounded to the next lower cardinal value if the discount applies or "0" if discount does not apply. <cF> is the amount due after subtracting the discount.

Following each invoice are two blank lines followed by a return to the input sequence for the next order.

ERRORS

If an order greater than one truck load (500 total cases) is input, then no invoice is output, but instead the following message is displayed. In this case the program voids this order, expecting the order to be reentered correctly.

```
Order exceeds one truck - reorder in parts
```

EXAMPLE

The example program execution below shows all input via highlighting.

```
Fruit Type? (A,B,O,P,E,X) >>A
Quantity? >>2

Fruit Type? (A,B,O,P,E,X) >>E


     Item    Quantity    Cost

     Apples      2        50
     Bananas     0         0
     Oranges     0         0
     Peaches     0         0

             Total        50
             Discount      0
             Amount due   50


Fruit Type? (A,B,O,P,E,X) >>P
Quantity? >>4

Fruit Type? (A,B,O,P,E,X) >>B
Quantity? >>1

Fruit Type? (A,B,O,P,E,X) >>P
Quantity? >>6

Fruit Type? (A,B,O,P,E,X) >>E
```

```
Item    Quantity   Cost
----    --------   ----

Apples     0         0
Bananas    1        18
Oranges    0         0
Peaches   10       380

          Total    398
          Discount   0
          Amount due 398


Fruit Type? (A,B,O,P,E,X) >> a
Quantity? >> 100

Fruit Type? (A,B,O,P,E,X) >> b
Quantity? >> 400

Fruit Type? (A,B,O,P,E,X) >> a
Quantity.? >> 2

Fruit Type? (A,B,O,P,E,X) >> E

Order exceeds one truck - reorder in parts

Fruit Type? (A,B,O,P,E,X) >> O
Quantity? >> 100

Fruit Type? (A,B,O,P,E,X) >> x

Order Voided!

Fruit Type? (A,B,O,P,E,X) >> B
Quantity? >> 428

Fruit Type? (A,B,O,P,E,X) >> E


Item    Quantity   Cost
----    --------   ----

Apples     0         0
Bananas  428      7704
Oranges    0         0
Peaches    0         0

          Total    7704
          Discount  385
          Amount due 7319
```

(* the program continues *)

4. Write a program to solve the following problem. Be certain to make effective use of the data abstraction tools presented in this chapter. (Note: Enumerated types are particularly helpful.)

TITLE
    Calculate long distance phone charges for calls

DESCRIPTION
    This program inputs a sequence of start and finish times for long distance phone calls and outputs the charge for each. There is a basic long distance fee of $1.50 for the first three minutes (or any part thereof) and $0.30 for any portion of a minute after the first three. Furthermore, rates are reduced according to their starting time (in terms of Eastern Standard Time). The following chart shows the reduced rates and times (all charges rounded to the nearest cent):

Starting time (EST)	Monday thru Friday	Saturday	Sunday
prior to 8am	40% off	60% off	60% off
8am to 4:59pm	basic rate	60% off	60% off
5pm to 10:59pm	30% off	60% off	40% off
11pm & after	40% off	60% off	60% off

INPUT
    Input consists of one or more lines of phone calls. Each line represents a single call. The last line is signified by beginning with an "X" character, unlike any other input line. The form of all other lines is as follows:

    <day> <time zone> <start time> <end time>

WHERE:
    <day> indicates the weekday of the start of the call. ("S" = sunday, "M" = monday, "T" = tuesday, "W" = wednesday, "H" = thursday, "F" = friday, "A" = saturday)
    <time zone> indicates the time zone in which the time is expressed. ("E" = eastern, "C" = central, "M" = mountain, "P" = pacific) — note charges are calculated accoring to start in terms of Eastern time zone.
    <start time> indicates the starting time of the call in terms of the specified time zone. This time is expressed as "Military time". In military time, the minutes are concatenated after the hours (3:45 am is expressed as 345, 10:03 am is 1003 and 12:25 am is 0025), and pm times begin at 1200 (1:24 pm is 1324 and 10:09 pm is 2209)
    <end time> indicates the time the call was completed in military time.
    <day> and <time zone> must be the first two characters on the input line.
    <start time> and <end time> may be preceded and/or followed with blanks, but there must be at least one blank between them.

OUTPUT

Prior to all input the following message is displayed:

Input phone call info (X to terminate)

A blank line follows the above prompt. After each input line, the next line contains the charge for the call in the form indicated below:

COST: <xxx>

where <xxx> is the cost (in cents) for the call as computed using the basic rate and discounts as indicated above.

A blank line separates each output line from the next input line.

ERRORS

1) All of the errors described below cause the normal output line to be replaced with the indicated output:
    a) any invalid <day> input character causes display of BAD DAY CODE
    b) any invalid <time zone> input character causes display of BAD TIME ZONE SPEC
    c) any invalid time (invalid hours or minutes) causes display of BAD TIME
2) Any other errors not described in (1) produce undefined results.

EXAMPLE

Below is a sample execution with input highlighted.

Input phone call info (X to terminate)

ME 810 815
COST: 210

WE 1700 1703
COST: 105

SE 1010 1013
COST: 60

SM 1558 1601
COST: 90

AP 2358 02
COST: 72

AE 2359 02
COST: 60

FC 2301 2304
COST: 60

FP 1200 1303
COST: 1950

tC 1601 1604
BAD DAY CODE

TZ 1601 1604
BAD TIME ZONE SPEC

TC 1601 2402
BAD TIME

TC 1601 1663
BAD TIME

X

12 INTRODUCTION TO STRUCTURED DATA: THE ONE-DIMENSIONAL ARRAY

12.1 WHY ARE STRUCTURED TYPES NECESSARY?

Objects are often collected, classified, and cataloged into groups. Many times the operations performed on or by a particular group are similar. The ultimate in processing by group is called "mass production."

When a computer is involved in mass production, the result is automation. Medical record keeping is automated. Magazine subscriptions are automated. Even income tax collection is automated. All of this automation involves large groups of data and operations that are performed repetitively upon items of the group.

The Modula-2 simple types are **atomic**, because they are not readily separated into parts. Simple variables are useful for expressing many algorithms, but their expressive power is limited. A program for a company with three employees can store weekly salary information in three different variables and process each separately. However, for a company of 10,000 employees, a program with 10,000 different variables and 10,000 separate algorithms is impractical. Data structures more complex than those of simple type are needed for effective automation.

These more complex, non-atomic data types are referred to as **structured data types**. They are collections of simple types and/or other structured types. The advantages of structuring data are similar to those of structured control. Grouping items of data into a single structured type is like grouping repetitively-executed instructions into a procedure or loop body; both simplify the algorithm.

Some problems cannot be solved using only simple variables. One example is sorting. The algorithm to sort two simple variables is not difficult. Figure 12.1 contains a Modula-2 program to sort CardA and CardB so that the larger value of the two is placed in CardB and the smaller in CardA.

```
MODULE SortTwo;
    (* This program inputs two cardinals and outputs them *)
    (* in ascending order.                                 *)

    FROM InOut IMPORT ReadCard, WriteCard. WriteLn;

    VAR CardA : CARDINAL;
        CardB : CARDINAL;

    PROCEDURE Swap( VAR Card1 : CARDINAL;
                    VAR Card2: CARDINAL );
        (* PRE:  Assigned(Card1) & Assigned(Card2)          *)
        (* POST: Card1=Card2<entry> & Card2=Card1<entry> *)
        VAR TempCard : CARDINAL;
    BEGIN
        TempCard := Card1;
        Card1 := Card2;
        Card2 := TempCard
    END Swap;

BEGIN
    ReadCard( CardA );
    ReadCard( CardB );
    WriteLn;
    IF CardB<CardA THEN
        Swap( CardB, CardA )
    END;
    (* ASSERT: CardA <= CardB *)
    WriteCard( CardA, 0 );
    WriteLn;
    WriteCard( CardB, 0 );
    WriteLn
END SortTwo.
```

FIGURE 12.1 *SortTwo, a program to sort two cardinals*

Only one IF-THEN instruction is needed to sort two variables. Sorting three values is more complicated. Figure 12.2 contains a SortThree program that shows the necessary changes from the earlier SortTwo program.

```
MODULE SortThree;
    (* This program inputs three cardinals and outputs *)
    (* them in ascending order.                         *)

    FROM InOut IMPORT ReadCard, WriteCard, WriteLn;

    VAR CardA : CARDINAL;
        CardB : CARDINAL;
        CardC : CARDINAL;
```

(continued)

```
            PROCEDURE Swap( VAR Card1 : CARDINAL;
                           VAR Card2: CARDINAL );
              (* PRE:  Assigned(Card1) & Assigned(Card2)        *)
              (* POST: Card1=Card2<entry> & Card2=Card1<entry> *)
              VAR TempCard : CARDINAL;
            BEGIN
              TempCard := Card1;
              Card1 := Card2;
              Card2 := TempCard
            END Swap;

        BEGIN
            ReadCard( CardA );
            ReadCard( CardB );
            ReadCard( CardC );
            WriteLn;
            IF CardA>CardB THEN
                Swap(CardA, CardB);
            END;
            (* ASSERT: CardA <= CardB *)
            IF CardC<CardA THEN
                Swap(CardC, CardA);
                (* ASSERT CardA<=CardC<=CardB *)
                Swap(CardC, CardB)
            ELSIF CardC<CardB THEN
                Swap (CardC, CardB)
            END;
            (* ASSERT: CardA<=CardB<=CardC *)

            WriteCard( CardA, 0 ); WriteLn;
            WriteCard( CardB, 0 ); WriteLn;
            WriteCard( CardC, 0 ); WriteLn;
        END SortThree.
```

FIGURE 12.2 *SortThree program*

Continuing to increase the number of variables sorted in this way becomes increasingly difficult. Sorting four values in simple variables is impractical, requiring multiple nested IF instructions. Sorting more than four values is far worse. If the the exact number of values to be sorted is unknown, then it is *impossible* to sort in this way.

2.2 THE CONCEPT OF AN ARRAY

The **array** is the most frequently used of all structured data types. An array is a data structure for storing a group of items, where every item in the group has an identical data type. Each **array item** (also referred to as an **array element**) is a unique data structure; it may be manipulated the same way as any other data structure of the same type. The aggregate of all individual items constitutes the group known as the array.

Variables of simple type can be thought of as storage **cells**. Figure 12.3 contains a declaration for three simple variables and diagrams of their cellular representation. The cells show the contents of the variables after executing the three indicated assignment instructions. LetterGrade1 contains the character "C", LetterGrade2 contains "A", and LetterGrade3 contains "B".

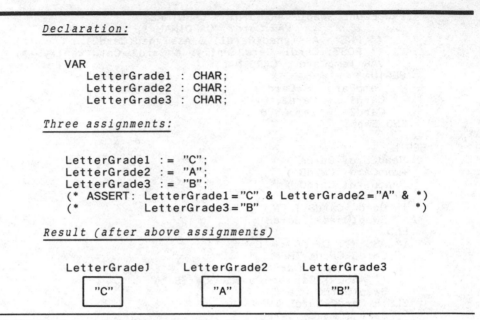

Declaration:

```
VAR
    LetterGrade1 : CHAR;
    LetterGrade2 : CHAR;
    LetterGrade3 : CHAR;
```

Three assignments:

```
LetterGrade1 := "C";
LetterGrade2 := "A";
LetterGrade3 := "B";
(* ASSERT: LetterGrade1="C" & LetterGrade2="A" & *)
(*         LetterGrade3="B"                        *)
```

Result (after above assignments)

LetterGradeJ	LetterGrade2	LetterGrade3
"C"	"A"	"B"

FIGURE 12.3 *Cellular representation of simple variables*

These three variables can be grouped together as a single array as shown in Figure 12.4. In this example, the three simple variables, LetterGrade1, LetterGrade2 and LetterGrade3, have been replaced by a single array, called LetterGrade, with three cells.

Declaration:

```
VAR
    LetterGrade : ARRAY[1..3] OF CHAR;
```

Three assignments:

```
LetterGrade[1] := "C";
LetterGrade[2] := "A";
LetterGrade[3] := "B";
(* ASSERT: LetterGrade[1]="C" & LetterGrade[2]="A" & *)
(*         LetterGrade[3]="B"                         *)
```

Result (after above assignments)

LetterGrade   [1]   [2]   [3]

"C"	"A"	"B"

FIGURE 12.4 *Example of cellular representation of array (similar to Figure 12.3)*

Every array consists of three parts:

1) Array name
2) Item type
3) Index set

The **array name** is the identifier used to refer to the entire group of array cells. Array names must be declared in VAR declarations. They follow the same rules of scope as other variables. The name of the array declared in Figure 12.4 is `LetterGrade`.

An array is a group of items. Every item in an array must have the same type. This data type is known as the **array item type**. For `LetterGrade`, the item type is CHAR, so each item cell stores one character. The item type is specified in the array declaration.

The cells of an array form a sequence. `LetterGrade` has a left cell, middle cell, and a right cell. The **index set**, or **index type**, provides the means for identifying particular items, (cells), of an array. The index set of `LetterGrade` is a subrange type

$$[1..3]$$

The possible values of this subrange type are 1, 2, and 3. Each of these values is used to identify a different item within the array. The complete name for an item consists of the array name and an **index**, one of the values from the index set.

Mathematicians have long used arrays for groups of variables. A mathematician might refer to a collection of four integer variables as a_1, a_2, a_3, and a_4. Each of the variables, collectively referred to as "a," has a unique subscript (1 to 4). The mathematical concept of a **subscript** is the same as that of a programmer's array index. In fact, many programmers refer to indices as "subscripts." The middle item of the `Letter-Grade` is described by all of the following:

"item 2 of `LetterGrade`"
"the `Lettergrade` item with index of 2"
"the `LetterGrade` item with subscript of 2"
"`LetterGrade` sub 2"

In Modula-2 the corresponding syntax is

`LetterGrade[2]`

12.3 ARRAY DECLARATION

Like any other Modula-2 data structure, an array must be declared before it is used. Figure 12.5 describes declaration of array types.

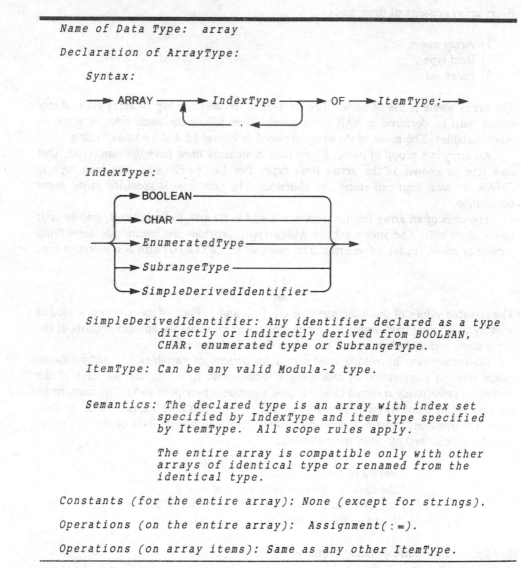

```
Name of Data Type:  array

Declaration of ArrayType:

    Syntax:

    ──→ ARRAY ──────→ IndexType ──────→ OF ──→ ItemType; ──→
                 ↑            ↓
                 └──── , ◄────┘

    IndexType:

              ┌──→ BOOLEAN ───────────────────────┐
              │                                    │
              ├──→ CHAR ──────────────────────────┤
              │                                    │
         ─────┼──→ EnumeratedType ────────────────┼──→
              │                                    │
              ├──→ SubrangeType ──────────────────┤
              │                                    │
              └──→ SimpleDerivedIdentifier ───────┘
```

    SimpleDerivedIdentifier: Any identifier declared as a type
              directly or indirectly derived from BOOLEAN,
              CHAR, enumerated type or SubrangeType.

    ItemType: Can be any valid Modula-2 type.

    Semantics: The declared type is an array with index set
          specified by IndexType and item type specified
          by ItemType. All scope rules apply.

          The entire array is compatible only with other
          arrays of identical type or renamed from the
          identical type.

Constants (for the entire array): None (except for strings).

Operations (on the entire array): Assignment(:=).

Operations (on array items): Same as any other ItemType.

FIGURE 12.5 *The array data type*

Both "IndexType" (the index set) and "ItemType" (the type for each array cell) are required in an array declaration. An array can have multiple index sets. Such an array is called a **multidimensional array**. An array with a single index set is known as a **one-dimensional array** or a **vector**. This chapter examines the use of vectors, while multidimensional arrays are presented in the next chapter.

Figure 12.6 contains several examples of array declarations. Below each declaration is a cellular picture of the array. The indices for each array item are shown above the corresponding cell. The type of the data within each cell is labeled "Cell type."

Declaration:

```
VAR
    LetterGrade  : ARRAY [1..3] OF CHAR;
```

LetterGrade   [1]   [2]   [3]

Cell type: CHAR

Declaration:

```
VAR
    DigCount : ARRAY ["0".."9"] OF CARDINAL;
```

DigCount
["0"] ["1"] ["2"] ["3"] ["4"] ["5"] ["6"] ["7"] ["8"] ["9"]

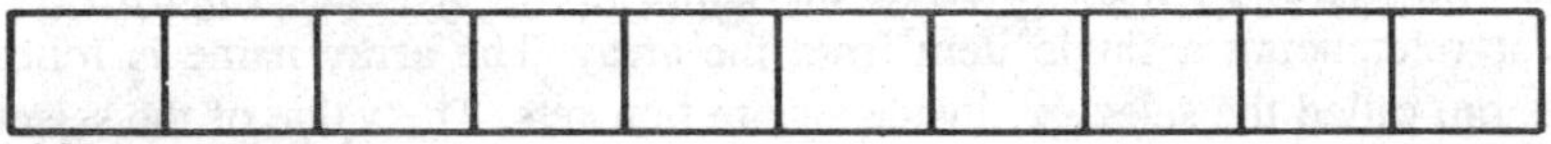

Cell type: CARDINAL

Declaration:

```
TYPE
    TwoContestants = (SamJones, MarkBlack);
VAR
    Contestant : ARRAY BOOLEAN OF TwoContestants;
```

Contestant   [FALSE][TRUE]

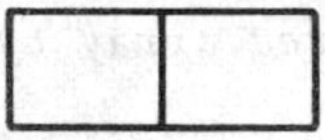

Cell type: TwoContestants *(may store either* SamJones *or* MarkBlack)

Declaration:

```
TYPE
    Employees = (Mae, Sue, Jim);
    EmpSalaryArray = ARRAY Employees OF REAL;
VAR
    Salary : EmpSalaryArray
```

Salary   [Mae] [Sue] [Jim]

Cell type: REAL

FIGURE 12.6 *Examples of array declarations*

The first declaration in Figure 12.6 is repeated from the earlier section. Letter-Grade is an array in which each of its three items stores a single CHAR value. The second example declares an array, named DigCount. The ten items of this array are indexed by the characters from "0" through "9", and each item stores a single cardinal value. The third example is an array named Contestant. The items of the array are indexed by the Boolean values TRUE and FALSE. Each item can store a value of the enumerated type called TwoContestants. The final example declares a type called EmpSalaryArray. This type is then used to declare an array data structure called Salary. Salary consists of three items. Each item stores a single REAL value. The indices of the items are the enumerated constants Mae, Sue, and Jim.

The index type specifies the **size of the array**, its number of items. The size of LetterGrade is 3, DigCount is 10, Contestant is 2 and Salary is 3. The size of an array is the number of elements in its index set. If the index set is BOOLEAN, then the array size is 2. If the index set is [1..10] then the array size is 10.

12.4 ACCESSING THE ITEMS OF AN ARRAY

An array name by itself refers to the entire group of items. Figure 12.7 shows the form for referencing a single item from the array. The array name is followed by an expression, called the **selector**, inside square brackets. The value of the selector expression is the index for the selected item. It must be within the index set.

```
Array item reference designator syntax:


  ──▶ ArrayName ──▶ [ ──▶ ItemExpression ──▶ ] ──────▶



ArrayName: A previously declared array type data structure

ItemExpression: Any expression compatible with ItemType for
                the specified array

Semantics: This reference is used to name an item from array
           ArrayName with index given by the value of
           ItemExpression.  The value of ItemExpression must
           be within the bounds of the ItemType or an
           execution error results.
```

FIGURE 12.7 *Syntax of a reference to a vector item*

Figure 12.8 contains several references to array items. Below each example is a picture of the cell that is referenced. The declarations from Figure 12.6 are assumed.

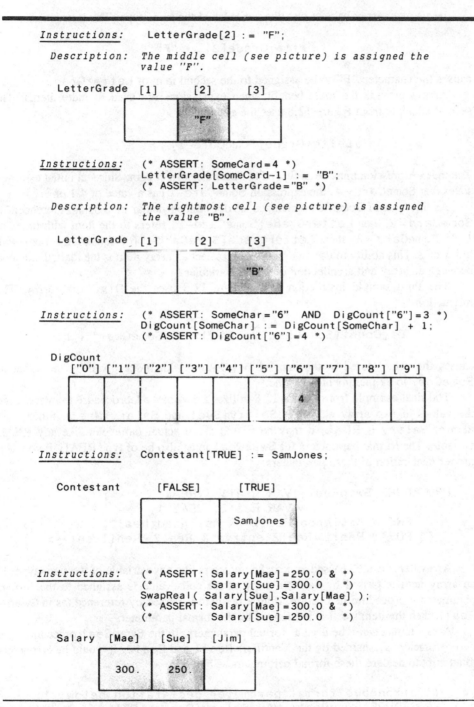

Instructions: LetterGrade[2] := "F";

Description: The middle cell (see picture) is assigned the
value "F".

LetterGrade   [1]   [2]   [3]

Instructions: (* ASSERT: SomeCard = 4 *)
LetterGrade[SomeCard-1] := "B";
(* ASSERT: LetterGrade="B" *)

Description: The rightmost cell (see picture) is assigned
the value "B".

LetterGrade   [1]   [2]   [3]

Instructions: (* ASSERT: SomeChar = "6"   AND   DigCount["6"]=3 *)
DigCount[SomeChar] := DigCount[SomeChar] + 1;
(* ASSERT: DigCount["6"]=4 *)

DigCount
   ["0"] ["1"] ["2"] ["3"] ["4"] ["5"] ["6"] ["7"] ["8"] ["9"]

Instructions: Contestant[TRUE] := SamJones;

Contestant   [FALSE]   [TRUE]

Instructions: (* ASSERT: Salary[Mae]=250.0 & *)
(*   Salary[Sue]=300.0   *)
SwapReal(Salary[Sue],Salary[Mae]);
(* ASSERT: Salary[Mae]=300.0 & *)
(*   Salary[Sue]=250.0   *)

Salary   [Mae]   [Sue]   [Jim]

FIGURE 12.8 *Examples of references to array items*

Items of an array behave just like variables of the same type. The instruction

```
LetterGrade[2] := "F";
```

causes the character "F" to be assigned to the second item of LetterGrade.

Arrays provide the most benefit when expressions are used to index items. The second example from Figure 12.8 uses the assignment

```
LetterGrade[SomeCard-1] := "B";
```

The index expression must be evaluated to select the correct item. Since an initial assertion states that SomeCard = 4, the expression SomeCard-1 has a value of 4-1 or 3.

As the value of SomeCard changes, so does the particular item being referenced. If SomeCard = 2, then LetterGrade[SomeCard-1] refers to the item with index of 1. If SomeCard = 3, then LetterGrade[SomeCard-1] refers to the item with index of 2. This ability to use an expression to select an array item is the main distinction between an array and a collection of simple variables.

The third sample instruction from Figure 12.8 uses the DigCount array. The instruction

```
DigCount[SomeChar] := DigCount[SomeChar] + 1
```

causes the value stored in the item of DigCount with index given by the value of SomeChar to be incremented by one.

The final example from Figure 12.8 utilizes a SwapReal procedure to interchange the values of two array elements (Salary[Sue] and Salary[Mae]). Since each item of Salary is REAL, it may be passed as an actual parameter like any REAL variable. The formal parameters for SwapReal must also be of type REAL. Below is a proper declaration of these parameters:

```
PROCEDURE SwapReal( VAR Real1 : REAL;
                    VAR Real2: REAL );
   (* PRE:   Assigned(Real1) & Assigned(Real2)         *)
   (* POST: Real1=Real2<entry> & Real2=Real1<entry> *)
```

Array items can be passed as actual parameters like any variable of the same type. If an array item is passed by value, a copy of the cells value is assigned to the formal parameter at procedure invocation. If an array item is passed by reference (as in Swap-Real), then the item's cell is referenced by the formal parameter.

Array items *cannot* be used as formal parameters. In the SwapReal procedure, the two parameters are named by the identifiers Real1 and Real2. It would be erroneous to attempt to declare these formal parameters as below

```
(* erroneous formal parameter declaration below: *)
PROCEDURE SwapReal( VAR Salary[Sue] : REAL;
                    VAR Salary[Mae] : REAL );
```

Care must be taken to ensure that an index expression is valid. An **array-index bounds violation** occurs at run-time when the value of an index expression is outside the range of the index set. Such an error occurs in a reference such as `LetterGrade[4]` or `LetterGrade[0]`. This variety of execution error is similar to boundary errors on simple variables. Typical error messages include:

```
INDEX VALUE OUT OF BOUNDS
INDEX RANGE VIOLATION
SUBCRIPT OUT OF BOUNDS
```

In some Modula-2 systems, array-index bounds violations are not detected. Still others offer bounds checking as an option that may be enabled or disabled. If bounds checking is not performed and a bounds violation occurs, almost anything can happen, so it is wise to use bounds checking.

12.5 USES OF VECTORS — RANDOM ACCESS

Two basic techniques for manipulating the items in an array are:

1) Random access
2) Sequential access

Sequential access is used whenever the items of an array are processed in some particular order. **Random access** occurs whenever array items are processed in no particular order.

An **array of counters** is a common application of arrays that involves random access. Each item of an array of counters serves as an individual counter. The indices of the array are used to specify the particular object being counted.

Suppose a psychologist is collecting favorite numbers of people. Figure 12.9 shows a section of Modula-2 code to read and count a favorite number within a range from 0 to 9. The associated declarations are also included. `PreferredNum` is an array that stores 10 counters, one for each possible favorite number. The user provides input to the `Preference` variable. The value of `Preference` is then used to select which item from the array to increment. If, for example, the user inputs the number 3, then `PreferredNum` is incremented.

```
Declarations:

        TYPE
            DecDigit = [0..9];
        VAR
            Preference : CARDINAL;
            PreferredNum : ARRAY DecDigit OF CARDINAL;
```

(continued)

Code:

```
WriteString( "Favorite number from 0 to 9?" );
ReadCard( Preference );
INC( PreferedNum[Preference] );
```

FIGURE 12.9 *Declarations and code to record favorite number*

These counters of `PreferredNum` are said to be "randomly accessed," because the order in which they are incremented depends upon the values input by the user.

An **array of BOOLEAN**, is a simplified version of a counter array. The items store a true/false, yes/no, on/off, 1/0 kind of situation.

For example, a program keeping track of which employees are available could use the following array:

```
VAR
    Available : ARRAY EmployeeIDs OF BOOLEAN;
```

where `EmployeeIDs` is some range of employee identifications. As an employee checks into the office, the corresponding `Available` item is assigned TRUE. When the employee checks out of the office, the correct item must be assigned FALSE.

Sometimes algorithms using arrays of counters increment or decrement by irregular values. This is the case when arrays of counters are used as storage for maintaining inventories. Figure 12.10 contains the problem definition for a swimming pool inventory problem that illustrates this array application.

TITLE
Swimming Pool Inventory

DESCRIPTION
The Sporty Submersion Swimming Pool Company needs a program to maintain its inventory. The company markets three swimming pool models: the Deluxe, the Grand Deluxe, and the Supreme Grand Deluxe.
The program repeatedly accepts commands of four types. They are:

1) Receive New Inventory
2) Ship Pools to Distributor
3) Query Inventory
4) Terminate Program Execution

When the "Receive New Inventory" or "ship pools to distributors" commands are input, the program must be able to update the inventory appropriately for some user-specified pool model. The "Query Inventory" command causes the program to display the current inventory for all models.
An important prerequisite of the program is that it must be easy to use. User input is largely in response to two menus. The first menu is the Command Menu, which prompts the user to specify an appropriate command. The second menu is the Pool Model Menu which prompts the user to specify a particular pool model. The only other input is made in response to a prompt for the quantity

(continued)

involved in either a "Receive New Inventory" or "Ship Pools to Distributor" command.

The program should assume that initially the inventories are all zero.

INPUT

The program repeatedly prompts for commands. Each command is specified by a single decimal digit from 1 to 4, where the correspondence of input to command is shown in the DESCRIPTION section. If the input supplied is "4," then the program terminates execution. If the input supplied is "3," then the current inventory is displayed and the program prompts for the next command. If the input supplied is "1" or "2," then the user is prompted to select a pool model and a quantity. The quantity must be a valid cardinal constant. The pool model specification is a single character, "A" for Supreme Grand Deluxe, "B" for Grand Deluxe, and "C" for Deluxe.

OUTPUT

There are three input prompts: the command menu, the pool model menu, and the prompt for quantity. Each of these prompts is preceded by a few blank lines. The prompts are shown below.

```
Command Menu:        Select One (1, 2, 3 or 4)
                     -------------------------
                       1) Receive New Inventory
                       2) Ship Pools to Distributors
                       3) Query Inventory
                       4) Terminate Program Execution

Pool Model Menu:     Select One (A, B or C)
                     ----------------------
                       A) Supreme Grand Deluxe
                       B) Grand Deluxe
                       C) Deluxe
```

Prompt for Quantity input: Indicate the quantity:

Following a successful inventory update (occurs for Commands 1 and 2), the following one-line message is displayed to show that the operation was completed

```
            Inventory Updated
```

A query command causes the following inventory report to be displayed.

```
        Inventory Report
        --------------------
        Supreme Grand Deluxe ... <S>
        Grand Deluxe .......... <G>
        Deluxe ................ <D>
```

In the form above <S> symbolizes the current inventory of the Supreme Grand Deluxe model, <G> symbolizes the Grand Deluxe, and <D> symbolizes the Deluxe. The above report is preceded by a few blank lines.

(continued)

ERRORS

One of the objectives of the program is robustness. The following input errors and unusual situations are handled:

1) Any input other than 1, 2, 3, or 4 to the command menu and A, B, or C to the pool models menu results in the following error message and a return to the command menu:

INCORRECT RESPONSE

2) Whenever a "Ship Pools to Distributor" command is given and the resulting inventory is below 100, the following message should be printed on the line following the "Inventory Updated" message:

WARNING – Inventory of this model is low

3) Any attempt to specify a "Ship Pools to Distributors" command with a quantity greater than the current inventory results in the following message in place of the "Inventory Updated" message:

INSUFFICIENT INVENTORY – command ignored.

The inventory remains unchanged in this case and the program returns to the command menu.

EXAMPLE

Below is an example execution. Input is signified by items that are highlighted.

```
            Select One (1, 2, 3 or 4)
            ---------------------------
              1) Receive New Inventory
              2) Ship Pools to Distributors
              3) Query Inventory
              4) Terminate Program Execution
          3

            Inventory Report
            -----------------
            Supreme Grand Deluxe ...     0
            Grand Deluxe ...........     0
            Deluxe .................     0

            Select One (1, 2, 3 or 4)
            ---------------------------
              1) Receive New Inventory
              2) Ship Pools to Distributors
              3) Query Inventory
              4) Terminate Program Execution
          1
```

(continued)

```
Select One (A, B or C)
----------------------
    A) Supreme Grand Deluxe
    B) Grand Deluxe
    C) Deluxe
A

Indicate the quantity: 200
Inventory Updated.


Select One (1, 2, 3 or 4)
-------------------------
    1) Receive New Inventory
    2) Ship Pools to Distributors
    3) Query Inventory
    4) Terminate Program Execution
1

Select One (A, B or C)
----------------------
    A) Supreme Grand Deluxe
    B) Grand Deluxe
    C) Deluxe
C

Indicate the quantity: 75
Inventory Updated.


Select One (1, 2, 3 or 4)
-------------------------
    1) Receive New Inventory
    2) Ship Pools to Distributors
    3) Query Inventory
    4) Terminate Program Execution
3

Inventory Report
----------------
Supreme Grand Deluxe ...   200
Grand Deluxe ...........     0
Deluxe .................    75


Select One (1, 2, 3 or 4)
-------------------------
    1) Receive New Inventory
    2) Ship Pools to Distributors
    3) Query Inventory
    4) Terminate Program Execution
2
```

(continued)

```
Select One (A, B or C)
----------------------
    A) Supreme Grand Deluxe
    B) Grand Deluxe
    C) Deluxe
A

Indicate the quantity: 25
Inventory Updated.


Select One (1, 2, 3 or 4)
-------------------------
    1) Receive New Inventory
    2) Ship Pools to Distributors
    3) Query Inventory
    4) Terminate Program Execution
1

Select One (A, B or C)
----------------------
    A) Supreme Grand Deluxe
    B) Grand Deluxe
    C) Deluxe
C

Indicate the quantity: 10
Inventory Updated.


Select One (1, 2, 3 or 4)
-------------------------
    1) Receive New Inventory
    2) Ship Pools to Distributors
    3) Query Inventory
    4) Terminate Program Execution
3

Inventory Report
----------------
Supreme Grand Deluxe ...  175
Grand Deluxe ...........    0
Deluxe .................   85


Select One (1, 2, 3 or 4)
-------------------------
    1) Receive New Inventory
    2) Ship Pools to Distributors
    3) Query Inventory
    4) Terminate Program Execution
2
```

(continued)

```
Select One (A, B or C)
----------------------
    A) Supreme Grand Deluxe
    B) Grand Deluxe
    C) Deluxe
C

Indicate the quantity: 20
Inventory Updated.
WARNING - Inventory of this model is low


Select One (1, 2, 3 or 4)
-------------------------
    1) Receive New Inventory
    2) Ship Pools to Distributors
    3) Query Inventory
    4) Terminate Program Execution
2

Select One (A, B or C)
----------------------
    A) Supreme Grand Deluxe
    B) Grand Deluxe
    C) Deluxe
A

Indicate the quantity: 300
INSUFFICIENT INVENTORY - command ignored.


Select One (1, 2, 3 or 4)
-------------------------
    1) Receive New Inventory
    2) Ship Pools to Distributors
    3) Query Inventory
    4) Terminate Program Execution
X
INCORRECT RESPONSE


Select One (1, 2, 3 or 4)
-------------------------
    1) Receive New Inventory
    2) Ship Pools to Distributors
    3) Query Inventory
    4) Terminate Program Execution
3

Inventory Report
----------------
Supreme Grand Deluxe ...   175
Grand Deluxe ..........     0
Deluxe ...............     65
```

(continued)

```
Select One (1, 2, 3 or 4)
------------------------
    1) Receive New Inventory
    2) Ship Pools to Distributors
    3) Query Inventory
    4) Terminate Program Execution
4
```

FIGURE 12.10 *Problem definition for swimming pool inventory*

Figure 12.11 contains a Modula-2 program for the swimming pool inventory problem.

```
MODULE PoolInventory;
        (* This program processes pool inventory *)
    FROM InOut IMPORT Read, ReadCard, WriteString, WriteCard,
                    WriteLn;
    CONST
        Supreme = "A"; (* Menu input for Supreme Grand Deluxe *)
        Grand = "B";   (*  "       "    "  Grand Deluxe       *)
        Deluxe = "C";  (*  "       "    "  Deluxe             *)
        ReceiveCmnd = "1";
        ShipOutCmnd = "2";
        QueryInvCmnd = "3";
        TerminateCmnd = "4";
    TYPE
        InventoryType = ARRAY [Supreme..Deluxe] OF CARDINAL;
    VAR
        QuantOnHand : InventoryType;
        Command : CHAR;

    PROCEDURE ZeroAllInventory( VAR Inventory : InventoryType );
        (* POST: All items of Inventory[Supreme..Deluxe] = 0 *)
    BEGIN
        Inventory[Supreme] := 0;
        Inventory[Grand] := 0;
        Inventory[Deluxe] := 0;
    END ZeroAllInventory;

    PROCEDURE DisplayCommandMenu;
        (* POST: Command menu is output. *)
    BEGIN
        WriteLn; WriteLn; WriteLn;
        WriteString("   Select One (1, 2, 3 or 4)"); WriteLn;
        WriteString("   ------------------------"); WriteLn;
        WriteString("     1) Receive New Inventory"); WriteLn;
        WriteString("     2) Ship Pools to Distributors"); WriteLn;
        WriteString("     3) Query Inventory"); WriteLn;
        WriteString("     4) Terminate Program Execution");WriteLn;
    END DisplayCommandMenu;

    PROCEDURE DisplayModelMenu;
        (* POST: Pool model menu is output. *)
    BEGIN
        WriteLn; WriteLn;
        WriteString( "   Select One (A, B or C)" ); WriteLn;
        WriteString( "   ---------------------" ); WriteLn;
        WriteString( "     A) Supreme Grand Deluxe" ); WriteLn;
        WriteString( "     B) Grand Deluxe" ); WriteLn;
        WriteString( "     C) Deluxe" ); WriteLn;
    END DisplayModelMenu;
```

(continued)

```
PROCEDURE ReceiveInventory( VAR Invnty : InventoryType );
        (* PRE:   Inventy is assigned                          *)
        (* POST: A char and a cardinal are input               *)
        (*     &  (Supreme <= input char <= Deluxe)            *)
        (*            IMPLIES Inventy[input char] is increased *)
        (*                   by input cardinal                 *)
        (*            OTHERWISE  an error message is output     *)
    VAR
        Model : CHAR;
        Quant : CARDINAL;
BEGIN
    DisplayModelMenu;
    Read( Model );
    WriteLn;
    Model := CAP(Model);
    IF  (Supreme<=Model) & (Model<=Deluxe)  THEN
        WriteString( "   Indicate the quantity: ");
        ReadCard( Quant );
        WriteLn;
        Invnty[Model] := Invnty[Model] + Quant;
        WriteString( "   Inventory Updated." )
    ELSE
        WriteString( "   INCORRECT RESPONSE")
    END
END ReceiveInventory;

PROCEDURE ShipToDistributor( VAR Invnty : InventoryType );
        (* PRE:   Inventy is assigned                          *)
        (* POST: A char and a cardinal are input               *)
        (*     &  (Supreme <= input char <= Deluxe)            *)
        (*            IMPLIES Inventy[input char] is decreased *)
        (*                   by input cardinal                 *)
        (*            OTHERWISE  an error message is output     *)
VAR
        Model : CHAR;
        Quant : CARDINAL;
BEGIN
    DisplayModelMenu;
    Read( Model );
    WriteLn;
    Model := CAP(Model);
    IF  (Supreme<=Model) & (Model<=Deluxe)  THEN
        WriteString( "   Indicate the quantity: ");
        ReadCard( Quant );
        WriteLn;
        IF  Invnty[Model]>=Quant  THEN
            Invnty[Model] := Invnty[Model] – Quant;
            WriteString( "   Inventory Updated." );
            IF  Invnty[Model]<100  THEN
                WriteLn;
                WriteString
                    ("WARNING – Inventory of this model is low");
            END
        ELSE
            WriteString
                ("INSUFFICIENT INVENTORY – command ignored");
        END
    ELSE
        WriteString( "   INCORRECT RESPONSE")
    END
END ShipToDistributor;
```

(continued)

```
PROCEDURE DisplayInventory( Inventory : InventoryType );
    (* PRE:    Inventory is assigned                    *)
    (* POST: a display of entire inventory output *)
BEGIN
    WriteLn; WriteLn;
    WriteString( "    Inventory Report" ); WriteLn;
    WriteString( "    ----------------" ); WriteLn;
    WriteString( "    Supreme Grand Deluxe ..." );
    WriteCard( Inventory[Supreme], 5); WriteLn;
    WriteString( "    Grand Deluxe ..........." );
    WriteCard( Inventory[Grand], 5); WriteLn;
    WriteString( "    Deluxe ................." );
    WriteCard( Inventory[Deluxe], 5)
END DisplayInventory;


BEGIN   (* PoolInventory mainline *)
    ZeroAllInventory( QuantOnHand );
    REPEAT
        DisplayCommandMenu;
        Read( Command );
        CASE Command OF
            ReceiveCmnd   : ReceiveInventory( QuantOnHand )
            ShipOutCmnd   : ShipToDistributor( QuantOnHand )
            QueryInvCmnd  : DisplayInventory( QuantOnHand )
            TerminateCmnd :   (* do nothing *)
        ELSE  (* erroneous input *)
            WriteString( "    INCORRECT RESPONSE");
            WriteLn
        END
        (* INV: The QuantOnHand array correctly stores the *)
        (*      current pool inventory for each pool type. *)
    UNTIL Command=TerminateCmnd
END PoolInventory.
```

FIGURE 12.11 *The PoolInventory program*

The PoolInventory program uses a three item array, called QuantOnHand to store the inventories of the three pool models. User input specifies each particular pool model as a single character ("A" for Supreme Grand Deluxe, "B" for Grand Deluxe and "C" for Deluxe). These three characters form the index set of QuantOnHand. Three constants, Supreme, Grand, and Deluxe, are declared globally to correspond to the user input selections. This permits the array type to be declared as follows:

```
TYPE
    InventoryType = ARRAY [Supreme..Deluxe] OF CARDINAL;
```

This program makes use of several procedures. A complete procedure hierarchy chart is shown in Figure 12.12. The mainline invokes ZeroAllInventory to initialize all inventory to zero. Within the REPEAT loop, the mainline uses DisplayCommandMenu to output the main menu to the user. The appropriate user-specified command is processed by either ReceiveInventory, ShipToDistributor, or DisplayInventory. Both ReceiveInventory and ShipToDistributor utilize a procedure, called DisplayModelMenu to output the pool model menu.

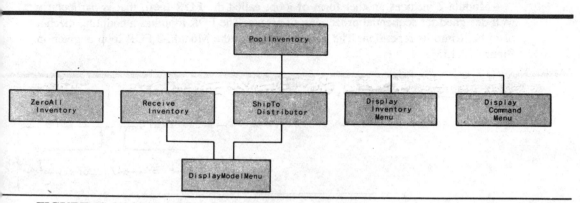

FIGURE 12.12 *Module hierarchy chart for PoolInventory*

Several of the procedures in the PoolInventory program pass the entire inventory array as parameters. For example, ZeroAllInventory is invoked by the mainline to initialize all inventory to zero. The QuantOnHand array is the actual parameter, and the corresponding formal parameter is Inventory. When an entire array is passed this way, any or all of its items may be used by the procedure.

The Modula-2 requirement that formal and actual parameters passed by reference have *identical* type is the reason that InventoryType is declared separately. Both QuantOnHand and Inventory are corerctly declared with the identical type InventoryType.

One of the appealing features of arrays is the ease with which they can be extended. Suppose the Sporty Submersion Swimming Pool Company decides to add a new intermediate quality model, called the "Semi-Grand Deluxe." The following programmer-defined constants are used to clarify the encoding of user input:

```
CONST
  Supreme = "A";  (* Menu input for Supreme Grand Deluxe *)
  Grand   = "B";  (*  "    "    "  Grand Deluxe          *)
  Semi    = "C";  (*  "    "    "  Semi-Grand Deluxe      *)
  Deluxe  = "D";  (*  "    "    "  Deluxe                 *)
```

With a few minor modifications, the PoolInventory program will work for all four pools. These modifications include changes to the pool model menu and the ZeroAllInventory and DisplayInventory procedures. Neither ReceiveInventory nor ShipToDistributor need to be altered in any way.

12.6 A CONTROL STRUCTURE FOR LOOP PROCESSING: THE FOR LOOP

Sequential array access is a technique of referencing the items of an array in sequence. Sequential access is used in algorithms that process array items like the articles on an assembly line, one right after another.

Modula-2 includes another form of loop, called the **FOR loop,** that is particularly well designed for sequential processing of arrays. The FOR loop has a counting mechanism built into its repetition. The general syntax of the Modula-2 FOR loop is given in Figure 12.13.

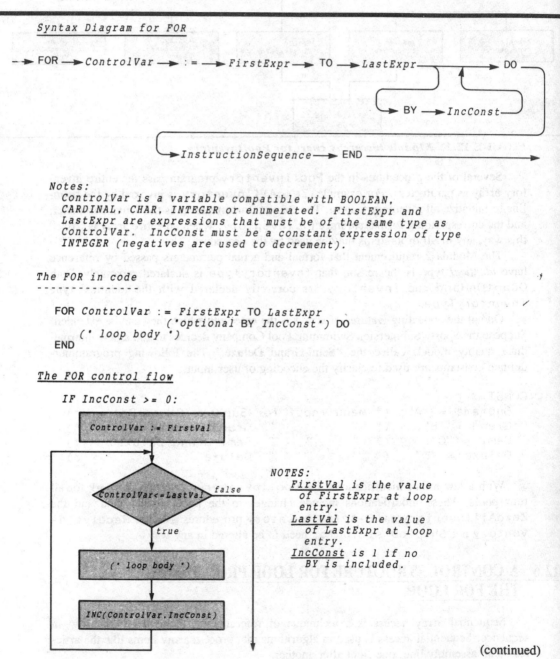

```
Syntax Diagram for FOR
```

Notes:
```
   ControlVar is a variable compatible with BOOLEAN,
   CARDINAL, CHAR, INTEGER or enumerated.  FirstExpr and
   LastExpr are expressions that must be of the same type as
   ControlVar.  IncConst must be a constant expression of type
   INTEGER (negatives are used to decrement).
```

The FOR in code

```
   FOR ControlVar := FirstExpr TO LastExpr
                   ('optional BY IncConst') DO
      (' loop body ')
   END
```

The FOR control flow

```
   IF IncConst >= 0:
```

NOTES:
```
   FirstVal is the value
      of FirstExpr at loop
      entry.
   LastVal is the value
      of LastExpr at loop
      entry.
   IncConst is 1 if no
      BY is included.
```

(continued)

IF IncConst < 0:

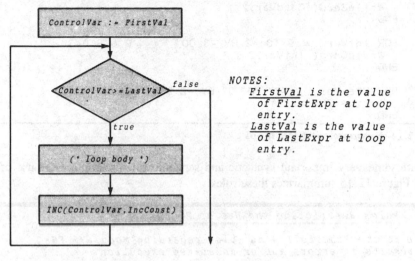

NOTES:
  FirstVal is the value
    of FirstExpr at loop
    entry.
  LastVal is the value
    of LastExpr at loop
    entry.

FIGURE 12.13 *Summary of FOR*

The FOR loop requires a **control variable**. As the loop is entered, FirstExpr and LastExpr are evaluated (in Figure 12.13 the resulting values are called "FirstVal" and "LastVal"). The control variable is assigned FirstVal for the first loop iteration. The control variable is automatically incremented after each loop iteration.

The amount of the increment can be varied by including a "BY IncConst," where InConst is some constant expression. If no "BY IncConst" clause is included then IncConst = 1 is assumed. After each loop iteration the control variable is incremented by IncConst.

The loop condition is tested at the top of a FOR loop. The loop will continue until the control variable has a value beyond LastVal. Figure 12.14 illustrates the execution of several FOR loops. For each FOR loop in this figure the output of the code is specified to the right.

Program Section	Output
FOR CardVar := 1 TO 4 DO WriteCard(CardVar,2) END	1 2 3 ·4
FOR CardVar := 1 TO 5 BY 2 DO WriteCard(CardVar,2) END	1 3 5
FOR CardVar := 0 TO 8 BY 3 DO WriteCard(CardVar,2) END	0 3 6
FOR CardVar := 4 TO 1 DO WriteCard(CardVar,2) END	(* no output *)

(continued)

```
FOR CardVar  : = 6 TO 2 BY −1 DO           6 5 4 3 2
   WriteCard( CardVar,2 )
END

FOR IntVar  : = 9 TO −3 BY −3 DO           9 6 3 0−3
   WriteCard( IntVar,2 )
END

FOR CharVar  : = "Z" TO "S" BY −2 DO       ZXVT
   Write( CharVar )
END
```

FIGURE 12.14 *Examples of FOR loops*

There are some very important syntactic and semantic rules restricting the use of FOR loops. Figure 12.15 summarizes these rules.

```
        Rules Restricting the Use of FOR Loops

Failure to obey the following rules regarding Modula-2 FOR
loops results in errors and/or undefined execution.

ControlVar rules
    1) None of the following may be used as control
       variables: a formal parameter, an imported
       variable, or any component of a structured variable.
    2) The value of the control variable should not be
       altered within the body of a FOR loop.
    3) The value of a control variable upon loop
       termination must be assumed to be unassigned.

FirstExpr and LastExpr rules
    1) The type of FirstExpr and LastExpr must be
       compatible with the control variable.
    2) FirstExpr and LastExpr are evaluated immediately
       before loop execution and not reevaluated after loop
       iterations.  Any code executed in the loop body that
       alters the value of these expressions will have no
       effect on the loop iteration mechanism.

IncConst rules
    1) IncConst must be of type CARDINAL or INTEGER.
    2) IncConst must be a constant expression (i.e., contain
       only constants as operands).
```

FIGURE 12.15 *Important rules about the use of FOR loops*

To further illustrate the complete semantics of the FOR loop, Figure 12.16 shows a typical FOR loop and a functionally equivalent WHILE loop. TempLastVal is included to illustrate that LastExpr is evaluated prior to the loop execution and cannot be altered within the loop.

A FOR loop

```
(* ASSERT: IncConst>=0 *)
FOR ControlVar := FirstExpr TO LastExpr BY IncConst DO
    LoopBody
END
```

A functionally equivalent WHILE loop

```
ControlVar := FirstExpr;
TempLastExpr := LastExpr;  (* TempLastExpr is a new var. *)
                           (* not used elsewhere         *)
WHILE ControlVar<=TempLastExpr DO
    LoopBody;  (* must not alter ControlVar *)
    INC( ControlVar, IncConst )
END
(* ControlVar assumed unassigned at this point *)
```

FIGURE 12.16 *The semantics of FOR in terms of WHILE*

The ZeroAllInventory procedure from Figure 12.11 procedure is rewritten using a FOR loop as shown in Figure 12.17.

```
PROCEDURE ZeroAllInventory( VAR Inventory : InventoryType );
    (* POST: all items from Inventory = 0 *)
VAR
    Model : [Supreme..Deluxe];
BEGIN
    FOR Model := Supreme
        (* INV: All Inventory items with indices <Model are =0 *)
        (*       & Model <= the character following Deluxe      *)
    TO Deluxe DO
        Inventory[Model] := 0
    END
END ZeroAllInventory;
```

FIGURE 12.17 *The ZeroAllInventory procedure using a FOR loop*

This procedure illustrates the use of a loop invariant in a FOR loop. Invariants should be placed just after the initial assignment of the control variable, but before the TO phrase. Initialization of the invariant may assume that the first control variable value is assigned.

The automatic control variable increment of the FOR loop must be remembered. The loop invariant must be preserved after executing the loop body *and then* incrementing the control variable.

The finalization argument may assume the control variable has been incremented once past the LastExpr value (If the increment value is 1, this means that the control variable is $> =$ LastVal + 1). [Caution: This assumption about the value of the control variable after the loop is valid only for purposes of arguing for finalization. The actual value assigned to a control variable is undefined outside the loop.]

Programming-with-Style

Using the FOR Loop

The FOR loop should *not* be considered a general purpose control structure. It should be used only when there is clear evidence that the loop meets both of the following requirements.

1) The number of iterations can always be determined when the loop begins to execute.
2) The loop condition is conveniently expressed in terms of an initial and final value.

The FOR loop is particularly useful in sequential processing of arrays, or when a loop needs to be iterated some predetermined number of times.

The best style for a FOR loop is shown below:

```
FOR ControlVar := FirstExpr (* INV: the invariant *)
TO LastExpr (* optional BY *) DO
  (* loop body *)
END
```

12.7   USES OF VECTORS: SEQUENTIAL ACCESS

The ZeroAllInventory procedure (see Figure 12.17) is an example of sequential array access. ZeroAllInventory assigns 0 to the item with the smallest index value, then the middle index, and finally the greatest index.

Sequential array access can be expressed by a general algorithm. Assuming an array called SomeArr, with index type of [Lo..Hi], the style of processing used in sequential access is generalized as shown by the loop invariant below.

```
FOR sub:=Lo  (* INV: all items of SomeArray[Lo..sub-1] *)
             (*      are processed   AND   sub<=Hi+1      *)
TO Hi  DO
  (* process SomeArr[sub] *)
END
```

The notation SomeArray[Lo..sub-1] used in this invariant is a convenient method for abbreviating a consecutive collection of array items. This notation is not valid for code, but often is useful in assertions.

This algorithm causes every item of SomeArr to be processed proceeding from the first (with index Lo) to the last (with index Hi). A general algorithm to process items in the opposite order is shown on the opposite page.

```
FOR sub:=Hi      (* INV: all items of SomeArray[sub+1..Hi] *)
                 (*       are processed  AND  sub>=Lo¦1      *)
TO Lo  BY -1  DO
    (* process SomeArr[sub] *)
END
```

BUFFERS AND PARTIALLY-USED ARRAYS

One common application of sequential algorithms is input or output buffering. A **buffer** is a vector used to store a collection of input values prior to processing or a collection of output values prior to writing. The loop from Figure 12.18 can be used to input all of the characters of a single line into an array (the input buffer) called Line-Buf. LineBuf is assumed to have an item type of CHAR and an index set of a sufficient subrange of cardinals.

```
NextIndx := 1;
Read( LineBuf[NextIndx] );
WHILE (* INV: LineBuf[1..NextIndx] stores the portion of *)
      (*        input line read thusfar and doesn't       *)
      (*        contain EOL                               *)
(LineBuf[NextIndx] # EOL)  DO
    INC( NextIndx );
    Read( LineBuf[NextIndx] );
END;
(* ASSERT: The past input line is buffered up through EOL *)
(*         in  LineBuf[1..NextIndx]                       *)
```

FIGURE 12.18 *A loop to buffer a single line of input*

The code in Figure 12.18 also illustrates an application of a **partially-used array**. When the code completes execution, NextIndx has become the subscript of the LineBuf array item containing the EOL character. The algorithm has used only the LineBuf[1..NextIndx] portion of the array. Suppose LineBuf is declared as follows:

```
CONST
    MaxInputLine = 80;
TYPE
    BufferRange = [1..MaxInputLine+1];
    LineBufType = ARRAY BufferRange OF CHAR;
VAR
    LineBuf : LineBufType;
```

If the input line is only 35 characters long, then only the first 36 items from the array are assigned values by the loop. The unused items of the array are necessary to permit buffering of the longest possible line.

Once an input line has been buffered as shown in Figure 12.18, it can be processed in many ways. One simple sequential access algorithm that can be performed on such a line buffer is to output it. The code below accomplishes this task.

```
FOR i:=1 (* INV: LineBuf[1..i-1] is output & i<=NextIndx *)
TO NextIndx-1 DO
    Write( LineBuf[i]);
END;
WriteLn;
```

SEARCHING ALGORITHMS: THE LINEAR SEARCH

Another important class of sequential array algorithms is known as **searching algorithms**. One type of searching algorithm sequentially processes an array, examining the contents of array cells for values with particular characteristics. The CapCount function of Figure 12.19 searches for and counts the number of uppercase letters stored in its parameter array.

```
PROCEDURE CapCount( CharArr : LineBufType;
                    LastItem : BufferRange )
: [0..MaxInputLine];
    (* PRE:  LastItem and CharArray[1..LastItem] are assigned *)
    (* POST: RESULT = number of upper case letters in         *)
    (*                CharArray[1..LastItem]                   *)
    VAR
        CapsFound : [0..MaxInputLine];
        i : BufferRange;
BEGIN
    CapsFound := 0;
    FOR i:=1 (* INV: CapsFound=number of upper case letters in *)
             (*      CharArray[1..i-1]  AND   i<=LastItem+1     *)
    TO LastItem  DO
        IF  ("A"<=CharArr[i]) & (CharArr[i]<="Z")  THEN
            CapsFound := CapsFound + 1;
        END;
    END;
    RETURN CapsFound
END CapCount;
```

FIGURE 12.19 *The CapCount function*

The Capcount function *searches* through all array items with a FOR loop. Every item that is found to store an uppercase letter causes the CapsFound variable to be incremented.

The **linear search** is the best known of all searching algorithms. A linear search scans through an array from the first item to the last, probing each item until it encounters one with an appropriate value or until it has examined all items without success. Figure 12.20 contains a procedure, called SearchBuffer that performs a linear search on an array for an item with value equal to SearchVal.

```
PROCEDURE SearchBuffer(    CharArr : LineBufType;
                           LoSub : [1..MaxInputLine];
                           HiSub : [1..MaxInputLine];
                           SearchVal : CHAR;
                       VAR MatchSub : BufferRange );
(* PRE:  LoSub, HiSub, SearchVal and CharArr[LoSub..HiSub]  *)
(*       are all assigned                                    *)
(* POST: MatchSub = smallest index >=LoSub such that this    *)
(*                      item of CharArr stores SearchVal     *)
(*                    = HiSub+1, if no CharArr item = SearchVal*)
BEGIN
    MatchSub := LoSub;
    WHILE  (* INV: no item from CharArr[LoSub..MatchSub-1]   *)
           (*         is =SearchVal    AND    MatchSub<=HiSub+1 *)
    (MatchSub<=HiSub) AND (CharArr[MatchSub]#SearchVal)  DO
        INC( MatchSub )
    END;
END SearchBuffer;
```

FIGURE 12.20 *The SearchBuffer procedure*

SearchBuffer examines the items of CharArr beginning with a subscript of LoSub and continuing consecutively to higher subcripts. When the first item storing the value SearchVal is found, its index is returned via the MatchSub parameter. If no such item is found, then MatchSub will be HiSub + 1 when the procedure returns.

MERGE ALGORITHMS

The **merge algorithms** make up still another variety of array processing. A merge algorithm processes multiple vectors and combines (merges) their item values into one array. There are many ways to merge. Two vectors can be merged so that the first portion of the resulting vector is from one of the originals and the last portion from the other. It is also possible to merge two vectors in such a way as to remove duplicate item values.

One merging algorithm, known as **interleaving**, takes two vectors and merges their contents alternately, preserving the order of the original vectors. Figure 12.21 on the following page, diagrams this algorithm. The arrows indicate the assignment of items from the two original arrays, Org1 and Org2, to the interleaved result, Intrlv. Figure 12.22 on the following page, shows a procedure for interleaving two arrays of four items each.

SHIFT ALGORITHMS

Yet another class of sequential array processing algorithms is known as **shifts**. A shift causes the contents of vector items to be assigned, or shifted, to their neighbors according to some pattern.

Figure 12.23 on page 415, diagrams the action of a **shift right** by one. When shifting right by one, each cell value is assigned to its neighbor to the right (the neighbor with next larger index). The rightmost original cell value is lost because it has no right neighbor. This version of the algorithm causes the leftmost cell to remain unchanged.

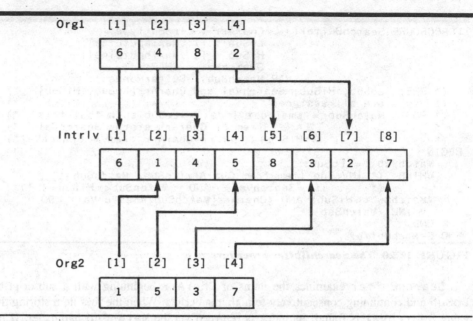

FIGURE 12.21 *Interleaving Org1 and Org2 to form Intrlv*

```
Assumed declarations for the Interleave2by4 procedure:

    TYPE
        FourItemArray  = ARRAY[1..4] OF CARDINAL;
        EightItemArray = ARRAY[1..8] OF CARDINAL;
```

```
PROCEDURE Interleave2by4(      Org1 : FourItemArray;
                               Org2 : FourItemArray;
                           VAR Intrlv : EightItemArray );
    (* PRE:  Org1[1..4] & Org2[1..4] are assigned              *)
    (* POST: Intrlv[1..8] contains Org1[1..4] and Org2[1..4]   *)
    (*       interleaved   i.e., Intrlv[1]=Org1[1],            *)
    (*       Intrlv[2]=Org2[1], Intrlv[3]=Org1[2], ...         *)
    VAR
        OrgI : [1..5];
BEGIN
    FOR OrgI:=1
        (* INV: Intrlv[1..2*(OrgI-1)] contains the interleave  *)
        (*      of Org1[1..OrgI-1] and Org2[1..OrgI-1]         *)
        (*      & OrgI <= 5                                     *)
    TO 4  DO
        Intrlv[OrgI*2-1] := Org1[OrgI];
        Intrlv[OrgI*2]   := Org2[OrgI];
    END
END Interleave2by4;
```

FIGURE 12.22 *The Interleave2by4 procedure*

Diagram of data movement:

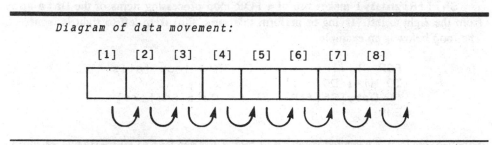

FIGURE 12.23 *Diagram of data movement for shift right*

Figure 12.24 illustrates the shift right operation on an array called Data. The result of this shift causes Data[2] to receive a copy of the original Data[1]. Data[3] receives a copy of the original Data[2], and so on.

Sample array, called "Data" (before shift right):

Data [1]   [2]   [3]   [4]   [5]   [6]   [7]   [8]

| 7 | 2 | 3 | 6 | 6 | 4 | 1 | 9 |

The Data array (after shift right):

Data [1]   [2]   [3]   [4]   [5]   [6]   [7]   [8]

| 7 | 7 | 2 | 3 | 6 | 6 | 4 | 1 |

FIGURE 12.24 *The results of shifting data right by one*

Figure 12.25 contains a ShiftRightBy1 procedure. ShiftRightBy1 shifts the Data array (its first parameter) right by one cell. Only the region of the array from index of Lo to index of Hi is shifted right.

```
PROCEDURE ShiftRightBy1( VAR Data : CardArrayType;
                             Lo : CARDINAL;
                             Hi : CARDINAL  );

    (* PRE:  CardArrayType is a vector with CARDINAL items   *)
    (*          AND  Data[Lo..Hi] is assigned                *)
    (* POST: For all subscripts, s, such that (Lo<=s<=Hi-1) *)
    (*          Data[s+1]=Data[s]<entry>                     *)
    VAR
        ShiftPt : CARDINAL;
BEGIN
    FOR ShiftPt:=Hi-1 (* INV: For all s, such that (ShiftPt+1<=s<=Hi-1),*)
                      (*         Data[s+1]=Data[s]<entry> & ShiftPt>=Lo-1  *)
    TO Lo BY -1 DO
        Data[ShiftPt+1] := Data[ShiftPt]
    END
END ShiftRightBy1;
```

FIGURE 12.25 *The ShiftRightBy1 procedure*

ShiftRightBy1 makes use of a FOR loop processing items of the Data array from the right to left. Trying to perform this same shift from left to right is incorrect. The loop below is an example.

```
FOR ShiftPt := Lo (* This loop fails *)
TO Hi-1 DO
    Data[ShiftPt+1] := Data[ShiftPt]
END
```

Suppose this loop is executed when ShiftPt = 3. Then Data[4] := Data[3] during the loop iteration. The next loop iteration performs Data[5] := Data[4], but Data[4] stores the previous value of Data[3] and not Data[4] <entry>. A trace of this new loop reveals that its postcondition is:

```
(* Assert: For all subscripts, s, such that  (Lo<=s<=Hi) *)
(*                  Data[s]  =  Data[Lo] <entry>                    *)
```

There are numerous other shifting algorithms. A vector can be shifted to the left, instead of right. It is also possible to shift a vector by more than one cell, where shifting by n cells is equivalent to n consecutive shift by one operations. Other modifications to shifting permit new value assignments to the cells normally unassigned by a shift. For example, a circular shift right by one performs a normal shift right by one with the modification that the final value of the leftmost cell is the original value of the rightmost cell.

12.8 AN EXAMPLE OF A SORTING ALGORITHM: THE INSERTION SORT

Sorting is the operation of rearranging the values of a collection of objects in some particular order. A sort is a boring and repetitious process that is well designed for computer processing. It is one of the most often used of all computer applications.

Values are sorted in either **ascending order** or **descending order**. Data that is arranged from smallest to largest is in ascending order. The words of a dictionary are sorted in ascending order. Sorting examination scores so that the highest scores are first is an example of a descending sort.

There are many sorting algorithms in use today. One of them is known as **insertion sort**, or **linear insertion sort**. The concept of an insertion sort algorithm is illustrated by considering the task of sorting five quizzes in ascending order across a desk top. Suppose the scores (8, 7, 5, 9, and 7) are written on the tops of the quiz papers. The insertion sort algorithm considers each quiz score separately and *inserts* it into the appropriate position.

To begin, the "8" quiz is considered. Since it is the only score examined, the quiz sheet is simply placed at the left edge of a desk top as shown on the opposite page.

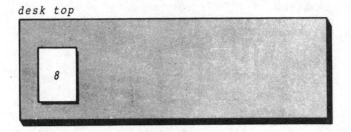

desk top

The second quiz score is 7. In order to insert this quiz into its proper position, the 8 quiz must be shifted to the right to make room. The result of this shift is shown below

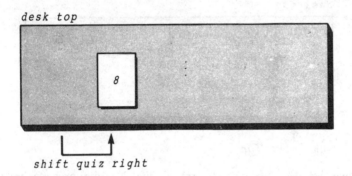

desk top

shift quiz right

Once the 8 quiz is shifted right, the 7 quiz is inserted in its proper place. Now the desk looks like this:

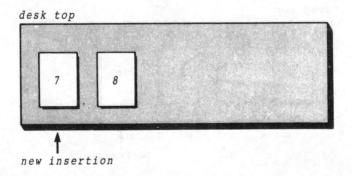

desk top

new insertion

The next quiz has a score of 5. In order to place the 5 quiz in the correct location, both of the previous quizzes must be shifted right and the 5 quiz placed at the left end of the desk. This shift and insert are shown in two steps on the following page:

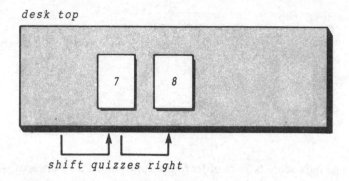

desk top

shift quizzes right

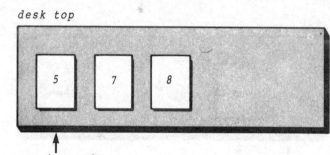

desk top

new insertion

Examining the next quiz score, 9, reveals that it is the largest examined thus far. Therefore, the 9 quiz is simply inserted on the right.

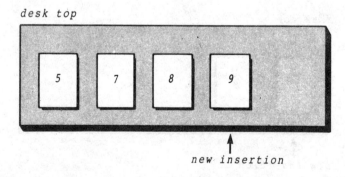

desk top

new insertion

The final quiz to consider has a score of 7. In order to insert this quiz properly, the 8 and 9 quizzes on the desk top must be shifted right, and then the new quiz inserted.

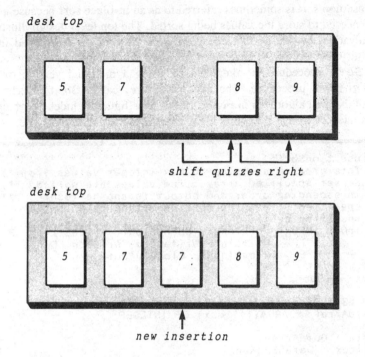

desk top

shift quizzes right

desk top

new insertion

This same insertion sort algorithm can be applied to a vector of values, Data-[1..Last]. Each of the items from the vector is examined from lowest index (1) to highest (Last). The items previously examined are maintained in ascending order in the first portion of the vector. This top level of the insertion sort algorithm is contained in Figure 12.26.

```
PROCEDURE Sort( VAR Data : DataArray;
                    Last : INTEGER  );
   (* PRE:  Data[1..Last] is assigned                      *)
   (* POST: Data[1..Last] contains the same values as      *)
   (*       Data[1..Last]<entry> except in ascending order *)
BEGIN
   FOR SortHi:=2 (* INV: Data[1..SortHi-1] contains its values from *)
                 (*      entry, rearranged in ascending order        *)
                 (*      & Data[SortHi..Last] is unchanged from entry *)
                 (*      & SortHi<=Last+1                             *)
   TO Last DO
        (* shift portion of Data[1..SortHi-1] that is greater
           than Data[SortHi] to the right then insert
           Data[SortHi] in its proper place *)
   END
END Sort;
```

FIGURE 12.26 *Top level of Sort (insertion) procedure*

The insertion sort is sometimes referred to as an **in-place sort** because no additional arrays are needed to store the values being sorted. The top level design illustrates this in the loop invariant by stating that one portion of the array is rearranged in ascending order and the other portion is unchanged from procedure entry.

The Sort procedure is completed by using a modified version of the earlier ShiftRightBy1 procedure. The new procedure, called ShiftRightToVal, is shown with the final algorithm in Figure 12.27. This figure includes Sort in a program that inputs integers from a file, sorts them and writes them to another file.

```
MODULE InsertionSort;
    (* This program sorts up to Max integer values from *)
    (* a user specified array.  The values are sorted   *)
    (* in ascending order and output to another user    *)
    (* specified file.  The sorting method used is the   *)
    (* insertion sort.                                   *)
    FROM InOut IMPORT OpenInput, OpenOutput, WriteString, ReadInt,
                   WriteInt, WriteCard, WriteLn, Done,
                   CloseInput, CloseOutput;
    CONST
        Max = 100;
    TYPE
        DataSizeRange = [0..Max];
        DataArray = ARRAY[1..Max] OF INTEGER;
    VAR
        Data : DataArray;
        HiIndx : DataSizeRange;

    PROCEDURE InputArray( VAR Data : DataArray;
                          VAR Last : DataSizeRange );
        (* PRE:  An input file must be opened                  *)
        (* POST: Data[1..Last] contain the integer values from *)
        (*       the input file                                *)
        (*    &  Last = number of inputs preceding end of file *)
        (*            = Max,  if more than Max inputs           *)
    BEGIN
        Last := 0;
        REPEAT
            INC( Last );
            ReadInt( Data[Last] );
            (* INV: Data[1..Last-1] contain the integer values *)
            (*      from the input file                         *)
            (*    & ( Data[Last] contains last input  OR  EOF) *)
            (*    & Last<=Max                                   *)
        UNTIL (NOT Done) OR (Last=Max);
        IF  NOT Done  THEN
            DEC( Last )
        END
    END InputArray;
```

(continued)

```
PROCEDURE OutputArray( Data : DataArray;
                       Last : DataSizeRange );
      (* PRE:  Data[1..Last] is assigned  *)
      (* POST: Data[1..Last] is output     *)
   VAR
      J : [0..Max+1];
BEGIN
   FOR J:=1  (* INV: Data[1..J-1] is output & J<=Last+1 *)
   TO Last  DO
      WriteInt( Data[J], 10 );
   END
END OutputArray;

PROCEDURE Sort( VAR Data : DataArray;
                    Last : CARDINAL );
      (* PRE:  Assigned( Data[1..Last] )               *)
      (* POST: SortedAscending( Data[1..Last] )        *)
      (*       AND ValuesMaintained( Data[1..Last] )  *)
   VAR
      SortHi : CARDINAL,
      CurrentVal : INTEGER;
      LowShift : CARDINAL;

   PROCEDURE ShiftRightToVal( VAR Data : DataArray;
                                  Hi : CARDINAL;
                                  Val : INTEGER;
                                  VAR LowShift : CARDINAL );
      (* PRE:  (1<Hi<=Max) & Data[1..Hi-1] is ascending          *)
      (* POST: For all subscripts, s, (LowShift+1<=s<=Hi-1)      *)
      (*              Data[s+1] = Data[s]<entry>                   *)
      (*         & LowShift = highest index of Data[1..Hi-1] for *)
      (*                  an item that is <= Val                  *)
      (*                = 0, if all Data[1..Hi-1] items > Val    *)
   BEGIN
      LowShift := Hi-1;
      WHILE (* INV: For all subscripts, s, (LowShift+1<=s<=Hi-1) *)
            (*          Data[s+1] = Data[s]<entry>                *)
            (*       & all items from Data[LowShift+1..Hi] are > Val *)
            (*       & LowShift>=0                                 *)
      (LowShift>=1) AND (Data[LowShift]>Val) DO
         Data[LowShift+1] := Data[LowShift];
         DEC( LowShift );
      END
   END ShiftRightToVal;

BEGIN (* Sort *)
   FOR SortHi:=2 (* INV: Data[1..SortHi-1] contains its values from *)
                 (*      entry, rearranged in ascending order        *)
                 (*    & Data[SortHi..Last] is unchanged from entry  *)
                 (*    & SortHi<=Last+1                               *)
   TO Last DO
      CurrentVal := Data[SortHi];
      ShiftRightToVal( Data, SortHi, CurrentVal, LowShift );
      Data[LowShift+1] := CurrentVal
   END
END Sort;
```

(continued)

```
BEGIN (* InsertionSort mainline *)
    WriteString( "This program sorts up to " );
    WriteCard( Max,0 );
    WriteString( " integers from one file to another " ); WriteLn;
    WriteString( "Please specify the original file of integers." );
    OpenInput( " " );
    InputArray( Data,HiIndx );

    Sort( Data,HiIndx );
    (* SortedAscending( Data[1..HiIndx] ) *)

    WriteLn; WriteLn;
    WriteString( "Please specify the new file for sorted integers.");
    OpenOutput( "" );
    OutputArray( Data,HiIndx );
    CloseInput;
    CloseOutput
END InsertionSort.
```

FIGURE 12.27 *The InsertionSort program*

The body of the Sort procedure saves each new value to be inserted in a variable called CurrentVal. Next, ShiftRightToVal is invoked, causing the sorted portion of Data to be shifted right to make room for CurrentVal. The ShiftRight-ToVal procedure assigns to LowShift the subscript that is 1 less than the lowest shifted item. Sort then inserts the value of CurrentVal into Data[Low-Shift + 1]. This process is repeated until all array items have been inserted into their correct location.

12.9 TREATING ARRAYS AS AGGREGATES

Sometimes it is convenient to manipulate the entire aggregate of array items as a single unit. Modula-2 includes two facilities for processing array aggregates:

1) An array can be assigned to another array.
2) An array can be passed as a parameter.

When one array is assigned to another, all of the item contents are copied. The arrays involved must be *assignment compatible*, for arrays this means they have identical types or are renamings of the same type.

Figure 12.28 illustrates an array assignment. The algorithm in this figure compares the monthly sales of two agents, Sales1 and Sales2, and assigns the sales of the agent with the greater total sales to an array called TopAgent.

Declarations used:

```
TYPE
    ThreeMonthSales = ARRAY (Jan, Feb, Mar) OF CARDINAL;
VAR
    Sales1 : ThreeMonthSales;
    Sales1 : ThreeMonthSales;
    TopAgent : ThreeMonthSales;
```

section of code

```
(* ASSERT: Sales1[Jan..Mar] and Sales2[Jan..Mar] *)
(*         are assigned                           *)
IF  Sales1[Jan]+Sales1[Feb]+Sales1[Mar]
    >  Sales2[Jan]+Sales2[Feb]+Sales2[Mar]
THEN
    TopAgent := Sales1
ELSE
    TopAgent := Sales2

END
(* ASSERT: TopAgent = Sales1,  if sum of Sales1[Jan..Mar] *)
(*                                > sum of Sales2[Jan..Mar] *)
(*                    = Sales2,  otherwise                 *)
```

FIGURE 12.28 *An example of an aggregate array assignment*

In an aggregate-array assignment instruction, the entire array is known by its array name; no index or index range is included. The example assigns the contents of all four items of Sales1 to the corresponding cells of TopAgent with the single instruction:

TopAgent := Sales1;

While Modula-2 does not permit a function to return a structured type, an array may be passed as a parameter. Every procedure in the InsertionSort program, Figure 12.27, uses an aggregate array parameter. When the entire array is passed by value, as in the OutputArray procedure, then the called routine receives a copy of the aggregate. The called routine has access to all of the item values of the array, but any changes to these values within the procedure occur only to the copy. When a procedure has an array parameter that is passed by reference, as in the InputArray, Sort, and ShiftRightToVal procedures, then the called routine is given access to the actual parameter array.

Compatibility rules require that actual and formal aggregate array parameters be of identical type or a renaming of the same type. (Renaming is allowed only for value parameters). This limits the flexibility of procedures to handle various array sizes. A procedure that can sort any sized array of INTEGERs is more flexible than a procedure that requires a single array size.

*P*rogramming-with-*S*tyle

When to Pass Array Aggregates by Reference

Parameter passage by value always causes the actual parameter to be copied into a data structure for the formal parameter. This copy operation takes execution time and also requires extra data space for the copy. The loss of execution speed is insignificant for simple variables. However, for large arrays the story is different. When arrays have a large number of items, it is always better to use parameter passage by reference. This is a reasonable concession to execution efficiency.

OPEN ARRAY PARAMETERS

An **open array parameter** is a Modula-2 feature that allows for different sized arrays, through a relaxation of the type checking rules of strong data typing. Figure 12.29 describes this method of declaring formal parameters.

Formal Parameter Declaration Syntax

Semantics

```
The formal parameter, called FormParmIdentifier is
declared to be an array.  FormParmIdentifier is
compatible with any array that has identical ItemType
(for VAR parameter) or compatible ItemType (for value
parameters).  The actual index set for the formal
parameter is the same size as the index set for the
actual parameter. The formal parameter index set is
always [0..HIGH(FormalParmIdentifier)].
```

FIGURE 12.29 *Open array parameter declarations*

The index set is completely omitted from an open array parameter declaration. Any array identifier with the same item type can be used as an actual parameter.

The index set for the formal parameter always has a lowest index of 0 and a size equal to the actual parameter. If the index type for the actual parameter is

$$[2..5]$$

then the corresponding formal open array parameter will have the following range of indices:

$$[0..3]$$

where the item from the actual array with subscript 2 has a subscript of 0 in the formal parameter. Likewise, the item of the actual parameter with index of 3, has an index of 1 for the formal parameter.

If the actual parameter is an array with this index set

$$[\text{"A"}..\text{"E"}]$$

then the formal parameter's index set is

$$[0..4]$$

In this case the actual parameter uses characters for subscripts, while the formal parameter uses the translated cardinal subscripts.

The procedure needs a way to determine the upper bound on indices of a formal open array parameter, because this value can change from one invocation to the next. The **HIGH** function, described in Figure 12.30, is included in Modula-2 for this purpose.

```
HIGH
    desc: determine the upper bound on open array parameter
    type: function
    spec: PROCEDURE HIGH( Arr : ARRAY OF AnyType )
        : CARDINAL;
            (* POST: RESULT=count of indices of Arr - 1 *)

    e.g.: (* ASSERT: Data declared with index type of     *)
          (*               [1..100]          AND           *)
          (*         Rainfall declared with index type of *)
          (*         [Spring, Summer, Winter, Fall]       *)
          DataMax := HIGH(Data);
          RainMax := HIGH(Rainfall);
          (* ASSERT: DataMax=99 & RainMax=3 *)
```

FIGURE 12.30 *Definition for the built-in HIGH function*

The value of HIGH(FormalOpenArrayParm) is always one less than the size of the actual parameter. The value of HIGH(FormalOpenArrayParm) can be different for different invocations of the procedure.

Figure 12.31 contains a procedure called BlankOut that accepts any array of CHAR type items and assigns all of the items the blank character. BlankOut makes use of an open array parameter, and the HIGH function to compute the upper bound on its subscripts.

```
PROCEDURE BlankOut( VAR CharArray : ARRAY OF CHAR );
       (* POST: all items from                        *)
       (*              CharArray[0..HIGH(CharArray)]=" " *)
    VAR
       I : CARDINAL;
    BEGIN
    FOR I:=0  (* INV: All items of CharArray[0..I-1]=" " *)
             (*      AND  I <= HIGH(CharArray)+1        *)
       TO HIGH(CharArray)  DO
          CharArray[I] := " "
       END
    END BlankOut;
```

FIGURE 12.31 *The BlankOut procedure*

*P*rogramming-with-*S*tyle

When to Use Open Array Parameters

Open array parameters are a breach of the strongly typed nature of Modula-2. However, they are a useful breach and should be used whenever avoiding their use results in duplicating code or copying arrays to achieve index type compatibility.

It should also be noted that the declaration form for open array parameters is allowed only for formal parameter declarations. The following declaration:

ARRAY OF SomeType

is *not a general type*. It cannot be used in TYPE or VAR declarations.

12.10 STRINGS

A sequence of consecutive characters is known as a **string**. Many programs, such as text editors, manipulate strings.

In Modula-2 a string is a special case of a vector. It is special because it is the only case of a structured data type that has a constant for the aggregate type. A string constant is any collection of characters enclosed by single or double quotation marks. The item type for a string is CHAR, and the index set consists of the cardinal values from 0 through the string's length. String constants of length one are assignment compatible with the simple type CHAR. Figure 12.32 shows several example string constants and their understood types.

Constant	*Understood type*
"Hi there."	ARRAY [0..9] OF CHAR
"Modula-2 isn't easy!"	ARRAY [0..20] OF CHAR
'ABC'	ARRAY [0..3] OF CHAR
"X"	ARRAY [0..1] OF CHAR
	or
	CHAR

FIGURE 12.32 *Examples of string implicit types*

Modula-2 string types contain one more cell than necessary. For example the string constant

"Hi there."

contains 9 characters, while its understood type

ARRAY [0..9] OF CHAR

contains 10 items. This discrepancy occurs because Modula-2 appends an extra **null character**, the character 0C, at the end of every string. Below is a diagram of the CHAR cells for storing the string ''Hi there.''

[0]	[1]	[2]	[3]	[4]	[5]	[6]	[7]	[8]	[9]
H	i		t	h	e	r	e	.	0C

The usual programming convention is to treat the null character as the end of a string and never to include null characters within strings. An appended null character allows algorithms to check for the end of strings.

Figure 12.33 contains a StrAssign procedure that assigns the value of one character string parameter, SourceStr, to another, DestStr. If SourceStr is shorter than DestStr, then its value is copied through the null character. If SourceStr is longer than DestStr, then DestStr is assigned the leading substring of SourceStr (with a null character appended).

```
PROCEDURE StrAssign( VAR DestStr : ARRAY OF CHAR;
                         SourceStr : ARRAY OF CHAR );
    (* PRE:  For some s, SourceStr[0..s] is assigned          *)
    (*           & SourceStr[0..s-1] does not contain OC       *)
    (*           & SourceStr[s] = OC                           *)
    (* POST: DestStr[0..s] = SourceStr[0..s], if s<=HIGH(DestStr)*)
    (*        DestStr[0..HIGH(DestStr)-1] = SourceStr[0.. ]    *)
    (*           & DestStr[HIGH(DestStr)] = OC,  otherwise      *)
    VAR
       I : CARDINAL;
BEGIN
    I := 0;
    WHILE  (* INV: DestStr[0..I-1]=SourceStr[0..I-1]        *)
           (*        & SourceStr[0..I-1] does not contain OC *)
           (*        & I <= HIGH(DestStr)+1                  *)
    (I<=HIGH(DestStr) & (SourceStr[I]#OC) DO
        DestStr[I] := SourceStr[I];
        INC(I);
    END;
    IF  I>HIGH(DestStr) THEN
        DestrStr[HIGH(DesStr)] := OC
    ELSE
        DestStr[I] := OC
    END
END StrAssign;
```

FIGURE 12.33 *The StrAssign procedure*

Figure 12.34 shows the results of three example invocations of StrAssign, illustrating the result for strings of equal and unequal length.

```
Use the following declaration:
        VAR
            TenChars : ARRAY [0..10] OF CHAR;

    First example invocation:
        StrAssign( TenChars, "abcdefghij" );
        (* ASSERT: TenChars = "abcdefghij"                    *)
        (*            (i.e., TenChars[0]="a", TenChars[1]="b", *)
        (*                        ... TenChars[9]="j"          *)
        (*            and TenChars[10] = OC)                   *)

    Second example invocation:
        StrAssign( TenChars, "abcdefghijklmnopqrstuvwxyz" );
        (* ASSERT: TenChars = "abcdefghij"                    *)
        (*            (same result as 1st example above)       *)

    Third example invocation:
        StrAssign( TenChars, "a" );
        (* ASSERT: TenChars = "a"                             *)
        (*            (i.e., TenChars[0]="a" & TenChars[1]=OC  *)
```

FIGURE 12.34 *Examples of invocations of StrAssign*

InOut contains two procedures for performing I/O of strings. The WriteString procedure is one. Figure 12.35 contains a WriteString procedure that duplicates the algorithm of the InOut procedure. The use of an open array parameter permits string constants or arrays of CHAR of various sizes to be output by WriteString.

```
PROCEDURE WriteString( Str : ARRAY OF CHAR );
        (* PRE:  For some s, Str[0..s] is assigned *)
        (*          & Str[0..s-1] does not contain OC *)
        (*          & Str[s] = OC                    *)
        (* POST: Str[0..s-1] output in order        *)
        (* NOTE: This code duplicates that of the   *)
        (*        same procedure from InOut          *)

BEGIN
    I := 0;
    WHILE   (* INV: Str[0..I-1] output and contains no OC *)
    Str[I] # OC   DO
        Write( Str[I] );
        INC(I)
    END
END WriteString;
```

FIGURE 12.35 *Code for the WriteString procedure*

In many Modula-2 systems another procedure, called **ReadString** is also included. The ReadString procedure, duplicated in Figure 12.36, inputs a string of characters. ReadString is designed to ignore leading non-printable characters and blanks. The following printable, non-blank character sequence (up to a character < = a blank) is input. The string returned is the printable, non-blank sequence of characters with OC appended. The last character input (it is non-printable or a blank) is assigned to **termCH**. The ReadString procedure and termCH variable can both be imported from InOut.

```
PROCEDURE ReadString( VAR Str : ARRAY OF CHAR );
        (* PRE:   input string must be shorter than     *)
        (*          HIGH(Str) - 1                        *)
        (* POST: Str is assigned input according to the  *)
        (*        following rules:                       *)
        (*    1) Leading non-printable chars & blanks are *)
        (*       ignored                                 *)
        (*    2) The input string consists of the first  *)
        (*       sequence of 1 or more non-blank,        *)
        (*       printable characters that are input     *)
        (*       (OC is appended)                        *)
        (*    3) Input terminates with a character <= " " *)
        (*       This character is assigned to termCH    *)
        (* NOTE: This code duplicates that of the same   *)
        (*        procedure from InOut                    *)
    VAR
        I : CARDINAL;
```

(continued)

```
BEGIN
   REPEAT
      Read( Str[0] );
      (* INV: all input chars from entry up to Str[0] *)
      (*        are <= " "                             *)
   UNTIL Str[0] > " ";
   I := 0;
   REPEAT
      INC( I );
      Read( Str[I] );
      (* INV: Str[0..I] stores current input string *)
   UNTIL Str[I]<=" ";
   termCH := Str[I];
   Str[I] := OC;
END ReadString;
```

FIGURE 12.36 *Code for the ReadString procedure*

12.11 INTRODUCTION TO TABLE DRIVEN CODE

Table driven code is a way of using an array to control the execution of a program. One form of table driven code is to replace certain types of multi-way selection with a single array access. Consider an algorithm to convert weight from "Earth weight" to the equivalent weight on another planet in the solar system. Since the gravitational force on each plant is different, equivalent weight differs. A table approximating the gravitational force of several planets relative to the gravitational force of earth is given in Figure 12.37.

Force of Gravity on Planets (relative to earth)

Earth	1.00	Pluto	0.05
Jupiter	2.64	Saturn	1.16
Mars	0.38	Uranus	1.07
Mercury	0.37	Venus	0.78
Neptune	1.21		

FIGURE 12.37 *Relative force of gravity on different planets*

If Planet, is declared as shown below:

```
TYPE
   PlanetType = (Earth, Jupiter, Mars, Mercury, Neptune,
                 Pluto, Saturn, Uranus, Venus);
VAR
   Planet : PlanetType;
```

then the algorithm from Figure 12.38 assigns to the variable PlanetWeight the weight equivalent to EarthWeight for the planet stored in variable Planet. This same problem is solved using the table driven code presented in Figure 12.39.

```
    (* ASSERT: Planet & EarthWeight are assigned *)
    CASE Planet OF
        Earth   : PlanetWeight := EarthWeight      |
        Jupiter : PlanetWeight := EarthWeight*2.64  |
        Mars    : PlanetWeight := EarthWeight*0.38  |
        Mercury : PlanetWeight := EarthWeight*0.37  |
        Neptune : PlanetWeight := EarthWeight*1.21  |
        Pluto   : PlanetWeight := EarthWeight*0.05  |
        Saturn  : PlanetWeight := EarthWeight*1.16  |
        Uranus  : PlanetWeight := EarthWeight*1.07  |
        Venus   : PlanetWeight := EarthWeight*0.78
    END;
    (* ASSERT: PlanetWeight = equivalent of EarthWeight *)
    (*                         for Planet              *)
```

FIGURE 12.38 *Using a CASE to convert planet weights*

```
Table Driven Code

    (* ASSERT: Planet & EarthWeight are assigned *)
    PlanetWeight := EarthWeight * RelativeWeight[Planet];
    (* ASSERT: PlanetWeight = equivalent of EarthWeight *)
    (*                         for Planet              *)

RelativeWeight declaration

        VAR
            RelativeWeight : ARRAY PlanetType OF REAL;


Array initialization

            RelativeWeight[Earth] := 1.00;
            RelativeWeight[Jupiter] := 2.64;
            RelativeWeight[Mars] := 0.38;
            RelativeWeight[Mercury] := 0.37;
            RelativeWeight[Neptune] := 1.21;
            RelativeWeight[Pluto] := 0.05;
            RelativeWeight[Saturn] := 1.16;
            RelativeWeight[Uranus] := 1.07;
            RelativeWeight[Venus] := 0.78;
```

FIGURE 12.39 *Using table driven code to convert relative weights*

The table driven version consists of a single assignment instruction. The work of selecting the appropriate multiplier in the assignment is done by a vector, called RelativeWeight, instead of a CASE. RelativeWeight must be properly initialized. The assignment instructions to perform this initialization are included at the bottom of Figure 12.39.

Another example of replacing CASE instructions with arrays in table driven fashion is found in an algorithm to calculate an automobile insurance premium. Auto insurance premiums are often determined by the age of the drivers using the car. Suppose a company uses the following schedule for increasing premium cost when adding an additional driver to an existing policy.

Driver's age	Percent increase in premium
16	85%
17	75%
18	70%
19	60%
20	45%
21	30%
22	20%
over 22	normal rates

The premium cost of an auto insurance policy caused by adding a new driver is calculated as follows:

```
NewPremium := OldPremium + ( OldPremium *
                             PercentIncrease[Age]/100.0 );
```

This calculation assumes that Age is assigned the age of the new driver, and OldPremium is the current premium cost. The PercentIncrease vector is used to store the percentages of increase from the above table and must have been so initialized. Using PercentIncrease avoids the need to select the increase percentage with a CASE instruction.

Programming with Style

Replacing a CASE With a Table

CASE instructions (and sometimes IFs with numerous ELSIF clauses) should be scrutinized for possible replacement with table driven code, especially if the individual selection clauses are similar. The advantages of a table over a CASE are:

1) The table is less code and generally more readable.
2) The table algorithm is usually more efficient.

Readability of an algorithm is enhanced, because the table driven algorithm is more succinct. Readability is also enhanced by choosing a good table name.

Table driven code often replaces CASE instructions. The execution of a CASE instruction often causes the CASE expression to be compared to every CASE selector. The table driven code eliminates comparisons, so it executes faster.

One disadvantage of table driven code is a requirement for extra data space to store the table. For large tables this may cause a CASE to be preferable. Another disadvantage is that the table must be initialized. If a table lookup is performed only once, the time required to initialize the entire table does not justify its use.

On the average, the advantages of table driven code outweigh the disadvantages. Consideration should always be given to simplifying code by the use of such tables.

12.12 SUMMARY

Arrays are the most commonly used of all structured data types. They are ideally suited to the ability of computers to process large amounts of data repetitiously.

Modula-2 provides many facilities for the manipulation of arrays. Individual items of arrays can be accessed by using expressions for indices. Both array items and the aggregate array can be passed as actual parameters. Open array parameters are an extension of aggregate array parameters that provide additional flexibility with a small concession in strong typing. The FOR loop is a control structure well suited to many sequential array access algorithms.

This chapter examines one-dimensional arrays, or vectors. There are many common applications for vector storage. Vectors can be used to store a group of counters or Booleans. Vectors can be used to buffer data for input or output. Vectors can be used to store character strings. Vectors can even be used in table driven fashion to replace multi-way selection.

A large class of algorithms exists for processing vectors. These algorithms make use of random and sequential access to array items. The algorithms examined in this chapter include the linear search, array merging, vector shifting, and sorting (in particular the insertion sort).

Many algorithms and programming techniques rely upon the array. However, learning to use arrays is somewhat like learning to use loops. Wise use requires careful thought and practice.

||| KEY TERMS

atomic data	size of an array	interleaving
structured data type	selector	shift algorithms
array	array-index bounds	shift right (or left)
item (of an array)	violation	sorting algorithms
element (of an array)	sequential array access	ascending order
array cell	random array access	descending order
array name	array of counters	insertion sort (linear insertion)
item type	array of BOOLEAN	in place sort
index set	FOR loop	open array parameter
index type	control variable	HIGH
index	buffer	string
subscript	partially-used array	null character
multidimensional array	array searching algorithms	ReadString
one-dimensional array	linear search	termCH
vector	merge algorithms	table driven code

‖ ‖ Exercises

Use the declarations below to complete Problems 1 through 3.

```
TYPE
    LiquidMeasure = (Gill, Pint, Quart, Gallon, Barrel);
    UpperAlpha = ["A".."Z"];
    CapCountArray = ARRAY UpperAlpha OF CARDINAL;
    RelWeightType = ARRAY [-5..5] OF BOOLEAN;
VAR
    CapCount. : CapCountArray;
    IsRelWeight : RelWeightType;
    Contents : ARRAY [0..100] OF LiquidMeasure;
    LiqMeasureEncoding : ARRAY LiquidMeasure OF CHAR;
```

1. Define the item type for each array declared in the VAR declaration above.

2. Specify the array size (number of items) for each of the arrays declared in the VAR above

3. Write an instruction(s) to perform the following tasks. You may assume that SomeChar is a CHAR variable.
   a) Assign the value 17 to the item of CapCount with index of "T".
   b) Copy the value of the item from IsRelWeight with subscript 3 into the item of the same array with a subscript of 5.
   c) Assign to all of the items of CapCount the value zero (0).
   d) Assign all of the items of LiquidMeasureEncoding the value " + ".
   e) Assuming the item of CapCount with index of "W" is between 0 and 100 in value, use this item value as the subscript into the Contents array and assign the specified item the value Gallon.

4. Write a separate FOR loop for each of the parts (a) through (f). The loop should produce the indicated output from the iterations of its body. In each case, the loop should produce output every iteration and use more than a single iteration. You may assume that Some- Char is a CHAR variable and SomeCard is a CARDINAL variable.

   a) 6 7 8 9 10 11 12 13 14 15 16 17 18 19 20 21 22 23 24

   b) 3 5 7 9 11 13 15 17 19 21 23 25 27 29 31 33 35 37 39

   c) 7 6 5 4 3 2

   d) CDEFGHIJKL

   e) ZWT

   f) 1 2 4 5 7 8 10 11 13 14 16 17 19 20

5. Each of the Modula-2 code segments below contains an error. Identify what the error is. You must assume that I and N are both variables of type CARDINAL.

a)
```
FOR I := 1 TO 10 BY N DO
   WriteCard( I, 0 )
END;
```

b)
```
I := 0;
FOR I := 0 TO N DO
   WriteCard( I, 0 ):
   INC( I )
END;
```

c)
```
FOR I := -3 TO -22 BY -1 DO
   WriteCard( I, 0 )
END;
```

d)
```
I := 52;
WriteCard( I, 0 );
FOR I := 50 to 10 BY -3 DO
   WriteCard( I, 0 )
END;
WriteCard( I, 0 );
```

Use the array declaration below to complete Exercise 6.

```
VAR A : ARRAY [1..200] OF INTEGER;
```

6. For each part below, a FOR loop invariant (INV) and the postcondition (POST) for the FOR loop are specified. Assuming no precondition, write the appropriate FOR loop.

a)
```
(* INV: For all subscripts, s, such that (1<=s<=Cur-1) *)
(*          A[s] = 0                                    *)
(*       & Cur <= 201                                   *)
(* POST: For all subscripts, s, such that (1<=s<=200)   *)
(*          A[s] = 0                                    *)
```

b)
```
(* INV: For all subscripts, s, such that (Cur+1<=s<=200)*)
(*          A[s] = 0                                    *)
(*       & Cur >= 0                                     *)
(* POST: For all subscripts, s, such that (1<=s<=200)   *)
(*          A[s] = 0                                    *)
```

c)
```
(* INV: For all subscripts, s, such that (1<=s<=Cur-1) *)
(*          A[s] = s+1                                  *)
(*       & Cur <= 201                                   *)
(* POST: For all subscripts, s, such that (1<=s<=200)   *)
(*          A[s] = s+1                                  *)
```

```
  d) (* INV: For all subscripts, s, such that (1<=s<=Cur-1) *)
     (*            ( A[s*3-2]=0 & A[s*3-1]=1 & A[s*3]=2 )     *)
     (*      & Cur <= 31                                      *)
     (* POST: For all subscripts, s, such that (1<=s<=30)    *)
     (*            ( A[s*3-2]=0 & A[s*3-1]=1 & A[s*3]=2 )     *)
```

7. Write the body of the Interleave4by5 procedure as specified below:

```
PROCEDURE Interleave4by5(     Org1 : FiveItemArray;
                              Org2 : FiveItemArray;
                              Org3 : FiveItemArray;
                              Org4 : FiveItemArray;
                          VAR Intrlv : TwentyItemArray );
  (* PRE:  Org1[0..4], Org2[0..4], Org3[0..4] & Org4[0..4] *)
  (*       are all assigned                                *)
  (* POST: For all cardinals, c, such that (0<=c<=4)       *)
  (*          ( Intrlv[c*4]=Org1[c]                        *)
  (*          & Intrlv[c*4+1]=Org2[c]                      *)
  (*          & Intrlv[c*4+2]=Org3[c]                      *)
  (*          & Intrlv[c*4+3]=Org4[c])                     *)
```

8. Write the body of the ShiftLeftCirc procedure below to shift a vector, Data, circula.ıy to the left by one cell.

```
PROCEDURE ShiftLeftCirc( VAR Data : CardArrayType;
                             Hi : CARDINAL  );
  (* PRE:  CardArrayType is some assigned vector with      *)
  (*            CARDINAL items                             *)
  (*        AND 1<Hi<=HIGH(Data)                           *)
  (*        AND Assigned( Data[1..Hi] )                    *)
  (* POST: For all subscripts, s, such that (1<=s<=Hi-1),  *)
  (*            Data[s] = Data[s+1]<entry>                 *)
  (*        & Data[Hi] = Data[1]<entry>                    *)
```

9.
```
PROCEDURE SortNoDups( VAR Data : DataArray;
                      VAR Last : DataSizeRange  );
  (* PRE:  Last and Data[1..Last] are assigned             *)
  (* POST: Data[1..Last] contains the same values as       *)
  (*       Data[1..Last<entry>]<entry>, but the values     *)
  (*       are sorted in ascending order with all          *)
  (*       duplicates removed. Note: Last is updated        *)
```

SortNoDups must sort the Data array (see Figure 12.27 for type definitions) in ascending order, removing all duplicate values. The value returned for the Last parameter is updated by SortNoDups to reflect the number of unique values in the resulting array.

10. Below is a section of Modula-2 code that converts nautical measures of distance to feet. Replace this code with table-driven code to perform the same task. Include the declaration for the vector used and the code to initialize it properly.

```
(* ASSERT: NauticalDistance is assigned a value *)
(*          of the following enumerated type:    *)
(*          (Span, Fathom, NauticalMile, League)*)
CASE NauticalDistance OF
  Span : DistanceInFeet := 0.75 |
  Fathom : DistanceInFeet := 6.0 |
  NauticalMile : DistanceInFeet := 6076.1 |
  League : DistanceInFeet := 18228.3
END;
(* ASSERT: DistanceInFeet = equivalent of      *)
(*          NauticalDistance expressed in feet *)
```

11. Below is a section of Modula-2 code that converts a compass direction heading into the appropriate cardinal degrees. Replace this code with table-driven code to perform the same task. Include the declaration for the vector used and the code to properly initialize it.

```
(* ASSERT: Direction is assigned a value of the *)
(*          following enumerated type:           *)
(*          (North, Northeast, East, Southeast,  *)
(*          South, Southwest, West, Northwest)   *)
CASE Direction OF
  North :      InDegrees :=   0 |
  Northeast :  InDegrees :=  45 |
  East :       InDegrees :=  90 |
  Southeast :  InDegrees := 135 |
  South :      InDegrees := 180 |
  Southwest :  InDegrees := 225 |
  West :       InDegrees := 270 |
  Northwest :  InDegrees := 315
END;
(* ASSERT: InDegrees = Direction measured in degrees *)
```

12. On the following page is a section of Modula-2 code that calculates the annual value of an average dairy cow of some breed. The particular breed is specified by the variable Breed. A cow's value is calulated by the expected butterfat percentage for that breed, times the AnnualBfatValue, plus the average pounds of milk that cows of that breed produce annually, times, the CurrentMilkPrice (per pound). Replace this code with table-driven code to perform the same task. Include the declaration for the vectors used and the code to execute them properly.

```
(* ASSERT: Breed is assigned a value of the following *)
(*          enumerated type:                           *)
(*              (Ayrshire, BrownSwiss, Guernsey, Holstein,*)
(*              Jersey)                                *)
CASE  Breed  OF
    Ayrshire    : Value := 4.0*AnnualBfatValue +
                          6500.0*CurrentMilkPrice |
    BrownSwiss  : Value := 4.0*AnnualBfatValue +
                          7000.0*CurrentMilkPrice |
    Guernsey    : Value := 4.9*AnnualBfatValue +
                          5750.0*CurrentMilkPrice |
    Holstein    : Value := 3.7*AnnualBfatValue +
                          8500.0*CurrentMilkPrice |
    Jersey      : Value := 5.3*AnnualBfatValue +
                          5350.0*CurrentMilkPrice
END;
(* ASSERT: Value = expected annual value of a dairy *)
(*         cow of type Breed                         *)
```

||| PROGRAMMING PROJECTS

1. Given two vectors that are already sorting, it is possible to merge the two vectors into another sorted vector that consists of all the item values from the first two. This type of merge selects the value for the new vector by examining the smallest value of the two original vectors not yet copied to the new vector. Because the original vectors are sorted, this merge algorithm is simpler than a complete sort. Write such a merge procedure to merge any two vectors of INTEGERS, regardless of their size. Include a test driver to complete the program.

2. The InsertionSort program from Figure 12.27 contains a procedure, called Sort, that sorts an array of INTEGERS in ascending order. Modify Sort to sort an array of CHAR in *descending* order, and use *an open array parameter* to sort the entire actual array parameter. (Last can be dropped from the parameter list.)

3. Write a program to fit the following problem definition.

TITLE
    Keeping baby statistics

DESCRIPTION
    A hospital wants to perform a study of the lengths and weights of the newborns. A program is needed to input the weight and length of each newborn and display the total number of newborns at each size and length. The hospital has never delivered a newborn shorter than 10 inches or longer than 33 inches. Neither has the hospital delivered a baby under one pound or over 16 pounds.

INPUT

Input consists of pairs of cardinal values where the first value of each pair is the length of a baby (from 10 to 33 inches) and the second is its weight (from one to 16 pounds). The end of input is signified by a 0,0 pair.

OUTPUT

Prior to all input, the following message should be printed to prompt the user for input:

Please input the length and weight of each baby on a separate line. Length (in inches) and weight (in pounds) should be rounded to the nearest unit. When all input is finished type a line with two 0s.

After all input is complete a blank line is printed followed by frequency tables for the various baby lengths and weights. These frequency tables appear as below, where <Li> indicates the number of input babies that are i inches long and <Wi> inidicates the number of babies that weigh i pounds.

```
Summary of Newborn Lengths:
---------------------------
         10 ......  <L10>
         11 ......  <L11>
                .
                .
                .
         33 ......  <L33>

Summary of Newborn Weights:
------------------------------
         1 ......  <W1>
         2 ......  <W2>
                .
                .
                .
         16 ......  <W16>
```

ERRORS

All input is assumed to be correct. Undefined results occur for erroneous input.

EXAMPLE

Below is a sample execution with all input highlighted:

Please input the length and weight of each baby on a separate line. Length (in inches) and weight (in pounds) should be rounded to the nearest unit. When all input is finished type a line with two 0s.

```
                              20   8
                              22   9
                              21   8
                              18   6
                              19   7
                              20   7
                              20   8
                              20   6
                              22   8
                              23  10
                              19   7
                              18   6
                              17   5
                              20   7
                              23   9
                              21   7
                               0   0
```

Summary of Newborn Lengths
```
--------------------------
                   10 ...... 0
                   11 ...... 0
                   12 ...... 0
                   13 ...... 0
                   14 ...... 0
                   15 ...... 0
                   16 ...... 0
                   17 ...... 1
                   18 ...... 2
                   19 ...... 2
                   20 ...... 5
                   21 ...... 2
                   22 ...... 2
                   23 ...... 2
                   24 ...... 0
                   25 ...... 0
                   26 ...... 0
                   27 ...... 0
                   28 ...... 0
                   29 ...... 0
                   30 ...... 0
                   31 ...... 0
                   32 ...... 0
                   33 ...... 0
```

Summary of Newborn Weights
```
--------------------------
                    1 ...... 0
                    2 ...... 0
                    3 ...... 0
                    4 ...... 0
                    5 ...... 1
                    6 ...... 3
                    7 ...... 5
                    8 ...... 4
                    9 ...... 2
                   10 ...... 1
                   11 ...... 0
                   12 ...... 0
                   13 ...... 0
                   14 ...... 0
                   15 ...... 0
                   16 ...... 0
```

4. Write a program to fit the following problem definition.

TITLE

Beer Barrel Sales Accounting

DESCRIPTION

Billy Bawble sells used beer barrels. He needs a program to consolidate the daily proceeds from his business. Billy sells five different sizes of beer barrels. The biggest barrel sells for $25, the next smaller for $23, the middle sized barrel for $19, the next-to-the-smallest for $18, and the smallest for $16. Billy wants to identify the barrels with numbers from 1 for the biggest barrel, to 5 for the smallest.

INPUT

After a prompt, Billy should input all sales so that one sale is on a single line. Each sale line contains a character from 1 to 5 in the first column, to signify the type of barrel in the sale, and a cardinal value after it, to signify the quantity of that barrel sold. These input lines are terminated by any line that has some character other than 1...5 in the first column. The final line is signified includes just a single "0."

OUTPUT

Prior to all input, the following message should be printed to prompt the user for input.

    Please specify barrel sales in the form <type> <quant> with
    one sale per line below.

Additionally, each input line is prompted as follows:

                    type, quantity?

After all input, the following summary is printed

        Huge barrels : <hugetot>
        Big barrels : <bigtot>
        Middle barrels : <midtot>
        Small barrels : <smalltot>
        Tiny barrels : <tinytot>

        Total barrels : <tot>
        Total Monetary Receipts: $<income>

The notation above uses <hugetot>, <bigtot>, <midtot>, <smalltot> and <tinytot> to denote the respective total numbers of each type of barrel sold, as specified by the input. <tot> = <hugetot> + <bigtot> + <midtot> + <smalltot> + <tinytot>. The total value of all sales is output as <income>

ERRORS

All input is assumed to be correct. Undefined results occur for erroneous input.

EXAMPLE

Below is a sample execution with all input highlighted.

```
Please specify barrel sales in the form <type> <quant> with
one sale per line below:

type, quantity? 1 10
type, quantity? 4 1
type, quantity? 5 3
type, quantity? 2 8
type, quantity? 1 5
type, quantity? 2 2
type, quantity? 0
```

After all input the following summary is printed:

```
Huge barrels : 15
Big barrels : 10
Middle barrels : 0
Small barrels : 1
Tiny barrels : 3
---------------------------
Total barrels : 29
Total Monetary Receipts: $671
```

5. Write a program to fit the following problem definition.

TITLE

Pig Latin Creation

DESCRIPTION

A word game often played by elementary age children is to speak in "Pig Latin." Pig Latin is abusive of the English language. In Pig Latin every word that begins with a consonant is transformed into a hyphenated word with the first portion coming from the original word less its first character and the portion after the hyphen is the first letter followed by "ay." For example, "pig" is transformed into "ig-pay" and "latin" into "atin-lay."

This program is supposed to automate the translation. Input to the program will be several English sentences. The program should output the Pig Latin equivalent after each. Input terminates when a line with no input characters is encountered. Note that words beginning with the vowels "a", "e", "i", "o", or "u" remain unchanged. The program considers a word to be any consecutive sequence of alphabetic letters.

INPUT

Input consists of several lines of text. It can be assumed that input lines are short enough so their translation will fit into 80 characters or fewer. The final input line contains no characters (i.e, two consecutive EOL characters occur).

OUTPUT

Prior to all input, the following message should be printed to prompt the user for input:

                Please specify English text below:

After each input line is echoed, the Pig Latin translation of the line is printed on a separate line. A blank line precedes the next input line.

ERRORS

All input is assumed to be correct. Undefined results occur for erroneous input.

EXAMPLE

Below is a sample execution with all input highlighted:

Please specify English text below:

This program is supposed to automate the
his-Tay rogram-pay is upposed-say o-tay automate he-tay

translation. Input to the program will be
ranslation-tay. Input o-tay he-tay rogram-pay ill-way e-bay

several English sentences. The program should
everal-say English entences-say. he-Tay rogram-pay hould-say

output the Pig Latin equivalent after each.
output he-tay ig-Pay atin-Lay equivalent after each.

6. Write a program to fit the following problem definition.

TITLE

Word Reverse

DESCRIPTION

Tiring of the Pig Latin (described in Project 5), a clever fourth grader devised a scheme of speaking English by pronouncing each word as though its characters were reversed.

This program accepts input lines and outputs the transformed lines (all characters in each word are exactly reversed). The end of input is signified by an input line with no characters in it. The program considers words to consist only of upper-case and lowercase alphabetic characters. Other characters are treated as punctuation. Punctuation remains unaltered and serves to separate words.

INPUT

Input consists of several lines of text. Each line must be 60 characters or fewer in length. The final input line contains no characters (i.e., two consecutive EOL characters occur).

OUTPUT

Prior to all input, the following message should be printed to prompt the user for input:

Please specify English text below:

After each input line the same line is displayed with all words reversed. Each output line is followed by a blank line prior to the next input.

ERRORS

All input is assumed to be correct. Undefined results occur for erroneous input.

EXAMPLE

Below is a sample execution with all input highlighted.

Please specify English text below:

This program accepts input lines and outputs the
sihT margorp stpecca tupni senil dna stuptuo eht

transformed lines (all characters in each word are
demrofsnart senil (lla sretcarahc ni hcae drow era

exactly reversed). The end of input is signified by an
yltcaxe desrever). ehT dne fo tupni si deifingis yb na

input line with no characters in it. Note "doesn't".
tupni enil htiw on sretcarahc ni ti. etoN "nseod't"

7. Write a program to fit the following problem definition.

TITLE

Perfect Numbers

DESCRIPTION

   The Greeks began an examination of numerology by classifying all positive integers as either *perfect*, *abundant*, or *deficient*. This classification scheme is based upon the factors (even divisors) of the number. If the sum of all of the factors of a number (excluding the number itself) equals the number then it is said to be "perfect." For example, the factors of 6 are 1, 2, 3, and 6. Therefore, the number 6 is a perfect number. The total of the factors of 6 (excluding 6) is $1 + 2 + 3 = 6$. An abundant number is one in which this sum of factors (excluding the number itself) is greater than the number. An example of an abundant number is 12, because $1 + 2 + 3 + 4 + 6 = 16 > 12$. All numbers that are neither perfect nor abundant are deficient.

This program accepts a sequence of cardinal values and classifies each as abundant, perfect, or deficient. The program also displays the factors of the number. Input is terminated by an input value of zero.

INPUT

Prompted input consists of single cardinal values. An input of zero (0) signals termination.

OUTPUT

Each input value is prompted by the following output line:

```
Specify a positive integer:
```

Following the input a line like the following is output, where <type> is either "abundant," "perfect," or "deficient" as is appropriate for the input value:

```
This number is <type> (factors given below).
```

The next line output is a list of the factors of the number in ascending order, one per line. A blank line precedes the next input prompt.

ERRORS

All input is assumed to be correct. Any incorrect input produces undefined results.

EXAMPLE

Below is a sample execution with all input highlighted.

```
Specify a positive integer: 6
This number is perfect (factors given below).
1
2
3

Specify a positive integer: 12
This number is abundant (factors given below).
1
2
3
4
6

Specify a positive integer: 333
This number is deficient (factors given below).
1
3
9
37
111
```

```
Specify a positive integer: 18
This number is abundant (factors given below).
1
2
3
6
9

Specify a positive integer: 16
This number is deficient (factors given below).
1
2
4
8

Specify a positive integer: 28
This number is perfect (factors given below).
1
2
4
7
14

Specify a positive integer: 0
```

8. Write a program to fit the following problem definition.

TITLE

Right justification of input file text

DESCRIPTION

Word processors usually incorporate the ability to right justify a given passage of text. Right justified text is broken into lines so that the order of words is preserved and each word is entirely on a single line. Each line of text has the greatest number of words possible. To be right justified means that the words are spread across the line so that the first character of the leftmost word is in the leftmost line column and the last character of the rightmost word is in the rightmost line column.

For this program, the user is asked to specify the name of a text file to be right justified, and the number of columns in the length of each justified line. The program then reads the specified text file, splits this input into lines, right justifies the lines, and outputs the results. For purposes of this program, a word is assumed to be any non-blank sequence of characters.

INPUT

The user is first prompted for the line length to use in right justification. This line must be some cardinal value less than 81. Then the user is prompted to specify the file for input. This file name must represent some text file.

OUTPUT

The prompt for line length is as follows:

```
Please input the desired line length:
```

The prompt for input text file specification is as follows:

```
Please input name of text file to justify:
```

Following the second prompt a blank line preceeds the right justified text. This right justified text must consist of the exact input text redistributed onto lines so that each line contains as many words as possible and so that the output lines are right justified to the user specified line length.

ERRORS
If the specified file is not a text file, then undefined results occur.

If there is only one word that will fit on a line it must be left justified and not right justified.

All words must be shorter than the user-specified line length or undefined results occur.

EXAMPLE
The input below uses the following text file, called "Problem"

The Problem file:

```
Word
      processors usually
incorporate the          ability to right
justify a given passage of text.
Right justified text is
broken into lines so that the order of words
is preserved
and
each word is entirely on a single line.
```
Below is a trace of a program execution with the user input highlighted.

```
Please input the desired line length: 20
Please input name of text file to justify: Problem

      Word          processors
      usually  incorporate
      the ability to right
      justify    a    given
      passage   of   text.
      Right justified text
      is broken into lines
      so that the order of
      words   is   preserved
      and   each   word   is
      entirely on a single
      line.
```

13 ||| THE MULTIDIMENSIONAL ARRAY

13.1 THE NEED FOR MORE ARRAY DIMENSIONS

Many collections of information are naturally organized into two dimensions. A chess board is a two-dimensional grid of eight columns and eight rows. Statistics are frequently represented in two-dimensional diagrams such as histograms and line graphs. Two-dimensional tax tables are used to determine the correct income tax bracket.

Physical objects are three-dimensional. Every box has length, width and height. Buildings have rooms arranged in a three-dimensional organization, where each room can be identified by its floor number and its two-dimensional position on the floor.

Sometimes three dimensions are too few. Consider a grocery store check out. Each customer checks out with one or more purchases. The items purchased by a single person can be thought of as a one-dimensional array, a vector. There are often several customers in a single check out line. This line is another vector: a vector of customers. Since large grocery stores have many check out stations, one store can be thought of as a vector of check outs.

From the perspective of the owner of a chain of grocery stores, this system has a four-dimensional model. The owner sees:

> The chain is a vector of grocery stores.
> Each grocery store is a vector of check out lines.
> Each check out line is a vector of customers.
> Each customer has a vector of purchases.

This grocery example illustrates the complexity of real world systems. Since computer programs model real world systems, programming languages must provide the tools for representing these complex systems. A multidimensional array is one such tool.

13.2 VECTORS OF ARRAYS

The grocery store example illustrates one method of viewing multidimensional arrays, as a **vector of arrays**. A vector of arrays is a one-dimensional array in which each item is an array by itself. In Modula-2, a vector of arrays is declared by specifying an item type that is an array.

An array of strings is an example of such a data structure. The declaration in Figure 13.1 is appropriate for an array to store 26 identifiers, each eight characters (plus an extra character for OC) or fewer in length.

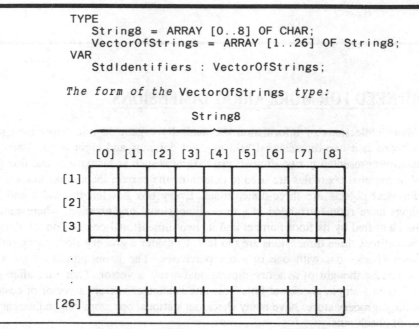

```
TYPE
    String8 = ARRAY [0..8] OF CHAR;
    VectorOfStrings = ARRAY [1..26] OF String8;
VAR
    StdIdentifiers : VectorOfStrings;
```

The form of the VectorOfStrings *type:*

FIGURE 13.1 *Declaration of StdIdentifiers*

The diagram in Figure 13.1 illustrates the form of the StdIdentifiers array. Each horizontal row of the figure represents the cells of a single string. Each string is also a vector, declared as String8. The columns across each row represent the cells of CHAR type that store each of the characters of a string.

The StdIdentifiers array is a **two-dimensional array** because its atomic cells, of CHAR type, can be arranged in rows and columns as a rectangular matrix. However, it is declared and used as though it were a vector of vectors, or more specifically, a vector of strings. Figure 13.2 shows an example of an assignment of the string constant "BOOLEAN" to the third string of StdIdentifiers. This illustrates how one array may be assigned to an item of another, as long as the item is an assignment compatible array.

```
Stdldentifiers[3] := "BOOLEAN";
(* results are shown for the portion of Stdldentifiers *)
(* diagrammed below                                    *)
```

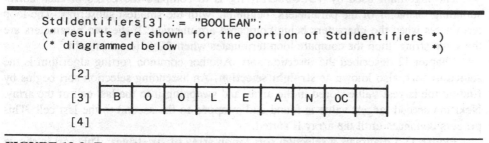

FIGURE 13.2 *Example of assignment to a row of an array*

Figure 13.3 contains two additional instructions involving Stdldentifiers. The first instruction assigns the contents of one row of Stdldentifiers (with index of 13) to another row (with index of 10). This assignment causes all nine of the characters of the row to be copied. The second example contains an invocation of Write-String to output the string from Stdldentifiers[4].

```
(* ASSERT: Stdldentifiers[13] is assigned *)
Stdldentifiers[10] := Stdldentifiers[13];
(* ASSERT: Stdldentifiers[13]=Stdldentifiers[10] *)

WriteString( Stdldentifiers[4] );
(* ASSERT: The string from Stdldentifiers[4] is *)
(*         output                               *)
```

FIGURE 13.3 *Two examples of uses of StdIdentifiers*

Modula-2 does not permit relational operators, like = or <, to be applied to aggregate arrays. In order to compare two values of type String, the programmer must write a comparison algorithm. Figure 13.4 contains an IsLessString function that checks for "less than."

```
PROCEDURE IsLessString( A : ARRAY OF CHAR;
                        B : ARRAY OF CHAR )
   : BOOLEAN;
      (* PRE: A and B contain assigned Modula-2 strings,     *)
      (*        including a OC terminating character          *)
      (* POST: RESULT = the value of string A alphabetically *)
      (*                precedes the value of B              *)
VAR
   Probe : CARDINAL;
BEGIN
   Probe := 0;
   WHILE (* INV: CAP(A[0..Probe-1])=CAP(B[0..Probe-1]) *)
         (*       & A[0..Probe-1] doesn't contain OC    *)
   (CAP(A[Probe])=CAP(B[Probe])) & (A[Probe]#OC)   DO
      Probe := Probe + 1
   END;
   RETURN A[Probe]<B[Probe]
END IsLessString;
```

FIGURE 13.4 *IsLessString procedure*

The algorithm used by IsLessString is to compare the CAPs of each corresponding character of the parameters, beginning with the smallest subscripts. The loop terminates when the characters being compared are unequal. If the two parameters are the same string, then the compare loop terminates when 0C is found in both.

Chapter 12 described the insertion sort. Another common sorting algorithm is the **selection sort**, also known as **straight selection**. An ascending selection sort begins by finding the largest value stored in the array and swapping it to the last cell of the array. Next the second largest value is found and swapped to the second to the last cell. This process continues until the array is sorted.

Figure 13.5 diagrams a selection sort for an array of six strings. This sort is shown in a sequence of six snapshots. The first snapshot shows the unsorted array. Each row of the array stores one string, using the Modula-2 convention of including 0C as a terminating character.

Snapshot 1

[0]	h	a	m	0C					
[1]	e	g	g	s	0C				
[2]	p	a	n	c	a	k	e	s	0C
[3]	w	a	f	f	l	e	s	0C	
[4]	s	a	u	s	a	g	e	0C	
[5]	t	o	a	s	t	0C			

} *Unsorted*

Snapshot 2

[0]	h	a	m	0C					
[1]	e	g	g	s	0C				
[2]	p	a	n	c	a	k	e	s	0C
[3]	t	o	a	s	t	0C			
[4]	s	a	u	s	a	g	e	0C	
[5]	w	a	f	f	l	e	s	0C	

} *Unsorted* (rows [0]–[4])

} *Sorted* (row [5])

Snapshot 3

[0]	h	a	m	0C					
[1]	e	g	g	s	0C				
[2]	p	a	n	c	a	k	e	s	0C
[3]	s	a	u	s	a	g	e	0C	
[4]	t	o	a	s	t	0C			
[5]	w	a	f	f	l	e	s	0C	

} *Unsorted* (rows [0]–[3])

} *Sorted* (rows [4]–[5])

(continued)

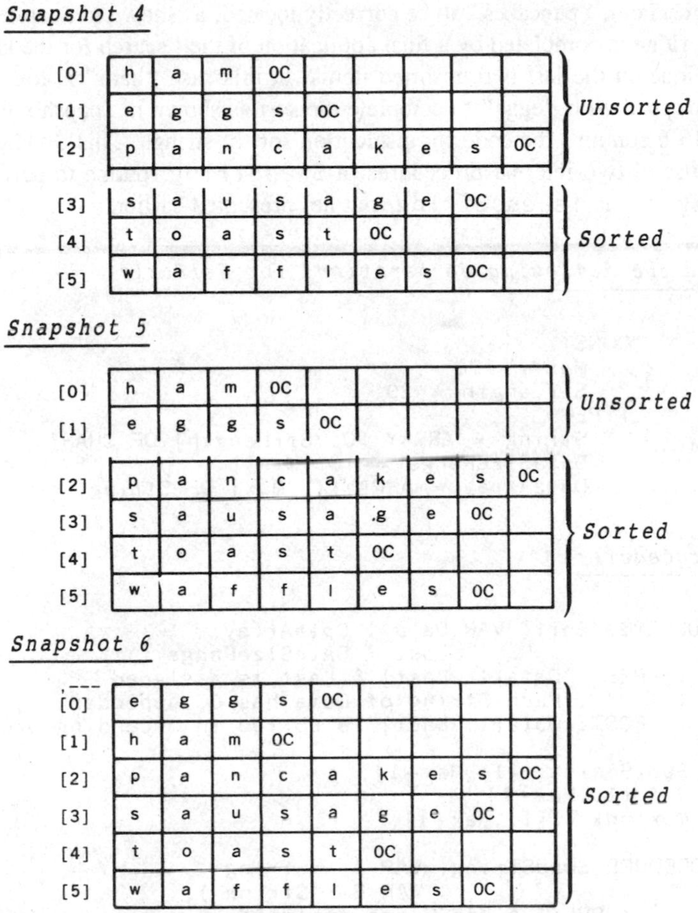

Snapshot 4

[0]	h	a	m	OC					
[1]	e	g	g	s	OC				
[2]	p	a	n	c	a	k	e	s	OC

Unsorted

[3]	s	a	u	s	a	g	e	OC	
[4]	t	o	a	s	t	OC			
[5]	w	a	f	f	l	e	s	OC	

Sorted

Snapshot 5

[0]	h	a	m	OC					
[1]	e	g	g	s	OC				

Unsorted

[2]	p	a	n	c	a	k	e	s	OC
[3]	s	a	u	s	a	.g	e	OC	
[4]	t	o	a	s	t	OC			
[5]	w	a	f	f	l	e	s	OC	

Sorted

Snapshot 6

[0]	e	g	g	s	OC				
[1]	h	a	m	OC					
[2]	p	a	n	c	a	k	e	s	OC
[3]	s	a	u	s	a	g	e	OC	
[4]	t	o	a	s	t	OC			
[5]	w	a	f	f	l	e	s	OC	

Sorted

FIGURE 13.5 *Diagram of a selection sort in snapshots*

The first task is to identify the item (string) with the largest value. In this case "waffles," the item with index of 3, is the largest string because it would come last alphabetically. The selection sort places it in its proper position by swapping it with the last item of the array as shown in Snapshot 2.

Now the last item contains the largest value of the array. This item is sorted and need not be considered further. Each snapshot separates the array diagram into two parts, one for the sorted portion of the array and one for the unsorted portion.

The selection sort next proceeds to identify the largest item in the unsorted (top five strings) portion of the array. The value of the third item, "toast," is the largest in this case. This item is swapped with the second to the last, the item with Index 4. The result appears in Snapshot 3.

After the swap, the sorted part of the array has an index range of [4..5]. The next search for the largest item in the unsorted portion finds that the largest item, "sausage," is in the correct location. Snapshot 4 shows the result of this step. Similarly, another search finds the largest item, "pancakes," to be correctly located, as shown in Snapshot 5.

The algorithm is completed by a final application of the "search for the largest, then swap" technique on the last two unsorted items. In this case "ham" is found to be the larger and swapped with "eggs" to complete the sort as shown in Snapshot 6.

Figure 13.6 contains the code for a selection sort of strings. This SelSort procedure makes use of two internal procedures, a SwapString routine to perform necessary swapping and the IsLessString routine, presented earlier.

Assume the following declarations for SelSort:

```
CONST
    Max = 100;
    StrLength = 20;
TYPE
    String = ARRAY [0..StrLength] OF CHAR;
    DataSizeRange = [0..Max];
    DataArray = ARRAY[1..Max] OF String;
```

The procedure:

```
PROCEDURE SelSort( VAR Data : DataArray;
                        Last : DataSizeRange );
    (* PRE:  Data[1..Last] & Last is assigned          *)
    (*       Each String of Data has OC appended        *)
    (* POST: Data[1..Last] is sorted in ascending order *)
VAR
    SortStart : [1..Max+1];
    J : [1..Max+1];
    MaxIndx : [1..Max+1];

    PROCEDURE SwapString( VAR A : String;
                          VAR B : String );
        (* PRE:  A and B are assigned       *)
        (* POST: A=B<entry> & B=A<entry>    *)
    VAR
        Temp : String;
    BEGIN
        Temp := A;
        A := B;
        B := Temp
    END SwapString;
```

(continued)

```
      PROCEDURE IsLessString( A : ARRAY OF CHAR;
                              B : ARRAY OF CHAR )
        : BOOLEAN;
          (* PRE: A and B contain assigned Modula-2 strings,      *)
          (*        including a 0C terminating character           *)
          (* POST: RESULT = the value of string A alphabetically *)
          (*                precedes the value of B                *)
      VAR
        Probe : CARDINAL;
      BEGIN
        Probe := 0;
        WHILE (* INV: CAP(A[0..Probe-1])=CAP(B[0..Probe-1]) *)
              (*      & A[0..Probe-1] doesn't contain 0C     *)
        (CAP(A[Probe])=CAP(B[Probe])) & (A[Probe]#0C)  DO
            Probe := Probe + 1
        END;
        RETURN A[Probe]<B[Probe]
      END IsLessString;


    BEGIN (* SelSort *)
      SortStart := Last + 1;
      WHILE (* INV: Data contains the same values as at entry,  *)
            (*      except rearranged so that all items from    *)
            (*      Data[1..SortStart-1] are <= Data[SortStart] *)
            (*      & Data[SortStart..Last] is sorted ascending *)
            (*      & SortStart>=2                                *)
      (SortStart>=3)  DO
          MaxIndx := 1;
          FOR J:=2 (* INV: Data[MaxIndx] is the largest item *)
                   (*      of Data[1..J-1]                    *)
                   (*      &  J <= SortStart                  *)
          TO SortStart-1  DO
              IF  IsLessString( Data[MaxIndx],Data[J] )  THEN
                MaxIndx := J
              END
          END;
          SortStart := SortStart - 1;
          SwapString( Data[SortStart], Data[MaxIndx] )
      END
    END SelSort;
```

FIGURE 13.6 *The SelSort procedure*

13.3 TWO-DIMENSIONAL ARRAYS

Two-dimensional arrays are called **matrices** (the singular form is "matrix"). A vector of vectors is one view of a matrix.

A two-dimensional array, or matrix, has two index sets, one to select a row and a second to select a column. The SelSort procedure makes use of a vector of strings called Data. In this code the item

Data[3]

is a vector of type String (an array of 21 CHAR items). The following expression can be used to refer to the sixth character (with subscript of 5) from the third string:

Data[3][5]

This notation treats Data as a matrix, where each row is a string and each column a character position within the string. Data[3][5] selects the character from Row 3, Column 5. An equivalent notation for this reference is:

Data[3,5]

This last notation is the more standard notation for identifying items of a matrix. Figure 13.7 describes this form further.

Syntax:

> → *ArrayName* → [→ *FirstInd* → , → *SecndInd* →] →

    ArrayName: *The identifier declared as the name of the*
        matrix
    FirstInd: *An expression with the same type as the first*
        index for the array ArrayName
    SecndInd: *An expression with the same type as the*
        second index for the array ArrayName

Semantics:
    This notation specifies a reference to the item from
    the matrix named ArrayName with a row number given by
    FirstInd and a column number given by SecndInd.

FIGURE 13.7 *Description of a matrix item reference*

Matrices do not have to be declared as a vector of vectors. It is also possible to declare matrices in more nearly the form used to reference them. Figure 13.8 repeats the syntax diagram for array declarations given in the previous chapter. For a two-dimensional array, two consecutive IndexTypes are included, one to declare the row indices and a second to declare the column indices.

ArrayDecl:

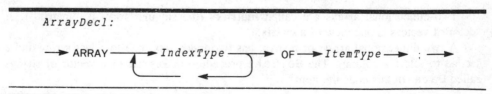

FIGURE 13.8 *Syntax of an array type*

Figure 13.9 contains several matrix declarations. After each set of declarations a picture of the matrix is included.

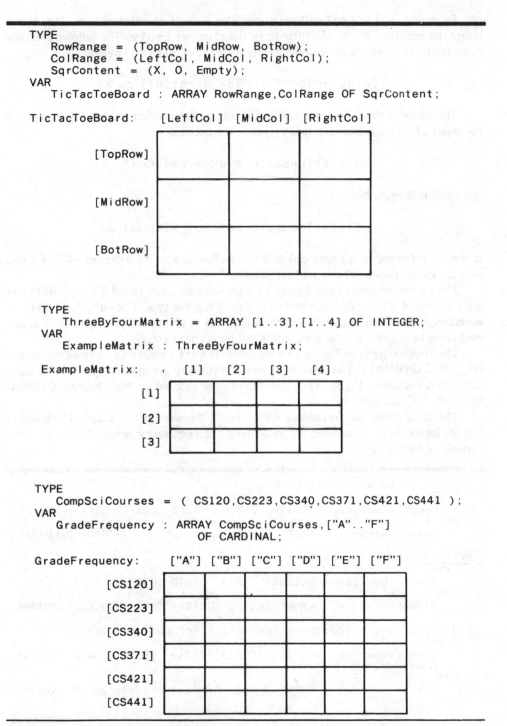

```
TYPE
    RowRange = (TopRow, MidRow, BotRow);
    ColRange = (LeftCol, MidCol, RightCol);
    SqrContent = (X, O, Empty);
VAR
    TicTacToeBoard : ARRAY RowRange,ColRange OF SqrContent;
```

TicTacToeBoard: [LeftCol] [MidCol] [RightCol]

[TopRow]

[MidRow]

[BotRow]

```
TYPE
    ThreeByFourMatrix = ARRAY [1..3],[1..4] OF INTEGER;
VAR
    ExampleMatrix : ThreeByFourMatrix;
```

ExampleMatrix: [1]   [2]   [3]   [4]

[1]

[2]

[3]

```
TYPE
    CompSciCourses = ( CS120,CS223,CS340,CS371,CS421,CS441 );
VAR
    GradeFrequency : ARRAY CompSciCourses,["A".."F"]
                     OF CARDINAL;
```

GradeFrequency: ["A"] ["B"] ["C"] ["D"] ["E"] ["F"]

[CS120]

[CS223]

[CS340]

[CS371]

[CS421]

[CS441]

FIGURE 13.9 *Example of declarations of matrices*

Each item of `TicTacToeBoard` stores an item of enumerated type. The item is either the identifier `X`, the identifier `O`, or the identifier `Empty`. The following assignment instruction assigns an X to the top right corner of `TicTacToeBoard`:

```
TicTacToeBoard[TopRow,RightCol] := X;
```

The order of the index expressions given in an array reference must *exactly match* the order of the corresponding index types in the declaration.

```
TicTacToeBoard[MidRow,LeftCol]
```

is a valid reference, but

```
TicTacToeBoard[LeftCol,MidRow]
```

is not. A reference to a single cell of `TicTacToeBoard` must consist of first a row selector index, *then* a column selector index.

The second example from Figure 13.9 declares an array called `ExampleMatrix` with a type of `ThreeByFourMatrix`. Declaring the type `ThreeByFourMatrix` separately permits the declaration of other matrices of identical type. This allows aggregate array operations such as assignment and parameter passage.

The final example of Figure 13.9 declares `GradeFrequency`, a two-dimensional array of CARDINALs. The rows of `GradeFrequency` are indexed by the `CompSci-Courses` enumerated type, while the columns are indexed by the subrange of characters from "A" through "F".

There are numerous techniques for declaring the same array. Figure 13.10 shows five different ways to declare the same `GradeFrequency` array. There are other variations not shown.

Option 1 (same as Figure 13.9):
```
TYPE
    CompSciCourses = (CS120, CS223, CS340, CS371, CS421, CS441);
VAR
    GradeFrequency : ARRAY CompSciCourses,["A".."F"] OF CARDINAL;
```

Option 2 (using 2 subranges):
```
TYPE
    CompSciCourses = (CS120, CS223, CS340, CS371, CS421, CS441);
VAR
    GradeFrequency : ARRAY [CS120..CS441],["A".."F"] OF CARDINAL;
```

Option 3 (using 2 programmer-defined types for indices):
```
TYPE
    CompSciCourses = (CS120, CS223, CS340, CS371, CS421, CS441);
    GradeRange = ["A".."F"];
VAR
    GradeFrequency : ARRAY CompSciCourses,GradeRange OF CARDINAL;
```

(continued)

```
Option 4 (using a programmer-defined type for matrix);
    TYPE
        CompSciCourses = (CS120, CS223, CS340, CS371, CS421, CS441);
        GradeArray = ARRAY CompSciCourses,["A".."F"] OF CARDINAL;

    VAR
        GradeFrequency : GradeArray;

Option 5 (using ARRAY OF ARRAY form)
    TYPE
        CompSciCourses = (CS120, CS223, CS340, CS371, CS421, CS441);
    VAR
        GradeFrequency : ARRAY CompSciCourses OF
                            ARRAY ["A".."F"] OF CARDINAL;
```

FIGURE 13.10 *Equivalent ways to declare the GradeFrequency matrix*

Option 3 declares both index types more abstractly than Options 1 or 2. The details of the precise ranges are not contained within the declaration of GradeFrequency in Option 3. Instead, they are declared as separate programmer-defined types. Using programmer-defined types for index sets helps to describe their purpose. Option 4 abstracts the entire array template as a programmer-defined type. This option hides even more detail than the others, and it is necessary if other arrays of identical type are required. Option 5 illustrates the notion that a matrix is nothing more than a vector of vectors, but it is probably the least attractive alternative presented.

Programming with Style

Style of Matrix Declaration

Matrix declaration style is an excellent example of the choices and tradeoffs in abstraction. Very little abstraction is used when the types of the index sets and the item type are all specified in detail within the array declaration. Option 2 from Figure 13.10 is a good example. This lack of abstraction makes the precise structure and all its detail immediately obvious and provides the complete array in the most condensed form.

Using programmer-defined types for index sets increases the abstraction. Option 3 of Figure 13.10 illustrates this case. Here the intent of the subscripts has become more clear. The first subscript selects from CompSciCourses and the second selects from a GradeRange. The details of the precise definition of these two types are described elsewhere. The definition is much like a footnote.

Even more abstraction is used when the entire template for an array is declared as a programmer-defined type. Option 4 illustrates this. So much abstraction occurs in this option that it is possible to identify neither the type of the items nor the form of the array (vector or matrix, ranges on indices, etc.) directly from the array declaration.

The choice of style is up to the programmer. Here are some useful things to remember.

1) Increased abstraction tends to improve readability by adding "meaning" for the reader.
2) It is possible to overuse abstraction. After a while it seems as if the footnotes contain other footnotes.
3) If an array is to be used in parameter passage, then it *must* be declared by a programmer-defined type.

13.4 SEQUENTIAL ACCESS OF MATRICES

Because a matrix has two index sets, there are two basic techniques for processing a matrix sequentially. A matrix is said to be **processed by rows** whenever the primary sequential processing is done on the first (row) subscript. The earlier SelSort procedure processed a matrix by rows (strings). A matrix is **processed by columns** whenever the primary sequential processing is done on the last (column) subscript.

A typical video computer display consists of 24 rows of characters with 80 characters per row. The screen image can be stored conveniently in the Screen matrix declared in Figure 13.11.

```
CONST
     MaxRow = 24;
     MaxCol = 80;

TYPE
     ScreenRows = [1..MaxRow];
     ScreenCols = [1..MaxCol];
     ScreenImage = ARRAY ScreenRows,ScreenCols OF CHAR;

VAR
     Screen : ScreenImage;
```

FIGURE 13.11 *Declaration of Screen matrix*

The DisplayScreen procedure from Figure 13.12 assumes Figure 13.11 declarations. DisplayScreen contains two FOR loops. The outer loop is designed to output another row (the one subscripted by Row) for each iteration. The inner loop outputs a single character with row of Row and column of Col for each iteration. This form of nested loops is a common algorithm for sequential processing of matrices.

```
PROCEDURE DisplayScreen( Screen : ScreenImage );
     (* PRE:   Screen[1..MaxRow,1..MaxCol] is assigned *)
     (* POST: Screen is displayed by rows              *)
   VAR
     Row : ScreenRows;
     Col : ScreenCols;
BEGIN
   FOR Row:=1 (* INV: the rows from Screen[1..Row-1] *)
             (*      are output   AND   Row<=MaxRow+1 *)
   TO MaxRow  DO
     FOR Col:=1 (* INV: Screen[Row,1..Col-1] is output *)
               (*      AND Col<=MaxCol+1              *)
     TO MaxCol  DO
       Write( Screen[Row,Col] )
     END;
     (* Assert: One more row of Screen has been output    *)
     (* Note: If no auto carriage return then WriteLn here *)
   END
END DisplayScreen;
```

FIGURE 13.12 *The DisplayScreen procedure*

DisplayScreen is an example of processing a two-dimensional array by rows. An example of an algorithm that processes by columns is the totaling of columns in a general ledger. The declarations used for this problem are given in Figure 13.13.

```
CONST  .
    ColCount = 12;
    NumberOfEntries = 100;

TYPE
    OneRowVector = ARRAY [1..ColCount] OF REAL;
    LedgerForm = ARRAY [1..NumberOfEntries],[1..ColCount]
                 OF REAL;
```

FIGURE 13.13 *Declarations for ColumnTot procedure*

The ColumnTot procedure, shown in Figure 13.14, has two formal parameters, called Ledger and ColSums. An invocation of ColumnTot totals each of the columns from the Ledger matrix and stores the resulting sum in the corresponding entry of the ColSums array. The Ledger parameter is passed by reference only because of the inefficiency of passing such a large data structure by value.

```
PROCEDURE ColumnTot( VAR Ledger : LedgerForm;
                     VAR ColSums : OneRowVector );
    (* PRE:  Ledger[1..NumberOfEntries,1..ColCount] is assigned  *)
    (* POST: For all subscripts, s, such that (1<=s<=ColCount)    *)
    (*         ColSums[s] = sum of Ledger[1..NumberOfEntries,s]   *)
    VAR
        Row : [1..NumberOfEntries];
        Col : [1..ColCount];
BEGIN
    FOR Col:=1 (* INV: For all subscripts, s, such that (1<=s<Col-1),*)
                 (*ColSums[s]=sumofLedger[1..NumberOfEntries,s]       *)
                 (*     & Col <= ColCount+1                            *)
    TO ColCount  DO
        ColSums[Col] := 0;
        FOR Row:=1 (* INV: ColSums[Col] = sum of Ledger[1..Row-1,Col] *)
                   (*     & Row <= NumberOfEntries+1                   *)
        TO NumberOfEntries  DO
            ColSums[Col] := ColSums[Col] + Ledger[Row,Col]
        END
    END
END ColumnTot;
```

FIGURE 13.14 *The ColumnTot procedure*

13.5 MULTIDIMENSIONAL ARRAYS

While most computer programs are able to represent data in vectors or matrices effectively, arrays of higher dimension are sometimes preferable.

The declaration form for additional dimensions is consistent with that of one- and two-dimensional arrays, except for additional index type specifications. The reference form for multidimensional arrays is also analogous. The restrictions on a reference to a particular cell of any array are summarized as follows:

1) The number of index selector expressions must be *exactly* the same as the number of index types declared in the array declaration.
2) The type of each index selector expression must be *assignment compatible* with the corresponding index type from the array declaration.

Figure 13.15 contains an example of a three-dimensional array declaration. The TicTacToeBoards array is designed to store up to twenty tic tac toe boards. This array could be used to store up to twenty different games, or it could store the board images from up to twenty moves of a single game. A picture of the image of this array is included in the figure.

```
TYPE
    RowRange = (TopRow, MidRow, BotRow);
    ColRange = (LeftCol, MidCol, RightCol);
    SqrContent = (X, O, Empty);
    TicTacToeBoardForm = ARRAY RowRange,ColRange
                         OF SqrContent;
VAR
    TicTacToeBoards : ARRAY [1..MaxBoards] OF TicTacToeBoardForm;
```

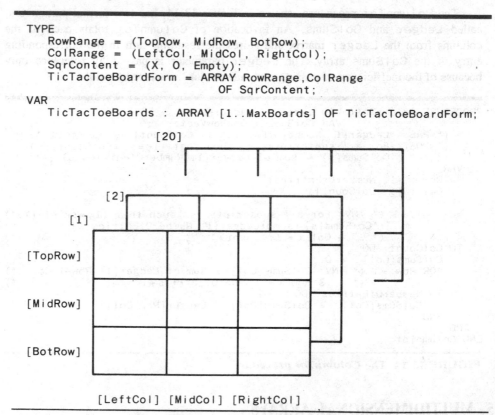

FIGURE 13.15 *Example of declaration and form of TicTacToeBoards*

The declaration of TicTacToeBoards suggests viewing the structure as a vector of tic tac toe boards—in other words, "a vector of matrices." Using such a declaration provides the opportunity to pass a single board (a two-dimensional array) as a parameter or to assign one board image to another. It is also possible to access individual items of the structure. For example, the following assignment instruction assigns the enumerated constant X to the bottom row of the middle column of Game Board three.

```
TicTacToeBoards[3,BotRow,MidCol] := X;
```

Figure 13.16 contains a second example declaration of a three-dimensional array. In this case, the form of the array is not a vector of matrices, nor matrix of vectors, but simply a three-dimensional grid. Rainfall is an array designed to store the rainfall amounts for a particular community for every day from the year 1921 until 1990.

```
TYPE
    YearRange = [1921..1990];
    MonthType = (Jan, Feb, Mar, Apr, May, Jun,
                 Jul, Aug, Sep, Oct, Nov, Dec);
    DayRange = [1..31];
VAR
    Rainfall : ARRAY YearRange,MonthType,DayRange OF REAL;
```

FIGURE 13.16 *Declaration of the Rainfall array*

The following assignment instruction can be used to add one to the rainfall total stored for March 27, 1951.

```
(* Assert: Rainfall[1951,Mar,27] is assigned *)
Rainfall[1951,Mar,27] := Rainfall[1951,Mar,27] + 1.0;
```

Rainfall is an example of a partially-used multidimensional array. Several months have no 31st day (February has no 30th day and seldom a 29th!). The array makes space for these non-existent days because it is impossible to declare an array with a subscript of 31 for some months and not for others. Declaring space for 31 days in every month wastes only a small portion of the total number of Rainfall items.

The size of an array is the number of items, or cells, in the entire structure. The size of an array with two or more dimensions is calculated by multiplying the range of the index types. The size of TicTacToeBoards is the number of boards (20) times the number of rows per board (3) times the number of columns per board (3), or 20*3*3 = 180.

Similarly, the size of Rainfall is calculated by multiplying the number of indices in YearRange (70), times the number of indices in MonthType (12), times the number of indices in DayRange (31), 70*12*31 = 26040. Sometimes the size of multidimensional arrays is deceptive. The declaration of Rainfall tends to hide its size from an unwary observer.

13.6 USING ARRAYS AS FUNCTIONS

A function is a mapping that translates a value of one type into some other value of the same or possibly different type. Modula-2 includes standard functions such as TRUNC and ORD. In addition, programmers can declare their own functions as procedures that return a value.

Arrays are another method of implementing functions. Any array can be thought of as a function that maps from an index value to the value stored in the corresponding array item. In mathematical terms, the indices serve as the "domain" of the function, and the item values are the "range."

Exclusive OR is a Boolean function that returns TRUE when exactly one of its two operands is TRUE. Modula-2 does not include an exclusive OR operator. Figure 13.17 is a Modula-2 function that implements the exclusive OR.

```
PROCEDURE XOR( Expr1 : BOOLEAN;
                 Expr2 : BOOLEAN )
  : BOOLEAN;
BEGIN
    RETURN  Expr1 # Expr2
END XOR;
```

FIGURE 13.17 *The XOR function*

Once this XOR function is defined, the programmer utilizes it by supplying appropriate actual parameters. The exclusive OR of the BOOLEAN type variables Boo1 and Boo2 is expressed as:

```
XOR( Boo1, Boo2 )
```

It is also possible to implement the exclusive OR operation as an array. Figure 13.18 declares and initializes the XOR matrix.

```
Required declaration:

VAR
    XOR : ARRAY BOOLEAN,BOOLEAN OF BOOLEAN;

Initialization code:

XOR[ TRUE , TRUE   ] : = FALSE ;
XOR[ TRUE , FALSE  ] : = TRUE  ;
XOR[ FALSE , TRUE  ] : = TRUE  ;
XOR[ FALSE , FALSE ] : = FALSE ;
```

FIGURE 13.18 *Declaration and initialization of XOR array*

The XOR array (Figure 13.17) is a good alternative to the XOR procedure (Figure 13.18). The following array reference serves to calculate the exclusive OR of Boo1 and Boo2.

```
XOR[ Boo1, Boo2 ]
```

Except for the use of square brackets in place of parentheses, the XOR array is interchangeable with the XOR function. Any expression that is a valid actual parameter to the XOR function is also a valid index expression for the XOR array.

The main difference between the function and the array is execution speed. It is much faster to retrieve an item value from an array than to invoke a procedure, calculate the value of a Boolean expression, and return.

A second example using arrays to implement functions is shown in the MorseCode program from Figure 13.19. MorseCode inputs a character string from a user-specified file and translates the each character into an International Morse Code encoding—a character string. The output of the program produces hyphens for the "dashes" and periods for "dots."

```
MODULE MorseCode;
      (* This program reads a message from a user specified *)
      (* file and displays it in Morse code.                 *)
   FROM InOut IMPORT Read, WriteString, OpenInput, CloseInput,
                     Write, WriteLn, Done;
   TYPE
      String6 = ARRAY [0..6] OF CHAR;
      ArrayOfString6 = ARRAY CHAR OF String6;
   VAR
      Code : ArrayOfString6;
      InChar : CHAR;

   PROCEDURE InitializeCodes( VAR Code : ArrayOfString6 );
         (* POST: All characters defined by International Morse*)
         (*        code are properly assigned, others are      *)
         (*        assigned a blank character. (NOTE: Lowercase *)
         (*        letters are not defined since no separate   *)
         (*        definition occurs in Morse Code.)           *)
      VAR
         I : CARDINAL;
      BEGIN
      FOR I:=0   (* INV: All items of Code[CHR(0)..CHR(I-1)] *)
            (*              are = " "    &  I<=128            *)
      TO 127  DO
         Code[CHR(I)] := " "
      END;

      Code["A"] := ".-";           Code["B"] := "-...";
      Code["C"] := "-.-.";         Code["D"] := "-..";
      Code["E"] := ".";            Code["F"] := "..-.";
      Code["G"] := "--.";          Code["H"] := "....";
      Code["I"] := "..";           Code["J"] := ".---";
      Code["K"] := "-.-";          Code["L"] := ".-..";
      Code["M"] := "--";           Code["N"] := "-.";
      Code["O"] := "---";          Code["P"] := ".--.";
      Code["Q"] := "--.-";         Code["R"] := ".-.";
      Code["S"] := "...";          Code["T"] := "-";
      Code["U"] := "..-";          Code["V"] := "...-";
      Code["W"] := ".--";          Code["X"] := "-..-";
      Code["Y"] := "-.--";         Code["Z"] := "--..";
      Code["0"] := "-----";        Code["1"] := ".----";
      Code["2"] := "..---";        Code["3"] := "...--";
      Code["4"] := "....-";        Code["5"] := ".....";
      Code["6"] := "-....";        Code["7"] := "--...";
      Code["8"] := "---..";        Code["9"] := "----.";
      Code["."] := ".-.-.-";       Code[","] := "--..--";
      Code[":"] := "---...";       Code[";"] := "-.-.-.";
      Code["'"] := ".-..-.";                                 (continued)
   END InitializeCodes;
```

```
BEGIN (* MorseCode mainline *)
   InitializeCodes( Code );
   WriteString( "Please specify input file." );
   OpenInput( " " );
   WriteLn; WriteLn;
   WriteString( "The file in Morse Code is as follows:");
   WriteLn;

   Read( InChar );
   WHILE (* INV: previous codes output for all previous inChars *)
     Done  DO
        WriteString( Code[CAP(InChar)] );
        Write( " " );   (* to separate consecutive codes *)
        Read( InChar )
   END
END MorseCode.
```

FIGURE 13.19 *The MorseCode program*

Using arrays as functions is a form of table driven code. As with other table driven code, it is necessary to initialize the array before it is used. The MorseCode program illustrates that this initialization can be lengthy; see the InitializeCodes procedure. If the array is accessed only a few times, all of the extra assignment instructions and the time required to execute them is probably not worth the bother. However, if the files translated by MorseCode contain many characters, then the increased efficiency of translating with the Code array more than offsets the time taken to initialize it.

Sometimes functions require more than a single parameter. These functions are often implemented as multidimensional arrays. Nutritionists frequently use expected weight tables to inform clients of their proper weight. Typical weight tables are organized by gender, height, and body type. Figure 13.20 declares an array, Expected-Weight, that could be used for this purpose.

```
CONST
    MinHeight = 51;
    MaxHeight = 80;
TYPE
    Gender = ( Female,Male );
    Build = ( SmallFrame, MedFrame, LargeFrame );
    Height = [MinHeight..MaxHeight];    (* in inches *)
    WeightTables = ARRAY Gender,Build,Height OF CARDINAL;
VAR
    ExpectedWeight : WeightTables;
```

FIGURE 13.20 *Declaration of ExpectedWeight array*

The size of ExpectedWeight is 180 items. A reasonable initialization technique for this array is to store all of the data (the expected weight values) in a file and to read them into the array with a loop. For example, the expected weights can be stored in a file of two separate tables, a female table followed by a male table. Each table consists of 30 rows of three cardinals per row (corresponding to the thirty heights and three body frames). The InitializeWeight procedure from Figure 13.21 is designed to initialize an array from this file.

```
PROCEDURE InitializeWeight( VAR ExpectedWeight : WeightTables);
    (* POST: ExpectedWeight initialized from user-specified  *)
    (*       file  (file should contain data in female table *)
    (*       followed by male; each table should be 30 rows  *)
    (*       for 30 heights and 3 frame size weights per row  *)
    VAR
      Sex : Gender;
      Hght : Height;
      Bld : Build;
BEGIN
    WriteString("File name of expected weight tables?");
    OpenInput;
    FOR Sex:=Female to Male DO
      FOR Hght:=MinHeight TO MaxHeight DO
        FOR Bld:=SmallFrame TO LargeFrame DO
            ReadCard( ExpectedWeight[Sex,Bld,Hght] );
          END;
        END;
      END;
    CloseInput;
END InitializeWeight;
```

FIGURE 13.21 *InitializeWeight procedure*

Once the ExpectedWeight array is initialized, it is possible to retrieve table values. The following output instruction is used to display the appropriate weight table value for a male, five foot ten inches tall (70 inches) and of a medium build:

```
WriteCard( ExpectedWeight[Male,MedFrame,70],0 );
```

The option of creating such a large data structure, coding the Initialize-Weight procedure, and setting up the data file may seem like a considerable effort. However, if this function were to be implemented in code, it would require complex control structures. A collection of CASE instructions to divide a request into 180 separate cases is lengthy and complicated.

The use of arrays as functions can also simplify the output of enumerated type values. Figure 13.22 shows an array, called BaseballPositionStr, that translates data of the enumerated type, BaseballPosition, into an appropriate character string for output.

Required declarations:

```
TYPE
    BaseballPosition = ( Catcher, Pitcher, FirstBase,
                         SecondBase, ShortStop, ThirdBase,
                         LeftField, CenterField, RightField );
    String12 = ARRAY [0..12] OF CHAR;
VAR
    BaseballPositionStr : ARRAY BaseballPosition OF String12;
```

(continued)

Initialization code:

```
BaseballPositionStr[ Catcher     ] := "catcher";
BaseballPositionStr[ Pitcher     ] := "pitcher";
BaseballPositionStr[ FirstBase   ] := "first base";
BaseballPositionStr[ SecondBase  ] := "second base";
BaseballPositionStr[ ShortStop   ] := "shortstop";
BaseballPositionStr[ ThirdBase   ] := "third base";
BaseballPositionStr[ LeftField   ] := "left field";
BaseballPositionStr[ CenterField ] := "center field";
BaseballPositionStr[ RightField  ] := "right field";
```

FIGURE 13.22 *Declaration and initialization of BaseballPositionStr array*

Using the declarations and initializations from Figure 13.22, and assuming that Position is a variable of type BaseballPosition, the following WriteString procedure invocation causes an appropriate string to be displayed:

```
WriteString( BaseballPositionStr[Position] );
```

Programming-with-Style

The Use of Arrays as Functions

An array is a very useful and efficient technique for implementing a function. Avoiding the use of arrays as functions often leads to complex, unreadable, unmodifiable code.

The main disadvantage to this application of arrays is the need to initialize the array. Files provide one alternative for initializing large arrays by abstracting the details of the function values from the code. If properly organized, a file also provides for easy modification of the values of the function by using an editor.

Space and initialization time requirements of arrays must be considered before implementing functions in this way. Large arrays occupy large amounts of memory and require execution time for initialization. These factors must be considered along with the number of times the function is used and how complicated it is to design an alternative algorithm.

13.7 DEBUGGING ARRAYS

Thinking of an array as merely a group of simple variables often provides the key to debugging. The main difficulty posed by the inclusion of arrays in code is their size. It is common to have arrays with hundreds or thousands of individual items. Many debugging techniques become cumbersome for such large amounts of data.

For any trace, a programmer needs to decide which variables are key, and to examine only those variables. Selecting a few items from an array for examination is the only practical trace for a large array. Sometimes there are certain key items that should be examined. For example, the first or last item or some particular item that seems to be causing problems may prove useful. Other times it is sufficient to consider a "typical" array item.

Another debugging issue for arrays is the subscript that goes out of bounds. A trace should search for such errors.

A display of the entire contents of an array is known as an **array dump**. Debugging a large system often requires the use of procedures that are sometimes called **dump routines**, which produce array dumps at various points during execution. A programmer may include dump routines, that are invoked only in the case of a severe execution error. During the debugging process, dump routines may be called more frequently in an attempt to uncover errors.

For large arrays, the output of dump routines may be voluminous. Sending such output to a video screen is often impractical. Printing large volumes creates large listings that are slow to complete and that require large amounts of paper. Because of these problems, dumping large arrays should be used with caution.

13.8 SUMMARY

Arrays come in boxes of different shapes and sizes. In Modula-2 there is considerable flexibility in the number and type of array index, as well as item type. The one-dimensional array, or vector, suffices for many program applications. However, many times two-dimensional arrays (matrices) and other multidimensional arrays are more useful.

Two-dimensional arrays can be viewed as a grid of rows and columns, like a chess board. Multidimensional arrays open up new possibilities for creating three, four, or more dimensions.

The TYPE declarations of Modula-2 permit flexibility in processing arrays and subarrays. A matrix can be treated as though it were a vector of vectors. In this form, an item of the matrix is an array that can be processed individually.

The algorithms used in conjunction with multidimensional arrays are analogous to those used with vectors. Multiple dimensions increase the loop nesting for many algorithms.

The use of a constant array as a function is yet another programming tool. This tool provides easy representation of tables of data. The constant array is also convenient for translation of enumerated types.

| | | KEY TERMS

vector of arrays
two-dimensional array
selection sort (straight selection)
matrix
matrix processing by rows

matrix processing by columns
multidimensional array
exclusive OR
array dump
dump routine

||| EXERCISES

Use the declarations below to complete Exercises 1 through 7.

```
TYPE
    DepartmentCodes = (Biol, Comp, Chem, Math, Phys);
    CourseNumbers = [100..499];
    Str20 = ARRAY [0..20] OF CHAR;
VAR
    SumMatrix : ARRAY [1..20],[1..50] OF INTEGER;
    CourseTitle : ARRAY DepartmentCodes,CourseNumbers OF Str20;
    I : CARDINAL;
    J : CARDINAL;
    RowTotal : CARDINAL;
TYPE
    CardVal = (two,three,four,five,six,seven,
               eight,nine,ten,jack,queen,king,ace);
    Suit = (Hearts,Diamonds,Clubs,Spades);
VAR
    IsCardInHand : ARRAY [two..ace],Suit OF BOOLEAN;
    FaceValue : CardVal;
    SomeSuit : Suit;
TYPE
    Divisions = (Johnson,Knudson,Michelson,Olson,Sorenson);
    SectorRange = [1..10];
    LotNumberRange = [1..100];
    Dimensions = ARRAY (Length,Width) OF CARDINAL;
                        (*dimensions in feet*)
    CityLotArray = ARRAY Divisions,SectorRange, LotNumberRange
                        OF Dimensions;
VAR
    CityLot : CityLotArray;
```

1. How many dimensions are there to the atomic items of the following arrays?
   a) SumMatrix
   b) CourseTitle
   c) IsCardInHand
   d) CityLot

2. What is the size (number of atomic items) of each of the following arrays?
   a) SumMatrix
   b) CourseTitle
   c) IsCardInHand
   d) CityLot

3. Write a segment of Modula-2 code to perform each of the following:
   a) Increment by one the value of the SumMatrix item in the third row and fifteenth column.
   b) Assign the title "Organic Chemistry II" as the course title of Chemistry course No. 202.
   c) Assign to city lot number 73 of sector 5 of the Olson division the size 150 (length) by 200 (width) feet.
   d) Assign 0 to every item of SumMatrix.

4. Assume that a TRUE value for an item in the IsCardInHand array means that the playing card with that subscript is in your hand of cards, and that a FALSE value means it is not in your hand. Write a segment of code that assigns IsCardInHand properly for the following hand of cards (Note: Remember to assign FALSE items as well as TRUE.)

   Queen of Hearts
   Ace of Spades
   Nine of Hearts
   Jack of Diamonds
   Ace of Clubs

5. Write a segment of code to output all of the course titles for the Biology department, assuming all permissible course numbers are used.

6. Write a procedure that will output the total square area of all city lots, assuming that all cells of CityLotArray are assigned.

7. Write a segment of code to output the sum of each row of the SumMatrix.

8. A rental car company rents five type of vehicles: subcompacts, compacts, sedans, station wagons, and vans. Their fleet consists of four cars of each type. Design a matrix (i.e., specify its declarations) to store the mileage for all cars of the fleet.

9. A triangular track meet involves high school teams from the towns of Holmen, Onalaska, and West Salem. The field events coach wants a program to store the points scored by each team in the triangular for each field event, as well as the total. The field events for this meet are the shot put, discus, pole vault, high jump, long jump, triple jump, and javelin. Design a single array to store each team's points in each event, as well as its total score.

10. A post office rents five hundred post office boxes. The boxes are arranged in rows, numbered from "A" through "J" and in columns numbered from 1 to 50. Design an array to store the last names (up to 20 characters) of the post office box owners. The array should be designed so that it resembles the row and column arrangement of the actual boxes for simplicity in changing the names of the owners.

11. A program is being written to maintain stock market prices for both common stock and preferred stock for the following companies: Burroughs, Control Data, Digital, IBM, and Sperry. Design a data structure that can maintain up to four years of all daily stock market prices.

12. Mid-continent to Overseas Majestic airlines, known affectionately as "MOM" needs to design a new program to maintain its plane reservation system. You must design the data structure to store seat assignments. MOM flies 124 flights daily; each flight has a number from 201 to 324; and the same flight numbers are used every day. Each plane MOM flies has 29 rows of five seats. The rows are numbered from 1 to 29 and the seats are lettered "A" through "E" accross a row. MOM wants a single array large enough to store the names (up to 25 characters) of each passenger for their particular seat assignment. The array need only store seat assignments for five days. Furthermore, the array must be organized so that the seat assignments from any one plane can be easily copied in their entirety, to another, since MOM has constant mechanical failures that necessitate such activity.

13. Design an array and specify all necessary initializations to implement the Boolean implication (→) function.

14. Design an array and specify all necessary initializations to implement the following mileage chart as a matrix representation of a function:

TO / FROM	Chicago	Los Angeles	Miami	New York
Chicago	0	2048	1397	809
Los Ang.	2048	0	2716	2794
Miami	1397	2716	0	1334
New York	809	2794	1334	0

15. Design an array and specify all necessary initializations to translate a variable of the following enumerated type into the character string corresponding to the enumerated constant value.

```
TYPE FavoriteComposers = (Bach, Beethoven, Brahms,
                          Haydn, Mozart);
```

16. Complete the code for the following procedure.

(* Use the following declarations *)

```
TYPE
    SomePoets = (Bates,Crane,Frost,Moore,Riley,Wylie);
    String5 = ARRAY[0..5] OF CHAR;
```

```
PROCEDURE FindPoet( VAR EnumPoet : SomePoets;
                    VAR Valid : BOOLEAN ;
                        StrPoet : String5 );
(* PRE:  StringPoet is assigned                      *)
(* POST: Valid = TRUE,   if StrPoet is "Bates", "Crane",  *)
(*                       "Frost", "Moore", "Riley" or     *)
(*                       "Wylie"                          *)
(*             = FALSE,  otherwise                        *)
(*     & EnumPoet is assigned the enumerated type         *)
(*                       corresponding to StrPoet if Valid *)
```

17. In matrix algebra the sum of two matrices is computed by summing the corresponding row and column positions of the two. Below is the definition of a matrix summing procedure. Complete the code for this procedure.

(* Use the following declaration *)

```
TYPE
    MatrixForm = ARRAY [1..RowDim],[1..ColDim] OF INTEGER;
```

```
PROCEDURE AddMatrices(    Srce1 : MatrixForm;
                          Srce2 : MatrixForm;
                      VAR MatrixSum : MatrixForm );
(* PRE:  Srce1 and Srce2 are completely assigned        *)
(* POST: For all subscripts, r & c, such that            *)
(* (1<=r<=RowDim) & (1<=c<=ColDim)  the following        *)
(*     results:  MatrixSum[r,c]=Srce1[r,c]+Srce2[r,c]    *)
```

18. In matrix algebra, the result of multiplying two matrices is another matrix where an entry in Row R and column C of the result comes from summing the product of the first item, Row R, of the first matrix times the first item, column C, of the second matrix; plus the second item, Row R, of the first matrix times the second item, Column C, of the second matrix; ... ; plus the last item, Row R, of the first matrix times the last item, Column C, of the second matrix. Complete the code for the MultiplyMatrices procedure below to perform this task.

(* Use the following declaration *)

```
TYPE
    MatrixForm = ARRAY [1..MaxDim],[1..MaxDim] OF INTEGER;
```

```
PROCEDURE MultMatrices(      Srce1 : MatrixForm;
                             Srce2 : MatrixForm;
                      VAR MatrixProduct : MatrixForm );
   (* PRE:  Srce1 and Srce2 are completely assigned       *)
   (* POST: For all subscripts, r & c, such that           *)
   (* (1<=r<=MaxDim) & (1<=c<=MaxDim)  the following *)    *)
   (*       results:  MatrixSum[r,c] =                     *)
   (*                     Srce1[r,1]*Srce2[1,c]            *)
   (*               + Srce1[r,2]*Srce2[2,c]  + ...         *)
   (*               + Srce1[r,MaxDim]*Srce2[MaxDim,c]      *)
```

||| PROGRAMMING PROJECTS

1. Write a program to solve the following problem.

TITLE
Simple Graphics Editor

DESCRIPTION
Much graphics work is performed on picture elements, or "pixels" for short. A pixel is merely a dot on the graphics screen that can be dark or light. In colored screens pixels may be assigned different colors. This program simulates a small graphics editor on a 20 by 20 grid of pixels. Each pixel is addressed by an ordered pair (row,col) and both rows and columns are numbered from the upper left as pictured below:

```
the grid  0 ------------------> 19 columns
          0
          |
          |
          V
          19
          rows
```

The program must maintain the status of the pixel grid at all times in a matrix of the following form:

TYPE
GridType = ARRAY [0..19],[0..19] OF BOOLEAN;

Any pixel that is "lit" corresponds to a TRUE value in the grid while any unlit pixel is left FALSE. Initially all pixel are assumed to be unlit.

The program repeatedly accepts user commands to manipulate this grid.

INPUT

The user enters the following commands, one per line. Each command begins with a single letter (either uppercase or lowercase) and is completed in different ways depending upon which command is chosen. Commands are input repeatedly until an "X" command is input to terminate the program. Note: All bracketed values below (<row>, <col>, <row1>, <row2>, <col1>, <col2>) signify cardinals in the range from 0 to 19.

L . . . Form: L <row> <col>

Meaning:

Light the single pixel specified by the ordered pair (<row>,<col>).

U . . . Form: U <row> <col>

Meaning:

Reset to Unlit the single pixel specified by the ordered pair (<row>,<col>) to Unlit.

H . . . Form: H <row> <col1> <col2>

Meaning:

Light a Horizontal line with endpoints specified by (<row>,<col1>) and (<row>,<col2>)

V . . . Form: V <col> <row1> <row2>

Meaning:

Light a Vertical line with endpoints specified by (<row1>,<col>) and (<row2>,<col>).

R . . . Form: R <row1> <col1> <row2> <col2>

Meaning:

Light the boundary of a rectangle with opposite corners specified by the ordered pairs (<row1>,<col1>) and (<row2>,<col2>).

C . . . Form: C <row1> <col1> <row2> <col2>

Meaning:

Clear (reset to unlit) all pixels within and on the boundary of the rectangle with opposite corners specified by the ordered pairs (<row1>,<col1>) and (<row2>,<col2>).

P . . . Form: P

Print the entire grid (see OUTPUT section for display form).

X . . . Form: X

Terminate program execution

OUTPUT

The only output produced by the program is the printed image of the grid (in response to a "P" command). This output image consists of 23 lines. Each lit pixel is displayed as an asterisk, "*", and each unlit pixel is blank. The grid is bordered by " + " symbols, acounting for two of the 23 output lines. The grid is also labeled above and on the right by the last digit of the pixel number.

ERRORS

All input may be assumed valid. Undefined results occur for invalid input.

EXAMPLE

In the example below all input has been highlighted.

```
              L 2 2
              H 4 5 11
              P
                01234567890123456789
                + + + + + + + + + + + + + +
              0 +                          +
              1 +                          +
              2 +    *                     +
              3 +                          +
              4 +         *******          +
              5 +                          +
              6 +                          +
              7 +                          +
              8 +                          +
              9 +                          +
              0 +                          +
              1 +                          +
              2 +                          +
              3 +                          +
              4 +                          +
              5 +                          +
              6 +                          +
              7 +                          +
              8 +                          +
              9 +                          +
                + + + + + + + + + + + + + +
              U 4 6
              U 1 1
              H 7 13 11
              R 10 12 14 15
              P
```

```
  0123456789012345678 9
  + + + + + + + + + + + + + + +
0 +                             +
1 +                             +
2 +    *                        +
3 +                             +
4 +         * *****             +
5 +                             +
6 +                             +
7 +              ***            +
8 +                             +
9 +                             +
0 +              ****           +
1 +              *  *           +
2 +              *  *           +
3 +              *  *           +
4 +              ****           +
5 +                             +
6 +                             +
7 +                             +
8 +                             +
9 +                             +
  + + + + + + + + + + + + + + +
V 19 0 15
C 2 3 4 8
C 7 11 6 10
C 14 14 14 14
P
  0123456789012345678 9
  + + + + + + + + + + + + + + +
0 +                          * +
1 +                          * +
2 +    *                     * +
3 +                          * +
4 +              ***         * +
5 +                          * +
6 +                          * +
7 +               **         * +
8 +                          * +
9 +                          * +
0 +         ****      **      * +
1 +         *  *      *       +
2 +         *  *      *  *    * +
3 +         *  *      *  *    * +
4 +         ** *      *  *    * +
5 +                          * +
6 +                          * +
7 +                          * +
8 +                          * +
9 +                          * +
  + + + + + + + + + + + + + + +
V 6 19 10
H 10 18 4
P
```

```
     01234567890123456789
     + + + + + + + + + + + + + + + +
  0 +                          * +
  1 +                          * +
  2 +    *                     * +
  3 +                          * +
  4 +              * * *        * +
  5 +                          * +
  6 +                          * +
  7 +                 * *       * +
  8 +                          * +
  9 +                          * +
  0 +     * * * * * * * * * * * * * +
  1 +        *      *   *       * +
  2 +        *      *   *       * +
  3 +        *      *   *       * +
  4 +        *      * *  *       * +
  5 +        *                  * +
  6 +        *                    +
  7 +        *                    +
  8 +        *                    +
  9 +        *                    +
     + + + + + + + + + + + + + + + +
  X
```

2. Write a program to solve the following problem.

TITLE
The Game of Life

DESCRIPTION
A mathematician by the name of John H. Conway invented a game (see *Scientific American*, Oct. 1970) called "The Game of Life." The Game of Life models the manner in which certain life forms change over time. Mr. Conway's model uses a two-dimensional grid. Every cell on the grid is either alive or dead. The game is played by generations. A cell's existence is defined by the previous generation. In particular, the cell depends on its "neighbors" from the previous generation. The neighbors of a cell are the eight cells that surround its border (note that cells on the boundaries of the grid have fewer neighbor cells).

The rules for the next generation in the Game of Life are as follows:

A birth occurs (a dead cell becomes alive) whenever exactly three of its neighbor cells were alive in the previous generation.

A death occurs (a live cell becomes dead) whenever it had four or more live neighbor cells in the previous generation (death by overcrowding) or whenever it had zero or one live neighbor cells in the previous generation (death by loneliness).

In all other cases, cells remain unchanged in the next generation.

This program should simulate the game of life on a ten by ten grid. The user must initialize the grid and specify the number of generations to be displayed. The program should then display in pictorial form each consecutive generation.

INPUT

The user is prompted for all input. The first ten lines of input are each ten characters long and represent the initial image of the Game of Life grid. A dead cell is represented by a blank and a live cell by a "#" character. Following the ten grid initialization lines, the eleventh input line contains a single cardinal value to specify the number of generations to be displayed after the first (an input of 0 indicates to display only the initial configuration).

OUTPUT

The two input prompts are as follows:

```
Specify initial form of Life Grid.
Type ten lines of ten chars (''#'' for live cell).

Specify number of generations to be displayed:
```

Each generation is output in the form shown below, where #'s symbolize live cells and blanks dead cells, <n> is the generation number, and a border is drawn around the grid:

```
Generation: <n>
```

ERRORS

All input is assumed correct. Incorrect input produces undefined results.

EXAMPLE

For the example on the following page all input is highlighted.

```
Specify initial form of Life Grid.
Type ten lines of ten chars (''#'' for live cell).
```

```
        #        #
        #
        #


      ###
      ###
      ###
        ##
        ##
```

Specify number of generations to be displayed:

2

Generation: 0
```
.-----------.
| #       # |
| #         |
| #         |
|           |
|           |
|    ###    |
|    ###    |
|    ###    |
|      ##|
|      ##|
"-----------'
```

Generation: 1
```
.-----------.
|           |
|###        |
|           |
|           |
|    #      |
|   # #     |
|  #   #    |
|   # #     |
|    #   ##|
|        ##|
"-----------'
```

Generation: 2
```
.-----------.
| #         |
| #         |
| #         |
|           |
|    #      |
|   ###     |
|  ## ##    |
|   ###     |
|    #   ##|
|        ##|
"-----------'
```

3. Write a program to solve the following problem.

    TITLE
        Cross Balance Sheet

    DESCRIPTION
        Many times it is convenient to make use of a cross balance sheet in summarizing statistics. Such a sheet can be used to summarize income, expenses, budgets, and the like. The basic idea of a cross balance is an arrangement of rows and columns of numbers. Each row has some particular meaning, such as some particular type of expense. Each column has a different particular meaning, such as some month of the year.

    This program is designed to manage a general cross balance sheet. Labels for rows and columns, and the data are input from a user-specified file. The program outputs this data along with totals for all rows and columns.

    INPUT
        The only input supplied by the user is the name of the file containing all cross balance sheet data.

    This input file begins with two cardinal values greater than 0. The first cardinal indicates the number of rows (represented as "m" in the output section) in the cross balance and the second indicate the number of columns (represented as "n" in the output section). The program should accommodate up to 20 rows and nine columns. The next input in the file consists of one label for each specified row. Subsequently there is one label for each specified column. Each label consists of from one to eight characters enclosed in double quotation marks. The remainder of the file input consists of the cross balance data, all integer constants, in row by row order.

    OUTPUT
        The user is prompted to specify the input file as follows:

        Name of file containing cross balance data?

    The program then summarizes the results in the following output form, where <ColLabi> indicates the ith column label, <RowLabj> indicates the jth row label and <Datji> indicates the input data for Row j, Column i, <RowSumj> is the sum of all <Datji> for the jth row, <ColSumi> is the sum of all <Datji> for the ith column and Sum is the sum of all <RowSumj> (also the sum of all <ColSumi>). Note: Column labels must be right justified.

    <ColLab1>   <ColLab2> ... <ColLabn>   Totals

    <RowLab1>   <Dat11>   <Dat12> ... <Dat1n>   <RowSum1>
    <RowLab2>   <Dat21>   <Dat22>   <Dat2n>   <RowSum2>
        .   .   .
        .   .   .
        .   .   .

    <RowLabm>   <Datm1>   <Datm2> ... <Datmn>   <RowSumm>
    Totals   <ColSum1> <ColSum2> ... <ColSumn> <SUM>

ERRORS

Any input not conforming to specifications produces undefined results.

EXAMPLE

The contents of the file, named "Budget" are as follows:

```
5 4
"Food" "Util." "Taxes" "Recreation" "Misc."
"January" "February" " March"   " April"
100 120 120 130
250 240 150 125
0 0 0 0
150 150 150 150
100  95 185 210
```

Below is a sample program execution using the file above. The user input is highlighted.

```
Name of file containing cross balance data? Budget

            January February March April  Totals

Food          100     120     120    130     470
Util.         250     240     250    125     865
Taxes           0       0       0      0       0
Recreation    150     150     150    150     600
Misc.         100      95     185    210     590
Totals        600     605     705    615    2525
```

4. Write a program to solve the problem below.

TITLE

Word Finder

DESCRIPTION

Word find games are popular and can often be found in newspapers. The idea of a word find is to locate particular words in a two-dimensional grid of letters. For this program, the grid of letters (8 by 8) will be supplied by the user and the program will search for occurrences of the word "HELP." All occurrences of HELP must either be horizontal (left to right) or vertical (top to bottom). Diagonal occurrences are not located. The program must report each occurrence, beginning and ending.

INPUT

The user is prompted to supply eight lines of characters, exactly eight characters per line.

OUTPUT
The input prompt is as follows.

Please specify 8 lines (8chars/line) to search:

Following the input, each horizontal and each vertical forward occurrence of HELP is identified as follows, where <row1> <col1> specifies one endpoint and <row2>, <col2> the other.

HELP found from, <row1>,<col1> to <row2>,<col2>

ERRORS
Insufficient input on a line results in the following message, followed by program termination.

All input lines must be 8 chars long! - ABORTING

Any additional input after eight characters on a line is ignored.

EXAMPLE
All input below is highlighted.

Please specify 8 lines (8 chars/line) to search:

```
HELPHHHH
ELPHHHHE
LH E HEL
PELLLEPP
PLLHELPH
*PPPPPPE
HHHHHHHL
EEEEHELP
HELP found from 1,1 to 1,4
HELP found from 5,4 to 5,7
HELP found from 8,5 to 8,8
HELP found from 1,1 to 4,1
HELP found from 2,3 to 2,6
·HELP found from 6,3 to 6,6
HELP found from 8,1 to 8,4
HELP found from 8,5 to 8,8
```

14 ||| THE RECORD DATA STRUCTURE

14.1 NON-HOMOGENEOUS DATA

Arrays are the most commonly used structured data type. However, arrays have one significant restriction: Every item of an array must have a type identical to every other item. Arrays are referred to as **homogeneous data types** because of this characteristic.

It is often advantageous to group together different types of data. A single data structure to store all information for a one employee is an example. This information might include the employee's name (a string type), the employee's age (a cardinal type), the employee's gender (an enumerated type), and the employee's hourly wage (a real type). The homogeneous nature of arrays makes an array impractical for storing all of these different data.

14.2 THE RECORD

Modula-2 includes a data type, called a **record**, to overcome this restriction of the array. Records are **heterogeneous structured data types** because they may combine data of different types.

Records are structured types. They group together different items, called **fields**. Figure 14.1 describes a record type. Each field has a **field type** (FieldType) and a name, called a **field identifier** (FieldId). Each field identifier must be different from all other field names of the same record so that no confusion results.

Name of data type: record

Declaration of RecordType:

Syntax:

→ RECORD → *FieldSequence* → END →

(continued)

FieldSequence:

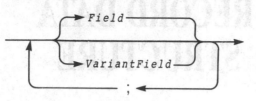

Field:

⟶ *FieldId* ⟶ : ⟶ *FieldType* ⟶

 FieldId: Any unambiguously declared identifier

 FieldType: Any valid data type

 *VariantField: See Figure 14.20 for description of variant
 records*

 *Semantics: The declared type is a record with fields named
 by FieldIds and types given by FieldTypes.*

 *Note: FieldId is localized to the record in which it is
 declared. FieldId may be declared elsewhere in the
 same scope without producing ambiguity.*

 Constants (for the entire record): none

 Operations (for the entire record): assignment (:=)

 *Operations (for the fields of the records): same as any other
 FieldType*

FIGURE 14.1 *The record data type*

Figure 14.2 declares CustomerType. CustomerType is a record type with five
fields. The FirstInit and LastInit fields are CHAR in type. The ID field has a
CARDINAL type. The Gender field is of the enumerated type called GenderType.
The AmountDue field is REAL.

```
TYPE
    GenderType = (Male, Female, Unknown);

    CustomerType = RECORD
                    FirstInit : CHAR;
                    LastInit : CHAR;
                    ID : CARDINAL;
                    Gender : GenderType;
                    AmountDue : REAL
                   END;
```

FIGURE 14.2 *Declaration of CustomerType*

Like any other programmer declared type, CustomerType is a template. Below is an example declaration for two customers called PreferredCust and Deferred-Cust that use CustomerType:

```
VAR
    PreferredCust : CustomerType;
    DeferredCust  : CustomerType;
```

This declares PreferredCust as a record. PreferredCust has the four fields specified in the declaration of CustomerType. DeferredCust has an identical type. Figure 14.3 diagrams the structure of DeferredCust.

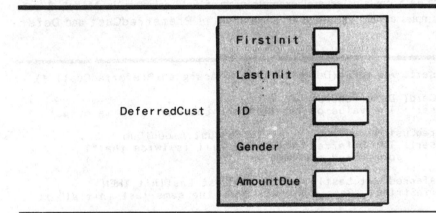

FIGURE 14.3 *The DeferredCust data structure*

After a record has been declared, its individual fields may be accessed using a **field selector**. The notation of a field selector consists of a record identifier followed by a period (".") followed by the field identifier. This syntax is shown in Figure 14.4.

FieldSelector:

$\longrightarrow$ *RecordName* $\longrightarrow$ $\longrightarrow$ *FieldId* $\longrightarrow$

RecordName: A reference to a record data structure

FieldId: One of the field identifiers from the declared
record data type corresponding to RecordName

FIGURE 14.4 *Syntax of FieldSelector*

Once a field has been selected from a record, it may be used like any variable of the same type. The field selector

DeferredCust.ID

selects the field of the DeferredCust that stores the customer's ID number, some cardinal value. DeferredCust.ID may be used like any other variable of type CARDINAL.

Field selectors belong to a class of references known as **qualified identifiers**. The name "qualified identifier" is appropriate, because it is necessary to qualify a field name with a record name in order to reference the field.

Figure 14.5 contains several example uses of field selectors in Modula-2 code. These examples assume the previous declarations of PreferredCust and DeferredCust.

```
(* Assert: Assigned(DeferredCust) & Assigned(PreferredCust) *)

WriteCard( DeferredCust.ID, 0 );
(* Assert: The value of the deferred customer's ID is output. *)

DeferredCust.AmountDue := PreferredCust.AmountDue * 2.0;
(* Assert: The deferred customer's bill is twice the *)
(*         preferred customer's.                      *)

IF PreferredCust.LastInit=DeferredCust.LastInit THEN
   WriteString( "Both customers have the same last initial" );
END;

INC( PreferredCust.ID );
(* Assert: The preferred customer's ID number has been *)
(*         increased by 1.                              *)

IF PreferredCust.Gender=Male THEN
   WriteString( "The preferred customer is a male." )
ELSIF PreferredCust.Gender=Female THEN
   WriteString( "The preferred customer is a female." )
ELSE
   WriteString( "The preferred customer's gender is unknown." )
END;
```

FIGURE 14.5 *Examples of record field selectors*

Because fields of records are named by qualified identifiers, it is possible to reuse a field name, such as ID. The only valid uses of ID, given the previous declarations, is either DeferredCust.ID or PreferredCust.ID. Therefore, it is possible to declare some other object with the name ID without confusion. In addition, other record types may also be declared with ID as a field name. Figure 14.6 shows an acceptable collection of declarations where ID is used to name a field of CustomerType, PresidentType and a cardinal variable. All of these declarations could be made within a single Modula-2 procedure or program.

```
TYPE
    GenderType = (Male, Female, Unknown);

    CustomerType = RECORD
                        FirstInit : CHAR;
                        LastInit : CHAR;
                        ID : CARDINAL;
                        Gender : GenderType;
                        AmountDue : REAL
                    END;
VAR
    PreferredCust : CustomerType;
    DeferredCust  : CustomerType;


TYPE
    PresidentType = RECORD
                        ID : CARDINAL;
                        Gender : GenderType;
                        AnnualWage : REAL
                    END;
VAR
    Pres : PresidentType;
    ID : CARDINAL;
```

FIGURE 14.6 *Example of redeclaration of field identifiers*

A fraction consists of two parts — numerator and denominator. This makes fractions good candidates for the record data type. Figure 14.7 contains a program that reads a fraction and outputs the equivalent fraction in simplest form (numerator and denominator with no common integer multiples except 1).

The SimplifyFraction program illustrates several different uses of records. It is possible to read into the field of a record:

```
ReadInt( InFrac.Numerator );
```

to write from the field of a record:

```
WriteInt( InFrac.Numerator,0 );
```

and to use record fields in assignment instructions:

```
Frac.Denominator := Frac.Denominator DIV PotentialDivisor;
```

In addition to accessing fields, it is also possible to pass an entire record as a single parameter:

```
Simplify( InFrac );
```

```
MODULE SimplifyFraction;
      (* This module inputs the value of a single fraction *)
      (* and outputs the simplified form of the fraction.  *)
   FROM InOut IMPORT Write, WriteCard, WriteInt, WriteString,
                     WriteLn, ReadCard, ReadInt;

   TYPE
      Fraction = RECORD
                    Numerator : INTEGER;
                    Denominator : CARDINAL
                 END;

   PROCEDURE Simplify( VAR Frac : Fraction );
      (* PRE:  Frac is assigned                           *)
      (* POST: Frac.Numerator DIV Frac.Denominator is the *)
      (*       same value as at procedure entry           *)
      (*    &  No cardinal>1 evenly divides both          *)
      (*       Frac.Numerator and Frac.Denominator        *)
   VAR
      SmallerMagnitude : CARDINAL;
      PotentialDivisor : CARDINAL;
   BEGIN
      IF CARDINAL(ABS(Frac.Numerator))<Frac.Denominator THEN
         SmallerMagnitude := ABS(Frac.Numerator);
      ELSE
         SmallerMagnitude := Frac.Denominator;
      END;
      (* Assert: No cardinal value can be greater than    *)
      (*         SmallerMagnitude and also evenly divide   *)
      (*         both Frac.Numerator and Frac.Denominator. *)

      FOR PotentialDivisor := SmallerMagnitude
         (* INV: No cardinal value can be greater than    *)
         (*      SmallerMagnitude and also evenly divide   *)
         (*      both Frac.Numerator and Frac.Denominator. *)
      TO 2 BY -1  DO
         IF (Frac.Numerator MOD INTEGER(PotentialDivisor) = 0)
            AND (Frac.Denominator MOD PotentialDivisor = 0)
         THEN
            Frac.Numerator := Frac.Numerator DIV INTEGER(PotentialDivisor);
            Frac.Denominator := Frac.Denominator DIV PotentialDivisor;
         END;
      END;
   END Simplify;

   VAR
      InFrac : Fraction;
```

(continued)

```
BEGIN (* SimplifyFraction mainline *)
    WriteString( "Please specify a fraction -> ");
    ReadInt( InFrac.Numerator );
    Write( "/" );
    ReadCard( InFrac.Denominator );
    WriteLn;
    Simplify( InFrac );
    WriteLn; WriteLn;
    WriteString( "The same fraction in simplest terms: ");
    WriteInt( InFrac.Numerator,0 );
    Write( "/" );
    WriteCard( InFrac.Denominator,0 );
    WriteLn;
END SimplifyFraction.
```

FIGURE 14.7 *SimplifyFraction module*

14.3 RECORDS WITH STRUCTURED FIELDS

In previous examples, the fields of records have all been of simple type. Record fields can also have structured type. It is often the case that one or more record fields are arrays or other records.

Figure 14.8 contains the Modula-2 declaration for a record called StudentType. StudentType consists of a Name field (a record), a Classification field, a SocialSecurityNumber field (an array), a Gender field, and a Grade-PointAverage field. This figure includes a declaration of a data structure, called Student, that has a type of StudentType.

```
TYPE
        GenderType = (Male, Female, Unknown);
        String9 = ARRAY [0..9] OF CHAR;
        String15 = ARRAY [0..15] OF CHAR;
        ClassType = ( freshman, sophomore, junior, senior,
                      graduate, special );

        NameType = RECORD
                      First : String15;
                      MiddleInit : CHAR;
                      Last : String15
                   END;

        StudentType = RECORD
                         Name : NameType;
                         Classification : ClassType;
                         SocialSecurityNumber : String9;
                         Gender : GenderType;
                         GradePointAverage : REAL
                      END;
        VAR
            Student : StudentType;
```

FIGURE 14.8 *Declaration of StudentType and Student*

The `SocialSecurityNumber` field of `StudentType` is a vector of nine characters. This vector, along with the remainder of the Student structure, is pictured in Figure 14.9. Any reference to

`Student.SocialSecurityNumber`

refers to this nine character string field as an aggregate array. As with any other array, individual items of `Student.SocialSecurityNumber` are referenced by including an index specification as a suffix. For example, the reference

`Student.SocialSecurityNumber[3]`

refers to the character with index of 3 from the `SocialSecurity` field of `Student`.

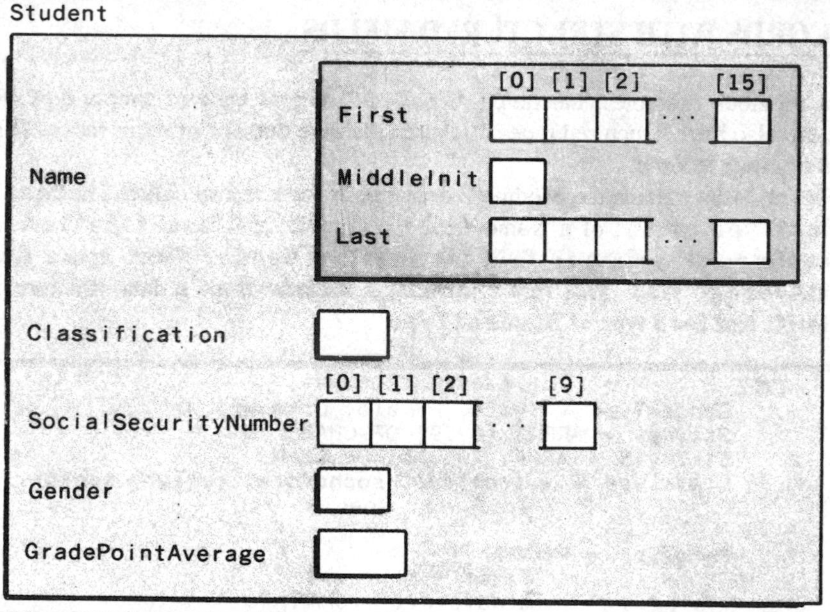

Student

FIGURE 14.9 *The Student data structure*

The Name field of `Student` is a record within a record. The qualified identifier `Student.Name` refers to this record type field. `Student.Name` has three fields corresponding to the first name, middle initial, and last name of the student. These fields of Name are actually **subfields** of `Student`.

The notation used to select subfields of a record is an extension of the notation to select fields. Any field of any record is referenced by appending a period ("."), then the field identifier to the reference form for the record. The following qualified identifier refers to the middle initial subfield:

```
Student.Name.MiddleInit
```

Figure 14.10 illustrates several references to portions of the Student record.

Reference form	Data structure referenced
Student	the entire Student record (' type: a record ')
Student.GradePointAverage	the GradePointAverage field of Student (' type: REAL ')
Student.SocialSecurityNumber	the SocialSecurityNumber field of Student (' type: String9 ')
Student.SocialSecurityNumber[0] .	the first char of the SocialSecurityNumber field of Student (' type: CHAR ')
Student.Name	the Name field of Student (' type: a NameType ')
Student.Name.MiddleInit ..	the MiddleInit field of the Name field of Student (' type: CHAR ')
Student.Name.First ...	the First field of the Name field of Student (' type: String15 ')
Student.Name.Last[2] .	the char with index of 2 from the Last field of the Name field of Student (' type: CHAR ')

FIGURE 14.10 *References to fields and subfields fo the Student record*

*P*rogramming-with-*S*tyle

Style of a Record Declaration

Records form a naturally hierarchical data structure. Each record has fields. Some or all of the fields may contain subfields. Subfields may contain subsubfields and so on. Because of the natural hierarchy, there are two main issues to remember in the style of declaring records.

The first issue is to use intelligent indentation in the form of a record declaration. The name of the record should be on one line with each of the fields on the indented on succeeding lines. Fields should be declared on separate lines. All fields of the same record should be indented as all other fields are.

The second issue to remember when declaring records is that it is generally preferable to declare the records within other records as a separate type. Trying to declare one record within another record results in awkward indentation patterns like the one below:

```
TYPE
   RecordType =
      RECORD
         FieldName :
            RECORD
               SubFieldName : SubFieldType;
               AnotherSubField : AnotherType
            END;
         AnotherFieldName : ...
```

The preferable form for the above declaration is given below:

```
TYPE
   ExtraType =
      RECORD
         SubFieldName : SubFieldType;
         AnotherSubField : AnotherType
      END;
   RecordType = RECORD
                   FieldName : ExtraType;
                   AnotherFieldName :
```

There are two advantages to using separate type declarations for fields that are records. Such a style of declaration avoids some of the indentation problems that occur when records are declared directly within records. The other advantage is that separate type declarations provide the opportunity to declare other data structures with identical type.

14.4 AGGREGATE RECORD OPERATIONS

Aggregate records, like aggregate arrays, can be assigned to other aggregate data structures. Using the declarations from Figure 14.6, the following assignment instruction causes the values of all fields of DeferredCust to be assigned to the corresponding fields of PreferredCust:

$$PreferredCust := DeferredCust$$

Two structured types are assignment compatible if and only if they have identical type or if the type of one is a renaming of the other. Consider Figure 14.11. It contains the declaration for four types: BeefCowType, BeefCattleRecord, MilkCow-Type, and DairyCattleRecord.

```
TYPE
    BeefVarieties = (Angus, Brahman, Hereford,
                     LongHorn, ShortHorn, OtherBeef);
    String8 = ARRAY [0..8] OF CHAR;

    BeefCowType = RECORD
                    Name : String8;
                    Breed : BeefVarieties;
                    Weight : CARDINAL;
                    Age : CARDINAL
                  END;
    BeefCattleRecord = BeefCowType;

    MilkVarieties = (BrownSwiss, Guernsey, Holstein,
                     Jersey, OtherDairy);
    MilkCowType = RECORD
                    Name : String8;
                    Breed : MilkVarieties;
                    DailyMilkProduction : CARDINAL;
                    Age : [0..12]
                  END;
    DairyCattleRecord = RECORD
                          Name : String8;
                          Breed : MilkVarieties;
                          DailyMilkProduction : CARDINAL;
                          Age : [0..12]
                        END;
VAR
    BeefCow1 : BeefCowType;
    BeefCow2 : BeefCowType;
    BeefCow3 : BeefCattleRecord;
    MilkCow1 : MilkCowType;
    MilkCow2 : DairyCattleRecord;
```

FIGURE 14.11 *Declaration of cattle records*

Any two data structures are identical, only if they have the same type. Since Beef-Cow1 and BeefCow2 are both declared to be of type BeefCowType, they have identical type. No other pair of data structures declared in Figure 14.11 has identical type.

Since BeefCow1 and BeefCow2 have identical type, they are assignment compatible. BeefCow3 is also assignment compatible with BeefCow1 and BeefCow2. This is because the type of BeefCow3, namely BeefCattleRecord, is a renaming of BeefCowType.

MilkCowType and DairyCattleRecord are incompatible, despite their identical fields, because they are neither identical nor renamed types. This incompatibility underscores the importance of declaring separate types to ensure type compatibility.

14.5 ARRAYS OF RECORDS

A program to store information about a company's employees is likely to use a vector to store this information. Each item in this vector contains the information for a single employee. Since the company stores several pieces of information about each employee, this suggests a vector of records. Figure 14.12 contains such a Modula-2 declaration.

```
TYPE
    GenderType = (Male, Female, Unknown);
    EmployeeType = RECORD
                        FirstInit : CHAR;
                        LastInit : CHAR;
                        Age : CARDINAL;
                        Gender : GenderType;
                        HourlyWage : CARDINAL
                    END;
    OneHundredEmployees = ARRAY [1..100] OF EmployeeType;

VAR
    Employee : OneHundredEmployees;
```

FIGURE 14.12 *Declaration of Employee array of records*

The Employee array from Figure 14.12 is a vector of 100 employees. The information stored for each employee includes FirstInit, LastInit, Age, Gender and HourlyWage. A diagram of this storage is shown in Figure 14.13 with the form of Employee[3] elaborated. All other items have the same form.

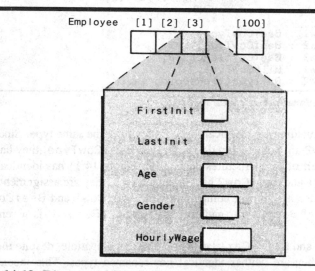

FIGURE 14.13 *Diagram of Employee array*

Since each item of Employee is a record, the form for accessing a field of an item uses the item selector with a qualifier appended. For example, the Age of the third employee is denoted:

Employee[3].Age

Figure 14.14 contains a procedure, called ReadEmployee, that inputs a single employee and stores the input results in the item of the EmpVec parameter as subscripted by EmpNo.

```
PROCEDURE ReadEmployee( VAR EmpVec : OneHundredEmployees;
                            EmpNo : CARDINAL );
      (* PRE:  1<=EmpNo<=100                                *)
      (* POST: EmpVec[EmpNo] is assigned from user input    *)
      (* NOTE: ReadOneEmployee (Figure 14.15) is a          *)
      (*       better alternative                           *)
   VAR
      GenderChar : CHAR;
BEGIN
   WriteString("Please specify info for employee number ");
   WriteCard( EmpNo,0 );
   WriteString(" below:");
   WriteLn;

   WriteString("  First and Last Initials -> ");
   Read( EmpVec[EmpNo].FirstInit );
   Read( EmpVec[EmpNo].LastInit );
   WriteLn;
   WriteString("  Age -> ");
   ReadCard( EmpVec[EmpNo].Age );
   WriteLn;

   WriteString("  Gender (M, F or ?) -> ");
   Read( GenderChar );
   WriteLn;
   CASE CAP(GenderChar) OF
     "M" : EmpVec[EmpNo].Gender := Male   |
     "F" : EmpVec[EmpNo].Gender := Female
   ELSE
      EmpVec[EmpNo].Gender := Unknown
   END;

   WriteString("  Hourly Wage (to nearest dollar) -> ");
   ReadCard( EmpVec[EmpNo].HourlyWage );
   WriteLn;
END ReadEmployee;
```

FIGURE 14.14 *ReadEmployee procedure*

ReadEmployee must be invoked with two actual parameters. The first parameter is a vector of employee records, like the Employee data structure declared in Figure 14.12. The second specifies a particular item from the vector represented by the first parameter that is used both in prompting the user and in indexing EmpVec.

There is no reason to pass the entire EmpVec record in order to read just one item. The ReadOneEmployee procedure from Figure 14.15 is a better alternative.

```
PROCEDURE ReadOneEmployee( VAR SomeEmp : EmployeeType;
                               EmpNo : CARDINAL );
      (* PRE:  Assigned(EmpNo)                       *)
      (* POST: SomeEmp is assigned from user input *)
   VAR
      GenderChar : CHAR;
BEGIN
   WriteString("Please specify info for employee number ");
   WriteCard( EmpNo,0 );
   WriteString(" below:");
   WriteLn;

   WriteString("  First and Last initials -> ");
   Read( SomeEmp.FirstInit );
   Read( SomeEmp.LastInit );
   WriteLn;
   WriteString("  Age -> ");
   ReadCard( SomeEmp.Age );
   WriteLn;

   WriteString("  Gender (M, F or ?) -> ");
   Read( GenderChar );
   WriteLn;
   CASE CAP(GenderChar) OF
     "M" : SomeEmp.Gender := Male   |
     "F" : SomeEmp.Gender := Female
   ELSE
     SomeEmp.Gender := Unknown
   END;

   WriteString("  Hourly Wage (to nearest dollars -> ");
   ReadCard( SomeEmp.HourlyWage );
   WriteLn;
END ReadOneEmployee;
```

FIGURE 14.15 *ReadOneEmployee procedure*

The SomeEmp parameter of ReadOneEmployee is used to pass a single employee. This avoids the need to pass all employees just to input one. ReadOneEmployee is also easier to read than ReadEmployee, because the length of the qualified identifiers is shorter. However, both procedures perform the same task when correctly used. Below are two invocations that both cause the sixth item from Employee to be assigned from input.

```
   (* Example invocation of ReadEmployee *)
   ReadEmployee( Employee, 6 );
   (* Assert: Employee[6] assigned from input *)
   (* Equivalent example invoking ReadOneEmployee *)
   ReadOneEmployee( Employee[6], 6 );
   (* Assert: Employee[6] assigned from input *)
```

14.6 SORTING RECORDS

Arrays of records can be sorted just like any other array. Since there are often several fields for every item being sorted, there are many ways to sort arrays of records. The most common way to sort arrays of records is to reorder items — whole records — so that one particular field is sorted. This is called **sorting on a field**. The Employee array declared in Figure 14.12 could be sorted on the FirstInit field or sorted on the Age field, as long as the record of information for each employee remains intact.

Figure 14.16 contains a sorting procedure, called SortEmployees that is used to sort any OneHundredEmployees type structure. SortEmployees performs its sort on the HourlyWage field.

```
PROCEDURE SortEmployees( VAR EmpVec : OneHundredEmployees );
     (* PRE:  EmpVec[1..100] is assigned            *)
     (* POST: EmpVec[1..100] is sorted in ascending *)
     (*       order on the HourlyWage field         *)
     (* NOTE: This uses a selection sort            *)
     VAR
         TempEmp : EmployeeType;
         SortStart : CARDINAL;
         j : CARDINAL;
         MaxIndx : CARDINAL;
BEGIN
     SortStart := 101;
     WHILE (* INV: EmpVec contains the same values as at entry,   *)
           (*      except rearranged so that all items from       *)
           (*      EmpVec[1..SortStart-1] are <= EmpVec[SortStart]*)
           (*    & EmpVec[SortStart..100] is sorted ascending on  *)
           (*      the HourlyWage Field                           *)
           (*    & SortStart>=2                                   *)
     (SortStart>=3)  DO
         MaxIndx := 1;
         FOR j:=2 (* INV: EmpVec[MaxIndx] has the greatest   *)
                  (*      HourlyWage field of EmpVec[1..j-1]  *)
                  (*    & j <= SortStart                      *)
         TO SortStart-1 DO
             IF EmpVec[MaxIndx].HourlyWage < EmpVec[j].HourlyWage THEN
                 MaxIndx := j
             END
         END;
         SortStart := SortStart - 1;
         TempEmp := EmpVec[MaxIndx];
         EmpVec[MaxIndx] := EmpVec[SortStart];
         EmpVec[SortStart] := TempEmp;
     END;
END SortEmployees;
```

FIGURE 14.16 *Procedure SortEmployees*

14.7 THE WITH STATEMENT

Programs often make repeated references to the same portion of a record. For example, the following code could be used to assign to the 34th item of the Employee vector a 35 year old male with the initials "D.R." who earns $7 per hour.

```
Employee[34].FirstInit := "D";
Employee[34].LastInit := "R";
Employee.[34].Age := 35;
Employee[34].Gender := Male;
Employee[34].HourlyWage := 7;
```

Modula-2 includes a facility to abbreviate access to records. This facility is known as the **WITH statement**. The section of code above is written equivalently, incorporating a WITH statement, as shown below:

```
WITH Employee[34] DO
    FirstInit := "D";
    LastInit := "R";
    Age := 35;
    Gender := Male;
    HourlyWage := 7;
END;
```

This WITH statement simplifies the notation by specifying the name of a record, Employee[34]. Within the body of the WITH, references to fields of the record, such as FirstInit and LastInit do not require full qualification, but are merely specified by their field names.

Figure 14.17 contains the syntax and semantics for the general form of the WITH statement. The "RecordRef" between WITH and DO denotes a reference to some record. The **body of a WITH statement** consists of an InstructionSequence enclosed by DO and END. Within the body of the WITH, the "RecordRef" prefix can be omitted from a reference to any field of the associated record.

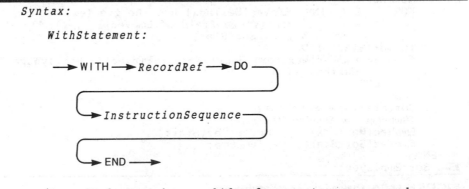

```
Syntax:

    WithStatement:

    ──▶ WITH ──▶ RecordRef ──▶ DO ──┐
                                     │
        ┌────────────────────────────┘
        │
        └─▶ InstructionSequence ──┐
                                   │
        ┌──────────────────────────┘
        │
        └─▶ END ──▶

    RecordRef: Must be a valid reference to some record

Semantics:
    RecordRef need not be included in references to its
    fields inside InstructionSequence.  For example, a
    reference like "RecordRef.Field" can be abbreviated as
    "Field".  When WITH instructions are nested, the
    innermost WITHs take precedence.
```

(continued)

Note:
RecordRef is evaluated at entry to the WITH statement.
Altering any data structure that might affect the data
referenced by RecordRef is prohibited within the body of
the same WITH statement.

FIGURE 14.17 *Syntax and semantics of the WITH statement*

There are two advantages to using WITH statements. The obvious advantage is the simplification of lengthy notation. A fully qualified reference to a record field can become long and cumbersome, particularly if records are used as fields within other records.

The second advantage of the WITH statement is the increased efficiency from certain uses of the WITH. In the earlier example

WITH Employee[34] DO

improves the efficiency of the code by evaluating Employee[34] just once and using it in four instances within the body of the WITH. If a WITH statement were not used, then four separate evaluations of Employee[34] would occur. Such efficiency gains occur when the record specified by the WITH is an item of an array.

There are two cautions to observe when using a WITH statement. The first caution is to remember that nesting the WITH statement can produce confusing code. Figure 14.18 repeats the Employee vector declaration along with a declaration of a single record called TheBoss.

```
(* Assume the following declarations *)
(*-----------------------------------*)
     TYPE
        GenderType = (Male, Female, Unknown);
        EmployeeType = RECORD
                          FirstInit : CHAR;
                          LastInit : CHAR;
                          Age : CARDINAL;
                          Gender : GenderType;
                          HourlyWage : CARDINAL
                       END;

        OneHundredEmployees = ARRAY [1..100] OF EmployeeType;
     VAR
        Employee : OneHundredEmployees;
        EmpNo : CARDINAL;
        TheBoss : EmployeeType;

(* Consider the following code using the above declarations *)
(*-------------------------------------------------------*)
     WITH Employee[EmpNo] DO
        WITH TheBoss DO
           Age := 55
        END
     END
```

FIGURE 14.18 *Example of nested WITH statements*

This figure contains an example of two nested WITH statements. The outer WITH references the item of the Employee vector indexed by EmpNo. The inner WITH references the record structure called TheBoss. Both WITH statements reference records of type EmployeeType. Inside the WITH instructions is an assignment instruction to the identifier Age. Confusion may result from whether this assignment instruction should be interpreted as:

```
Employee[EmpNo].Age := 55
```

or should be interpreted as:

```
TheBoss.Age := 55
```

The rule used by Modula-2 is that, for nested WITH instructions, the *innermost WITH takes precedence*. In other words, the second interpretation above is the correct one. Even though the language includes rules to handle confusing cases, they are still best avoided for the sake of readability.

The second caution for the use of WITH concerns the manner in which the record reference of WITH is established. Figure 14.19 illustrates a potential source of confusion.

```
FOR EmpNo := 1 TO 100 DO
    WITH Employee[EmpNo] DO
        HourlyWage := 0
    END
END;

(* an erroneous attempt at the above code *)
WITH Employee[EmpNo] DO
    FOR EmpNo := 1 TO 100 DO
        HourlyWage := 0
    END
END;
```

FIGURE 14.19 *Example of difficulties with WITH record referencing*

The WITH instruction (at the bottom of Figure 14.19) looks similar to the FOR loop. However, the WITH is incorrect, because the value of EmpNo changes within the body of the WITH. Since the value of EmpNo changes, the record referenced by Employees[EmpNo] correspondingly changes. This violates the rule that the record reference of a WITH is evaluated when the WITH is entered, and it must not be altered within the WITH body.

*P*rogramming-with-*S*tyle

Handle WITH Care!

WITH statements are useful in simplifying notation for improved code readability. WITH statements can also provide some measure of increased execution efficiency. However, WITH statement must be used with caution. Below are several rules to observe in their use.

1) Always indent the body of a WITH to indicate the range of the WITH clearly.
2) Never include code, within a WITH body, that can alter the particular record referenced by that WITH.
3) Keep the body of a WITH short. Long WITH bodies make it difficult to find the WITH that is being used, negating any advantage from the abbreviation.
4) Avoid nesting WITH statements. Nested WITHs force the reader to sort out which WITH applies in each instance.

14.8 VARIANT RECORDS (OPTIONAL)

One variation of the record data type is known as a **variant record**. Variant records are more pliable than other records, because the exact form of the record's fields can be chosen at execution time.

Variant records in Modula-2 are declared by including one or more variant fields in a declaration. The syntax and semantics of a variant field are summarized in Figure 14.20.

Syntax:

VariantField:

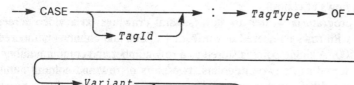

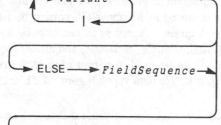

Variant:

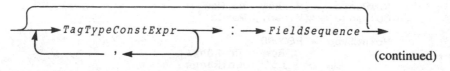

(continued)

FieldSequence: Defined in Figure 14.1

TagId: Any unambiguously declared identifier

TagType: Either BOOLEAN, CARDINAL, CHAR, INTEGER,
enumerated, or subrange type

TagTypeConstExpr: A constant expression of type TagType

*Semantics: The form of the field is taken from exactly one of
the variant FieldSequences or the* ELSE. *TagId
behaves like a field at the same level of the
record as VariantField. If TagId is included, then
the particular form chosen for the field is the
one that has a TagTypeConstExpr equal to TagId.
If none of the TagTypeExprs equal TagId, then the
ELSE is chosen for the field's form. If TagId is
omitted, then the form chosen depends on the
FieldId used in a reference.*

*Note: Each FieldId within a single variant field must be
different from other FieldIds within the same variant
field.*

FIGURE 14.20 *Syntax and semantics of VariantField*

Variant fields permit a fixed number of alternate forms for a single field of the record. The desired form can be selected at execution time by the program. The syntax of a variant record uses a form similar to the CASE instruction. This form shows that variant records permit choices in alternate data structures much as CASE instructions permit choices among alternate flows of control.

Suppose a program is written to store several drawings on a video screen. This screen is a grid with rows numbered down from 1 to 500 and columns numbered left to right from 1 to 500. A single point is stored as a row number and column number pair. A line segment is stored as its two endpoints, two pairs of row and column numbers. A triangle is stored as three vertex points, three pairs of row and column numbers. A rectangle with horizontal orientation is stored as its upper left corner, its length (left to right), and its height (top to bottom). A circle is stored as its center point and a radius.

Each drawing figure type (point, line, triangle, rectangle, and circle) requires different data to be stored. A variant record can be used to permit each of the five different drawing figure types to be stored by a single data type. Figure 14.21 declares such a type, called DrawingType.

```
CONST
      MinRow = 1;   MaxRow = 500;
      MinCol = 1;   MaxCol = 500;

TYPE
      RowRange = [MinRow..MaxRow];
      ColRange = [MinCol..MaxCol];

      PointType = RECORD
                     Row : RowRange;
                     Col : ColRange
                  END;
```

(continued)

```
    DrawingFig = (Point, Line, Triangle, Rectangle, Circle);

    DrawingType =
      RECORD
         CASE DrawTag : DrawingFig OF
            Point :
               Location : PointType   |
            Line :
               LeftEnd : PointType;
               RightEnd : PointType   |
            Triangle :
               Vertex1 : PointType;
               Vertex2 : PointType;
               Vertex3 : PointType    |
            Rectangle :
               UpperLeft : PointType;
               Length : CARDINAL;
               Width : CARDINAL   |
            Circle :
               Center : PointType;
               Radius : CARDINAL
         END (* CASE *)
      END; (* RECORD *)

VAR
    Drawings : ARRAY [1..100] OF DrawingType;
```

FIGURE 14.21 *Declaration of DrawingType and Drawings*

Drawings is an array that can store up to one hundred different drawings. Each item of Drawings is of type DrawingType, so each can store any of the five different drawing types.

DrawingType includes a **tag field**, sometimes called a **discriminator**. The tag field for DrawingType is called DrawTag. Tag fields behave like a field of the record at the same level as the variant. The reference Drawings[44].DrawTag refers to the tag field of the item of Drawings with index of 44.

The value of the tag field serves to select the particular option or **variant** for the field form. If Drawings[2].DrawTag equals Circle, then the second item of the Drawings array stores a circle and the item's form corresponds to the Circle variant. If Drawings[5].DrawTag equals Rectangle, then the fifth item stores a rectangle with the form given by the Rectangle variant. The value of the tag field should always be assigned before any variant field is referenced.

The form of each variant follows a list of one or more constant expressions used to select the variant. Each variant of a single variant field consists of zero or more fields. Figure 14.22 shows all five possible forms for this record.

```
    If Drawings[i].DrawTag=Point, the Point variant, then
    the form of Drawings[i] is:

        RECORD
            DrawTag : DrawingFig;
            Location : PointType
        END
```

(continued)

If Drawings[i].DrawTag=Line, *the* Line *variant, then the form of* Drawings[i] *is:*

```
RECORD
    DrawTag : DrawingFig;
    LeftEnd : PointType;
    RightEnd : PointType
END
```

If Drawings[i].DrawTag=Triangle, *the* Triangle *variant, then the form of* Drawings[i] *is:*

```
RECORD
    DrawTag : DrawingFig;
    Vertex1 : PointType;
    Vertex2 : PointType;
    Vertex3 : PointType
END
```

If Drawings[i].DrawTag=Rectangle, *the* Rectangle *variant, then the form of* Drawings[i] *is:*

```
RECORD
    DrawTag : DrawingFig;
    UpperLeft : PointType;
    Length : CARDINAL;
    Width : CARDINAL
END
```

If Drawings[i].DrawTag=Circle, *the* Circle *variant, then the form of* Drawings[i] *is:*

```
RECORD
    DrawTag : DrawingFig;
    Center : PointType;
    Radius : CARDINAL
END
```

FIGURE 14.22 *The form of the variants of DrawingType*

Assigning a value to a variant record with a tag field requires that the tag field be assigned first. Below is a section of code that assigns to the seventh item of Drawings a circle with center at Row 100 and Column 250 and a radius of 75:

```
WITH Drawings[7] DO
    DrawTag := Circle;
    Center.Row := 100;
    Center.Col := 250;
    Radius := 75
END;
(* Assert: Drawings[7] stores a circle with    *)
(*         center at (100,250) and radius of 75 *)
```

DrawingType is a type where the entire structure consists of a single variant field. Modula-2 permits each field of a variant record to be a variant independent of other fields. Figure 14.23 contains such a declaration for AnimalType.

```
TYPE
      String20 = ARRAY [0..19] OF CHAR;
      AnimalVarieties = (Fish, Birds, Insects, Reptiles);

      AnimalType =
        RECORD
           Name : String20;
           MaxWeight : REAL;
           CASE LegTag : ["A".."D"] OF
              "A", "B", "D" :
                 LegCount : CARDINAL  |
              "C" :
           END;
           CASE PoisonTag : [1..10] OF
              3, 7 :
              ELSE
                 Poisonous : BOOLEAN;
           END;
           CASE AnimalTag : AnimalVarieties OF
              Fish :
                 Habitat : (FreshWater,SaltWater);
                 Edible : BOOLEAN  |
              Birds :
                 MaxWingSpan : REAL;
                 WaterFowl : BOOLEAN;
                 CanFly : BOOLEAN  |
              Insects :
                 AverageLifeSpan : CARDINAL  |
              Reptiles :
                 MaxLength : REAL;
                 RepKind : (Turtle,Snake,Lizard)
           END
        END;
```

FIGURE 14.23 *Declaration of AnimalType*

AnimalType has three variant fields. The first variant field includes a single LegCount subfield for animals coded as type "A", "B", or "D". In this first variant field, there is no field specified for type "C" animals, so none exists. The second variant field declares no field for animals of Type 3 or 7 and a Poisonous field for all other animal types. The final variant field specifies from one to three different fields for each animal variety.

Any variable of type AnimalType can take on numerous different forms. Figure 14.24 illustrates two possible alternatives.

```
        Let Animal be a variable of AnimalType.


    If (Animal.LegTag="B") and (Animal.PoisonTag=7) and
    (Animal.AnimalTag=Fish) then the form of Animal is:
        RECORD
            Name : String20;
            MaxWeight : REAL;
            LegTag : ["A".."D"];
            LegCount : CARDINAL;
            PoisonTag : [1..10];
            AnimalTag : AnimalVarieties;
            Habitat : (FreshWater,SaltWater);
            Edible : BOOLEAN;
        END;


    If (Animal.LegTag="C") and (Animal.PoisonTag=4) and
    (Animal.AnimalTag=Birds), then the form of Animal is:
        RECORD
            Name : String20;
            MaxWeight : REAL;
            LegTag : ["A".."D"];
            PoisonTag : [1..10];
            Poisonous : BOOLEAN;
            AnimalTag : AnimalVarieties;
            MaxWingSpan : REAL;
            WaterFowl : BOOLEAN;
            CanFly : BOOLEAN;
        END;
```

FIGURE 14.24 *Two possible forms of the AnimalType variant record*

Programming-with-Style

Pitfalls of the Variant Record

The variant record provides considerable power to the programmer. If used wisely, variant records are useful types. However, the price of the power of variant records is a great potential for misuse. Some rules to help avoid potential pitfalls in the use of variant records are given below:

1) Don't overuse variant records. Variant records are always difficult to code and to maintain. If a suitable non-variant alternative exists, use it.
2) Carefully indent declarations to illustrate the form of the variant record as well as possible. There is no single best technique for indenting variant records because of the myriad of options.
3) Avoid using too many variant fields within a single record. The single variant field of the DrawingType is much easier to understand than the three variant fields of AnimalType.
4) Avoid nesting variant records within variant records. The complexity of a nested variant is far greater than consecutive variants.

5) Always use a tag field on a variant field. The fact that all field identifiers must be unique in a variant record makes the tag field (but not the tag type) optional. However, omitting the tag field makes the code accessing the record more difficult to read.
6) Never store data in a variant record with one value for a tag field and access it using a different value for the same tag field. This is a cheap programming trick to convert data from one type to another. Such code obscures the algorithm, providing a fertile climate for bugs.

14.9 SUMMARY

Records comprise another tool for data abstraction. It is possible to store a vector of fractions as two vectors of integers, one vector to store numerators and one for denominators. These numerator and denominator vectors are parallel in the sense that the Ith numerator and Ith denominator form the Ith fraction. Parallel arrays do not clearly indicate to the reader of a program their parallel nature. A better abstraction is to store a single fraction as a record with one field for numerator and another for denominator. Declaring the vector of fractions as a single vector of records where each record contains a numerator and denominator fields is much closer to the desired concept of storing several fractions, each with a numerator and denominator.

Records are more flexible than arrays because fields of records can be of differing type. However, selecting a field of a record is more restrictive than selecting an item of an array. No variables may be used to identify fields, but variables may be used as index values to select array items.

Fully-qualified field selectors can be clumsy. When the identifiers used for record or field names are long or when records are nested within records, field selectors can become very lengthy. The WITH statement is a programming language facility for abbreviating lengthy references. If used sparingly, the WITH statement improves the readability of clumsy record references.

The variant record adds pliability to the record type. A variant field has multiple possible forms. The precise form used for a variant field is controlled by the value of the tag field during program execution. Variant records are a powerful feature whose wise use requires caution.

Many collections of information are naturally modeled with records. For this reason, records are a significant structured data type.

||| KEY TERMS

homogeneous data type	field selector	variant record
record	qualified identifier	tag field
heterogeneous data type	subfields	discriminator
field	"sort on" some field	variant
field type	WITH statement	
field identifier	WITH statement body	

||| EXERCISES

1. Use the declarations below to complete parts (a) through (o).

```
CONST
    ProfessorCount = 203;

TYPE
    ScienceDepts = ( Biology, Chemistry, CompSci,
                     Geology, Math, Physics );
    ValidCourseNumbers = [100..799];
    String20 = ARRAY [0..20] OF CHAR;
    NameType = RECORD
                   FirstInit : CHAR;
                   Last : String20
               END;

    CourseType = RECORD
                     Dept : ScienceDepts;
                     Number : ValidCourseNumbers
                 END;

    CoursesRec = RECORD
                     Count : [1..5];
                     Course : ARRAY [1..5] OF CourseType;
                 END;

    ProfType = RECORD
                   Name : NameType;
                   Age : [20..90];
                   HomeDept : ScienceDepts;
                   CurrentCourseLoad : CoursesRec;
                   AnnualSalary : CARDINAL;
               END;

VAR

    VisitingProf: Professor;
    ScienceProfs : ARRAY [1..ProfessorCount] OF ProfType;
```

a) Specify a field selector for the age field of the record for the visiting professor.
b) Specify a field selector for the first initial of the name of the visiting professor.
c) Specify a field selector for the last name of the visiting professor.
d) Specify a field selector for the number of courses being taught by the visiting professor.

e) Specify a field selector for the department of the first course being taught by the visiting professor.

f) Specify a field selector for the Age field of the fifth science professor.

g) Specify a field selector for the "Home department" of the science professor with index of 173.

h) Specify a field selector for the course number of the second course taught by the third science professor.

i) Specify a collection of assignment instructions without a WITH statement to assign the information below to the visiting professor data structure:

```
Name: Marian Roecker
Age: 52
Home Department: Chemistry
Annual Salary: $31000
Current teaching load: Chemistry 100
                       Chemistry 203
                       Math      161
```

j) Repeat the task from (i) above, using a WITH statement.

k) Specify a collection of assignment instructions without a WITH statement to assign the information below to the professor with index of 31:

```
Name: Albert Becker
Age: 35
Home Department: Computer Science
Annual Salary: $38000
Current teaching load: Comp.Sci. 110
                       Comp.Sci. 222
```

l) Repeat the task from (k) above, using a WITH statement.

m) Write the code for a procedure, called WriteProf, that will output the information stored for a single professor in the format used above in parts (i) and (k). The header for WriteProf is given below:

```
PROCEDURE WriteProf( Prof : ProfType );
    (* PRE:  Prof is assigned.                        *)
    (* POST: Info stored for Prof is output in form *)
    (*       shown in part (k) above                  *)
```

n) Write a procedure that will output all professors by repeatedly invoking WriteProf from part (m).

o) Write a procedure that swaps the information for any two science professors whose indices are passed as parameters.

2. Specify an appropriate collection of Modula-2 declarations to declare a data structure f each of the following.

   a) A structure to store a single vegetable by storing its variety (such as corn, bean, tomato), its growing period (number of days), and the color of its edible portion.

   b) A structure to store a triangle by storing the measure of its three angles (in degrees and the length of its longest side. (Note: The measure of any angle of a triangle mu be between 0 and 180. Furthermore, assume that the length is stored as an integer number of centimeters between 1 and 5000.)

   c) A structure to store up to 500 common stocks. For each stock, the following must l stored: its name (up to 15 characters), its highest value per share, its lowest value p share, its current value per share, its change in value per share (positive or negativ from the previous day.

   d) A structure to store the typical weather for each of the past thirty days. For each da the average barometric pressure, average wind speed, most common wind directior and sky conditions (overcast, clear, or partly cloudy) should be stored.

   e) A structure to store an index for a book. This index must be capable of storing up t 1000 entries. Each entry consists of the name of the entry word (up to 20 character and a list of up to 15 page numbers where the word is found.

   f) A structure to store the library catalog information for a single book. This informat should include: a title (up to forty characters), a catalog number (three digits, a dec mal point and two more digits), the author's name (up to 30 characters), the publisl (up to 20 characters), a brief description (up to 80 characters), and two subjects (u to 25 characters each).

   g) A structure to store up to 100 invoices. Each invoice consists of a date, the origina dollar amount of the invoice, the dollar amount of the total amount paid to date on invoice, and a list of up to 15 items included in the invoice; where each item has a description of up to 40 characters, a dollar cost, and a quantity.

3. Use the declarations below to complete parts (a) through (i):

```
CONST
    MaxBelongings = 200;

TYPE
    MajorBelongingsType = ( Home, Auto, Appliance,
                            Furniture, Other );

    DateType = RECORD
                    Month: [1..12];
                    Day: [1..31];
                    Year: [1900..2000];
               END;
```

```
HouseType = (Ranch, TwoStory, Split, Condo);
ColorType = (Red, Orange, Yellow, Green, Blue, Brown,
             Purple, White, Black);
CarType = (Sedan, StaWagon, Van, Sport, OffRoad, Pickup);
ApplianceType = (Range, Dishwasher, Washer, Dryer);
FurnitureType = (Sofa, Table, Chair, Bed, Desk, Cabinet);
String40 = ARRAY [0..40] OF CHAR;
BelongingsInfoType =

    RECORD
        PurchaseDate : DateType;
        HundredsVal : CARDINAL;  (* value in units of $100 *)
        CASE  Article : MajorBelongingsType  OF
            Home  :
                HouseStyle : HouseType;
                SquareFeet: CARDINAL;
                BuildingDate : DateType  |

            Auto :
                AutoStyle : CarType;
                CarColor : ColorType  |

            Appliance :
                ApplianceItem : ApplianceType ;
                ApplianceColor : ColorType  |

            Furniture :
                FurniturePiece : FurnitureType

            Other :
                Description : String40

        END
    END;

AllBelongingsType =

    RECORD
        Quantity : CARDINAL;
        Belongings : ARRAY [1..MaxBelongings]
                     OF BelongingsInfoType;

    END;

VAR
    MajorPossessions : AllBelongingsType;
    MostImportantPossession : BelongingsInfoType;
```

a) If the most important possession stores an appliance, specify a field selector for the year in which the appliance was purchased.

b) If the most important possession stores an auto, specify a field selector for the color of the car.

c) If the most important possession stores a home, specify a field selector for the number of square feet in the home.

d) If the most important possession stores a home, specify a field selector for the month in which the house was built.

e) Specify an assignment instruction to cause the most important possession to use the appropriate variant for a home.

f) Specify an assignment instruction to cause the first item of the major possessions to use the variant that is appropriate for furniture.

g) Specify a collection of assignment instructions to cause the most important possession to be a desk purchased on May 9, 1951 and worth $500.

h) Specify a collection of assignment instructions to cause the third item of the major possessions to be a green range purchased on Jan. 4, 1986 and valued at $900.

i) Specify a collection of assignment instructions to cause the items listed below to be the complete collection of major belongings.
   (1) A condominium with 1200 square feet of living space, built in 6/8/82 and purchased on 8/9/84 with a current value of $64,000.
   (2) A blue pickup purchased on 7/16/81 and worth $2500.
   (3) A sofa purchased on 8/10/84 and worth $400.

4. Figure 14.21 declares a vector, called Drawings, that stores various types of drawing images. For each part below, specify the assignment instructions to cause the third item of this array to store the indicated drawing image (Note: Points are sometimes indicated as (R,C) where R is the row number and C the column number of the point.)
   a) A point in row 123 and column 321.
   b) A circle with center at (55,55) and radius of 10.
   c) A line from (5,10) to (20,50).
   d) A triangle with vertices at (2,2), (10,10) and (4,9).
   e) A rectangle with vertices at (100,10), (100,175), (180,10) and (180,175).

5. Modify the SortEmployees procedure from Figure 14.16 to sort in *descending* order *on the* Age *field* instead of ascending order on the HourlyWage field.

|||PROGRAMMING PROJECTS

1. Write and test a procedure to sort the ScienceProfs vector from Exercise 1 in descending order on the salary field. Use an insertion sort algorithm. You may assume that the entire vector is assigned.

2. Write and test a procedure to sort the `MajorPossessions` vector from Exercise 3 in ascending order on the date field.

3. Write and test a program for the following problem.

TITLE

Motorcycle shop inventory

DESCRIPTION

A motorcycle shop needs a program to maintain its inventory. This program must interactively permit the shop owner to enter newly purchased motorcycles, indicate when a motorcycle is sold, and show the current display inventory and statistics about the shop. As the program begins, the shop has an empty inventory and $10000 on hand.

The program must maintain the total profit made to date and cash on hand in addition to the inventory. The information stored for each motorcycle in the inventory includes its brand (only BMW, Honda, Suzuki and Yamaha cycles are sold), its model year, its engine displacement (50 cc. to 1200 cc.) and its cost to the shop. The shop never maintains more than one cycle of any brand, model year and engine displacement at a time and never has an inventory of more than 100.

INPUT

All input is in the form of commands. Each command is one line long with separate data separated by one or more blanks. Below is a list of the valid input commands, their syntax and semantics.

Purchase command:

Syntax : ⟶ P ⟶ Brand ⟶ Year ⟶ Displ ⟶ Cost ⟶

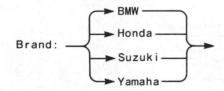

Brand:
- BMW
- Honda
- Suzuki
- Yamaha

Year: A cardinal constant

Displ: A cardinal constant

Cost: A cardinal constant

Semantics: Add the cycle with the given brand, model year, engine displacement, and purchase cost to the inventory.

Sell command:

Syntax: ⟶ S ⟶ Brand ⟶ Year ⟶ Displ ⟶ Price −

Price : A cardinal constant

Semantics: The indicated cycle is sold to a customer. It must be removed from inventory and profit calculated.

Display command:

Syntax: ⟶ D ⟶

Semantics: The complete inventory, profit to date and cash on hand is displayed.

Terminate command:

Syntax: ⟶ T ⟶

Semantics: Terminate program execution.

OUTPUT

The command prompt is specified below. It is always preceded by a blank line:

Command?

The form of the display produced by the display command is a list of cycles in the inventory, one per line, with the following information left to right on the line: model year, brand, displacement, cost. Following the inventory, the following two lines are displayed, where <cash> and <profit> are dollar values for current cash on hand and profit to date, respectively.

```
On Hand :    <cash>
Profit :   <profit>
```

ERRORS

This early version of the program makes no attempt to identify invalid input form, producing undefined results. The following cases are detected and the indicated error message issued:

1) If insufficient cash on hand exists to purchase the cycle in a purchase command, then the cycle is not added to the inventory and the following message is issued: INSUFFICIENT FUNDS.

2) If the inventory already includes a cycle with the same brand, year and displacement as one specified in a purchase command, then the cycle is not added to the inventory, and the following message issued: DUPLICATE CYCLE IN INVENTORY.

3) If there is no cycle matching the one indicated in a purchase command, then the following message is issued: NO SUCH CYCLE IN INVENTORY

EXAMPLE

Below is a sample execution of the program with all input highlighted.

```
Command? D


On Hand :   10000

Profit :        0


Command? PHonda 1983 250 700


Command? PYamaha 1985 350 1000


Command? D
```

```
       1983 Honda    250    700

       1985 Yamaha   350   1000

       On Hand :    8300

       Profit :        0

Command? PSuzuki 1981 250 300


Command? SYamaha 1985 350 1200


Command? D

       1983 Honda    250    700

       1981 Suzuki   250    300

       On Hand :    9200

       Profit :      200


Command? SSuzuki 1981 250 600


Command? PHonda 1983 1000 2000


Command? PHonda 1982  250 600


Command? D


       1983 Honda    250    700

       1983 Honda   1000   2000

       1982 Honda    250    600

       On Hand :    7200

       Profit :      500


Command? PHonda 1983 1000 1800

DUPLICATE CYCLE IN INVENTORY
```

```
Command? SBMW 1980 750 2000

NO  SUCH  CYCLE  IN  INVENTORY


Command? T
```

4. Write and test a program for the following problem.

TITLE
File system simulator

DESCRIPTION
One of the tasks typically performed by an operating system is to maintain a file system. This program is to simulate some of the workings of such a system. The file system to be simulated maintains information up to 50 files. This information consists of the file name (up to 10 characters), the file type (either a program source file, a program object file or a data file), and the file size (between 1 and 30000 bytes).

Initially the simulator program has no files entered in its directory. The user provides input to the simulator to specify one of three operations: (1) Add a new file to the directory; (2) Delete a file from the directory; and (3) List the entire directory. All I/O is interactive.

INPUT & OUTPUT
All input is prompted so a description of input has been integrated with a description of output. All prompts are preceded by one blank line.

The first output is the command menu as shown below:

```
Command Menu: A)dd file, D)elete file, L)ist all, Q)uit
```

After each command from the command menu completes (except a final Quit command), the simulator returns to this command menu. Each command input consists of a single character (either uppercase or lowercase). An input of "A" or "a" invokes the add file command. An input of "D" or "d" invokes the delete file command. An input of "L" or "l" invokes the list file command. An input of "Q" or "q" invokes the quit command.

The add command causes a file name prompt, as shown below, to be displayed:

```
Please specify file name:
```

The user must input a name of 1 to 10 characters followed by a carriage return in response to the file name prompt. If the file to be added is not already in the file directory, then the user is prompted to select the file type from the following menu:

```
File type menu: S)ource, O)bject, D)ata
```

The user inputs a "y" or "s" to specify a program source file type, "O" or "o" to specify a program object file type and "D" or "d" to specify a data file type. Next the user is prompted to specify the file size as follows:

> File Size? (1 to 30000):

After the user specifies a cardinal value from 1 to 30000, the simulator makes a new file entry in the directory for the specified file.

The delete file command also begins with the file name prompt. If the specified file is in the directory, then it is removed.

The list command lists all of the files currently in the directory. This list should be alphabetized by file name and have the following form, where <name> is the file name, <size> is the file size and <type> is the file type.

> <name> <size> <type>

The quit command prompts the user to be certain the user has not erroneously struck a "Q." The following prompt is output:

> Are you sure (Y or N)?

If the user responds with a "Y" or "y" input then the program terminates; otherwise the program returns to the command menu.

ERRORS
1) When a file name is input in the add file command and that file is already in the directory, then the following message is displayed and control returns to the command menu: ERROR – duplicate file name!
2) When a file name is input in the delete file command and that file is not in the directory then the following message is displayed and control returns to the command menu: ERROR – file not in directory!
3) Any other invalid input produces undefined results.

EXAMPLE
Below is a sample execution of this program with the input highlighted.

> Command Menu: A)dd file, D)elete file, L)ist all, Q)uit A

> Please specify file name: DrawingSO

> File type menu: S)ource, O)bject, D)ata S

> File Size? (1 to 30000): 3978

Command Menu: A)dd file, D)elete file, L)ist all, Q)uit A

Please specify file name: DrawingOB

File type menu: S)ource, O)bject, D)ata O

File Size? (1 to 30000): 1024

Command Menu: A)dd file, D)elete file, L)ist all, Q)uit L

    DrawingOB 1024 Object

    DrawingSO 3978 Source

Command Menu: A)dd file, D)elete file, L)ist all, Q)uit A

Please specify file name: Animals

File type menu: 'S)ource, O)bject, D)ata O

File Size? (1 to 30000): 2048

Command Menu: A)dd file, D)elete file, L)ist all, Q)uit a

Please specify file name: Text

File type menu: S)ource, O)bject, D)ata D

File Size? (1 to 30000): 10199

Command Menu: A)dd file, D)elete file, L)ist all, Q)uit L

    Animals   2048 Object

    DrawingOB 1024 Object

    DrawingSO 3978 Source

    Text   10199 Data

Command Menu: A)dd file, D)elete file, L)ist all, Q)uit A

Please specify file name: Text

ERROR – duplicate file name!

Command Menu: A)dd file, D)elete file, L)ist all, Q)uit D

Please specify file name: DrawingOB

Command Menu: A)dd file, D)elete file, L)ist all, Q)uit L

Animals   2048 Object

DrawingSO   3978 Source

Text   10199 Data

Command Menu: A)dd file, D)elete file, L)ist all, Q)uit D

Please specify file name: DrawingOB

ERROR – file not in directory!

Command Menu: A)dd file, D)elete file, L)ist all, Q)uit Q

Are you sure (Y or N)? z

Command Menu: A)dd file, D)elete file, L)ist all, Q)uit Q

Are you sure (Y or N)? Y

15 MORE PROGRAMMING TOOLS

15.1 RECURSION

What happens when a procedure invokes itself? Not only is it possible in Modula-2 for such an invocation to occur, but it also results in an important form of control, known as **recursion**. Figure 15.1 illustrates a recursive procedure called EchoReversed.

```
PROCEDURE EchoReversed;
      (* POST: One input line (up to EOL) is output *)
      (*         in the reverse order of input.       *)
    VAR InChar : CHAR;
BEGIN
    Read(InChar);
    IF InChar=EOL THEN
        WriteLn;  (* separates input line from output line *)
    ELSE
        EchoReversed;
        Write(InChar);
    END;
END EchoReversed;
```

FIGURE 15.1 *EchoReversed procedure*

To trace the execution of a recursive procedure, it is useful to borrow a concept gaining widespread popularity as a computer user environment: **windows**. A window mimics a memo lying on top of a desk. New memos may be laid on top of the desk, just as a new window may be opened on a computer display. The new window, like a new memo, is the one on top that is currently in use. Previous windows, like old memos, are somewhere underneath and partially covered by newer ones.

Suppose the EchoReversed program is about to be invoked and the following input supplied:

FUM

Figure 15.2 diagrams a trace of this execution of EchoReversed in eight distinct steps. The state of computation shown in Step 1 supposes that EchoReversed has been invoked and the Read instruction just executed. This diagram uses a window enclosed in a rectangle to depict the current execution environment.

STEP 1

input: FUM < EOL >

```
                                    Activation #1
  InChar  'F'

  BEGIN
      Read (InChar);
      IF InChar = EOL THEN
          WriteLn;
      ELSE
  ───►    EchoReversed;
          Write(InChar);
      END:
  END Echo Reversed;
```

STEP 2

input: FUM < EOL >

```
                                    Activation #1
  InChar  'F'

          ...
  ───► EchoReversed; ──────────────────┐
       Write(InChar);                  │
                                       │
                                       ▼
                                    Activation #2
       InChar   ?

       BEGIN
  ───►    Read(Inchar);
          IF InChar = EOL THEN
             ...
```

STEP 3

input: FUM < EOL >

```
                                    Activation #1
  InChar  'F'
  ──► EchoReversed; ───────────────────┐
      Write(InChar);                    │
                                        │
                                        ▼
                                    Activation #2
       InChar  'U'
  ───► EchoReversed; ─────────────────────┐
       Write(InChar);                      │
                                           │
                                           ▼
                                    Activation #3
          InChar   ?

          BEGIN
  ───►       Read(InChar);
             IF InChar = EOL THEN
                ...
```

(continued)

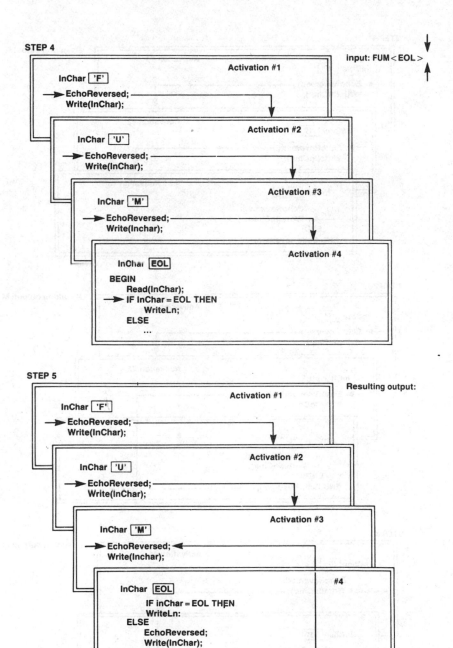

STEP 4

input: FUM < EOL >

Activation #1

InChar `'F'`

→ EchoReversed;
Write(InChar);

Activation #2

InChar `'U'`

→ EchoReversed;
Write(InChar);

Activation #3

InChar `'M'`

→ EchoReversed;
Write(Inchar);

Activation #4

InChar `EOL`

BEGIN
    Read(InChar);
→   IF InChar = EOL THEN
        WriteLn;
    ELSE
        ...

STEP 5

Resulting output:

Activation #1

InChar `'F'`

→ EchoReversed;
Write(InChar);

Activation #2

InChar `'U'`

→ EchoReversed;
Write(InChar);

Activation #3

InChar `'M'`

→ EchoReversed; ◄
Write(Inchar);

#4

InChar `EOL`

        IF inChar = EOL THEN
            WriteLn:
        ELSE
            EchoReversed;
            Write(InChar);
        END:
    END EchoReversed;

(continued)

STEP 6

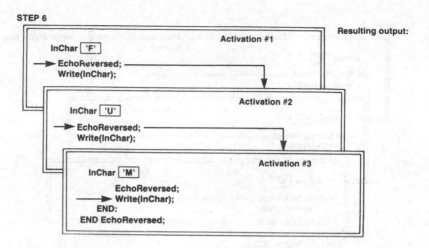

Resulting output:

STEP 7

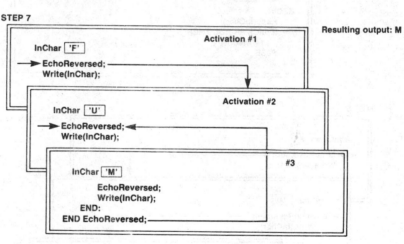

Resulting output: M

STEP 8

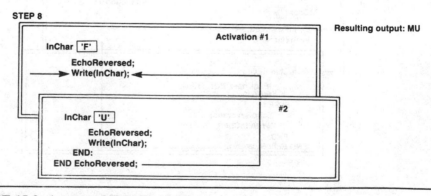

Resulting output: MU

FIGURE 15.2 *A trace of EchoReversed*

Each time a procedure is invoked, the invocation is referred to as an **activation**, and the environment of the activation is called the **activation frame** or **activation record**. The window in Step 1 of Figure 15.2 is labeled "Activation #1." The important contents of any activation frame are its local data (including parameters) and the instruction it is about to execute. The activation frame in Step 1 shows that the local InChar variable stores "F", the first character input, and that the instruction to be executed next (arrow to its left) is EchoReversed.

When this next instruction executes the result is a recursive invocation of EchoReversed. This is the second activation of the procedure. Step 2 depicts the result as a second window laid on top of the first. It is important to notice that each activation frame is a completely separate environment. The first activation is currently executing a recursive call to EchoReversed, while the second activation is about to execute its first instruction. Each activation frame has its own copy of local variables and parameters as well. The first activation frame stores "F" in InChar, while in the second activation frame, InChar is unassigned (denoted by a question mark). The most recent activation of a procedure is the one executing at any point in time. Therefore, the second activation of EchoReversed will read the next character, "U," and proceed to activate the procedure another time recursively. This situation is shown in Step 3.

By Step 4, the third activation has already input "M" and performed the fourth activation. This fourth activation has input EOL and is about to execute the IF instruction. Since the fourth activation executes the THEN clause, it will output an end of line (via WriteLn) and return.

Notice that the return from the fourth activation goes back to the place where it was invoked (i.e., within the third activation). Step 5 of Figure 15.2 illustrates this return. In Step 6, the fourth window has been removed because the fourth activation is complete. This causes the third activation to be the current activation, and it resumes execution from the point where it performed Activation 4. The third activation next executes Write(InChar) and returns to the second activation. See Step 7. In similar fashion, Step 8 shows the situation after the second activation has output its value of InChar and is returning to the first activation. Finally, the first activation will output InChar and return, completing the entire trace. Since each InChar value was output *after* the return from the subsequent activation, the characters are output in the reverse of the input order, "MUF" for this trace.

Functions can also be recursive. Figure 15.4 contains a recursive function to return a Fibonacci number. This sequence of numbers begins as shown in Figure 15.3.

```
1st Fibonacci  =  1
2nd Fibonacci  =  1
3rd Fibonacci  =  2    (1+1)
4th Fibonacci  =  3    (2+1)
5th Fibonacci  =  5    (3+2)
6th Fibonacci  =  8    (5+3)
7th Fibonacci  = 13    (8+5)
8th Fibonacci  = 21    (13+8)
               .
               .
               .
```

FIGURE 15.3 *The start of the Fibonacci sequence*

The Fib function in Figure 15.4 returns the Fibonacci number that has a sequence position given by the Position parameter. In other words, Fib(1) returns 1, Fib(6) returns 8, and so on.

```
PROCEDURE Fib( Position : CARDINAL )
: CARDINAL;
    (* PRE:  Position is assigned.                     *)
    (* POST: RESULT is the Position-th Fibonacci number *)
    (* NOTE: This function is inefficient.              *)
BEGIN
  CASE Position OF
      0 : WriteString("There is no 0th Fibonacci"); WriteLn|
      1,2 : RETURN 1
  ELSE
      RETURN  Fib(Position-1) + Fib(Position-2);
  END;
END Fib;
```

FIGURE 15.4 *Fib function*

The recursive Fib function looks very much like the definition for Fibonacci numbers. When Position equals 1 or 2, corresponding to the first and second Fibonacci numbers, Fib returns the value 1 immediately. If Position>2, then Fib returns the sum of the Fibonacci numbers at positions Position-1 and Position-2.

The execution of Fib(5) illustrates how the Fib function makes use of recursion. Since Position = 5 for this first activation, the ELSE clause is executed. This causes the following:

$$RETURN \ Fib(4) + Fib(3);$$

Before this return can occur, it must first calculate the value of the expression to be returned. This calculation produces two additional Fib activations. As each of these activations executes, it causes still other activations. Figure 15.5 diagrams the activations and their return values in a tree-like form, where the downward arrows represent activations, and the upward arrows show the values returned.

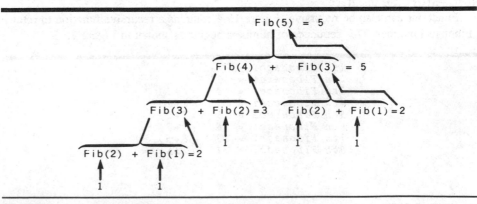

FIGURE 15.5 *Activations created by Fib(5)*

15.2   A COMPARISON OF REPETITION AND RECURSION

Recursion is an control method alternative to repetition. Consecutive activations of a procedure are comparable to consecutive iterations of a loop. In fact, any loop can be rewritten recursively. Figure 15.6 diagrams a WHILE loop and a functionally-equivalent

Some WHILE loop	An equivalent recursive procedure
| ```
WHILE LoopCond DO
     LoopBody;
END;
``` | ```
PROCEDURE RecWHILE;
BEGIN
     IF LoopCond THEN
     LoopBody;
     RecWHILE;
     END;
END RecWHILE;
``` |

FIGURE 15.6 Mimicking the WHILE recursively

recursive procedure called RecWHILE.

The RecWHILE procedure, like the corresponding WHILE loop, first checks the expression LoopCond. Both the WHILE loop and RecWHILE terminate when Loop-Cond is initially FALSE. When LoopCond is TRUE, then the LoopBody is executed by RecWHILE, followed by an activation that repeats the same task. The RecWHILE procedure activations all return whenever LoopCond is found to be FALSE.

One of the dangers programmers avoid is that of the infinite loop. **Infinite recursion**, executing activation after activation without returning, is a similar problem. A programmer must ensure that there are activations that initiate a return sequence for any invocation of a recursive procedure. The EchoReversed procedure will return as long as an EOL character is eventually encountered. The Fib function always returns, because its recursive activations use ever-decreasing parameter values, and any parameter value < = 2 produces an immediate return. RecWHILE mimics the WHILE loop. As long as the corresponding WHILE loop terminates, so does RecWHILE.

Another issue raised by the RecWHILE procedure is **execution efficiency**, the speed of program execution. In general, algorithms that use repetition are more efficient (require less time to execute) than those using recursion. This is because recursive procedures require time to invoke, allocate local data, establish parameter passage, deallocate local data, and return.

The RecWHILE procedure mimics the WHILE loop, but must be expected to execute more slowly. Similarly, there are non-recursive algorithms for computing Fibonacci numbers that are more efficient than the Fib procedure.

15.3   POINTERS AND DYNAMIC DATA

Recursion can be used to design algorithms that are very difficult to express and debug by any other means. The EchoReversed procedure works regardless of the length of the input line it reads. Any non-recursive solution to this problem must declare a data structure in which to place each character until it needs to be output. If an array is used, then it is declared to some specific size, imposing a constraint on the maximum number of characters that can be input.

Part of the difficulty with the data types examined thus far is that their form is fixed at the time of declaration. Arrays are more restrictive than EchoReversed because any array declaration must specify its exact size. Data types that are required to be of a single fixed form throughout execution are called **static data**. An alternative to static data structures is known as **dynamic data**. Dynamic data is allocated and deallocated under the explicit control of the program. When the program requires additional data storage, it executes an instruction to allocate more storage. When the program no longer needs the use of some dynamic storage, it can relinquish the space to the operating system.

Modula-2 uses a mechanism to support dynamic data structures called a **pointer**. A pointer is not a dynamic variable itself, but rather a simple variable that is an access mechanism for accessing dynamic variables. A description of the POINTER data type is given in Figure 15.7.

```
Name of the Data Type:  Pointer

Declaration form of PointerType:

  Syntax:

      ───────► POINTER ────────► TO ──────► NodeType ──────►

      NodeType: any valid data type

  Semantics: A variable of Pointer type is an access
             mechanism to dynamic data.

    Constant: NIL (' a special Pointer addressing nothing ')

    Operations: := (assignment) requires identical types or NIL
```

FIGURE 15.7 The Pointer data type

Dynamic variables are like lock boxes. You can access the contents of the lock box (the value of the dynamic variable) only if you have the key. Pointer variables are analogous to lock box keys. No dynamic variable can be assigned a new value unless the program accesses the variable with the correct pointer variable, or key. Neither can the value of any dynamic variable be examined without a pointer to it. Furthermore, the lock for each dynamic variable is different. A single pointer variable can only "point to" (serve as a key for) only a single dynamic variable at a time.

Pointer variables are frequently diagrammed as rectangles with arrows going from each rectangle to the dynamic data pointed to by the variable. Below is the declaration for a simple pointer variable, called MyPointer.

```
(* Assert: MyNodeType is a previously declared type *)
VAR
    MyPointer : POINTER TO MyNodeType;
```

During program execution MyPointer is permitted to point to a data structure of the form specified as MyNodeType. This situation is diagrammed as follows:

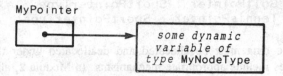

There are actually three different kinds of values for a pointer variable. The variable can

1) Be unassigned (like any other variable).
2) Store a pointer (as pictured above).
3) Store the value NIL.

The constant **NIL** may be assigned to any pointer variable. NIL points to nothing, like a blank key incapable of opening any lock. The reason for including NIL is to be able to identify a pointer that does not currently point to any variable. There are two commonly used techniques for diagramming pointers whose value is NIL, sometimes called **NIL pointers**. These two techniques are diagrammed below. The form on the left is used throughout the remainder of this text.

Pointer variables are strongly typed, which makes them consistent with other Modula-2 data. A pointer variable can point only to data that have the type specified in the pointer variable's declaration. Consider the declarations below:

```
VAR
    GolfPointer : POINTER TO Golf;
    TennisPointer : POINTER TO Tennis;
```

The variables GolfPointer and TennisPointer are of incompatible type. Even if both Golf and Tennis are compatible types, such as

```
TYPE
    Golf = INTEGER;
    Tennis = INTEGER;
```

GolfPointer and TennisPointer are still incompatible. Pointer variables are compatible only if they have identical type. The declarations on the following page, make Golf and Tennis compatible:

```
TYPE
    SportPointerType = POINTER TO CARDINAL;
VAR
    GolfPointer : SportPointerType;
    TennisPointer : SportPointerType;
```

Since dynamic data must be allocated and deallocated under the control of the program, languages include appropriate mechanisms. In Modula-2, allocation and deallocation of dynamic data are accomplished through procedure calls. These Modula-2 procedures are **ALLOCATE** and **DEALLOCATE**, as they are defined in Figure 15.8. (Note: Some versions of Modula-2 also use the procedures NEW and DISPOSE.)

```
PROCEDURE ALLOCATE( VAR P : SomePointerType;
                        S : CARDINAL );
    (* POST: A new unassigned data structure of size S is *)
    (*       allocated  AND   P points to the structure   *)
    (* NOTE: ALLOCATE must be imported from Storage        *)

PROCEDURE DEALLOCATE( VAR P : SomePointerType;
                          S : CARDINAL );
    (* PRE:  P points to some dynamic data structure       *)
    (* POST: The data structure, which should be of size S, *)
    (*       that is pointed to by P is deallocated,       *)
    (*       AND   P should be considered unassigned.      *)
    (* NOTE: DEALLOCATE must be imported from Storage.     *)
```

FIGURE 15.8 *ALLOCATE and DEALLOCATE*

Both ALLOCATE and DEALLOCATE require two parameters. The first actual parameter must be a pointer variable. This variable is assigned to point to a newly allocated data structure (data node) after ALLOCATE. For the DEALLOCATE procedure, this variable specifies the dynamic node to be disposed of.

The second parameter of ALLOCATE and DEALLOCATE specifies the size of the dynamic data node to be allocated or deallocated. This value *should always be equal to the size of the data type pointed to by the first parameter*. Modula-2 includes a built-in function called **SIZE** that is used to supply the actual second parameter for ALLOCATE and DEALLOCATE. The following invocation returns the size of any standard or programmer-defined type supplied as SomeType:

SIZE(SomeType)

Figure 15.9 on the opposite page, contains declarations along with a section of the program code that illustrates the ALLOCATE procedure.

Below are declarations used by the program segment that follows.

```
TYPE
      CardPointer = POINTER TO CARDINAL;
      String9 = ARRAY [0..9] OF CHAR;
      Str9Pointer = POINTER TO String9;
VAR
      MyAge : CardPointer;
      YourAge : CardPointer;
      Temporary : CardPointer;
      MyName : Str9Pointer;
      TheHorsesName : Str9Pointer;
```

This segment of Modula-2 code is described by the assertion.

```
ALLOCATE( MyAge, SIZE(CARDINAL) );
ALLOCATE( MyName, SIZE(String9) );
TheHorsesName := NIL;
(* Assert the following diagram:                    *)
(*                                                   *)
(*   MyName         MyAge              TheHorsesName *)
(*                                                   *)
(*                                                   *)
(*                                                   *)
(*                                                   *)
(*                                                   *)
(*          [0] [1] [2] [3] [4] [5] [6] [7] [8] [9]  *)
(*                                                   *)
(*                                                   *)
(*                                                   *)
```

FIGURE 15.9 *Illustration of ALLOCATE procedure*

The code in Figure 15.9 first invokes ALLOCATE, with MyAge as actual parameter. This causes a dynamic structure to be allocated and MyAge to be set to point to it. The second parameter specifies SIZE(CARDINAL) as the size of the dynamic data structure. This is correct, since MyAge is declared as a pointer to CARDINAL.

The second invocation of ALLOCATE in Figure 15.9 allocates an array of 10 characters (type String9) and assigns MyName to point to it. Again it is important that the size of the structure allocated by the same as what MyName is permitted to point to.

DEALLOCATE is used to deallocate dynamic variables. When the variable pointed to by MyAge is no longer needed by the program, the following instruction should be issued:

```
DEALLOCATE( MyAge, SIZE(CARDINAL) )
```

Following this instruction, the CARDINAL variable pointed to by MyAge is relinquished by the program. Since DEALLOCATE leaves its parameter unassigned, it is impossible to use the value of MyAge without assigning another value or using it in another ALLO-CATE invocation.

Every program that invokes ALLOCATE and DEALLOCATE must include a declaration at the start of the program similar to the InOut declaration. The exact form of this declaration is shown on the following page:

FROM Storage IMPORT ALLOCATE, DEALLOCATE;

One pointer variable can be assigned to another. For example, the assignment instruction

TheHorsesName := MyName;

causes a copy of the pointer stored in MyName to be assigned to TheHorsesName. This instruction does not alter the contents of the dynamic data structure, but rather sets both variables to point to the same dynamic structure.

In order to access the value of the dynamic variable, it is necessary to use a **dereferencing expression**. Figure 15.10 describes the Modula-2 dereferencing expression to consist of some expression of pointer type followed by a **dereferencing operator**, ^.

Syntax of DereferencingExpression:

⟶ *PointerExpression* ⟶ ⟶

PointerExpression: Any expression that yields an assigned pointer value other than NIL

Semantics: This expression denotes the data structure pointed to by PointerExpression.

FIGURE 15.10 *Description of DereferencingExpression*

The three variables, MyAge, YourAge, and Temporary are declared in Figure 15.9 to be of type POINTER TO CARDINAL. The following instructions allocate dynamic data and assign values:

```
ALLOCATE( MyAge, SIZE(CARDINAL) );
MyAge^ := -33;
ALLOCATE( YourAge, SIZE(CARDINAL) );
```

The following picture describes the result of these instructions:

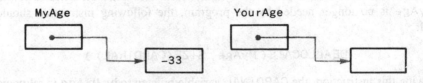

Both MyAge and YourAge are assigned to point to newly allocated CARDINAL variables by ALLOCATE invocations. In addition, the instruction MyAge^ := -33; causes the value of the variable pointed to by MyAge to be assigned -33. The dynamic variable pointed to by YourAge is as yet unassigned.

Continuing with this example, the following instruction is executed:

$$WriteCard(\ MyAge^\wedge,\ 0\ );$$

This instruction causes the value of the data structure pointed to by MyAge, -33, to be output.

Next assume that the instructions below are executed:

$$YourAge^\wedge\ :=\ MyAge^\wedge;$$
$$Temporary\ :=\ MyAge;$$

Below is a picture diagramming the result.

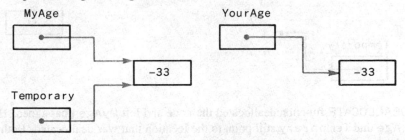

The instruction YourAge$^\wedge$: = MyAge$^\wedge$; causes the value of the cardinal pointed to by MyAge, -33 to be copied into the cardinal pointed to by YourAge. The second assignment instruction copies the pointer value of MyAge into Temporary, assigning both variables to point to the same cardinal node.

There are two traps programmers must avoid when using pointer variables and dynamic data.

        1) Creating inaccessible nodes
        2) Leaving dangling references

An **inaccessible node** is created whenever a node remains allocated without any pointer pointing to it. Suppose after the instructions above the following instruction was executed:

$$YourAge\ :=\ MyAge;$$

Now all three pointer variables point to the same node as shown below.

The dynamic cardinal node to the right has now been orphaned as an inaccessible node. This program cannot utilize or deallocate this node.

A **dangling reference** is an unassigned pointer variable that addresses a node that has been deallocated. Continuing the example, the following instruction is executed:

```
DEALLOCATE( MyAge, SIZE(CARDINAL) );
```

The result of this instruction is pictured below:

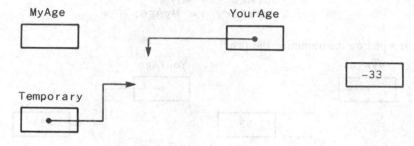

The DEALLOCATE function deallocated the node and left MyAge unassigned. However, YourAge and Temporary still point to the location that was deallocated. Both of these variables are now dangling pointers. Dangling pointers are a special problem because they often go undetected. If the programmer attempts to dereference a dangling pointer in an instruction such as

```
WriteCard( YourAge^, 0 );
```

it is likely that the computer will not generate an error message, but will allow YourAge to point to some meaningless data. This makes debugging extremely difficult.

Designing-with-Wisdom

Suggestions for Using Dynamic Variables

Pointers and dynamic variables add complexity to a program. They can make debugging and maintaining more challenging. The dangers of using dynamic variables can be manageably reduced by following these rules:

Before invoking ALLOCATE, remember to check whether the actual parameter points to another node that is pointed to by no other. If so, then DEALLOCATE the old node or reuse it rather than make it inaccessible.

After invoking ALLOCATE, remember that a pointer to this new node has been assigned, but the entire content of the node remains unassigned.

Before dereferencing, be certain to check that the pointer being dereferenced is assigned and not NIL; otherwise, run time errors will occur.

Before invoking DEALLOCATE, remember to locate all other pointers that address the node to be deallocated. Assigning all these pointers NIL, rather than letting them dangle, is a better practice.

Assigning them NIL clarifies the situation for maintenance programmers and provides a condition that is testable. (You can compare a pointer to NIL, but there is no way to identify a pointer that is dangling.)

After invoking DEALLOCATE, remember that the pointer that is the actual parameter is once again unassigned.

When assigning a new pointer to a pointer variable, make certain that it doesn't already point to a node that will become inaccessible.

When a procedure returns with local pointer variables, beware. These local pointers are deallocated automatically with the procedure activation frame. However, dynamic data are deallocated only by DEALLOCATE. Any dynamic data pointed to solely by local pointers become inaccessible when the procedure returns.

15.4 LINKED LISTS

Pointers and dynamic data are building blocks that can be used to construct more complicated data structures. These data structures are built from nodes containing pointers to other nodes. Figure 15.11 shows the declarations for one such node type and pointer.

```
TYPE
     CardNodePointer = POINTER TO CardNode;

     CardNode = RECORD
                     CardVal : CARDINAL;
                     Next : CardNodePointer
                  END;

VAR
     FirstNode : CardNodePointer;
     TempNode : CardNodePointer;
```

FIGURE 15.11 *Examples of linked list declarations*

The declarations from Figure 15.11 specify a dynamic data node, with CardNode type, that is a record with two fields. The CardVal field stores a single cardinal, and the Next field stores a pointer to the same type of node. If the following instruction is executed

ALLOCATE(FirstNode, SIZE(CardNode));

then the resulting situation can be depicted as shown below

FirstNode

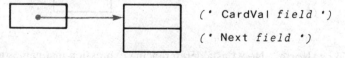

(* CardVal *field* *)

(* Next *field* *)

Figure 15.12 illustrates various identifiers and dereferencing expressions to show how this new node may be accessed.

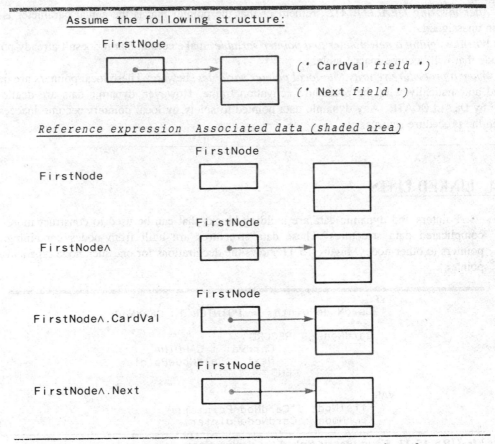

```
Assume the following structure:
    FirstNode
                                        ('CardVal field ')

                                        ('Next field ')


Reference expression  Associated data (shaded area)

                        FirstNode

FirstNode


                        FirstNode

FirstNode^


                        FirstNode

FirstNode^.CardVal


                        FirstNode

FirstNode^.Next
```

FIGURE 15.12 *Example of dereferencing expressions in dynamic nodes*

Below is an example of how to assign the value 791 to the cardinal field and N I L to the pointer field of the dynamic node:

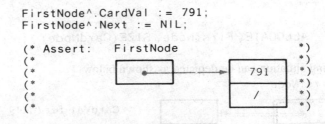

```
FirstNode^.CardVal := 791;
FirstNode^.Next := NIL;

(* Assert:    FirstNode              *)
(*                                   *)
(*                             791   *)
(*                                   *)
(*                              /    *)
(*                                   *)
```

Since F i rstNode^ . Next is a dereferencing expression that names a data field of pointer type, the following instruction is also possible at this point in the execution.

```
ALLOCATE (FirstNode^. Next, SIZE (CardNode));
```

```
(* Assert:     FirstNode                                    *)
(*                                                          *)
(*                                                          *)
(*                                                          *)
(*                                                          *)
(*                                                          *)
```

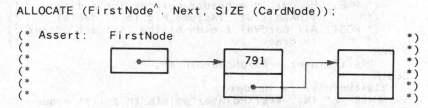

Now a second dynamic node has been allocated. It is pointed to by the Next field of the first dynamic node. Furthermore, the fields of this new node can be accessed as shown below.

```
FirstNode^.Next^.CardVal := 248;
FirstNode^.Next^.Next := NIL;
```

```
(* Assert:     FirstNode                                    *)
(*                                                          *)
(*                                                          *)
(*                                                          *)
(*                                                          *)
```

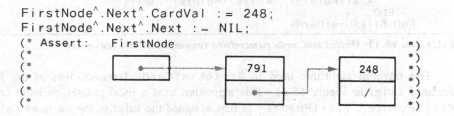

The structure described above belongs to a class of structures known as **linked lists**. A linked list is an ordered collection of dynamic nodes that are connected by pointers within the nodes. The most common of all linked lists is the **singly linked list**. A singly linked list consists of a **header** and a list of nodes. The header of a singly linked list is a pointer variable that points to the first node of the list. The name "singly linked list" is derived from a requirement that each node must contain a single list pointer field. The pointer field of each node, except the last, points to the next node in the list. The pointer field of the last node is NIL. In the previous example, the FirstNode variable serves as the header for a singly linked list of two nodes.

There are three common algorithms for processing linked lists:

1) Traversing the list.
2) Inserting a new node.
3) Deleting a node.

Traversing a list consists of beginning at the header and visiting every node of the list in order. Various types of processing can be performed on a node when it is visited. For example, Figure 15.13 on the following page, contains an algorithm of list traversal where the CardVal field of each node is output. This algorithm works regardless of the number of nodes in the list.

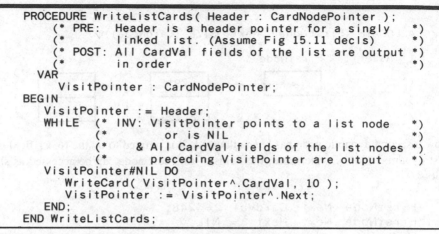

```
PROCEDURE WriteListCards( Header : CardNodePointer );
    (* PRE:  Header is a header pointer for a singly  *)
    (*       linked list. (Assume Fig 15.11 decls)    *)
    (* POST: All CardVal fields of the list are output *)
    (*       in order                                 *)
  VAR
     VisitPointer : CardNodePointer;
BEGIN
   VisitPointer := Header;
   WHILE   (* INV: VisitPointer points to a list node  *)
           (*           or is NIL                       *)
           (*      & All CardVal fields of the list nodes *)
           (*          preceding VisitPointer are output  *)
   VisitPointer#NIL DO
     WriteCard( VisitPointer^.CardVal, 10 );
     VisitPointer := VisitPointer^.Next;
   END;
END WriteListCards;
```

FIGURE 15.13 *WriteListCards procedure (example of list traversal)*

The traversal algorithm used in WriteListCards traverses lists of the form declared earlier in Figure 15.11. This algorithm uses a local pointer variable called VisitPointer. VisitPointer is first assigned the value of the list header and is advanced node by node until it reaches the last node and finally is assigned NIL. Advancing VisitPointer is similar to incrementing an array index variable using INC(SomeVar), because each advances access to the next item or node. The key instruction that performs the advance for VisitPointer is:

$$VisitPointer := VisitPointer^\wedge.Next;$$

Inserting a new node within a list is pictured in Figure 15.14. This operation requires a pointer to the node preceding the list position of the insertion.

Inserting a node from within a list

The algorithm below assumes CardPointerType *(Figure 15.11) and uses* PrePointer *and* NewPointer, *variables of type* CardPointerType.

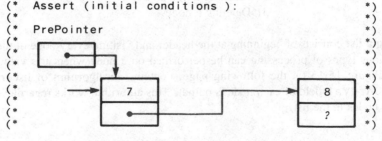

```
(*   Assert (initial conditions ):                *)
(*                                                *)
(*   PrePointer                                   *)
(*                                                *)
(*                                                *)
(*                                                *)
(*                                                *)
(*                                                *)
(*                     7                    8     *)
(*                                                *)
(*                                          ?     *)
(*                                                *)
```

```
ALLOCATE( NewPointer, SIZE(CardNode) );
NewPointer^.Next := PrePointer^.Next;
PrePointer^.Next := NewPointer;
NewPointer^.CardVal := 111;
```

(continued)

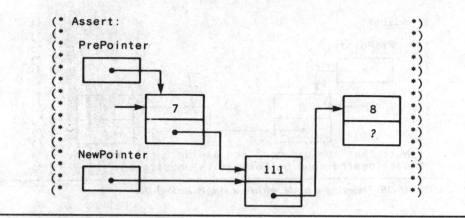

FIGURE 15.14 *Inserting a node within a single linked list*

Inserting a new node always requires the same four operations:

    1) Allocate the new node (using ALLOCATE)
    2) Link the new node to its successor
    3) Link the predessor to the new node
    4) Assign values to the fields of the new node

These four operations are performed by the four instructions shown in Figure 15.14. Notice that the algorithm fails unless the first three instructions are performed in this order.

Deleting a node from within a linked list requires a pointer to the node *preceding* the one to be deleted. Figure 15.15 illustrates this deletion algorithm.

Deleting a node from within a list

The algorithm below assumes CardNodePointer *(Figure 15.11) and uses* PrePointer *and* DelPointer, *variables of type Card NodePointer.*

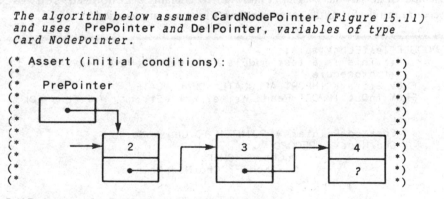

```
DelPointer := PrePointer^.Next;
PrePointer^.Next := DelPointer^.Next;
DEALLOCATE( DelPointer, SIZE(CardNode) );
```

(continued)

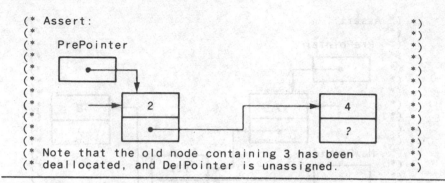

```
(* Assert:                                              *)
(*                                                      *)
(*     PrePointer                                       *)
(*                                                      *)
(*                                                      *)
(*                                                      *)
(*                                                      *)
(*                                                      *)
(*                                                      *)
(*                                                      *)
(*                                                      *)
(* Note that the old node containing 3 has been         *)
(* deallocated, and DelPointer is unassigned.           *)
```

FIGURE 15.15 *`eleting a node within a singly linked list*

Three steps are always required to delete an existing node of a linked list.

1) Save a pointer to the node to be deleted (delete node).
2) Link the node preceding the delete node to the node following it.
3) Deallocate the delete node.

These three steps correspond to the three instructions from Figure 15.15, and they must be performed in this order to work properly.

Inserting the first node of a linked list or deleting the first node from a list requires slight modifications to the insert and delete algorithms. These operations require that the header be updated, in place of the Next field of a list node.

15.5 ECHOREVERSED REVISITED

The singly linked list provides another solution to the EchoReversed procedure presented earlier in the chapter. Figure 15.16 contains a EchoReversedViaList procedure that performs the same task without the use of recursion.

```
MODULE TestEchoViaList;
        (* This is a test module for the EchoReversedViaList *)
        (* procedure                                          *)
    FROM Storage IMPORT ALLOCATE, DEALLOCATE;
    FROM InOut IMPORT Read, Write, WriteString, WriteLn, EOL;

    TYPE
        CharNodePointer = POINTER TO CharNode;
        CharNode = RECORD
                       InChar  : CHAR;
                       NextNode : CharNodePointe,
                   END;
```

(continued)

```
      PROCEDURE EchoReversedViaList;
          (* POST: One input line (up to EOL) is output *)
          (*        in the reverse order of input.         *)
        VAR
          InputLineHeader : CharNodePointer;
          NewNode : CharNodePointer;
          NextNodeToOutput : CharNodePointer;
          PastNode : CharNodePointer;
      BEGIN
        InputLineHeader := NIL;
        (* Assert: The list contains no nodes initially. *)

        REPEAT
          ALLOCATE( NewNode, SIZE(CharNode) );
          NewNode^.NextNode := InputLineHeader;
          InputLineHeader := NewNode;
          Read( InputLineHeader^.InChar );
          (* INV: All characters input so far are stored in  *)
          (*      reverse order in the singly linked list     *)
          (*      with InputLineHeader as a header.           *)
        UNTIL InputLineHeader^.InChar = EOL;
        WriteLn;  (* terminate input line *)
        (* Assert: Complete input line, including EOL, is        *)
        (*         stored in reverse by the InputLineHeader list. *)

        NextNodeToOutput := InputLineHeader^.NextNode; (*skip EOL*)
        DEALLOCATE( InputLineHeader, SIZE(CharNode) );
        WHILE    (* INV: All chars preceding NexNodeToOutput from  *)
                 (*      the linked list have been output in order  *)
        NextNodeToOutput#NIL DO
          Write( NextNodeToOutput^.InChar );
          PastNode := NextNodeToOutput;
          NextNodeToOutput := NextNodeToOutput^.NextNode;
          DEALLOCATE( PastNode, SIZE(CharNode) );
        END;
      END EchoReversedViaList;

BEGIN (* TestEchoViaList *)
  WriteString("Please specify an input line below:"); WriteLn;
  WriteString("It will be output in reverse."); WriteLn;
  EchoReversedViaList;
  WriteLn;
END TestEchoViaList.
```

FIGURE 15.16 *TestEchoViaList module, including EchoReversedViaList procedure*

The EchoReversedViaList procedure reverses an input line in two steps. In the first step, the characters are input, one at a time, and each character is inserted at the front of the list. This technique of inserting new nodes at the front of the list is convenient because this end of the list is easier to locate. (InputLineHeader points to the list front.) In this case, it is more important that inserting characters at the front of the list has the effect of reversing the characters, so that the first character is in the last node and the last character input (EOL) is in the first node.

The second step of the EchoReversedViaList algorithm is to traverse the list and output each character from first to last. After a node value is output, the node is deallocated to avoid inaccessible nodes.

*D*esigning-with-*W*isdom-

There Is No Such Thing As a Free Algorithm

Recursion and dynamic data structures allow for the solution of some problems that could not be otherwise coded. For example, the problem solved by EchoReversed and EchoReversed-ViaList cannot be accomplished, given techniques presented prior to this chapter.

Comparison of the recursive EchoReversed procedure and the linked list implementation of EchoReversedViaList reveals other recurrent issues in algorithms. It is often the case that recursion produces a shorter (in terms of line of code) solution. For this reason many programmers think of recursion as more "elegant."

However, any algorithm using recursion or dynamic data structures is complicated. Perhaps recursive algorithms are better at camouflaging their complexity than algorithms using dynamic data, but both are difficult to read, trace, debug, and maintain. Furthermore, both tend to be inefficient. Creating and eliminating activation frames consumes execution time in recursive algorithms. Allocating, deallocating and locating dynamic data also consumes extra execution time.

Keep language features in perspective. Recursion & dynamic data are powerful tools, but they are easily abused.

15.6 STACKS AND QUEUES

Two data structures with numerous applications in computer algorithms are **stacks** and **queues**. Neither of these data structures is a standard type within Modula-2, but each can be implemented as a dynamic data structure.

A stack is a last-in, first-out (**LIFO**) storage device. The name is appropriate, because this data structure behaves like a stack of papers. Only the **Top** paper in the stack is completely accessible at any point in time. It is possible to **Push** (place) new papers on top of the stack or to **Pop** (remove) papers to reveal a sheet somewhere below.

Similarly, a stack is a collection of objects. Four operations on the stack are possible.

1) **Push** places a new object atop the stack. (Push(S,x) denotes pushing object x on stack S)

2) **Pop** removes the top object from the stack, leaving the one below the top as the new top. (Pop(S) denotes popping one object from stack S.)

3) **Top** retrieves the top object from the stack. (Top(S) denotes the value of the object atop stack S.)

4) **IsEmptyStack** is a Boolean test that is TRUE exactly when the stack contains no more objects. (IsEmptyStack(S) is TRUE exactly when stack S is empty.)

The EchoReversed algorithm can be conveniently solved using stacks. Figure 15.17 illustrates a stack algorithm for the solution of this problem.

A Stack Algorithm to Output an Input Line in Reverse:

```
    PROCEDURE EchoReversedViaStack;
        (* This algorithm assumes a stack called "S"     *)
        (* and the related operations of Push, Pop, Top   *)
        (* and IsEmptyStack have been created elsewhere.  *)
        (* PRE:   IsEmptyStack(S)                         *)
        (* POST: Next input line is output in reverse.    *)
    VAR
        InChar : CHAR;
    BEGIN
        Read( InChar );
        WHILE  (* INV: Each input character prior to InChar    *)
               (*      has been pushed on S in order of input.*)
        InChar#EOL DO
            Push( S,InChar );
            Read( InChar );
        END;
        WriteLn;
        (* Assert: All input excepting the last EOL is stored   *)
        (*         in stack S; order of input is bottom to top. *)

        WHILE  (* INV: Input line output in reverse *)
               (*      back to Top(S)               *)
        NOT IsEmptyStack(S) DO
            Write( Top(S) );
            Pop(S);
        END;
    END EchoReversedViaStack;
```

FIGURE 15.17 *EchoReversedViaStack procedure*

Singly linked lists are handy for implementing stacks. The standard stack implementation uses a singly linked list with the front of the list as the top of the stack. The contents of each list node are the values from the stack. Figure 15.18 illustrates this implementation, along with the associated operations for stacks of INTEGER objects.

Stack declarations:

```
    TYPE
        Stack = POINTER TO StackNode;
        StackNode = RECORD
                        Object : INTEGER;
                        NextObject : Stack
                    END;
    VAR
        SomeStack : Stack;
```

(continued)

Diagram of stack implementation:

SomeStack

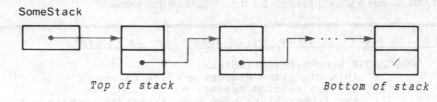

Top of stack   *Bottom of stack*

Initialization of a stack, SomeStack *to empty:*

```
SomeStack := NIL;
```

IsEmptyStack operation:

```
PROCEDURE IsEmptyStack( S : Stack )
: BOOLEAN;
    (* PRE:  S is assigned                    *)
    (* POST: RESULT = (S contains zero objects) *)
BEGIN
    RETURN  (S = NIL);
END IsEmptyStack;
```

Push operation:

```
PROCEDURE Push( VAR S : Stack;
                     NewObject : INTEGER );
      (* PRE:  S points to a singly linked list *)
      (* POST: NewObject is pushed on stack S    *)
    VAR NewPointer : Stack;
BEGIN
    ALLOCATE( NewPointer, SIZE(StackNode) );
    NewPointer^.NextObject := S;
    S := NewPointer;
    NewPointer^.Object := NewObject;
END Push;
```

Top operation:

```
PROCEDURE Top( S : Stack )
: INTEGER;
      (* PRE:  NOT IsEmptyStack(S)              *)
      (* POST: RESULT = the top object of stack S *)
BEGIN
    RETURN S^.Object;
END Top;
```

Pop operation:

```
PROCEDURE Pop( VAR S : Stack );
      (* PRE:  NOT IsEmptyStack(S)              *)
      (* POST: The top object is popped off stack S *)
    VAR OldTopOfStack : Stack;
BEGIN
    OldTopOfStack := S;
    S := S^.NextObject;
    DEALLOCATE( OldTopOfStack, SIZE(StackNode) );
END Pop;
```

FIGURE 15.18 *Implementation of stack as a singly linked list*

A queue is a first-in, first-out (**FIFO**) store. Objects are removed from a queue in the same order as they are added. A waiting line in a supermarket, an assembly line in a factory, or a group of program listings waiting in order to be printed by an operating system are all examples of queues.

The **front** of the queue is taken to be the oldest object in the queue, and the **back** of the queue is the most recently added. The four operations associated with queues are

1) **Enqueue** places a new object at the back of the queue. (Enqueue(Q,x) denotes adding object x to queue Q.)
2) **Dequeue** removes the front (oldest) object from the queue. (Dequeue(Q) denotes removing the front of queue Q.)
3) **Front** retrieves the front (oldest) object from the queue. (Front(Q) denotes the value of the front object of queue Q.)
4) **IsEmptyQueue** is a Boolean test that is TRUE exactly when the queue contains no more objects. (IsEmptyQueue(Q) is TRUE exactly when queue Q is empty.)

When a queue is implemented as a singly linked list, it is most efficient to maintain a pointer to the front and a pointer to the back of the queue. The order of objects in the queue is the same as the nodes of the list. Figure 15.19 illustrates the typical singly linked list implementation of a queue of integers.

Queue declarations:

```
TYPE
    QueNodePointer = POINTER TO QueNode;
    QueNode = RECORD
                    Object : INTEGER;
                    NextObject : QueNodePointer
              END;
    Queue = RECORD
                 Front : QueNodePointer;
                 Back : QueNodePointer
            END;
VAR
    SomeQue : Queue;
```

Diagram of queue implementation:

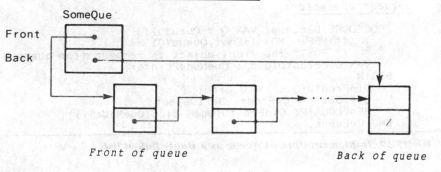

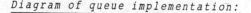

(continued)

Initialization of a stack, SomeQue *to empty:*

```
SomeQue.Front := NIL;
```

IsEmptyQueue operation:

```
PROCEDURE IsEmptyQueue( Q : Queue )
: BOOLEAN;
    (* PRE:  Q is assigned                        *)
    (* POST: RESULT = (Q contains zero objects) *)
BEGIN
    RETURN  (Q.Front = NIL);
END IsEmptyQueue;
```

Enqueue operation:

```
PROCEDURE Enqueue( VAR Q : Queue;
                       NewObject : INTEGER );
    (* PRE:  Q.Back points to the last list node *)
    (*        if the list is not empty           *)
    (* POST: NewObject is enqueued on queue Q     *)
VAR NewPointer : QueNodePointer;
BEGIN
    ALLOCATE( NewPointer, SIZE(QueNode) );
    NewPointer^.NextObject := NIL;
    IF IsEmptyQueue(Q) THEN
        Q.Front := NewPointer;
        Q.Back := NewPointer;
    ELSE
        Q.Back^.NextObject := NewPointer;
        Q.Back := NewPointer;
    END;
    NewPointer^.Object := NewObject;
END Enqueue;
```

Front operation:

```
PROCEDURE Front( Q : Queue )
: INTEGER;
    (* PRE:  NOT IsEmptyQueue(Q)                  *)
    (* POST: RESULT = the front object of queue Q *)
BEGIN
    RETURN Q.Front^.Object;
END Front;
```

Dequeue operation:

```
PROCEDURE Dequeue( VAR Q : Queue );
    (* PRE:  NOT IsEmptyQueue(Q)                     *)
    (* POST: The front object is removed from queue Q *)
    VAR OldFrontOfQue : QueNodePointer;
BEGIN
    OldFrontOfQue := Q.Front;
    Q.Front := Q.Front^.NextObject;
    DEALLOCATE( OldFrontOfQue, SIZE(QueNode) );
END Dequeue;
```

FIGURE 15.19 *Implementation of queue as a singly linked list*

5.7 THE SET DATA TYPE

There is one standard data type included in Modula-2 that has not yet been presented, the **SET**. The Modula-2 implementation of set parallels that of the mathematical notion. Figure 15.20 describes this type.

```
Name of Data Type: set

Declaration of SetType:

    Syntax:


          ──────▶ SET ──────▶ OF ──────▶ UniverseType ──────▶


          UniverseType is an enumeration or subrange type

    Semantics: A set may contain any or all of the elements
               of UniverseType, similar to a mathematical set.

    NOTE: Implementations are permitted to restrict
          UniverseType.  In many implementations, it is
          required that every constant in UniverseType have
          ordinal value in the range from 0 to 15.

    Constant syntax:

  ──────▶ SetType ─▶ { ─────────────────────────────────── } ──▶

                        ┌──▶ UniverseConstant ──┐

                        └──▶ UniverseSubrange ──┘


    SetType: the identifier used to name this set type

    UniverseConstant:  some constant of type UniverseType

    UniverseSubrange:  any subrange over UniverseType
                       (older compilers may not support
                        this addition of the 1985 revision)

  Operations (on 2 sets yielding another set)
     + ... union (the set including all elements in either
             or both original sets)
     * ... intersection (the set including only elements in
             both original sets)
     - ... set subtraction (the set including only elements
             from the first set not in the second)
     / ... symmetric set difference (the set including all
             elements that are in exactly one of the
             two original sets)

                                              (continued)
```

```
Operations (comparing 2 sets to yield a Boolean value)
  =  ... set equality
  #  ... set inequality
  <> ... set inequality
  <= ... subset  (TRUE when all elements of the first set
                        are also included in the second)
  >= ... superset (TRUE when the second set <= the first)

Operation (on a set element and a set yielding a Boolean)
  IN ... membership (TRUE when the element is contained
                        in the set)

The assignment operation (:=)

Standard procedures for manipulating sets
  EXCL ...  PROCEDURE EXCL( VAR S : SetType;
                                E : UniverseType );
                (* PRE:  S and E are assigned          *)
                (* POST: S is the set formed by S<entry> *)
                (*        with element E removed        *)

  INCL ...  PROCEDURE INCL( VAR S : SetType;
                                E : UniverseType );
                (* PRE:  S and E are assigned          *)
                (* POST: S is the set formed by S<entry> *)
                (*        with element E included        *)
```

FIGURE 15.20 *The SET data type*

Figure 15.21 contains a collection of declarations that declare set types and variables.

```
TYPE
    DigitSet = SET OF [0..9];

VAR
    OddDigits : DigitSet;
    SquareDigits : DigitSet;
    OctalDigits : DigitSet;
    SomeDigits : DigitSet;

TYPE
    StereoEquipment = ( TurnTable, Amplifier, CDdiskPlayer,
                        Receiver, CassetteDeck, Speakers );
    EquipSet = SET OF StereoEquipment;

VAR
    MyStereo : EquipSet;
    EdsStereo : EquipSet;
```

FIGURE 15.21 *Examples of set declarations*

Every set must be specified with a universe. The universe establishes what constants may be elements of the set. DigitSet is a universe of

$$\{0..9\}$$

so any cardinal constant from 0 to 9 may be an element of any variable of type Digit-Set. Likewise, EquipSet variables may include any or all of the enumerated constants from StereoEquipment as set elements.

A common misconception is that SET variables are automatically assigned the value of their universe. After the declarations from Figure 15.21, none of the set variables are assigned. The universe type included in their declaration only specifies *potential*, not actual values of the variables. Figure 15.22 contains several examples of how to assign values to these variables.

```
OddDigits := DigitSet{1, 3, 5, 7, 9};
SquareDigits := DigitSet{ 0, 1, 4, 9 };
OctalDigits := DigitSet{ 0..7 };
MyStereo := EquipSet{Receiver, Speakers};
EdsStereo := MyStereo;
(* Assert: OddDigits = {1,3,5,7,9}                      *)
(*         & SquareDigits = {0,1,4,9}                    *)
(*         & OctalDigits = {0,1,2,3,4,5,6,7}             *)
(*         & MyStereo = EdsStereo = {Receiver,Speakers} *)
(*         & SomeDigits is unassigned                    *)
```

FIGURE 15.22 *Examples of set assignments*

Sets are very strongly typed in Modula-2. Every set constant is prefixed by the name of the type of the set, such as DigitSet{1,3,5,7}. Furthermore, two different set variables are incompatible unless they share the same type.

The sets assigned in Figure 15.22 could be manipulated using any of the set operations shown below.

```
(* Assert: OddDigits = {1,3,5,7,9}           *)
(*         & SquareDigits = {0,1,4,9}         *)
(*         & OctalDigits = {0,1,2,3,4,5,6,7} *)
SomeDigits := OddDigits + SquareDigits;
(* Assert: SomeDigits = {0,1,3,4,5,7,9}  [UNION] *)
SomeDigits := OddDigits + DigitSet{8,9};
(* Assert: SomeDigits = {1,3,5,7,8,9}  [UNION] *)
SomeDigits := OddDigits * OctalDigits;
(* Assert: SomeDigits = {1,3,5,7}  [INTERSECTION] *)
SomeDigits := SquareDigits - OddDigits;
(* Assert: SomeDigits = {0,4}   [SET DIFFERENCE] *)
SomeDigits := OddDigits / SquareDigits;
(* Assert: SomeDigits = {0,3,4,5,7} [SYMMETRIC DIF.] *)
SomeDigits := DigitSet{};
(* Assert: SomeDigits = the empty set *)
```

In addition to the set operations, union (+), intersection (*), set difference (−) and symmetric difference (/) Modula-2 also permit two sets to be compared for equality (=), inequality (# or <>), subset (<=) and superset (>=). The operations of proper subset and proper superset (you might guess < and >) are *not* included.

Modula-2 also permits testing an element for membership in a set through the IN operator. For example, the following section of code outputs all of the elements stored in OddDigits (i is some cardinal variable).

```
FOR i:=0 TO 9 DO
    IF i IN OddDigits THEN
        WriteCard( i,2 );
    END;
END;
(* Assert: if OddDigits={1,3,5,7,9} then the *)
(* following is output: 1 3 5 7 9            *)
```

Even with all these operations, certain manipulations of set type data are difficult. For example, suppose a program has read some cardinal into a variable called SomeCard, and the program must assign to SomeSet the set consisting of the value of SomeCard as its lone element. The following assignment seems reasonable:

```
SomeSet := DigitSet{ SomeCard };
(* The above instruction is invalid! *)
```

However, this instruction fails on a syntax error because the set constant on the right side of the assignment contains the *variable* SomeCard. Set constants may not contain variables. They may contain only constants or constant subranges.

Modula-2 incorporates two procedures to alleviate the difficulty of including or excluding variable values as set elements, **INCL** and **EXCL**. The INCL procedure updates the value of its set parameter to be the union of this parameter at procedure entry together with the set containing the single value as specified by the second parameter. INCL can be used to perform the problematic assignment above successfully.

```
(* Assert: SomeCard is assigned some cardinal digit *)
SomeSet := DigitSet{};
INCL( SomeSet, SomeCard );
(* Assert: SomeSet = the set containing the single   *)
(*             element given by the value of SomeCard *)
```

The use of sets can improve code readability. Unfortunately, Modula-2 sets are limited by the original definition of the programming language. Modula-2 compilers can, and generally do, limit the possibilities for permissible universe types. In some implementations of the language, no element of the universe type for a set may have an ordinal value outside the range from 0 to 15. This kind of restriction effectively limits universe types for sets to enumerated types, since few other useful universes exist.

15.8 SUMMARY

Recursion is a powerful tool for expressing certain algorithms. When used appropriately, recursive procedures and functions result in clear and concise algorithms. Recursion can be a difficult tool to master, but the technique exposes new horizons of problems that can be solved by programs.

Dynamic data gives a programmer more control over data. Programs may allocate and deallocate new data structures during their execution. Two data structures, stacks and queues, are conveniently implemented through linked lists and related algorithms.

Programs make frequent use of sets. It is natural that a set data type should be a useful tool for the programmer.

While this chapter completes the presentation of programming tools for this book, this is not an exhaustive presentation. Computer science includes countless programming tools and techniques. New ideas are always being developed. Programmers must be perpetual students if they are to remain current with their craft.

||| KEY TERMS

recursion	DEALLOCATE	stack operations (Push,
window	SIZE	Pop, Top,
activation	dereferencing expression	IsEmptyStack)
activation frame	dereferencing operator ($^\wedge$)	FIFO
activation record	inaccessible node	front (of a queue)
infinite recursion	dangling reference	back (of a queue)
execution efficiency	linked list	queue operations
static data	singly linked list	(Enqueue, Dequeue,
dynamic data	header	Front, IsEmptyQueue)
pointer	list traversal	SET
NIL	stack	INCL
NIL pointer	queue	EXCL
ALLOCATE	LIFO	

||| EXERCISES

1. Below are two virtually identical recursive procedures, excepting that they use different parameter passage techniques. Use them to complete parts (a) and (b).

```
PROCEDURE MysteryIncl( Blacker : CHAR );
BEGIN
    IF Blacker<"Z" THEN
        INC(Blacker);
        MysteryIncl(Blacker);
    END;
    Write(Blacker);
END MysteryIncl;
```

```
PROCEDURE MysteryInc2( VAR Blackest : CHAR );
BEGIN
    IF Blackest<"Z" THEN
        INC(Blackest);
        MysteryInc2(Blackest);
    END;
    Write(Blackest);
END MysteryInc2;
```

a) Show the output produced by the following invocation assuming SomeChar is a global CHAR variable:

```
SomeChar := "X";
MysteryInc1( SomeChar );
```

b) Show the output produced by the following invocation assuming SomeChar is a global CHAR variable:

```
SomeChar := "X";
MysteryInc2( SomeChar );
```

2. Use the recursive procedure below to answer parts (a) through (c).

```
PROCEDURE Wuzzles( BumbleLion : INTEGER );
    (* PRE & POST:   ???????   *)
BEGIN
    WriteInt( BumbleLion, 5 );
    IF BumbleLion<10 THEN
        Wuzzles( BumbleLion+3 )
    END;
    WriteInt( BumbleLion, 5 );
END Wuzzles;
```

a) Show the output produced by the following invocation:

```
Wuzzles( 4 )
```

b) Show the output produced by the following invocation:

```
Wuzzles( -2 )
```

c) Show the output produced by the following invocation:

```
Wuzzles( 11 )
```

3. Use the recursive procedure below to answer parts (a) and (b).

```
PROCEDURE Smurfs( Vanity : CHAR );
   (* PRE & POST:  ??????  *)
BEGIN
   Write( Vanity );
   IF Vanity>"C" THEN
      Smurfs( CHR(ORD(Vanity)-1) );
      Smurfs( CHR(ORD(Vanity)-2) );
   END;
END Smurfs;
```

a) Show the output produced by the following invocation:

Smurfs("E")

b) Show the output produced by the following invocation:

Smurfs("G")

4. Use the recursive function below to answer parts (a) through (c).

```
PROCEDURE WreckMult( A : CARDINAL;
                     B : CARDINAL )
 : CARDINAL;
   (* PRE & POST:  ??????  *)
BEGIN
   IF B>0 THEN
      RETURN( A*WreckMult(A,B-1) )
   ELSE
      RETURN( 1 );
   END;
END WreckMult;
```

a) Show the value output by the following instruction:

WriteCard(WreckMult(3,2), 0);

b) Show the value output by the following instruction:

WriteCard(WreckMult(2,9), 0);

c) Show the value output by the following instruction:

WriteCard(WreckMult(8,0), 0);

5. Write a procedure that is equivalent to Fib (See Figure 15.4), but that does not use recursion. Discuss the advantages and disadvantages of each version.

6. For each of the explicit code sections below, write a recursive procedure or procedures to accomplish the same task without using any loop instructions. Assume that I and N are INTEGER type variables.

a)
```
FOR I := 1 TO N DO
    WriteInt( I,0 );
END;
```

b)
```
ReadInt( I );
ReadInt( N );
REPEAT
    WriteInt( I,0 );
    DEC( I );
    INC( N );
UNTIL I<N;
```

Use the Declarations below to complete Exercises 7 through 9.

```
TYPE
    CharPointer = POINTER TO CHAR;
VAR
    PointerA : CharPointer;
    PointerB : CharPointer;
    PointerC : CharPointer;
    PointerD : CharPointer;

TYPE
    IntNodePointer = POINTER TO IntNode;
    IntNode = RECORD
                 Int : INTEGER;
                 Next : IntNodePointer
              END;
VAR
    IntHeader1 : IntNodePointer;
    IntHeader2 : IntNodePointer;
```

7. Assume that the picture below depicts the configuration of storage just prior to each part (a) through (g), and redraw the picture as it should appear after the code.

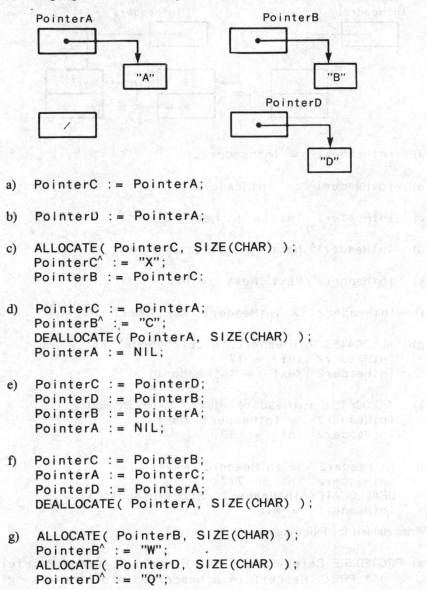

a) PointerC := PointerA;

b) PointerD := PointerA;

c) ALLOCATE(PointerC, SIZE(CHAR));
   PointerC^ := "X";
   PointerB := PointerC;

d) PointerC := PointerA;
   PointerB^ := "C";
   DEALLOCATE(PointerA, SIZE(CHAR));
   PointerA := NIL;

e) PointerC := PointerD;
   PointerD := PointerB;
   PointerB := PointerA;
   PointerA := NIL;

f) PointerC := PointerB;
   PointerA := PointerC;
   PointerD := PointerA;
   DEALLOCATE(PointerA, SIZE(CHAR));

g) ALLOCATE(PointerB, SIZE(CHAR));
   PointerB^ := "W";
   ALLOCATE(PointerD, SIZE(CHAR));
   PointerD^ := "Q";

8. Assume that the picture below depicts the configuration of storage just prior to *each* part (a) through (i), and redraw the picture as it should appear after the code.

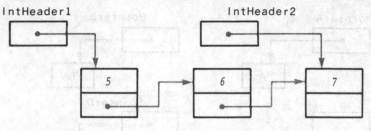

a) IntHeader1 := IntHeader2;

b) IntHeader1^ := IntHeader2^;

c) IntHeader1^.Int := IntHeader2^.Int;

d) IntHeader1^.Next := IntHeader2^.Next;

e) IntHeader1^.Next^.Next := NIL;

f) IntHeader2 := IntHeader1^.Next^.Next;

g) ALLOCATE(IntHeader2, SIZE(IntNode));
    IntHeader2^.Int := 17;
    IntHeader2^.Next := IntHeader1;

h) ALLOCATE(IntHeader1^.Next, SIZE(IntNode));
    IntHeader2 := IntHeader1^.Next;
    IntHeader2^.Int := -33;

i) IntHeader2 := IntHeader1^.Next;
    IntHeader2^.Int := 777;
    DEALLOCATE(IntHeader1, SIZE(IntNode));
    IntHeader1 := NIL;

9. Write and test the following procedures.

a) PROCEDURE DeleteFirst(VAR Header1 : IntNodePointer);
      (* PRE: Header1 is a header pointer for a singly *)
      (*   linked list with one or more nodes.   *)
      (* POST: Header1 is a header for the list at entry *)
      (*   with the first node deleted.   *)

b) PROCEDURE DeleteLast(Header1 : IntNodePointer);
       (* PRE: Header1 is a header pointer for a singly *)
       (*   linked list with one or more nodes.   *)
       (* POST: Header1 is a header for the list at entry *)
       (*   with the last node deleted.   *)

c) PROCEDURE InsertNewFirst(VAR Header1 : IntNodePointer
                         NewInt : INTEGER);
       (* PRE: Header1 is a header pointer for a singly *)
       (*   linked list with zero or more nodes.   *)
       (* POST: Header1 is a header for the list at entry *)
       (*   with a newly inserted first node   *)
       (*   containing the value of NewInt.   *)

d) PROCEDURE InsertNewLast(Header1 : IntNodePointer
                       NewInt : INTEGER);
       (* PRE: Header1 is a header pointer for a singly *)
       (*   linked list with zero or more nodes.   *)
       (* POST: Header1 is a header for the list at entry *)
       (*   with a newly inserted last node   *)
       (*   containing the value of NewInt.   *)

e) PROCEDURE Append(Header1 : IntNodePointer;
                Header2 : IntNodePointer);
       (* PRE: Header1 and Header2 are both header pointers *)
       (*   for separate singly linked lists of zero or *)
       (*   more nodes.   *)
       (* POST: The entire list from Header2 has been   *)
       (*   appended to the rear of the list from Header1 *)
       (*   without any allocation or deallocation.   *)

10. Assume that a stack, called IntStack, of integers initially contains 15 as the top value, 16 as the second, and 17 as the third. This situation can be pictured as a sequence of these three values enclosed in angle brackets as shown below:

$$<15, 16, 17>$$

This notation shows the integers left to right as they occur top to bottom in the stack. Assume that IntStack stores these three values just before each sequence of operations below, and show the stack resulting from the operations. Use this sequence notation to express your answers.

a) ```
Pop(IntStack);
Pop(IntStack);
Push(IntStack, 77);
```

b) ```
Push( IntStack,201 );
Push( IntStack, 202 );
Pop( IntStack );
Push( IntStack, 203 );
```

c) ```
Push(IntStack,100);
IF Top(IntStack)<0 THEN
    Push(IntStack,999);
END;
Pop(IntStack);
Pop(IntStack);
Push(IntStack, 203);
```

d) ```
WHILE NOT IsEmptyStack(IntStack) DO
    Pop(IntStack);
END;
```

11. Assume that a queue, called CardQueue, of cardinals initially contains the values 31, 32, 33 and 34, from front to back. This situation can be pictured as a sequence of these three values enclosed in angle brackets as shown below:

$$<31, 32, 33, 34>$$

This notation shows the cardinals left to right as they occur in the queue. Assume that CardQueue stores these four values just before each sequence of operations below, and show the queue resulting from the operations. Use this sequence notation to express your answers.

a) ```
Enqueue(CardQueue, 2222);
Dequeue(CardQueue);
```

b) ```
Enqueue( CardQueue, 3333 );
Enqueue( CardQueue, 4444 );
Dequeue( CardQueue );
Enqueue( CardQueue, 5555 );
```

c) ```
IF Front(CardQueue)=31 THEN
    Enqueue(CardQueue,12);
END;
IF IsEmptyQueue(CardQueue) THEN
    Enqueue(CardQueue,13);
ELSE
    Dequeue(CardQueue);
END;
```
```

12. It is possible to implement a queue, and all of its operations, using two stacks. This technique requires upsetting one stack onto the other for certain operations. Using this idea with stacks S1 and S2, give pseudocode for each of the four queue operations on a queue, Q, using exclusively the stack operations of Push, Pop, Top and IsEmptyStack and appropriate control structures.

Use the Declarations below to complete Exercises 13 through 15.

```
TYPE
    FastFood = (CheeseBurger, Chips, Coke);
    DinerSet = SET OF FastFood;
VAR
    YuppyFood : DinerSet;
    YummyFood : DinerSet;
TYPE
    HexNumSet = SET OF [0..15];
VAR
    HexSet1 : HexNumSet;
    HexSet2 : HexNumSet;
    HexSet3 : HexNumSet;
```

13. Using the notation of Modula-2 express the value of each expression below.

   a) DinerSet{CheeseBurger,Chips} + DinerSet{Chips,Coke}
   b) DinerSet{CheeseBurger,Chips} + DinerSet{}
   c) DinerSet{CheeseBurger,Chips} * DinerSet{Chips,Coke}
   d) DinerSet{CheeseBurger,Chips} − DinerSet{Chips,Coke}
   e) DinerSet{CheeseBurger,Chips} / DinerSet{Chips,Coke}
   f) DinerSet{CheeseBurger,Chips} = DinerSet{Chips,CheeseBurger}
   g) DinerSet{CheeseBurger,Chips} # DinerSet{CheeseBurger,
      CheeseBurger,Chips}
   h) DinerSet{CheeseBurger,Chips} <= DinerSet{Chips,Coke}
   i) DinerSet{Coke,Chips} <= DinerSet{Chips,Coke,CheeseBurger}
   j) DinerSet{Coke,Chips} >= DinerSet{Chips,Coke}
   k) Coke IN DinerSet{Chips}

14. For each part below specify the values of YuppyFood and YummyFood after the code.
   a) YuppyFood := DinerSet{Coke};
      YummyFood := DinerSet{CheeseBurger,Coke,Chips};
      INCL(YuppyFood,Chips);

   b) YuppyFood := DinerSet{Coke};
      YummyFood := DinerSet{CheeseBurger..Coke};
      EXCL(YummyFood,Chips);

c) YuppyFood := DinerSet{Coke};
YummyFood := DinerSet{CheeseBurger,Coke,Chips};
INCL(YummyFood,CheeseBurger);
EXCL(YummyFood,CheeseBurger);

d) YuppyFood := DinerSet{Coke};
YummyFood := DinerSet{CheeseBurger..Chips};
EXCL(YuppyFood,Chips);
EXCL(YuppyFood,CheeseBurger);

15. Write a single assignment instruction to complete each of the following. (You may assume that HexSet2 and HexSet3 are assigned.)

a) Assign to HexSet1 the set consisting all even integers in the range from 4 to 12.

b) Assign to HexSet1 the set consisting of all prime numbers in the HexNumSet universe.

c) Assign to HexSet1 the set consisting of all integers from the HexNumSet universe that are evenly divisible by 3.

d) Assign to HexSet1 the null or empty set.

e) Assign to HexSet1 the union of HexSet2 and HexSet3.

f) Assign to HexSet1 the intersection of HexSet2 and HexSet3.

g) Assign to HexSet2 its previous value with the element 7 included in the new set.

h) Assign to HexSet2 its previous value with the element 9 removed from the new set.

A

SYNTAX DIAGRAMS FOR MODULA-2

This Appendix defines the Modula-2 programming language through syntax diagrams. Each diagram is labeled with a name. Non-highlighted identifiers refer to other diagrams, while highlighted identifiers refer to actual syntactic entitities.

Table of syntax diagrams

OctalDigit

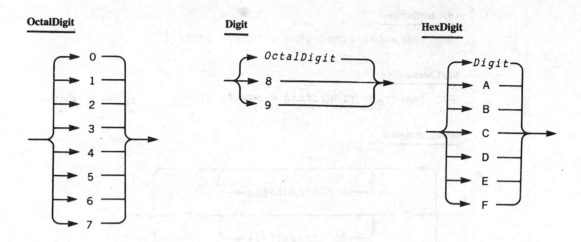

Digit

HexDigit

AlphaChar

Any uppercase or lowercase alphabetic character.

Identifier

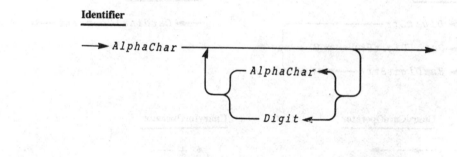

OctalDigitStr

DigitStr

HexDigitStr

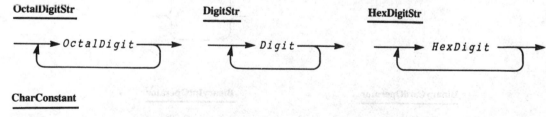

CharConstant

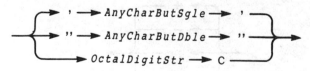

AnyCharButSgle

Any character other than a single quote (').

AnyCharButDble

Any character other than a double quote (").

StringConstant

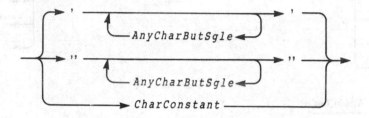

CardinalConstant

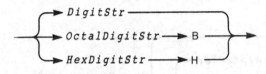

IntegerConstant

→ *CardinalConstant* →

UnaryCardOperator

→ + →

UnaryIntOperator

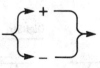

BinaryCardOperator

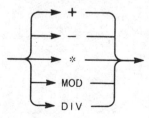

BinaryIntOperator

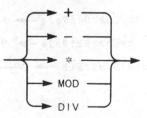

RealConstant

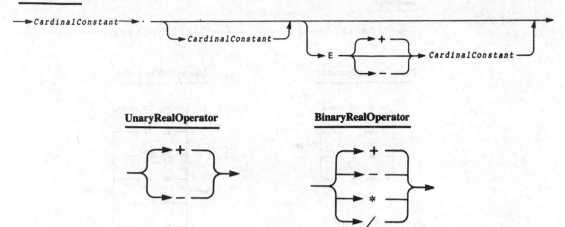

UnaryRealOperator

BinaryRealOperator

BitsetConstant

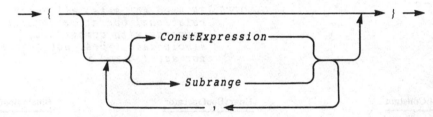

SetConstant

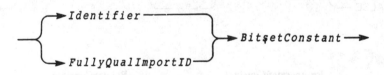

Subrange

$\longrightarrow ConstExpression \longrightarrow .. \longrightarrow ConstExpression \longrightarrow$

BinaryBitsetOperator

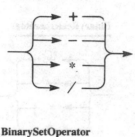

BinaryRelOperator

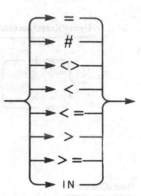

BinarySetOperator

$\longrightarrow BinaryBitsetOperator \longrightarrow$

```
NOTES: IN used for sets; all other
       relational operators require
       operands with compatible,
       simple data types; not available
       for sets: < and >
```

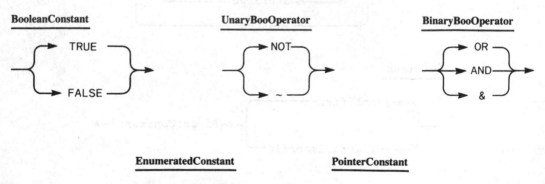

BooleanConstant

TRUE

FALSE

UnaryBooOperator

NOT

~

BinaryBooOperator

OR

AND

&

EnumeratedConstant

$\longrightarrow Identifier \longrightarrow$

PointerConstant

$\longrightarrow NIL \longrightarrow$

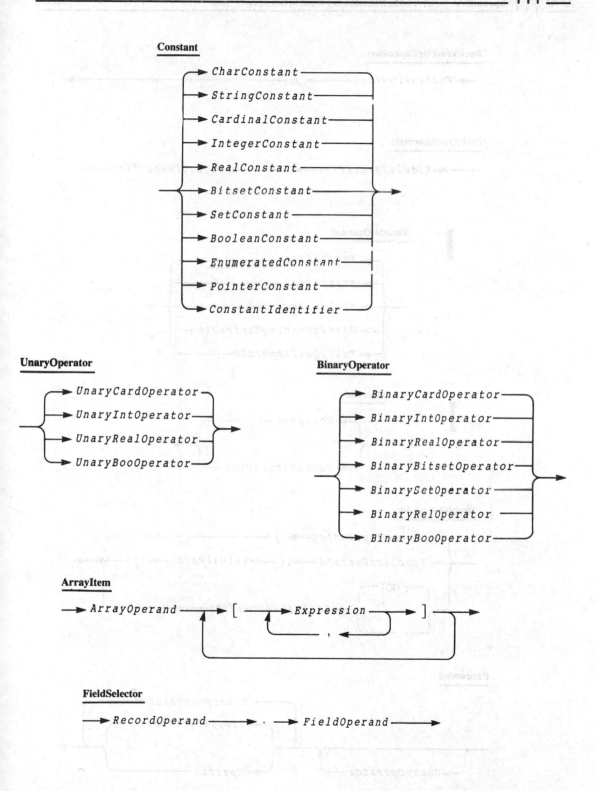

Constant

- CharConstant
- StringConstant
- CardinalConstant
- IntegerConstant
- RealConstant
- BitsetConstant
- SetConstant
- BooleanConstant
- EnumeratedConstant
- PointerConstant
- ConstantIdentifier

UnaryOperator

- UnaryCardOperator
- UnaryIntOperator
- UnaryRealOperator
- UnaryBooOperator

BinaryOperator

- BinaryCardOperator
- BinaryIntOperator
- BinaryRealOperator
- BinaryBitsetOperator
- BinarySetOperator
- BinaryRelOperator
- BinaryBooOperator

ArrayItem

ArrayOperand [Expression ,]

FieldSelector

RecordOperand . FieldOperand

DereferencingExpression

→ *PointerOperand* → ∧ →

FullyQualImportID

→ *ModuleIdentifier* → . → *ObjectIdentifier* →

VariableOperand

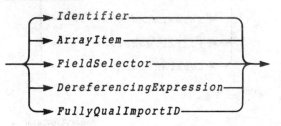

→ *Identifier*
→ *ArrayItem*
→ *FieldSelector*
→ *DereferencingExpression*
→ *FullyQualImportID*

Operand

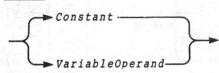

→ *Constant*
→ *VariableOperand*

SimpleExpression

(→ *Expression* →)

→ *FunctionOperand* → (→ *ActualParms* →) →

NOT

~ → *BooleanExpression*

Expression

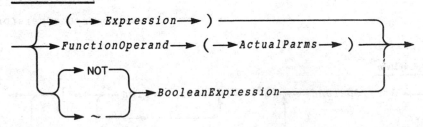

BinaryOperator
→ *SimpleExpression*
→ *UnaryOperator*
→ *Operand*

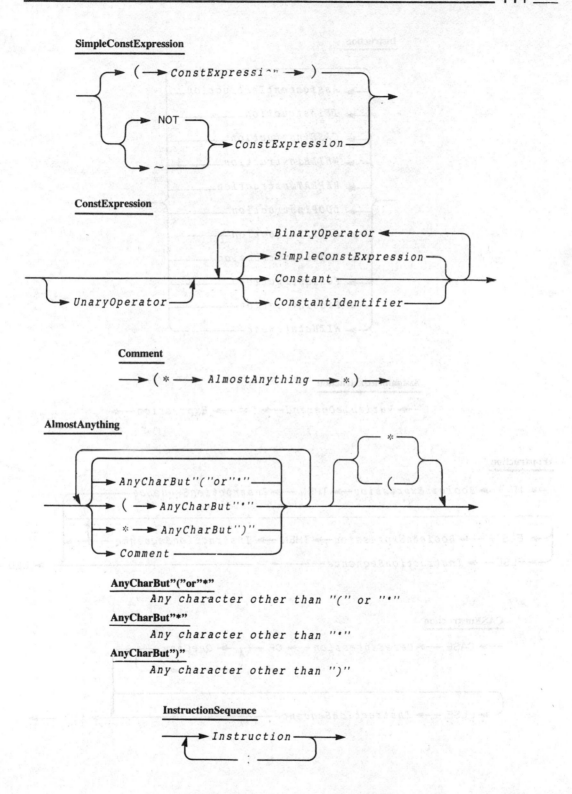

SimpleConstExpression

ConstExpression

Comment

AlmostAnything

AnyCharBut"("or"*"
  Any character other than "(" or ""*

AnyCharBut"*"
  Any character other than ""*

AnyCharBut")"
  Any character other than ")"

InstructionSequence

Instruction

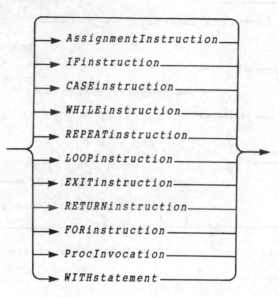

AssignmentInstruction

$$\rightarrow VariableOperand \rightarrow := \rightarrow Expression \rightarrow$$

IFinstruction

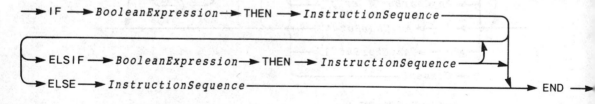

CASEinstruction

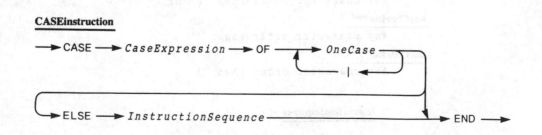

OneCase

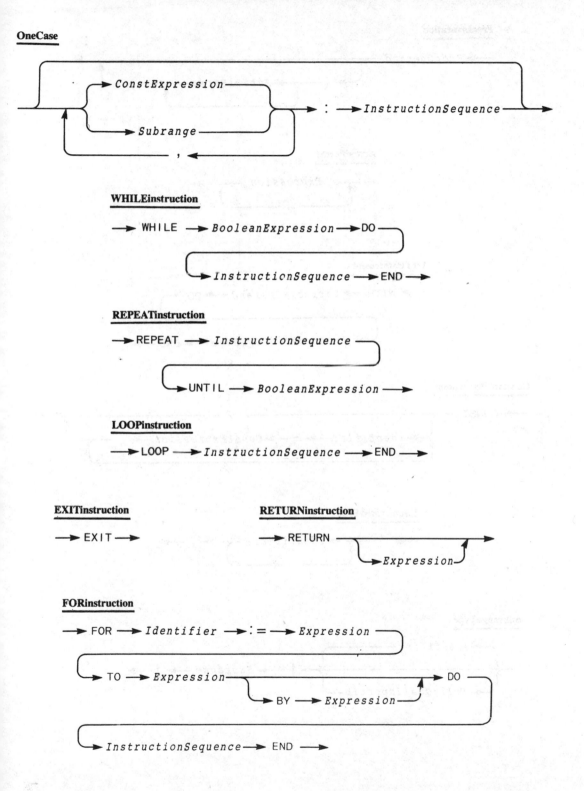

WHILEinstruction

REPEATinstruction

LOOPinstruction

EXITinstruction

RETURNinstruction

FORinstruction

ProcInvocation

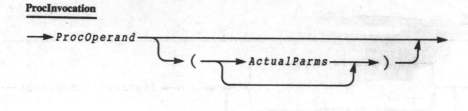

ActualParms

→ *Expression* →
,

WITHstatement

→ WITH → *VariableOperand* → DO
→ *InstructionSequence* → END →

ConstantDeclaration

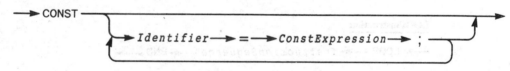

→ CONST
→ *Identifier* → = → *ConstExpression* → ;

EnumeratedType

→ (→ *Identifier* →) →
,

SubrangeType

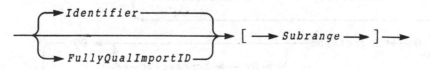

→ *Identifier*
→ *FullyQualImportID* → [→ *Subrange* →] →

ArrayType

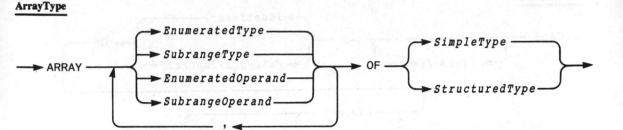

OpenArrayParmDecl

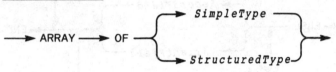

RecordType

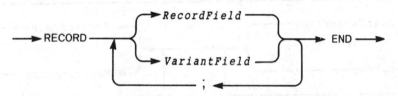

RecordField

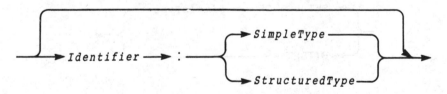

VariantField

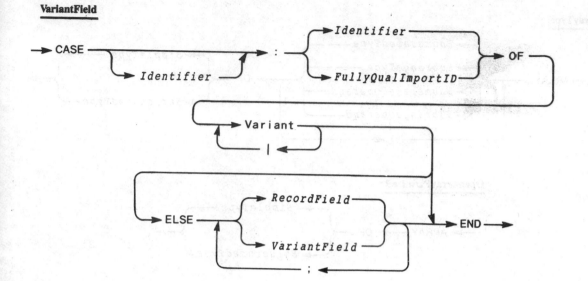

Variant

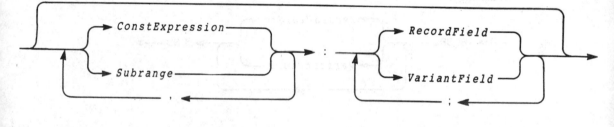

SetType

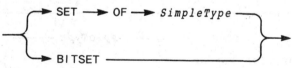

PointerType

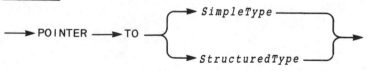

ProcedureType

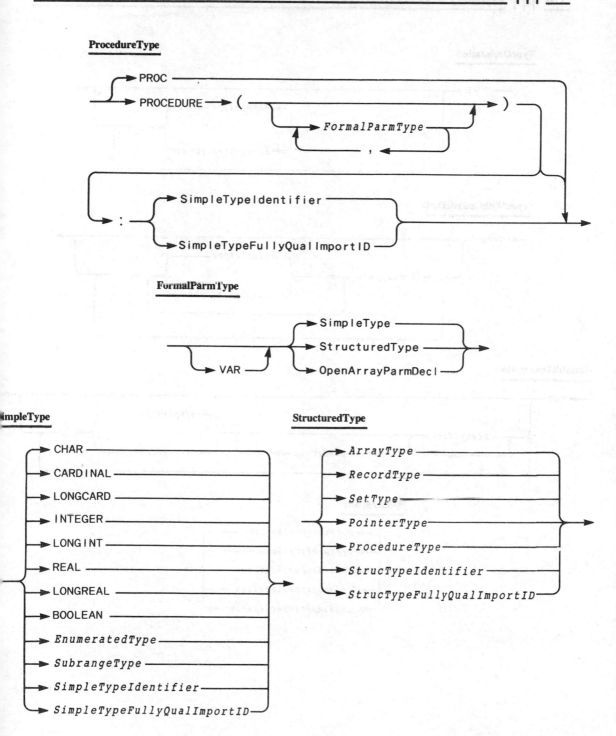

FormalParmType

SimpleType

CHAR
CARDINAL
LONGCARD
INTEGER
LONGINT
REAL
LONGREAL
BOOLEAN
EnumeratedType
SubrangeType
SimpleTypeIdentifier
SimpleTypeFullyQualImportID

StructuredType

ArrayType
RecordType
SetType
PointerType
ProcedureType
StrucTypeIdentifier
StrucTypeFullyQualImportID

NOTE: LONGCARD, LONGINT & LONGREAL *not supported by all implementations.*

TypeDeclaration

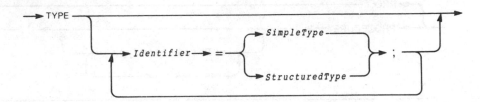

TypeWithOpagueDecl

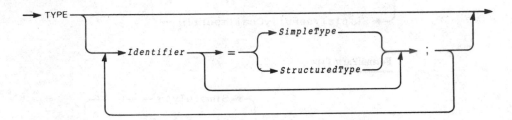

VariableDeclaration

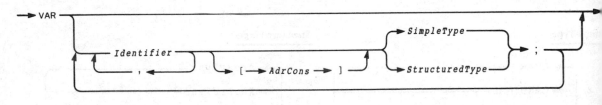

Declarations

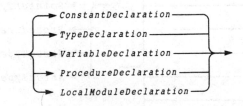

ProcedureHeader

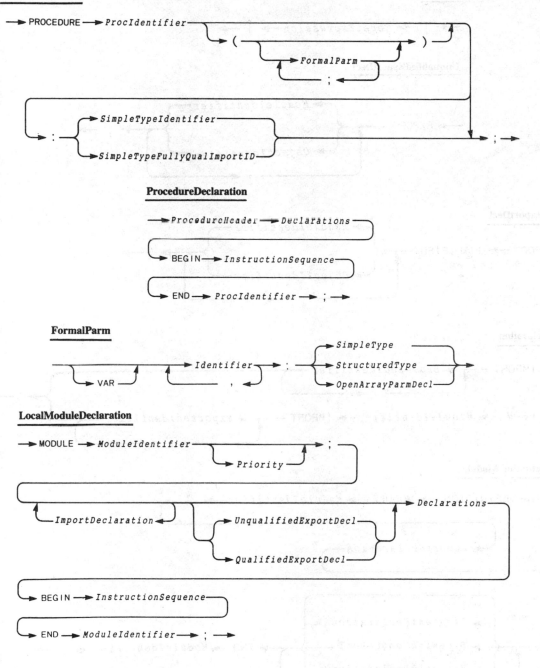

ProcedureDeclaration

FormalParm

LocalModuleDeclaration

Priority

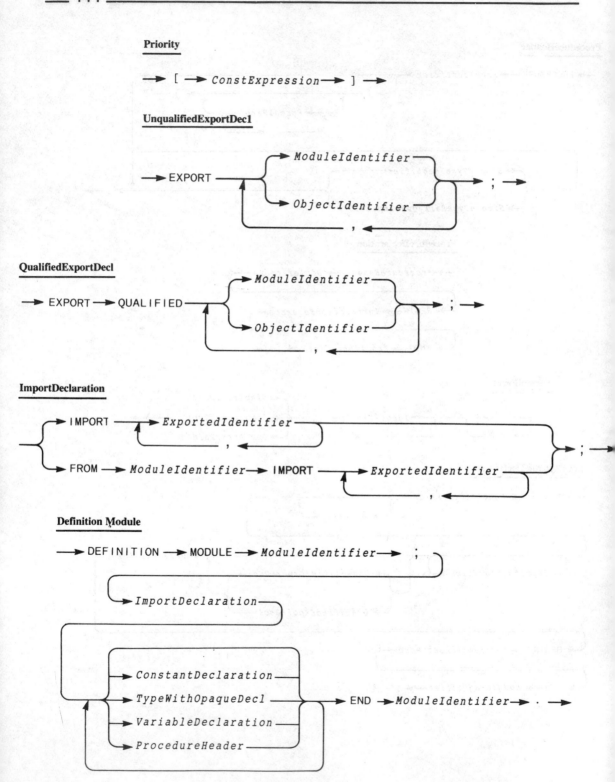

UnqualifiedExportDecl

QualifiedExportDecl

ImportDeclaration

Definition Module

ProgramModule

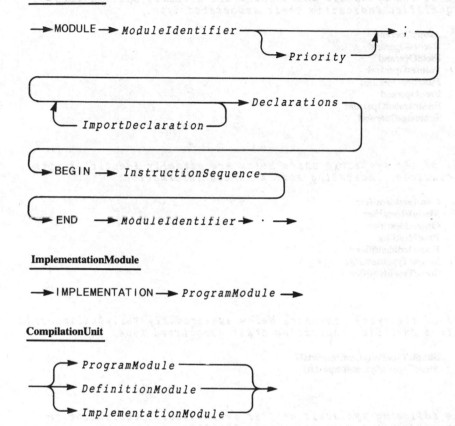

ImplementationModule

CompilationUnit

All of the syntactic units below are actually Operand with a qualifier indicating their associated type:

> **ArrayOperand**
> **RecordOperand**
> **FieldOperand**
> **PointerOperand**
> **FunctionOperand**
> **ProcOperand**
> **EnumeratedOperand**
> **SubrangeOperand**

All of the syntactic units below are actually Identifier with a qualifier indicating some semantic information:

> **ConstantIdentifier**
> **ModuleIdentifier**
> **ObjectIdentifier**
> **ProcIdentifier**
> **ExportedIdentifier**
> **SimpleTypeIdentifier**
> **StrucTypeIdentifier**

All of the syntactic units below are actually FullyQualImportID with a qualifier indicating their associated type:

> **SimpleTypeFullyQualImportID**
> **StrucTypeFullyQualImportID**

The following syntactic unit is syntactically equivalent to Expression, but must be of type BOOLEAN:

> **BooleanExpression**

The following syntactic unit is syntactically equivalent to Expression, but must be one of type CHAR, CARDINAL, INTEGER, LONGINT, BOOLEAN, or enumerated:

> **CaseExpression**

AdrCons *is an absolute address constant. The syntax of this is implementation dependent, and may not even be supported on certain systems.*

B MODULA-2 RESERVED WORDS

Below is a list of reserved words in Modula-2. These identifiers have predefined meaning for Modula-2 compilers and may not be declared for other uses by Modula-2 programs.

AND	ELSIF	LOOP	REPEAT
ARRAY	END	MOD	RETURN
BEGIN	EXIT	MODULE	SET
BY	EXPORT	NOT	THEN
CASE	FOR	OF	TO
CONST	FROM	OR	TYPE
DEFINITION	IF	POINTER	UNTIL
DIV	IMPLEMENTATION	PROCEDURE	VAR
DO	IMPORT	QUALIFIED	WHILE
ELSE	IN	RECORD	WITH

Below is a list of standard identifiers in Modula-2. These identifiers have predefined meaning for Modula-2 compilers but may be redefined by declarations.

ABS	EXCL	LONGCARD	PROC
BITSET	FALSE	LONGINT	REAL
BOOLEAN	FLOAT	LONGREAL	SIZE
CAP	HALT	MAX	TRUE
CARDINAL	HIGH	MIN	TRUNC
CHAR	INC	NIL	VAL
CHR	INCL	ODD	
DEC	INTEGER	ORD	

Below is a list of single and double character combinations that have predefined meaning for Modula-2 compilers.

+	;	^	|
-	(	~	:=
*	)	=	<>
/	[	#	<=
&	]	<	>=
.	{	>	..
,	}	:	

C

ASCII CONVERSION TABLE

Dec	Octal	Char	Dec	Octal	Char	Dec	Octal	Char	Dec	Octal	Char
0	0C	<NUL>	35	43C	#	70	106C	F	105	151C	i
1	1C	<SOH>	36	44C	$	71	107C	G	106	152C	j
2	2C	<STX>	37	45C	%	72	110C	H	107	153C	k
3	3C	<ETX>	38	46C	&	73	111C	I	108	154C	l
4	4C	<EOT>	39	47C	'	74	112C	J	109	155C	m
5	5C	<ENQ>	40	50C	(	75	113C	K	110	156C	n
6	6C	<ACK>	41	51C	)	76	114C	L	111	157C	o
7	7C	<BEL>	42	52C	*	77	115C	M	112	160C	p
8	10C	<BS>	43	53C	+	78	116C	N	113	161C	q
9	11C	<HT>	44	54C	,	79	117C	O	114	162C	r
10	12C	<LF>	45	55C	–	80	120C	P	115	163C	s
11	13C	<VT>	46	56C	.	81	121C	Q	116	164C	t
12	14C	<FF>	47	57C	/	82	122C	R	117	165C	u
13	15C	<CR>	48	60C	0	83	123C	S	118	166C	v
14	16C	<SO>	49	61C	1	84	124C	T	119	167C	w
15	17C	<SI>	50	62C	2	85	125C	U	120	170C	x
16	20C	<DLE>	51	63C	3	86	126C	V	121	171C	y
17	21C	<DC1>	52	64C	4	86	127C	W	122	172C	z
18	22C	<DC2>	53	65C	5	88	130C	X	123	173C	[
19	23C	<DC3>	54	66C	6	89	131C	Y	124	174C	|
20	24C	<DC4>	55	67C	7	90	132C	Z	125	175C	]
21	25C	<NAK>	56	70C	8	91	133C	[	126	176C	~
22	26C	<SYN>	5	71C	9	92	134C	\	127	177C	<DEL>
23	27C	<ETB>	58	72C	:	93	135C	]			
24	30C	<CAN>	59	73C	;	94	136C	^			
25	31C	<EM>	60	74C	<	95	137C	_			
26	32C	<SUB>	61	75C	=	96	140C	`			
27	33C	<ESC>	62	76C	>	97	141C	a			
28	34C	<FS>	63	77C	?	98	142C	b			
29	35C	<GS>	64	100C	@	99	143C	c			
30	36C	<RS>	65	101C	A	100	144C	d			
31	37C	<US>	66	102C	B	101	145C	e			
32	40C	SPACE	67	103C	C	102	146C	f			
33	41C	!	68	104C	D	103	147C	g			
34	42C	''	69	105C	E	104	150C	h			

Notes:

1) SPACE refers to a single blank (space) character.
2) "Dec" column is the ordinal value in decimal.
3) "Octal" column is used for C notation.
4) Unprintable characters, <XX>, described as follows.

Further description of unprintable characters:

Symbol from ASCII table	Keystroke	Meaning
\<NUL\>	. . Ctrl-@	Null or Idle character
\<SOH\>	. . . Ctrl-A	Start of header
\<STX\>	. . . Ctrl-B	Start of text
\<ETX\>	. . . Ctrl-C	End of text
\<EOT\>	. . . Ctrl-D	End of transmission
\<ENQ\>	. . Ctrl-E	Enquiry
\<ACK\>	. . Ctrl-F	Acknowledgement
\<BEL\>	. . . Ctrl-G	Bell character (audible beep)
\<BS\>	. . . . Ctrl-H	Back space
\<HT\>	. . . . Ctrl-I	Horizontal tab
\<LF\>	. . . . Ctrl-J	Line feed
\<VT\>	. . . . Ctrl-K	Vertical tab
\<FF\>	. . . . Ctrl-L	Form feed
\<CR\>	. . . . Ctrl-M	Carriage return
\<SO\>	. . . . Ctrl-N	Shift out
\<SI\>	. . . . . Ctrl-O	Shift in
\<DLE\>	. . . Ctrl-P	Data link escape
\<DC1\>	. . . Ctrl-Q	Device control one (resume transmission)
\<DC2\>	. . . Ctrl-R	Device control two
\<DC3\>	. . . Ctrl-S	Device control three (stop transmission)
\<DC4\>	. . . Ctrl-T	Device control four
\<NAK\>	. . Ctrl-U	Negative acknowledgement
\<SYN\>	. . . Ctrl-V	Synchronous idle
\<ETB\>	. . . Ctrl-W	End of transmitted block
\<CAN\>	. . Ctrl-X	Cancel
\<EM\>	. . . Ctrl-Y	End of medium
\<SUB\>	. . . Ctrl-Z	Special sequence
\<ESC\>	. . . Ctrl-[	Escape
\<FS\>	. . . . Ctrl-\	File separator
\<GS\>	. . . . Ctrl-]	Group separator
\<RS\>	. . . . Ctrl-^	Record separator
\<US\>	. . . . Ctrl-—	Unit separator
\<DEL\>	. . . Del	Delete or Idle

The keystroke column indicates the computer keystroke that most often produces the associated character for input. The notation "Ctrl-?", where ? is some character denotes depressing the "Ctrl" key and striking the key labeled ? at the same time. Many of these unprintable characters are assigned special meanings that differ from one computer system to another.

D AXIOMS AND THEOREMS

Idempotent Axioms
P OR P = P   P & P = P

Identity Axioms
P OR FALSE = P   P OR TRUE = TRUE
P & FALSE = FALSE   P & TRUE = P

Commutative Axioms
P OR Q = Q OR P   P & Q = Q & P

Associative Axioms
(P OR Q) OR R = P OR (Q OR R)
(P & Q) & R = P & (Q & R)

Complementing Axioms
P OR (NOT P) = TRUE   P & (NOT P) = FALSE
NOT TRUE = FALSE   NOT FALSE = TRUE

Axiom of Double Negation
NOT (NOT P) = P

Distributive Axioms
P OR (Q & R) = (P OR Q) & (P OR R)
P & (Q OR R) = (P & Q) OR (P & R)

DeMorgan's Laws
NOT (P OR Q) = (NOT P) & (NOT Q)
NOT (P & Q) = (NOT P) OR (NOT Q)

Implication Definition
P→Q = (NOT P) OR Q

Contrapositive Axiom
P→Q = (NOT Q) → (NOT P)

Equivalence Definition
P=Q = (P→Q) & (Q→P)

E

STANDARD MODULA-2 PROCEDURES AND FUNCTIONS
(Including Storage & InOut)

The procedures and functions that are standard in Modula-2 implementations are described below. These routines may be used without import. The notation "type1 | type2" denotes the fact that either "type1" or "type2" may be used.

ABS
```
desc: absolute value conversion
type: function
spec: PROCEDURE ABS( x : INTEGER  |  REAL )
    : INTEGER  |  REAL;
      (' PRE:  x is assigned          ')
      (' POST: RESULT  = x, if x>=0   ')
      ('               = -x, otherwise ')
      ('                              ')
      ('         RESULT is same type as x ')

e.g.: OneBound := -5;
      AnotherBound := 2;
      Range := ABS( OneBound - AnotherBound );
      (* ASSERT:Range = 7 *)
```

CAP
```
desc: capitalize letters
type: function
spec: PROCEDURE CAP( x : CHAR )
    : CHAR;
      (' PRE:  x is assigned                          ')
      (' POST: RESULT  = uppercase for x,  if "a"<=x<="z" ')
      ('               = x,  otherwise                ')

e.g.: CapInitial := CAP( "t" );
      (* ASSERT: CapInitial = "T" *)
```

CHR
```
desc: convert ordinal to character
type: function
spec: PROCEDURE CHR( x : CARDINAL )
    : CHAR;
      (' PRE:  x is assigned                    ')
      (' POST: RESULT = character with ordinal value x  ')

e.g.: aChar := CHR( 65 );
      (* ASSERT: ORD( aChar ) = 65 *)
```

```
DEC  (* alternative #1 *)
    desc: immediate predecessor
    type: procedure
    spec: PROCEDURE DEC( VAR x : CHAR  |  CARDINAL  |
                                  INTEGER  | enumerated );
          (* PRE:  x-1 >= MIN(type of parameter x)            *)
          (* POST: x = VAL( T, ORD(x<entry>)-1)               *)
          (*                 where x<entry> denotes the value *)
          (*                 x when DEC is invoked AND x is   *)
          (*                 of type T                        *)

    e.g.: aChar := "Z";
          DEC( aChar );
          (* ASSERT: aChar = "Y" *)


DEC  (* alternative #2 *)
    desc: more general predecessor
    type: procedure
    spec: PROCEDURE DEC( VAR x : CHAR  |  CARDINAL  |
                                  INTEGER  | enumerated );
                             s : CARDINAL );
          (* PRE:  x-s >= MIN(type of parameter x)            *)
          (* POST: x = VAL( T, ORD(x<entry>)-s)               *)
          (*                 where x<entry> denotes the value *)
          (*                 x when DEC is invoked AND x is   *)
          (*                 of type T                        *)

    e.g.: AnInt := -4;
          DEC( AnInt, 3);
          (* ASSERT: AnInt = -7 *)


EXCL
    desc: remove element from a set
    type: procedure
    spec: PROCEDURE EXCL( VAR s : SET OF ElementType;
                              e : ElementType );
          (* PRE:  Assigned(s) & Assigned(e) *)
          (* POST: s = s<entry> - {e}        *)

    e.g.: (* ASSERT: aBitset = {2,3,7} *)
          EXCL( aBitset, 1+2 );
          (* ASSERT: aBitset = {2,7} *)


FLOAT
    desc: convert CARDINAL to equivalent value as a REAL type
    type: function
    spec: PROCEDURE FLOAT( x : CARDINAL )
          : REAL;
          (* PRE:  x is assigned *)
          (* POST: RESULT =  x   *)

    e.g.: aReal := FLOAT( 65 );
          (* ASSERT: aReal = 65.0 *)
```

HALT
    desc: *terminate program execution*
    type: *procedure*
    spec: *PROCEDURE HALT;*
        (' POST: transfer control to the end of the   ')
        ('   program (often a dump of run time info ')
        ('   is produced)   ')

    e.g.: HALT

HIGH
    desc: *returns highest index from open array parm (assuming*
          lowest index is adjusted to 0)
    type: *function*
    spec: *PROCEDURE HIGH(a : ARRAY OF AnyType)*
          : CARDINAL;
            (' POST: RESULT = highest index for actual parm a ')
            ('   if lowest index is adjusted to 0 ')

    e.g.: *Suppose the Test procedure is invoked as follows:*

        Test(Array1);

    Also assume that Array1 is declared as follows:

        VAR Array1 : ARRAY [1..10] OF SomeType;

    Then the following is true for this invocation of Test:

        PROCEDURE Test(SomeArray : ARRAY OF SomeType);
            VAR ArrayBound : CARDINAL;
        BEGIN
            ArrayBound := HIGH(SomeArray);
            (* ASSERT: ArrayBound=9 for Array1 as actual parameter *)

INC *(' alternative #1 ')*
    desc: *immediate successor*
    type: *procedure*
    spec: *PROCEDURE INC(VAR x : CHAR | CARDINAL |*
                              INTEGER | ¬enumerated);
            (' PRE: x+1 <= MAX(type of parameter x)   ')
            (' POST: x = VAL(T, ORD(x<entry>)+1)   ')
            ('   where x<entry> denotes the value ')
            ('   x when INC is invoked AND x is   ')
            ('   of type T   ')

    e.g.: aCard := 3;
          INC(aCard);
          (* ASSERT: aCard = 4 *)

```
INC   (* alternative #2 *)
    desc: more general successor
    type: procedure
    spec: PROCEDURE INC( VAR x : CHAR  |  CARDINAL  |
                                         INTEGER  |  enumerated;
                              s : CARDINAL );
             (* PRE:   x+s <= MAX( type of parameter x )        *)
             (* POST:  x = VAL( T, ORD(x<entry>)+s)             *)
             (*                where x<entry> denotes the value *)
             (*                x when INC is invoked AND x is   *)
             (*                of type T                         *)

    e.g.: aChar := "b";
          INC( aChar, 4 );
          (* ASSERT: aChar = "f" *)


INCL
    desc: include an element in a set
    type: procedure
    spec: PROCEDURE INCL( VAR s : SET OF ElementType;
                              e : ElementType );
             (* PRE:  Assigned(s) & Assigned(e) *)
             (* POST: s = s<entry> union {e}     *)

    e.g.: (* ASSERT: aBitset = {2,3,7} *)
          INCL( aBitset, 4 );
          (* ASSERT: aBitset = {2,3,4,7} *)


MAX
    desc: returns largest possible constant of given type
    type: function
    spec: PROCEDURE MAX( t (* see PRE below *) )
          : t ;
             (* PRE:  The actual parameter for t must be some valid *)
             (*       type identifier, either standard or declared  *)
             (* POST: RESULT = largest possible value of type t      *)

    e.g.: aCard := MAX(CARDINAL);
          (* ASSERT: aCard = largest possible value of type CARDINAL *)


MIN
    desc: returns smallest possible constant of given type
    type: function
    spec: PROCEDURE MIN( t (* see PRE below *) )
          : t ;
             (* PRE:  The actual parameter for t must be some valid *)
             (*       type identifier, either standard or declared  *)
             (* POST: RESULT = smallest possible value of type t     *)

    e.g.: aReal := MIN(REAL);
          (* ASSERT: aReal = smallest possible value of type REAL *)
```

ODD
```
    desc: return whether parm is odd (not even)
    type: function
    spec: PROCEDURE ODD( x : CARDINAL  |  INTEGER );
          :BOOLEAN
             (* PRE:  Assigned(x)              *)
             (* POST: RESULT = (x MOD 2) # 0 *)

    e.g.: IF ODD(3) THEN
             WriteString("3 is odd");
          ELSE
             WriteString("3 is even");
          END;
          (* ASSERT: "3 is odd" is output *)
```

ORD
```
    desc: convert to ordinal value
    type: function
    spec: PROCEDURE ORD( x : CHAR  |  CARDINAL  |
                               INTEGER  |  enumerated;
          : CARDINAL ;
             (* PRE:  x is assigned                        *)
             (* POST: RESULT = ordinal value of the machine*)
             (*       representation for x  (ordinal values *)
             (*       are numbered beginning with 0)       *)
             (* NOTE: VAL provides an inverse for ORD      *)

    e.g.: WriteCard( ORD("B"),0 );
          (* ASSERT: ordinal of "B" (66 for ASCII) is output *)
```

SIZE
```
    desc: return size of storage for a variable of given type
    type: function
    spec: PROCEDURE SIZE( x : (* may be any type *) )
          : CARDINAL;
             (* POST: RESULT = number of storage units   *)
             (*                required for the single    *)
             (*                variable x                 *)
             (* NOTE: This is especially useful for       *)
             (*       allocating and deallocating storage *)
             (*       (see the Storage module)            *)

    e.g.: ALLOCATE(VarPointer, SIZE(SomeVar));
          (* ASSERT: a "chunk" of storage of the same      *)
          (*         memory size as SomeVar is allocated *)
          (*         and VarPointer points to it           *)
```

TRUNC
```
    desc: return whole part of a REAL value
    type: function
    spec: PROCEDURE TRUNC( x : REAL )
          : CARDINAL ;
             (* PRE:  x >= 0                         *)
             (* POST: RESULT = integer portion of x *)

    e.g.: aCard := TRUNC( 7.9 );
          (* ASSERT: aCard = 7 *)
```

VAL
    desc: return value of specified type with given ordinal
          value
    type: function
    spec: PROCEDURE VAL((' first parm must be CHAR or CARDINAL ')
                     (' or INTEGER or some enumerated type ')
                     x : CARDINAL);
         : CHAR | CARDINAL | INTEGER | enumerated;
          (' PRE: MIN(first parm) <= x <= MAX(first parm) ')
          (' POST: ORD(RESULT)=x where RESULT has the type ')
          ('   indicated by the first   ')
          ('   parameter   ')

    e.g.: aChar := VAL(CHAR, 65);
          (* ASSERT: ORD(aChar) = 65   *)
          (* NOTE: VAL(CHAR,x) same as CHR(x) *)

NOTES: (1) Any standard or declared type identifier can be used as
            a function to defeat type checking without altering data
            encoding.
       (2) LONGINT, LONGCARD, and LONGREAL are available on some Modula-2
            SYSTEMS and may be used in place of INTEGER, CARDINAL,
            and REAL for some purposes.

Standard Modules

    The Storage and InOut modules defined below are more or less standard in Modula-2 systems. There may be minor differences from one implementation to the next.

DEFINITION MODULE Storage;

    (* This module is required for dynamic data allocation *)
    (* and deallocation.   *)
    (* NOTE: some Modula-2 systems may also include NEW and *)
    (*   DISPOSE procedures, but these are non-standard *)
    (*   as of the 1985 language definition revision.   *)

FROM SYSTEM IMPORT ADDRESS;

PROCEDURE ALLOCATE(VAR SomeAddress : ADDRESS;
                    Size : CARDINAL);
    (* PRE: Assigned(Size)   *)
    (* POST: Size storage units are available for allocation *)
    (*   -> Size units allocated   *)
    (*   AND SomeAddress points to the allocated *)
    (*   storage   *)
    (*   AND   *)
    (*   Size storage units not available for allocation *)
    (*   -> EXECUTION ERROR   *)
    (* NOTE: ADDRESS may be any POINTER type   *)

```
    PROCEDURE DEALLOCATE( VAR SomeAddress : ADDRESS;
                               Size : CARDINAL );
      (* PRE:  Assigned(Size) & Assigned(SomeAddress)      *)
      (* POST: Returns Size storage units pointed at by     *)
      (*       SomeAddress to available pool of storage space *)
      (* NOTE: ADDRESS may be any POINTER type              *)

    PROCEDURE Available( Size : CARDINAL )
    : BOOLEAN;
      (* PRE:  Assigned( Size )                             *)
      (* POST: RESULT = Size storage units are available for *)
      (*                allocation                          *)

END Storage.


DEFINITION MODULE InOut;
    (* This module defines stream style I/O for a single input *)
    (* file and a single output file. The standard input   *)
    (* device (usually the keyboard) and the standard output *)
    (* device (usually the display) are the initial defaults *)
    (* for these files.                                    *)

    CONST
       EOL = 15C; (* The precise constant value is system *)
                  (* dependent.                          *)

    VAR
       Done: BOOLEAN;   (* Assigned TRUE for success FALSE *)
                        (* for failure.                    *)
       termCH : CHAR;   (* used by ReadString *)

    PROCEDURE OpenInput( DefExt : String );
      (* POST: Done = TRUE,  if UserFileName is acceptable *)
      (*            = FALSE,  otherwise                    *)
      (*       & Done  ->  the file named UserFileName     *)
      (*                   is opened for future input from *)
      (*                   the beginning of the file       *)
      (*                                                   *)
      (* NOTES: UserFileName denotes a name specified by   *)
      (*        the user via the standard input device.    *)
      (*        DefExt is the default file name extension.  *)
      (*        "acceptable" means the operating system    *)
      (*        successfully opened the file. Likely       *)
      (*        error: non-existent file                   *)

    PROCEDURE OpenOutput( DefExt : String );
      (* POST: Done = TRUE,  if UserFileName is acceptable *)
      (*            = FALSE,  otherwise                    *)
      (*       & Done  ->  the file named UserFileName     *)
      (*                   is opened for future output from *)
      (*                   the beginning of the file (new  *)
      (*                   file has been created)          *)
      (*                                                   *)
      (* NOTES: UserFileName denotes a name specified by   *)
      (*        the user via the standard input device.    *)
      (*        DefExt is the default file name extension.  *)
      (*        "acceptable" means the operating system    *)
      (*        successfully opened the file. Likely       *)
      (*        errors: invalid file name or no available  *)
      (*        space for file storage                     *)
```

```
PROCEDURE CloseInput;
   (* PRE:  The InOut input is coming from an opened   *)
   (*       data file not yet closed                   *)
   (* POST: The InOut input file is closed & subsequent *)
   (*       input comes from the standard input device. *)
   (* NOTE: All "opened" files must be closed.         *)

PROCEDURE CloseOutput;
   (* PRE:  The InOut output is going to an opened      *)
   (*       data file not yet closed                   *)
   (* POST: The InOut output file is closed & subsequent *)
   (*       output goes to the standard output device. *)
   (* NOTE: All "opened" files must be closed.         *)

PROCEDURE Read( VAR InChar : CHAR );
   (* Post: InChar = next input character              *)
   (*     & Done = TRUE,   if successful input occurred *)
   (*            = FALSE,  if end of file at entry      *)
   (* Note: In many systems no output echo is produced *)

PROCEDURE ReadCard( VAR InCard : CARDINAL );
   (* POST: InCard = cardinal value of input string    *)
   (*      & Done = TRUE,  if cardinal is read         *)
   (* NOTE: This procedure causes all leading blanks and *)
   (*       control characters to be consumed. A valid  *)
   (*       cardinal input consists of all consecutive  *)
   (*       characters in the range from "0" through "9".*)
   (*       In many systems only numeric digits are     *)
   (*       output echoed.                             *)

PROCEDURE ReadInt( VAR InInt : INTEGER );
   (* POST: InInt = integer value of input string      *)
   (*      & Done = TRUE, if cardinal is read          *)
   (* NOTE: This procedure causes all leading blanks and *)
   (*       control characters to be consumed. A valid  *)
   (*       cardinal input consists of all consecutive  *)
   (*       characters in the range from "0" through "9" *)
   (*       optionally preceded by "+" or "-".          *)
   (*       In many systems only numeric constant       *)
   (*       characters are output echoed.              *)

PROCEDURE ReadString( VAR Str : ARRAY OF CHAR );
   (* PRE:  input string must be shorter than          *)
   (*       HIGH(Str) - 1                              *)
   (* POST: Str is assigned input according to the     *)
   (*       following rules:                           *)
   (*    1) Leading non-printable chars & blanks are   *)
   (*       ignored                                    *)
   (*    2) The input string consists of the first     *)
   (*       sequence of 1 or more non-blank,           *)
   (*       printable characters that are input        *)
   (*       (0C is appended)                           *)
   (*    3) Input terminates with a character <= " "   *)
   (*       This character is assigned to termCH       *)

PROCEDURE Write( OutChar : CHAR );
   (* PRE:  OutChar is assigned                        *)
   (* Post: OutChar appended to previous output *)
```

```
PROCEDURE WriteCard( OutCard : CARDINAL;
                     FieldWidth : CARDINAL );
     (* PRE:  OutChar and FieldWidth are assigned           *)
     (* POST: The value of OutCard as a string of decimal    *)
     (*       digit characters is appended to previous output *)
     (*       within a field specified by FieldWidth          *)
     (*                                                        *)
     (* FieldWidth: specifies the minimum number of           *)
     (*        characters that are output. OutCard is         *)
     (*.       preceded by blanks as necessary.               *)

PROCEDURE WriteInt( OutInt : INTEGER;
                    FieldWidth : CARDINAL );
     (* PRE:  OutInt and FieldWidth are assigned             *)
     (* POST: The value of OutInt as a string of decimal digit*)
     (*       characters (preceded by "-" for a negative) is  *)
     (*       appended to previous output within a field      *)
     (*       specified by FieldWidth.                        *)
     (*                                                        *)
     (* FieldWidth: specifies the minimum number of           *)
     (*        characters that are output. OutInt is          *)
     (*        preceded by blanks as necessary.               *)

PROCEDURE WriteString( OutString : ARRAY OF CHAR );
     (* PRE:  OutString is assigned                          *)
     (* POST: The characters from OutString are appended     *)
     (*       to previous output.                            *)
     (* NOTE: ARRAY OF CHAR is compatible with a string      *)
     (*       constant                                       *)

PROCEDURE WriteLn;
     (* POST: The EOL character is appended to previous      *)
     (*       output.                                        *)
     (* NOTE: In some Modula-2 systems the output of a       *)
     (*       line does not occur until WriteLn executes.    *)

END InOut.
```

SOLUTIONS TO
SELECTED EXERCISES

SOLUTIONS FOR CHAPTER 1 EXERCISES

1. a) 1. Define the problem.
      2. Design a solution.
      3. Code the program.
      4. Maintain the program.

   b) User, systems analyst (defines the problem together with the user,) designer (designs a solution, an algorithm,) coder (translates algorithm to code,) maintenance programmer (maintains the code.)

   c) 1. problem definition (after defining the problem)
      2. algorithm - pseudocode (after designing a solution)
      3. program (after coding the program)

   d) Documentation is ongoing and an integral part of each step.

2. Pseudocode is used by the systems anyalyst and coder to express the algorithm. It cannot be executed by a computer like a program.

4. It should be:
      1. complete
      2. precise
      3. understandable

5. a) 1. problem title - single sentence or phrase that captures the basic nature of the problem succinctly.
      2. general description - describes problem more completely, but does not include all of the detail for input form, output form or error cases.
      3. input form - fills in specifics for expected input.
      4. output form - fills in specifics for expected output
      5. errors - lists erroneous and unexpected input cases and resulting output
      6. example - illustrates a typical example program execution

7. a) top down
   b) bottom up

PROGRAMMING PROJECT SOLUTION

1. *Input*

Input consists of two or more integers, one per line. The first integer must be less than or equal to the second, because they establish the range. Input is terminated by a 0 input. This input is not processed.

Def: integer - 1 or more consecutive decimal digits optionally preceded by a plus sign " + " or minus sign "–".

Output

The first output line is:

The range is <lb> to <ub>

where <lb> denotes the first input integer and <ub> is the second.

Every input integer after the first two which has a value that is greater than or equal to the first input and less than or equal to the second causes an additional line to be output with the following form:

<inp> is within the range

where <inp> denotes the input integer.

SOLUTIONS FOR CHAPTER 2 EXERCISES

1. An unassigned variable is one which has not yet been assigned a value during execution.

2. a) halcost is not a declared variable (Note: Modula-2 is case sensitive.)
   c) A variable must appear to the left of : = .
   e) -4 is an INTEGER constant, but
   g) ** is not a valid operand
   i) There is a type mismatch because 17 is a CARDINAL and 2.0 is a REAL.

3. VAR
       Answer : CHAR;
       Profit : REAL;
       StoreNum : CARDINAL;

4. a) CARDINAL
   b) CHAR

5. a) correct, CHAR type
   c) correct, REAL type
   e) correct, CHAR type

6. a) 66

7. a) 1.1+2.25*4.0+(-6.4)*5.0/3.2*3.7-2.8
        6   2   7 1   3   4   5   8

   c) (((6+2)*(7-3)) MOD (5+(6+4)))+3
       1   4 2   6   5   3   7

8. a) -28.7
   c) 5

9. a) dBsSold = 15 & dBsOnHand = 1 & DiFisSold = 30

10. a) TotalIncome + 17
    b) TRUNC(IncomePerWeek)
    d) ORD(dBCode) + ORD(DiFiCode) + ORD(HalCode)
       + ORD(WORDCode) + ORD(TempCode)

11. a) IncomePerDay := FLOAT(CARDINAL (TotalIncome))
                           /FLOAT(Days)

14. a) FROM InOut IMPORT ReadInt, Write;

15. a) !?
    XXXYY

16. a) input file: source file
    output file: compiled image

    b) no input file - input is typed by the user
    output file: source file

17. a) execution
    b) syntax

18. a) executing code
    b) compiler

SOLUTIONS FOR CHAPTER 3 EXERCISES

1. There are many ways to complete the parts of this problem. The solutions below illustrate with a single possibility.

   a) (* examine past education records *)
      (* examine past work related experiences *)

   b (* prepare milker *)
      (* position cow in stanchion *)
      (* clean udder *)
      (* place milker on cow *)
      (* take milker off cow *)
      (* place milk in cooler *)

4. This would save the one level of refinement that replaces a left turn by 3 RightTurns with this new LeftTurn.

SOLUTIONS FOR CHAPTER 4 EXERCISES

1. a) Sequence-the "first step" followed by the "second step"
      Abstraction-"The first step is..."
      Selection-"If hubcap is removed..."
      Repetition-"All lug nuts must be replaced..."

2. a) XHERE
      THERE
   c) 131

3. a) part (a) has no parameters
      part (c) Char1, Char2 and Sum
   b) part (a) has no parameters
      part (c) "A", "B" and Total for SumOfOrds Total; and 0
      for WriteCard

4. a) part (c) Char1 and Char2
   b) part (c) Sum

5. & 6.
   a) PROCEDURE WriteHERE;
      (* PRE: no precondition =TRUE   *)
      (* POST: "HERE" is output on the next line *)

```
c) PROCEDURE SumOfOrds(  Char1 : CHAR;
                         Char2 : CHAR;
                    VAR Sum : CARDINAL );
```
(* PRE: Char1 & Char2 are assigned *)
(* POST: Sum = ORD(Char1) + ORD(Char2) *)

SOLUTIONS FOR CHAPTER 5 EXERCISES

1. a) CDXYXYXYXYXYXY
   c) Z

2. a)
```
IF Hrs > 40.0 THEN
    Wages = Hrs * HrWage
ELSE
    Wages = ((Hrs-40.0)*1.5 + 40.0) * HrWage
END
```

   c)
```
IF Age> 65 THEN
    (* Cost is discounted *)
END
```

   d)
```
IF Single THEN
    (* use single tax table *)
ELSE
    (* use married tax table *)
END
```

   g)
```
IF (* ProgramDue *) THEN
    (* don't go to class *)
END
```

3. Loop 2 has a different loop condition than Loop 1 or Loop 3. Loop 3 does not alter the value of OutCount within the body of the loop. The result is...

Loop 1 outputs: 5	Loop 3 outputs: 5
6	5
7	5
8	5
9	.
10	.
	. (* an infinite loop *)

Loop 2 outputs: 5
6
7
8
9

4. a)
```
Counter := 5;
WHILE Counter<=12 DO
    WriteCard( Counter, 0 );
    WriteLn;
    Counter := Counter + 1;
END
```

   c)
```
Counter := 2;
WHILE Counter <=64 DO
    WriteCard( Counter, 0 );
    WriteLn;
    Counter := Counter * 2;
END
```

5. a) trailer loops: i)
        counter loop: iii)

   b) i) WHILE InputChar # " " DO
       iii) WHILE InputCount < = 50 DO

   c) i) Read(InputChar)
       iii) Read(InputChar);
            InputCount := InputCount +1

   d) i) Read(InputChar);
       iii) InputCount := 1;

SOLUTIONS FOR CHAPTER 6 EXERCISES

1. a)

P	Q	(NOT P) OR (P&Q)
F	F	T
F	T	T
T	F	F
T	T	T

   c)

P	Q	R	(P→Q) & ((Q→P) OR R)
F	F	F	T
F	F	T	T
F	T	F	F
F	T	T	T
T	F	F	F
T	F	T	F
T	T	F	T
T	T	T	T

d)

P	Q	(P & (NOT Q))	=	((NOT P) OR Q)
F	F			F
F	T			F
T	F			F
T	T			F

2. a) ZeroCounter AND Max99
   b) Max99 OR InOrder
   f) (NOT ZeroCounter) $\rightarrow$ Max99

3. a) Distributive

4. (NOT P) OR Q

6. a) (A<B) AND (B<C) AND (C<D)
   c) (IsRound AND (Count = 17)) OR (NOT IsRound AND (Count = 0))

SOLUTIONS FOR CHAPTER 7 EXERCISES

1. a) FrstParm & ScndParm
   b) Thrd Parm & Frth Parm
   c) D23A
      AB3A
   d) Actual parameters for parameters passed by value *must* be variables.
      "3" and "4" are constants, not variables.
   e) PRE: FrstParm and FrthParm must be assigned
   f) POST: A line is output containing FrstParm<entry>,
            "2", "3", FrthParm<entry>
            & FrthParm=FrstParm<entry>
            & ThrdParm="3"

3. a) 14
   c) "G"

4. a) 4
   b) They both may increase the value of their parameter by one.
   c) INC is a procedure, while Increase is a function. INC can operate on CHAR
      or CARDINAL or INTEGER, not just INTEGER like Increase.

5. a)

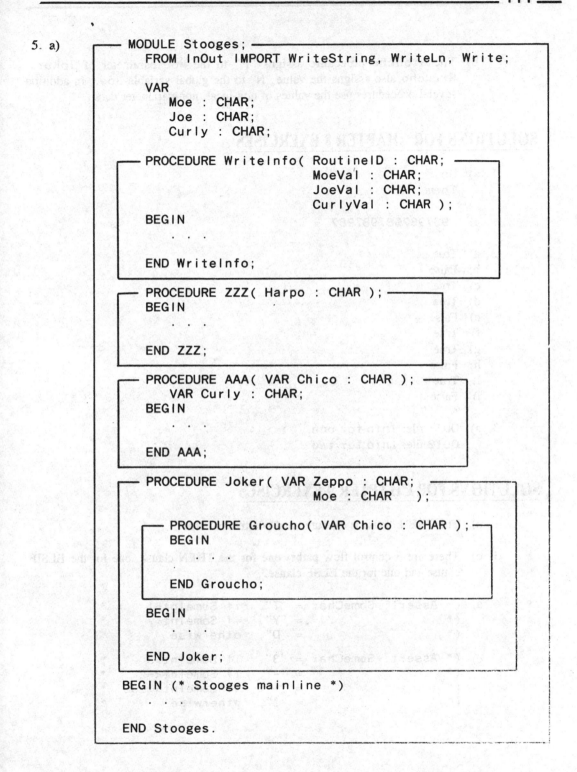

```
MODULE Stooges;
    FROM InOut IMPORT WriteString, WriteLn, Write;

    VAR
        Moe : CHAR;
        Joe : CHAR;
        Curly : CHAR;

    PROCEDURE WriteInfo( RoutineID : CHAR;
                         MoeVal : CHAR;
                         JoeVal : CHAR;
                         CurlyVal : CHAR );
    BEGIN
        . . .

    END WriteInfo;

    PROCEDURE ZZZ( Harpo : CHAR );
    BEGIN
        . . .

    END ZZZ;

    PROCEDURE AAA( VAR Chico : CHAR );
        VAR Curly : CHAR;
    BEGIN
        . . .

    END AAA;

    PROCEDURE Joker( VAR Zeppo : CHAR;
                     Moe : CHAR     );

        PROCEDURE Groucho( VAR Chico : CHAR );
        BEGIN

        END Groucho;

    BEGIN
        . . .

    END Joker;

BEGIN (* Stooges mainline *)
    . . .

END Stooges.
```

b) The Groucho procedure assigns "F" to the Moe parameter of Joker. Groucho also assigns the value "N" to the global variable Joe. In addition several procedures use the values of non-local, non-parameter data.

SOLUTIONS FOR CHAPTER 8 EXERCISES

1. a) Us
      Them

   c) 987987987987987

2. a) True
   b) False
   c) True
   d) True
   e) False
   f) True
   g) True
   h) False
   i) True
   j) False

3. a) OUT1 file: Info for one.
      Out2 file: Info for two.

SOLUTIONS FOR CHAPTER 9 EXERCISES

1. a) The THEN clause is executed and positive is output.

3. c) There are 3 control flow paths, one for the THEN clause, one for the ELSIF clause and one for the ELSE clause.

6. a)
```
(* Assert: SomeChar = "T",   if SomeInt=1       *)
(*                  = "Y",   if SomeInt=7       *)
(*                  = "D",   otherwise          *)
```

   c)
```
(* Assert: SomeChar = "3",   if SomeInt=3       *)
(*                  = "-",   if SomeInt<=2      *)
(*                  = "+",   if SomeInt>=100    *)
(*                  = "?",   otherwise          *)
```

```
7.
PROCEDURE YearAttending( SemesterAttending )
:   CARDINAL;
        (* PRE:   SemesterAttending is assigned                    *)
        (* POST: RESULT = 1,   if SemesterAttending is 1 or 2      *)
        (*             = 2,   if SemesterAttending is 3 or 4      *)
        (*             = 3,   if SemesterAttending is 5 or 6      *)
        (*             = 4,   if SemesterAttending is 7,8 or 9    *)
        (*             = 0,   otherwise                          *)
BEGIN
    CASE  SemesterAttending  OF
        1,2    : RETURN 1  |
        3,4    : RETURN 2  |
        5,6    : RETURN 3  |
        7,8,9  : RETURN 4
    ELSE
        RETURN 0
    END
END YearAttending;
```

SOLUTIONS FOR CHAPTER 10 EXERCISES

```
1. a)  024681012141618
   b)  34

2. a)  (* Assert: Suma = 0+2+4+ ... +18 = 90 & CountByTwo = 20 *)

3. a)  (* INV: Suma = 0+2+4+ ... + (CountByTwo−2) *)
       (*        AND CountByTwo MOD 2                *)
       (*        AND CountByTwo< = 20               *)

5. b)  (* ASSERT: Number is a cardinal & Number>1 *)
       Divisor := Number − 1;
       IF Number MOD Divisor # 0 THEN
           REPEAT
               DEC( Divisor );
               (* INV: No cardinal in the range between Divisor *)
               (*        and Number evenly divides Number       *)
               (*      & 1<=Divisor<Number                     *)
           UNTIL Number MOD Divisor = 0
       END
       (* ASSERT: Divisor is the greatest even divisor of *)
       (*          Number                                 *)

6. a)  4
```

```
7. a) ReadInt( LastIn );
      WHILE (* INV: LastIn is the last input integer *)
            (*       & All input prior to LastIn #-33 *)
      LastIn#-33 DO
         ReadInt( LastIn );
      END;
      (* Assert: LastIn is the last input integer & LastIn=-33
      (*          & All input prior to LastIn#-33
```

8. a) REPEAT because the loop must be executed at least once.

SOLUTIONS FOR CHAPTER 11 EXERCISES

1. a) ShipType, MilitaryShip, FamousVessel, MerchantFleetRange

   b) SOS, MerchantFleetMax, Trawler, Freighter, OilTanker, TowBoat, Cargo, Liner, PTboat, Cruiser, Destroyer, Battleship, Clermont, Constitution, Lusitania, Maine, Monitor, Merrimack, Titanic

   c) ShipA may store any of the following:

   Trawler, Freighter, OilTanker, TowBoat, Cargo, Liner, PTboat, Cruiser, Destroyer, Battleship

   ShipB may store any of the following:

   Clermont, Constitution, Lusitania, Maine, Monitor, Merrimack, Titanic

   Warship may store any of the following:

   PTboat, Cruiser, Destroyer, Battleship

   d) ShipA := TowBoat

   e) WriteString(SOS);
      WriteString(SOS);
      WriteString(SOS);

2. Below is a list of the invalid instructions with reasons.

   a) Cent has an enuerated type, but "Steel" is a string type constant. The double quotes must be removed.
   c) valid

e) Dollar is a constant and can not be assigned a value.

g) valid

i) Programmer defined types are not permitted as actual parameters for INC.

k) The first actual parameter of VAL must be a type, not a a variable.

m) Subranges are types. A subrange cannot be assigned to a variable.

o) Barber is not within the range of constants allowed for NewQuarters

q) valid

s) Addition is not a valid operation for enumerated type constants, such as Large.

u) Programmer defined types, like QuarterType, cannot be assigned values.

3. a) *never* results in a bounds violation

d) *never* results in a bounds violation

e) *never* results in a bounds violation

g) *may* result in a bounds violation (when Cent > Eagle)

i) *never* results in a bounds violation

k) *may* result in a bounds violation (when Change = 100)

m) *may* result in a bounds violation (when PrewarCent = Large)

o) *may* result in a bounds violation (when Int = MIN(INTEGER))

q) *may* result in a bounds violation (when Card > 100)

s) *may* result in a bounds violation (when Int < 0)

u) *never* results in a bounds violation

w) *definitely* results in a bounds violation

4. a) incompatible

c) identical

e) assignment compatible

g) compatible

i) compatible

5. The invalid declarations and reasons are listed below:

a) valid

c) valid

e) valid

g) A subrange type, like [2..25], cannot be the value of a constant.

i) valid

k) A programmer defined type cannot be declared as a constant, such as OrchestraSeats.

m) valid

o) A programmer defined type cannot be declared as an expression. You may also note that the expression is invalid.

q) The square brackets [ ] must be replaced by parentheses ( ) for an enumerated type.

s) An enumeration is a list of undeclared identifiers, but BrassFamily and StringFamily are already declared as programmer defined types.

u) Coronet, Trombone, and Tuba are constants of another type and cannot be redeclared within the same program unit.

6. The first set of declarations includes a separate programmer defined type, TurtleType. This can be used to specify the type of additional variables or formal parameters. Without this separate type it is impossible to have any other identifiers of identical type, and compatible types are only possible as a subrange.

7. TYPE
```
DeciduousVarieties = [Ash..Maple];
```

10. a) CONST
```
LitersPerGallon = 3.785;
```
c) CONST
```
TwentyBlanks = "
```

11. a) TYPE
```
PlanetType = (Mercury, Venus, Earth, Mars, Jupiter,
              Saturn, Uranus, Neptune, Pluto);
```
f) TYPE
```
SmallLetters = ["a".."z"];
```

12. PROCEDURE ReadDirection(VAR Dir : Directions);
```
          (* POST: A single input character, InChar, is read *)
          (*       Dir = North,  if Inchar is "N" or "n"      *)
          (*           = East,   if Inchar is "E" or "e"      *)
          (*           = South,  if Inchar is "S" or "s"      *)
          (*           = West,   if Inchar is "W" or "w"      *)
          (*           = DirectionUnknown,  otherwise         *)
    VAR
       InChar : CHAR;
    BEGIN
       Read( InChar );
       CASE CAP(InChar) OF
          "N" :  Dir := North  |
          "E" :  Dir := East   |
          "S" :  Dir := South  |
          "W" :  Dir := West
       ELSE
          Dir := DirectionUnknown
       END
    END ReadDirection;
```

SOLUTIONS FOR CHAPTER 12 EXERCISES

1. Every item of CapCount is of type CARDINAL.
   Every item of Contents is of type LiquidMeasure.

2. The size of CapCount is 26 items.
   The size of Contents is 101 items.

3. a) `CapCount["T"] : = 17;`

   c) (* assume SomeChar is a CHAR variable *)
      ```
      FOR SomeChar: ="A" TO "Z" DO
          CapCount[SomeChar] : = 0;
      END;
      ```

4. a)
   ```
   FOR SomeCard : = 6 TO 24 DO
       WriteCard( SomeCard,3 );
   END;
   ```

   d)
   ```
   FOR SomeChar : = "C" TO "L" DO
       Write( SomeChar );
   END;
   ```

5. a) The BY clause contains a variable, N. This clause may only contain a constant.

   c) The control variable, I, is of CARDINAL type, but all of the values in the FOR
      are negative.

6. a)
   ```
   FOR Cur:=1    (* INV: For all subscripts, s, such that      *)
                 (*        (1<=s<=Cur-1)  A[s]=0     AND   Cur<=201 *)
   TO 200 DO
       A[Cur] := 0;
   END;
   ```

   c)
   ```
   FOR Cur:=1    (* INV: For all subscripts, s, such that      *)
                 (*         (1<=s<=Cur-1)  A[s]=s+1  AND   Cur<=201 *)
   TO 200 DO
       A[Cur] := Cur+1;
   END;
   ```

10. Use the following declarations:

    ```
    TYPE
        NauticalMeasures =
             (Span, Fathom, NauticalMile, League);
    VAR
        FeetEquivalent : ARRAY NauticalMeasures OF REAL;
    ```

    The above array is initialized as shown on the opposite page:

```
FeetEquivalent[Span]  := 0.75;
FeetEquivalent[Fathom]  := 6.0;
FeetEquivalent[NauticalMile]  := 6076.1;
FeetEquivalent[League]  := 18228.3;
```

The translation of the code from the problem is:

```
DistanceInFeet := FeetEquivalent[NauticalDistance];
(* ASSERT: DistanceInFeet = equivalent of        *)
(*          NauticalDistance expressed in feet *)
```

SOLUTIONS FOR CHAPTER 13 EXERCISES

1. a) SumMatrix has 2 dimensions.
   c) IsCardInHand has 2 dimensions.

2. a) SumMatrix contains 1000 INTEGER items.
   c) IsCardInHand contains 65 BOOLEAN items.

3. a) SumMatrix[3,15] := SumMatrix[3,15] + 1:
       OR
       INC(SumMatrix[3,15]);

4. FOR FaceVal := two TO ace DO
       FOR SomeSuit := Hearts TO Spades DO
           IsCardInHand[FaceValue,SomeSuit] := FALSE;
       END:
   END;
   (* Assert: All of IsCardInHand[two..ace,Hearts..Spades] =FALSE *)
   IsInCardHand[queen,Hearts] := TRUE;
   IsInCardHand[ace,Spades] := TRUE;
   IsInCardHand[nine,Hearts] := TRUE;
   IsInCardHand[jack,Diamonds] := TRUE;
   IsInCardHand[ace,Clubs] := TRUE;

6. PROCEDURE WriteTotalLotArea(VAR Lots : CityLotArray);
           (* PRE: All of the following items are assigned: *)
           (*   Lots[Johnson..Sorenson,1..10,1..100,Length..Width] *)
           (* POST: The total square feet of all above lots is   *)
           (*   output   *)
```
```

```
        VAR
            Div : Divisions;
            Sec : SectorRange;
            Num : LotNumberRange;
            TotalSqFeet : CARDINAL;
    BEGIN
        TotalSqFeet := 0;
        FOR Div := Johnson TO Sorenson DO
            FOR Sec := 1 TO 10 DO
                FOR Num := 1 TO 100 DO
                    TotalSqFeet := TotalSqFeet+(Lots[Div,Sec,Num,Length]
                                             * Lots[Div,Sec,Num,Width]);
                END;
            END;
        END;
        WriteCard( TotalSqFeet,0 );
    END WriteTotalLotArea;
```

8. TYPE
```
        VehicleType = (Subcompact, Compact, Sedan, StWagon, Van);
        RentalFleetType = ARRAY VehicleType,[1..4] OF CARDINAL;
    VAR
        FleetMileage = RentalFleetType;
```

10. TYPE
```
        String20 = ARRAY [0..20] OF CHAR;
        BoxNameArray = ARRAY ["A".."J"],[1..50] OF String20;
    VAR
        POBoxOwner : BoxNameArray;
```

13. Use the following declartion:

```
        VAR
            Implies : ARRAY BOOLEAN,BOOLEAN OF BOOLEAN;
```

Implies can be used as (→) after these initializations:

```
    Implies[TRUE,TRUE]      := TRUE;
    Implies[TRUE,FALSE]     := FALSE;
    Implies[FALSE,TRUE]     := TRUE;
    Implies[FALSE,FALSE]    := TRUE;
```

```
17. PROCEDURE AddMatrices(        Srce1 : MatrixForm;
                                  Srce2 : MatrixForm;
                              VAR MatrixSum : MatrixForm );
        (* PRE:  Srce1 and Srce2 are completely assigned      *)
        (* POST: For all subscripts, r & c, such that          *)
        (*         (1<=r<=RowMax) & (1<=c<=ColMax)  the following *)
        (*         results:  MatrixSum[r,c]=Srce1[r,c]+Srce2[r,c] *)
    VAR
      R : CARDINAL;
      C : CARDINAL;
    BEGIN
      FOR R:=1  (* INV: MatrixSum[1..R-1,1..ColMax] properly *)
                (*        assigned  AND  R <= RowMax+1          *)
      TO RowMax DO
        FOR C:=1  (* INV: MatrixSum[R,1..C-1] properly *)
                  (*        assigned  AND  C <= ColMax+1 *)
        TO ColMax DO
          MatrixSum[R,C] := Srce1[R,C] + Srce2[R,C];
        END;
      END;
    END AddMatrices;
```

SOLUTIONS FOR CHAPTER 14 EXERCISES

1. a) VisitingProf.Age
   c) VisitingProf.Name
   e) VisitingProf.CurrentCourseLoad.Course[1].Dept
   g) ScienceProf[173].HomeDept

   i) VisitingProf.Name.FirstInit := "M";
      VisitingProf.Name.Last := "Roecker";
      VisitingProf.Age := 52;
      VisitingProf.HomeDept := Chemistry;
      VisitingProf.AnnualSalary := 31000;
      VisitingProf.CurrentCourseLoad.Count := 3;
      VisitingProf.CurrentCourseLoad.Course[1].Dept := Chemistry;
      VisitingProf.CurrentCourseLoad.Course[1].Number := 100;
      VisitingProf.CurrentCourseLoad.Course[2].Dept := Chemistry;
      VisitingProf.CurrentCourseLoad.Course[2].Number := 203;
      VisitingProf.CurrentCourseLoad.Course[3].Dept := Math;
      VisitingProf.CurrentCourseLoad.Course[3].Number := 161;

```
j) WITH VisitingProf DO
       Name.FirstInit := "M";
       Name.Last := "Roecker";
       Age := 52;
       HomeDept := Chemistry;
       AnnualSalary := 31000;
       CurrentCourseLoad.Count := 3;
       CurrentCourseLoad.Course[1].Dept := Chemistry;
       CurrentCourseLoad.Course[1].Number := 100;
       CurrentCourseLoad.Course[2].Dept := Chemistry;
       CurrentCourseLoad.Course[2].Number := 203;
       CurrentCourseLoad.Course[3].Dept := Math;
       CurrentCourseLoad.Course[3].Number := 161;
    END;

n) PROCEDURE WriteAllProfs;
           (* PRE:  ScienceProfs[1..ProfessorCount] is  *)
           (*       completely assigned                 *)
           (* POST: ScienceProfs[1..ProfessorCount] are *)
           (*       output                              *)
           (* NOTE: This accesses ScienceProfs as a     *)
           (*       GLOBAL DATA STRUCTURE!!             *)
       VAR
           Prof : CARDINAL;
    BEGIN
       FOR Prof:=1    (* INV: ScienceProfs[1..Prof-1] are    *)
                      (*      output & Prof<=ProfessorCount+1 *)
       TO ProfessorCount DO
           WriteProf(ScienceProfs[Prof]);
       END;
    END WriteAllProfs;

2. a) TYPE
       VegetableType = (Corn, Bean, Tomato, Carrot, Pea, Other);
       FruitColor = (Yellow, Orange, Red, Green, OtherColor);
       OneVegieType = RECORD
                          Variety : VegetableType;
                          GrowingPeriod : CARDINAL;
                          EdibleColor : FruitColor
                      END;
    VAR
       OneVegetable : OneVegieType;
```

c) TYPE
```
        String15 = ARRAY [0..15] OF CHAR;
        StockType = RECORD
                        Name : String15;
                        High : REAL;
                        Low : REAL;
                        Change : REAL
                    END;
        ArrayOf500Stocks = ARRAY [1..500] OF StockType;
    VAR
        Stocks : ArrayOf500Stocks;
```

e) TYPE
```
        String20 = ARRAY [0..20] OF CHAR;
        IndexEntryType = RECORD
                            Word : String20;
                            ReferenceCount : [1..15];
                            References : ARRAY [1..15] OF CARDINAL
                        END;
        IndexArrayType = ARRAY [1..1000] OF IndexEntryType;
    VAR
        Index : IndexArrayType;
```

3. a) MostImportantPossession.PurchaseDate.Year
   c) MostImportantPossession.SquareFeet
   e) MostImportantPossession.Article := Home;

   g) WITH MostImportantPossession DO
```
        Article := Furniture;
        FurniturePiece := Desk;
        PurchaseDate.Month := 5;
        PurchaseDate.Day := 9;
        PurchaseDate.Year := 1951;
        HundredsVal := 5;
    END;
```

4. a) WITH Drawings[3] DO
```
        DrawTag := Point;
        Location.Row := 123;
        Location.Col := 10;
    END;
```

```
c) WITH Drawings[3] DO
       DrawTag  := Line;
       LeftEnd.Row  := 5;
       LeftEnd.Col  := 10;
       RightEnd.Row := 20;
       RightEnd.Col := 50;
   END;
```

SOLUTIONS FOR CHAPTER 15 EXERCISES

1. a) ZYX
   b) ZZZ

2. a)   4   7 10 10   7   4
   b) −2   1   4   7 10 10   7   4   1 −2
   c) 11 11

6. a) The procedure below must be invoked with RecFOR(N) to duplicate the
       required task:

```
PROCEDURE RecFOR( N : INTEGER );
   (* PRE:  N is assigned                          *)
   (* POST: all integers from 1 thru N are output *)

   PROCEDURE RecursiveLoop( I : INTEGER;
                            N : INTEGER );
   BEGIN
      IF I>N THEN
   RETURN
      ELSE
         WriteInt( I,0 );
         RecursiveLoop( I+1,N );
      END;
   END RecursiveLoop;

BEGIN (* RecFor *)
   RecursiveLoop(1,N);
END RecFor;
```

7. a)

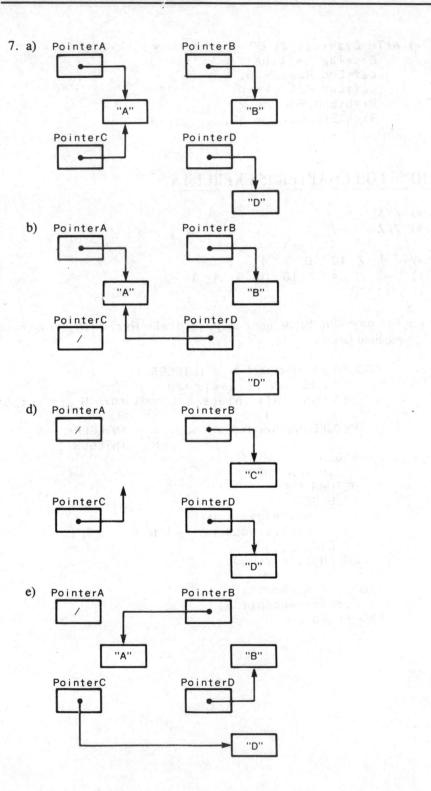

b)

d)

e)

8.

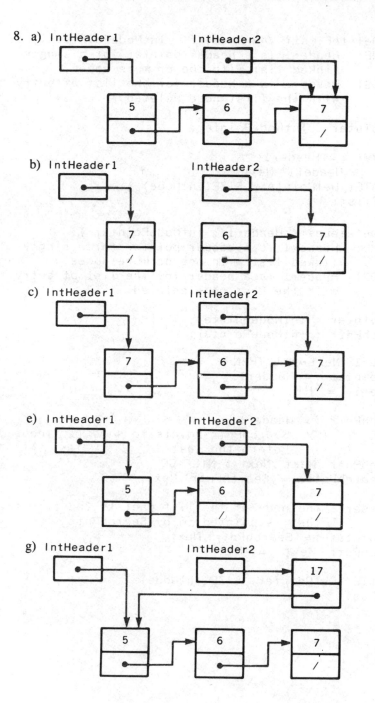

```
9. a) PROCEDURE DeleteFirst( VAR Header1 : IntNodePointer );
            (* PRE:  Header1 is a header pointer for a singly  *)
            (*       linked list with one or more nodes.       *)
            (* POST: Header1 is a header for the list at entry *)
            (*       with the first node deleted.              *)
      VAR
         DelPointer : IntNodePointer;
      BEGIN
         DelPointer := Header1;
         Header1 := Header1^.Next;
         DEALLOCATE( DelPointer, SIZE(IntNode) );
      END DeleteFirst;


   b) PROCEDURE DeleteLast( Header1 : IntNodePointer );
            (* PRE:  Header1 is a header pointer for a singly  *)
            (*       linked list with one or more nodes.       *)
            (* POST: Header1 is a header for the list at entry *)
            (*       with the Last node deleted.               *)
      VAR
         DelPointer : IntNodePointer;
         SearchPntr : IntNodePointer;
      BEGIN
         IF Header1^.Next=NIL THEN
            DelPointer := Header1;
            Header1 := NIL;
         ELSE
            SearchPntr := Header1;
            WHILE  (* INV: SearchPntr points to some list node *)
                   (*          before the last                 *)
            SearchPntr^.Next^.Next # NIL  DO
               SearchPntr := SearchPntr^.Next;
            END;
            (* Assert: The node of the list that is 2nd from the *)
            (*         last is pointed to by SearchPntr          *)
            DelPointer := SearchPntr^.Next;
            SearchPntr^.Next := NIL;
         END;
         DEALLOCATE( DelPointer, SIZE(IntNode) );
      END DeleteLast;
```

10. a) < 77, 17 >
    c) < 203, 16, 17 >

11. a) < 32, 33, 34, 2222 >

13. a) DinerSet{CheeseBurger,Chips,Coke}
    c) DinerSet{Chips}
    e) DinerSet{CheeseBurger,Coke}
    g) FALSE
    i) TRUE

14. a) YuppyFood = DinerSet{Coke,Chips}
        YummyFood = DinerSet{CheeseBurger,Coke,Chips}

    c) YuppyFood = DinerSet{Coke}
        YummyFood = DinerSet{Coke,Chips}

15. a) HexSet1 : = HexNumSet{4, 6, 8, 10 '2};
    d) HexSet1 : = HexNumSet{}
    e) HexSet1 : = HexSet1 + HexSet2;

GLOSSARY

abstraction Emphasizing important concepts, while hiding unnecessary details. (See also control abstraction and data abstraction.)

activation One invocation of a procedure. Recursive procedures may have several activations in existence simultaneously.

activation frame Environment of the procedure invocation, including all local variables, parameters and the location of the next instruction to execute for this activation.

activation record Environment of the procedure invocation, including all local variables, parameters and the location of the next instruction to execute for this activation.

actual parameter The value, variable or expression passed as a parameter when a procedure is invoked.

adding operators Addition, subtraction, and OR. All of these operations have equal precedence in Modula-2.

algorithm A set of instructions (not necessarily from any programming language) that will perform some prescribed task.

allocation The creation of a previously non-existent data structure during program execution.

AND A logical operation that evaluates to TRUE exactly when both of its operands are TRUE (also known as & and "conjunction").

array A data structure consisting of a sequence of items each with identical type.

array cell The storage occupied by one array item.

array dump An algorithm for writing the entire contents of an array.

array index bounds violation A run-time error that occurs when the expression used to index an array is outside the range of the index set.

array name The identifier used to refer to the entire group of array cells.

array of counters Each item of an array serves as an separate counter variable.

array searching algorithms A class of algorithms that sequentially examines the value of array items to locate an item(s) with particular characteristics.

ascending order Arranged from least to greatest.

ASCII American Standard Code for Information Interchange. The most popular character set used for CHAR constants. (See also Appendix C.)

assertion A logical statement that describes the values of program data at a particular point of execution. Assertions are normally written as (* Assert: ... *) comments and placed in the code at the location where they are TRUE. Preconditions, postconditions and loop invariants are special types of assertions.

assignment compatible type This is a property of any two data types that are either

1) Compatible
2) One is compatible with INTEGER and the other is compatible with CARDINAL
3) One is CHAR and the other is a string of length one

Assignment compatibility is required for all of the following:

1) The variable and expression of an assignment instruction
2) Actual and formal parameters that are passed by value
3) The expression in a RETURN instruction and the function type
4) An array index expression and the index type

assignment instruction An instruction that causes an expression to be evaluated and the result assigned to a variable.

automatic data Data structures that are automatically allocated when a procedure is invoked and deallocated when it returns. Local variables and formal parameters have this characteristic.

back (of a queue) Most recently added object in a queue.

binary file Files that store numeric encodings intended for computer, not human consumption.

black box A typical user's view of a computer, emphasizing what it does, not how it works.

block structured language A programming language that defines identifier scope according to program "blocks", like procedures and modules. These blocks define the scope of visibility for identifiers.

Boolean expression A statement that can be evaluated to either TRUE or FALSE, also called a **logical expression**.

Boolean variable A variable that must be either TRUE or FALSE. In Modula-2 the corresponding standard type is BOOLEAN.

bounds checking A special test on each newly assigned variable value to see that it is within proper range, and report an error message if it is not. Many Modula-2 systems will perform this check automatically, or optionally.

bounds violation An execution error that occurs when a value is outside some prescribed range.

branch instruction A selection control structure.

buffer An array used to store a collection of input values prior to processing or a collection of output values prior to writing.

bug An error in a program (See also **syntax error**, **execution error**, **logical error**, and **fatal error**.)

built-in procedure Any standard procedure or function, included within the language without being written by the programmer, also called an "intrinsic" procedure (See also Appendix E).

call (of a procedure) Initiating the execution of a procedure, also called a "procedure invocation."

cardinal A positive valued integer (i.e., a number 0 or greater with no fractional, decimal part).

case expression The expression between CASE and OF that is used to select which clause of a CASE instruction is executed.

case label The constant expression that is compared to the case expression during the execution of a CASE. When they are equal, the corresponding case clause is executed.

case sensitive A language characteristic that identifies every lower-case letter to be different from every upper-case letter.

character string A sequence of consecutive characters.

close (a file) To perform all housekeeping functions necessary to complete a program's use of a file.

coder An individual who translates algorithms into computer programs.

coding The process of translating an algorithm into program instructions.

comment A remark inserted within a program that does not effect the code's execution but that can improve readability.

compatible type A property of any two data types that have one of the following characteristics:

1) Identical type
2) One or both are programmer defined types, as long as they are derived from some identical type
3) One or both are subranges of identical types

Compatibility is required for all of the following:

1) Any two operands of an expression
2) The initial and final expressions of a FOR instruction and its control variable

Compile, link, and go The three step process to compiling then linking and finally loading and executing a program.

compiled image A file produced by a compiler that stores the translation of a program into a low-level language that can be understood by the computer hardware, also called "object code."

compiler A program to translate a program into a form that can be executed by a computer.

compound logical expression A logical expression that contains other logical expressions.

conditional evaluation A method for evaluating AND or OR where the value of the left operand is calculated first. If the expression's value can be determined from the left operand value then the right operand is not evaluated.

conditional operators AND (&) and OR are operators that are evaluated by the conditional evaluation technique.

conjunction The AND operation

constant A symbol whose value is fixed throughout a program execution. Modula-2 includes standard constants, like 77, 64.33, "?", that are understood by the compiler. Modula-2 also permits the user to declare identifiers as constants.

control abstraction Procedures and functions allow a complicated algorithm to be broken into separate tasks. A procedure or function invocation is an abstraction because it contains only the routine name and parameter list and not all of the details.

control character Any of the unprintable characters (in ASCII these characters have ordinal values less than 32). Unprintable character constants must use the "C" notation.

control flow The order in which instructions are executed.

control structure An instruction that controls the execution sequence of other instructions. The three major classes of control structures are selection, repetition and procedure invocations.

control variable A variable that is automatically incremented or decremented after each loop iteration in a FOR loop.

correct algorithm An algorithm that performs precisely the task it was designed to perform.

counter loop A loop in which the number of iterations is controlled by a counter.

counter variable A variable used to count something. For example, it could count the number of value input or the number of times a loop is iterated, etc.

dangling reference A pointer variable that points to a dynamic data structure that has been deallocated.

data Information stored within a computer.

data abstraction The selective suppression of the details of data. This includes ideas such as well-chosen variable names, programmer-defined constants and types, and enumerated types.

data structure An organizational technique for storing data.

deallocation (of data) Relinquishing a data structure so that the program can no longer validly access it.

debugging The process of searching for a an error, or bug, in a program.

declaration A non-executable statement that specifies characteristics of a variable, constant, type or procedure.

dereferencing expression An expression that is used to name the data pointed to by a pointer.

descending order Arranged from greatest to least.

design (of programs) The process of transforming a problem definition into an algorithm.

design quiescence The time at which the job of designer is complete.

design review Examining an algorithm to ensure that it's precise, complete, and correct.

designer An individual who is responsible for designing algorithms to solve problems.

discriminator The tag field of a variant field. This is used to select a particular form of the field.

disjunction The OR operation.

documentation Written descriptions of how a program works, what the program does, or how to use a program. (See also **internal documentation**, **reference manual**, and **tutorial**.)

dump routine A procedure to output the contents of an array.

dynamic data Data that is allocated and deallocated under the explicit control of the program. Dynamic data in Modula-2 is allocated via ALLOCATE, deallocated via DEALLOCATE and accessed via pointer variables.

echo Writing precisely what has been input.

editor A program that assists an individual to create or modify a text file.

element (of an array) One of the component objects of an array, an array item.

ELSE clause The collection of instructions that are executed when the selection conditions of an IF-THEN-ELSE is FALSE.

encoding (of data) Representing data in a different form. For example, a Social Security Number is an encoding to represent a person.

enumerated type Allows a programmer to declare a type by specifying a list of identifiers that become the constants of the type.

equivalence A logical operator that evaluates to TRUE exactly when its two operands have the same value (both TRUE or both FALSE).

exclusive OR A logical operation that evaluates to TRUE exactly when one or the other, but not both, of its operands are TRUE. This operator is not directly supported within Modula-2.

executable image A program that has been prepared, after linking, to be executed. This consists of the complete collection of machine code.

execution efficiency The speed and amount of storage required for program execution.

execution error An error that occurs during the execution of a program and that could not be detected during compilation.

execution trace The process where an individual imitates how a computer would execute a program, especially with respect to the values assigned to variables during execution.

expression A combination of operands and operations that will be evaluated when the program executes.

fatal error An error that causes a program to terminate execution.

field A component part of a record.

field identifier Identifier used to name a field of a record.

field selector An expression used to completely identify a field of a record. The selector must include both the name of the record and the field name, with a period between.

file One unit of information on secondary storage. Files are used to store source programs, object programs, and collection of data.

file I/O When input comes from a file or output is stored in a file.

file name The identifier by which a file is known.

FIFO First-in, first-out. This form of storage is exhibited by a queue.

floppy diskette A form of secondary storage that consists of a thin, flexible platter on which magnetic encodings can be stored and later retrieved.

flow (of control) The order in which instructions are executed.

formal parameter The identifiers declared as parameters within a procedure. This is the name that identifies the parameter within the procedure.

front (of a queue) The object that has remained in the queue the longest time.

function A procedure that returns a value. The value returned by a function must be of simple type in Modula-2.

functionally equivalent Two code segments are functionally equivalent (with respect to I/O) if they each produce the same output for identical input.

generic procedure A procedure that accepts an actual parameter of more than one type.

global identifier An identifier declared just inside the module. Global identifiers are visible throughout the program in which they are declared.

guard The Boolean expression of an IF or ELSIF, or the CASE label of a CASE, that governs when the corresponding clause is executed.

hard disk A form of secondary storage that consists of a rigid platter on which magnetic encodings can be stored and later retrieved.

header A pointer variable that points to the first node of a linked list.

heterogeneous data type The component parts of the data structure have differing types. A record is a heterogeneous data type because each field has its own type.

high-level language Programming language that is closer to English than to something that can be directly executed by a computer.

homogeneous data type The component parts of the data structure have the same type. An array is a homogeneous data type because each item has the same type.

identical type Two types that are the same. The types of formal and actual parameters passed by reference must have identical type.

identifier A sequence of one alphabetic letter followed by zero or more letters and/or numeric digits. In Modula-2 identifiers are used to name variables, procedures, modules, and some types and constants.

IF instruction The most commonly used form of selection in algorithms and programming languages. The Modula-2 version requires a THEN-clause and includes optional ELSIF and ELSE clauses.

IF-THEN instruction A version of the IF instruction with only a THEN clause (i.e., no ELSIF or ELSE clauses).

IF-THEN-ELSE instruction A version of the IF instruction with both a THEN clause and an ELSE clause, but not ELSIF clauses.

implication A logical operation that evaluates to TRUE exactly when its first operand is FALSE or else both of its operands are TRUE. This operation is similar to an "IF-THEN" statement in English. P implies Q is sometimes symbolized "P → Q". The operator is not directly supported in Modula-2.

in place sort A sorting algorithm that is able to perform the sorting operation on a data structure with little additional storage.

inaccessible node A dynamic node that has been allocated, but during execution all pointers to it have been lost.

inclusive OR A logical operation that evaluates to TRUE exactly when at least one of its two operands is TRUE. This is the standard Modula-2 OR operator.

incompatible types Any two types that are in no way compatible (See also assignment compatible, compatible and identical types.)

index An expression used to distinguish one particular item from an array, also called a "subscript." Multidimensional arrays require multiple indices.

index set The range of permissible array indices. This is declared along with an array and fixed throughout the array's existence.

index type The range of permissible array indices. This is declared along with an array and fixed throughout the array's existence.

indices Plural of **index**.

infinite loop A loop which is performed over and over with no provision for completing its execution.

infinite recursion Executing activation after activation with no means for completing.

information processor A name often used to describe computers, because of their ability to process large amounts of data, or information.

InOut(I/O) This is a standard module of procedures, etc. that is the most common collection of input and output facilities used in Modula-2. InOut can work interactively or with text files.

input Any data that is read by an executing program into some variable. The data may be read from any external device, such as a keyboard or a secondary storage device.

input/process/output algorithm A class of algorithms that follow the pattern of first reading data, then manipulating the data and finally writing the results. This is a common form for many algorithms.

integer A positive or negative whole number (i.e., has no fractional or decimal part.)

interactive I/O The input/output style in which input comes from a keyboard and output goes to a display, that is like a dialogue between computer and user.

internal documentation Comments included in a program to assist individuals reading the code.

interpreter A program that examines instructions in the sequence in which they are to be executed; checks syntax; decodes semantics; and causes the task performed by an instruction to occur.

intrinsic procedure Any standard procedure or function, included within the language without being written by the programmer, also called a "built-in" procedure (See also Appendix E).

intrinsic type A type recognized by the language without a TYPE declaration, also called a "standard type."

invocation (of a procedure) Initiating the execution of a procedure, also called a procedure "call."

item (of an array) One of the component members of an array data structure.

item type The data type of every item in an array.

iteration A single instance of performing a loop body.

LIFO Last-in, first-out. Stacks are LIFO data structures.

lead designer An experienced designer responsible for the topmost levels of a program design.

line oriented (programming language) A language that utilizes ends of lines as separators for program units, (i.e., the end of an instruction or declaration is denoted by the end of a line).

linear search A searching algorithm that scans for the first occurrence of a value within some array by probing items in sequence.

linked list An ordered collection of nodes that connects by pointers within the nodes.

linker A program that performs the necessary linking of the compiled image to produce an executable image. This program is responsible for integrating external module code, such as InOut, with the main program code to produce a complete program.

linking The process of combining the various sections of compiled code into a single executable image.

list traversal Beginning at the header of a linked list and visiting (processing) every node of the list in order.

loader A program that retrieves the machine code from the executable image file and places this in the memory of the computer so that it may be executed. This program is usually executed automatically when a programmer requests a program execution.

local identifier An identifier declared within a procedure. The scope of this identifier is the procedure in which it is declared.

logic A system where every expression evaluates to either true or false.

logic error An error in a program that occurs because of a faulty algorithm. Logic errors result in undesired program output, but not necessarily computer generated error messages.

logical assertion A type of comment that describes what has happened in previous code (See also **assertion**.)

logical axioms Rules of logic (See also Appendix D.)

logical expression A statement that can be evaluated to either TRUE or FALSE, also called a "Boolean expression."

logical negation NOT

logical theorems Rules of logic (See also Appendix D.)

logical variable A variable that must be either TRUE or FALSE. In Modula-2 the corresponding standard type is BOOLEAN.

loop A program control structure that causes a group of instructions, the loop body, to be executed repeatedly.

loop body The group of instructions performed by each repetition, iteration, of a loop.

loop condition A logical expression that is evaluated after each loop body iteration and determines when loop repetition completes.

loop finalization Showing that the desired result occurs when a loop completes its execution. This is usually done by combining what is known about the loop condition upon loop completion with the loop invariant.

loop initialization Showing that the loop invariant must be TRUE the first time it is encountered.

loop invariant A condition, written in the form of an assertion, that is TRUE just before the loop condition is tested.

loop preservation Showing that the loop invariant remains TRUE after a loop iteration when it is TRUE before.

loop termination Showing that a loop completes execution, does not execute infinitely.

low-level language A programming language with primitive instructions that computers can execute, but that are often hard for people to read.

machine language The set of instructions a particular computer can execute. Machine instructions are usually stored in a numeric encoding that is virtually unreadable.

mainline routine The main algorithm or driver. This is the portion of the program that begins executing first.

maintenance programmer An individual responsible for alterations to an existing computer program. Maintenance programmers fix bugs in programs and add new features.

matrices Plural of matrix.

matrix A two dimensional array (i.e., items are arranged in a grid of rows and columns.) A matrix has 2 index sets.

merge algorithms A type of the sequential array processing algorithm that processes multiple vectors and combines their item values into one.

multidimensional array Arrays of two or more dimensions.

multiplying operators All multiplication, division, and AND operations for BOOLEAN type variables. These operators have equal precedence in Modula-2.

multiway selection A selection structure with many control path alternatives (e.g., a CASE instruction or and IF instruction with several ELSIF clauses).

natural language A language used for written and/or spoken communication between people, such as English, Spanish, Russian, etc.

nested comments Entirely enclosing one comment within another.

nested control structures When one control instruction is contained within the body or some clause of another.

NOT A logical operation that evaluates to TRUE if its operand is FALSE and is FALSE if its operand is TRUE. This is also symbolized with the Modula-2 ~ operator.

null instruction This has no characters and represents nothing to be executed. Null instructions result from placing unneeded semicolons within code.

object code A file produced by a compiler that stores the translation of a program into a low-level language that can be understood by the computer hardware, also called "compiled image."

one-armed branch Another name for an IF-THEN instruction.

one-dimensional array An array with a single index set, so items are arranged in a single sequence (also called a "vector.")

open a file To initialize a file so that the program can read from it or write to it.

open array parameter A formal parameter that is declared without specifying an index set. The actual parameter may be any array with the same item type. When the procedure is invoked the index set will be the subrange [0..HIGH(FormalParameterName)].

operating system The collection of software that together with hardware, forms the nucleus of facilities upon which all other software relies. The operating system controls all computer functions, including file management, program execution and I/O device access.

operation An action or calcualtion that is performed during the evaluation of an expression.

operator overloading The practice of allowing the same operator symbol to express different functions for different variable types. For example the * symbol denotes CARDINAL multiplication, INTEGER multiplication, REAL multiplication and set intersection in Modula-2.

operator precedence Rules that establish the order of evaluation of the operations in an expression.

optimizing (a program) Improving a program so it will execute faster and/or occupy less computer storage space.

OR A logical operation that evaluates to TRUE exactly when at least one of its two operands is TRUE.

ordinal value A cardinal value uniquely associated with a particular character or enumerated constant. These constants are numbered beginning with an ordinal value of 0.

outline style pseudocode A representation of top down design that places pseudoinstructions in proper sequence with heading levels indicating design levels.

output Any data that is written by an executing progan external device such as a computer screen, printer or secondary storage device.

output line A row of characters written by a program.

overflow An execution error that results when the value of some calculation is too large for the computer.

parameter passage A programming mechanism that permits sharing of data between two routines.

parameter passage by reference (VAR parameter) Where the calling routine supplies the address rather than value of the actual parameter at the time of invocation. A subsequent reference to the formal parameter will use the actual parameter.

parameter passage by value The value of the actual parameter is copied to the formal parameter when the routine is invoked. Subsequent reference to the formal parameter uses only this local copy.

pointer A simple variable required to gain access to dynamic data structures.

priming read The process of reading an initial value before executing a loop. This operation is often required to initialize a trailer style loop.

printable character Any character that can be displayed or printed by a computer terminal (in ASCII these characters have ordinal greater than 31.)

problem definition A description of the task a program must perform which serves as the contract between the user and programmer.

problem solving The process of reaching an accurate conclusion for something that must be done. In computer programming this is the process of designing a working program.

procedure A Modula-2 subprogram that consists a group of instructions that are executed as a single unit (See also invoke.)

procedure body The collection of instructions executed by a procedure.

procedure hierarchy chart A graphical model of the control relationships among the routines of a program.

procedure postcondition An assertion that states what is true when a procedure completes execution.

procedure precondition An assertion that describes the condition that must be true prior to procedure execution in order for the post condition to be true upon procedure completion.

procedure stub An unrefined shell of a procedure used to test and debug programs.

program A sequence of instructions that, when executed, causes a particular task to be carried out by a computer.

program maintenance An ongoing process of correcting program deficiencies and adding new features.

program module Another name for a Modula-2 program.

program specification The definition of the task to be performed by a program.

programmer An individual who designs and/or codes programs.

programmer-defined constant An identifier declared in a CONST instruction or within an enumeration of a Modula-2 program. The values of these identifiers are fixed throughout their scope.

programmer-defined type A data type that is declared in a TYPE declaration of a Modula-2 program.

programming language A means to express programs.

pseudocode A sequence of pseudoinstructions that constitute an algorithm to solve some problem.

pseudolanguage A language for expressing algorithms that does not include all the syntactic detail of a programming language.

qualified identifier A reference with a suffix following a period. This form is used to refer to a field of a record.

queue A data structure used to store objects so that the first objects inserted (enqueued) are also the first removed (dequeued.)

random array access This occurs when an algorithm processes array items without any regular pattern.

range of existence The execution time during which an identifier has been allocated but not deallocated.

real Numeric data type consisting of postive and negative numbers permitting fractional, or decimal, parts.

record A structured data type that consists of one or more fields, each with its own independent type.

recursion A form of control where a procedure invokes itself. Recursion can be used as a replacement for repetition.

reference manual A document that can be used to locate information about a piece of software.

relational expression The comparison of two expressions of compatible type. Relational expressions are of type BOOLEAN in Modula-2.

repetition A control flow options that indicates some task is to be performed over and over.

reserved word An identifier that is a standard part of the programming language and cannot be redefined (See Appendix B for a list of Modula-2 reserved words.)

RESULT A notation often used in postconditions to refer to the value returned by a function.

robust (program) A program that produces reasonable output for unreasonable input.

routine A separate algorithm designed to perform some subtask of the complete algorithm.

scalar type An atomic data type where the constants of the type can be ordered. In Modula-2 the scalar data types include BOOLEAN, CARDINAL, CHAR, enumerations, INTEGER, LONGINT, LONGCARD, and subranges.

scope of visibility The program region in which an identifier can be referenced.

secondary storage A long term memory where data may be stored after program termination, such as magnetic tape, floppy disk or hard disk.

selection A control structure that permits a choice between alternate instruction sequences (e.g., If and Case).

selection condition Some expression contained within a selection control structure. The value of this expression determines which option is selected by the instruction.

selector Another name used for the expression used to index or subscript an array.

semantics The *meaning* of a computer program.

sequence A list of instructions performed one after another in order.

sequential array access Any algorithm that processes items of an array in a regular pattern.

sequential execution In this form of execution each instruction begins immediately after the preceding instruction completes.

sequential I/O Reading or writing data in order.

shift algorithms A class of sequential array processing algorithms that causes the contents of vector items to be assigned to their neighbors according to some regular pattern.

short-circuit evaluation A method for evaluating AND or OR where the value of the left operand is calculated first. If the expression's value can be determined from the left operand value then the right operand is not evaluated.

side effect Assigning a value to any non-local and non-parameter data structure (bad program style).

simple type An atomic data type. In Modula-2 the scalar data types include BOOLEAN, CARDINAL, CHAR, enumerations, INTEGER, LONGINT, LONGCARD, LONGREAL, REAL and subranges.

singly-linked list An ordered collection of dynamic nodes that are connected by pointers. All nodes but the last contain a pointer to the next node in the list and the pointer of the last node is NIL.

size of an array The number of items in an array.

software A collection of programs.

sorting algorithms Operations for reordering a collection of data so that they are arranged from least to greatest (ascending) or greatest to least (descending).

source code The form of the original program before it has been compiled.

stack A data structure used to store objects so that the last objects inserted (pushed) are also the removed (popped.)

standard input device The device from which the program normally receives input, usually the user's keyboard.

standard output device The device that normally receives program output, usually the user's video screen.

standard procedure Any standard procedure or function, included within the language without being written by the programmer, also called a "built-in" or "intrinsic" procedure (See also Appendix E).

standard type A type recognized by the language without a TYPE declaration (See also simple type and structured type.)

state of computation A snapshot of the execution environment, including data values and point location of next instruction to be performed, at some instant during the execution of a program.

static data Data that exists throughout a program's execution.

static scope Scope of an identifier is determined by the placement of its declaration and can be described regardless of the program's control flow.

stepwise refinement The process of repeatedly refining large problems into successively smaller ones in steps, where each step is another complete algorithm that supplies more detail than the previous.

string A sequence of consecutive characters of any data of type ARRAY [0...x] OF CHAR, where x is the maximum string length. String constants in Modula-2 consist of a sequence of characters bracketed by either single or double quotation marks.

strongly typed A programming language characteristic that requires different types of data to be carefully distinguished from each other.

structured data types A type that contains other component data. In Modula-2 these types include ARRAY, RECORD, SET, POINTER and PROCEDURE types.

structured programming An approach to program design representing a disciplined style of program development concentrating on control of flow of an algorithm and relying on top down design.

subprogram A programming language feature for control abstraction. In Modula-2 the PROCEDURE is a subprogram.

subrange type A data type that consists of a consecutive collection of constants from some other type.

subscript An expression used to distinguish one particular item from an array, also called an "index." Multidimensional arrays require multiple subscripts.

syntax The rules of form and punctuation for a programming language.

syntax diagram A graphical structure used to describe programming language syntax (See Appendix A for a syntax diagram for the complete Modula-2 programming language.)

syntax error Errors caused by incorrect program syntax. These errors are detected during compilation.

systems analyst An individual who works with the user and designer to arrive at a suitable problem definition.

table driven code The use of an array to direct program activity in place of a more complex control structure.

tag field A special field of a variant record whose value selects the form of the data structure at execution time.

test at the bottom of the loop The loop condition is tested after the loop body is executed (e.g., REPEAT loop).

test at the top of the loop The loop condition is tested before the loop body is executed (e.g., WHILE loop).

test driver A mainline whose sole purpose is to test a procedure in an effort to uncover bugs.

test oracle A collection of acceptable program input along with the expected output.

text file Files designed for human consumption containing only characters.

THEN clause The collection of instructions that are executed when the selection condition of an IF-THEN-ELSE is TRUE.

top down design The process, beginning with a single large problem, then repeatedly refining into collections of smaller subproblems. The result of a top down design should be an algorithm that can be easily coded.

trailer loop A loop that examines a collection of values up to but not including some particular value.

transfer of control An abrupt change from the execution of a particular sequence of instructions to a different sequence located elsewhere in the program.

truncate (a real value) The process of retaining only the integer portion of a REAL value. In Modula-2 there is a standard TRUNC type conversion function that converts a REAL expression into a CARDINAL value.

truth table A diagram for listing all possible cases for values of a logical expressions.

tutorial Documentation that teaches how to use some software.

two armed branch Another name for an IF-THEN-ELSE instruction.

two-dimensional array An array with a two index sets, so items are arranged in a rectangular grid of rows and columns (also called a "matrix.")

two-way selection Selection option with two control path alternatives (e.g., IF-THEN and IF-THEN-ELSE).

type conversion function A function that accepts an expression of one data type and returns a corresponding value of another data type. Standard Modula-2 type conversion functions include CARDINAL, CHR, FLOAT, INTEGER, ORD and TRUNC.

unassigned variable (undefined value) A variable that has yet to be assigned a value by an assignment instruction, input instruction or parameter passage.

underflow An execution error that results when the value of some calculation is too small for the computer.

user Anyone who uses computers or computer programs.

VAR parameter The parameter passage style where the calling routine supplies the address rather than value of the actual parameter at the time of invocation. A subsequent reference to the formal parameter will use the actual parameter. This style of parameter passage is known as "parameter passage by reference."

variable A unit of storage capable of storing a data value.

variable name The identifier used to refer to a variable within a program. Variable names must be declared in a VAR declaration.

variable value The data value stored by a variable.

variant One of the optional forms of a variant record field.

variant record A record data structure that can take different forms, call variants chosen at execution time.

vector A one dimensional array (i.e., items are arranged in a single sequence.) A vector has a single index set.

vector of arrays A multidemensional array that is treated as though it were a one dimensional array with every item is also an array.

Wirth, Niklaus The creator of the Modula-2 language.

INDEX

Assignment Instruction

→ *VarOperand* → : = → *Expression* →

CASEinstruction

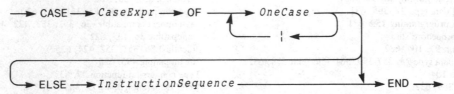

EXITinstruction

→ EXIT →

FORinstruction

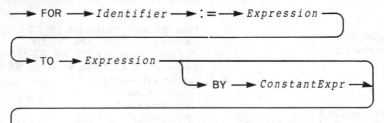

HALTprocedure

→ HALT →

IFinstruction

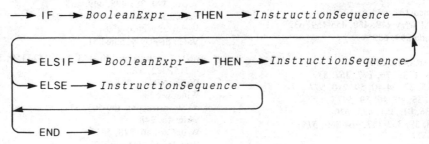